Roland M HANSEN JR.
4132 Regent St.

Government

in the Fifty States

Government

NEW YORK

in the Fifty States

WILLIAM ANDERSON

University of Minnesota

CLARA PENNIMAN

University of Wisconsin

EDWARD W. WEIDNER

Michigan State College

HOLT, RINEHART AND WINSTON

December, 1960

Copyright 1951, © 1960
by Holt, Rinehart and Winston, Inc.
Library of Congress Catalog Card Number: 60–9131
20414–0810
Printed in the United States of America

Preface

MORE THAN TWO YEARS AGO William Anderson, senior author of *State and Local Government in the United States* (1951), asked me to undertake a revised edition of the text. Respect and esteem for Professor Anderson as a person and a scholar as well as interest in state government made it easy for me to decide to accept the task.

The change in title to *Government in the Fifty States* reflects the change in emphasis of the revised edition to state government. Local government, however, has not been ignored. Chapter 5 gives particular attention to metropolitan areas as the special, growing problem of state-local relations. The data throughout the text have been revised to record the changes that have taken place since 1951. Material on Alaska and Hawaii has been added to the discussion of the other states. As an example of the problems encountered in writing a state constitution, the writing of the Alaska constitution has been reported in a special case study. The text of the constitution is included in an Appendix. It is not only one of the latest state constitutions but also an excellent specimen indicating the nature and scope of such a document. Students can compare it with the constitution of their own state.

A short case history of a bill before the Wisconsin legislature, written by a former member of that legislature, is included in Chapter 11, "Legislative Organization and Procedure," to aid the student in understanding legislative activity.

A number of tables and figures have been included to highlight certain important topics. Among the figures are two political cartoons that relate the subject matter of the text to contemporary events. References for further reading are to be found at the end of each chapter.

The revised edition continues the assumption that students in state government courses are near the beginning of their work in political science and need to gain a knowledge of the legal and institutional framework of state government. But the chapter bibliographies and some of the analyses of political parties, voting, legislative process, and so forth call attention to the importance of the behavioral studies for an understanding of state government today.

As one would expect, Professor Anderson has given generously of his time in offering advice and suggestions for this revision without insisting on his own point of view. Professor Weidner also helpfully discussed some of the possible approaches to the revision. Neither has any responsibility for errors of judgment or fact in the specific revisions that have been made.

Special thanks are owed to Mrs. Leone Suttie for an excellent job of manuscript typing.

C.P.

Madison, Wis.
January 1960

Contents

List of Tables

List of Figures

PART ONE

Intergovernmental Relations

CHAPTER 1

Each State a Community

AMERICAN STATE and local governments are spending about thirty billion dollars annually. They employ more than six million individuals. Their expenditures for education, highways, social services, public health contribute to the welfare of agriculture, business, and labor and of men, women, and children. Voters, political parties, interest groups, legislators, and governors choose the items for expenditure, the total to be expended, and the types of taxes to provide the revenues. No citizen can escape responsibility for the decisions made. Citizen disinterestedness, ignorance, and inactivity influence government action just as do political party, interest group, or active individual work.

You have obligations and opportunities to participate in state and local government. You will vote, you may become active in politics, and you may find a career in either state or local government. Right now you can walk out of the classroom and attend a city council meeting or a hearing. Many students can go directly to the state capitol and attend sessions and committee meetings of the legislature and of the state administrative commissions and agencies. Local, state, and federal courts are sitting nearby. You may find a congenial pressure group with which to work. You can attend political-party meetings. In fact, any student seriously interested in party politics and willing to work probably will find more opportunities for ac-

3

tivity than he has time in his college curriculum. State and local governments also offer rich opportunities for study and research. You do not need to go to Washington or New York to learn about voting behavior. Local studies in voting behavior, legislative behavior, or administrative behavior may make significant contributions to the literature.

You will find a warmer welcome from men in government and parties if your questions, your comments, and your actions reflect a knowledge of government and politics. You will be a better contributing citizen if you understand something of the organization of government and the problems you are asking your elected representatives to solve. And a research student in government needs a background of state government for his special area of interest for future investigation.

This book attempts to provide the needed description of the framework and institutions of state government and an introduction to an analysis of how men and women as voters, politicians, legislators, governors, and administrators have worked within that framework.

Differences among the States

No general state government book can convey the full flavor of the government and politics of an individual state. The states differ. Similar formal institutional arrangements may become quite different institutions in practice. The French heritage of Louisiana and the Spanish background in California affect laws and institutions differently from the English traditions of Virginia. Some differences can be measured, others cannot.

★ Statistical differences among the states

Although in all essential respects *legally equal* and under equal responsibility to govern and to provide public services, *the states are in almost all other respects unequal*. They differ in location, area, shape, topography, geology, resources, fertility, climate, rainfall, length of growing season, plant life, animal life, latitude, altitude, and other physical characteristics. They differ in population composition: race and national origins; age and sex distribution; urban and rural residence; educational preparation; scientific, industrial, and commercial skills; religious affiliations; and others. The states differ in history, tradition, political parties, constitutions, forms of government, types of local institutions, industrial pursuits, wealth, income, taxing systems, and many other features that are important for state and local government.

Almost every state, of course, has a little of every factor of which some other states have more. There is at least a little agriculture in every state and also at least a little industry and a little commerce. Differences in race and in national origins, in religion, in levels of education, and so on do not closely follow state lines. And all states have *similar* if not identical problems in government, in taxation, and in the performance of public services. The differences from state to state are not absolute but relative.

It is important, however, to get some sense of these *relative differences* among the state. Differences in area, population, income, and governmental expenditures place wide gulfs between the largest and smallest state, the most populous and the least populous state, the most wealthy and the poorest, and the most urban and most rural state. Public policy and the operations of government will vary considerably from state to state in some relation to these factors. Note your own state and the extremes among the states in Table 1 (p. 18). Such a table presents a good introductory guide to every state.

★ *Less measurable differences*

Statistics seldom suggest the subtle distinctions among the states. The authors of the study, *Presidential Nominating Politics in 1952,* commented:

> The economic development of a state and the cultural factors of race, religion, and population origins, all affect the way in which it participates in the presidential nomination process. These factors underlie and have helped to shape the political traditions of the nature of the two-party balance in each state. Every state has its own political institutions that are in some degree distinctive.[1]

To understand politics and government in Wisconsin, one must know the influence of the La Follette family, especially Robert M. LaFollette, Sr. California politics are more comprehensible when one knows about Hiram Johnson and his role in the early decades of this century. Other states have had other individual political leaders who have left similar impress on the politics and government. Different individuals and groups in different periods and with different aims have affected the growth of each state.

States may show different stages of development in political and administrative practices. Some states conduct government today in terms of political patronage, rudimentary fiscal controls, political boss rule, and general governmental ethics along the lines and standards common to other states in the nineteenth century. Citizens in such states have accepted and retained the older tradition of government practices and generally have

[1] Paul T. David, Malcolm Moos, Ralph M. Goldman, *Presidential Nominating Politics in 1952, The National Story,* Vol. 1 (Baltimore: The Johns Hopkins Press, 1954), pp. 157, 158.

made fewer demands on government for services (both because philosophically they may not wish government to assume these responsibilities and because they do not trust the government now operating to carry out such responsibilities).

Not only do standards of governmental services and the place of governmental services differ among the states, but the ethics of governmental personnel and political leaders also differ from state to state. There was a time in the nineteenth century when it was a common political practice for the state treasurer personally to keep all interest on state fund deposits. His political party, of course, expected a substantial contribution. Minnesota, Wisconsin, and many other states made an abrupt change in this custom about the end of the nineteenth century. Today any state treasurer pursuing such a course would probably end up behind bars and his party would find itself out of office. Yet some of the states still pay particular officials with fees that are collected instead of putting all full-time officials on a salary. In some instances, the result is not too different from the old case of interest payments and the state treasurer. Often, the fees received are unreasonably large for the duties performed. The post is recognized as a political plum, and the recipient is expected to contribute handsomely to his party.

Reformers have often advocated nonpartisan selection of the judiciary. The "nonpartisan" election of judges in Wisconsin means that the judicial candidates are nominated at primaries on ballots which do not indicate any party affiliation, and they are elected at a nonpartisan election in the spring. In Michigan the "nonpartisan" election of judges means that judicial candidates are nominated at party conventions but appear on the final ballot without any party designation. In Arizona "nonpartisan" election means that judicial candidates are nominated in party primaries but appear on the final ballot without any party designation. The same term has a significantly different meaning in practice in three states.

But the States Are Alike

Recognizing that the states differ in practices and institutions, we still know that they are similar. They are all a part of a common union. They share much common history and tradition. Their citizens have a common loyalty beyond the state. *Government in the Fifty States* describes and analyzes the general governmental arrangements, practices, and problems that the states share in common. A table of contents might read:

This book is about human freedom—freedom of thought, freedom of religious belief, and all the other great freedoms that some men and women try to preserve through their own acts and through the government;

It is about human aspirations for equality and justice—to be treated as equals before the law, in legislative representation, in voting rights, in access to public employment, and in the use and benefits of public institutions;

It is about voting and campaigning, about primaries and elections, about people participating in politics and government, about lay citizens, and about officials;

It is about public opinion, how it is made, how it is measured, and how it works to influence government and about political parties and their roles in government;

It is about pressures in government—pressures of every kind by individuals, small groups, large and powerful organizations, pressures on all branches of government—and about conflicts of interest and lobbying activities;

It is about honesty and ethics in government;

It is about constitutions and laws and other regulators of the state's public business, how these constitutions and laws are made and changed, and how the courts interpret and apply them;

It is about the branches of government—legislative, executive, judicial —how they are set up, how they divide the labors of government among them, how they work together and how they check each other, how they have grown and changed, what their techniques of internal operation are and how they work;

It is about the many public services, great and small—the way they have grown, the needs they are expected to meet, how they are carried on;

It is about public administration in the states—the daily performance of countless services, the departments and bureaus, and some of their technical operations;

It is about public personnel—nearly 30,000 in the average state, 1,500,-000 in all fifty states, and another 4,400,000 in local governments;

It is about the material necessities of government—taxation and budgets, expenditures and accounting, how the necessary money is raised, and who shall pay it;

It is about intergovernmental relations, how the state governments work, and sometimes collide, with the national government, their local governments, and the governments of other states;

It is about individual responsibility, too—for personal conduct bears a share in preserving and promoting the public welfare, the rights of others, and the strength and integrity of the government in all its processes and institutions; in short, it is about *you and your role in government,* for no citizen can escape being involved with his state government.

Two Political Cases

Of course, these "abouts" and the chapters of the book do not describe individual events. Each political incident shows a meshing of most of the factors we describe separately. To show these interrelationships, we have summarized these recent political decisions in California and Wisconsin.

★ *Cross-filing in California*[2]

A few Republicans joined Democrats in eliminating Hiram Johnson's "reform" of cross-filing. State Democrats were especially happy to see the demise of a system that had worked to their disadvantage for twenty years. These two sentences tell a story of great political import for California.

California had had an insurgent Republican political reform movement in the early part of the twentieth century led by Hiram Johnson. Attacking the special "interests" and in particular the Southern Pacific Railroad, the reformers first attempted to secure changes from within the Republican party, then worked as a third party, and later returned as a Progressive faction within the Republican party. In establishing a third party the reformers did not wish to lose the support of individuals who sympathized with their cause but were unwilling to vote outside the Republican primary. To meet this situation, they secured state legislation that permitted a candidate for public office to file in one or more party primaries as he desired. A Republican voter then could continue his registered affiliation with the Republican party and vote in the Republican primary, but he could choose from among the candidates listed those who represented the reform, Progressive policies. The system worked reasonably well for its authors. The Progressives shortly returned to the Republican party and the system continued to work better and better for the Republicans.

From the advent of the New Deal, a majority of California's voters registered in advance of the primary elections as Democrats. Yet again and again these same registered Democrats went into the primaries, examined their ballots, apparently voted for the names they knew best, and frequently nominated Republicans (especially incumbent Republicans) for the Democratic ticket in November. Republican voters, probably also voting for the names they knew best, nominated these same Republicans for their

2 Summarized from article by Gordon E. Baker and Bernard Teitelbaum, "An End to Cross-filing," *National Civic Review*, Vol. 48 (June 1959), 286-291.

ticket in November. The outcome of the general election in such cases was decided before it was held. In 1952, both the Democrats and Republicans nominated the Republican incumbent, William Knowland, for the United States Senate. The Democratic party, in effect, had no candidate for the United States Senate in the November election.

Quite understandably the Democrats did not like the cross-filing system. Others with a less immediate partisan interest also objected to cross-filing as destructive of party responsibility and party competition. If democracy requires opportunities for voters to make choices and if meaningful choices are possible only through party competition, then California needed a change in its primary law to achieve political responsibility and accountability.

Finally, citizens desiring repeal of cross-filing secured 134,000 signatures on a petition which would force the legislature to act. Under California law, the legislature could pass the law requested by this initiative petition or it could propose a different measure and put both items on the next ballot. Over 70 percent of the members of the legislature had cross-filed and won the nomination of both parties in 1952, and they did not propose to vote themselves out of office. As an alternative proposal, the legislature submitted to a referendum a proposal to retain cross-filing but to require each candidate to indicate his party affiliation on the ballot. To the surprise of many Californians, the legislature's proposal passed overwhelmingly. (The indirect-initiative proposal eliminating cross-filing almost won. In other words, California voters could—and many did—vote "yes" on both the legislative proposal to require party designation of candidates on primary ballots *and* the citizen initiative petition to eliminate cross-filing entirely.)

The result of this proposal produced even greater surprises. It soon became evident that a registered Democrat voting in the Democratic primary usually did not want to vote for a Republican candidate, and most registered Republicans did not support Democrats who appeared on their primary ballot. There were exceptions, but the pattern was clear. November general-election ballots showed fewer and fewer candidates entered in both the Republican and Democratic columns. The Democrats now, more often than the Republicans, became the beneficiaries of the cross-filing system. Five Democratic Congressional candidates in 1958 won both the Democratic and Republican primaries.

Yet the Democrats, more than the Republicans, wished to be rid of cross-filing. They believed the system had delayed their rise to power in the state and they saw it as a possible barrier in the future. Controlling the governorship and both houses of the legislature in 1959, they easily passed legislation to outlaw cross-filing. How California party politics will develop in the future cannot be forecast. But California voters will choose their representatives from the two political parties in the November general elections and not in the primaries.

★ *Apportionment in Wisconsin*[3]

DEMOCRATS ELECT GOVERNOR AND ASSEMBLY MAJORITY, FIRST TIME IN TWENTY-SIX YEARS

Political successes in the recent election suggest the possibility that the governorship and both houses of the legislature will be controlled by the Democrats in 1960.

Headlines and stories similar to these appeared in most Wisconsin newspapers in November 1958. The news meant not only that the Democratic party was showing new strength in the state by its election of a governor and an assembly majority but that the legislative redistricting effective in 1954 had played a part in this shift of power. Wisconsin could have elected a Democratic governor any year that a majority of voters so decreed. It would have taken much more than a simple majority of voters, however, to have secured a Democratic assembly under the former legislative districts.

> No consequential reapportionment of seats in either house [occurred between 1921 and the 1950 census]. The continuing urbanization of the population, therefore, had been inadequately reflected in the distribution of legislative representation. Assembly districts in 1951 ranged in size from 13,715 to 95,534 and Senate districts from 61,795 to 191,588. The under-represented populations were virtually all in the large urban and industrial regions of the state and the over-represented populations were in the agricultural and "cut-over" regions. The under-represented peoples had also shown a fondness for Democratic or Progressive candidates for office while the over-represented peoples, especially those in agricultural areas, preferred Republicans. (Pp. 398, 399.)

Both parties pledged action on reapportionment in their 1950 platforms. The Legislative Council proceeded to appoint a committee, headed by the former chief justice of the state supreme court, to study and make a report on reapportionment in the state. The committee subsequently recommended to the Legislative Council a plan for redistricting which recognized the constitutional provision that after each centennial census, "the legislature shall apportion and district anew the members of the Senate and Assembly, according to the number of inhabitants." Meanwhile rural Republicans and some urban Republicans became disturbed at the political

[3] Summarized from article by William H. Young, "Court Settles Apportionment," *National Municipal Review*, Vol. 43 (September 1954), 398-402.

implications of reapportionment. The Republican majority in the Legislative Council did not want either to disavow the report of the committee they had appointed or to approve it. They solved their dilemma by throwing the problem back into the hands of the legislature as a whole. They forwarded to the legislature the committee's report without comment and also a proposed amendment to the state constitution which would, if adopted, permit consideration of area as well as population in later reapportionments.

The two houses of the legislature considered the two reapportionment proposals: Failure to do anything about apportionment left the Republican party open to the charge of violating their campaign pledge. Acceptance of their committee's report opened the way for a greater legislative voice by the urban, industrial areas of the state with the probability of more Democratic representation. Failure to accept the committee's report, however, implied a lack of faith in their own appointments and an unwillingness to give Republicans in the urban areas a one-to-one voice with Republicans in urban areas—yet acceptance of the report would antagonize rural Republicans. It was a situation not easily solved.

The governor, although not unalterably opposed to some area recognition, supported the committee's report. Urban Republicans generally supported the committee. Most Democrats in the legislature also supported the report. Finally, the legislature put the problem to the voters for a decision, by presenting an advisory referendum to the voters in 1952. At that time the voters were asked whether they wished to make area as well as population a factor in subsequent redistrictings. An affirmative vote would prevent the committee's recommended plan for excluding area in redistricting from going into effect. At the same time, however, the legislature passed a constitutional amendment making area a factor in redistricting. Amendments in Wisconsin require a second passage by the legislature (in this case, in 1953) and approval by a majority of the voters. In the 1952 election, urban voters succeeded by a vote of 753,092 against 689,615 in defeating the proposal to recognize area as well as population in legislative districts.

Rural and conservative Republican legislators, however, had now rallied their forces. Despite the advisory referendum results, the legislature passed the constitutional amendment for area representation a second time and placed it on the April election ballots. Spring elections do not bring out a large vote and particularly do not bring out a large urban vote. This election followed the pattern: 433,043 citizens approved the area amendment and 406,133 citizens opposed it. The legislature was now free to repeal the earlier redistricting statute and to enact legislation reducing even the older urban representation in the state senate. In effect, Wisconsin might have even less population representation in the legislature after these maneuvers than in the 1930s and 1940s. But now the State Supreme Court intervened. In a case brought by the attorney general against an action of the secretary of state which ignored the amendment passed by the legislature in 1953 the court held that (1) the legislature "had exhausted its constitutional authority to reapportion again before 1961 by its passage of the committee's recommendations" and that (2) the language of the constitutional amendment itself was technically incorrect and its passage therefore invalid.

The state now had to return to its population-districting plan based on the 1950 census, and the 1954 elections for the legislature were held on the new basis.

Several unusual items characterized this episode: (1) The division within the Republican party as to the desirability or undesirability of increased urban representation; (2) The attempts to give both sides an opportunity to argue their case first within the legislative council, then within the legislature, and finally before the voters; (3) The fall general election and then the spring election represented urban and then rural victories in the legislature; (4) The influence of the governor in his support of the committee's report for population redistricting; (5) The intervention of the court with its decision in effect that the constitutional amendment was unconstitutional. A difference on any one of these points could have produced a different result. And a different result that brought area representation would have affected subsequent Democratic legislative control. It could be said that many Republicans, in the legislature, in the governor's chair, and on the Supreme Court bench, believed sufficiently in the people and the two-party system to be willing to give their opponents a chance. Or it could be said that the rural and conservative Republicans simply were outmaneuvered.

Conclusion

In the succeeding chapters on state government, keep in sight the overall goal of understanding the whole political process. Constitutions and laws do not alone describe government. No state institution stands by itself nor gives by itself an understanding of the state's operating government. The political process in some states makes apparently outdated institutions work well. Elsewhere the latest governmental machinery may work poorly. Individual citizens and groups work within the constitution, the laws, and the institutions to secure their purposes and goals. Understanding of state government includes knowledge of constitutions, laws, and institutions; knowledge of the political organization and behavior of individuals, parties, and groups; and knowledge of the purposes and goals of groups and individuals.

REFERENCES

The Forty-eight States; Their Tasks as Policy Makers and Administrators, The American Assembly, Graduate School of Business, Columbia University, 1955.

Tompkins, Dorothy Louise, *State Government and Administration: A Bibliography.* Chicago: Public Administration Service, 1955.

Periodicals

National Civic Review (formerly the *National Municipal Review*). The National Municipal League, monthly.

Public Administration Review. The American Society for Public Administration, quarterly.

Recent Publications on Government Problems. Joint Reference Library, Chicago, weekly.

State Government. The Council of State Governments, quarterly.

Studies of states

Buckley, William E., *Connecticut: The State and Its Government.* New York: Oxford Book, 1953.

Crouch, Winston W., and Dean E. McHenry, *California Government: Politics and Administration.* Berkeley, Calif.: University of California Press, 1949.

Crowell Publishing Company series, *The Government and Administration of . . . ,* now including Delaware, Florida, Georgia, Illinois, Iowa, Mississippi, Montana, New Jersey, New York, North Carolina, Ohio, and Wyoming.

Donnelly, Thomas Claude, *The Government of New Mexico.* Albuquerque: University of New Mexico Press, 1953.

Erickson, Elmer J., *California Government, State and Local.* New York: American Book, 1955.

The Government of Louisiana. Baton Rouge, La.: Legislative Council, 1959.

Mack, Effie Mona, *Nevada Government: A Study of the Administration and Politics of State, County, Township, and Cities.* Caldwell, Ida.: Caxton, 1953.

CHAPTER 2

The States and Their Local Units

WHAT IS A STATE in the Union? What is a county or any other unit of local government? To understand state and local governments, you should keep in mind what these units of government are. By a unit of government is usually meant a resident population that occupies a definite land area, that is legally organized for government and for the rendering of public services, and that has authority to exercise certain public powers and to perform one or more public functions. Among the *powers* that are usually possessed in some degree are taxation, eminent domain, police power, and penal power. Among the *functions* to be performed (which for any unit of government may be one, a few, or many) are provision for law enforcement, education, public health, social welfare, and highways, and regulation and promotion of the welfare of such interests as agriculture, labor, industry, and commerce. The steps involved include the passage of laws and subordinate regulations, the day-to-day administration of the public services in accordance with the laws, the adjudication of disputes arising under the laws, and the enforcement of rights and punishment of offenders.

Every unit of government is a complex thing with various characteristics that can best be visualized if the units are considered by separate classes. We are therefore going to consider, in turn, the states, the counties, and minor civil divisions such as towns and townships, incorporated places, and special districts. The factors to be studied fall partly in the realm of what formerly was called political arithmetic, or "statistics" in the older sense of that word, and partly in the field of political and administrative geography.

The Fifty States

★ *Area and population data*

The fifty states are the principal territorial divisions of the United States. In *area* the largest states today are far larger than the original states and much larger than many independent foreign nations. Texas is over five times as large as such original states as New York and Pennsylvania, while California, Montana, and other Western states are also considerably larger. Alaska is more than twice as large as Texas, and hence more than ten times as large as New York and Pennsylvania. But it is in *population* that the increase in scale is most striking (see Fig. 1). Today each of ten states has more population than all the original thirteen had at the first census in 1790, and the average state today (out of fifty instead of thirteen states) has more than ten times the original average state population.

The states may also be compared with all but the larger national states that make up the United Nations. In general, the South American, African, and Asiatic nations have larger areas than the individual states of the United States. Compared in area with European nations, Texas is larger than France or Spain; California nearly equals Sweden; Montana is larger than Norway; Arizona, Colorado, Nevada, and New Mexico each occupies an area comparable to that of Italy or Finland; each of the foregoing states as well as Oregon or Wyoming has an area greater than that of the British island of England, Wales, and Scotland; and the median American state (over 56,000 square miles) has an area four to five times that of Belgium, the Netherlands, or Switzerland.

Using population as a measure, New York in 1958 ranked with Canada; California with Colombia and the Union of South Africa; Pennsylvania with the Netherlands; Illinois with Belgium or Portugal; Ohio or Texas with Australia, Hungary, or Peru; Michigan with Bulgaria or Sweden; New Jersey and Missouri with Switzerland and Finland; Georgia, Minnesota, Tennessee, Virginia, or Wisconsin with Guatemala or Norway; and Connecticut, Kansas, or South Carolina with New Zealand or Puerto Rico; and so on down through states of smaller population. In area the American states generally exceed those of comparable population in Europe.

When compared with the member states or provinces of such federations as Canada or Australia, the American states are not only more numerous (50 to 10 and 6, respectively) but are also far more populous, the *average* American state equaling or exceeding the most populous Australian state and being nearly equal to the two most populous Canadian provinces. In area, however, the American states are relatively smaller.

Figure 1. POPULATION GROWTH, 1790-1958 [a]

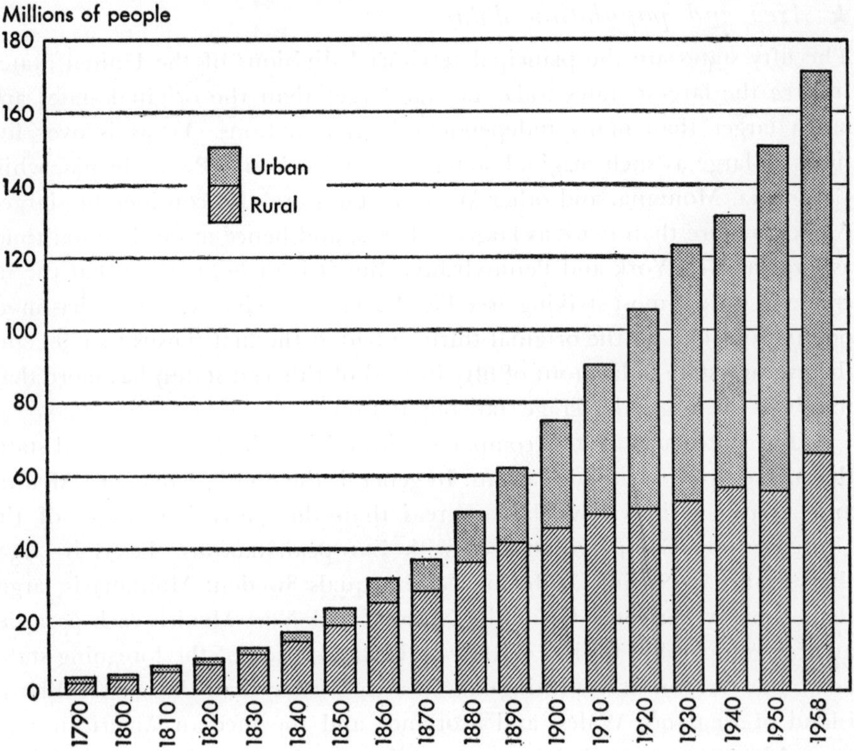

Millions of people

Source: U. S. Department of Commerce, Bureau of the Census, *Statistical Abstract of the United States, 1959*, and *Current Population Reports, Population Characteristics*, Series P-20, No. 88, November 17, 1959.

a The 1958 population estimate includes continental United States only (as do the earlier figures) and only those members of the armed forces living off the post or with their families on the post. The 1958 estimate, moreover, is based on "the new Census definition of urban."

There is no need for you to try to remember these specific population and area comparisons. They are but details to illustrate and emphasize the important fact that American state government is *big government*. It is *big democracy*.

In land area, Alaska is the largest state with 571,065 square miles of territory, and Rhode Island is the smallest with 1058 square miles. The difference is 571 to 1. In population, New York is the largest with 16,229,000, and Alaska is smallest with 211,000, a spread of over 16 million. The median state area figure is 56,154 square miles, and the median state population is 2,400,000. The average population is 3,465,180.

The differences among the states in area and in population do not coincide. Some of the largest in area, such as Alaska, Montana, Nevada, and Wyoming, are relatively small in population. Indeed the Great Plains and Mountain states generally are characterized by large areas and relatively small and sparse populations. In such states the average greater distances between families and between communities add considerably to the difficulty and the cost of providing highways, schools, and other public services. In addition these states have some of the handicaps of states like Rhode Island, Delaware, and Vermont, where both the area and the population are small. Assuming a reasonable equality of income per capita among the states, all states of small population find less need for and more difficulty in providing services such as higher education and institutions to provide specialized services for handicapped persons or the mentally deficient. In general the states of small population and correspondingly small staffs of state employees conduct their services on a smaller scale and on a less professional basis than the more populous states. They cannot afford, nor do they feel the need for, as many different classes of specialists. This difference seems to hold true to some extent in legislative and judicial work as well as in the administrative branch. After all, states like New York, Pennsylvania, and California are truly big states in the sense that they both need and can afford public services which states at the other end of the population scale cannot seriously contemplate. It does not follow that the mere existence of a large population in a state results in that state's establishing all the major services earlier than smaller states. Small states, influenced by progressive ideas, in some instances undertake services before they can really afford them, whereas large states may, because of local conditions and peculiar policies, be laggard in certain fields. Thus many frontier states hastened to establish universities before they could adequately support them—partly because of the dearth of private colleges—whereas older, more populous, wealthier states like Massachusetts and New York were late in creating state universities, partly because, within their areas, there seemed to be adequate private colleges and universities.

★ *Per-capita income*

The discussion up to this point has assumed that the ability to support services varies with the population. This would be substantially true if the income received by the people in all states were practically equal on a per-

Table 1. STATE AREAS, POPULATIONS, AND EXPENDITURES

Region and state	Population 1958 estimate[a]	Population rank	1958 State General Expenditures (in thousands)	1957 State and Local General Expenditures (in thousands)[b] [c]	Per-capita 1957 State and Local General Expenditures
United States total	174,084,000		$23,712,962	$40,419,627[c]	$237.35
New England					
Maine	952,000	36	125,101	196,870	209.66
New Hampshire	584,000	45	78,700	139,165	242.87
Vermont	372,000	47	65,508	92,212	249.22
Massachusetts	4,862,000	9	698,609	1,411,382	292.39
Rhode Island	875,000	37	124,291	179,252	209.16
Connecticut	2,316,000	26	495,016	736,586	324.63
Middle Atlantic					
New York	16,229,000	1	2,289,239	4,780,568	296.05
New Jersey	5,749,000	8	446,403	1,330,158	236.81
Pennsylvania	11,101,000	3	1,236,357	2,163,420	196.48
East North Central					
Ohio	9,345,000	6	1,143,266	2,052,132	222.91
Indiana	4,581,000	10	498,236	931,815	206.75
Illinois	9,889,000	4	1,139,490	2,208,771	227.73
Michigan	7,866,000	7	1,259,354	2,024,970	262.81
Wisconsin	3,938,000	14	491,563	937,552	242.83
West North Central					
Minnesota	3,375,000	18	485,856	851,729	256.70
Iowa	2,822,000	23	380,479	656,926	236.05
Missouri	4,271,000	13	476,418	833,922	196.78
North Dakota	650,000	44	120,069	166,845	258.67
South Dakota	699,000	40	94,574	169,568	244.69
Nebraska	1,457,000	33	142,597	290,831	202.39
Kansas	2,116,000	29	277,911	572,860	272.79
South Atlantic					
Delaware	454,000	46	116,423	105,643	243.42
Maryland	2,956,000	22	407,113	695,800	240.35
Virginia	3,935,000	15	452,996	716,695	187.22
West Virginia	1,969,000	30	245,836	303,885	154.81
North Carolina	4,549,000	11	542,040	723,506	161.79
South Carolina	2,404,000	25	270,118	366,602	154.82

Georgia	3,818,000	16	474,761	700,863	185.86
Florida	4,442,000	12	606,856	993,122	235.95
East South Central					
Kentucky	3,080,000	21	317,544	469,160	154.18
Tennessee	3,469,000	17	372,624	563,631	163.70
Alabama	3,211,000	19	383,590	563,018	178.06
Mississippi	2,186,000	28	262,533	328,895	151.84
West South Central					
Arkansas	1,766,000	32	222,322	262,656	147.56
Louisiana	3,110,000	20	691,322	847,904	276.55
Oklahoma	2,285,000	27	410,967	561,024	248.57
Texas	9,377,000	5	1,054,048	1,869,994	203.81
Mountain					
Montana	688,000	41	108,844	189,039	281.73
Idaho	662,000	42	94,388	150,458	233.27
Wyoming	320,000	48	83,620	104,131	328.49
Colorado	1,711,000	33	292,559	467,424	281.07
New Mexico	842,000	39	196,885	226,311	278.37
Arizona	1,140,000	35	188,755	294,271	272.98
Utah	865,000	38	127,912	195,216	232.40
Nevada	267,000	49	60,379	96,339	367.71
Pacific					
Alaska	211,000	50	40,044	d	d
Washington	2,769,000	24	575,549	779,885	286.20
Oregon	1,773,000	31	301,885	473,563	271.69
California	14,337,000	2	2,606,131	4,457,889	321.20
Hawaii	613,000	43	135,931	d	d

Source: U. S. Department of Commerce, Bureau of the Census, *Current Population Reports, Population Estimates Series P-25*, No. 189 (Washington, D.C.: Government Printing Office, November 12, 1958); *Compendium of State Government Finances in 1958*, G-SF58-No. 2 (Washington, D. C.: Government Printing Office, 1959); *State and Local Government Finances in 1957*, G-CGA-No. 8 (Washington, D. C.: Government Printing Office, February 1959).

a Includes District of Columbia: Area 69 sq. mi.; 1958 pop. est. 825,000. Alaska and Hawaii have been added to reported 48-state totals in each column as applicable.

b This column of state and local government expenditures is not comparable with the preceding column of state government expenditures because the first is for 1958 and this one is for 1957. The separate presentations of state government expenditures and state and local government expenditures are given since the two serve separate purposes. Whereas the state government necessarily must worry more about sufficient revenues to meet its own expenditures, the taxpayer in any community is paying his share on the combined total. In terms of comparing tax burdens or expenditures among states, the state and local figure has more meaning.

c Includes $185,169,000 of general expenditures for the District of Columbia.

d Census did not include Alaska and Hawaii in 1957 expenditure reports.

capita basis. In fact this is far from being true (see Fig. 2). Every thorough study of the income of the people of the United States has revealed striking differences from state to state. In 1957, for example, the average per-capita income in the United States was $2027. The range was from $2821 in Connecticut, $2740 in Delaware, and $2578 in New York to $1151 in Arkansas and $958 in Mississippi. In general the Middle Atlantic and Pacific Coast states were at the top and the South Atlantic and Southeastern states at the bottom of the scale, with differences as much as 3 to 1 between top and bottom, while the New England and Middle Western states held in general a midway position.

Three important bases for measuring differences among the states have now been presented: area, population, and per-capita income. The fifty states can be ranked from number 1 to number 50 on each of these scales, with rather significant results. New York, with the largest state population, practically the highest per-capita income, and a smaller-than-average area to serve, clearly stands out as the most fortunate of states from the viewpoint of supporting the public services. Other highly fortunate states are California, Illinois, Massachusetts, Michigan, Ohio, and Pennsylvania, not to mention some of smaller population. It is very difficult to give an exact ranking on the composite basis of even these three factors; and, when other factors are considered, the ranking becomes still more difficult.

Do these differences actually show up in the quantity and quality of governmental services and in the financial efforts made by the people in the various states? That would be hard indeed to prove. As already indicated, some states low in the income scale make greater efforts to support education, for example, than states of seemingly greater financial ability. One index that is of some significance is the amount per capita spent on general services. Both New York and California have over $2-billion annual state budgets, but how do they stand on a per-capita basis? Here the data in Table 1 again give us some light. We have used expenditure data for governments in each state at both the state and local level. Since states divide responsibilities differently state expenditures alone may give a distorted comparative picture.

Against an average per-capita state expenditure of $237 in 1957, New York spent $296, and California $321. These figures are high, but not the highest. Nevada led with $368, Wyoming was next with $328, Connecticut had $325, and thirty-one other states exceeded $200. At the same time the Southern states were in general at the bottom of the scale (Arkansas $148, Mississippi $152, South Carolina $155, and Virginia $187), but some favorably situated Northern states were also far below average (Indiana $207, Pennsylvania $197). Obviously many factors besides area, population, and

Figure 2. GROUPING OF STATES ACCORDING TO 1957 PER-CAPITA INCOME PAYMENTS [a]

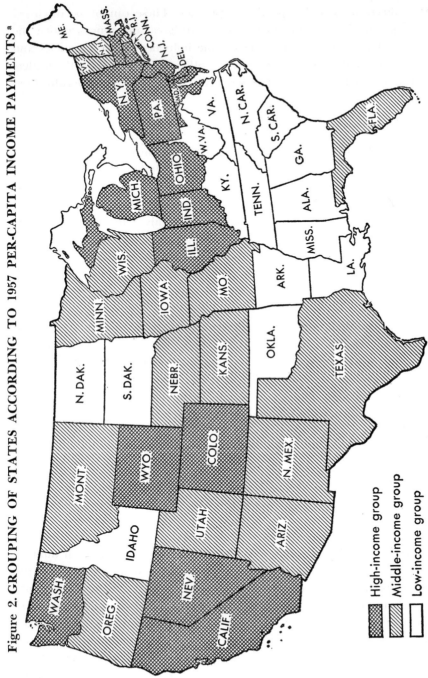

High-income group
Middle-income group
Low-income group

[a] Hawaii's per-capita income places it in the middle third. Alaska's per-capita income is not available from the Census data.

income affect the states' expenditure policies. These cannot be discussed here; it is enough to point out that there are great differences among the states and that these differences have some influence on their policies and budgets. Every state is different from every other one, and it is for the leaders in each state to know its distinctive needs and capacities and its peculiarities.

The Counties

The major territorial divisions of the state for state purposes are the counties (called parishes in Louisiana and boroughs in Alaska) (see Table 2). All states, except Connecticut (which eliminated its counties in 1959) and Rhode Island utilize such major divisions for some purposes, but the emphasis varies considerably. Rhode Island, itself only a little larger in area than an average American county, has five counties, but these are not organized for local self-government; they serve primarily as state judicial districts. In the other New England states, the counties are also relatively unimportant because the towns and cities are the principal local governments that serve as agents of the state. From New York, New Jersey, and Pennsylvania westward through the northeastern quarter of the country to and including the Dakotas, Nebraska, and Kansas, there are both counties and systems of township government to compete with each other for the right to serve as agents of the state in the handling of various services. Elsewhere —in the Southern, Mountain, and Pacific Coast states—the counties are the principal local agencies of the states and almost the exclusive ones in rural areas. Counties in the United States are both agents of the state and also, as a rule and in varying degrees, units of self-government for local purposes. Taken together, their areas cover, in most cases and to all practical purposes, the entire area of the state.

The organized *county areas* for the whole United States number 3042 or about 60 to the average state, with variations from 3 in Delaware to 254 in Texas. The average county area is about 960 square miles, but the average is brought to this high figure by the existence of a rather small number of very large counties in the Mountain and Pacific states. About half the counties are under 600 square miles in area, so that the median county area is about 600 square miles. In general the smallest counties in area are in the East and Southeast, the largest in the Mountain and Pacific Coast states, as already indicated. San Bernardino County in the mountainous and desert area of California east of Los Angeles is the largest, with 20,131 square miles of area, while several small city-counties of Virginia have only about one square mile of area each (see Fig. 3). (Alaska no doubt may eventually have the largest counties in its borough organization.)

Figure 3. COMPARISON OF AREAS OF THE LARGEST, AVERAGE, AND SMALLEST STATES AND COUNTIES, 1959

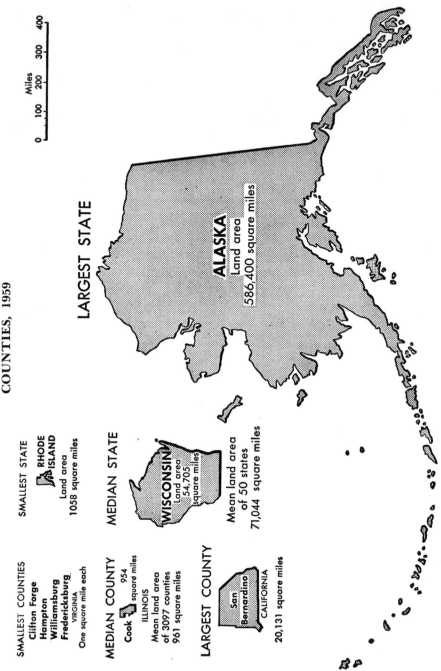

SMALLEST COUNTIES
Clifton Forge
Hampton
Williamsburg
Fredericksburg
VIRGINIA
One square mile each

SMALLEST STATE
RHODE ISLAND
Land area
1058 square miles

MEDIAN STATE
WISCONSIN
Land area
54,705
square miles

LARGEST STATE
ALASKA
Land area
586,400 square miles

MEDIAN COUNTY
Cook 954
square miles
ILLINOIS
Mean land area
of 3097 counties
961 square miles

Mean land area
of 50 states
71,044 square miles

LARGEST COUNTY
San
Bernardino
CALIFORNIA
20,131 square miles

Miles
0   100 200 300 400

Source: William Anderson, *Units of Government in the United States*, Chicago: Public Administration Service, 1949, p. 22, and updated from the *1957 Census of Local Governments*.

Table 2. GOVERNMENTAL UNITS BY STATES AND REGIONS, 1957

Region and state	All govern- mental units	Counties	Municipalities	Towns and townships	Special districts	School districts
United States total	102,384 a	3042 b	17,215	17,198 c	14,424	50,454
New England						
Maine	645	16	42	471	107	8
New Hampshire	545	10	12	222	80	220
Vermont	409	14	68	238	72	16
Massachusetts	573	12	39	312	205	4
Rhode Island	91	—	7	32	51	—
Connecticut	376	—	33	152	187	3
Middle Atlantic						
New York	4,189	57	611	932	924	1,664
New Jersey	1,217	21	333	233	140	489
Pennsylvania	5,073	66	991	1,564	34	2,417
East North Central						
Ohio	3,667	88	915	1,335	160	1,168
Indiana	2,989	92	544	1,009	313	1,030
Illinois	6,510	102	1,181	1,433	1,800	1,993
Michigan	5,160	83	498	1,262	102	3,214
Wisconsin	5,781	71	547	1,276	78	3,758
West North Central						
Minnesota	6,298	87	826	1,828	92	3,464
Iowa	4,906	99	942	—	199	3,665
Missouri	5,307	114	803	328	827	3,234
North Dakota	3,968	53	356	1,392	168	1,998
South Dakota	4,808	64	306	1,080	69	3,288
Nebraska	6,658	93	534	478	610	4,942
Kansas	6,214	105	610	1,550	808	3,140
South Atlantic						
Delaware	132	3	49	—	64	15
Maryland	328	23	149	—	155	—
Virginia	367	98	228	—	40	—
West Virginia	362	55	219	—	32	55
North Carolina	624	100	412	—	111	—
South Carolina	503	46	235	2	112	107
Georgia	1,121	159	508	—	255	198
Florida	672	67	310	—	227	67

East South Central						
Kentucky	822	120	323	—	157	221
Tennessee	560	95	255	—	195	14
Alabama	617	67	318	—	119	112
Mississippi	672	82	262	—	248	79
West South Central						
Arkansas	1,127	75	374	—	254	423
Louisiana	584	62	237	—	217	67
Oklahoma	2,332	77	506	—	105	1,643
Texas	3,485	254	793	—	645	1,792
Mountain						
Montana	1,503	56	123	—	174	1,149
Idaho	843	44	199	—	431	168
Wyoming	489	23	86	—	133	246
Colorado	1,666	62	246	—	421	936
New Mexico	317	32	77	—	112	95
Arizona	367	14	52	—	50	250
Utah	398	29	210	—	118	40
Nevada	110	17	17	—	58	17
Pacific						
Alaska	42	—	31	69	2	8
Washington	1,577	39	252	—	745	471
Oregon	1,526	36	213	—	550	726
California	3,879	57	331	—	1,650	1,840
Hawaii	22	3	1	—	17	—

Source: U. S. Department of Commerce, Bureau of the Census, *Governments in the United States, 1957 Census of Governments*, Vol. 1, No. 1 (Washington, D.C.: Government Printing Office, 1957), Table 1, p. 14. Census data for 1957 has been adjusted to reflect: (1) elimination of counties as governmental units in Connecticut in 1959; (2) admission of Alaska and Hawaii as new states, but number of governmental units in each follows 1957 census (some boroughs [counties] are having organized governments under new Alaska law).

a Includes federal government, Washington, D. C., and the fifty states, not shown in distribution by type.

b Excludes areas corresponding to counties but having no organized county government. In some states, e.g., South Dakota this means identified but unorganized county governments not included. In some states, e.g., Louisiana where Orleans Parish is consolidated with the City of New Orleans and East Baton Rouge Parish with Baton Rouge, cities are counted but not counties. Also see above note.

c Includes "towns" in the six New England states, New York, and Wisconsin.

These are the county areas in which the states organize and administer many of their financial, administrative, and judicial functions that must reach out to all the people of the state. But the number of people per county varies just as surprisingly as the county areas. In 1950 Cook County, Illinois, including Chicago, had about 4,500,000 inhabitants, in contrast to Cook County, Minnesota, with less than 3000, while Alpine County, California, had 236 and Loving County, Texas, had 227. The range here of about 14,000 to 1 in population is rather striking but also misleading. While the average county then had about 42,000 inhabitants, over four fifths of all counties had less than 40,000, and the median had about 17,000. Several hundred very populous counties, from Cook County, Illinois, down, supplied the population to pull the average county population so far above the median.

It is interesting to note, also, that the counties of largest population in most cases had rather small areas. This suggests that counties fall into a number of distinct classes, as they do. There are first the several hundred highly urban, industrial, and commercial counties of small areas, large populations, and great concentrations of wealth. At the other extreme are another several hundred counties in mountainous, semiarid, or forested regions, with large areas, sparse populations, and usually little wealth. Between these extremes lie the great majority of the county areas, largely agricultural but with some urban population, whose populations, areas, and wealth are generally medium to small.

Such are the diversities among the county areas that serve the states as local districts for certain state services. But the counties are also organized for local self-government. They have their governing bodies, certain elective officers, and an organized and usually corporate status. In some states, such as Wisconsin, the counties perform a wide range of local services as well as having numerous state responsibilities. In other states both state and local government responsibilities in the counties are few. In part the differences in roles of counties reflect tradition; in part the differences relate to the degree of urbanization in the state, with the counties tending to have a lesser role in the more highly urbanized states.

Minor Civil Divisions

★ Towns and townships

In the present day of telephones, automobiles, and airplanes, counties are often described as being uneconomically small, mere relics of the "horse-

and-buggy" days. There is some truth in this observation. When horses provided the most rapid means of local travel, the distance that a remote settler could conveniently drive or ride in one day from his home to the county seat and back again was a factor to consider in laying out the counties. Even so, many a county seemed then a rather large area to the man who had to go on foot. For this and other reasons, some of which involved tradition, geography, and other factors, all states in the northeastern part of the country provided for dividing the counties up into smaller civil divisions for services considered to be of a more local character.

New England towns.   In New England the towns were practically coeval with the colonies. They were divisions of land set off for local settlement and for the management of the local church, school, roads, and other services. Fairly large in area at first when population was scanty, they were in many cases subdivided into two, three, or more towns, often bearing a common name prefixed by North, East, South, or West. The New England colonies and states, however, as a rule did not separate the rural area from the built-up commercial center, which in other states tended to become a separate village or city. Instead they kept the rural and urban people together in town governments under their town meetings. The average areas of these New England towns have fluctuated little in recent years—from under 25 square miles in Massachusetts to just under 37 in Vermont, or about 30 square miles for the whole region. In population (excluding cities) towns have averaged from 1097 in Maine to 6347 in Rhode Island, while median populations have been even smaller, ranging from 754 in Vermont to 4400 in Rhode Island. Total and per-capita wealth is not reported by towns, but one may reasonably assume that wealth is not great in the towns of the hills and the forested areas, and that it rises to substantial figures in the more populous industrial towns. At best, however, the majority of the over 1400 New England towns are rather small units of government. Nevertheless, as units of government they are relatively strong, and it has been a matter of both state and town policy to keep them so by preventing the rise of the counties as rival effective units of government.

Middle Atlantic towns.   New York, New Jersey, and Pennsylvania also have systems of town government, but these operate within or alongside a fairly vigorous system of county governments. The towns of these three states are in general like those of New England in having irregular shapes and rather unequal areas, but toward the west both New York and Pennsylvania tend to have a checkerboard layout that anticipates to some extent the 6-x-6-mile squares of the public land townships farther west. In New Jersey and Pennsylvania the towns average in area about the same as in New England, but in New York they average over 48 square miles, or more than 50 percent larger. Pennsylvania alone has more towns (1564) than all New England, while New York has nearly a thousand (932). In population these towns and those of New Jersey average out fairly well with those of New England.

Middle Western townships. The New England-Middle Atlantic idea of town government was carried by early settlers into Ohio in the Old Northwest Territory. Here towns were established along with counties, and both were endowed with powers of self-government. Most of Ohio was affected by the system of public land surveys then being established; thereafter, and from Ohio westward, the square 6-x-6-mile areas laid out by the surveyors on east-west and north-south lines came to dominate the area pattern of town government.

These normally 36-square-mile areas, laid out by the surveyors in advance of population, were designated as "townships" on the map. Later, when they acquired population and were organized for local government, the designation of "township" clung in the people's minds, whatever the law might call them. Thus today it is still common to speak of the New England "town system" and the Middle Western "township system."

Generally speaking, in the states north of the Ohio River and west through Kansas, Nebraska, South and North Dakota, town governments were established in addition to county governments. As a rule the 6 x 6, or 36-square-mile area of the public land survey, became the area of the organized township. As a result a number of Midwestern state maps look like giant checkerboards, the counties being simply bigger squares or rectangles that are made up of a number of township squares. From this general pattern there are numerous departures. In many places major streams, lakes, badlands, arid stretches, and mountainous areas led the surveyors to accept the boundaries set by nature in place of their own straight lines. Later, local populations, with legislative approval, added to or subtracted from the normal township area when organizing or reorganizing township government to make many organized townships larger and some smaller than 36 square miles. Many surveyed townships, for lack of population or other reason, were not organized for township government. In spite of all appearances on the maps, also, there are many other differences among organized townships—differences in population, in local conditions, in wealth, and in services. In general, organized townships in the Middle West are rural and have much smaller average populations than do those in the industrial parts of New England and the Middle Atlantic states. Their number is very considerable, however—12,971 in the North Central states compared with 4156 towns in the New England and Middle Atlantic states.

The *1957 Census of Governments* continues to show that organized town and township governments are found in, roughly, the northeastern quarter of the United States, plus a few counties in the state of Washington. Even in the states where they occur, however, they do not cover the entire state, being ousted by incorporated places in the urban centers and absent for other reasons in heavily forested, cut-over, and thinly populated regions, as well as by local choice in parts of Illinois, Missouri, and some other states.

In the states south of the Mason and Dixon Line and the Ohio River, and also generally in the West, small units of rural government like the towns and townships of the Northeast do not exist. There were early experiments with parish government in Virginia and a few other states, but these have long since been abandoned in favor of leaving the counties as the only local governments for general purposes in rural areas. For judicial and census purposes, for conducting elections, assessing property for taxation, and administering other county functions, there are subdivisions of the counties in all states. They are called by a variety of names: *beats* in Mississippi, *districts* (civil, election, judicial, magisterial, militia, representative, school, and supervisorial districts) in over a dozen states, *precincts* (commissioners, election, justices) in another dozen, and *police-jury wards* in Louisiana. In these administrative areas will be found one or a few resident officials of the county or state, but the areas and the people therein are not organized as separate units of local government. Except in urban places, therefore, almost the entire emphasis in local government in these states is on the counties.

★ *Incorporated places*

In all countries it is recognized to some extent that the populations of urban places require separate local governments or administrations of their own. There are special needs arising out of the concentration of populations in small areas that cannot easily be met by governments like those of counties that are designed primarily to perform functions of state-wide concern over larger and more rural areas. Besides, the people in urban centers easily make vocal and persuasive their demands for separate local governments. All states in the United States recognize this need, but no two of them set identical standards of minimum population for establishing such urban governments or provide identically for their organization, powers, and functions. When organized, such units are variously called towns, incorporated towns, villages, boroughs, and cities. As a rule (except in Virginia), they remain within and are a part of the county for county purposes, but they are separated from such other minor civil divisions as towns or townships.

At the last census of governments (1957), there were 17,215 such incorporated places, of which 3926 had over 2500 population. By states their numbers ranged from 1181 in Illinois, 991 in Pennsylvania, and 915 in Ohio, down to 12 in New Hampshire, 7 in Rhode Island, and 1 in Hawaii. Their land areas are usually small, and all told they probably occupy less than 2 percent of the national area. On the other hand, their populations, although varying from small to very large, accounted in 1950 for over 64 percent of the nation's people—97,130,000 out of 151,000,000, of whom over 87,000,000 lived in the more strictly "urban" places of over 2500 inhabitants.[1] In many states the urban population now far outnumbers the rural—an important fact for state as well as local politics and government. Here we are mainly concerned with the fact that in the state-and-local framework of government there are many urban units to be considered. In population and in wealth they reach all the way from those with a mere handful of people and very little per-capita wealth to great and wealthy cities such as New York, Chicago, Philadelphia, and Los Angeles. While the smallest places provide only the most essential services, and that only with great difficulty, the large and wealthy cities are financially capable of performing a wide range of expensive functions that conduce to the comfort and convenience of the citizens.

Counties (called parishes in Louisiana) usually cover the entire state area and are consequently available for the performance of services that require state-wide provision. In contrast to counties, incorporated places are scattered about the state in a seemingly haphazard way. Taken by themselves these incorporated places cannot be used by the state for services that are needed by all the people and over the entire state area. However, the larger cities, say, those of 50,000 population and over, can provide such state services as education, public health, and law enforcement for their people easily on a par with the counties. Furthermore, the states that rely on town or township organizations for state functions utilize incorporated places plus the towns or townships to supply such state-wide services for practically all the people of the state. An important question then is: How effectively can this network of minor civil divisions perform a function as compared with the counties—generally much larger in area and far fewer in number?

---

[1] U. S. Department of Commerce, Bureau of the Census, *Governments in the United States, 1957 Census of Governments*, Vol. 1, No. 1 (Washington, D. C.: Government Printing Office, 1957), Table 1, p. 19, Alaska and Hawaii have been included in the analysis.

★ Ad hoc *or special districts*

Not content to assign all functions of local government and administration to the counties and the minor civil divisions, the states have created in varying numbers many classes of governmental units that are *ad hoc* or special districts for special purposes. Most widely utilized and most numerous of these are the school districts. Although reduced in numbers very considerably since the census enumeration of 1942, there still are close to 50,000 school districts in operation as units of government throughout the United States—more than all other types of local governments combined. They vary in size from petty areas that operate a single one-room school which may not have enough children to fill it, to immense districts like that of Chicago with hundreds of schools and hundreds of thousands of schoolchildren.

Besides the school districts the states have each from one or two to hundreds of other special districts in operation. These exist for water control, irrigation, roads and bridges, urban improvements, urban utilities, public housing, soil conservation, port development and administration, and many other purposes. All told these seem to number over 14,000. They vary among themselves in area, population, and available resources almost as much as other classes of local governments do. What they have in common is that each supplies only one or at most a few related services, and that their areas have been defined with an eye to the service to be performed. Some are called districts, some authorities, some boards or commissions, but all are more or less autonomous units of local government.

★ *Other areas and agencies*

The full richness and complexity of the apparatus through which state and local governments carry out their functions is only partly revealed by the foregoing sketch of the units of local government. *First*, there are many *districts* or areas laid out for purposes of elections, judicial administration, civil administration (as of highways, law enforcement, tax assessment and collection, relief, public health, school attendance, and so on), and local improvements that are not separately organized with governing bodies of their own. Police precincts and election precincts in cities are good examples. *Second*, there are uncounted numbers of *boards, commissions,* and *committees* connected with state and local government that are not separate units of government but eyes and ears and arms of the state, city, or county to which they are attached. Finally, *third*, there are other uncounted numbers of borderline agencies that perform important public and semipublic services in agricultural and consumers' credit, rural electrification, veterans' needs, charity, and other fields too numerous to attempt to list. Some of these seem outwardly to be mere private associations, but many receive public funds and perform public services.

At this point all we aim to present is a broad and comprehensive view, as from an airplane, of a teeming and diversified multitude of governments, groups, and agencies that operate in the region we are about to explore.

REFERENCES

U. S. Department of Commerce, Bureau of the Census, *Governments in the United States, 1957 Census of Governments.* Washington, D. C.: Government Printing Office, 1957.

CHAPTER 3

The States and the
Union

OUR FEDERAL ". . . SYSTEM has characteristically been very flexible, leaving
a great deal of room for argument and adjustment. The division of powers
between the Nation and the States leaves substantial authority with each,
but the use and relative importance of powers may shift." [1] Federalism is
not an exact and invariable division of powers between two levels of government. The national Constitution sets the framework of federalism, but
the political process determines the boundaries of state and national power
at any given moment. And the boundary lines permit joint occupancy of
many areas. Understanding federalism and the role of the states in the union *begins* with a knowledge of the pertinent Constitutional provisions and
their interpretations in practice and by the federal courts, but it is *completed* only with appreciation of the variety of factors molding it. Emphasis
merely on legal provisions and formal structure will prevent understanding
of federalism. *Legally* the national government has had power to establish
a national system of education or at least to provide grants-in-aid for education with specific national standards. *Politically* this has been a function
largely reserved to local governments with some state participation.

1 The Commission on Intergovernmental Relations, *A Report to the President for Transmittal to the Congress* (Washington, D. C.: Government Printing Office, 1955), p. 11.

The Constitutional Position of the States

With the adoption of the Articles of Confederation, the states accepted a confederate government under which each state still retained ". . . its sovereignty, freedom and independence, and every power, jurisdiction and right, which is not by this confederation expressly delegated to the United States, in Congress assembled." What aspects of "sovereignty, freedom and independence" and so forth that the states gave up with the adoption of the Constitution have been the subject of continuing debate. The Constitution laid out some prohibitions on state action and delegated to the new national government more powers than the Congress under the Articles had had. The Civil War decided the right of secession against the states. Beginning with the 13th Amendment, most of our formal Constitutional changes have tended to restrict the states. Many of the Supreme Court's decisions have limited the states first in substantive matters and later in procedural ways. Twentieth-century Presidents and Congresses have, by expanding national programs, increased the role of the national government and thereby decreased at least the prestige of the states. Yet in some ways all of these things add up to this summary: the role of government generally is greater today; the national government has increased its functions and asserted its superior sovereignty; but the states still have responsibility for more services today than at any time in the past.

★ Early position

A convention of delegates from the several states drew up the Constitution in 1787. Congress submitted the Constitution to specially called conventions in the states, and these conventions ratified the Constitution during the years 1787-1788.

According to the preamble of the Constitution, "We the people of the United States" ordained and established the Constitution in order to form a more perfect union, and for other purposes, but specified ratification by "the conventions of nine states" as necessary to place the Constitution in effect. Thus the act was done in the name of the whole people but by special conventions in the states. The regular state authorities, legislatures and executives, were not directly consulted, nor was the Constitution submitted to a vote of the people.

Instead of "articles of confederation" the new document called itself a "constitution." Nowhere does the Constitution designate the "more perfect union" as either a confederation or a federation. It uses only the terms *Union* and *United States*. There are no words to designate the Constitution as a treaty, compact, or confederation of the states. Furthermore, the Constitution declares itself to be "the supreme law of the land," and also puts into the supreme-law category "laws of the United States which shall be made in pursuance" of the Constitution and "all treaties made, or which shall be made, under the authority of the United States." Nowhere in the document are there any words that assert the sovereignty or independence of the states or that limit the national government to the powers expressly granted. Indeed, the Constitution binds all judges, legislators, and executive officers of the states, along with those of the nation, to take an oath to support the Constitution. Taken all together, these clauses indicate a very substantial change in the position of the states as a result of the transition from the Articles of Confederation to the Constitution.

Another great change took place in the form of the central government and in the relations of the states to it. Under the Articles there was only one organ of central authority, the Congress of the United States, and its members were under the control of the state legislatures. The Constitution, on the other hand, provided for a complete central government of three branches, legislative, executive, and judicial, with ample powers for each. Only one half of one of these branches, the Senate, was left to be chosen directly by the state legislatures, and even its members were not made subject to recall by the states or dependent upon them for their remuneration. The members of the House of Representatives were to be chosen directly by the voters in each state, while the President was to be elected by Presidential electors, not by any branch of the state governments, and the members of the courts were to be appointed by the President with Senate approval. Thus the scales were tipped heavily in favor of an autonomous national government, one that stood on its own feet, not dependent upon the state governments, while the states lost their top-dog position of control over the central government.

With great wisdom and patience the early leaders of the republic under the Constitution gave the central government the authority and responsibility necessary for an effective national existence and this without any unnecessary affronts to the states. The two levels of government operated to a large extent in separate channels, sufficiently removed from and parallel to each other, so that open conflicts were very few, and those few were in part resolved by Supreme Court decisions.

Then the disentanglement of the national from the state governments was carried further. The Presidential electors came to be chosen in all states by popular vote, no longer by state legislatures as some had been in the early days. National-party nominating conventions arose to eliminate any serious possibility of state legislatures trying to nominate Presidential candidates. Much later some states provided for popular votes on United

States Senators, and in 1913 the states completed ratification of the 17th Amendment by which the voters in all states were authorized to elect the Senators. Thus the last important vestige of control by the state governments over the government of the United States was eliminated. In the meantime various Supreme Court decisions had somewhat limited the power of the states to control national elections, including primaries, and had asserted the power of Congress to regulate campaign expenditures and various other aspects of national campaigns and elections.

The 14th Amendment, adopted in 1868, made other significant changes in the position of the states in the Union. It imposed on them several new restrictions—due process and equal protection, for example. It also established national citizenship for all persons born or naturalized in the United States and subject to the jurisdiction thereof and made that citizenship primary, so that state citizenships became only secondary and derivative. The bearing of this change on the position of the states in the Union will be discussed later.

★ The present constitutional position of the states

Just as the position of the states in the Union is an ever-changing one, and partly for that reason, there is constant disagreement among publicists as to the nature of the Union and as to the states' position therein. In the next few paragraphs we summarize the now-prevailing theory on the subject, without denying that other views may be held or without attempting to argue against any contrary views. After all, a theory is a general proposition that conforms as nearly as possible to the facts, and men will always differ in their views of the facts. The following statements turn upon the written Constitution of the United States as interpreted and applied in Supreme Court decisions and the actions and acquiescences of both national and state authorities.

1. The people as the source of the Constitution. "We the people of the United States . . . do ordain and establish this Constitution for the United States of America." This proposition from the preamble asserts the official theory of the popular origin of the Constitution. In fact a convention of delegates from the states drew up the Constitution, and conventions in the several states approved it. The theory of such constitutional conventions is that in the making of constitutions they represent the people more fully than any other type of representative body could possibly do. The people did not vote on the Constitution, and no one knows how they would have voted if they had had the opportunity. It is important, however, that at the time the Constitution (including the statement quoted) was accepted and acquiesced in by all the state legislatures, governors, and other officials of the states, and that it came in a relatively short time to have widespread popular support. Furthermore, a constitution as a body of rules for government receives its force and sanction not from the original act of adopting a certain document but from the people who operate it and live under its rules at any particular time. Since 1788 the people of the United States have become a nation with national citizenship. It is their acceptance and support of the Constitution today, as modified and interpreted by the theory of popular sovereignty, that give the Constitution its sanction and support. It is the people of 1960 who in 1960 are the source and strength of the Constitution as it is in 1960—and so on for every year in the future that the Constitution shall endure. This is, we believe, the accepted theory of the popular source of the Constitution.

2. The states under the Constitution. By its own words the Constitution declares itself to be a constitution "for the United States of America" and also "the supreme law of the land, . . . any Thing in the Constitution or Laws of any State to the Contrary notwithstanding" (Art. VI, par. 2). All state officers, legislative, executive, and judicial, must take an oath to support the Constitution as such supreme law. From these and other parts of the written Constitution as now interpreted, it follows that in constitutional theory (1) no state may legally do anything that is not authorized for states to do or that is forbidden to them by the Constitution and (2) that, in the constitutional sense, all the states derive their powers *from the United States Constitution*. Whatever may have been the situation at the Declaration of Independence in 1776, when the states claimed to have inherent, original, and sovereign powers, the adoption of the United States Constitution changed the constitutional situation beginning in 1788. Thereafter their powers derived from the Constitution, and no change in constitutional practice and theory since then has detracted from this central principle. It is interesting but futile to hark back to the situation before 1788 to find the constitutional position of the states today.[2]

---

[2] Attempts have been made in several states to get the courts to say that because towns existed and exercised powers in those places before the colonies and later states were formed, those towns never gave up their sovereign right of local self-government to the colony or state. The facts vary and are somewhat disputed in these cases, but the parallel between them and the historical claims for state sovereignty against the national government because of the prior exercise of powers by the states is obvious. In the local self-government cases the decisions have been almost uniformly against the claims of the towns. State of Connecticut *ex rel.* Bulkeley *v.* Williams, 68 Conn. 131 (1896); City of Newport *v.* Horton, 22 R. I. 196 (1900); and see Howard Lee McBain, "The Doctrine of an Inherent Right of Local Self-government," 16 *Col. Law Rev.*, 190, 299 (1916).

3. The states as agents of the nation. For its own enforcement, and for the conduct of government under it, the Constitution recognizes and establishes both a national government and the state governments. The officers of both are required to swear to uphold the Constitution. Their respective powers and functions in government are set forth, and thus their duties as distinct agents of the nation—that is, of the American people—are approximately defined. In short, the state governments, acting within their powers and their respective land areas, are as much agents of the people of the United States as the national government is.

"The Constitution, in all its provisions, looks to an indestructible Union, composed of indestructible states." [3] This is true, but it is not the whole truth. It suggests a fixed and static situation. The states and their governments have also a positive role in the performance of governmental services for the American people under the Constitution. While each state government has a special responsibility for the people within its own state's area, it has also certain duties (to be dealt with hereafter) toward the nation or people as a whole. The role of the state governments is different from that of the national government, but in a constitutional sense it is no less important and no less firmly established by the Constitution.

This general view was clearly asserted at the very beginning. Considering whether the national or the state governments would have the greater support from the people, James Madison said in *The Federalist,* No. 45:

> Notwithstanding the different modes in which they are appointed, we must consider both of them as substantially dependent on the great body of citizens of the United States. . . . The federal and state governments are in fact but different agents and trustees of the people, constituted with different powers, and designated for different purposes. The adversaries of the Constitution seem to have lost sight of the people altogether, in their reasoning on this subject; and to have viewed these different establishments, not only as mutual rivals and enemies, but as uncontrolled by any common superior, in their efforts to usurp the authorities of each other. These gentlemen must here be reminded of their error. They must be told, that the ultimate authority, wherever the derivative may be found, resides in the people alone.

4. The equality of the states. The states are constitutionally equal, one to another, no matter what their areas or populations. In proof of this equality it is customary to refer to the equal votes of the states in the Senate. This is by no means the only respect in which the states are constitutionally equal, but it is an important point and one that is constantly in evidence. Furthermore, the amending article of the Constitution emphasizes its im-

---

[3] C. J. Chase in Texas *v.* White, 7 Wall. 700 (1869).

portance by providing "that no State, without its Consent, shall be deprived of its equal Suffrage in the Senate" (Art. V).

In addition to (1) equality of representation in the Senate, as noted above, the states are equal in the following respects, among others: (2) in the adoption of amendments to the United States Constitution, each state counts as one; (3) in the election of the President by the House of Representatives, in case the electors fail to make a choice, each state delegation in the House counts as one.

Every state is guaranteed a minimum of one Representative in Congress, and a minimum of three Presidential electors. These provisions assure each state of not complete equality but of an equal minimum with every other state.

In other provisions, also, the Constitution clearly evinces an intention of the framers that no favoritism should be shown by the central government to particular states over others. They are all and equally guaranteed a republican form of government, protection in case of invasion and domestic violence, assurance against the ports of any state being given preferential treatment by Congress over the ports of other states, the preservation of their territorial limits except as changed with their own consent, at least initial control over elections, and an equal reservation of the powers not delegated by the Constitution to the United States. Likewise the states are all equally under the same Constitutional restrictions and prohibitions. In short, the Constitution does not discriminate for or against any state or states by name or by region. Except for representation in the House of Representatives and the proportionate number of Presidential electors, both of which vary with population, the Constitution treats all states as legally equals.

This rule of equality covers the states later admitted as well as the original states. Although the words "New states may be admitted by the Congress into this Union" do not explicitly assert a necessary equality between newer and older states, the Supreme Court insists that no state can be more or less than a state, and that *this Union* means a union of constitutionally equal states.[4]

★ *The autonomy of the states*

At the present time the states appear to be autonomous and self-governing but not independent or sovereign units within the Union. They are autonomous in the sense that whatever powers and functions they have under the Constitution they may exercise on their own initiative and responsibility,

[4] Coyle *v.* Smith, 221 U. S. 559 (1911); United States *v.* State of Texas, 339 U. S. 707 (1950).

They do not need to get enabling legislation from Congress or executive approval from the President to utilize the powers that they possess. The normal presumption is that they will act lawfully, according to the Constitution, laws, and treaties of the United States, and that if they overstep their authority so as to invade the rights of others, they will in due time be checked by action in the courts or in Congress or elsewhere. Included among their powers are those of making and changing their own constitutions and laws, setting up and operating their own legislative, administrative, and judicial systems, and establishing and operating such functions, services, and institutions as they deem best.

Under the United States Constitution every state is free to pass such laws and undertake such functions and enterprises as the proper authorities of the state deem best. State powers and functions are largely undefined and residual, including all those powers of government that are left over after the Constitutional grant of certain powers to the national government. Except that it may not tax imports, exports, and instrumentalities of the national government, a state may adopt any system of taxation that is consistent with ordinary due process. Keeping only within the rule that its government must be republican in form, a state may alter its government as it sees fit and may set up such systems of local government and administration as it chooses. Every state has, in short, a very wide range of choices with respect to what it shall do, how it shall organize its government, and how it shall finance its services. The states have also a recognized position in and under the United States Constitution so that only by Constitutional amendments that would require approval of three fourths of the states could the states be deprived of any of their present autonomy. And the United States Congress and Supreme Court have shown a respect for state autonomy that promises it a long continuance.

Counties and other local governments, on the other hand, are legally inferior to the states on all the points mentioned and on a number of others. They have only such powers and functions as the state has clearly conferred upon them, and in most cases these may be modified or withdrawn by simple legislative act. Local governments have hardly any freedom in the matter of tax systems or the sources and amounts of their revenue. Except in a few states where there is a broad grant of county or municipal home rule, counties and other local units must accept the forms of government, official salary scales, the range of functions, and even the minute procedural regulations that are laid down for them by their states. They are also legally agents of the state, and as such are required to perform the services set for them by state law. For failure to perform their duties properly they can be sued in ordinary courts without their own consent.

The Role of the States in the National Government

It is clear that the framers of the Constitution and its amendments, at least down to the Civil War, tried to keep the state and national governments in somewhat separate channels so that neither could interfere seriously with the other. Nevertheless there has always been and there still is some interdependence among them. Let us now consider what the states and their governments have to do with the conduct of the national government as such.

★ Suffrage and elections

The Constitution does not explicitly define what persons may vote for Representatives and Senators in Congress. Instead it stipulates that "the Electors in each State shall have the Qualifications requisite for Electors of the most numerous Branch of the State Legislature" (Art. I, sec. 2, par. 1; 17 Amend., par. 1). This ties the national voting requirements to those of the states, so that the same lists of voters may be used and the state and national elections may be readily conducted at the same time and place. The clause does not permit any state to define separately who may vote for members of Congress. Moreover, those who favor Congressional legislation to outlaw the poll tax have raised the question as to what "qualifications" for voting the states are entitled to fix. Is payment of a poll tax an actual qualification or test of ability that shows a man to be able to vote intelligently and responsibly? Or is it just a tax on voting, an obstacle to voting, that may not be imposed upon citizens who are actually qualified? As yet there is no answer to this question, but there is still a desire in some quarters for Congressional legislation that will outlaw the poll tax as an improper "qualification" for voting.

The actual conduct of elections for members of Congress is in practice left in the hands of the states. This does not seem to be required by the Constitution. In the words of the Constitution: "The Times, Places and Manner of holding Elections for Senators and Representatives, shall be prescribed in each State by the Legislature thereof; but the Congress may at any time by Law make or alter such Regulations . . ." (Art. I, sec. 4, par. 1). This clause is a direct delegation by the Constitution to the state legislatures of the power to pass laws for the election of members of Congress, and a delegation of power to Congress to override such laws by laws of its own. Nothing is said about the administration of such elections. As a matter of convenience the state and local officers who conduct state and local elections are left to handle the national elections also, but there is nothing in the Constitution that specifically authorizes or requires this. Except for the long continuance of the practice and the admitted convenience of it, the assumption might well be that national officials should conduct national elections and state officials, state elections. Congress has, in fact, passed some legislation to regulate Congressional elections, and state election officials who violate such laws are subject to national penalties. In conducting national elections they are, so to speak, officers of the national government. Furthermore, should any states ever fail to cooperate loyally in the conduct of Congressional elections, it almost certainly lies in the power of Congress to provide for direct national administration of such elections, as was done in the Civil War and Reconstruction period. The right of the national government to protect and preserve itself has been asserted many times by Presidents and the Supreme Court.

The choice of Presidential electors is provided for in different constitutional language. "Each State shall appoint [note the word] in such Manner as the Legislature thereof may direct, a Number of Electors, equal to the whole Number of Senators and Representatives to which the State may be entitled in the Congress . . ." (Art. II, sec. 1, par. 2). This language lays a duty upon each state to see that its quota of electors is appointed or elected for each Presidential election, but it also seems to give state legislatures great freedom in the choice of methods of appointing or electing them. At one time many Presidential electors were chosen by the legislatures themselves, but today all the states devolve this duty and power upon the voters at general elections. Any attempt by a state legislature to withdraw this power from the voters and take it back into its own hands would arouse great public opposition. There are proposals, indeed, to eliminate the Presidential electors and to have the voters cast ballots directly on Presidential and Vice Presidential candidates. For the time being this seems to be the more likely direction of reform. In the meantime, the states perform a national constitutional duty in providing for the choice of Presidential electors.

★ Filling of vacancies in Congress

The Constitution lays several express duties upon the governors of the states to provide for filling Congressional vacancies. As to Representatives it provides that "When vacancies happen in the representation from any State, the Executive Authority thereof shall issue Writs of Election to fill such Vacancies" (Art. I, sec. 2, par. 4). As to Senate vacancies the wording is that "When vacancies happen in the representation of any State in the Senate, the executive authority of such State shall issue writs of election to fill such vacancies: *Provided,* that the legislature of any State may empower the executive thereof to make temporary appointments until the people fill the vacancies by election as the legislature may direct" (17 Amend., par. 2). The power to fill United States Senate vacancies until the next regular election is now generally vested in the governors by state law.[5]

★ Amendment of the Constitution

The state legislatures have one certain but weak and one contingent but potentially decisive power with respect to amending the United States Constitution (Article V). The *first* is the power to apply to Congress for the calling of a convention to propose Constitutional amendments. A legislature may do this at any time, but Congress may ignore the request—as it may ignore any other petition—unless two thirds of all the state legislatures make it. Even then there is no definite way whereby Congress can be compelled to call such a convention, and if Congress does issue the call, it is still doubtful whether the convention called will propose any amendments of the kinds that the state legislatures might desire.

The *second* power is that of ratifying or rejecting any Constitutional amendments that Congress itself may submit to the state legislatures. If Congress does make such a submission, the approval of three fourths of the state legislatures suffices to make the amendment a part of the Constitution, as with the 22d Amendment (1951), whereas if just one legislative house in each of one fourth plus one of the state legislatures (thirteen states out of fifty) refuses to ratify, the amendment fails. However, Congress may, if it so chooses, get around the state legislatures entirely by submitting proposed amendments to conventions in the states, as it did in submitting the 21st Amendment to repeal the 18th. Thus, while the states in a sense participate in amending the United States Constitution, the regular branches of the state government are not guaranteed any direct part in the process. The governors are not consulted, and the legislatures may be ignored.

★ Ceding of lands to the national government

From time to time the national government needs to acquire additional land within the states for various public purposes. The Constitution includes the following pertinent provision among the powers of Congress:

> The Congress shall have Power . . . To exercise exclusive Legislation in all Cases whatsoever, over such District (not exceeding ten Miles square) as may, by Cession of particular States, and the acceptance of Congress, become the Seat of the Government of the United States, and to exercise like Authority over all Places purchased by the Consent of the Legislature of the State in which the Same shall be, for the Erection

[5] See the collection of state regulations on this subject in *Senate Election Cases from 1913 to 1940*, Senate Document 147, 76th Cong., 1st Sess., pp. 748-757.

of Forts, Magazines, Arsenals, dock-Yards, and other needful Buildings; . . . (Art. I, sec. 8, pars. 1, 17).

Aside from the amending clause, this is the one provision of the Constitution that calls for concurrent state and national action in the exercise of any power set forth in the Constitution. Both clauses provide for changes in the existing constitutional rules, and we might generalize by saying that in the performance of their separate functions the state and national governments are separate and autonomous, whereas any change in the basic rules that will affect both calls for some sort of joint or concurrent action. As a matter of fact the effect of the clause concerning territorial jurisdiction is far more limited than might be supposed. The national government has the power to acquire what land it needs in any state by either purchase or condemnation. Its priority of right is such that it may in certain instances even take land that is already devoted to a state or local public use. It appears that only when the national government desires any considerable tract of land and wants to exercise exclusive jurisdiction over the tract does it proceed by the method of asking state consent. The states have in some cases granted exclusive jurisdiction and in other instances have reserved some measure of state control.

★ Joint control of state militia

The militia clauses of the United States Constitution suggest one other instance of a state check upon a national power. These clauses read that "Congress shall have power"

> To provide for calling forth the Militia to execute the Laws of the Union, suppress Insurrections and repel Invasions;
> To provide for organizing, arming, and disciplining the Militia, and for governing such Part of them as may be employed in the Service of the United States, reserving to the States respectively, the Appointment of the Officers, and the Authoriy of training the Militia according to the discipline prescribed by Congress; . . . (Art. I, sec. 8, pars. 15, 16).

Evidently these clauses assume the militia to be both a national and a state force, and give Congress a substantial priority in control. The states may appoint the militia officers and train the militia according to a discipline prescribed by Congress, but they have no Constitutional power to obstruct national control of the militia or to veto national use of the militia forces. This is not a clear instance, therefore, of state consent being required for the exercise of a national power.

★ *Conclusions*

In general the government of the United States is not Constitutionally dependent upon state help or state consent in the performance of any of its functions. Even in the conduct of elections, Congress may at any time resort to national legislation and national administration, and if it ever does so, it will probably find some way to define the qualifications of voters in accordance with the Constitution. Be that as it may, the state legislatures and governors serve to some extent now as agents of the nation for election purposes.

The Role of the National Government in the Government of the States

If the state governments play only a minor role in the operation of the national government, the reverse is not true. Most of the time and in most of their actions the states suffer but little direct intervention from the central authorities. In the following pages we deal mainly with certain Constitutional provisions that bring the national authorities into direct contact with the states and their governments. The far more extensive contacts that occur in the daily operations of national and state authorities, including administration of the grant-in-aid programs, without special Constitutional provisions will be dealt with in later chapters.

★ *Admission of new states*

The framers provided that the Constitution should be in effect among the ratifying states as soon as nine states had ratified. As a matter of fact the leaders hoped and expected that all thirteen original states would promptly come under "the new roof." There was also some hope that Canada, as then organized, might desire to enter the Union, and there were the growing settlements in the western lands. As to the latter the old Congress had made several ordinances for temporary territorial government and ultimate statehood. In the Northwest Ordinance (July 1787), for example, Congress provided that from three to five states were to be formed in the Northwest Territory, north of the Ohio and east of the Mississippi, and that "whenever any of the said states shall have sixty thousand free inhabitants therein, such state shall be admitted, by its delegates, into the Congress of the United States, on an equal footing with the states, in all respects whatever; and shall be at liberty to form a permanent constitution and state government: Provided, The constitution and government so to be formed, shall be republican . . ." (Art. V of the compact clauses in par. 14).

Thus the pattern was set for the provision in the Constitution (Art. IV, sec. 3, par. 1) worded as follows:

> New states may be admitted by the Congress into this Union; but no new State shall be formed or erected within the Jurisdiction of any other State; nor any State be formed by the Junction of two or more States, or parts of States, without the Consent of the Legislatures of the States concerned as well as of the Congress.

Thirty-seven states have been brought into the Union by Congress under this provision, but the procedure has not in all cases been the same. Vermont came in with the consent of New York, which had claimed the Vermont area; Maine, which had been a separate province of Massachusetts, became a state with the latter's consent; and Congress during the Civil War accepted the legislature set up in West Virginia, while Virginia was in secession, as the legislature authorized to consent to the admission of West Virginia as a separate state. Texas, after revolting from Mexican rule, operated for nearly ten years as an independent republic and then entered the Union under a joint resolution of Congress. Each of these four admissions had unique features and reveal the flexibility of the admissions clause.

The other thirty-three states have in general been carved out of or set up in lands acquired by the United States as parts of its public domain, but the circumstances and procedures have varied. For example, California, like Texas, came into the Union without preliminary status as a territory.

The original states came in with boundaries already established simply by accepting the Constitution. Nearly all the others have had their boundaries set by Congress and have been admitted to the Union by Congressional acts of admission that stipulated one or more conditions. In many cases the acts of admission have been preceded by "enabling acts" passed by Congress to permit the people within described boundaries to hold a constitutional convention, draft and adopt a state constitution, and petition for entry into the Union thereunder. A state constitution so formulated usually contained clauses expressing the state's acceptance of the boundaries set by Congress and any other stipulated conditions (such as the nontaxability of United States lands within the state), and this document was before Congress when the act of admission was being discussed. Parts of the proceedings had the appearance of a treaty negotiation between Congress and the embryonic state, but under the Constitution the result was not a treaty at all but an act of Congress setting up a new state and admitting it to the Union. Congress and the population of the area seeking statehood were not like two equal and independent nations making a treaty, although in the admission of Texas there was a semblance of such a relationship. On the other hand, the new state did not make any partnership or federative arrangement with the states already in the Union. It had no direct negotiations with them.

In the view of the Supreme Court of the United States, an act of Congress admitting a state to the Union is the exercise of a specific power granted to Congress by the American people through the Constitution. That power is the power to admit states, and, as previously stated, every state admitted to the Union, including each original state, is the Constitutional equal of every other one—no more and no less. Congress may set conditions for admission, such as boundaries, that are completed in the act of admission. Every state must have boundaries, and there is no discrimination against any incoming state in insisting that it accept certain territorial limits. Congress may also make property arrangements with any state, such as granting it certain lands, reserving others for national ownership, and preventing state taxation of United States property. The latter is in fact a Constitutional rule that hardly needs to be stated in the act of admission. But Congress may not limit the political or law making powers of any state so as to leave it with fewer powers than other states have. When in the admission of Oklahoma Congress stipulated that the state capital should not be moved from its then location for a period of ten years, and Oklahoma moved it anyway, the Supreme Court held that Congress had exceeded its powers.[6] Similarly under present Constitutional doctrines Congress presumably could not limit any incoming state to one United States Senator or limit its powers to amend its own constitution, to give but two examples.

★ National guarantees to the states

On entering the Union under the Constitution the original states gave up the power to raise their own troops, to keep troops and ships of war in time of peace, and various other rights they had previously claimed. In partial recompense for these sacrifices they received the following assurances in the Constitution (Art. IV, sec. 4):

> The United States shall guarantee to every State in this Union a Republican Form of Government, and shall protect each of them against Invasion; and on Application of the Legislature, or of the Executive (when the Legislature cannot be convened) against domestic Violence.

Republican form of government. The Constitution does not define a republican form of government, but one is safe in surmising that at a mini-

[6] Coyle v. Smith, 221 U. S. 559 (1911).

mum it implies a nonmonarchical form. Beyond that one can do little more than guess. If it means government under popular control, then dictatorships, whether fascist or communist ("dictatorship of the proletariat"), would probably also be disapproved. The Supreme Court seems to consider the question of republican form to be essentially a "political" rather than a judicial question, and it refused to invalidate the state-wide initiative and referendum when they were attacked as being "democratic" in the old sense of direct, popular government instead of "representative" or republican.

The "hands-off" policy of the Supreme Court raises the question: Who is responsible for guaranteeing to each state a republican form of government? The provision on this subject is almost unique in its language. Instead of saying that Congress or the President or the courts shall do something, it says *the United States shall*. This leaves the matter at large, at least to the extent of not specifying whether Congress or the President shall do it. Actually it may mean that each may do what is appropriate within the range of its or his powers, and that an act of Congress defining and authorizing what is to be done, to be enforced by the President, would probably meet the Constitutional requirements. There is no such statute, and in the absence thereof it is assumed that the houses of Congress might do something to bring a state back to a republican form by refusing to seat members sent up from such a state. This would be a very mild penalty, and in the sense of a tough dictatorship set up in a particular state—not an impossible event, by the way—far more drastic action might be needed. This would be especially true if the dictatorship in a state represented a political party that was spreading its control to other states.

Except in the Civil War and Reconstruction period the national government of the United States has not had to face seriously the problem of intervention in state affairs in order to preserve a republican form in every state. This appears to be a fortunate circumstance, but it should not be allowed to lull the people into thinking that revolutionary dictatorships "cannot happen here." General public education, a high standard of living, and a strong spirit of liberty and local self-government appear to be excellent preventives of antidemocratic movements, but they offer no absolute guarantees. Congress and the President may at any time have to face the issue of how to assure every state of a republican form of government.

Protection against invasion and domestic violence.   The overthrow of a government sometimes accompanies an armed invasion, and in other cases it is brought about by internal violence. The preservation of republican government may be closely tied to the prevention of such disasters. With practically complete control over the nation's military might, the national government has a clearly marked responsibility for defense of all states and all the people against foreign invaders. But evidently the framers of the Constitution feared every sort of intervention by the national government in the affairs of the states. For cases of domestic violence they provided that the national authorities were to interfere to protect the states on application of the state legislature or the state executive. Does this mean that the President may not act to restore order by force without a request from the state concerned? The practice seems to be against this interpretation.[7] Domestic violence interferes with national responsibilities such as the postal service, collection of taxes, and regulation of commerce as well as with state and local functions. Congress may provide for such situations, and, even in the absence of legislation, the President may act to see that the laws are enforced. To some extent the President has implied powers to act in such emergencies.[8]

Territorial integrity. The clause already quoted on the admission of new states is in part a Constitutional guaranty of the territorial integrity of each state within its present boundaries. Without a state's consent—and in practice that means without a state government's consent—Congress may make no change in a state's boundaries or area, nor may Congress acquire exclusive jurisdiction over any land within a state without its consent. These provisions are entirely consistent with the power of the Supreme Court to decide boundary disputes between states. In a number of interstate lawsuits to settle boundary disputes, Supreme Court decisions have established various rules that protect state boundaries and ward off interstate violence.

Equality in the Senate. No state may without its consent be deprived of its equal suffrage in the Senate. Such a guaranty might, of course, be eliminated in fact by revolutionary action, but is there any Constitutional means by which the change may be made? Suggestions have been made that it might be done by two Constitutional amendments in succession, the first simply eliminating the guaranty from Article V of the Constitution and the second introducing whatever change is desired in Senate representation. This suggestion outlines a possibly correct procedure, but it overlooks im-

[7] See Bennett M. Rich, *The Presidents and Civil Disorder* (Washington, D. C.: Brookings Institution, 1941).
[8] *In re* Neagle, 135 U. S. 1 (1890); *In re* Debs, 158 U. S. 564 (1895). When President Eisenhower sent troops into Little Rock in 1957 to protect Negro children attending Central High School (and to prevent state troops from barring their attendance), the state of Arkansas did not attempt to contest in the courts the President's authority to use the troops in the enforcement of a federal right.

portant factors. If there is in the Constitution any element of a compact or solemn moral agreement among the states, it is the agreement for equal representation of the states in the Senate. Many citizens would experience a strong feeling of revulsion against a suggested breach of this long-established understanding. Furthermore, if the action were to be taken by having Congress propose the amendments, it is most unlikely that two thirds of the Senators could be induced to approve. And at present, certainly, there is no important agitation for such a change.

Regulation of interstate relations. Under its power to enact necessary and proper laws for making effective the United States Constitution and other powers vested by the Constitution in the national government, Congress has legislated for the carrying out of the "full-faith-and-credit" idea, for the return to the state of the crime of persons accused of crime, for making interstate compacts possible, and for regulating interstate commerce (which has been described broadly as intercourse among the states). There is a respectable body of Congressional legislation for the regulation of such interstate affairs. These laws will be discussed in a later chapter.

Grants-in-aid and interdependent legislation. An important recent development not mentioned in the Constitution is the grants-in-aid system for such functions as highways, welfare, and public health, which the nation helps to support and the states administer. To facilitate national-state cooperation in these and other fields, state laws have been enacted in many instances to conform to and support Congressional enactments. In all such cases the national authorities exercise a certain amount of supervision over what the states do.

National Restrictions on the States

The Constitution not only makes guarantees to the states and by the 10th Amendment places the reserve powers of government in the hands of the states, but it also lays down some important restrictions on the states and confines the stream of their activities. Also not expressly mentioned in the Constitution is the power, and practice, of the United States courts to decide in appropriate cases whether specific state laws and the actions of state administrators and judges in enforcing them conform to the Constitution of the United States both as to the powers given exclusively to the national government and the prohibitions laid on the exercise of state authority.

The practice of judicial review is one of the most pervasive and searching types of national supervision over the states that can be imagined. It has been a factor in molding the federal system and in fitting the states into their proper place in the Union from the very earliest years under the Constitution. What Justice Oliver Wendell Holmes of the Supreme Court once said may be taken as a common opinion: "I do not think the Constitution would come to an end if we lost our power to declare an act of Congress void. I do think the Union would be imperiled if we could not make that declaration as to the laws of the several states."

★ Accepted restrictions

It is perhaps a part of the maturity or aging of the nation that today makes many of the national Constitutional limitations on the states simply facts not to be questioned but part of the established boundaries of state action. What governor would argue that he ought to have a right to enter into a treaty with a foreign nation on behalf of his state? Or that to raise adequate state revenues, the state legislature ought to be permitted to levy general tariffs on goods coming into the state? These and many other Constitutional restrictions normally never arise as problems to disturb governors or legislators.

The national courts are seldom troubled by attempted usurpations on the part of states to (1) ". . . enter into any Treaty, Alliance, or Confederation . . ."; (2) ". . . without the Consent of Congress . . . enter into any Agreement or Compact with another State, or with a foreign Power . . ."; (3) ". . . grant Letters of Marque and Reprisal"; (4) ". . . without the Consent of Congress . . . keep Troops, or Ships of War in time of Peace . . . or engage in War, unless actually invaded, or in such imminent Danger as will not admit of delay" (Art. I, sec. 10). Neither are the calendars of the national courts filled with cases of states which have tried to (1) ". . . coin Money; emit Bills of Credit; or make any Thing but gold and silver Coin a Tender in Payment of Debts . . ."; (2) ". . . without the Consent of Congress lay any Imposts or Duties on Imports or Exports, except what may be absolutely necessary for executing its inspection Laws; (3) ". . . without the consent of Congress, lay any duty of Tonnage . . ."; (4) . . . pass any Bill of Attainder, ex post facto Law, or Law impairing the Obligation of Contracts"; (5) . . . grant any Title of Nobility." (All again from Art. I, sec. 10).[9]

9 In some instances, these apparently now settled prohibitions became established doctrine with necessary interpretations only in the course of a number of court cases. For example, in the instance of the contract clause major cases would include: Trustees of Dartmouth College v. Woodward, 4 Wheat. 518 (1819); Fletcher v. Peck, 6 Cranch, 87 (1810); Laramie County v. Albany County, 92 U. S. 307 (1876); City of Trenton v. State of New Jersey, 262 U. S. 182 (1923); Home Building and Loan Association v. Blaisdell, 290 U. S. 398 (1934).

★ *Restrictions still debated*

On the other hand, some of the restrictions on the states continue in a rather active category of differences between the states and the nation. Much of the field of civil rights as affected by state action has come up for judicial review and/or Congressional and Presidential attention.

Limitations in the Bill of Rights.   The so-called Bill of Rights embodied in the first ten amendments to the United States Constitution was construed originally as being applicable solely against the national government. After the 14th Amendment was adopted (1868), however, some lawyers began to think differently. The 14th Amendment says that "No State shall . . . deprive any person of life, liberty, or property, without due process of law." What is this *liberty* if it is not the group of civil liberties set forth in the 1st Amendment—freedom of speech, press, religion, and assembly? How can due process be defined any better than in the terms of Amendments 4 to 8 inclusive, with their provisions on unreasonable searches and seizures, self-incrimination, grand and petty juries, right of counsel in criminal trials, excessive bail, and cruel and unusual punishments? In short, why not construe these earlier amendments as restrictions on the states as well as on the national government?

The debate over this question has resulted in the decision that freedom of speech, press, religion, and assembly, as set forth in the 1st Amendment, are parts of the *liberty* guaranteed by the 14th Amendment against the states. This subject is referred to again in Chapter 18.

As to the procedural rights in Amendments 4 to 8, the decisions have been mainly the other way—that is, that the states are not bound by all the specific protections for the individual set up therein against the national government. This subject is discussed further in Chapter 18.

Limitations in the 13th Amendment.   The 13th Amendment (1865), the first of the three Civil War amendments, provides that

> SECTION 1. Neither slavery nor involuntary servitude, except as a punishment for crime whereof the party shall have been duly convicted, shall exist within the United States, or any place subject to their jurisdiction.
>
> SECTION 2. Congress shall have power to enforce this article by appropriate legislation.

Although this 13th Amendment is directed against the evils named, no matter by whom practiced, it was obviously aimed in large part against the states, since they were the governmental units that had formerly authorized slavery. Following the Amendment, Congress enacted a statute against certain forms of involuntary servitude, and there have been a number of prosecutions under it against individuals. The states have not frequently transgressed the prohibition through the passage of legislation, but there have been a few cases. Thus a statute in Alabama under which a man could be fined and imprisoned for not fulfilling a labor contract after accepting an advance in wages, and under which he was not entitled to present testimony to prove that he did not intend to defraud the employer when he took the money, was held unconstitutional.[10] Using a criminal punishment as an alternative to forcing a person to work out a debt was held to be a form of involuntary servitude like peonage.

It must be remembered, however, that compulsory service in such public services as road repair, jury service, fire fighting, and *posse comitatus,* like military service, are not forbidden by the Amendment.

Limitations in the 14th Amendment. It was the 14th Amendment (1868) that introduced the most sweeping changes into the relations between the national government and the states. One of these changes made national citizenship paramount over that of the states and thus opened the door to Congressional enactment of a whole code of citizenship and nationality laws. Most of the oft-cited first section of the Amendment consists, however, of prohibitions upon the states and not of direct grants of power to the national government.

> No state shall make or enforce any law which shall abridge the privileges or immunities of citizens of the United States; nor shall any State deprive any person of life, liberty, or property, without due process of law; nor deny to any person within its jurisdiction the equal protection of the laws.

Of the three clauses in this sentence, the "due process clause" has been used most often and most effectively in decisions that deny certain powers to the states. Next in importance is the "equal protection clause," while the "privileges or immunities clause" has had but little effect. The "due process clause" has given citizens generally many of the same protections against state and local government action that they have had under the 1st Amendment, for example, against the national government. In civil rights matters, the "equal protection clause" has assumed great stature recently. The use of the courts in the enforcement of restrictive covenants was denied as a matter of equal protection; restrictions on race for admission to state institutions of higher education and racial segregation in public elementary and secondary schools have been held violations of the equal protection

10 Bailey *v.* Alabama, 219 U. S. 219 (1911).

clause.[11] Similarly, the Supreme Court has held segregated public beaches, golf courses, parks, and buses to be violations of equal protection.[12] The Supreme Court, however, has not as yet changed its early interpretation that Congress may enact laws to overcome state laws which authorize discrimination; but if the discrimination is practiced privately, that is, by hotel or theater owners and managers (but not by private transportation companies engaging in interstate commerce), there is no power granted by the 14th Amendment to Congress to correct the evil by sweeping general legislation. In short, the Amendment forbids public action—state and local government action—but not private misdeeds; and in the early view of the court it was not the intent of the Amendment to transfer from the states to Congress the power to pass and enforce laws concerning private conduct in the whole field of civil rights.[13]

Regulations of the suffrage.   At one time the states were free to make any rules they saw fit for determining who might vote, whether in national or in state or local elections. Aliens might be and were in many states admitted to the suffrage, while many citizens might be and were excluded. After property tests were on the wane, the most common tests for voting were age (21), sex (male), color (white), citizenship, and residence. The states still have a wide choice in these matters, but on two points the United States Constitution restricts them. The 15th Amendment (1870) provides that "The right of citizens of the United States to vote shall not be denied or abridged by the United States or by any State on account of race, color, or previous condition of servitude." The 19th Amendment, adopted fifty years later, starts off in the same way and ends up "on account of sex." In effect these two Amendments forbid the states to discriminate against Negroes and women in fixing their suffrage qualifications.

After some early grumbling objections, woman suffrage came to be widely accepted, but not so Negro suffrage. A number of Southern states have tried and some still practice various methods of excluding Negroes from effective participation in voting. The Eighty-fifth Congress (1957) provided national investigatory machinery and also authorized the Attorney General to bring suit to enjoin any person from depriving an individual of his voting rights for the reason of color, race, religion, or national

11 Shelley *v.* Kraemer, 334 U. S. 1 (1948); McLaurin *v.* Oklahoma State Regents of Higher Education *et al.*, 339 U. S. 637 (1950); Sweatt *v.* Painter *et al.*, 339 U. S. 629 (1950); Brown *v.* Board of Education of Topeka, 347 U. S. 483 (1954); Pennsylvania *v.* Board of Directors of City Trusts of Philadelphia, 353 U. S. 230 (1957).
12 Mayor and City Council of Baltimore *v.* Dawson, 350 U. S. 877 (1955); Holmes *v.* City of Atlanta, 350 U. S. 879 (1955); Gayle *v.* Browder, 352 U. S. 903 (1956); South Carolina Electric and Gas Co. *v.* Flemming, 351 U. S. 901 (1956).
13 Civil Rights Cases, 109 U. S. 3 (1883).

origin in any election ". . . for the office of President, Vice President, Presidential elector, member of the Senate or member of the House of Representatives. . . ." The investigations of the commission and the activity of the Attorney General's office may be the basis of subsequent national legislation to enforce Constitutional voting rights. (See Chapter 7 for further discussion.)

Conclusions

The role of the national government in the government and protection of the states has now been briefly outlined. The methods used by the national government leave the states generally free to go ahead on their own initiative to pass and enforce such laws as they think best, subject to later check. Even so there are many fields in which the Constitution and laws of the United States mark the channels in which the states may operate, and there are both administrative and judicial agencies of the national government to induce or compel the states to stay within them. Such are the facts of political life in the United States that such phrases as the sovereignty and independence of the states must be construed as nostalgic hyperboles uttered by those who do not know the facts or who wish to preserve an ancient myth for some ulterior purposes. The careful and objective student will not be misled by them, and there well may be cause to believe that the role of the states in the Union can mean more for democratic government, if the states do not pursue the false hopes of sovereignty and independence but devote themselves to more constructive efforts.

REFERENCES

Anderson, William, *The States and the Nation, Rivals or Partners?* Minneapolis: The University of Minnesota Press, 1955.

Clark, Jane Perry, *The Rise of a New Federalism.* New York: Columbia University Press, 1938.

Commission on Intergovernmental Relations, *A Report to the President for Transmittal to the Congress.* Washington, D. C.: Government Printing Office, 1955, Ch. 1 and 2.

Hamilton, Alexander, James Madison, and John Jay, *The Federalist.* Many editions. See especially essays 44-46.

MacMahon, Arthur W. (ed.), *Federalism Mature and Emergent.* New York: Doubleday, 1955.

White, Leonard D., *The States and the Nation.* Baton Rouge, La.: Louisiana State University Press, 1953.

CHAPTER 4

State Constitutions

EACH OF THE FIFTY STATES has a document known as the state constitution. It represents in theory, if not in historical fact, a sort of original agreement of the people. It continues in effect, although amended from time to time, as a superior law—superior to the legislature, the governor, and the courts, and superior also to the ordinary laws enacted by the legislature, but necessarily subordinate to the United States Constitution. It retains its superior position largely by being accepted, as a routine matter, by public officers and the general public.

The idea of such a superior written agreement, separate from the ordinary laws, for the purpose of regulating a government did not originate with the American states, but they were the first in modern times to make general application of it. Most nations and communities of earlier times, even when they had written laws, did not always distinguish between the constitution and the other laws. The ancient Greeks, for example, in their numerous city-states and colonies, in many cases employed outstanding statesmen like Solon as legislators or lawgivers. These men drew up, for adoption by the people, the basic laws of the community. In these laws they dealt not only with the rules of governance but also with religion, property rights, marriage, the family, the punishment of crimes, and other matters that are today considered more suitable for regulation by ordinary statutes. In Great Britain to this day there is no legal differentiation between the two levels of law, but statesmen and scholars everywhere are fully cognizant that a distinction exists. Furthermore, most of the nations have by now, as in the case of the United States, adopted written constitutions. This is not so generally true of the member-states in federal systems. In Canada, for example, most of the so-called provinces do not have separate written constitutions.

Development of Written Constitutions

How did the American states get started in the other direction? When the English began to colonize the American Atlantic coast in the seventeenth century, their central government issued various charters and other legal documents that were the forerunners of present-day state constitutions. Certain companies, such as the Massachusetts Bay and Virginia companies, received land grants in America and charters from the king for colonizing the lands that were assigned to them and for governing the people who settled there. Proprietary grants were made also to certain individuals for colonizing and developing lands (William Penn and Lord Calvert). These various charters and grants provided for the rudiments of government in the colonies and defined the limits of the powers of those who governed. As the populations of the colonies increased and called for more government, additional instructions went out from England that modified and enlarged the governing powers of the companies and proprietors. Later, when most of the colonies fell under more direct royal control, the company charters had less effect, except in Rhode Island and Connecticut, while the written instructions issued in the king's name to the governors sent out from England assumed controlling importance as constitutions for the government of most of the colonies. Some of the old charters were revoked.

In all the colonies there was some provision for popular participation in the colonial governments, especially through the election of one house of the colonial legislative body. So far so good! But these arrangements did not satisfy all the colonists. Many of them, imbued with ideas of popular self-government, thought of constitutions as properly emanating only from the people. They looked upon constitutions of government as compacts among the people, like the Mayflower Compact or the Fundamental Orders of Connecticut. These were documents concerning government that had been drawn up by or in the name of groups of colonists and had been approved by them. In short, the theory that a constitution is a higher law— a people's law—and that it should be written out as a sort of agreement was already strong in America long before the War for Independence.

The revolutionary "conventions of the people" that took over the government in one colony after another after 1774 and that served as legislatures for the colonies in 1775 and 1776 sought advice from the Continental Congress as to what to do about their permanent governments. On May 10, 1776, nearly two months before the Declaration of Independence, the Congress advised all colonies that were as yet unprovided with permanent constitutions to adopt such governments as would best conduce to the happiness and safety of the people. This the conventions proceeded to do.[1] As a matter of fact, some of the state conventions had already taken such steps. In Massachusetts the old charter of 1691 was revived; in Connecticut and Rhode Island the existing charters were continued without substantial change. The other colonies did not have such documents conveniently at hand. They did not wish to use the instructions previously issued to their governors by the British government; these smacked of autocracy rather than of popular rule. Their revolutionary governing bodies proceeded, therefore, to draw up state constitutions. In most cases they did not have the advance approval of the people to make a constitution nor did they submit their work to the voters for ratification. In five states in 1776 and 1777 they did consult the people in advance, but they did not submit the constitution to the people for their approval.

By 1777 all thirteen of the former colonies, already called states or commonwealths, had acquired written charters or constitutions for their government. Each had come, however, from the legislature, the same body that passed the ordinary laws for the state. Except by title and contents, the constitutions were not very clearly set apart from the ordinary statutes. Not one could be described as truly a higher law, a people's law or a compact or agreement of the people. They were even amendable by the ordinary legislature. These deficiencies were to be corrected later. In the meantime each state had a temporary working constitution, and every state that entered the Union later came in with a written constitution.

★ Nature of earliest state constitutions

By present standards the first state constitutions of 1776 and 1777 were very short and very incomplete. In contents they varied considerably. All provided for a legislature, a governor or president, and judicial courts. A few asserted adherence to the doctrine of separation of powers. A majority included some provisions for civil liberties or what men usually call a "bill of rights." The suffrage provisions were only slightly more liberal than those that had prevailed in the colonies. Terms of office were generally

[1] See Alan Nevins, *The American States during and after the Revolution, 1775-1789* (New York, 1927), Ch. 4, "The Writing of the State Constitutions."

short. In practice the form of government set up by these first state constitutions was one of almost complete legislative control. Whatever was said in some constitutions about the separation of powers among the three branches, the governors and the courts were actually inferior in powers and in status to the legislatures. Revolting colonists who had resented the powers and the policies of the British colonial governors and the decisions of Crown-appointed judges were in no mood to give real strength to the executive and judicial branches against the still-popular legislature. Or, shall we say, the legislative bodies that drew up and put into effect these first state constitutions were not inclined to give the other branches of government any effective check upon their own authority. That change had to wait until there was more popular control of constitution-making.

★ Rise of constitutional conventions

In Massachusetts and New Hampshire the people were not content to accept a constitution from the hands of the regular legislative body. They believed too firmly in the theory that a constitution is a higher law, a compact of the people, and that it must receive its sanction from the people. In 1778 the people of Massachusetts, in town meetings assembled, rejected a constitution that had been drafted and submitted to them by the legislature to replace the colonial charter of 1691. The town meetings expressed objections not only to the contents of the proposed constitution but also to the way in which it had been prepared and submitted to them.

Thereupon the legislature took a new tack. After first securing the approval of the town meetings for the purpose, it ordered the election of a special constitutional convention. Every town was entitled to representation in this body, and every adult freeman resident in a town had a right to vote for its delegates. The body so elected met in September 1779; a similar body for New Hampshire had met in June of that year. These were the first constitutional conventions, properly so called, in the history of the United States. John Adams did much of the drafting for the Massachusetts convention. When the proposed constitution had been approved by the convention, it was printed and submitted to the town meetings for debate, revision, and approval or rejection. From the town meetings came a number of objections to specific articles, but the document as a whole was approved by a majority. The constitutional convention then met again, in June 1780, canvassed the town votes, considered the objections to certain articles, and declared the document in effect as the state constitution.

The people as the source of constitutions. Massachusetts thus became the first state to complete the drafting and adoption of a constitution through a separate constitutional convention and a popular referendum. As New Hampshire soon followed, these two states set the pattern for later state constitution-making. By their procedure, the "constituent power"—the power to frame and adopt constitutions—is withdrawn from and is set above the ordinary legislative power. A constitutional convention is chosen as the special representative of the people for the sole purpose of framing the constitution.

Spread of conventions. One after another most of the original states fell into line with the Massachusetts and New Hampshire constitutional theories and practices for the framing and adoption of new constitutions. In addition, when new states were being formed in the territories, Congress generally provided that the nascent states should hold constitutional conventions and adopt their constitutions by popular vote. These had to be acceptable to Congress also before the state could be admitted to the Union. All told, there have been about 200 state constitutional conventions, ranging from only one each in seventeen states up to fourteen in New Hampshire, thirteen in Georgia, eleven in Vermont, and ten in Louisiana. The number of completely new or thoroughly revised constitutions that have been adopted, however, is considerably less than 200.

The Present Written Constitutions

A state constitution is a set of limitations on the state and local governments of the state concerned. If it were not for this controlling document, every state legislature could exercise to the fullest extent all the powers permitted to any state under the United States Constitution. Viewed in general, the constitutions of the several states contain many restrictions on state and local governments of which some are out of date, others protect special interests as against broader public interests, and others stand in the way of improved government. Yet the broad theory of putting limitations on the powers of government is one that is deeply engrained in the American people and is reflected in constitutional documents and court decisions affecting every level of government.

★ *General characteristics*

Fashions in constitutions, as in women's clothes, vary with the years, and state constitutions tend to reflect the dominant political thought of their birth time. Constitutions written after some states had had unfortunate experiences in building canals or railroads include prohibitions against the state engaging in internal improvements. Unamended constitutions influenced by the Jacksonian approach to government will likely name a long list of state and county officials to be elected by the voters. Late nineteenth-century constitutions, following a number of scandals in misuse of funds and reckless appropriations, tend to restrict state legislatures. The "model state constitution," reflecting more recent approaches to government, attempts to meet any recurrence of earlier court intransigence toward legislative delegation of rule-making power; blesses the one-house legislature, beloved by the rationalist in government organization; and gives constitutional status to the reforms of merit-system selection of personnel, a limited number of departments for reasonable control by the governor, a unified court system, and the establishment of legislative and judicial councils.

If one assumes the objective of state government is to fulfill all those governmental requirements of its citizens which the national Constitution and Congress do not lodge in Washington, then a state constitution should lay down some general principles of government without tying down either future legislatures or future generations too closely. Current state constitutional provisions frequently (1) dilute the authority of the governor through the election of other state administrative officials; (2) restrict unduly the legislature in its decisions on raising revenue—in types of taxes permitted or in the use of borrowing—or in spending money by the establishment of large and possibly numerous segregated funds; (3) prevent local experimentation in governmental structure. Other provisions in state constitutions may produce legislatures unlikely to be representative of state majorities and may make constitutional changes improbable by requiring unusual pluralities for their approval. Such details in state constitutions limit the responsiveness and flexibility of state governments and promote what their sponsors often most fear—recourse to the national government on the part of seriously disaffected groups.

Age. One of the striking things about the present fifty state constitutions is their age. This is figured from the official date of the adoption of the current basic document and is not affected by subsequent amendments, no matter how important. Including Alaska's constitution which is technically one year old in 1960, and Hawaii's, just born, the average age of our state constitutions is about 83 years. The oldest constitution is that of Massachusetts written in 1780, but twelve others are over a hundred years of age. Aside from Alaska and Hawaii, the youngest constitutions are those of Georgia and Missouri (revised in 1945) and the New Jersey constitution written in 1947.

Length. In length the present written state constitutions range from under 7000 words (Rhode Island, 6650; Connecticut, 6741) to over 201,000 words (Louisiana) and over 75,000 (California), with a median figure of 19,797 (North Dakota). This median is about three times the length of the national Constitution. In general it is the newer state constitutions (excluding Alaska with 12,000 and Hawaii with 11,412 words) of the West and South that are the longest. Even when greatly increased in length, as we shall see below, no written constitution of any state includes all the rules of the working constitution. Indeed the longer they are the more the documents seem to need amendment, while short constitutions that deal only with fundamentals, like the Ten Commandments, are far less in need of change.

Principal contents. The arrangement of the constitutions into articles and sections is, of course, considerably varied. In the newer constitutions will be found, also, a number of subjects not dealt with in the majority. The standard subjects—that is, those that are dealt with to some extent in nearly all the constitutions—are as follows:

1. Bill of rights
2. Suffrage and elections
3. Separation of powers
4. Legislative organization and procedure
5. Executive officers and power
6. Judiciary—organization, jurisdiction, procedure
7. Military powers and militia
8. State finances and taxation
9. Local government—counties, cities, towns, etc., their officers and powers
10. Public education
11. Public highways
12. Miscellaneous restrictions on legislative powers
13. Miscellaneous provisions on corporations, banks, railroads, public utilities, monopolies, and trusts
14. Amendment and revision of the constitution.

The Alaskan constitution. The Alaskan Territorial Legislature in 1955 issued the call for a state constitutional convention to open on November 8 at the University of Alaska. Of the 55 elected delegates, 31 came from the cities of Anchorage, Fairbanks, and Juneau. The others claimed homes in 19 communities scattered from Kotzebue in the northwest to Ketchikan in the southeast. Following the usual pattern of American constitutional conventions, law was the largest occupational group represented (13 out of the

55) by the convention members.[2] Several of the delegates had served in the territorial legislature and others had held territorial or local offices.

A review of the document produced by the Alaska constitutional convention gives some idea of the forces at work in the writing (or revising) of a state constitution.[3] Any constitutional convention in part copies and builds on the past. The Alaskan delegates consciously drew upon the national Constitution, the Model State Constitution, the constitutions of the states (some of the most recent, those most familiar to convention members, those of leading states, and those of states accounted to have similar problems), and ideas expressed in the literature on state constitutions. Locke, Jefferson, and Hamilton—among others—no doubt would own the Constitution with its ideas of natural rights, the consent of the governed, separation of church and state, and a "government that is energetic in fostering the growth and development of the whole state and the welfare of all the people." Naturally the Convention needed to produce not only a document recognizing "the best of America's 180 years of experience in self-government" but also one to "fit the special needs and traditions of Alaska." [4]

Constitutions tend to be personal to each state's situation. Internal pressures in Alaska made apportionment, natural resources, and segregated funds lively issues. Fish traps, transportation rates, absentee ownership, undeveloped resources were old sources of controversy. The Constitutional Convention members, moreover, had some sense of Congress looking over their shoulder—a problem accepted states do not face. Too many innova-

[2] Nine convention members were store owners; 4, mining men; 4, fishermen; 3, housewives; 2, ministers; 2, freighting operators; 2, hotel men. Other occupations included news distributor, city planner, editor, architect, homesteader, real estate dealer, banker, publicity man, photographer. John E. Bebout, "Charter for Last Frontier," *National Municipal Review,* April 1956, p. 159.

[3] As yet, no detailed analysis of the proceedings of the Alaskan Constitutional Convention has been made nor has there been analysis of the voting record of the convention members nor of the interested pressure groups. Elaborate answers cannot be made to questions of the background and experience of the delegates; what or whom they might be assumed to represent; what information and ideas they had access to; or questions of underlying socio-economic interest conflicts. It is possible, nevertheless, to achieve some understanding of influences from the available writings and the specific constitutional provisions. See: Public Administration Service, *Constitutional Studies,* 3 vols., 1955 (mimeo.), prepared on behalf of the Alaska Statehood Committee for Alaska Constitutional Convention, Chicago, 1955; Victor Fischer, "Alaska Constitutional Convention Meets in November," *National Municipal Review* (September 1955), pp. 423-424; Unsigned, "Convention Completes Constitution for Alaska," *National Municipal Review* (March 1956), p. 124; John E. Bebout, "Charter for Last Frontier," *National Municipal Review* (April 1956), pp. 158-163. See also the Autumn 1958 issue of *State Government,* articles by Robert B. Atwood, "Alaska's Struggle for Statehood," pp. 202-208; William A. Egan, "The Constitution of the New State of Alaska," pp. 209-214; Thomas B. Stewart, "The Meaning of Statehood to Alaska," pp. 215-219. Pertinent Congressional hearings as well as Department of Interior reports on the Territory of Alaska supply further background data.

[4] The quotations are from *A Report to the People of Alaska,* issued by the Constitutional Convention on the completion of its duties.

tions, radical policies relative to land and mineral resources, any failure to recognize rights of the national government in its land ownership or in its defense needs, or any failure to secure the rights of minority groups would delay Congressional approval of the constitution and statehood.

Alaska's constitution then is a composite of many influences. All of the "standard subjects" (p. 62) except highways are included. It is a relatively short constitution with a limited number of restrictions. The "Declaration of Rights" is substantially a modern phrasing of the rights guaranteed by our original national Constitution and in the appropriate amendments (1 to 10, 13, and 14). The effect of a two-house legislature is modified by the use of joint sessions for review of gubernatorial vetoes and approval of gubernatorial appointments. The governor has a four-year term and shares his elected status with only one other official—a secretary of state who must be elected as a running mate of the governor. The judicial article recognizes the desirability of "a united judicial system" under the State Supreme Court and provides for gubernatorial appointment of judges from the judicial council's list of nominees and with eventual referendum to the voters.

Voting rights are given to United States citizens, 19 years of age, who have been residents of Alaska for at least one year and of their election district for 30 days. Ability to read and write English is also a prerequisite. Initiative (with some restrictions), referendum, and recall are provided. Constitutional amendments take a two-thirds vote of each house of the legislature and a majority vote of the voters at the next state-wide election. The question of a new constitutional convention must be put to the voters at least every ten years. The "new ideas" are represented.

Constitutional limitations include: the governor may have only one successive re-election; state and local debts are restricted to capital improvements and require majority-vote approval in state or local referendums[5]; state-dedicated (or segregated) funds are constitutionally limited to those existing at the time of ratification and those required by federal grant-in-aid programs.[6] Article XII, section 4 provides: "No person who advocates, or who aids or belongs to any party or organization or association which advocates, the overthrow by force or violence of the government of the United States or of the State shall be qualified to hold any public office of trust or profit under this constitution."

---

[5] Anticipation of revenues by the government and revenue bonds by public enterprises or public corporations as well as indebtedness by special assessment to benefited property are not included in the restriction.

[6] Article IX, section 7 does not establish any segregated funds but in its general prohibition of dedicated funds exempts those in existence and those required by the federal government. A future legislature could eliminate the former funds and at least restrict the second group.

Three of the most interesting sections of the constitution cover (1) apportionment, (2) local government, and (3) natural resources. Concentration of Alaska's population in a few cities with scattered settlements throughout vast stretches of land together with the fact that the minority groups in the state are largely outside the cities made apportionment particularly complex. In the calling of the convention, 7 delegates were elected at large, 31 delegates were elected from the four territorial judicial divisions, and 17 delegates were elected by local districts. As might have been expected, representation in the new legislature continues to recognize some of these lines. Lower-house districts are substantially set up on the basis of population, but upper-house representation gives emphasis to area—socioeconomic lines which roughly correspond to the four territorial judicial divisions. Reapportionment is made more or less automatic through the device of a reapportionment commission, the governor's determination, and the ease of taxpayer suits to command the governor to act.

The first sentence of Article X reads: "The purpose of this article is to provide for maximum self-government with a minimum of local governmental units, and to prevent duplication of tax-levying jurisdictions." This introductory statement lays the groundwork for some innovations in local government. The borough replaces the county, so criticized in the literature, and only the borough and the city will have taxing powers. A state commission on local boundaries, subject to local referendum and legislative veto, will have authority to change boundaries of cities or boroughs. Boroughs may establish service districts under their supervision and make charges for special services but the taxing power is reserved to the boroughs. Much of Alaska will remain in unorganized boroughs with the actual government and the functions of special service districts the province of the state government until increased population justifies local government.

Most Alaskans probably want both to develop quickly and substantially their land and resources and to avoid exploitation and monopoly in so doing.[7] Alaska's full endowments remain unknown. Salmon and seal fishing, forests, gold, copper, coal, and iron ore are known to be present. The line between development and exploitation often seems clearer in retrospect than at the time. Constitutional statements that "The legislature shall

[7] Alaskans have frequently criticized past federal policies as the following comment reflects: "The citizen of Alaska is only too well aware of the stifling effect of federal red tape upon the development of Alaskan land and resources. His own industry and intiative have frequently been curtailed by agencies over which he exercised no control and whose decisions he was powerless to appeal. He has seen, on more than one occasion, the policy of federal agencies serving as protection for interests which did not want to see Alaskan resources developed because of competition with those outside interests or for other reasons." (Public Administration Service, *Constitutional Studies*, Vol. III, p. 54.)

provide for the utilization, development, and conservation of all natural resources belonging to the State, including lands and waters, for the maximum benefit of its people" are likely to be variously interpreted by the legislators and the public. And the courts are not likely to interfere. On the other hand, the provision, "No exclusive right or special privilege of fishery shall be created or authorized in the natural waters of the State" would appear as a real limitation on future legislative action. Attempts were also made to prevent possibilities of fraud by requiring public notice "and other safeguards of the public interest" in all sales or leases of public lands or interests therein. And there was preacceptance of Congressional restrictions: "All sales or grants shall contain such reservations to the State of all resources as may be required by Congress or the State and shall provide for access to these resources." [8] (See Appendix.)

The Hawaii constitution. The Hawaii constitution, written in 1950 in anticipation of statehood, contains 11,412 words. Like the Alaska convention, the Hawaii convention accepted a number of the current ideas of state constitution-making. The constitution is general, provides for only the governor and lieutenant governor as state-wide elected officers, emphasizes the breadth of the executive responsibility of the governor, and gives the governor a four-year term with no limitation on re-election. The legislature will meet annually but even-numbered-year sessions will be restricted to budget matters. The governor is empowered to reapportion the lower house decennially according to a formula recognizing population. If the governor does not act or errs in acting, suit may be brought in the state supreme court to compel him to act or correct an error. The geographic problems of an island state served to justify to the constitutional convention a static representation in the state senate. As in Alaska, the convention gave special attention to conservation, development of resources, and the Hawaiian home lands.[9]

How Written Constitutions Can Be Changed

The Hawaii constitution and the Alaska constitution reflect both the traditional conceptions of state government and some of the "new ideas." Both constitutions are relatively short and in other ways meet the usual stand-

8 The quotations are from Article VIII, sections 2, 15, 10, and 9.
9 House of Representatives, 86th Cong., 1st Sess., *Report No. 32.* (Washington, D. C.: Government Printing Office, February 11, 1959). This *Report* reviews the history of Hawaii's petitions for statehood and includes a copy of the state constitution.

ards of state constitutions. Older states could, of course, change their constitutions to reduce the detail and to meet more easily present conditions. By specific constitutional provision or court interpretation, states may change their constitutions by one or more of three different methods (1) the calling of a new constitutional convention; (2) legislative proposal of amendments; or (3) a petition signed by a certain percentage of the voters.

★ Constitutional-convention method

Thirty-nine of the present state constitutions specifically authorize the calling of constitutional conventions to propose changes in the state constitution. In New Hampshire the convention method is the only one permitted. The eleven states whose constitutions do not expressly provide for conventions are not necessarily excluded from using this method. The usual ruling of the state supreme courts on this point (as in Rhode Island in 1935) is that the right to hold constitutional conventions is inherent in the people and that such conventions may be provided for by legislative action. The legislators, rather than constitutional provisions, in these states then determine the membership, election, and work of constitutional conventions.

Seventeen state constitutions require the approval of two-thirds of both houses of the legislature before the question of whether a constitutional convention shall be held can be submitted to the voters. Eight other states permit the legislature to do this by a simple majority and one by a three-fifths vote. In Georgia and Maine a two-thirds vote and in Mississippi and Montana a majority vote in the legislature alone, without submitting the question to the voters, is sufficient to call a convention. In nine other states it is mandatory for the legislature to submit the question of calling a convention to the voters at fixed intervals of time—in New Hampshire every seven years, in Alaska, Hawaii, and Iowa every ten years, in Michigan every sixteen years, and in Maryland, Missouri, New York, and Oklahoma every twenty years. These periods are not always followed exactly, and in some instances, as in Maryland in 1951, even when the voters approve the calling of a convention the legislature may not issue the call. On the other hand, submitting the question more frequently does not seem to be forbidden in these states.[10]

Cumbersomeness of conventions. Following the legislature's preliminary action, the usual next step is to hold an election or referendum on the simple question whether a convention shall be held. If the vote is favorable, the legislature must proceed to arrange for the convention. This requires

[10] Information in this section from *Book of the States, 1958-1959*, pp. 11, 12.

legislation as to the composition, election, and time and place of meeting of the convention, and the appropriation of the necessary funds. Unless the constitution specifically regulates the matter, there can be considerable strife in the legislature over the size of the convention and the apportionment of its members among the different parts of the state. Following this legislation, there is the popular election of the convention's members and then at last the meeting of the convention. By this time from two to four years may have elapsed, but the procedure is not ended. The convention must meet, deliberate, draft and discuss proposals, and then approve a new constitution or amendments to submit to the voters. These in turn must go to an election for approval or rejection and, if adopted, must usually be put into effect by subsequent legislation.

In the course of these proceedings, if all the steps are taken, the legislature will have had to act on three different matters, and the voters will have participated in three separate elections. Since regular state elections and legislative sessions are ordinarily biennial, and special sessions and elections are both expensive and unpopular, five or six years may elapse between the beginning and the conclusion of the modern constitutional convention process. The federal Constitutional Convention of 1787 and the state ratifying conventions of 1787 and 1788 required, all told, less than two years to frame and adopt the national Constitution. In short, the very cumbersomeness of the state-convention process is one reason why the states have sought other means of revising and amending their constitutions.

Usefulness of conventions. Constitutional conventions were very useful in the early and formative period of the states, and their numbers then in proportion to the number of states were much greater than today. Actually the theory of the constitutional convention was developed primarily to support popular control in the making of the original compact or constitution of the state community. That theory is still pertinent and cogent whenever major changes in a constitution are required.

A legislature may become, or at least many individual members of it may become, representative of vested interests, of the *status quo*. The majority of the people may be in effect disfranchised by the method of apportionment in the legislature, for example, and thus the legislative majority may stand between the people and the achievement of true majority rule. Such a legislature cannot be expected to propose a constitutional amendment to bring about fair representation. Whether a constitutional convention can meet such a challenge depends upon the base of its representation and, of course, unfettered freedom to rewrite and revise the existing constitution.

A political act. The decision to call a constitutional convention is a political act. The political wisdom of seeking or opposing a constitutional convention depends upon how individuals and groups are affected by the existing constitution and how likely they are to control the convention. Legislators may fear that a constitutional convention would get into "dangerous" hands and make "radical" proposals. A convention might propose, for instance, legislative redistricting, reduction in the size of the legislature, or even a unicameral system. Even where a legislature has set in motion a call for a convention, it may attempt to restrict consideration. Thus in the New Jersey convention of 1947, changes in legislative apportionment arrangements were placed out-of-bounds.[11] In their fears of "radical" proposals, the legislators are joined by many citizens and by various special interests— liquor interests, taxpayer interests, commercial and industrial interests, perhaps—which have adjusted themselves to existing constitutional requirements and do not wish to be disturbed.

"Reformers" and "good-government people" also may have an interest in not calling a constitutional convention. Given the normal distribution of political influence in a state, many legislators are likely to run for and be elected to any constitutional convention. And they are not likely to stand for different things in the constitutional convention from those they stood for in the state legislature. Pressure groups or special interests will be just as active, if not more so, in a constitutional convention as in the legislature. Because the voters must subsequently accept or reject the constitution as a whole, the convention may make certain compromises which the majority of voters would reject if they could register their opposition to separate provisions.

Possible improvement of convention method. For the future of democratic government in the American states, the constitutional convention should not only be kept alive but strengthened and improved or else an equally good substitute should be found. Those states that require the submission to the voters at regular intervals of the question whether a constitutional convention shall be held seem to be on the right track. Do they go far enough? We have suggested that they do not. More needs to be done to simplify the whole process of calling and holding constitutional conventions to assure that such conventions will be called at regular intervals and

11 Voters on the New Jersey ballot had a choice of voting "against such a constitutional convention" or voting "for such a constitutional convention, instructed to retain the present territorial limits of the respective counties and the present basis of representation in the Legislature." Each delegate to the convention was required to take an oath to abide by the ballot instructions of the voters. Bennett M. Rich, *The Government and Administration of New Jersey* (New York: Thomas Y. Crowell Company, 1957), p. 25.

that, when called, they will truly represent a majority of the people and be unobstructed by the legislature and other branches of the government. Since the legislature is too much an interested party, the constitution might make it the mandatory duty of the secretary of state or the state election board to place the question of calling a constitutional convention on the ballot every twelfth or sixteenth year. The constitution could also provide for a fair distribution of the delegates throughout the state on a population basis, authorize a minimum appropriation for convention expenses, and set a limit to the size of the convention. (To secure such provisions would require political activity of a high order.)

The size of most state constitutional conventions has been greater than was necessary or desirable for effective work. Most of them have run well over a hundred members, whereas the national Constitutional Convention of 1787 had only fifty-five members. (Alaska chose this magic number.) The average caliber of the members would probably be considerably higher if fewer delegates were elected. It would be advisable, also, to break away from the practice of electing one delegate from each state legislative district. Larger districts are desirable, and a substantial group of delegates might be elected at large. In this way a fairer representation of the whole people might be achieved, a representation that is not tied to existing legislative districts.

In recent decades conventions have had to give careful thought to their public relations and to consider seriously how best to submit their work to the voters. When a new state was being formed, almost a complete constitution had to be submitted; today, when it is a question of revising an existing constitution, the convention needs to consider whether it should not submit a series of amendments rather than a completely new document. Highly controversial matters could then be decided separately and would not defeat an otherwise satisfactory document nor increase the frustrations of conscientious citizens.

Information for constitutional conventions. Coming only at long intervals and lacking experience in what they are to do, constitutional conventions are greatly handicapped if they must "start from scratch" in the matter of getting needed information. Recognizing this difficulty, a number of states, when about to hold constitutional conventions, have provided for preparatory commissions to collate much of the needed information before the convention meets. Notable examples of informational commissions of this type have been those of Alaska (1955-1956), Massachusetts (1917-1918), New York (1937-1938 and 1956-1957), and Missouri (1942-1944). The research staffs of these commissions have included a number of men with training in political science, law, and other fields. Their work involved first the preparation and printing of numerous special studies on questions likely to come before the convention, and later the gathering of further information for convention members as the work proceeded. In view of the tremendous amount of information now available on problems of state government, it is doubtful whether any constitutional convention in the future can perform its functions acceptably without the aid of such a research staff.

Constitutional commissions. The research bodies mentioned in the preceding paragraphs, though variously named, are usually called *constitutional convention commissions.* They should not be confused with another type of organization, the *constitutional commission.*[12] In several states where it has been difficult to convene a constitutional convention but where the constitution has needed an extensive overhauling, this type of agency has appeared in the states, off and on, for over a century. It is obvious that no legislature can take the time from its other duties to make a complete study of the state constitution with a view to revising it. This situation led in New Jersey to a legislative act in 1941 creating a Constitutional Revision Commission, and a similar situation in Georgia led the legislature in 1943 to establish a Commission to Revise the Constitution.[13] In New Jersey there had been only four amendments to the constitution since 1875, whereas in Georgia there had been over 300, of which about 200 were of primarily local concern. Both constitutions needed revision, but partly for opposite reasons. In each case the commission did its work and submitted it to the legislature, which in turn sent it on to the voters for approval, although in New Jersey the legislature first made substantial changes in the proposal. Thus these commissions merely served as advisers to the legislature. The Georgia revision was approved by the voters in 1945; that of New Jersey was defeated in 1944, but its work was one of the factors which led to the holding of a constitutional convention later and the adoption of a new constitution by the voters late in 1947. Other recent commissions of this type have been those of Minnesota (1947-1949) and North Carolina (1948-1949).

This approach—the employment of a commission of leading citizens and experts to assist the legislature on constitutional revision—holds forth considerable promise for improving the legislative proposal of amendments,

[12] See Bennett M. Rich, "Convention or Commission?", *National Municipal Review,* 37 (March 1948), 133-139. Also reprinted in a National Municipal League pamphlet, *Modernizing State Constitutions,* 1948.
[13] Just as New Jersey legislators labeled reapportionment a forbidden subject in the 1947 convention so there is the view that Georgia used the Revision Commission method to avoid consideration of the subject.

the topic next to be discussed. It should be added, however, that many variations of the constitutional-commission idea are possible, such as (1) a joint interim legislative committee (California, 1947), (2) a commission appointed by the governor on his own responsibility (Kentucky, 1949) or on authorization by the legislature (Tennessee, 1945), (3) assignment of the research and drafting work needed to a state law institute (Louisiana, 1946), or (4) assignment of the task by the state's legislative council to its own staff (Oklahoma, 1947).

What interests, pressures, and arguments lead to the selection of one method over another for studying constitutional questions would be an interesting study. One thing is certain: legislative leaders do not approach constitutional revision in an abstract and academic manner.[14]

★ Legislative-proposal method

While Massachusetts and New Hampshire between 1776 and 1784 were working out the idea of the state constitutional convention, the other states, less doctrinaire, accepted constitutions that were prepared and in some cases put into effect by their ordinary legislatures. The Delaware (1776) and South Carolina (1778) constitutions also permitted the legislature to amend the constitution at any session, though by a majority somewhat higher than was required for making ordinary laws. Maryland (1776) authorized legislative amendment of the constitution, provided the measure was passed at two successive sessions by majority vote and with publication of the proposal for three months before the election of the second legislature. None of these required a popular vote of approval. It was Thomas Jefferson who, in 1776, first suggested a procedure by which the legislature could propose amendments and the voters approve them, and it was the state of Connecticut in 1818 that first put this plan into a constitution. Since then the idea has been placed in the constitutions in all states except New Hampshire, where only a constitutional convention, meeting usually every seventh year, may propose amendments. Thus, as far as authorizations are concerned, the method of legislative proposal and popular approval of constitutional amendments is far in the lead of the constitutional-convention method.

Thirty-five states permit a single session of the legislature to propose constitutional amendments. Of these, nineteen require a two-thirds vote, seven a three-fifths vote, and nine a majority vote. Thirteen states, on the other hand, require the proposed amendment to be passed in two sessions

14 For recent and current developments in state constitutional revision, consult *State Government* (quarterly), *The Book of the States* (biennially), and the *National Municipal Review* (now *National Civic Review*) (monthly).

before it can go to the voters, and one of these states requires a two-thirds vote in each session. This leaves two states unaccounted for. Of these New Hampshire, as previously noted, does not permit the legislature to propose amendments, while Delaware, at the other end of the scale, authorizes the legislature by a two-thirds vote in each of two sessions to *adopt* constitutional amendments without referring them to the voters.

Difficulty of change. In the long history of the development of human laws there are records of various attempts to make the basic laws wholly unchangeable—by engraving them in bronze or by placing a halter around the neck of any citizen who, in the public assembly, proposed any change, so that he might be hanged forthwith if the populace turned against his proposal. It is an evidence of great advance in man's concept of the dynamic and changeable character of laws and institutions that states should make definite provisions for deliberate change in their constitutions. In this advance the American states and the United States as a whole have certainly been outstanding leaders. At the same time the obstacles to constitutional change are very great in a number of states.

Mention has been made of the great difficulties in the convention process of constitutional revisions. Some state constitutions present similar obstacles to change by the process of legislative proposal. For example, the Tennessee constitution, adopted in 1870, has been amended only eight times. One reason is that the constitution provides that no amendment may be proposed except by a majority of all the members of each house at one session and then at the next session "by two-thirds of all the members elected to each house"; that no amendment so proposed shall be considered adopted unless approved "by a majority of all the citizens of the State voting for governor."

The Illinois constitution, also adopted in 1870, has been amended only thirteen times in almost ninety years. Until 1950, in that state it took two thirds of all the members elected to each house of the legislature to propose amendments and a majority of the electors voting at the next regular election to approve them—substantially the same as in Tennessee. But, in addition, the legislature had "no power to propose amendments to more than one article of this constitution at the same session, nor to the same article oftener than once in four years" (Art. XIV, sec. 2). With fourteen articles in the constitution it would have taken fifty-six years to get around to making amendments to all parts of the document. Fortunately this provision was changed in 1950 by the adoption of the so-called Gateway Amendment, and the amending process is now much easier.

In Indiana, where favorable action in two successive sessions is required to propose amendments, "no additional amendment or amendments shall be proposed," while an amendment or amendments agreed upon by one legislature are awaiting the action of a succeeding legislature or of the voters (Indiana Constitution, 1851, Art. XVI, sec. 2). This in effect limits new proposals to once in four years—and the Indiana constitution has been amended only eighteen times in over 100 years.

Reasons for difficulty. The reasons for restrictions upon the number of amendments to be submitted or upon the frequency of proposals reflect in part the concept that the adopted constitution is an interlocking series of agreements not to be tampered with too frequently. "Be slow about changing the handiwork of the past." This is the argument of all who are satisfied with the *status quo* and wish to delay change through the erection of all possible barriers.

Even those who remain less fearful of change might, however, accept reasonable limitations on the number of submitted amendments on the same grounds as they might support the short ballot. Numerous amending proposals may produce voter apathy or contribute to uninformed voting. Constitutional amendments typically draw less voter interest (and understanding?) than elections of officials. Between 1921 and 1958, Louisiana submitted more than ten amendments on an average each year to its electorate. The 1956 ballot in Louisiana carried more than fifty! California's *average* of amendments proposed each year from 1879 to 1958 is more than six. Again many ballots would have carried many more than six. It is possible that unrestrained submission of amendments to the voters may produce as equally unfortunate minority control as in the instance of amendment limitations.[15]

The arguments for extraordinary majorities stem from the theory that a written constitution is a higher form of law, a compact of the people concerning fundamental principles and one in which an overwhelming majority presumably concurred. The supporters argue that to retain this superior and sanctified character a written constitution should not be easily changed by the chance majority of the day, and to protect all members of the compact, including minorities, a higher-than-usual majority should be required in order to make any change in the constitution.

In answer to this it has been argued: (1) A compact of fifty, seventy-five, or a hundred or more years ago is not a compact of the present generation. This is the same argument as above. (2) The process of constitutional

15 The most satisfactory safeguard against too numerous amendments no doubt is a broadly framed constitution. The Louisiana constitution contains much detail that would preferably be found in the statutes. California's constitution is also detailed and the situation is further confused by rather wide use of the initiative for amendments.

amendment, which involves proposal by the legislature or by a convention and approval by vote of the people, already involves a more deliberative process than ordinary legislation. This process in itself distinguishes legislation from constitutional change by requiring a popular vote of approval. (3) Whenever an extraordinary majority is required for any purpose, a minority is in a position to rule the majority. In voluntary societies which members can join or leave as they see fit, the rule of a minority is not as serious as in a state or government where membership is practically unavoidable. If state constitutions dealt with only the fundamentals of the so-called "social compact," a difficult amending process could be defended more logically than it can when applied to modern state constitutions, many of which include much legislative detail about specific offices, elections, functions, and even official salaries.

Desirability of restrictions. The majoritarian in government, as well as others, believes that the people are sufficiently protected in any state where a legislative majority is required to propose a constitutional amendment and where a majority of the voters, voting on the question, need to vote favorably to put it into effect. This is especially true in the United States, where, under the national Constitution, states are forbidden to take life, liberty, or property without due process of law and to deny to any person within their jurisdiction the equal protection of the laws. The states that have liberal procedures for changing their state constitutions have not, on the record, violated the rights of life, liberty, or property any more than those in which the written constitutions are difficult to amend.

In those states where altering the written constitution ranges from the difficult to the nearly impossible, public needs are met in part by simply winking at the document. Constitutional prohibitions against incurring public debt, for example, have been circumvented in a number of states. The fiction of a strict debt limitation is retained, while borrowing with the blessing of the courts goes merrily on. Other parts of the constitution, such as the requirement of decennial redistricting for the legislature, are also ignored when they prove to be inconvenient to the prevailing legislative majority.

★ *Constitutional initiative method*

A generation or more ago, when it was found that constitutions could not be easily enforced or changed, leaders in certain states sought new and more democratic methods of altering their constitutions. They reasoned that if the legislature would not act because of its own special interests or the other special interests that dominated it, the voters should themselves have some means of initiating changes. Thus arose what is known as the constitutional initiative. This, in short, is the power of a given number or percent of the voters of a state to draw up and to submit to the entire body of voters proposals for constitutional amendments.

Oregon became in 1902 the first state to adopt a constitutional provision for the constitutional initiative. Incidentally, it was the state legislature in Oregon and in a number of other states that proposed most of the amendments to authorize this new amending process. The pressure upon legislatures for such a method during the early "progressive" years of the twentieth century was very great. While the drive for this new amending method continued in strength, fourteen states introduced it into their constitutions. Massachusetts, the last state to join the group, in 1918 adopted the constitutional initiative in a diluted form, while the constitutional provision in Idaho appears to be inoperative. The remaining twelve states in which the ordinary constitutional initiative is operative extend westward from Michigan and Ohio through Missouri, North Dakota, Nebraska, Arkansas, and Oklahoma to include Colorado, Arizona, Nevada, California, and Oregon.

The requirements for initiating constitutional amendments vary from state to state. In most states 8 or 10 percent of the number of voters who voted for governor or justice of the supreme court at the last election must sign a petition to make it effective. In Arizona and Oklahoma it takes 15 percent, and in North Dakota it takes 20,000 voters. Several states require a definite distribution of signers among the counties or Congressional districts. A petition that is found by the designated state officials to have enough legal signers has the effect of requiring the state election officials to place the proposition on the ballot for the next regular election. To be adopted, the proposal must be approved by a majority of the voters as defined in the constitution.

Although in operation for two generations, the constitutional initiative has not seriously rivaled the legislative method of proposing constitutional amendments. It has produced no successful amendments to date in three states, while the legislative process in the same three has brought forth a great many. The legislature probably stole the thunder of the leaders of initiative groups by proposing similar amendments before the initiative petitions could be completed. But it also happens that the voters rejected a higher percentage of initiated proposals. To some extent, therefore, the initiative on constitutional amendments has served as a means for permitting minorities to "let off steam," while attempting to get public acceptance of their proposals. The value of the initiative method as a threat and warning and sometimes as a corrective to legislative leadership cannot be entirely ignored, however.

From the viewpoint of democratic and majoritarian theory, the initiative process has something to commend it. At least in those cases where the legislature is bound to certain special interests and refuses to recognize the legitimate demands of a majority of the citizens, the initiative on constitutional amendments is partially justified. On the other hand it opens the door to proposals from various and conflicting groups and by that much reduces or prevents the harmonious development of the state constitution. The legislature, executive, and courts are left to put into effect proposals that were not planned by any of them and that do not necessarily fit well into the developing pattern of state government.

★ *Ratification of constitutional amendments*

A number of state constitutions, especially in the South after the end of Reconstruction, were put into effect by constitutional conventions without submission to the voters. Today, except in Delaware, all state constitutions require that constitutional amendments proposed by the legislature or by the constitutional initiative shall be approved by the voters at an election.

The size of the popular majority required for the approval of amendments is an important factor in determining the difficulty of any state's amending process. Ordinarily a simple majority of the voters voting on the question is all that is required—that is, if more voters vote "yes" than vote "no," the amendment is declared adopted. This is the ordinary principle of majority rule in legislative bodies as well as in popular elections. It assumes that members or voters who fail to vote either "yes" or "no" thereby tacitly accept the decision reached by those who do vote. Under this rule decisions can be reached and the government can go on, even if many individuals fail to perform their duties.

Those who tried to make it more difficult to amend state constitutions soon learned to stipulate higher popular majorities. In this case, however, instead of saying three fifths or two thirds, as in legislative proceedings, they put in such words as "a majority voting at the next general election" or "a majority voting at the next election for members of the general assembly." What practical difference do such words make? This depends in part on how the courts construe the words. As a rule "voting at the election" means voting for any purpose or on any office at the election. Thus, if we assume a general election (which is the most common case), a million voters all told might vote for various candidates for the general assembly or for governor. This figure then becomes the basis for determining a majority, and a majority would be 500,001. But suppose 200,000 voters neglect to mark the ballot on constitutional amendments. That makes no difference in determining the number needed for a majority under this rule; the number is still 500,001, or a majority of the entire million. To see what a difference this makes, compare the results below.

Table 3. ADOPTION OF A CONSTITUTIONAL AMENDMENT

	By majority voting on the question	By majority voting at the (general) election
Total number of voters voting at election	1,000,000	1,000,000
Number voting on amendment	800,000	800,000
Number of "yes" votes required to adopt amendment	400,001	500,001
Actual number of "yes" votes	450,000	450,000
Actual number of "no" votes	350,000	350,000
Amendment adopted or defeated?	Adopted by 100,000 majority ("yes" over "no" votes)	Defeated by 50,001 votes (the number short of constitutional requirement)

Recent Trends in Constitutional Revision

★ *Agitation for revision*

Since World War II there has been a decided wave of movements in the states to revise their constitutions. About half of the states have either taken some official steps toward revision or at least developed strong citizen groups that look toward revision of the constitution.

These movements have not all arisen from or been opposed by one source. Every organized interest group—political, economic, or moral—that feels itself adversely affected by anything in a state's constitution may begin an agitation for change. Bar associations, legislative and judicial councils, taxpayers' organizations, leagues of voters, and other types of groups give stimulus or lend support to proposed revisory action. When enough such pressures are felt, legislatures are likely to act in some way to stave off or to try to satisfy the demands, although strong pressures may also be felt from those who find existing provisions advantageous.

Many of the same or similar defects are found in the written constitutions of all states. Because most constitutions are now several generations old, many of their provisions are archaic or obsolete. Public needs have changed and so have the prevailing opinions as to how to satisfy needs. The Commission on Intergovernmental Relations called attention to the defects in state constitutions as a barrier to the states in meeting their partnership share in federalism. In many states the executive branch of government appears to be unduly disintegrated and headless, and the organization of the judicial branch is also rather chaotic and unsystematic. Attacks have also been made upon the bicameral system of legislative organization, upon the large size of one or both chambers, upon the inequitable apportionment of their members, and upon the internal organization and procedure of the legislatures. Then, too, in many states the constitutional provisions dealing with local government stand in the way of systematic reorganization in that field. Bills of rights are found to be somewhat inadequate, and other provisions, too, are found to be in need of alteration. Extensive alteration or complete revision is frequently needed.

★ Character of constitutions

Is it possible to find any definite trends in the development of the written constitutions of the states? Unfortunately for the student the trends, as they sometimes say of the stock market, are considerably "mixed." In general, the written constitutions tend to lag behind the needs of the times. Furthermore, some states lag behind far more than others; they seem to be almost immobile and wholly resistant to change. Tennessee and Indiana are current examples. Actually, however, by ignoring the words of the constitution or because of "political" decisions of their supreme courts, these states are able to get along without formal amendments. Louisiana is the leading example of a state which includes much of its ordinary law in the constitution. There are long passages on the government of New Orleans, on the details of highway financing including full details on the gasoline tax, on all the different minor courts, on parish (county) officers and government, on the registration of voters, on school finances down to exact millage rates, and on levees and breaks therein.

★ The "working" constitution

A state constitution, as the national Constitution, consists of all the formal and informal interpretations made by the executive, legislative, and judicial branches of government. Sometimes this means custom. Sometimes it means statutory law. Sometimes it means judicial decision.

In the background for all the states is the Constitution of the United States, with all the political practices, important statutes, and Supreme Court decisions that help to round out and fill in that instrument of government. All the powers of a state are controlled to some extent by the United States Constitution; and in recent years the rise of grants-in-aid and of extensive cooperation between national and state governments on important programs of social security and highways, for example, has brought the states more and more into conformity with national requirements.

No written state constitution can possibly change any important part of these national controls.

Within each state, also, there are important political customs, practices, and understandings that make the machinery go and determine its results. Party machinery, the regional distribution of appointments to office, labor unions and church groups, and many other things help to shape the government almost as much as the written constitution does.

And then there are the principal statutes—on the state budget and personnel systems, on state departmental organization, on local government, on the courts, and so forth. These are in many cases as important and as permanent as provisions of the written constitution.

It is only when all these parts are viewed together, in their proper relationships, that the full outlines of the actual working constitution of a state can be seen. The United States Constitution as a whole, the state's written constitution, state political customs, practices, and understandings, the party system, the important state statutes and departments, the system of local government—all these and possibly others are important elements in the *working* constitution of a state. It is not the document in which a thing is written so much as it is the intrinsic and extrinsic importance of the thing itself that determines whether it should be considered a part of a state's total constitution.

For a constitution consists of *all* the rules, both legal and customary, that establish and organize a state and its government, define their powers, and express the fundamental liberties of individuals with respect to the government.

REFERENCES

Burdine, J. Alton, "Basic Materials for the Study of State Constitutions," *American Political Science Review* (December 1954), 1140-1152.

Havard, William C., "Notes on a Theory of State Constitutional Change: The Florida Experience," 21 *Journal of Politics* (February 1959), 80-104.

Legislative Drafting Fund of Columbia University, *Index-Digest of State Constitutions*. New York: Oceana, 1960.

Model State Constitution, with Explanatory Articles, fifth ed. New York: National Municipal League, 1948.

National Civic Review (monthly). Current notes and articles on state constitutional revision and amendment.

State Government (now published quarterly by Council of State Governments, Chicago). Many recent articles and notes.

Sturm, Albert, *Methods of State Constitutional Reform.* University of Michigan Governmental Studies, No. 28. Ann Arbor: University of Michigan Press, 1954.

Wheeler, John P. Jr. and John E. Bebout, *Recent Thinking About State Constitutions*. Unpublished paper presented at the annual meeting of the American Political Science Association, September 1959.

See also the publications of recent constitutional commissions and constitutional convention commissions in Alaska, Florida, Louisiana, New Hampshire, New Jersey, New York, and others.

CHAPTER 5

Interstate Relations

ATTEMPTS HAVE BEEN MADE to compare interstate relations under the Constitution with international relations. These comparisons have arisen because the states, like nations, are governmental units of equal status with each other and have common problems of boundaries, migration of peoples, trade with each other, and other forms of intercourse. In addition many writers have looked upon the states as sovereign in about the same sense that nations are. There is a basic difference, as we saw before, in that nations have their own powers of defense, war, and foreign affairs and have no superior authority over them with a monopoly of these powers. The states are under a Constitution and a central government with powers to regulate their interrelations, to declare what their rights are, by judicial decision and otherwise, and to utilize superior force if necessary to compel each of them to respect the rights of other states. Even under the Articles of Confederation the states were not in the position toward each other of truly independent nations.

One evidence of this great difference is that the states do not have departments of foreign affairs, ambassadors, and ministers for maintaining "diplomatic relations" with each other. Instead, on all important matters that call for negotiation with one or more other states, they must have action by their legislatures and, for many matters, the consent of Congress. In fact the number of matters that call for this procedure are very few in the total of their governmental transactions, whereas minor matters are dealt with in large numbers directly and more or less informally by the administrative departments concerned. More of this later. In the meantime let us look at the constitutional provisions on interstate relations, including settlement of disputes, interstate compacts, comity, full faith and credit, and interstate rendition.

Settlement of Interstate Disputes

In setting up a true central government, with legislative, executive, and judicial departments, the framers of the Constitution were faced with the problem of providing for a simple method of judicial settlement of interstate disputes if the federal system were to remain stable. The pertinent Constitutional provisions are:

> The judicial Power [of the United States] shall extend . . . to Controversies between two or more States;—between a State and Citizens of another State;—between Citizens of different States;—between Citizens of the same State claiming Lands under Grants of different States, and between a State, or the Citizens thereof, and foreign States, Citizens or Subjects.
>
> In all Cases . . . in which a State shall be a Party, the supreme Court shall have original Jurisdiction (Art. III, sec. 2, pars. 2, 3).

Thus many types of disputes in which states are parties are brought under judicial review and are subject to judicial settlement. Direct controversies between state and state are especially mentioned but so also are other cases in which states have an indirect interest because their citizens or their land grants are involved.

★ Subjects of interstate disputes

The settlement of interstate disputes by the Supreme Court through regular judicial process has become so much a routine matter that little attention is paid to it any more. Up to the present time the court has rendered about one hundred decisions in some fifty disputes directly between two states—that is, where one state was the plaintiff and the other the defendant —and there have been uncounted decisions in which the laws and rights of different states were indirectly involved. Many of the cases have involved disputes over interstate boundaries arising out of conflicts and ambiguities in land-grant boundaries, errors in surveys, and the shifting of boundary river beds and channels. A famous case that was before the Supreme Court a number of times arose out of Virginia's attempt to compel West Virginia to pay an agreed portion of the state debt, a case that ended only when West Virginia finally decided to pay. Other decisions have involved rights to common waters for irrigation and other purposes, the pollution of waters, the flooding of lands in one state due to dams and other works in a neighboring state, and the repayment of bonds issued by one state and bought by another.

★ Some rules of interstate litigation

In the course of settling these and other disputes the Supreme Court has firmly maintained its right to exercise jurisdiction over states without their consent.[1] In this respect, the states stand before the Supreme Court in a position similar to but not identical with that of municipal corporations. A municipal corporation is ordinarily suable by anyone in any court of competent jurisdiction. A state may be sued by the United States or by any other state without its own consent but only in the Supreme Court.

Under the 11th Amendment (1798), "The Judicial power of the United States shall not be construed to extend to any suit in law or equity, commenced or prosecuted against one of the United States by Citizens of another State, or by Citizens or Subjects of any Foreign State." Consequently a state may not be sued without its own consent in federal courts by any private citizen or group of citizens from other states or from foreign countries. But now suppose that a state by flood control work inside its own boundaries causes water to flow into an adjoining state so as to cause damage to farms and other property there.[2] In these cases a state representing its own people as *parens patriae* (the father of his country or people) may sue the other state in the Supreme Court to recover for past damages and to prevent further damages even though its individual citizens, who are the main sufferers, could not do so. However, the court has ruled that where certain persons in one state held the bonds of another state, to enforce the payment of which they could not sue the state that sold them, their own state could not step in and sue for them as state against state.[3] Otherwise the 11th Amendment forbidding suits by outside private persons against the state in federal courts could be circumvented completely. Furthermore, the mere failure of a state to enforce its laws fairly, to the injury of the citizens of another state, does not give the latter state a right to sue the offending state.[4]

[1] See New Jersey v. New York, 5 Peters 284 (1831); on the power of the court to settle boundary disputes between states, see Rhode Island v. Massachusetts, 12 Peters 657 (1838).
[2] North Dakota v. Minnesota, 263 U. S. 365 (1923).
[3] New Hampshire v. Louisiana, 108 U. S. 76 (1883).
[4] Louisiana v. Texas, 176 U. S. 1 (1900).

The Supreme Court has firmly asserted also its power to issue judicial process against a state to compel it to obey a Supreme Court decision.[5] In most instances these decisions are accepted by the losing states; in other cases no doubt some way could be found to compel the appropriate state officers to carry out the court's decree. Up to now, however, the court has not found a practicable way to compel a state to pay money to another state.

Interstate Compacts

The danger that groups of states dissatisfied with the general national policy might form blocs and alliances against the central authorities was foreseen by the framers of both the Articles and the Constitution. The provision in the Articles read that

> No two or more states shall enter into any treaty, confederation or alliance whatever between them, without the consent of the United States in Congress assembled, specifying accurately the purposes for which the same is to be entered into, and how long it shall continue (Art. VI, par. 2).

This sentence clearly has no reference to interstate agreements about bridges, ferries, mutual assistance in law enforcement, and other minor matters. It seems to be directed entirely at such general political agreements for joint action as have long been known internationally under the designations of alliances and confederations.

The same general idea was taken over into the Constitution, but the wording was altered. "No State shall, without the Consent of the Congress, . . . enter into any Agreement or Compact with another State, or with a foreign Power . . ." (Art. I, sec. 10, par. 3). Just what was meant by "agreement or compact" is not entirely clear. Possibly these words were intended to be even broader and more inclusive than those used in the Articles. Surely they would *include* confederations and alliances, because the intent certainly was in large part to forbid the states to split the Union by forming smaller alliances or groups among themselves that might be used against other members of the Union and even against the Union itself. But how much farther do the terms "agreement or compact" go? Do they include agreements by states as to boundary disputes, bridges and ferries on boundary waters, reciprocity in taxation, interstate parks, and other such minor matters?

The Supreme Court has not had to answer this question directly as yet,

5 Virginia *v.* West Virginia, 246 U. S. 565 (1918).

but it is conceivable that if two or more states made some compact without the consent of Congress, any other states that felt themselves endangered thereby, or the United States government itself, might bring a case before the Supreme Court to invalidate the agreement. It is generally agreed that the action of the Southern states in forming the Confederate States of America was an unconstitutional compact, for although each had first gone through the form of seceding from the Union, the acts of secession were themselves unconstitutional. As the Supreme Court said in the leading case, "the ordinance of secession, adopted by the convention and ratified by a majority of the citizens of Texas, and all the acts of her legislature intended to give effect to that ordinance, were absolutely void." [6]

The practical judgment on the compact clause is that it requires the consent of Congress for only such agreements among states as might have some general political significance—for example, by increasing the power of the states concerned, or their unity of action, against other states or against the United States as a whole, or by making joint resolve to obstruct the national government or even to secede from the Union. Such compacts would require the consent of Congress, and such consent would normally not be forthcoming. On all less important matters—that is, on all that do not threaten other states or the national government or the Union under the Constitution—the principle of maximum freedom and self-government for the states would seem to apply.[7]

★ *The compact device in practice*

For almost a century and a half, the compact was used essentially as a means for recording settlement of boundary disputes among the states. Such compacts clearly called for Congressional approval and generally received it without delay. Beginning in the 1920s and especially in the 1950s, interstate compacts have dealt largely with aspects of administration and services.[8] Zimmerman and Wendell, the leading authorities in the field, classified interstate compacts in 1951 as: (1) boundary jurisdictional compacts,

6 Texas *v.* White, 7 Wall. 700 (1869).
7 This is the gist of the dictum in Virginia *v.* Tennessee, 148 U.S. 503 (1893), where an interstate agreement settling a boundary question without the express consent of Congress was upheld.
8 The standard references on interstate compacts are: Felix Frankfurter and James M. Landis, "The Compact Clause of the Constitution—A Study in Interstate Adjustments," 34 *Yale Law Journal* (1925), 685 and accompanying tables; *Report* of the Committee on Inter-State Compacts to the National Conference of Commissioners on Uniform State Laws (1921); Frederick L. Zimmerman and Mitchell Wendell, *The Interstate Compact Since 1925* (Chicago: The Council of State Governments, 1951); The Council of State Governments, *Interstate Compacts 1783-1956* (Chicago: 1956); and *The Book of the States* (biennial).

(2) boundary administrative compacts, (3) regional administrative compacts, and (4) administrative-recommendatory compacts. But in 1958 these authors saw the principal uses of compacts as: (1) establishment of joint agencies and institutions, (2) provision of common services, (3) meeting jurisdictional questions, and (4) providing interstate equity.[9] In other words boundary compacts were things of the past and the new compacts looked to the meeting of common service needs.

The states uncovered broad uses of the interstate compact beginning in the 1940s. The landmark compact was the earlier Port of New York Authority Compact, agreed to by New York and New Jersey and approved by Congress in 1921. The success of the New York Port Authority as an interstate administrative agency eventually encouraged other compact experimentation. There are now such compacts as the Ohio River Valley Water Sanitation Compact, the Upper Colorado River Basin Compact, the Great Lakes Basin Compact, the Pacific Marine Fisheries Compact, the Northeastern Forest Fire Protection Compact, the Interstate Oil Compact, the Interstate Compact for the Supervision of Parolees and Probationers, the Interstate Compact on Juveniles, the Southern Regional Educational Compact, the Interstate Compact on Mental Health, the South Central Corrections Compact, and the New York-New Jersey Waterfront Compact, as well as the classic Port of New York Authority Compact.

Some of the compacts include only two states as parties; the Parolee and Probationer Compact includes all fifty states and Puerto Rico; and the relatively new Interstate Detainers Agreement is open to participation by the national government as well as all of the states and territories. And as the title indicates, the Government of Canada-New York, Buffalo and Fort Erie Public Bridge Authority Compact is a compact between a state and a foreign power.

Substantively, the New York Port Authority operates the numerous services—tugboats, piers, bridges, and so forth—required by a major world port; the Waterfront Commission is regulating labor arrangements for the port area. Through the Southern Regional Educational Compact (as well as the Western Interstate Higher Educational Compact and the New England Higher Educational Compact), the party states have attempted to provide a student exchange means which would permit full utilization of special educational facilities such as medical or dental school without each state establishing its own. The South Central Corrections Compact provides arrangements for the cooperative use of existing prisons for women to avoid duplicate building in adjoining states.

[9] *The Book of the States, 1958-59,* Vol. XII, p. 213.

★ The national government and compacts

During the early decades under the Constitution, various states made a number of agreements with each other without troubling to ask the consent of Congress. In the same period other states began the practice of asking the consent of Congress for agreements of no great intrinsic importance. No doubt many legal advisers of the states looked upon the compact clause as essentially negative, a direct discouragement to such agreements, and when they were called to advise on interstate arrangements even of small import, out of excess of caution they recommended that the states concerned apply to Congress for consent. Recently the National Association of Attorneys General emphasized the right of states to enter into many agreements and urged that the states avoid going to Congress needlessly to seek consent.

Congressional approval of earlier boundary compacts tended to be automatic. In the instance of the Interstate Compact for the Supervision of Parolees and Probationers, Congress gave its consent in advance. Again Congress has given a general consent in an area but with the requirement that the actual compact be referred to Congress for approval. In the instance of the Republican River Compact, Congress approved the compact, but President Roosevelt vetoed it. The Southern Regional Educational Compact was approved in the House, but referral to a committee avoided a decision in the Senate. (Some Senators feared approval of the compact also meant approval of segregated education.) The context of the referral suggested that the Senate did not oppose the compact, and the states proceeded as if approval had been given. It is believed then that Congress may give its consent either before or after the participating states have signed, and by implication or by practical recognition of what has been done as well as by express resolution. Congressional (and Presidential) approval, however, is not automatic and the increasing number of interstate compact proposals seems to have stimulated Congressional review.

In general the interstate compact may be looked upon as one method of achieving certain regional and even nation-wide results. It is by no means the only method. In cases where Congress has a keener interest, it usually achieves nation-wide results with state administration through a grant-in-aid system, as in the cases of highways, unemployment compensation, and old-age assistance. Congress has shown in the Tennessee Valley Authority (TVA) how regional or river-basin results can be attained under national control through the use of the government-owned corporation. Wide use of the interstate compact along the lines of the New York Port Authority and the New York-New Jersey Waterfront Commission might produce problems not substantially different from those of functional districts at the local government level. These have been much criticized on such grounds as lack of clear, responsible control; tax inequities; and overemphasis on a single function to the detriment of consideration of the total needs of the community. Yet to the degree that the states can cooperatively meet mutual problems of their citizens without resort to national revenues or national regulation, the partnership status of the states in the federal system is strengthened.

Interstate Comity

From their colonial experience the framers of both the Articles of Confederation and the Constitution knew that men, vessels, vehicles, goods, and communications would move in large numbers back and forth across state lines. Striving for perpetual union among the states, they realized the necessity for protecting citizens and their possessions in all states equally, no matter where they might move or reside. Under the Articles they did not forbid interstate tariffs on goods, but they did offer protection for citizens. As stated in Article IV:

> The better to secure and perpetuate mutual friendship and intercourse among the people of the different states in this union, the free inhabitants of each of these states, . . . shall be entitled to all privileges and immunities of free citizens in the several states; and the people of each state shall have free ingress and regress to and from any other state, and shall enjoy therein all the privileges of trade and commerce, subject to the same duties, impositions and restrictions as the inhabitants thereof respectively. . . .

This, the so-called "comity clause" of the Articles of Confederation, has been praised as one of the most important steps toward the establishment of nationhood. At a time when men of all states were highly provincial if not parochial, and when there was much misunderstanding and even contempt and hatred among men of different states (yes, even in Washington's "continental" army!), the comity clause indeed stands out as intelligent and broad-minded.

More brief than the provision in the Articles, the comity clause of the Constitution (Art. IV, sec. 2) apparently was intended to achieve the same purpose and cover the same ground. "The Citizens of each State shall be entitled to all Privileges and Immunities of Citizens in the several States."

Over a century ago the United States Circuit Court, through one of the Supreme Court justices, said that the privileges and immunities so guaranteed to state citizens in all states are limited to those "which are, in their nature, fundamental; which belong, of right, to the citizens of all free governments. . . ." [10] Without attempting to enumerate all such fundamental rights, the court said that they fall under the headings of protection by the government, the enjoyment of life and liberty, with the right to acquire and possess property of every kind and to pursue and obtain happiness and safety, subject to reasonable laws.

> The right of a citizen of one state to pass through, or to reside in any other state, for purposes of trade, agriculture, professional pursuits, or otherwise; to claim the benefit of the writ of habeas corpus; to institute and maintain actions of any kind in the courts of the state; to take, hold and dispose of property, either real or personal; and an exemption from higher taxes or impositions than are paid by the other citizens of the state. . . .

These were some specific fundamental rights that the court took time to mention.

It is generally agreed, however, that in each state there are certain special rights connected with a state's own property, institutions, or services that a state may reserve solely for its own citizens or that it may concede to others only on their payment of higher charges. Thus state colleges and universities may exclude nonresidents, or they may charge higher fees to nonresident students. The right to hunt or fish, to be admitted to state hospitals and sanatoriums, to work for the state or local governments, and to obtain public assistance are other examples of special or local privileges that may be similarly restricted to citizens or residents of the state. Since under the 14th Amendment any citizen of the United States may become a citizen of any state by merely residing therein, the restriction of these special privileges to a state's own citizens is not usually a serious hardship on outsiders.

The tremendous volume of travel, shipping, and communications that crosses state lines results in a host of interstate legal complications. Under the Constitution each state is a source of law, and every state has its own system of laws. Not only the statutes but also the court decisions and rules of common law differ from state to state. Now consider a few fact situations. (1) A man in state A buys insurance on his car from a company in state B and has an accident in state C calling for an insurance settlement. The words of the policy are clear enough, but are they to be interpreted by the common law rules of state $A, B,$ or C? (2) A workman resident in state E is employed by a company incorporated and situated in state F and is injured while working for the company in state G. The workmen's compensation

---

[10] Corfield v. Coryell, 4 Wash. C. C. 371 (1825).

laws of the three states differ considerably. Which one shall apply? (3) A man leaves his residence and family in state *M*, obtains a divorce from his wife in state *N*, and then marries again in state *O*. Which state's law shall control his former wife's rights and his rights to the family property and the children? Indeed, shall his divorce in such circumstances be recognized as valid? If he returns, married or unmarried, to state *M*, the situation is even more complicated. To provide a rule for decision of such cases the Constitution includes the "full-faith-and-credit" clause.

Full Faith and Credit

The full-faith-and-credit clause of the Constitution was preceded by the following sentence in the Articles of Confederation: "Full faith and credit shall be given in each of these states to the records, acts and judicial proceedings of the courts and magistrates of every other state" (Art. IV, par. 3). This requirement was limited to the acts and records of judges and courts, whereas the provision put into the Constitution obviously provides for broader coverage, as follows:

> Full Faith and Credit shall be given in each State to the public Acts, Records, and judicial Proceedings of every other State. And the Congress may by general Laws provide the Manner in which such Acts, Records and Proceedings shall be proved, and the Effect thereof (Art. IV, sec. 1).

Congress has passed several statutes for defining how legislative acts may be authenticated and judicial proceedings and judgments proved. But as to the effect such documents shall have when presented in evidence in the courts of other states, it has provided merely, in the most recent revision, that they "shall have the same full faith and credit in every court within the United States and its territories and possessions as they have by law or usage in the courts of such state, territory or possession from which they are taken." [11]

As to judicial proceedings, this statute almost completely avoids the main issue. In the first Congress James Madison and James Wilson supported the proposal that authenticated decisions by a court in any state should be executed or enforced by the courts in any state where presented without any further questions asked. Thus if *A* got a judgment against *B* for a sum of money in state *X*, and *B* moved with his possessions to state *Y* before paying, all that *A* would have to do would be to present the judgment to a proper court in *Y* and that court would have to get the sheriff or other

[11] 28 *U.S. Code* (1946 ed., Supplement II, 1949), sec. 1738, as revised in 1948.

officer to collect on the judgment, and not hold a new trial of the case. This is substantially what is done among the states of Australia, the provinces of Canada, and, in fact, throughout other parts of the British Commonwealth of Nations.[12]

★ Conflict of laws

Congress having failed to enact such a requirement, the state courts and the United States Supreme Court have had to work out the full-faith-and-credit principle in their own way. As a matter of fact, long before this clause was formulated in the Articles and the Constitution, the courts had begun to work out rules for giving effect in their own decisions to the statute laws and judicial decisions of other jurisdictions. This is an ever-present concern of the courts. To take a single current example, if two men form a partnership in New York and get into a dispute about some aspect of their business in New Jersey or any other state, either party may appeal to the court in the state where the dispute arises, and that court will take jurisdiction but faces the question of what law it shall apply. In so far as there is a question arising out of the partnership agreement, it is obvious that the law of New York, the law under which the agreement was made, should control. There are probably thousands of such cases in the courts every year where the laws of two or more states are involved. For several centuries jurists and writers on legal subjects have been developing the rules in this field, which is called "conflict of laws." It presents one of the most complicated subjects of study in the law schools.[13] Even without a full-faith-and-credit clause in the Constitution, this development in the law would undoubtedly have taken place very much as it has. Indeed, many such cases are tried and decided in the courts without either the lawyers or the judges mentioning the full-faith-and-credit section. Thus a certain respect for the statutes and decisions of other jurisdictions in cases where they apply is accorded as a matter of course by all state and federal courts.

★ Questions raised

When state courts are asked to enforce decisions of the courts of other states, they may make inquiry as to the jurisdictional competence of the earlier court, whether the parties received procedural due process, and whether the first state's public policies accord with theirs. The courts of

12 See Robert H. Jackson, *Full Faith and Credit, The Lawyer's Clause of the Constitution,* New York: Columbia University Press, 1945, pp. 31-35.
13 See the articles on Conflict of Laws in *Encyclopedia of the Social Sciences,* Vol. 4, pp. 187-194, and the leading casebooks on the subject, such as those of Fowler V. Harper and Charles W. Taintor II; Joseph H. Beale; Ernest G. Lorenzen; and Elliott E. Cheatham and others.

one state do not enforce the penal laws of another state. Consequently if the judgment a party has won includes a penalty against the other party, at least that part of the judgment may not be enforced. As a matter of public policy, states frequently refuse to enforce gambling-debt judgments of a sister state with legal gambling.

It seems to be the general opinion of lawyers and judges who have written on the question that the law on full faith and credit is not in a satisfactory condition from the viewpoint of litigants, or when tested by the standard of efficient administration of the laws. Congress has not made full use of its power to regulate this aspect of interstate relations, and it is a reasonably safe prediction that it will be slow to make any major changes in present federal laws on this subject. In the meantime many persons must remain uncertain as to their legal rights when they move from state to state, and there will be many instances of trying over again cases that have already been decided in state courts. The difficulty remains, however, that states differ considerably in their policies on certain subjects and are not prepared fully to accept each other's standards in adjudications on such subjects as marriage and divorce. In the circumstances Congress could hardly be expected to legislate for more complete interstate acceptance of divorces, for example, without setting minimum standards for residence and notice to parties concerned. Such Congressional intervention in a field like divorce would be deeply resented by many persons and in many states.

Interstate Rendition

The general statement was made above that states do not enforce each other's criminal or penal laws. Among nations there is some practice of extraditing, or returning to the nation that claims them, escaped criminals and those accused of crime. Among the states in the Union a similar obligation has existed since the days of the Articles of Confederation. The provision in the Articles on the subject (Art. IV, par. 2) was almost the same as that put into the Constitution, as follows:

> A Person charged in any State with Treason, Felony, or other Crime, who shall flee from Justice, and be found in another State, shall on demand of the executive Authority of the State from which he fled, be delivered up, to be removed to the State having Jurisdiction of the Crime (Art. IV, sec. 2, par. 2).

In 1793 Congress passed a law to regularize the procedure of interstate rendition.[14] Under it, a governor who demands the return of a fugitive

14 18 *U. S. Code* (1946 ed., Supplement II, 1949), sec. 3182, as revised in 1948.

from justice from another state shall accompany his demand with an authentic copy of the indictment against him, or an affidavit made before a magistrate (judge) certifying to the charge against the person wanted. The governor must also send an officer or agent to bring back the person wanted. Then the "executive Authority" of the state—in practice, the governor—to whom the demand is sent is obligated to have the suspect arrested and turned over to the officer of the other state. All costs are to be paid by the demanding state.

The nature of the duty imposed on a governor to return such suspects on demand has been considerably discussed. To protect himself and the suspect, the governor certainly has the duty to examine the papers in order to assure himself that a crime is charged and that the person demanded is a fugitive from justice in the demanding state. Beyond that the governor or other executive authority has no discretion. The Constitution and the act of Congress place on him a positive duty of a nondiscretionary nature to hand over the suspect. But the act of Congress does not impose any penalty on a governor who fails to perform his duty. Sometimes a governor refuses to return a suspect, alleging that the person will not receive a fair trial or giving some similar explanation. The difficulty with such a position is that other states can quickly and easily retaliate against such a governor and his state. In practice, therefore, the procedure for rendition is fairly uniform and automatic. It is to some extent regulated by statute in each state, thirty-five states having adopted a uniform criminal extradition act, and an assistant to the governor usually handles most of the cases for him, reserving for the governor's personal decision only the most doubtful cases.

In a leading decision on the subject, just at the outbreak of the Civil War, Chief Justice Taney made some broad generalizations on the duties of the governors and on the lack of power in the national government to exercise any compulsion on the governors.[15] The case involved a man charged in Kentucky with the crime of helping a slave to escape, and the state of Kentucky tried to get a Supreme Court writ of mandamus against the governor of Ohio to compel him to return the fugitive. This writ the court refused to issue. The act of Congress made no express provision for any such writ to issue against a governor, and the Chief Justice asserted further: ". . . nor is there any clause or provision in the Constitution which arms the government of the United States with this power." Pointing out the danger that such a power, if vested in the central government, might enable it to dominate the states, the court concluded: "And we think it clear, that the federal government, under the Constitution, has no power to im-

15 Kentucky v. Dennison, 24 How. 66 (1861).

pose on a state officer, as such, any duty whatever, and compel him to perform it. . . ."

There is considerable doubt as to the validity of this argument. The only duty before the court in this case was one that is imposed on the states by the Constitution itself. The fugitive "shall . . . be delivered up," and Congress has the power to pass all necessary and proper laws for carrying into effect the powers vested by the Constitution in various departments and officers. The state does not need to designate its governor as its "executive authority" to carry out this power of returning fugitives to other states, but whatever officer a state does designate has a power and a duty under the United States Constitution that he presumably can be compelled to perform or punished for not performing. The analogy of state elections officers who also administer national elections is obvious. They are to that extent officers of the national government and subject to punishment for abuses in conducting such elections.

This argument goes to the nature of the Union and is necessarily somewhat academic in so far as any likelihood of Congress passing such a penal law against state governors is concerned. In practice Congress seems to prefer to tolerate some inefficiency and misuse of powers in the states, in order to keep them autonomous, to any program of using its powers to compel the states and their officers to perform to the full their constitutional duties.

Uniform State Legislation

One of the advantages claimed for a federal system of government is that it permits uniform legislation and administration on subjects that require it, while allowing state-to-state variations in laws and administration on all others. If the central government had full power to legislate on all subjects that to any extent required uniformity or in respect to which the public might gain a net advantage from uniformity, and if the central legislature used its powers to the hilt, then central legislation and administration would fulfill all the needs for uniformity. Also, then, it might be added, a federal system would be hardly distinguishable from a unitary one. It happens, however, that no central government in a federal system fulfills the two requirements of having all the power needed and of using it to the fullest extent possible. In the United States, for example, while we may concede that Congress has more powers than it has ever used, the fact that it has not used them indicates a policy of leaving many things to the states. Under its power to implement the full-faith-and-credit clause, for example,

Congress might conceivably enact a law setting the minimum standards requisite for a divorce before other states had to recognize it as valid, but Congress has chosen not to legislate in this field—hence the movement in certain states for a uniform divorce-recognition law, to be adopted by state legislatures.

It is in certain fields of business and commerce, however, that the diversity of laws among the states has come to be felt most widely. Hundreds of thousands of businesses doing business across state lines may be inconvenienced in various ways by the diversity of state statutes on sales, bills of lading, warehouse receipts, negotiable instruments, partnerships, business records, and property. Many other human activities and transactions might also benefit from greater uniformity of laws among the states, for example, judicial proceedings, public welfare and health legislation, tax administration, marriage laws, and guardianship. Many of the diversities that exist among state laws are of doubtful value even in the states concerned, whereas certain diversities permit some states to take advantage of others and encourage a lowering of legislative standards all around.

Recognizing the need for having the states themselves take steps for more uniformity in their laws, certain leaders in the American Bar Association seventy years ago started a movement that has brought into existence the National Conference of Commissioners on Uniform State Laws, which now usually includes commissioners from practically every state and territory and which has made considerable progress toward its goal. Each state establishes its own commission consisting usually of a few lawyers to work on uniformity of laws, and these commissioners meet in annual conference. At these meetings they decide on taking up new subjects for uniform laws and dropping others; they discuss, amend, and approve drafts of uniform and model laws that have been prepared by their various committees. The Council of State Governments serves as the secretariat for the conference as a whole and assists in informing state legislatures about the program.

Since its inception, the conference has sponsored about a hundred fifty uniform and model laws. Some of these have been dropped, leaving about a hundred that are currently active. The Negotiable Instruments Act dates back to 1896, but most of the proposals are of much more recent date. The best batting averages have been obtained by the Negotiable Instruments Act, approved in all fifty states, the District of Columbia, and Puerto Rico; the Warehouse Receipts Act with the same number of adoptions; and the Stock Transfer Act which has been approved by all except the Commonwealth of Puerto Rico. At least six other acts have forty or more adoptions, but from these high peaks the number of adoptions drops off considerably, down to a dozen or so acts that no state or territory has chosen to adopt.

The National Conference is not the only agency at work for uniform laws. The Council of State Governments itself has had a drafting commit- tee since 1940. These cover various subjects of war legislation (state coun- cils of defense, air-raid precautions, wartime speed limits, defense housing, for example) and special subjects in agriculture, aviation, crime control, public health, and other fields. Many national agencies such as the Depart- ment of Agriculture and the Public Health Service have also sponsored model laws, and so have numerous private organizations in their own fields of interest.

Infinite diversity and constant change appear to be laws of human activity. Uniformity is an ideal for which some persons strive with vigor, while others as strongly oppose it. Complete and perfect uniformity is clearly an unattainable ideal just as absolute diversity is. Give a number of men the same uniform ballot or income tax blank to fill out, and the re- sults will be somewhat different for every one. Even a uniform law enacted by Congress for the nation will be differently administered and enforced in different places. It is simply unrealistic to expect fifty different state legisla- tures with freedom of choice to reach identical results in legislation merely because a certain model law is placed before them. If in some cases they all adopt the same law without any initial amendments—which is almost unheard of—some will soon find reasons for amending it in different ways with resultant diversities. State-court interpretations of the same law will also vary. This has been the experience to date in the movement for uni- form state legislation.

If we put away childish ideas of perfection in the uniform-state-law movement and look rather to worthwhile practical results, the movement and the efforts that have gone into it have undoubtedly justified them- selves. There have been substantial reductions in the diversity of laws, and the movement for more uniformity steadily gains headway. Results seem to be best in certain common-law fields where controversy among special in- terests is at a minimum. So far, also, relatively short laws on limited sub- jects have had the most adoptions.

Reciprocal and Retaliatory Legislation

Without any concerted movement, most states have adopted a certain num- ber of laws for reciprocity in certain fields. Such laws are usually condi- tional upon what other states do. Thus state A will enact that physicians or other professional men licensed to practice in other states with licensing standards equal to those of state *A* may obtain licenses to practice in state *A*, provided their own state grants corresponding rights to physicians in state *A*. Some states have enacted reciprocal provisions in their inheritance and income tax laws so as to avoid double and treble taxation. Indeed, the principle of reciprocity will be found in many places in a code of state laws.

The opposite is, of course, retaliatory legislation. Where a state legislature believes that its own industries and citizens are being discriminated against in other states, it may pass laws designed to get some sort of revenge or to induce the other states to mend their ways. For example, where one state required all public buildings to be erected with locally produced stone, to the detriment of the quarrying industry in other states, one of the latter forbade its own institutions to buy any butter or other products from producers in the first state. Such measures of discrimination and retaliation seem rather puerile and are usually self-defeating. They do nothing to improve interstate relations except to teach the current body of legislators a lesson, that their successors will probably have to learn in their turn, that no state can substantially benefit itself by cutting off commerce and friendly relations with its neighbors. Leaders in the field of interstate relations are generally opposed to all such discriminatory and retaliatory laws.

Interstate Relations in Practice

In a sense the formal constitutional provisions for interstate relations and interstate cooperation are involved and cumbersome and if the states were to work together only in a manner provided by the Constitution and as enforced by the courts, our federal machinery would creak and groan indeed. The greasing of interstate relations comes out of voluntary and professional organizations, informal arrangements, and the personal cooperation of the individuals actually carrying on government in the several states.

★ *Organization for interstate cooperation*

The idea of nation-wide cooperation among state governments for the performance of state functions and the protection of general state interests, though not a new idea, has only recently received adequate implementation. Some earlier organizations of state officials in particular functional fields (public health, education, insurance, and railroad regulation) were followed by the creation in 1892 of the National Conference of Commissioners on Uniform State Laws and in 1908 by the Governors' Conference. Since about 1930 the number of these nation-wide organizations of state officials has increased considerably.

The organization of the American Legislators Association in 1925 and the absorption of its work into that of the Council of State Governments, organized in 1933, set the stage for a rapid increase in the number of organizations of state officials. Working through the Council of State Governments as a central secretariat are the following organizations, all based on state official membership and representing state interests:

American Legislators Association
The National Legislative Conference
The Governors' Conference
The Conference of Chief Justices
The National Association of Attorneys General
The National Conference of Court Administrative Officers
The National Association of State Budget Officers
The National Association of State Purchasing Officials
The Parole and Probation Compact Administrators Association
The Juvenile Compact Administrators Association

To some extent, also, the National Conference of Commissioners on Uniform State Laws works with and through the Council.

The Council of State Governments describes itself as "a joint governmental agency established by the states, supported by the states, for service to the states.[16] It is composed of "Commissions or Committees on Interstate Cooperation established in each of the forty-eight [now fifty] states." Its stated objectives are: clearing house for information, research, improving state legislative, administrative and judicial practices, encouraging interstate cooperation, and improving federal-state and state-local relations. It maintains a central office in Chicago, regional offices in New York and San Francisco, and a Washington office to look out for state interests at the national capital. It is a dynamic organization with a frankly state-oriented viewpoint, and it unquestionably carries a great deal of weight with members of Congress and national administrators.

There are a number of other official organizations in functional fields that stress the role of the states in American public life, but unquestionably the organizations listed above that are affiliated with each other through the Council of State Governments are the most active group in promoting interstate cooperation and in forwarding the interests of the states. They represent something new in American public life, new activities in drawing the states together as states, and so also setting up a counterweight to

16 *The Book of the States, 1958-59,* Vol. XII, p. 201.

the national government. In some ways the Council has a significance for public policy and for the federal system that would seem to call for a basis in an interstate compact approved by Congress.

★ Informal agreements and cooperation

Every working day the states collaborate with each other in making policies and in the financing and administration of public functions. State highway departments cooperate with other state highway departments and not only at the state boundaries. State health and welfare departments negotiate with each other about the residence, support, and care of the sick, the aged, and the dependent. Law-enforcement officers in every state cooperate with their "opposite numbers" in other states in making arrests, in detaining and in arranging to return to other states persons arrested, or in detaining for other states prisoners who are leaving penal institutions, and in exchanging information.

The national organizations of attorneys general, health officials, tax officials, and the like offer excellent opportunities for personal acquaintanceships which later smooth relations in each of their respective fields. Although there is little evidence to suggest refusal to cooperate or difficulties of cooperation among states as the result of differing political party control, there does occur, at least at times, a special comradeship between officials of states with similar party loyalties. Wisconsin's Democratic governor in 1959 was warmly welcomed by the Democratic governors of Michigan and Minnesota. Similarly Democratic governors in New York, New Jersey, and Connecticut had earlier shared a party faith. At the very least common regional problems may be more informally handled where confidence exists as to purposes.

Interstate relations then frequently necessitate agreements, but many of these are reached very informally—by conferences, telephone calls, letters, and other actions of various administrative agencies. These numerous and daily acts of collaboration of officials across state lines are of the very stuff of public administration.

★ Cooperation in the tax field

To illustrate some of the problems and solutions in interstate relations, the field of taxation is chosen. Any one of half a dozen others might have been used. Numerous examples of formal and informal agreements and practices occur among the states in the writing and administration of their tax laws. The National Tax Association and the National Association of Tax Administrators (which include many state tax administrators in their membership) from time to time have had committees on uniform tax laws or tax administration. Recommendations were made on such matters as uniform allocation formulas (in the case of corporations doing business in several states), reciprocity and tax credits, and exchange of information for administratives purposes. Adoption of uniform tax legislation in substantive tax law has stumbled on the same rocks as attempts at uniformity in many other fields. The tax interests of the states are not the same nor are the controlling political philosophies in tax matters. Reciprocity and information exchange do not so frequently affect the vital interests of the states in tax matters and so in practice (whether formally or not) receive more favorable attention.

Interstate comity and full faith and credit as concepts may come into play in the state's definition of its tax debts and in its attempt to collect taxes owing. In part these problems have been solved through reciprocal legislation as well as through more informal practices in tax administrators' organizations.

It is not illegal under the national Constitution or present Congressional acts for an individual to be subject to an income tax in the state where he lives and also to be subject to an income tax in another state on the same, or at least part of the same, income if he happens to work or have property income outside his state of residence. In practice states using the personal income tax tend to recognize the inequity of such a situation and to provide for adjustment if the sister state also provides for adjustment.[17] New York taxes all those who work within the State of New York regardless of their residence, but provides in effect for cancellation of this tax indebtedness if the individual is subject to an income tax in his state of residence.[18] As another example, if A works in Minnesota for a period but continues his permanent residence in Wisconsin, he can satisfy the Minnesota income tax law through filing (1) a statement of nonresidence and (2) a copy of his Wisconsin income tax return.

But how does Minnesota actually know that A filed the original of the return and paid a Wisconsin tax? On request, the Wisconsin Tax Department would check its files and advise Minnesota of the filing and paying by A of his income tax. New York has entered into formal agreements with

17 Widespread double and treble taxation of incomes by the states would probably bring about Congressional action to standardize residence definitions and the basis on which state income taxes could be levied. And taxpayers would more carefully choose their state of residence, work location, and property ownership to the possible detriment of one or more of the states levying the income taxes in an inequitable manner.
18 New York's generosity in providing for cancellation if the state of residence taxes the income earned in New York is somewhat marred in the case where the residence state has no income tax. Unlike its treatment of its own residents, such taxpayers may not offset New York income with the usual personal deductions for contributions to charity and so forth. This differential treatment has been subject to recent conferences between the governor of New York and the governors of Connecticut and New Jersey.

several states for exchange of information and even for inspection of returns by another state's tax employees. Most of the states, however, rely on the good will and reasonableness of other states to provide them with information as their need arises. The laws of Massachusetts, Missouri, and Utah, however, have provided no basis for reciprocal exchange of detailed information with other income tax states.

Another question. Can state *A* collect in state *B* a tax debt discovered after the taxpayer has removed himself and his property from state *A* to state *B*? No test in the United States Supreme Court has been made of the full-faith-and-credit doctrine as it might apply to a state tax-department determination of indebtedness. About half of the income tax states have written reciprocal legislation which grants comity to other states with similar legislation to use their courts for the purpose of collection. Missouri under a general statute permitted Oklahoma to use its courts to secure a tax judgment against a taxpayer formerly a resident of Oklahoma but at the time of the suit a resident of Missouri.[19] Without formal statutes state tax administrators may provide mutual assistance in bringing pressure on tax debtors. And tax debtors do not always raise the technical objections of jurisdiction.

REFERENCES

Leach, Richard H., "The Status of Interstate Compacts Today," 32 *State Government* (Spring 1959), 134-139.

————, and Redding S. Sugg, *The Administration of Interstate Compacts*. Baton Rouge, La.: Louisiana State University Press, 1959.

Report of the Joint Legislative Committee on Interstate Cooperation. Albany, New York, 1958.

Thursby, Vincent V., *Interstate Cooperation—A Study of the Interstate Compact*. Washington, D. C.: Public Affairs Press, 1953.

19 State of Oklahoma ex rel. Oklahoma Tax Commission *v.* Rodgers, 238 Mo. App. 1115, 193 S. W. 2d 919 (1946).

CHAPTER 6

Intergovernmental
Relations and Local
Governments

THE ORGANIZATION, structure, and functions of local governments frequently have old historical roots when community custom and law bound the individual. The fiercely independent Greek city-states gave way to the Roman Empire. The Empire dissolved into a congeries of rural strong men whose descendants acknowledged a succession of regional rulers. Nonetheless the king or emperor was a distant potentate who guarded the peace or involved his subjects in war, attempted to enforce particular uniformities demanded by powerful advisers, or otherwise affected the local citizen rather more at the periphery of his membership in the local community. Even taxes by the central government were, more often than not, levies on communities or classes rather than individualized impositions. Local governments—cities, towns, counties—often became centers of disaffection to the regime if any of its demands ignored local customs or interests too flagrantly. The City of London, more than once, showed such unmistakable objection to the acts of particular sovereigns that the king and household remained away from the city for varying periods. The Paris "mobs" were recognized opponents of the sovereign and the aristocracy on occasions long before the Revolution of 1789. Several other European cities had reputations for looking after the interests of their own citizens in defiance of royal command.

American local governments have had their times of resistance too.

Boston and Philadelphia provided centers for the growth of the American Revolution. Charleston, Richmond, and Atlanta helped feed the Southern cause in the Civil War. The moving frontier gave most American communities an individualistic, self-sufficing sense of meeting their own problems, even though the United States Army, marshals, military roads, and land grants contributed much to frontier development and growing rural communities. Local governments have also shown more seamy undercoats of political corruption: the misuse of public moneys, protection of crime, connivance at the avoidance or evasion of many local ordinances, and a strong tendency at times for government to be manipulated in the interests of the few. Nevertheless, local governments were necessary, and all states had to provide for them, both urban and rural.

The common strands of local loyalties, substantial local control, and some sense of general participation of the citizens in the Greek city-state, the old European city, and the American frontier community combine to influence our conceptions of local government. At the same time, the twentieth-century revolutions in industrialization, urbanization, transportation, and communication have radically changed the character and requirements of local governments. We need to avoid merely reciting older incantations when we consider local government in its modern context.

Are local governments carrying on functions as a matter of historic tradition or social inertia which in modern terms would be more effective or have a wider impact if carried on at the state level? How small, immediate, and personal does government need to be to secure not just the loyalty of citizens in the generalized sense but the type of interest and loyalty, so important in a democratic country, which will encourage substantial participation in the community's decisions? What are the breaking points in population concentration and other community characteristics at which the service demands of citizens change? Such questions and others lie in the background, if not on the surface, of discussions of local government.

Allocation of Responsibilities

Although the draftsmen of our national Constitution avoided reference to local governments, such governments already existed and there was an implicit assumption that they would continue to exist. The states were left to determine their degree of control, direction, or supervision. All states have cities and villages; all, except Connecticut, have counties (Louisiana has parishes and Alaska has boroughs). In a general sense the local governments of the fifty states have much the same organization, responsibilities, and opportunities.

If the analysis is not carried out too literally, it is possible to see a second set of federal relations between the state and its local governments.[1] The national Constitution divides responsibilities between the federal government and the states. State constitutions divide responsibilities between the state capital and local governments. In both instances, the division rests in part on theories of liberty and local self-government and in part on practical convenience. Thus defense and foreign relations are national matters, general regulation of elections and higher education have been a state responsibility, and immediate citizen protection has been a local matter. The national Constitution left all undelegated powers to the states (or to the people). But although state constitutions have usually left some room for local governments to determine the variety of responsibilities they wish to undertake, state legislatures have both assigned specific responsibilities to them and restricted their organization structure, revenue sources, and functions.

★ Legislative-local relations

Some nineteenth-century legislatures, often relying on older precedents, saw local governments as corporations to be organized and regulated by the state. Since different cities manifestly had different problems, different charters and regulations were called for. Special legislation for each organized community became common, and the local laws of most state legislatures might easily fill more pages in the statute books than would the general state laws. Individual charters and special legislation offered unexampled opportunities for logrolling and bribery. Reacting against these excesses opposition to special legislation often took the form of requirements for uniformity in new or revised state constitutions. "The legislature shall establish but one system of town and county government, which shall be as nearly uniform as practicable."[2] Such uniformity clauses made no distinction between the problems of rural and urban areas. "Reform" pressures of the late nineteenth and early twentieth centuries emphasized optional legislative provisions and home rule as antidotes for the extremes of special or uniform

---

[1] The concept of a state-local federal relation and the existence of inherent powers in local governments was stated in the much quoted, but less often applied, opinion of Judge Thomas M. Cooley in a Michigan State Supreme Court case, People *ex rel.* LeRoy *v.* Hurlbut, 24 Mich., 44. 9 Am. Rep. 103 (1871). A more recent and extreme statement of this position is that of Rodney L. Mott, *Home Rule for America's Cities* (Chicago: American Municipal Association, 1949).

[2] Wisconsin Constitution (1848), Art. IV, sec. 23.

legislation. Village and city governments in Wisconsin secured home rule and a variety of optional charters of general organization from which to choose. County governments in New York have available to them a great variety of forms of government as a result of a multiplicity of optional laws on the subject. Massachusetts cities are similarly situated. Most cities in Michigan and Minnesota and counties in Texas and California, for example, have home-rule authority, but some make no use of it.

Whether the legislature supposedly recognizes home rule or not, there usually exists a sizable body of legal restrictions which may be most limiting, the result of the piecemeal approach of legislative action. Borrowing and taxing restrictions have been adopted, often following taxpayer-group pressures and with little review of what functions are required or might reasonably be undertaken locally. Unrelated state laws may affect local organization structure. The Virginia law with a ceiling on school aids meant reduction in state aid to three communities if they accepted a metropolitan consolidation proposal of a few years ago. Wisconsin's formula for distributing its income tax has encouraged the separate organization of particularly wealthy suburbs.[3]

★ *State administrative supervision*

With the tremendous growth of functions of state governments in the last sixty years, the extent and variety of state administrative supervision over local governments has increased tremendously. Under the conditions of travel existing in the nineteenth century—poor roads and relatively few miles of railroad tracks—a county, school district, township, or city had to be quite independent of the state in terms of its day-to-day operations. Mail was slow, and long-distance telephone or telegraph nonexistent or not extensively used. While state legislatures controlled local governments by means of special legislation and other devices, state administrators, to the extent that there were any, had relatively little continuing contact with the localities. Intergovernmental relations were legislative, legal, formal, and sporadic.

Under present-day conditions travel is rapid and communication almost instantaneous. No county or city is too distant to escape rather frequent contact by mail, telephone, or travel with the state administrative offices. Add to this the fact that most state agencies, at least in the larger

[3] Wisconsin's personal and corporate taxes are collected by the state but shared with localities on a general 40-50-10 formula. After certain deductions, the state keeps 40 percent and returns to the taxpayer's home municipality 50 percent and to his county 10 percent. The formula traces back to the state's income tax law of 1911 when the modern suburban problem was unknown to the state.

states, have regional or district offices, and you will realize some of the potentialities of state-local relations. State supervision of an increasing number of functions may be advisory, inspectional, or a variety of compulsory devices. Grants-in-aid offer further opportunities for state direction. The contacts now are not between units of governments, far removed from each other, but to a large extent face-to-face contacts among officials. State-local relations today are primarily administrative, informal, and continuous.

Services of government.   While technological developments were facilitating better communication and travel, they were creating new problems for government. They changed the character of the economy. Large-scale business, mechanized agriculture, huge labor unions—all brought with them new demands for governmental services. A vast system of roadways, health, welfare, and education services, increased law enforcement activities, and inevitably knotty fiscal problems have been part of the last seventy years. Since the states generally were not equipped to perform all the services demanded and since the spirit of local self-government was strong, many of the functions added to state responsibilities were passed on to local governments, the state retaining a primarily supervisory role. The counties were chosen most frequently as the units to administer relief or welfare, health, and highway activities, and their participation in agriculture through the county agricultural agents is one of the oldest state-county administrative programs. In New England not the counties but the towns became the basic outposts of state-local administration. Education came to be handled by special units of government, the school districts, or alternatively by the cities, counties, or towns already existing. Other special districts were established from time to time also, such as irrigation districts, soil-conservation districts, and housing authorities.

Gradually during the last seventy years almost all state and local government services have become state-local in character, if not outright national-state-local. Joint administration by two or three levels of government is now necessary. Hardly a function of government can be named that belongs exclusively to the states, counties, or cities. Certainly all major functions of government are today administered by more than one unit of government, almost always as part of a joint program of intergovernmental cooperation. Since the problems government must face are not confined to the areas of specific counties or cities but are nation-wide (or even international), region-wide, or at least state-wide, the administration of governmental activities cannot be confined to single watertight compartments known as units of government. Cooperation has become the keynote in national-state-local relations.

Units versus functions. Cooperation and a feeling of good will between state and local officials in their functions may be desirable up to a point, but it is frequently true that the close collaboration of some individuals is looked upon askance by others. What has happened in part is that state and local officials in each of the various major fields, such as highways, welfare, and education, have built up close working relationships among themselves almost at the expense of their relations with those in general control of local government, such as city councils, mayors and managers, and county governing bodies and executives. There is a point at which the control of the general governing officers of local government over administration is weakened.

At the extreme this conflict between state functional administrator and locality involves independent units of government. Some state administrators would like nothing better than to have the function they supervise be performed by special or *ad-hoc* units of local government under their own supervision, bypassing the regular general-purpose units, such as cities, counties, and, in New England, towns. The picture drawn is one of the state department of education with its independent school boards, the health department with its local health boards, the welfare department with its welfare boards, the soil conservation service with its districts, and so on. The theory of this school of thought is that local integration is unnecessary, since the state integrates the various functions of government to the extent that integration is needed.

The unity of local government has been seriously impaired in many states by the complete or semi-independence of certain local administrative agencies that report only to the state. School districts in a major portion of the country are of the completely independent character, but most local boards have at least a tenuous relationship to the general governing body of the city or county.

Some restrictions on the activities and methods of state administrative departments do exist in practice. While state administrators have a genuine interest in securing the voluntary cooperation of local officials, they also play down and fail to use their powers of compulsion for another reason: local governments (if united) have considerable influence over state legislatures. Many state legislators have had municipal or county government experience and retain great sympathy for the local official's point of view. If a state agency were to go beyond the bounds of propriety, it might suffer a curtailment of its powers or budget or both in the next legislative session. To a certain extent the legislature acts as an intermediary between state administrative agencies and local governments, and it is not uncommon to find that on particular points which are crucial to them the latter can carry the day.

Lack of central state agency. State supervision, whether legislative or administrative, of local government might not seem so piecemeal and scattered if there were a central state agency in each of the states that had a general concern for local governments. Canadian and European experience has led to the establishment of departments of internal or municipal affairs, which supervise local government. As operating in Canadian provinces and in England, these departments seem quite compatible with extensive local self-government. It is possible, if such departments were established in the several states, county and city government as a whole might benefit by having a state agency interested in the entire unit of government rather than many state agencies each interested in only one function. Virginia, North Carolina, and New Jersey have had state agencies interested in the broader aspects of local government. The latter two have confined their activities to financial supervision for the most part, but Virginia has had a commission that has actively promoted better forms of county government.

Interlocal Relations

★ Local governments

No central intelligence, no state-wide planning board or commission on local government boundaries, ever planned our present jumble of counties, cities, villages, towns, school districts, and other government units with their overlapping, conflicting, and competing responsibilities and authorities. Yet in rural, nineteenth-century America, it is possible to distinguish a rationale. Urban, industrialized, twentieth-century America's loyalty to the old and the requirements of the new have produced a patchwork of compromises and concessions. Each group which senses real or imagined harm to its interests (whether these be economic, social, traditional, political, or whatever) stands athwart the road to fundamental changes in local-government organization and assignment of functions.

Nineteenth-century counties were generally laid out to permit every citizen to drive by horse and buggy to his county seat and to return in time for farm chores. Justice, official records of land transactions, and some road work were to be had from the county. The township (or, in its absence, the county) worried about farm roads and the welfare of newcomers or older inhabitants struck by catastrophe, and collected property taxes for the state, county, and school district as well as for itself. The incorporated village or city added a few other services for citizens—improved streets, fire and police protection, water, health, eventually some housing standards and parks. Transportation made visits between country and city cousins infrequent and effectively separated the service needs and political relations of urban and rural areas.

Recognizing mid-twentieth-century needs, one of the original authors of this text suggested in 1949 a "rationalized scheme" of local-government units[4]:

Units	Number
City-counties (each having a central city of at least 50,000 people)	200
Counties (rural and part rural)	2,100
Incorporated places (including the larger towns in New England)	15,000
Miscellaneous units	500
Total	17,800

These figures are in striking contrast to the actual number of units reported in 1957 by the Bureau of the Census[5]:

Units	Number
Counties	3,047
Townships	17,198
Municipalities	17,183
School districts	50,446
Special districts	14,405
Total	102,279

In the abstract, it is not difficult to secure agreement that some local governments have outgrown their usefulness entirely or in their present organizational form, that resources and responsibilities are not well matched, and that political control is often beyond the effective grasp of the citizens. Agreement does not so easily develop as to the particulars of a new plan of local governments. Every existing unit of local government has its loyal supporters. Encouragement for the consolidator lies mainly in the continu-

[4] William Anderson, *The Units of Government in the United States* (Chicago: Public Administration Service, 1949), p. 46.
[5] U. S. Department of Commerce, Bureau of the Census, *Governmental Units in the United States*, Vol. I, No. 1 (Washington: Government Printing Office, 1957).

ing reduction in the number of school districts in recent years (108,579 in 1942 and 50,446 in 1957).

★ Interlocal agreements

Without the formal sound of interstate compacts and with little indication of fear by state governments of local conspiracies, states grant formal and informal authority to local governments to make common agreements or to contract with each other for local services. A central city may contract to furnish water to a suburb. Some Wisconsin counties have hospitals for the aged; others which do not send their patients to institutions of adjacent counties at an agreed charge. Adjacent communities or even counties may establish a common planning authority.

Metropolitan Areas

State-local and interlocal headaches today center largely around the "metropolitan problem." Most state governments not only began existence in a period in which their local urban areas were small and disparate but have lived a good part of their lives with that condition as a fact. Without ignoring New York, Boston, Chicago, and a few other nineteenth-century metropolitan areas, only in this century and even more particularly since World War II have many states found that metropolitan development provides problems largely ignored under older theories of local-government relationships. Many of the shibboleths of the past rise up to haunt the modern exponent of action in the metropolitan field. Home rule, which under the good-government movement became a battle song for citizens disturbed by state legislative "interference" and direction of local affairs, is not quite so sweet to central cities when sung by their suburbs and county governments. Constitutional and statutory home-rule provisions and earlier legislation sharing state tax revenues or allotting state aids have sometimes had unforeseen consequences in encouraging separatism of suburb and central city. County governments in large metropolitan areas may largely duplicate functions already being performed or, in somewhat smaller metropolitan areas, draw most tax support from the central city and give services largely to rural areas. Professional educators (or welfare workers or sanitarians) intent on the needs of education (or welfare or sanitation) push their functional reforms oblivious to the complex of metropolitan problems. And perhaps worst of all, the metropolitan area refuses to stand still for diagnosis and medication. What we call the metropolitan problem tends to grow as we look at it.

★ Meaning of metropolitan area

Today most individuals using the term have reference to the 1950 Bureau of Census definition when they say metropolitan area. The Census defined a Standard Metropolitan Area as follows:

> Except in New England, a standard metropolitan area is a county or group of contiguous counties which contains at least one city of 50,000 inhabitants or over. In addition to the county or counties containing such a city or cities, contiguous counties are included in a standard metropolitan area if, according to certain criteria, they are essentially metropolitan in character and socially and economically integrated with the central city.[6]

★ Expanding metropolitan areas

Most of the population growth in the United States in the last two decades has taken place in and about the metropolitan areas, whereas most of the rural sections away from the metropolitan centers have lost population. Between 1940 and 1950, four fifths of the United States population growth was in metropolitan areas. Parts of the United States show signs of developing great chains of metropolitan areas. Thus it is not farfetched to suggest that a continuous metropolitan area may soon exist from above Boston down the Atlantic Coast to New York, Philadelphia, Baltimore, and Washington. Another such continuous metropolitan area seems likely to stretch westward from New York through Pennsylvania, Ohio, Indiana, to Chicago. Some writers have referred to such chains as a megalopolis.

In 1957 there were 174 metropolitan areas in forty-two states and the District of Columbia. Only Idaho, Montana, Nevada, North Dakota, Vermont, Wyoming had no city of 50,000 or more. Hawaii, but not Alaska, would now be added to the list of states with metropolitan areas. More than one half of the population of the United States lives in metropolitan areas. The statistics in the 1950 Census, the 1957 Census Estimates, and, without doubt, the 1960 Census emphasize the urbanization of the United States and the concentration of its people in large, sprawling metropolitan areas. Home builders and industry show little regard for city, county, state, or even international borders. And government then tries to catch up.

★ The "metropolitan problem"

We have created metropolises in large part by our increased technological knowledge and application of this knowledge to the world we live in. Increased agricultural productivity made it possible to feed more urban peo-

---

6 Bureau of the Census, *U. S. Census of Population: 1950*, Vol. 1, *Number of Inhabitants* (Washington: Government Printing Office), p. xxxiii.

Figure 4. REASONS WHY CITY RESIDENTS MOVE
TO THE SUBURBS

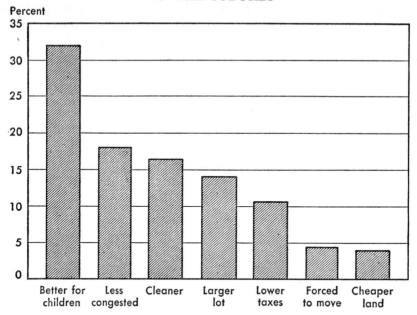

Source: Milwaukee County Regional Planning Department, *Residential Develop-*
ment in the Unincorporated Areas of Milwaukee County, Wisconsin (1946). Later
studies have included objections to new migrants moving to the city and the
quality of schools as reasons for moving to suburbs. It appears that the reasons
for moving to the suburbs are not constant but are related to: (1) the size of the
city; (2) the particular characteristics of the city; and (3) the situation at the time
the study is made.

ples and decreased the need for farm labor. Increased health knowledge
not only removed old scourges of cities but often made improvements in
health more practical in urban than rural living. Long-distance transmission
of power with little loss of energy as well as the quickened transportation
means lessened earlier needs of dense land use for urban population and
industry. The "new" city offered many people a higher standard of living
and interesting educational and recreational opportunities without the sac-
rifice of all the amenities of space in country living.

Metropolitan living has deepened some old problems—juvenile delinquency, adjustment of racial and national-group tensions, organized
crime, and mental health. The multiplication of governments within most
metropolitan areas has divided the attention given not only to this list of
problems but to general social and physical planning of the expanding,
interrelated area. Too often problems are seen as the province either of
professional administrators (such as education and welfare) or of separately
organized cities and villages. This restricted approach seeks answers in

piecemeal terms and leaves other problems to fall between the labeled stools of "function" or "government unit."

Thus the "metropolitan problem" is one of a substantive and structural nature. How can we make safe, comfortable, and attractive the extensive living and working space of our metropolises? What governmental arrangements will encourage civic responsibility and participation and match reasonably well community resources and responsibilities?

How many governments?   The fifty states of the union achieved their present borders from a mixture of the timing of their settlement, the boundaries already fixed for land acquired through purchase or conquest, and compromises in Congressional action. Counties and townships frequently followed survey lines or natural boundary lines of streams or lakes. On the other hand, eighteenth- and nineteenth-century villages and cities usually established community boundary lines.

The numbers and types of governments in nineteenth-century America, much more than today, corresponded with the differentiated responsibilites of distinguishable communities. The model pattern of governments (p. 110) would attempt to restore something of the earlier logic of differentiated responsibilities on today's tangled mass of governments. Several assumptions underlie the model. (1) With a few exceptions, the citizen today needs only one government between him and state government. A thoroughly unitary government may gain in its ability to act at the expense of losing contact with its citizens, but too many governments and governmental levels may stall all agreement and prevent the accomplishment of widely accepted goals. (2) Fewer local governments with general responsibilities would simplify the citizen's task in placing responsibility. The city council or county board could be held accountable for schools, parks, sanitation, water, planning, law enforcement, or whatever the rural or urban community requested. (3) Fewer local governments would bring into closer approximation the resources and responsibilities of the governmental unit. States would find it easier to develop shared-tax and grant-in-aid formulas for the benefit of local governments out of revenues raised by the state's greater tax-gathering ability without distorting either the organization of local government or the presumed equity of the tax shared or the aid distributed. (4) The reduced number of governments would again correspond to meaningful communities of interrelated social and economic activity. An unbroken rural area would be under a county government. An unbroken urban area would have a single city-county government.

The model does not give us a standard for every decision. Presumably if the unbroken rural area extended over tens of miles, or even hundreds of miles as in Alaska, it would be desirable to break it up into one or more separate counties. Likewise no one would suggest a single government for the Boston-New York-Washington area even when it meets the Census definition of a single metropolitan area. Should this string of continuous settlements be broken at the state boundary lines? More frequently? Less frequently? The unbroken urban area, with a readily identifiable metropolitan center, historic existence, and economic and social interdependence, seems a good candidate for a single metropolitan government in our model. But large, merging metropolises raise questions of size and number in their most aggravated form.

Citizen participation. In the metropolis as in other areas political participation may be identified both by its activity and the degree of its involvement. There is the nonvoter, the occasional voter, the habit voter, the informed voter. There is the self-motivated candidate for public office and the front candidate. There is the citizen who follows, the citizen who attempts to inform himself, and the citizen who is one of the decision-makers and who influences others. Metropolises, especially the central cities, exhibit the gamut of political participation; but the proportion of citizens reasonably involved—even in voting terms—is smaller than in rural and nonmetropolitan urban areas. Dispersion of leadership, the complexity of the government, the fluidity of the population, the absence of a sense of immediate responsibility and involvement, poverty, limited education—all reduce participation.

Metropolitan organization also contributes to reduced political activity. Multiple governments scatter leadership and dilute its attention. Interlocal administrative districts may remove activities from the direct pressure of the voter or may add so many decisions to the ballot that the voter gives up the attempt to become informed. Leading business and professional men may approach city government only as its activities encroach on their immediate economic interests; they will probably devote the balance of their public-affairs time to a dilettantish participation in the affairs of their suburban "village" with its emphases on the virtues of separateness and increased physical comforts for its citizens. In fact, whatever the income level of the suburb and wherever employment is found, the civic loyalty of residents may lie with the suburb rather than the central city or the general metropolitan area. Election statistics usually show that political participation is greater in the suburbs than in the central city, but this participation may never rise above a PTA concern for education, zoning related to property values, garbage disposal, and trash collection. The actual or forced homogeneity of many suburban communities may discourage political differences and political argument. Central-city redevelopment needs, racial, economic, and social adjustments, perhaps even governmental corruption and general metropolitan planning are considered by newspaper or television reports to be "foreign" news.

The suburban "greater democracy" omits from its concern the "tough" problems of the metropolis. It is bought at the price of leadership continuity and generalist emphasis. Suburbs often attract as residents many of those business and professional men who have the special talents for civic leadership. The central city, as a result, may have to depend on men with talents not as well adapted to the leadership needs of a community with growing problems. But, the suburban leaders may find that their time is largely invested in minor problems. In other words, the central cities often need the leaders who have moved to the suburbs; and these leaders in the suburbs may find it frustrating to work for the solution of only small problems. A reduction in the number of governmental units would make available a greater number and a greater variety of leaders to deal with interrelated problems.[7]

Resources and responsibilities. A look at the states has convinced most Americans not only that some states are more blessed with economic resources than others and that some states have fewer problems to meet, but that no state is sufficiently isolated not to be affected by the action or lack of action of other states. This description fits metropolitan governmental units as well. The disparities in resources and needs become clearer when they are observed in an area of a few miles. The central city may have a considerably lower per-capita wealth than its richest suburbs and yet find it necessary to provide more governmental services. It may have an aggravated slum and housing problem as well as special welfare and health needs. It is burdened with the necessity of providing police and fire protection, traffic control, pavements, and numerous other services not only for its own inhabitants but also for the thousands or even tens and hundreds of thousands of people who live beyond its limits but come and go each day for work, shopping and amusement. Residential suburbs of moderate- or low-income families may find that the absence of taxable industry makes their tax bill for a modest level of governmental service higher than the central city's. A few wealthy suburban areas may combine high-quality governmental services with a relatively low local tax rate.

[7] The assumption of more available leadership when there are fewer governmental units seems clear on its face. What is less clear is the question of continued participation of the general suburban citizenry if the suburb loses its political identity. Is the suburban citizen willing to act in politics only in a municipality of village or small-city size when the questions for his attention immediately concern his living pattern? Do the larger, more general questions of the metropolis weaken his political attention and interest? The authors are not acquainted with any studies of voting patterns in a community before and after consolidation or annexation with a central city which would help to supply an answer.

The state capitol. Equally important to joining economic resources for common goals may be the joining of political resources locally and at the state level. More and more studies and observations suggest that a *united* metropolitan delegation is seldom unsuccessful in the state legislature— even in a rural-dominated state legislature.[8] Chicago or Milwaukee or St. Louis usually sees legislation it does not want passed or legislation it wants fail to pass only when the central city and the suburbs or even the central city government and its legislative delegation are not in agreement.[9] If metropolitan legislative delegations could be as united as state Congressional delegations often are in matters of direct concern to the state, metropolitan areas might have less reason to complain about their state legislatures. Even differences in political party might have less untoward influence.

But again there is a circular problem. Where state legislation intentionally or unintentionally favors separatist organization of governments in the metropolitan areas, the metropolitan delegations are likely to continue to represent vested community interests and so fail to present a united front. In this situation, political-party differences between a central city and its suburbs may turn decisions on metropolitan issues before the legislature into tests of party strength.

★ Solutions to the metropolitan problem

Today's metropolis gives many of its residents a more varied and satisfying life than otherwise would be possible. Even for its newest and most trodupon citizens, the life may represent a step up even in physical conditions and almost certainly in future prospects. But it is as we stand apart and dream dreams that we are disturbed by much of the reality. There are great sections of some American cities where only a blessed fire (while all the residents and their most precious belongings were happily absent) could remove at least some of the dirt and ugliness. Post-World War II London and Berlin gained as well as lost from the bombing holocausts. It is not only the physical dirt and decay but the seemingly more evident spiritual tensions which disturb the city.

With even a modicum of respect for the traditional values of liberty, few people would desire that government should solve all the problems and

[8] See David R. Derge, "Metropolitan and Outstate Alignments in Illinois and Missouri Legislative Delegations," *American Political Science Review* (December 1958), pp. 1051-1065.

[9] The State League of Municipalities, with its dominance by small and medium-sized cities including metropolitan satellites, is not the answer to political action for the metropolis. The leagues, while asking for more state aid and shared taxes, have tended to cry "home rule" and oppose or at least fail to support legislation which would encourage citizens to avoid separate incorporations and to seek consolidation in metropolitan areas.

meet all the needs of metropolitan areas. While some needs can be solved or changed through the interaction of citizens and groups in ordinary living, others cannot. But government alone can meet some of the difficulties and can create the conditions under which citizens can meet others.

The first and the most appealing to our model approach is the establishment—initially, through annexation and consolidation, even through possible state action—of a single government for a metropolitan area. Special districts, federation, enlargement of county or state activities are most often cited as alternatives. Without planning and action, the present helter-skelter arrangements will continue.

1. Annexation and intercity consolidation. Annexation and intercity consolidation are simply means to achieve the single metropolitan government. Unfortunately in most states statutory provisions for home rule normally make all moves for annexation by the central city or consolidation with the central city very difficult. Statutes normally provide that consolidation can take place only by a majority vote of the citizens (or the governing boards) of each community. Citizens of each community lack equality in their influence upon decision-making, and even such matters as the desire of a village president (mayor) to retain his position may decide the issue.

The principal expansion of the boundaries of central cities comes through annexation—that is, through the attachment of unincorporated territory to the metropolis. The procedure is usually simpler than consolidation; the citizens of unincorporated areas have less of a veto power. Even where there must be a favorable majority for annexation, the boundaries can be established to include such a majority—sometimes forcing the other parts to seek annexation as a result of untenable tax and service situation. States providing for a very simple procedure for annexation, such as Virginia and Texas, have given their cities an effective tool to control the entire metropolitan area. However, annexation of unincorporated areas does not solve the dilemma of many large central cities which are hemmed in by a ring of incorporated suburbs. It is true that on occasion central cities have "jumped across" or gone around incorporated suburbs and taken in new territory. Some suburbs thus have become islands in the central city's territory. However, this procedure is frequently impossible for a city to follow either legally or practically. Several state supreme courts have ruled against it.

Suburban areas are not all alike—suburbs may be residential with high-income, middle-income, or low-income families; their residents may have few or many children; or suburbs may be largely industrial with few residents. The central city will find annexation or consolidation with some suburbs especially advantageous for tax, service, and planning purposes and annexation or consolidation with other areas disadvantageous. If homes are small and children many, for example, property tax income may be low in relation to the schools and other services that must be provided. Yet for general development and planning purposes, the city council may still seek and approve annexation or consolidation of both the high-tax, low-service areas and the low-tax, high-service areas.

2. **Extraterritorial powers.** Practically all large cities have already been given the power to acquire land outside their limits, either by purchase or by condemnation, for safeguarding or procuring a water supply, for providing parks and golf courses, or for establishing hospitals, airports, housing projects, workhouses, stone quarries, gravel pits, and other needed public facilities. Some cities are permitted or even required to spend money for the construction and maintenance of roads and bridges beyond the city limits, although the power to do this will not ordinarily be implied. Whenever it is proposed, however, to give the large city police powers over the adjacent area political opposition to the suggestion is usually too strong to be overcome. Furthermore, large cities seldom have much extraterritorial power over incorporated suburbs. For sparsely settled territory not yet ready for incorporation into the city, extraterritorial power for central cities might provide some measure of land-use control. It may be essential for some city services such as parks and airports, but it does not greatly reduce metropolitan disunity.

3. **City-county consolidation.** In a number of areas city-county consolidation has been proposed. The latest adoption of such a plan was in Baton Rouge, Louisiana, in 1948. Several of the larger cities in the country are both cities and counties—one government performs the usual functions of both units. San Francisco, Denver, New York, New Orleans, Philadelphia, Baltimore, St. Louis, Boston, and most of the larger cities of Virginia are in this category. Some of these city-county consolidations are complete, while others retain partial fragments of the former county governments. City-county consolidation achieves for local government a single general government in the same way that a state government and the national government each has general governing power.

The two principal difficulties of using city-county consolidation to solve metropolitan problems are (1) the political difficulties of securing state enabling legislation and local consent if each organized suburb must produce an approving majority (Louisiana legislation required merely majority approval of the total citizenry of the area); and (2) the difficulty in determining where the boundaries of the city-county should be drawn. A too-inclusive boundary line may add to the opposition. A tighter boundary line, without simplified annexation or consolidation procedures, merely gives new form to the metropolitan problem within a few years.

A variation of city-county consolidation (or perhaps of federalism) transfers designated common functions of the metropolitan communities to the county government. Where the boundaries of the metropolitan area and a single county are reasonably coterminous, this may be the easiest solution. Planning and zoning, parks, health, and welfare are among the functions commonly vested in urban counties. County assumption of some municipal functions has many of the strengths and weaknesses of metropolitan federalism. County government, under some state laws, also suffers from awkward executive-administrative arrangements.

4. Special districts. For many urban districts the simplest solution to a specific metropolitan-wide problem is to establish a special district for that purpose. Such a change involves no basic reorganization of the local governments of the area and is therefore more feasible politically than most alternatives. In some cases, such as the Port of New York Authority, a district may be given a number of functions to perform and become for these limited purposes a metropolitan-wide government. The difficulties of special districts are several, including such problems as (1) who will control the special district and the basis of representation if a special board is set up, (2) how to assure the responsibility of the officials of the special unit, and (3) how to coordinate the activities of the special district with the municipalities and other units of local government in the area.[10]

5. Federation. During the 1920s much attention was centered on metropolitan federation as a solution to urban organization. New York City with its five boroughs was cited as an example, although today it is essentially an integrated municipality and hardly represents federation, except perhaps for a few historical remnants. The idea of federation was to create a central government with certain powers for the entire metropolitan area, with the more local governments or boroughs retaining other powers. The 1950s have seen a resurgence of enthusiasm for federalism with the adoption of federal structures by Toronto, Canada, and Miami, Dade County, Florida.

In a sense a federal metropolitan government is a consolidation of special districts. Instead of dispersed agreements between the central city

[10] It is easier to justify the New York Port Authority on grounds of efficiency than it is on those of democratic planning and control.

and suburban communities to conduct this or that or a dozen functions on a metropolitan basis, there is one agreement for a federal government with authority over named functions. The central city and surrounding municipalities continue to maintain their governments as usual for any other functions they wish.

Supporters of metropolitan federation emphasize the opportunities for handling generally matters of metropolitan-wide concern without sacrificing the values of "village" local government. Federation promotes equalization of services and gives region-wide planning a chance. Some also see it as the necessary first step toward a desirable but distant single metropolitan government. Enthusiasm for federalism as a metropolitan solution may brush over some of the problems it does not solve. (1) It adds another governmental level which may increase costs and will almost certainly further complicate the voter's choice. (2) It usually means an allocation of representation on the federal council which recognizes incorporated units of government rather than number of voters. (3) It does not necessarily improve and may worsen equity in sharing costs of government. (4) It often is at least as awkward as the central city in attempting to keep its growth in line with the actuality of metropolitan living.[11]

★ Some last thoughts on the metropolis

The old adage of home rule needs to be restated or abandoned. State laws and state constitutions need to find a substitute for their piecemeal approach to metropolitan centers. It is not enough to ask the legislature to give local governments general powers. Wallace S. Sayre has commented on the New York City metropolitan problem and its relation to New York State:

> The State government has a clear and inescapable responsibility for leadership in the field of metropolitan problems. It is the only government in the State with adequate jurisdictional reach to grapple effectively with metropolitan decisions, the only government with a clear title for leadership, and the only government with the needed resources in staff and finances. It is further, the only government which can deal

11 Eric Hardy, "Progress in Toronto," *National Municipal Review* (October 1958), pp. 445ff. includes the above list and others as problems remaining unsolved after five years of federalism of Toronto. Since for many metropolitan areas these are the critical problems before federation, federation offers few solutions. And federalism may in fact delay the possibility of a single government. Wisconsin's sharing of its personal and corporate income taxes in terms of tax origin works to the advantage of its wealthy suburban communities. Only the financial pressures of independent school systems or independent water or sewage system may be incentives for consolidation. A federal metropolitan system under which the wealthy incorporated suburb may keep its high shared tax revenues and still secure the advantages of large-scale operation of schools, for example, assists the communities with the least need.

effectively with the governments of the adjoining states, which are involved in and have partial jurisdiction over many of the problems.[12]

Most states do not now face the problem of New York, but state responsibility is common. Legislatures (and governors) should take a new look at the responsibilities of the local citizen; assess the general type of area in terms of population and resources which is capable of doing this job; and then provide statutes written in organizational, functional, and fiscal power terms which will encourage or at least not discourage local initiative in meeting the problems identified.

President Eisenhower's establishment of a federal-state relations unit in the Executive Office might be worth emulating on the state level. State governors could set up coordinating executive agencies in the field of state-local relations. Legislatures, in interim committees or in legislative councils, may need to develop liaison committees with the governor's agency. The complex decisions required should recognize the impact of party politics. State legislatures with representation apportioned by population may find their task easier than states with area representation. The failure of states to assist metropolitan-area development is likely to result in the transfer of local functions to the state government or to an assumption of former state responsibilities by the federal government.

Urban sociologists and psychologists, however, have underscored our recognition that most urban dwellers give little attention to governmental arrangements. Urban residents seek to satisfy a variety of needs in their living accommodations that do not include government organization. The rural small town may restrict occupational opportunities, entertainment choices, and personal freedom. It offers friendship, a feeling of belonging (including participation in governmental affairs), aid in times of personal difficulty, and relaxation in emphasis on status symbols. The city offers wide occupational choices, varieties of entertainment, identification with a big and perhaps great community. Success in the city is writ large.

The city's values both attract and repel. The family frequently seeks the city for working and the "country" for family living. In the suburb are yards, neighborhood organizations, and possibilities for acquaintances and friends. The big central city government is set aside in favor of the smaller suburban government without the "politics" of the big city. Political parochialism follows with an emphasis on separateness not only from the central city but from other suburbs. The immediacy and interweaving of complex governmental problems involving the suburbs and central city are submerged in the emphasis on "small town" virtues, living and working with

12 New York State, New York City Fiscal Relations Committee, *A Report to the Governor of the State of New York and the Mayor of the City of New York* (November 1956), p. 62.

"our own kind," and vested interests in superior services and/or low tax rates. The values at stake in meeting the metropolitan's problems locally seldom receive recognition.

It is easy on paper to suggest the values of a single level of local government encompassing the metropolitan area in terms of participation, responsibility, resource use, service equalization, political effectiveness. But there remain questions for empirical investigation of the validity of these assumptions and, if valid, how to get there from here. Democratic thought assumes citizen participation, responsibility, and political effectiveness. Population and area size are factors in resource use and service equalization. We need more studies to assist in identifying the conditions for the marriage of optimum citizen participation and political effectiveness with optimum resource use and service equalization. As in any marriage, some compromise is necessary.

REFERENCES

Banfield, Edward C., "The Politics of Metropolitan Area Organization," I *Midwest Journal of Politics* (May 1957), 77ff.

Council of State Governments, *The States and the Metropolitan Problem; A Report to the Governors' Conference.* Chicago: Council of State Governments, 1956.

Dixon, Robert G., Jr., and John R. Kerstetter, *Adjusting Municipal Boundaries: The Law and Practice in 48 States.* Chicago: American Municipal Association, 1959.

Government Affairs Foundation, *Metropolitan Communities: A Bibliography.* Chicago: Public Administration Service, 1956.

Jamison, Judith Norvell, and Richard Bigger, "Metropolitan Coordination in Los Angeles," 7 *Public Administration Review* (Summer 1957), 164-169.

Lyon, Leverett S., *Governmental Problems in the Chicago Metropolitan Area.* Chicago: The University of Chicago Press, 1957.

Maass, Arthur L. (ed.), *Area and Power: A Theory of Local Government.* Glencoe, Ill.: The Free Press, 1959. Especially Ch. 1-4.

1959 Report of the Joint Legislative Committee on Metropolitan Areas Study. Albany, New York, March 20, 1959.

Robson, William A. (ed.), *Great Cities of the World; Their Government, Politics, and Planning.* New York: The Macmillan Company, 1957.

Wood, Robert C., "Metropolitan Government, 1975: An Extrapolation of Trends," 52 *American Political Science Review* (March 1958), 108-122.

Woodbury, Coleman, "Great Cities, Great Problems, Great Possibilities?," review of several books in 18 *Public Administration Review* (Autumn 1958), 332-340.

Zimmerman, Frederick L., and Mitchell Wendell, "Local Government and State Lines," 30 *State Government* (February 1957), 35-39.

PART TWO

The Voter and
Politics

CHAPTER 7

The Electorate and

Pressure Groups

ONE BASIC ELEMENT of democracy is popular participation in government. While there is some amount of participation in all forms of government, democracy prides itself upon the breadth and depth of popular participation in its governmental affairs. In a thriving democratic system there is maximum leeway for a citizen to discuss and criticize actions taken by government, to join or organize an opposition group, and to cast a secret ballot that expresses real choices between the ins and the outs.

Participation in Politics

Viewed broadly, politics is the control of government and the development of public policies. There are dozens of methods of participation in politics, and it would be difficult to say which of them is most important. If a citizen were to try to make as large a contribution to politics as laws and customs allowed, he could not exhaust the possibilities in all his waking hours during his lifetime. As long as men live in a society, the actions of all citizens will contribute toward governmental action in one direction or another, whether they will it or not.

Assuming, then, that a citizen wants to participate in politics in whatever ways his time, inclination, and ability permit, he or she has a wide variety of choices to make. While perhaps most citizens never go through a formal process of determining once and for all exactly how they are going to participate in politics, some realization of the opportunities available is necessary, if the role of the citizen in a democracy is to be evaluated.

★ Individual action

Perhaps the most common method of formal participation in politics is casting a vote. Voting is not by any means universal in this country, particularly for state and local elections. It is common to have less than 50 per cent of the qualified voters turn out for these contests. While nonvoting and the suffrage generally will be discussed more in detail later in this chapter, it is appropriate to point out here that voters use their right to vote in widely different ways. Some of them feel compelled to vote at every election on all issues, others only vote at elections or on issues that they consider crucial, and still others never bother to go to the polls. There is not only a difference in the number of votes cast by each voter over the years, but also a difference in the quality of the effort put forth. Some voters give extended consideration to the issues and candidates in an election, while others vote blindly for a "name" or follow without exception and question the recommendations of some group or individual.

Beyond casting a ballot, the individual has a wide variety of choices open to him for participation in politics more or less on his own. He may write letters to or telegraph or telephone his state legislators, the governor, mayor, or some department head or agency. He may read newspapers and periodicals, listen to broadcasts of political speeches, attend meetings, and talk to his friends and fellow workers about politics. An occasional citizen may even undertake individual research on one or more aspects of governmental problems. Appearing before legislative or administrative committees to give testimony is quite common, particularly on the local-government level. Many a voter even without political-party ties may urge his neighbors and friends to vote and offer them rides to the polls.

★ Pressure groups

More and more participation in politics is being funneled through groups with special interests to promote. Relatively seldom do citizens become concerned with government as a whole; they become interested in government as it affects a particular service or activity. It may be the street in front of the house or the road going past the farm; it may be veteran benefits or taxes or pensions or fish and game laws. Whatever the special area of concern, there is likely to be a pressure group already existing, or one can readily be formed, that will give added weight to the lobbying that needs to be undertaken to accomplish the specific end in view. It may be a neighborhood or district group, a veterans organization, taxpayers association, old-age-pension group, or sportsmen's club. Whatever its name or special interest, it is likely to be far more effective in appearing before official agencies than single individuals. Many citizens, therefore, are members of one or more such groups and consciously or unconsciously give their endorsement to the policies that the organization decides to promote. By being active members of a pressure group or even organizing a new one, some citizens exert considerable influence on the actions of government in particular functions.

★ The officeholder and employee

While there are relatively few officials on a national level who hold elective office, there are fairly large numbers on state and local levels. Indeed, in some states the number of members of school boards is greater than the number of teachers employed. When all the elected township, school-district, municipal, county, and state officers are taken into account, the possibilities of participating in politics through holding elective office are very real indeed for anyone who wants to expend the necessary time and energy. Nearly a million public positions are elective. Of course, in highly politically organized areas, such as Chicago or New York City, the chances of holding public office without working through a party over a period of years are rather slim. But, as a whole, running successfully for public office on a state or local level, especially the latter, is not difficult.

Governmental employment is not usually considered to be a method of participation in politics, but at the very least the employees holding the more important positions are concerned with public policy and hence with politics. A department head in a large city or state and even most professional employees at any level of government participate in many policy decisions. They help decide what recommendations are to be made to the county board, city council, or state legislature. They are entrusted by these bodies with rather extensive discretion. They help plan governmental policy for the future as well as shape it for the present in day-to-day administration. In a true sense they may be said to participate in politics.

★ Parties and campaigns

Almost anyone in any area can become an active member of a political party. There are no accurate statistics as to the exact number of active party members, but they probably number nearly a million if one counts as active those who attend one or more party meetings a year or who distribute party campaign literature. Political parties are discussed in Chapter 8, and here it is only necessary to point out that there are important opportunities for anyone who wants to participate in politics to expend much of his energy on political-party affairs.

Very similar to the kind of work carried out by some party members is the job assigned to campaign workers attached to individual candidates. In many states the main work of a political campaign is carried on by the followers of certain candidates and not by the members of political parties as such. Any candidate is happy to accept help of any kind, and as a result thousands of persons become involved in politics because of their allegiance to one or more candidates for public office. Here again the amount of time that may be spent can vary from occasional pamphlet distribution to leadership in organizing a campaign.

★ *Governmental research*

Governmental research agencies of a wide variety have been formed and try to influence the policies of official groups directly or indirectly by means of research and publication. Some of these are attached to universities. Others are citizen organizations operating in particular cities or states and, in a few instances, on a nation-wide scale. The total effect of research bureaus on governmental operations is very great in a few localities and rather negligible in others. There is opportunity for participation in politics by associating with the bureaus as an employee or as an interested citizen.

This list of areas in which participation in politics is possible does not begin to exhaust the possibilities. There are such organizations as the League of Women Voters and good-government groups locally and nationally. There are many volunteer advisory committees attached to government, some being concerned with specific departments, some with overall reorganization such as citizen committees to promote the revision of charters and constitutions. The purpose has not been to present as long a list as possible but rather to indicate some of the alternatives facing the citizen who would be active in politics. There are many more areas of participation than a single individual can possibly be active in. He must pick and choose those that appear of most interest and value to him. Furthermore, political participation is not the only activity that demands a citizen's attention. There are the demands of family, vocation, radio and television, comic strips, recreation of all sorts, clubs, and many others.

Because an individual chooses to concentrate his attention upon matters other than politics does not necessarily mean that he is a bad or ineffective citizen. He may influence public policy to a smaller extent than someone else, but that is to be expected in a division-of-labor society. The crucial point for democracy is not that everyone exerts the same amount of influence upon governmental affairs, but that everyone has an opportunity to exercise a large amount of influence and especially that everyone has open to him all the methods of participation in politics that others do, to as large extent as is possible. While all of us do not have an equal chance to become governor of a state, all of us should have the legal right to run for public office, including the governorship, if we so desire. Many methods of participation may lie dormant as far as most people are concerned for a number of years, but it is essential that the methods be available when the individuals concerned feel the need to make use of them. If the latter condition obtains, governmental action can be checked by an aroused citizenry.

The Electorate

Viewed in perspective, the casting of a ballot is not an adequate measure of the vigor of a democracy. If elections were the only form of participation in politics, government would not rest on a very firm foundation of popular support. Yet the casting of a secret ballot on which appear opposing candidates is a symbol of democracy, and it is an essential part of a free society. Small wonder that the right to cast such a ballot has been so highly prized for centuries that even armed conflict has arisen over it.

★ *Role of the voter*

The right to cast a vote on election day is the capstone of political participation. In the long run, if control of the majority of votes at elections is assured, control of governmental policy will almost surely follow. The stakes are thus high. But most members of the electorate are followers, not leaders, if they can be said to belong to any one group at all. The individual who casts his vote may have an entirely different view of what he is doing from that of the political strategist.

If its significance is to be understood, the action of the voter at election time must be considered in relation to other people and groups of people, not as an individual, atomistic act. The individual exists as part of a society, and there are countless groups that crisscross its fabric. Winning elections is a group process, not a haphazard collection of individual votes. It is essential in a democracy to permit the voter complete freedom and secrecy in voting for the candidates of his choice, but it is doubtful if any important office such as the governorship or mayoralty of a large city has ever been won without extensive group support and activity. In casting a ballot, the voter is responding in one way or another to group action. Voting is not a "final" response, either; rather, it is one stage of the continuous process of participation in politics.

The reasons why a voter turns out or fails to turns out on election day are both rational and nonrational. Among the factors illustrative of the latter are sheer habit, the weather, or emotion, such as liking of the looks of a candidate. Among rational factors are the desire to vote for a certain man or group because of the policies he or they support and the desire to vote against a group for similar reasons. The objective of the individual voter or the group he is supporting may not be to win the election at all. It may be to register a protest vote. Even a small protest vote can often be of some influence in governmental affairs; it indicates dissatisfaction. The intelligent political leader will pay attention not only to the majority of votes cast for the winning candidate but also to the trends that are evident in the proportion and distribution of votes received by losing candidates. If this is not done adequately, a majority party may find itself thrown out of power rather quickly.

Generally, however, the aim of a group in politics is to try to gain political power for whatever purposes it has in mind. No political party will be completely unified in what it hopes to accomplish, of course, nor will all individuals who support a candidate be equally satisfied with all aspects of his program. There will be a limited consensus, at least enough to warrant sticking together to try to win the election. Most voters are formal or informal members of some group that seeks political control. They may be members of a political party, or a labor union, farm organization, or chamber of commerce. The organization will usually send them an endorsed slate of candidates and urge them to vote the straight ticket. The number of voters who make independent choices, choices not endorsed by any group with which they happen to have some connection, are relatively few. They may be the crucial voters who determine which side is to be the winner.

The voter engages in the group process of political participation. Individually, his vote counts for little, at least where there are thousands of voters. It is voters who band together in groups that have real significance for modern politics. Since not all persons participate equally in the processes that lead up to elections, the voters who are content with merely casting a ballot find many of their choices already made, so to speak, and consequently they cannot register so effective a choice as those who have helped between elections to shape the issues and choose the candidates.

★ *Restriction of suffrage*

The history of the suffrage in America since the early colonial days has been one of gradual extension. It is a case study of the growth of one element of democracy, a growth that overcame many seemingly insurmountable obstacles. There was a theory underlying all these obstacles that was quite uniform. That theory was that there are two kinds of men as far as political participation is concerned, those who are good and those who are bad. Those who are "good" are presumed to have superior qualities in one way or another, such as superior intelligence, superior experience, or feelings that are important enough to be considered in determining public policy. Those who are "bad" are thought to be unfit for politics because of some native inability, such as lack of intelligence, inferior breeding, shiftlessness, or simple lack of political know-how.

Historically the states have determined our legal electorate. The 15th and 19th Amendments plus an occasional Congressional act constitute national action in defining the electorate. As long as a state does not preclude individuals from voting for reasons of sex, race, or religion, it has been free to decide issues of residence, literacy, age, and even poll taxes. In the eighteenth and nineteenth centuries, states frequently did not insist on U. S. citizenship and permitted aliens or at least declarants for citizenship to vote. National-state conflicts (and suits and court cases) arise over questions of legal intent, application, and result. But as long as the statute is *uniformly* applied, flaws are not likely to be found in laws which merely reduce the number of voters or even the number of Negro voters, for example. Uniformly administered literacy tests are Constitutional even though there may be a higher percentage of illiteracy among Negro than white adults. Questions and suits arise when literacy standards are adjusted to fit ideas of who are proper voters in terms of race.

For many years the Congress adopted a hands-off policy toward state actions restricting the electorate. Section 2 of the 14th Amendment was inoperative; Senators engaged in filibusters to prevent action on antipoll tax bills; the courts hesitated to look behind statutory words. Beginning in the 1930s, a series of Supreme Court cases narrowed the legal opportunities for avoiding the 15th Amendment, and in many southern states the electorate lost some of its earlier exclusiveness. Two Congressional acts have added to the trend—absentee balloting for the armed forces and the Commission on Civil Rights (1957). The former aided (although it did not guarantee) all citizen members of the armed forces to vote in the Presidential election of 1944 and subsequently. The latter has opened the way for federal officials to bring contempt proceedings against state officials suspected of bias in the application of state election laws.

The mere fact of greater numbers of voters does not assure better government, but the right to vote gives a badge of democratic equality and the possibility of changes in government direction. The states, on their own initiative or under national pressure, have relaxed suffrage restrictions in some directions while tightening them in others.

Religion, race, sex. The 15th and 19th Amendments to the national Constitution forbade depriving any citizen of the right to vote for reasons of race, creed, or sex. The states, in fact, had removed religious voting requirements earlier in the nineteenth century and many states had given women the right to vote before 1920. The northern states generally had removed the word "white" from their list of voter requirements before the Civil War.

Today there are few suggestions that a return to religious qualifications be made, although there is still important religious discrimination in the electoral process and elsewhere. For example, in many Protestant areas no Catholic or Jew could hope to be elected to office, and similarly, non-Catholics are frequently voted against in predominantly Catholic areas in favor of a "Ryan," "Murphy," or other such name. Intercultural relations are never made entirely smooth by a mere change in laws, and the fact that no religious qualification for suffrage exists today does not necessarily guarantee harmonious relations between different faiths.

Discrimination against women takes some of the same forms as religious discrimination. Any woman running for public office finds expressed or covert objection that suggests a woman's place is in the home or women don't understand government and politics.

Not only do minority racial groups suffer the same type of discrimination as do religious minorities or women, but suffrage legislation (or its administration) may be designed to prevent their casting a vote. Several of the next sections will suggest roadblocks which make it difficult for Negroes to vote.

Property. Religious qualifications for the suffrage were abolished early, but property qualifications remained and to a certain extent there was some relationship between the two. Puritans believed that the members of the elect were marked rather obviously by success in the temporal world. Therefore, those who owned property were men who could be trusted in the eyes of the church. Supplementary to this line of reasoning came another, that men who owned property paid taxes and therefore had a special stake in society, and also that those who did not own property were a shiftless lot, the ugly mass of men who had neither the ambition, industry, nor ability to acquire an estate or property of some kind. For local government there was the further consideration that in the early days localities performed services largely for property, not for men. Roads were for access to property, and law enforcement was for the protection of property. No need to consult the mass of propertyless men.

Vestiges of the property-tax requirement are still with us, since in some states on certain kinds of issues, such as approving bonds, property taxpayers only are permitted to vote. This is true in Texas, Utah, Nevada, New Mexico, Montana, and Michigan, for example. Slowly, however, the property qualification for general suffrage has disappeared; it became relatively unimportant as a suffrage requirement around the time of the Civil War, although Pennsylvania retained a taxpaying requirement as late as 1933.

Closely related to property tests is the question of permitting persons on relief to vote. Especially during the depression of the 1930s there was much discussion in some circles of limiting the elective franchise in this fashion. Ten or twelve states do legally prohibit paupers from casting votes. This seems rather unfair, since all groups receive special aid and subsidy from the government, including businessmen, farmers, and labor. A businessman going through bankruptcy receives more financial benefit from the government than most people on relief do in many, many years.

Poll taxes. The poll tax is a per-capita tax assessment that is found in a number of states. There is earnest debate over its merits as a tax, but its most vicious application has come in the southern states, where its payment is used as a requirement for voting. In the South the poll tax was enacted as a mechanism to keep the Negro from participating in elections.[1] Not only was this the original intent, but there is extensive evidence that states with poll-tax voting requirements have had considerably lower voter turnout than states without them. Nor is the effect of the poll tax felt only by Negroes, since many poor whites find it difficult to pay the tax, particularly if it is cumulative from years past.

Literacy. As another technique of discriminating against the Negro in voting, a number of southern states have adopted literacy tests that are administered rather severely for Negroes and very loosely for whites. But some Northern states (and Alaska and Hawaii) also have literacy tests, and

[1] Presently Alabama, Arkansas, Mississippi, Texas, and Virginia have a poll tax as a voting requirement.

theoretically for a quite different purpose. Illiterates, it is argued, should not be allowed to vote, because they cannot read the instructions and names on the ballot and cannot make available to themselves knowledge that appears in newspapers, periodicals, and campaign literature about the candidates and issues in the elections. Yet behind this seemingly plausible argument there is a deep suspicion that Northern and Western states which have literacy tests wanted not so much a minimum educational requirement as the exclusion of certain types of immigrants from the voting booth. This seems particularly likely since it is largely the coastal states in the East and West plus Southern states in which a literacy requirement is to be found. In states where immigrant or Negro populations are not large, the demand for literacy tests apparently is small.

That a certain degree of literacy is a necessary or desirable requisite of voting is arguable. To what extent do those who can read actually pay attention to political news and advertisements? In a modern age with radio and television is it not possible to listen to speeches and political argumentation and become as well or better informed as most do through reading? If a person does not spoil his ballot in marking it, what else should be required of him in registering his choice for public office? Fortunately, with the high degree of literacy in the country, not many persons are excluded from voting because of this test, but the basic theory underlying it—that for voting purposes there are two kinds of men defined by educational achievement—is a potentially dangerous philosophy to accept in a democracy.

As in the South with the Negroes, the literacy test is frequently administered in an arbitrary manner, and this has been its chief defect in practice. In states or areas where advance registration of voters is required, determination of literacy can rather objectively be undertaken at the same time. Abuses can easily occur if literacy tests are to be administered at the time of election. Election judges and clerks can discriminate against those they do not like by declaring that they cannot read or write well enough. There have been cases in which college graduates have been excluded and others with no education admitted to the polls on the basis of the literacy test.

It is generally agreed that the so-called "New York method" is about the best system of administering a literacy requirement. Under an act passed in 1923 a new voter in that state may present to the election inspectors as evidence of his literacy either a certificate or diploma showing he has completed the work of an approved eighth-grade elementary school or of a higher school in which English is the language of instruction, or he may present a certificate attesting to his literacy issued by the board of regents of the state. What is important in this law is that the test of literacy is to be given by the state school authorities and not by the election judges or clerks. The educational test is administered by the educational authorities.

Age. All states except Alaska (19 years old), Hawaii (20 years old), Georgia and Kentucky (18 years old) have a 21-years age requirement for voting. Georgia first reduced the voting age to 18 during World War II, partly in response to the slogan that if men were old enough to fight they were old enough to vote. Other states have argued the matter on a number of occasions. The reasons put forward for reduction on the age requirement were largely threefold: (1) if 18-year-olds are old enough to fight, they are old enough to vote; (2) 18-year-olds have voting ability equal to those over 21; and (3) high-school civics would have much more meaning if the students enrolled in it knew that they could vote within a year. The first argument is a *non sequitur*, although potentially a powerful argument politically; the second has been vigorously disputed, and the third largely ignored.

Residence. To facilitate orderly election procedure, prevent frauds and abuses, and make certain that only persons with some interest in the locality or state be allowed to vote, residence requirements for voting are in effect in every state in the union. As with almost all voting requirements, certain abuses have been associated with the stipulation of residence. A number of states have discovered that one or more rather unpopular minority groups are characterized by a tendency to move rather frequently. A simple way to disenfranchise them is to define residence for election purposes rather stringently, requiring a large number of months and years residence in the state, county, and election district. A glance at Table 4 will indicate the pattern. Southern states require the longest period of residence before the franchise is granted, two years in the state being common. This is followed by standards that make mandatory six-months to one-year residence in the county and several months to one year in the election district. These requirements are designed to prevent Negroes and undesirable poor whites from casting ballots. Because of the nature of their work and their living habits, many of these individuals do not have permanent places of residence, or at least frequently change them. The net result is that they have no voice in the governments under which they live.

Southern states are not the sole offenders, although they definitely represent the extreme in the matter. Industrial and seaboard states generally have the longest residence requirements next to the Southern states. It is fairly logical to assume that legislators had in mind the immigrant and the migratory worker when these residence laws were written. At any rate, it is striking that the Midwestern nonindustrial states as a group tend to have the lowest residence requirements to be found anywhere.

Justification for residence laws in terms of the citizen having time to gain knowledge and interest in the political affairs of his new community overlooks the Presidential election.[2] Connecticut and Wisconsin began a movement in the 1950s to permit U. S. citizens to vote for President even though they might not have the legal residence requirements for voting in state and local elections.

Registration. Some of the abuses that were a partial factor in the establishment and extension of residence requirements at a later date led to the idea of the registration of voters before election day. Registration insures that only those people whose names have been duly recorded can vote. When the country was primarily rural, residence and the right to vote in general were quite easily determined, since in small communities everyone knew everyone. As the country industrialized and urbanized, this became impossible. No longer did a man know all the people in his election district, and frequently he would know relatively few of them. Some proof of residence and other qualifications for the suffrage was therefore desirable, and the device that was adopted was the process of registration.

The registration of voters in advance of an election has spread in some form to almost every state in the union. While in some cases only urban areas are affected, increasingly both city and rural voters come under common registration requirements.

Because of the cost, inconvenience, and confusion of the periodic registration system, permanent and more or less centralized systems have been established in most states (see Table 4). The essentials of any such system are: (1) the keeping of a fairly permanent list of voters with the result that it can be made quite accurate and complete; (2) the creation of a special staff of clerks in a central place in the city, county, or town to be responsible for preparing and revising the list; and (3) relieving the voter from the necessity of having to register every year. In some states a voter may register at any time up until a few weeks before the election at some local registration office. In order to keep the list current a number of devices may be used. A frequent provision requires that voters who fail to cast a ballot during two consecutive calendar years are automatically dropped from the lists. Death notices may be checked systematically, and law-enforcement officials may make house-to-house canvasses. No system of registration is free of the dangers of fraud and political manipulation, but a

2 Or it makes the rather unreal assumption of the need of the voter to know the electoral-college candidates!

well-conceived plan will make these evils much less common. If a system of permanent registration is in operation with a special and permanent staff of registration officials and clerks, it would seem desirable to select them in accordance with merit principles. Similarly, if law-enforcement officials are used to check or help enforce the registration system, merit principles ought to be extended to them.

Absentee voting. In our age of increasing mobility, many citizens lose their voting rights when they move from one state to another and fail to meet residence requirements by election day. Other conscientious citizens may be unavoidably absent from their legal residences on election day. What provisions a state makes for permitting advance or absentee balloting will affect the make-up of the state's electorate.[3] Some states have no legislation permitting a qualified voter to vote at any time except on election days at the polling places. Other states require advance request of so many days, weeks, or even months for absentee ballots that voters with less planned lives become disenfranchised. In the nineteenth century, there was less need for absentee balloting and some of the state laws merely reflect a time lag. In other instances, the laws may be aimed at disenfranchising particular groups on the theory that certain racial and lower-income groups are more likely to be ill or absent or that absentee voting can not be as neatly policed as literacy tests, for example, on election day.

The series of Congressional acts in the 1940s and 1950s and the Federal Voting Assistance Act of 1955 have attempted to provide absentee voting privileges in national elections for all members of the armed forces.

★ *Actual voters of a state*

While legal stipulations and theoretical arguments may support a broad suffrage, there is usually a marked difference between the number of people who are legally permitted to vote and the number who actually cast ballots. Nation-wide figures are not available on nonvoting for different types of elections, but those that have been published for particular states or cities generally agree. On the average, the largest voter participation occurs in Presidential elections, the second largest in state-wide elections including the governorship, and the least participation in local elections. There are notable exceptions to the rule, of course, and it must be understood that these are *averages*. Nevertheless, the figures indicate that local government seems less important and less exciting to the voter than state or national government.

[3] The number of absentee ballots and their distribution have occasionally determined the outcome of particular elections, including the Nebraska gubernatorial election of 1958.

Table 4. RESIDENCE AND REGISTRATION VOTING REQUIREMENTS [a]

State	Residence in			Registration					Coverage	
	State	County	District	Permanent All areas	Permanent Some areas	Periodic All areas	Periodic Some areas	Periodic Frequency	All elections	Some elections
Alabama	2 yrs.	1 yr.	3 mo.	*					*	b
Alaska	1 yr.		30 da.	*					b	b
Arizona	12 mo.		30 da.	*					*	*
Arkansas	1 yr.	6 mo.	1 mo.	*					*	
California	1 yr.	90 da.	54 da.	*					*	
Colorado	1 yr.	90 da.	15 da.	*					*	
Connecticut	1 yr.		6 mo.	*					*	
Delaware	1 yr.	3 mo.	30 da.	*					*	
Florida	1 yr.	6 mo.		*					b	b
Georgia	1 yr.	6 mo.		*					*	
Hawaii	1 yr.			*					b	
Idaho	6 mo.	30 da.	30 da.	*					*	*
Illinois	1 yr.	90 da.	30 da.	*					*	*
Indiana	6 mo.	60 da.	10 da.		*		*	4 years	*	*
Iowa	6 mo.	60 da.	30 da.		*		*		*	
Kansas	6 mo.	30 da.	60 da.	*					*	
Kentucky	1 yr.	6 mo.	3 mo.	*	*		*	4 years	*	
Louisiana	1 yr.	1 yr.	3 mo.	*					*	
Maine	6 mo.	3 mo.	3 mo.	*	*		*		*	
Maryland	1 yr.	6 mo.	6 mo.	*					*	
Massachusetts	1 yr.		6 mo.	*	*		*		*	
Michigan	6 mo.		30 da.	*					*	
Minnesota	6 mo.		30 da.		*		*		*	
Mississippi	2 yrs.		1 yr.	*					*	
Missouri	1 yr.	60 da.	60 da.	*	*		*	4 years	*	*
Montana	1 yr.	30 da.			*		*		*	*
Nebraska	6 mo.	40 da.	10 da.					6 years	*	
Nevada	6 mo.	30 da.	10 da.	*					*	

State						Annual			Decennial		Every elec.		Every gen. elec.
New Hampshire	6 mo.		6 mo.										
New Jersey	1 yr.	5 mo.	30 da.										
New Mexico	12 mo.	90 da.	30 da.										
New York	1 yr.	4 mo.	30 da.										
North Carolina	1 yr.		30 da.										
North Dakota	1 yr.	90 da.	40 da.										
Ohio	1 yr.	40 da.	30 da.										
Oklahoma	6 mo.	6 mo.	30 da.										
Oregon	6 mo.												
Pennsylvania	1 yr.		2 mo.										
Rhode Island	1 yr.		6 mo.										
South Carolina	2 yrs.	1 yr.	4 mo.										
South Dakota	1 yr.	90 da.	30 da.										
Tennessee	12 mo.	6 mo.											
Texas	1 yr.	6 mo.	6 mo.										
Utah	1 yr.	4 mo.	60 da.										
Vermont	1 yr.		3 mo.										
Virginia	1 yr.	6 mo.	30 da.										
Washington	1 yr.	90 da.	30 da.										
West Virginia	1 yr.	60 da.											
Wisconsin	1 yr.		10 da.										
Wyoming	1 yr.	60 da.	10 da.										

Source: *The Book of the States*, 1958-59, pp. 20-21.

[a] No attempt has been made to show all exceptions to general provisions.

[b] The legislatures of Alaska and Hawaii had yet to act on these matters when this text was published.

It is not just the level of government that determines the extent of nonvoting. Many other factors are influential. The issues, candidates, and parties involved have much to do with nonvoting. The more crucial the issues seem to be, generally the larger the vote. The more attractive the candidates and the more active the parties, the larger the voter turnout. A heated and active campaign will help get out the vote, as will good weather on election day and a high degree of civic responsibility among the residents of a particular area.

No one would be concerned about nonvoting if the results of elections were not altered by the failure of large groups of people to vote. On several significant counts the composition of the electorate is different in elections with a high turnout from that in elections with a low turnout. Lower-income groups, for instance, tend to be disproportionately represented among the nonvoters when the turnout is light; the well-to-do apparently cast their ballots more frequently and more consistently. Since party and candidate preferences vary somewhat in accordance with economic status, one party or faction may lose the election because of a light voter turnout. There are similar differences in political preference and voter turnout between highly educated and poorly educated individuals. The less educated a group, the more likely it is to vote less frequently and regularly. Since both lower-income and more poorly educated groups tend to vote in somewhat greater proportions for the Democratic party than do the rest of the people, at least in the last three decades, nonvoting becomes an issue with partisan significance.

Women tend to vote to a lesser extent than men, and certain foreign-born citizens less than native-born. Minority groups such as Negroes and Japanese-Americans likewise vote less frequently than the general population. The problem of the Negro is partially regional in character, and it points up the variations in voter turnout from state to state. The southern states are, as a rule, far behind others in the number of ballots cast at both primaries and general elections in proportion to potential voters. There are often important geographical differences in voter participation within states—rural compared to urban and one ward or district compared to another, for example.

Interest and information or knowledge affect voting habits. Some potential voters see no difference between the "ins" and the "outs." It is a matter of slight concern to them if one or another party or faction has control, and they may have come to this conclusion only after long reflection. On the other hand, some voters think that there are vital issues at stake in the election or rejection of a certain group of candidates. For the peace and welfare of the body politic, it is probably highly desirable that the latter individual vote and express his opinion. For the indifferent voter, there will be no stresses and strains whoever gets elected, while the voter who sees vital issues at stake may react quite definitely to the election results. These thoughts do not mean that voting should be discouraged or that get-out-the-vote campaigns are harmful, but they do suggest a more moderate and basic approach to the problem of non-voting. The right of the eligible citizen to decide not to vote may be a choice he should have in a democracy. Australia, however, requires citizens to vote. Voting can become a ritual of mere approval of the leaders in power: 85-90 percent of the eligible voters in Germany under Hitler turned out and the Soviet Union reports even higher records. On the other hand, if only 25 percent of the electorate cast ballots on election day in a city election and only 40 percent in a state election, some basic questions need to be asked about the policies and methods of those governmental units. Perhaps there are no pressing problems facing them. On the other hand, perhaps those units are not meeting these problems or perhaps the electorate is not sufficiently informed about how they hope to meet these problems. (See pp. 201, 202.)

Public Opinion, Propaganda, and Pressure Groups

★ Public opinion

Does good representative state and local government mean that public opinion rules these units? A variety of writers have given a diversity of definitions for the term public opinion. Agreement seems to exist that the word "public" most often refers to a number less than the whole and normally less than a majority (frequently considerably less than a majority) and that the make-up and number of those who constitute the "public" will differ with issues. Even on matters which may assume great importance, there may be no public opinion in the general sense. Public-opinion polls on major foreign-policy matters, for example, have frequently produced a significant percentage of "no opinion" responses and of the people responding positively, there is evidence that the opinion on many is only an opinion of the moment without the depth of understanding or conviction which would assure their holding the same opinion a month, a week, or perhaps even an hour later. In other words, there is no organic public opinion that automatically forms on each issue.

Public opinion is atomistic and variable. It is atomistic to the extent that prevailing opinion varies with the individual, group, or area that is examined. There is seldom a general consensus on an important matter. Law enforcement and old-age pensions are two examples of state and local issues on which people take widely varying views. On such issues there may be a *prevailing* opinion, but there will be no single view that represents the thought of everyone. Even those who subscribe to the prevailing view will do so for a variety of reasons. Some may be for strict law enforcement because they have religious scruples about such matters. Others may favor the policy because it is to their economic advantage to do so; people may patronize a merchant who supports such "good" policies. There are those who want crime and its attendant social evils reduced because empirically they think that these are bad, and political groups may favor strict law enforcement to further their political future. Thus there are many reasons to explain the prevailing opinion. But it is possible that there may be no prevailing opinion whatsoever on some subjects. Each small group of people may have some different point of view on an issue, or the public in general may simply be uninformed about the matter and hence hold no individual opinions.

In addition to its atomistic qualities, public opinion is variable. It is variable in intensity and it is variable in time. If a cross section of the people in a state were polled on whether they approved or disapproved of the way in which a rather colorless governor carried out the duties of his office, it might be discovered that 40 percent disapproved and 60 percent approved of him. However, opinion concerning such a person would very likely be lightly held. A rather neutral, colorless, do-nothing governor does not offend many people, but neither does he create a band of zealous followers. A dynamic governor who takes positive steps is likely to be presented with a different situation. A poll might indicate that 40 percent disapproved and 60 percent approved of the way he was carrying out his job. However, it is possible, even probable, that the bulk of those who disapproved did so vehemently, while those approving his conduct in office were enthusiastic supporters. Thus, while prevailing opinion in the two cases would superficially appear to be the same, in actual fact there would be a great difference in the intensity with which opinions were held. A rival candidate for governor at the next election would have difficulty beating the dynamic governor, but it is very possible that a rival candidate could beat the colorless incumbent even though 60 percent approved more or less of the way he performed his duties.

The passage of time brings about changes in public opinion. A scandal in the attorney general's office may change a favorable prevailing opinion into an unfavorable one. A depression may change the prevailing opinion of a community as to the proper relationship of the national government to state and local governments. One practical significance of changes that occur in prevailing opinion is that the party or officeholder who sponsors or holds unpopular views may be re-elected to office if opinion changes before election time. Similarly, the officeholder who tries merely to record prevailing opinion may find that he is blamed for "not knowing better" when a sudden shift of public opinion alters previously held views.

There is no such thing as a prevailing or public opinion made up of the same individuals on all issues. No two people think exactly alike, and in the many issues of state and local government there is ample room for disagreement. An individual may agree with prevailing opinion on a law-enforcement issue, with the minority on a highway matter, and again with the majority on a health proposal. What might constitute a prevailing opinion is made up of different individuals for each small issue on which it forms. On some issues, of course, the public is not adequately informed, in which case there will probably be no meaningful prevailing opinion. Nor does a majority party and its members provide a constant prevailing opinion. Individuals within a political party vary in their views to a considerable extent, and under American conditions in states and localities it is common to see members of the majority party combining with members of the minority party to carry the day in the legislature or city council or popular referendum. Public opinion, prevailing opinion, and majority opinion are all abstractions and exist only in regard to particular issues at particular times.

We return to the question with which we started. How and to what extent is public opinion effective in state and local government? Public opinion is influential at every stage of the process of government—elections, parties, legislatures, administration, adjudication. However, it is frequently true that not the whole of public opinion has an influence on every individual concerned. A welfare department will be especially conscious of and responsive to the desires of relief recipients, for example, and fish and game officials to the wishes of sportsmen's groups. A certain assemblyman will be responsive to his constituency, and probably to only that part of it which supported him at election time. There is no guarantee, therefore, that just because 51 percent of the people favor a course of action that it will become the official course of action. The 51 percent may be made up primarily of minority party members, or they may hold their views very lightly. If the 49 percent hold their opinion vehemently, it is likely that they will prevail despite the opposition of 51 percent.

★ *Propaganda*

Often only a thin line exists between education and propaganda, and the side on which a particular message falls will depend on many circumstances. One writer has defined education as "the imparting of knowledge or skill considered to be scientific or to have survival value in a society at a particular time." Under this definition only a society with a complete dictatorship is without propaganda. Under such a dictatorship there is only one truth which has survival value and the imparting of this truth then is "education." [4] This definition, or a somewhat modified version, implies the need for skepticism and questioning. Harold Lasswell once suggested that in reading or listening we should ask who gets what, when, and how.

Opportunities for propaganda and the prizes for success in our world today inflate the necessity for each individual to distinguish areas of "the known," "the tentative," "the value judgment," "the misleading," and "the false." Subtle and blatant advertising which suggests that if we want to lead a glamorous life, we only need to choose the proper perfume, silver, or shirt carries over into government and politics. Repetition of the "big lie" (once popularized by Adolf Hitler—the most fantastic story is accepted because its very improbability makes it believed) and half-truths is a weapon of the cold war.

Interest groups and government may attempt to influence public opinion with propaganda. In these and other instances, the statements may be factually correct but stated in an especially persuasive manner (fully recognizing its target audience) and omitting information which might influence opinion in a different direction. Read, for example, the advertisements of the public utilities of America emphasizing the tax payments of privately owned utilities and suggesting that whereas the privately owned utility pays taxes into the public treasury, the publicly owned utility is merely a drain on the treasury. There is not necessarily any establishable factual error in the ad; but neither does it explain that the profits of the publicly owned utility go into the public treasury or that the possible lower rates of the publicly owned utility make the payment of taxes by utility consumers easier.

Every lawyer and every debater (which includes most of us) in our society has attempted on occasion to make his case convincing by presenting evidence in a certain way and by omitting information which does not contribute to the effect he wishes to produce. Such is propaganda. Detection of propaganda and production of counter propaganda are becoming professional skills badly needed in wartime. Their peacetime, domestic use raises questions for a democratic society.

★ Pressure groups

The individual participates in economic, social, and political life through groups and receives his opinions or contributes to the opinions of others in

[4] Leonard W. Doob, *Public Opinion and Propaganda* (New York: Henry Holt, 1948), Ch. 11.

his interaction with other members of groups. Each group is a series of power relations within and in its relations with other groups in the public or private sphere. Many groups at some point in their existence attempt to influence government. As government and the economy and our society generally have increased in size and complexity, the number and the extent of the activity of interest groups have also increased. But group organization is not new in the twentieth century, nor is it *per se* bad. De Tocqueville noted of the United States in the 1830s: "In no country in the world has the principle of association been more successfully used or applied to a greater number of objects than in America." Extensive group organization and democracy may be parallel developments as long as political parties retain their identity apart from the multiple interest groups and as long as groups generally are not arms of the government or of the party in power.

On the other hand the influence of group competition and conflict on government is not necessarily a full substitute for sensing the "public interest." Significant viewpoints and interests may be absent from the clamor of organized groups in particular situations.[5] In one sense all of the descriptions and analyses of government in this text are descriptions of what has been achieved or how something is achieved by the group process. Governments and their functions have not been prescribed from above nor given ready-made by this or that leader. For the study and understanding of government, it is necessary to keep group activity constantly in mind.

Interest groups affect every part of the government process—from influencing the opinion of citizens generally, platforms of parties, and pledges of candidates to public or private pressure on legislative, gubernatorial, and administrative decisions. Most debates over location of programs or regulation at the state or national level really are conflicts for advantage between groups which believe their relative advantage and strength lie at the state capitol or at Washington. Many programs have shifted to Washington, as particular groups found the conflict for their position too difficult in St. Paul, Albany, Springfield, or Salem. Cries of states rights often are shrillest from groups who find their influence greater at the state capitols.

Almost everyone is part of some interest group, and many belong to a number of them. Individuals may belong to a variety of groups to satisfy different areas or needs of life—a labor union, a church, a social club, a

---

[5] Little satisfaction exists among scholars as to a definition of "public interest," yet it seems impossible to discuss many matters without the conception that "public interest" does exist and that it is something more than an arithmetical average of the moment's power relations among groups. The "Consumer Counsel" case is an excellent example of compromise and adjustment among business and labor within the government framework and the ignoring of the interest of the consumer who often is the public. (See pp. 149, 150.)

PTA, and a political club. The active, competing centers of influence in each of these groups will differ and may produce public positions at variance with each other. Rarely does an individual belong only to groups holding identical positions with equal intensity. (Why should he? If such groups existed they would likely consolidate for greater strength.) It is not unusual for him to belong to groups which may be diametrically opposed on particular issues. Unless the issue has critical importance to him, he may well continue his multiple membership without having any great concern about the inconsistency of the public position of his several affiliations. And he may or may not work actively to change the positions of one or more of such organizations.

Some individuals would probably never be classified as "active" in their membership in any group. Others may be active at times and not at others. Individuals in their roles as group members as in their roles as citizens vary their efforts over time. Just as the citizen through indifference, satisfaction, or even dissatisfaction may not vote, so the group member may take no part in forming the position of the group to which he nominally belongs. The American Legion, for example, has hundreds of thousands of members. Yet in state and national conventions only a handful of members really direct, debate, and pass policy recommendations. The Legion representatives in legislative halls may then proceed to lobby for the program agreed upon in the name of *all* the members of the organization. An interview poll might establish that less than half of the Legion membership feels strongly about the issue, and part of this number would take a stand directly opposing the Legion's official position. The Legion, like most other pressure groups, overstates the picture of unity of thought among its members when it lobbies for its programs.

Many interest groups have become national in scope. Although these groups may have an apparent federal organization, in many instances the national organization and the national staff may tend to shape a uniform policy for application and support by each state and local unit. Certainly it was true during some of the discussions of public health programs that some city and county, and possibly even state, medical societies did not agree with the stand of the American Medical Association. But the power and influence of the American Medical Association prevented most expressions of local differences. Local, "grass-roots" government may find itself pressed to act on the basis of public policies framed by national pressure groups. The Farm Bureau's influence over most of the county agricultural agents in the county may be the classic example of this.[6]

6 See Charles M. Hardin, *The Politics of Agriculture; Soil Conservation and the Struggle for Power in Rural America* (Glencoe, Ill.: Free Press, 1952). Other studies of active in-

★ *Public interest*

Individual citizens, pressure groups, politicians, and political parties frequently call upon the image of the "public interest" to justify their position. At the very least none of them wishes to be tagged as opposed to the "public interest." And a special aura surrounds any argument that is supported by statements purporting it to represent the "public interest."

Defining the meaning of the term "public interest" from the written and spoken usages of the words is a near-impossible chore. There is no general agreement in practice as to its substantive meaning. The "public interest" has been equated with the general values of the society, with wisdom, with morality, and with the results of compromises in the political process. None of these meanings stands up well as an analytical conception. Community values do exist but they are not in the realm of contesting group interests in government. To deny a substantive meaning to public interest is not to deny the existence of community values generally held or of moral values possibly widely held but variously interpreted in terms of concrete issues.

Greater recent agreement among political science writers appears to lie in identifying the significant meaning of "public interest" as the democratic process of group accommodation.[7] Making decisions via the legal election process or through legally elected legislators acting within the established rules or through the chief executive and administrative officials elected or appointed according to law and who are acting within the law and accepted institutions constitutes the "public interest." The "public interest" so defined requires not only the use of the more formal legal and institutional procedures but also the use of the best available information. Again, it is not the decision itself that is the public interest but the method by which it is arrived at. The decision, in fact, may prove in practice to be unsatisfactory to a majority that then organizes to change it. The process of change, organized and accomplished through democratic procedures, again would represent the "public interest."

Defining the "public interest" in the above manner provides an operational definition. For any particular decision, we can check whether the legal rules, the established precedents, the accepted ways of doing things in a

---

terest groups would include: R. W. Gable, "NAM: Influential Lobby or Kiss of Death?" *Journal of Politics* (May 1953), pp. 253-273; Roscoe Baker, *The American Legion and American Foreign Policy* (New York: Bookman Associates, 1954); and Oliver Garceau, *The Political Life of the American Medical Association* (Cambridge, Mass.: Harvard University Press, 1941).

7 See the journal articles of Frank Sorauf and Glendon A. Schubert, Jr., in the list of bibliography references for this chapter.

democratic country have or have not been followed. We can check on how many people through how many groups participated. We can test the decision in the light of current knowledge. We can perhaps uncover majority approval or disapproval of the action. "Public interest" so defined can be tested in the legislative, judicial, and executive-administrative branches of government.

Conclusion

Although the American citizen has a variety of opportunities for influencing political decisions, he also faces barriers. If he is a member of a minority race or religious group, practical, legal, or political restrictions may apply. In any event, he usually finds that he can be effective only if he is willing to work through a group and to some degree accept the discipline of group action. He must work hard to understand issues and to avoid merely voting to match a hired publicity man's imposed picture of his interests and desires. Political science, in part, is a study of how the citizen acts within his opportunities, how he attempts to influence others, and how in turn he is influenced.

REFERENCES

Bernd, Joseph L. and Lynwood M. Holland, "Recent Restrictions upon Negro Suffrage: The Case of Georgia," 21 *Journal of Politics* (August 1959), 487ff.

Lane, Robert E., *Political Life: Why People Get Involved in Politics.* Glencoe, Ill.: The Free Press, 1959.

Ogul, Morris S., "Residence Requirements as Barriers to Voting in Presidential Elections," III *Midwest Journal of Political Science* (August 1959), 254-262.

Public Opinion Quarterly (periodical).

Schubert, Glendon A., Jr., " 'The Public Interest' in Administrative Decision-Making," 51 *American Political Science Review* (June 1957), 346-368.

———, "The Theory of 'The Public Interest' in Judicial Decision-Making," *Midwest Journal of Political Science* (February 1958), 1-25.

Sorauf, Frank J., "The Public Interest Reconsidered," 19 *The Journal of Politics* (November 1957), 616-639.

Truman, David B., *The Governmental Process.* New York: Alfred A. Knopf, 1951.

See also references at end of Chs. 8 and 9.

CHAPTER 8

Political Parties

THE NEED for political parties was not apparent to the leaders in the early years of democracy in the United States. Washington viewed opposition to his program as factionalism that was dangerous because it tended to divide the country. The idea of a *loyal* opposition did not gain acceptance until some years later.

Today political parties are organized on a local, state, and national basis and are accepted as essential to democracy, even though some people are cynical about the way they operate. The designation *political party* is somewhat vague. Does the term refer to all the voters who cast ballots for a party's candidates or does it refer merely to those voters active in the party's affairs between elections? Perhaps it refers only to the leaders or officers of the party or to the men it has successfully elected to public positions. For the present discussion *political party* is used in a general sense to refer to two or more of these groups.

Political parties are based in part upon a very practical, selfish consideration, namely, that different groups of citizens desire and strive for control of government. More than one party is needed in a democracy because all citizens do not naturally agree on political matters and because some alternative to those who hold political power is required, if citizens are to have an effective choice on election day. If opposition exists, those who

151

have political power will use it more carefully, more responsibly. They will realize that if they abuse the trust the voters have placed in them, their political opponents may take control of the government at the next election. And since a political party wants to maintain itself in power as long as possible, a great incentive arises for the majority party to give the voters a type of administration that will make them want to continue to support the party. Party government is thus to some extent responsible government—responsible at election time to voters or groups of voters who have at least one alternative choice to the "ins," a competing political party.

Between elections political parties are accountable to influential individuals, pressure groups, party members, and others. Furthermore, they play a positive role in keeping government accountable—they help to check state legislatures, city councils, and county governing bodies—they keep a close eye on the actions of the chief executives—governors, mayors, and managers, for example—and every aspect of the administrative process comes in for their attention from time to time.

The majority party, the party in control of the legislative and executive branches of government, tries to bring about unity and cooperation between these branches. To this end its leaders are frequently instrumental in encouraging members of the party who hold public office to support a common program or set of policies, and the rank-and-file party members or voters are encouraged to support the party program as a whole. The opposition party finds itself in the role of critic. It examines the record of the party in office with an eye to singling out aspects that it wishes to oppose. While neither the majority nor any opposition party may have a well-articulated program, the majority party commonly has a more developed one than its opponent, since it is faced with the necessity of taking action on the problems facing the government. To a very real extent political parties tend to bring voters and officeholders into somewhat homogeneous or compatible groups that proceed to select candidates for public office and adopt some kind of program of their own. In so doing they reduce the number of alternatives facing the voters both as to candidates for public office and as to issues. Such a reduction is necessary if the task of the voter is to be made manageable.

Because a political party wants to obtain or retain public office, it must appeal to a sufficient number of voters to make that possible. This tends to make a party a unifying organization. It cannot ignore pressure groups, of course, with their special interests. But it must have a sufficiently broad program or attraction for the voters to secure the preponderant number of votes. It must go beyond narrow geographical or occupational concerns. It must be an amalgamating force. In this process it performs a very valuable educational function. It stimulates interest in government as a whole, not just a particular aspect or activity of government.

Political parties and their leaders may perform other functions. They have organized "schools" in the art of politics. In some cities they have helped naturalize aliens in the hope of securing additional votes. Party leaders have acted on occasion as intermediaries between citizen and government, sometimes even resorting to "selling" their influence. Yet in the long run, in a democracy the most important functions that political parties perform are those of providing an orderly mechanism for securing control of government, for keeping government responsible, and for reducing the number of alternatives facing the voters as to candidates and issues.

Political-party Systems

When we talk about political-party activity and political-party systems, there is something of the abominable snow man about the discussion. Tracks of political parties and political activity are easily discernible. We can describe these tracks in great detail. Yet the total picture and life of politics and political parties often seems beyond the grasp of words. State politics and political parties have a special elusiveness when an attempt is made to generalize about the fifty states. A variety of statistical analyses provides an understanding of parties needful for study, but statistical analysis has its greatest value for the individual who has gained directly or vicariously a sensitivity and "feel" for politics. Good political biographies, acquaintance with knowledgeable politicians, and perhaps a bit of personal experience will fill in details of the life of politics that the following description necessarily omits.

State politics influence, and are influenced by, national politics. Strong state political opposition to such an item as raising the minimum unemployment compensation payment can offset the normal liberal economics of a Congress. The Southern states have repeatedly affected Democratic party stands on civil rights issues. The Republican foreign-policy position attempts to satisfy both the states of the Eastern internationalists and those of the midwestern isolationists. A meeting of the national committees of the Democratic and Republican parties bears some resemblance to an assemblage of foreign diplomats—looking for alliances but suspicious of each other. The classical British two-party system of substantial ideological agreement within each party might have developed in this country if we had not had a federated party system as well as a federal governmental system. If they can be separated, the dependence of the two national parties on the activities of the fifty state parties exceeds the dependence of the national government on the fifty states.

The century of Southern loyalty to the Democratic party, on the other hand, may merely recognize the felt need of these states to hold a sectional position in Congress and in national politics. The South has a one-party system not from choice but from its view of the necessities of national politics. The historic position of the Republican party on a few issues and the need for a united front made the Democratic party the only choice for the Southern states in the past. Here, as in many situations, the once adopted form persists. But the pressure of national interests not only limits the choice in matters of national politics but has fastened the one-party system on these states in state and local matters. So perhaps not state politics but national politics have created the one-party South.[1]

★ One-party areas

English and American democratic writers often have emphasized the desirability of a two-party system—criticizing multiparty systems as too often leading to deadlock and delay and suggesting that one-party systems obviously offer no choice and therefore by definition are nondemocratic. Nationally the United States has traditionally exhibited the proper two-party complexion; but in many states, in most counties and small cities, and in some large cities, an apparent one-party system prevails.[2] The Democratic party in Vermont and the Republican party in Mississippi have not led bustling lives in the last century.

A precise classification of one-party states is not simple. Of the ten Deep South states, only Florida (and then only once) has deviated in the twentieth century from the practice of electing Democratic governors. Democratic loyalty is so complete that the ten state legislatures in 1957 with a total of 1658 members had only thirty-three Republicans, divided among four states. The occasional backsliding which may give a southern state's electoral vote to a Republican Presidential candidate or elect a Republican Representative in North Carolina or Virginia does not remove the ten states from the one-party classification. Vermont's 1958 heretical election of a Democratic Representative to Washington, for the first time in more than a century, did not make that state a two-party state either. Some states, moreover, show swings in attachment from one party to the other. Thus in any analysis of party attachment, the years which are chosen for review may be critical and affect the conclusion.

[1] V. O. Key, Jr., *American State Politics: An Introduction* (New York: Alfred A. Knopf, 1956), Ch. 2.
[2] To the extent of at least three-parties, several states and communities have had multiparty systems in given periods of their history.

Using party control of the governorship in the fourteen years since World War II as the focus, fourteen states have never deviated from their loyalty to the Democratic party and five states have never deviated from their Republican-party affiliation.[3] Party control of the governorship, however, may understate one-party dominance for it is possible to gain the governor's chair for a term or two without securing the legislature. Both houses of the Connecticut legislature have had Republican majorities in twelve of the fourteen years from 1946-1960, whereas Republican governors have held office for only six of those years.[4] Detailed local investigation in many states would tend to show strong, continued ties to the majority party in county and local elections with a one-party dominance of even greater depth than is measured by the legislative majorities of other states.

The depth of agreement and the absence of political contests can be overdrawn. Factional fights within particular Southern states have had many of the characteristics of interparty contests—sometimes, in fact, a bit rougher as might behoove a family quarrel. The Long and anti-Long factions of the Louisiana Democratic party or the old La Follette and Stalwart groups of the Wisconsin Republican party gave each state's voters as meaningful choices as most Republican-Democratic contests. The anti-Long faction in 1952 and 1956 identified itself as Eisenhower Democrats and many of the descendants of La Follette Republicans now take active roles in the Wisconsin Democratic party. When deep factional disputes occur they may signal a disruption of the old one-party system. Certainly the Middle West states which displayed strong factionalism within the Republican party have tended to lose their one-party classification and to move toward a system of two-party competitive politics.

Wherever one party regularly wins elections with pluralities which make the minority's position seemingly hopeless, the voter's opportunity to choose shrinks. If strong, factional divisions exist, he may have a choice if he is willing to vote in the majority party's primary. In any event he has substantially no choice in the general election and may well have little choice in the primary. Under such circumstances, the controlling party often lacks the vigorous leadership and sense of party responsibility of the competitive two-party situation. No organized opposition stands ready to expose the faults of those who hold office. Casualness and perhaps a loose sense of ethics, if not corruption, permeate much of the administrative

3 The Democratic states were Alabama, Arkansas, Florida, Georgia, Kentucky, Louisiana, Mississippi, Missouri, North Carolina, Oklahoma, South Carolina, Tennessee, Texas, Virginia. The Republican states were Idaho, Montana, New Hampshire, North Dakota, and Vermont.
4 The Connecticut situation, as is usually true of split gubernatorial and legislative control, reflects a failure to relate representation to population.

structure of government. Although there are exceptions, one-party states have tended to make the fewest innovations of public policy, to review and revise their administrative structure least, and to make the fewest efforts toward selection of employees on a merit basis.[5]

★ Two-party areas

Continuing our use of gubernatorial control as the focus, there are fourteen states in which Democratic and Republican control has changed back and forth so that neither party has had the governorship for more than eight of the fourteen years.[6] These are the states, at least in gubernatorial terms, which most nearly approximate our usual democratic or national model of the two-party system. Here the voter presumably sees two well-organized parties actively competing for his vote and presenting him with a choice in each general election and frequently in each primary. About half the states and many medium- and large-sized cities and counties normally have two principal parties. Spirited contests are commonly found at election time, at least for the important posts. There will be some opposition for almost every candidate, no matter how insignificant the office.

The voter's opportunity for choice in the two-party states not only expands in the general election but frequently expands in the primary election. Closely contested general elections attract more candidates to the primaries of both parties.[7] In other words, where winning in the general election is quite certain (but not overwhelmingly certain) more individuals are interested in trying to win the party's nomination in the primary. As chances of winning the general election decrease, interest in contesting in the party's primary declines. Where election is overwhelmingly certain, factors such as the continued running of the incumbent appear to reduce primary contests in the dominant party. Opportunities for the voter to choose seem then to be at a maximum both in primary and general elections in states with definite two-party characteristics. The scent (but not the stench) of victory is needed to interest candidates.

Some evidence is at hand to indicate that voter participation is greater in highly contested elections. With an active opposition, a political party is anxious to get out the vote, and voters tend to believe that something is

[5] It is recognized, of course, that the lack of change in policy and administrative means may reflect generally held attitudes which are also the reason for the one party rather than that the *one-party* control produces fewer pressures for change.
[6] The fourteen states with changing control were Arizona, Connecticut, Delaware, Maine, Maryland, Massachusetts, Minnesota, Nevada, New Jersey, New Mexico, Ohio, Pennsylvania, Washington, and Wyoming.
[7] Leon D. Epstein, *Politics in Wisconsin* (Madison: The University of Wisconsin Press, 1958), pp. 132, 133. Key, *op. cit.*, Ch. 6.

at stake in the election that their vote may affect. While large voter turn-outs are not necessarily confined to two-party areas, they are more often found there than in areas with a one-party set-up.

What creates two-party competition? Key sees it as being often the result of metropolitan versus rural differences.[8] Not a simple city versus farm antagonism but a complex of the variety of urban interests line up with and against the rural interests to produce active political competition. Even in states with small urban development, traditional regional economic or social divisions may produce state-wide two-party competition, with one-party control being normal in many communities or areas.

★ Multiparty areas

Several cities and a few counties have more than two parties that occasionally are able to elect their candidates to public office. New York City with its Republican, Democratic, Liberal, and American Labor parties is an example. Yet in New York City this system has not generally prevented one set of candidates from obtaining a majority of all the votes cast at an election. While there has been some tendency toward coalition there and even in New York state, other localities and states with a multiparty system offer a few examples of a single party securing a majority of votes cast at an election without resort to coalition. Since experience with a multiparty system has been so limited in the United States, it is impossible to say what advantages or disadvantages might accrue from it. Judging from European experience, however, a multiparty system leads to rather unstable coalition government.

★ No-party areas

While at least one political party is active in every state, there are counties, cities, and school districts in which virtually no political-party activity is present in local elections. There are various reasons for this dearth of party life. "Nonpartisanship" explains a part: the predominant philosophy in some communities is that political parties have no place in local government; local issues are not partisan, it is said. A second factor is the extreme likemindedness of the local population. Where there are few differences to be represented, rival organization or any organization at all seems somewhat needless. A general lack of pressing issues or of political interest may be present. Many times there are special factions or groups in a locality around which a local election centers, so that the ordinary role of political

[8] Key, *Politics, Parties, and Pressure Groups,* 4th ed. (New York: Thomas Y. Crowell Company, 1958), p. 325.

parties may be performed by such factions. The chamber of commerce may be the center of one organization, the labor unions the center of another. Or rival farm groups may battle it out in a county election.

Whatever the reason for the absence of parties, a characteristic of cities and counties lacking parties is a greater emphasis on personalities or pressure groups. There is no amalgamating group, so that special interests largely determine the outcome of an election. These interests may be "good" or "bad," depending upon an individual's point of view, but that they exist is certain. A PTA may have its way in a school-district election, a taxpayers' group in a county election—the result is government by a special pressure group in any event. Individuals elected to office will credit either some special group or their own personalities for their success and act accordingly.

If these pressure groups or personal allegiances are strong enough and combine, they may approach the status of special political parties for local elections. Some communities do have special parties for local elections, and their situations frequently differ but little from the regular two-party cities or counties.

Party Organization

The organization of parties varies from state to state and locality to locality. Even the paper or formal organization of parties varies widely among the states, and everywhere the informal methods of using or getting around the formal organization are adapted by the leaders to local circumstances and desires. It seems accurate to say, at times, that one ought to know the details of party organization in order to ignore them. There are tightly organized parties and loosely organized parties. A few years ago in Wisconsin, any individual who expressed a single pleasantry on the state Democratic party might have received a telephone call inviting him to be a delegate to the state convention. Even in the successful 1958 gubernatorial campaign, the governor's campaign manager was a university student and a member of the Young Democrats and had probably not attended more than one state convention. To a New York Democrat or Republican such casualness would be unthinkable. State convention delegates are hand picked, trusted, and known individuals with long working acquaintance in the party.

Political organization has changed over the years. The old-time precinct worker generally has suffered technological unemployment. Governmental assumption of many welfare functions, the decline of immigration, and the decline in party patronage jobs with widespread adoption of merit systems have affected, if not entirely eliminated, the old-style political machine. Perhaps increased opportunities for face-to-face meetings of like-minded individuals throughout the state together with the wide rise of mass communication during election campaigns has also helped to account for the near revolution in party organization and activity. At any rate, party workers can pull strings of puppet government officeholders less frequently. Political bosses, in the Lincoln Steffens sense, have become almost extinct. Formal hierarchies of party structure, which may still exist in the state's statutes or even in practice, generally have lost their old meaning of tightly run organizations with status and influence directly related to some line on a chart.

With all of the strictures on the changing meaning of political organization, some knowledge of the statutory party (or formal party) organization is requisite.

★ Levels of organization

The precinct. The basic electoral division in the United States is the precinct or election district. In many cases political parties use the precinct as the basic unit in their organization. Some states specify that the declared or registered party voters in a direct primary shall elect a precinct committee or captain, but in other instances the party's precinct officials are selected by the county or district leaders or committees or elected at precinct conventions or caucuses. In any event, in the great majority of precincts in the United States there are officials of at least one of the major parties, and frequently there are representatives of both the Republicans and Democrats in the form of precinct captains or committees. But in states in which the county or district organization is left to appoint precinct officials or in which precinct caucuses perform this function, there are many instances in which no precinct organization exists at all. There is a striking difference, for example, between Chicago and Los Angeles, the former having an extensive system of active precinct captains and the latter having none, except occasionally at election time. Precinct organization is found more frequently in cities than in rural areas, although there are wide differences among counties. Contrast the virtually nonexistent precinct organization in many Southern rural counties with the almost complete precinct organization in rural counties in Illinois, Ohio, and New York.

An active precinct chairman will try to know every voter in his precinct by name, his party affiliation, his family, and a good deal about his job and personal affairs. He will be on the job every day of the year ministering to the needs of the voters of the district. He may use his influence to secure a job for Mr. X, help adjust the Ys' marital difficulties, and in general place himself at everyone's disposal. He may act as an intermediary between the citizen and the government, advising the citizen whom to see, what his rights are, or what procedure to follow. A citizen may want to apply for old-age assistance or to appeal the assessment upon his property. An active and available precinct captain can be helpful.

All these services, however, are secondary in importance as far as the party is concerned. Its real objective is to win more votes for the party so that political power can be achieved or continued. Therefore, the precinct captain will make sure that all voters in his district—at least all voters of his political faith—register. He will distribute literature, campaign from house to house for the party's candidates, circulate petitions, drive voters to the polls, serve on election boards, hold meetings—the list of activities is a long one.

The active year-round precinct chairman is becoming scarce, however. Even in New York City where house-to-house and apartment-to-apartment work was once so well organized, it is now easily possible to be a resident for several years without receiving a call from an election-district captain or assembly-district worker. Many precinct captains hold the office nominally but do virtually no work for the party except at election time. During an actual campaign, they may distribute a bit of literature and encourage a few of their friends and neighbors to vote, but they are a far cry from the "professionals" who so frequently occupied such posts in the days when boss and machine politics were at their height.

Ward, city, and district. Ward, city, and district organization is sometimes a substitute for precinct captains or committees, or alternatively, such an organization may represent an intermediate level between the precinct and county. Here again there are no hard and fast rules. In some cities, ward, legislative-district, and city committees are made up of precinct representatives. In other cities there are regular conventions at these levels for any party members who care to attend, or party officers may be directly elected at a primary. In rural areas the districts from which members of the county governing body are elected may serve as areas for party conventions or for the election or appointment of party leaders.

If there is no precinct activity, then ward, district, or city workers may perform duties similar to those performed by precinct captains in many areas. If a good measure of precinct work is being done, leaders at the intermediate level serve as go-betweens for the precinct and county organizations. For state and local elections, ward, legislative-district, township, city, and county organizations may play special roles in helping to nominate and elect the party's candidates for the city council, for city-wide offices generally, for the county governing body, for township offices, or for the legislature.

The county. The county organization of a political party is usually the strongest and most permanent part of its local organization. In almost every county in the United States at least one major party has a county chairman and a county committee. Probably over half the counties have both Republican and Democratic organizations of some permanence and activity.

The county committee of a political party may be directly elected by the voters at a party primary, may be composed of delegates from the precincts or districts of a county, or may be selected by the party's candidates for public office or by a county convention of party members. The county committee is in many places so large that it is unwieldy, and an executive committee is appointed to take any action that seems necessary between the very infrequent meetings of the entire committee. The committee usually elects a chairman (perhaps also a chairwoman), and it is usually the chairman who is the most active leader of the party in the county. Sometimes, however, the real leader is the man behind the chairman.

In two-party localities, county party positions are commonly highly prized and eagerly sought. Sometimes, particularly in one-party areas, county positions in the minority party go begging. In such circumstances a county convention may bring out only two or three people—such cases have been recorded.

The powers of the county organization typically include that of exercising at least a small amount of supervision over whatever party structure may be below the county level, helping to distribute the patronage that is frequently available from county governments, and conducting county-wide campaigns to nominate and elect candidates for county, state, and national office. Since it is quite traditional in the United States to concede to the party organization at each level a rather wide degree of independence, the county organization will usually find that it is not supervised very greatly by the state level, and that, in turn, it cannot exercise a great amount of supervision over precinct, ward, or city groups. The more active county organizations will decide and announce party policy on local issues on occasion and will issue many news releases.

The state. Between the county and state levels of party organization, there are sometimes to be found Congressional-district party conventions, committees, or chairmen, but these groups are largely for the purpose of promoting the candidacy of the party's nominee for Congress in the district. They do not have much importance in terms of running the party's general affairs, except that they may serve as units to elect members of the state committee. Similarly, there may be party organization in judicial districts, if such exist, for the purpose of endorsing and promoting certain candidates for judgeships.

In the South and in some of the strongest party states, the state central committee, usually recognized by the state's laws, governs the party's state activities. This is true no matter how the committee is selected or what the powers of the state convention or state chairman might be on paper. The exceptions to this generalization are (1) the occasional instance where the party is dominated by a state chairman or some other boss and (2) the situation, such as that in Wisconsin, where the formal statutory party organization has been largely replaced by a nonstatutory one.[9]

State central committees are constituted in many different ways. Some are selected by the state convention, some are made up largely of county chairmen or Congressional-district representatives; others are elected in direct primaries or appointed by the party's nominees for office. There are numerous combinations of these and other devices, the state convention and direct-primary systems being the most common. The size of state committees (where it is becoming standard to divide the membership equally between men and women) is frequently so large that executive committees are appointed to carry on much of the work. In many cases the state chairman is nominally appointed by the entire state committee but is actually the choice of the party's candidate for governor (as the national party chairman is the choice of the party's Presidential candidate).

The platform of a party is drawn up by the state convention, by the state central committee, or by a council of the party's candidates for office. More important than drawing up the platform are running campaigns, determining party policy from time to time, calling and managing of state conventions, and setting dates for county and precinct conventions. In many states it is the central committee that has power over these matters. If an internal split develops in a party, the state committee may endorse the candidates of one of the factions and not the other. Since the committee usually has prestige and some financial resources at its disposal, such a decision may mean the difference between victory and defeat for the factions concerned.

[9] Both the Republican and Democratic parties in Wisconsin work through state-wide groups known as the Republican Voluntary Committee and the Democratic Organizing Committee. The replacement of the statutory organization with these groups as the focus of party authority occurred (1) to avoid some of the state's legal controls over party activities and (2) to secure ideological control by a particular faction in each party.

The nation. National political-party committees are largely outside the scope of state and local government. In both of the major parties, the national committee is composed of one man and one woman from each state, plus some representation of the territories. On paper, the national committee is selected by the national convention. In practice, each state's committeemen are chosen by the state delegation to the national convention, by the state convention, or by direct primaries. The national chairman is chosen by the party's candidate for President, although technically he is an appointee of the national committee. As a generalization, the state central committee (if powerful at home) is likely to have more influence on the national committee through the state's committeemen than the national committee will have on the state. Although there are inevitable interrelations between the national committee and the state central committee and the margin of influence will vary in each, most often influence rises from the state rather than going down from national.

★ The use of organization

Organization is a means, not an end—and only one means among many. Therefore many mechanisms have developed for getting around the established political-party organization or for supplementing it. Many of the formally established officers or committees of parties do not function in actual fact, or do not function to the extent that they are empowered to do so.

There is a significant number of states and localities in which organization is somewhat personal. For example, while theoretically the state, county, and other committees should take a leading role in all political campaigns for all the party's candidates, actually they do so only occasionally. Individual candidates are frequently left to their own devices and set up their own campaign committees, which may be much more instrumental in their nomination and election than the general party organization. Some governors and many mayors or county officeholders have been essentially antiorganization men who have depended upon their own supporters almost entirely to maintain themselves in office.

The position of state committees has been weakened by state and national laws limiting the amount of money that any one organization may spend in an election. Before these laws were popular, state and national committees wielded power through their ability to grant or withhold campaign funds. Today many candidates must finance their campaigns through special fund-raising techniques of their own. If they get neither money nor many active house-to-house workers from the regular organization, they may owe very little to it for their election.

Political conventions or large committees have formal powers that are sometimes rather sweeping, but meetings of these groups are rarely deliberative. There is nothing quite so boring as a long-drawn-out meeting of a large number of people in which wrangling over details constitutes the bulk of action. Similarly, if there is conflict within an organization, there is nothing so dangerous for a faction that wants to capture or maintain itself in power as not to plan its strategy well in advance of a meeting of the whole committee or convention. Therefore, for one reason or another, most important meetings of political committees or conventions are preceded by informal caucuses of like-minded individuals or leaders who plan the strategy they are going to follow. The action of the formal meeting is thus a foregone conclusion, at least if one faction clearly has the most votes.

Much of the operation of party structure is to be explained in social and economic terms. The individuals who make up a party do not live in a vacuum. They meet each other in their labor unions, in their business or farm associations. They get together socially; perhaps some are even neighbors. Many may work for the same state or local governments. Through their many contacts with each other, they develop a spirit and friendship that help to make party affairs run smoothly. The various contacts of party members and workers do not take place only among members of a county committee, for example, or members of the state committee. Perhaps the precinct captain knows the state chairman well, or a county chairman lives next door to a ward leader. Friendships do not follow neat hierarchical lines, and they help to bypass the formal organization on numerous occasions.

Many political clubs of one kind or another have supplemented the political hierarchy from time to time. Some of the earliest of these were established by boss and machine systems in urban areas. They would hold parties, picnics, and meetings of all sorts; they would dispense information about government services or about jobs. The precinct or district club headquarters would be the headquarters nearly every evening for those wishing political advancement in the future. While political clubs have declined in influence and in number, some of them continue to be active. Also outside the usual hierarchy of party machinery are the various women's clubs or Young Democrats or Young Republicans. They hold many political forums or discussion meetings and provide a mechanism of keeping special groups of voters active in party affairs.

The *party*, meaning all party members, seldom takes any action unanimously. The Republican and Democratic parties, even most of the minor parties, are composed of such a variety of individuals that party unity is never achieved. There may be a unanimous vote formally recorded, yet behind the record may be strict machine control, compromise among discordant elements, or participation by only a very few party members.

Effects of Variations in Party Organization

★ *Political participation*

There are several important consequences of variations in party organization and in the use of party organization from state to state and community to community. Not the least of these involves personal participation in politics. If a novice in politics wishes to become an active party member in a highly organized area, he probably will have to start at the bottom. Obtaining the party's nomination for public office at a direct primary may be impossible for all except machine-endorsed candidates. Under such a system, the road to political preferment is long and hard. In sharp contrast are those states and communities in which political parties have a loosely knit fabric. A novice may start in such a system by running for mayor, even for governor or U. S. Senator, and get elected without any previous political experience. Such extreme cases are uncommon, but in a loosely knit political party an expression of interest in political activity to a county committee or a candidate for office may easily turn a political novice into a precinct captain or ward leader.

★ *Independence of candidates*

The less thoroughly organized an area is in terms of parties, the larger the role that personalities of candidates are likely to play in election results. A premium will be placed upon independence or even nonpartisanship in some instances. It becomes a virtue for a candidate to announce that he is an antimachine man. He will be nominated and elected depending upon his own personal strength as a candidate. If he is able to raise enough money to finance his campaign properly, if he can organize his own individual campaign adequately, and if above all he is attractive as an individual to the voters, he will be elected no matter what the formal leaders of the loosely organized party say or desire. A widely different system is likely to be in effect in a tightly and thoroughly organized party. A candidate, no matter how colorful or uncolorful, cannot be elected without endorsement of the regular party organization. He depends upon the party for finances, for house-to-house workers, and for advice on all matters of policy. If elected, he may not be as free an agent as the "independent" candidate; but he may well have the advantage of organized support for many of his policies.

★ Pressure groups and parties

Pressure groups will usually have much greater influence in areas in which political parties are weak than in areas in which political parties are very strong. Pressure groups are, of course, present everywhere. They are well organized in Virginia, New York, and Illinois, as well as in California, Minnesota, and Mississippi, but there is a world of difference between the political-party activity of these two groups of states. The former group is marked by parties of real strength and extensive organization, while the latter group has relatively weak political parties.

A pressure group in New York, Virginia, or Illinois usually finds it must work along with or through party groups in or out of office. Parties are stronger than any pressure group and can assure their candidates at least a minimum amount of support at the next election. A strong party is a protection for legislators and public officeholders generally, making it possible for them to resist the demands of lobbyists more frequently than would otherwise be the case. However, there have been instances where the reverse was true—strong parties used to enforce the demands of pressure groups.

A pressure group in California, Minnesota, or Mississippi finds that there is little reason for compromising with political parties. The individual public officeholder receives little support at election times from his party because its organization is so weak. (Minnesota legislators are elected on nonpartisan ballot without organized party support in usual sense.) Such an officeholder is "open game," and the lobbyist may be able to ignore party leaders or party organization and yet obtain what he wants.[10]

★ Majority rule

The kind of party organization that is found in an area affects majority rule. In a state or locality in which a well-disciplined party is operating, it takes just a preponderance of the party's votes, and not a majority of all the votes cast, to control elections. If a direct primary system is in effect, the results of the primary for party A might be as follows:

Candidate X	51 percent of party A's votes
Candidate Y	36 percent of party A's votes
Candidate Z	13 percent of party A's votes

Obviously, those supporting candidate X have won the party's primary. In a well-disciplined party, those supporting Y and Z will rally to the party's

---

[10] See, for example, Belle Zeller (ed.), *American State Legislatures*, Report of the Committee on American Legislatures, American Political Science Association (New York: Thomas Y. Crowell Company, 1954), pp. 190-191.

banner in the final election, voting for X. If X gets a preponderance of the votes cast at that time, he will be elected, even though his initial support came from only 51 percent of the members of his party alone, perhaps representing only 26 percent of the total votes cast for both parties' candidates in the primary. In a community in which party organization and affiliation is rather weak, many of the supporters of Y and Z might vote for the nominee of party B in the final election because they prefer him to candidate X. In such an instance candidate X might be defeated, even though he received a majority of the votes in the primary and even though his party technically has more registered voters who cast their ballots at the election. With fluid party lines it is not enough for a candidate to get a preponderant number of his party's votes. He must get a plurality of all votes cast in the final election. This may or may not depend on his being able to get a preponderant number of votes from the members of his party.

★ *Accountability*

The political party may be a mechanism for keeping government responsible; yet if a party abuses its power, it may be a means for preventing government from being highly responsible to the voters. The same may be said for keeping government close to the people, making government representative, or developing a critical and helpful opposition to those who have political power. Political-party organization is a means and not an end. As such, it is open to abuse at the same time that it offers many advantages to those who would use it responsibly. With all their actual and possible faults, political parties nevertheless have been our most satisfactory means to date for practicing democracy; but they do not guarantee responsible government, government close to the people, or representative government.

Having discussed some of the differences in party organization and some of the effects of these differences, let us turn to an examination of the individuals who compose political parties.

Composition of Political Parties

Are the voters given a real choice at election time when they can choose between the candidates of the two major parties? Are there any real differences involving issues or people in the Democratic and Republican parties? Is the choice one of Tweedledee and Tweedledum? These questions have bothered many a thoughtful voter as he goes about the task of deciding for whom to vote. Unfortunately, there is no pat answer. This is particularly true in the realm of state and local government, where it is easy to find a branch of the Democratic party in one community much more conservative than the local Republican party, while in another area the reverse is true.

★ The two major parties

Despite the diversity of state and local party organization and activity and the diversity in party issues and personalities, some generalizations may be made on the basis of available data. Since the ballot is secret, most of the data are in the form of voting records in legislatures and councils, public-opinion polls, case studies, and general impressions of certain writers. There is a measure of agreement on the following points:

1. Conservatism-liberalism. Neither the Republicans nor the Democrats can claim to be the conservative or liberal party in all of the many states and localities. While it is true that in the country as a whole the Democrats are looked upon as more liberal than the Republicans, three points must be kept in mind in interpreting this fact. First of all, the liberal-conservative difference between the parties, even nationally, is not large; secondly, there are important regional and local variations; and thirdly, there are many individual, personal differences.

These points may be illustrated by the policies established by state and local legislative bodies. If you think of a liberal as one who believes in equal representation for all, and you consider one particular party to be liberal, then that party should stand for periodic redrawing of the state legislative districts, from which are elected members of the legislature, so that each of them contains approximately the same number of inhabitants. Yet on this score it does not seem that the record of the Democrats is any better than that of the Republicans; narrow partisan advantage principally determines a party's stand on such a matter.

Perhaps a liberal is one who believes in equal opportunity. Can it be documented that one of the two major parties is less interested than another in supporting public education on a state and local level? Or maybe fair-employment-practices legislation, under which discrimination in hiring because of race, creed, or color is declared to be against public policy, is a better test. Such laws have been enacted under Republican leadership in the states of New York, New Jersey, and elsewhere, while Democrats in other states have enacted similar legislation. There may be some slight difference between the two major parties in issues of this kind, but it is so small and so variable from area to area and individual to individual that it would be hazardous, without detailed knowledge of the two parties in a given community, to wager what Republican and Democratic policies were.

Liberalism and social and economic legislation have been equated recently. Do you find reliable party differences here? It is tempting to give an unqualified affirmative answer to this proposition, and it is certainly true that you will find some differences between the two parties at these points. Yet enough exceptions to any rule can be formulated so that a strong caveat must be issued. For example, while Democrats are more frequently in favor of social insurance and public ownership of utilities than Republicans, you cannot assume that the position of all Democrats or all local branches of the Democratic party is one favoring these policies, or that the position of the Republican party members or groups is the reverse. Differences, if any, are small, and many regional and personal variations are to be found.

The absence of firm ideological differences between the two parties and the resulting untidiness moderates the degree of political antagonism and may be the only pragmatic solution to democratic governance of 175 million or more people. At least practicing politicians show little desire to change. Thomas E. Dewey, Republican Presidential nominee in 1944 and 1948 and three-time governor of New York, has succinctly stated the political case against neat liberal and conservative party divisions in the country:

> These impractical theorists with a "passion for neatness" demand that our parties be sharply divided, one against the other, in interest, membership, and doctrine. They want to drive all the moderates and liberals out of the Republican party and then have the remainder join forces with the conservative groups of the South. They then would have everything very neatly arranged, indeed. The Democratic party would be the liberal-to-radical party. The Republican party would be the conservative-to-reactionary party.
>
> The results would be neatly arranged, too. The Republicans would lose every election and the Democrats would win every election. It may be a perfect theory but it would result in a one-party system and finally totalitarian government. As you may suspect by now, I am against it.[11]

2. Kinds of people. Neither the Republican nor the Democratic party is a class party in any complete sense of the term. There are millionaires in both parties, and there are persons who are on relief in both. In the average state, however, the percentage of Republicans in the upper income groups is larger than the percentage in the lower income groups. Businessmen and professional people likewise tend to be Republicans more frequently than semiskilled and unskilled workers. Party affiliation seems to

---

11 From lecture by Thomas E. Dewey at Princeton University, February 8, 1950, quoted by Henry A. Turner in *Politics in the United States* (New York: McGraw-Hill Book Company, Inc., 1955), pp. 220-221.

be affected by other factors, such as size of city—the larger a city, the better off the Democrats tend to be. Republicans thrive in the rural North and West. Geographical location is also important. Cities in the South are more Democratic than cities in the Middle West, for example; and it is common to observe that the Republicans usually receive relatively more votes in a higher income residential suburb than in a central city. Older voters and those with more education favor the Republicans to a greater degree than do younger voters and those with less education, while in some states certain ethnic groups tend to favor one or another party from time to time. Affiliation with a labor union or the Roman Catholic Church frequently is associated with support of the Democrats. The general finding seems to be: the more closely the member of a minority group identifies with his group, the more likely he is to be a Democrat.

All these tendencies can be illustrated by public-opinion-poll data that seem quite reliable. While admitting local and regional differences, these organizations have found that party membership in this country is related to the many factors mentioned in the preceding paragraph. The largest, most significant differences found have been those related to income and occupation. But even these differences are not very great. Almost never is there a difference in excess of 50 percentage points (for example, 80 percent of members of lower-income groups are Democratic, 30 percent of upper income groups are Democratic), and much more frequently the differences are 30 or 40 percentage points or even smaller. All other factors except income, occupation, and geographical location seldom bring forth differences in party affiliation greater than 10 or 20 percent. Geographical location varies widely as an influence on party preference, producing differences from 10 to 20 percent up to 40 percent and beyond, depending upon the areas compared. However, the location of one's residence is closely related to income and occupation, as are other factors such as education.

★ The role of minor parties

Third parties have traditionally been parties of protest, whether their activities have been confined to a city or a county or have extended to entire states or the nation. Their leaders and adherents have felt that the two major parties did not represent their views adequately. There was too little difference between the two parties. Therefore, they turned to third parties as the only course of action open to those who wanted a real choice.

There is little doubt that third parties have usually had distinctive platforms and ideas. Generally their proposals have stood in marked contrast to the relative similarity of the Republican and Democratic platforms. Sometimes third parties have not had a rounded program but have stood for particular cures for the country's ills, such as action against monopolies or free silver.

While some of the protest parties have had a rather long life and continue in existence today, the tendency has been for them to begin quietly, extend their influence rather modestly on a state or local level, and then decline in importance or disappear. These parties generally decline because the Republican or Democratic party, or both, adopts a good part of its program or the difficulties that were responsible for its rise have been overcome. Thus third parties serve as measuring sticks of the dissatisfaction of the voters with the two major parties. If the Republicans and Democrats are wise, they can use these groups for their own purposes, adapting or changing their programs when they see that a third party is gaining strength.

★ Nonpartisanship

The rise of minor parties has been the result of dissatisfaction with the two major parties. For the same reason, particularly in state and local governments, another important movement has been aimed at both Republicans and Democrats—the movement for nonpartisanship. Regardless of the extent of the differences between the two major parties, advocates of this point of view proclaim that there is no room for partisanship in state and local government. There is no Democratic way to pave a street or highway, it is pointed out, nor any Republican way to run the state conservation department or the county schools. Partisan politics should therefore be put aside and the best man elected governor or legislator, no matter what his party affiliation. Furthermore, it is argued that local self-government must remain close to the people, and it is implied that somehow political parties are not close to or even of the people.

The nonpartisanship movement has been rather widespread. Two states—Nebraska and Minnesota—elect their legislatures on the basis of a nonpartisan (no party designation) ballot in both primary and general elections.[12] One quarter of the states provide for the election of most judges by this method, and about one half make some provision for cities, counties, school districts, or townships to nominate and elect their officials on ballots without party designation. As a result of the nonpartisan movement candidates for office have frequently found it to their advantage to campaign as nonpartisans, even if they have strong party affiliations. While

[12] See Chapter 9 for a discussion of nonpartisan primaries.

politicians have engaged in this practice for a long time, the nonpartisan movement has given encouragement to it. Thus the real beliefs and associations of a candidate may become lost from view and almost impossible to discover.

It must be admitted that the two major parties have very frequently offered nothing distinctive for state and local voters, and that sometimes they have been more or less local spoils offices of the national party. The remedy for the poor functioning of parties, however, is not to ignore their existence. To adopt such a course of action makes party responsibility all the more difficult to obtain. An attempt at reorganizing the major parties or forming a third party probably would have a much greater beneficial effect upon the politics of state or local government than the movement for a nonpartisan ballot.

The nonpartisan movement is based upon questionable premises as to the nature of state and local government and the federal system. State and local governments have numerous partisan matters that confront them nearly every day. At first glance it does appear that there is no Republican or Democratic position on streets and highways. A more careful view, however, will reveal that the question of when to build or repair public works of all kinds may very often be a partisan issue, with the liberal spenders on one side and their opponents on the other. Welfare is obviously a possible subject of partisan politics, with disagreement over the extent of old-age assistance, for example. State conservation departments confronted with public *versus* private use and development of natural resources, school boards with questions of the extent of the education program and the relationship of private and parochial to public schools, and almost all other functions with their policy implications present problems or issues that can readily be partisan.

As national, state, and local governments become even more interdependent, the issues confronting each become more and more similar. Furthermore, it has long been argued that one of the great advantages of a federal system and of local self-government is the political experience to be gained by those not in control of the national or central governments in the more numerous state and local governments. If the Congress and the Presidency are controlled by one party, how is the political opposition to get experience in running government except through state or local office? It is a healthy thing for the governmental system as a whole to have some cities or counties under control of the Democrats when the state government is Republican, and likewise to have some of the states under Republican control when the national administration is Democratic. New leaders are developed and interest in public affairs heightened.

Political Leadership

Popular sovereignty, democracy, or consent of the governed have not meant state or national mass meetings of citizens, carefully sifting problems and arriving at a common decision. Political leaders, in and out of the formal institutions of government and knowingly or unknowingly chosen by the voters, have made the decisions. Our understanding of political leadership as well as our acceptance of types of leaders has changed over the centuries. The eighteenth and early nineteenth centuries in the United States produced leaders largely in class terms. The Jeffersons and the Madisons might write and speak of the people governing. Yet in practice they assumed men of their class would be the leaders who would be responsive to the people but who would lead and secure their consent. The Revolutionary War leaders, the signers of the Declaration of Independence, the writers of the Constitution, and the officers of the early government came from the propertied classes. Most of them had wealth, education, and social standing much above the average.

America's early political leaders also had a sense of obligation—the French sense of *noblesse oblige* that the English upper classes developed more than the upper classes of other European nations. Apparently Washington wished to remain at Mt. Vernon and tend his estates, but he nevertheless accepted the call for national service in the Presidency. Not all of the leaders in those days were above reproach, never looked to their own advantage, and always saw and followed the public interest. Yet *noblesse oblige*, the obligation to serve (coupled with a faith in the common man and a belief in his political rights), gave the United States thirty or forty years of unusual leadership. Public service was a high calling that could not be refused.

Andrew Jackson set out to make the common man the political leader as well as the final arbiter of his government. The American governmental "aristocracy" faded out. Over the decades, the newer man in government often tended to lose control of the big decisions. Many citizens and groups used government but assumed little general responsibility. Rapidly growing and changing populations accepted (and helped to develop) the institution of the political boss. The political boss could interpret government and, for a price, could get favors from government. Government officials might be merely puppets of the big political boss who carried on an intricate business of granting favors and subsequently collecting, often with interest, for his gifts. Corruption on a small and grand scale permeated all levels of government by the late nineteenth century. A Henry Adams could complain of the absence of opportunity for the man who wished to serve the people in government.

By the latter part of the nineteenth century party leadership in many states and localities seemed almost confined to political bosses or leaders who vigorously and quite ruthlessly controlled the organization for personal, selfish, and frequently corrupt ends. Very few of these men held high office within their parties, preferring to direct their activities from a more secluded spot. Some did not even hold an elective public office, and when they did, they were responsible only to small coteries of their own followers.

Bossism has declined markedly in the last forty years, and particularly since 1930. First of all, the elaborate precinct organization that most bosses developed depended in large part upon lots of spoils, the existence of needy people, and immigrants who were new to the ways of life of this country. When spoils were progressively reduced by purchasing, contract, and personnel controls, when relief and welfare activities were assumed by government and immigration shut off, most bosses were unable to adapt themselves to the change. Population became more mobile; recreation facilities became more diverse, including radio and television in one's own home. Pressure groups, such as labor and farm organizations, came to be the intermediaries between party and individual.

Political reformers in the last of the nineteenth and the twentieth centuries contributed to the demise of the political boss. They held him up for scorn and ridicule, they brought adoption of the institutional procedures that reduced his power, and they emphasized government work as an obligation to serve. Now in a reversal of emphasis from the Jacksonian era, the increasing complexities of our world have shifted the emphasis from the role of the common man in government to the need for leaders and for professionalization. Governors should lead. Administrators should have experience and training. Personnel should be chosen for their *expertise*. The chief executive should have power commensurate with his responsibilities.

Just as some bosses accomplished many things in the public interest, some reformers had short visions or used the mantle of reform to cover grabs for power. Some of our strong governors do not meet the challenge of responsibility. Political leadership is not usually centered in a single person, and the governor and other elected officials may still be more subject to the influence of others than actively influential themselves. State traditions affect political leadership and political leadership may influence traditions. State voters do not demand or get the same caliber of leadership in every one of the fifty states. Yet political leaders in the twentieth century have regained some of the sense of *noblesse oblige* of the earlier period and, with lapses, recognize a higher minimum standard of conduct than what had been acceptable in the era of boss rule.

The identification of party and political leaders (the two are not always synonymous) and an analysis of their methods and their influence on political life is an important part of political science. The foregoing pages on political leadership have been impressionistic rather than analytical. To analyze political leadership in a given period much detailed research is needed. Crucial questions would include: (1) What type of men are party and political leaders? What are their occupations? Income? Personalities? Interests? (2) What is the extent of the leader's influence? With whom does he share power? How long has he been influential? (3) Where do leaders come from? What is the recruitment process used? How do leaders go up the ladder? (4) How do the answers to these questions vary for local, state, and national leaders? (5) What are the changes in types of party leaders over time? Any study, moreover, gains significance if it is not isolated but is part of a series. Lester G. Seligman has suggested the goals of the research:

> A politics-by-leadership conception would concern itself with generalizations concerning four types of relations: (1) the relations of leaders to led within particular political structures, (2) the relationship between leaders of political structures, (3) the relationship between leaders of one structure and the followers of another, and (4) the relationships between leaders and the "unorganized" or "nonaffiliated." [13]

REFERENCES

Eldersveld, Samuel J., "The Independent Vote: Measurement, Characteristics, and Implications for Party Strategy," 46 *American Political Science Review* (September 1952), 732-753.

Key, Valdimer O., Jr., and Alexander Heard, *Southern Politics in State and Nation.* New York: Alfred A. Knopf, 1949.

McKean, Dayton D., *The Boss, The Hague Machine in Action.* Boston: Houghton Mifflin, 1950.

Miller, Warren E., "One-Party Politics and the Voter," 50 *The American Political Science Review* (September 1956), 707-725.

Moscow, Warren, *Politics in the Empire State.* New York: Alfred A. Knopf, 1948.

Price, Margaret, *The Negro and the Ballot in the South.* Atlanta, Ga.: Southern Regional Council, 1959.

Price, Hugh Douglas, "The Negro and Florida Politics, 1944-1954," 17 *The Journal of Politics* (May 1955), 198-220.

[13] Lester G. Seligman, "The Study of Political Leadership," in *Political Behavior, A Reader in Theory and Research,* edited by Heinz Eulau, Samuel J. Eldersveld, and Morris Janowitz (Glencoe, Ill.: The Free Press, 1956), p. 182.

176 - THE VOTER AND POLITICS

Prothro, James W., Ernest Q. Campbell, and Charles M. Grigg, "Two-Party Voting in the South: Class vs. Party Identification," 52 *American Political Science Review* (March 1958), 131-139.

Steffens, Lincoln, *The Shame of the Cities*. New York: Doubleday, 1904.

See also references at end of Chs. 7 and 9.

CHAPTER 9

Nominations, Campaigns, and Elections

NOMINATIONS, CAMPAIGNS, AND ELECTIONS are colorful aspects of state and local politics as they are of national politics. General similarities in the views of candidates and parties do not mean it is unimportant who wins. One administration may keep its doors open for business, another for labor. One administration may have special sympathy for victims of mental illness, another may see the goal of tomorrow in the expansion of the schools. One administration may stress close regulation of public utilities, another may believe that the public welfare is best served when business is allowed to police itself. In any event, those who win on election day take control of government, along with the power, prestige, and emoluments that control carries.

Election results don't just happen. Much planning and preparation go into each campaign. The participating parties try to secure candidates who will be successful and who most clearly represent their views on important policies. They try to influence voters to vote for their candidates and, perhaps more important, on election day they try to get to the polls those voters who will vote for them. The nominating, campaign, and election machinery and methods they use depend in part upon the objectives they have and in part upon the history and environment of each state and community.

Nominations

The selection of nomination and election machinery is not entirely determined by abstract considerations. The requirements of democracy may have great weight in determining what methods are proper and legal, and so may certain principles or theoretical arguments. Competing with these considerations are others, such as who will receive the most benefit from the system that is adopted, who stands to lose, and how the system can be adapted to the exigencies that occur in politics.

For example, some states provide that political parties shall nominate their candidates for governor by means of a party convention, while others provide that a direct primary shall be held. Many arguments can be adduced for each of these systems and are presented in some of the pages that follow. However, the unstated arguments on both sides frequently involve personal or selfish factors. To the established political leader the convention system may seem preferable, since he can obtain what he wants from the delegates because of his control over party machinery. The political novice may feel that his only chance to have an effective voice in politics is by means of the direct primary. Votes, not organizational control, determine the outcome of direct primaries, he may feel. (These feelings may affect positions even where subsequent events prove that they are an inaccurate reflection of the true situation.) In addition to, if not apart from, theoretical democratic principles, Wisconsin adopted an open primary because Robert M. La Follette, in 1903, saw it as the mechanism by which he and his Progressive Republican followers could control Republican nominations. Under different political conditions in California, Hiram Johnson and his followers saw cross-filing (any candidate is permitted to file in both party primaries) as the means to their control of nominations and elections. In Wisconsin, La Follette needed merely to control Republican nominations to win elections, whereas Johnson in California needed influence in both parties to succeed. Both men were astute and for two or three decades they correctly forecast the usefulness of the different devices they chose. Under new conditions, the open primary in Wisconsin and the cross-filing system in the California primaries have sometimes proved troublesome to their ideological descendants.

Individuals use nomination and election machinery. A law student may make an excellent study of the laws and regulations governing elections, but he is likely not to grasp their real significance unless he goes beyond the statute books. The statute book or party regulation may say that the party convention adopts the state platform. Perhaps a platform committee is specified as the agency to draw up the document for presentation to the convention. During a convention the platform committee and the convention as a whole will undoubtedly give formal approval to the platform document, but action by these two groups probably does not explain how the document came to be adopted. It may be that the prevailing political leaders dictated the platform, or perhaps an informal caucus of a select number of people forced their views upon the party convention. It is likely that one or more pressure groups lobbied vigorously for the inclusion of specific planks that appealed especially to them. There may have been considerations in the mind of the chairman when he selected the committee that may not be obvious to the outsider. He may have "stacked" the committee in favor of his pet proposal or with partisans who do not represent a cross section of the active members of the party. In any event, the diaries of an "insider" in politics are likely to make valuable supplementary reading to the formal legal and party requirements concerning nominations, campaigns, and elections.

Individuals may secure nomination for public office with little or no effort on their part in relatively minor local elections through write-in votes of friends and neighbors. Or they may be nominated after great or moderate personal efforts by a caucus, convention, primary, petition, or some combination of these mechanisms. Whatever the nominating process, it is intended to reduce the voter's choices at the final election. Too long a list of candidates would confuse the voter or at least prevent him from obtaining adequate information to make an intelligent choice. A long list might also include a number of candidates who think alike. Splitting votes among these candidates may result in the election of the man with a minority view. If the final election puts fewer choices before the voter, it nevertheless may make the voter's choice more meaningful.

Once the policy of restricting the number of names on the final election ballot is accepted, every person or organization that wants to have influence in politics will try to control the process of restriction so that only candidates who are friendly to the group will be eligible or nominated. In politics control of the nominating process is fundamental. A political leader cannot always decide the results of the final election, but he may wield great power in making the nominations. Furthermore, a political group's standing and its ability to influence the government subsequently elected depend upon its success in the primaries. It has been difficult to make the voters aware of the importance of control over nominations; political experts have always been aware of it. Consequently in the United States the history of nominating methods has been a continuous struggle between political groups that have tried to keep the power of nomination in their own hands and those groups who have endeavored to place control of nominations with the rank-and-file membership of the party.

★ *The caucus*

Every American government textbook recites the history of the rise and fall of the caucus, especially the legislative caucus, as a nominating method. Unfortunately for its success, legislative caucuses never included representatives of important state and community groups, and these groups had the power to overthrow the caucus and secure the convention as more amenable to their interests. The caucus, an informal gathering of individuals of a particular group or leaders of several groups to agree on candidates and issues, existed before the advent of the legislative caucus and has continued to exist after its demise. The caucusing of convention delegations from the same geographic area or delegations with some other group interest is a recognized feature of party conventions. The much abused "smoke-filled room" refers really to the caucus of leaders—bargaining on candidates and policies. The caucus bargain may be a realistic adjustment of a variety of points of view in an effort to achieve at least half an apple rather than none at all. Occasionally it has been a callous sell-out. While today candidates are formally nominated by party conventions, direct primaries, or petitions, informal caucuses can influence a convention or direct primary or even those who file nominating petitions.

★ *The nominating convention*

The nominating convention generally had replaced the older legislative-caucus system by the middle of the nineteenth century. The state convention was the top of a pyramid: a precinct caucus selected delegates to a city convention, the city convention sent delegates to a county convention, and the county sent them to the state convention. The precinct caucus proved easy for nineteenth-century political bosses to control. In most states, rising groups unable to control the nominating convention turned to some form of the direct primary. A few states, such as New York, modified the convention system to permit the voters to select the nominating-convention delegates at a direct primary but left the final candidate selection with the convention. New York, Connecticut, and Indiana continue to use the nominating convention for state-wide offices and Michigan for state-wide offices except governor and lieutenant governor. Currently those states which have retained the convention system have had favorable experiences with it. Perhaps it was not the convention system which led to the bad results in the middle and latter parts of the nineteenth century but the general atmosphere of politics which has since changed. Or perhaps the mere existence of the direct primary is a sufficiently threatening check on convention behavior in those states with the convention system.

As caucuses did not disappear with the adoption of nominating conventions, so conventions have not disappeared with the rise of the direct primary. In many states the preprimary party convention carries on functions such as candidate endorsement not materially different from the old nominating convention. The official nomination in these circumstances, however, is made at the primary and not by such endorsement.

★ The direct primary

The overwhelming majority of states, counties, and cities now nominate candidates by direct primaries. This development occurred largely after the turn of the twentieth century, although direct primaries had been in existence for over fifty years before, mostly in the South. As the method spread from state to state and locality to locality, two points were stressed: the convention system leads to corruption, and the direct primary system is a needed extension of democracy. A condition frequently present but less often stressed was the absence of real two-party competition. With the virtual elimination of the Republican party in the South following Reconstruction, the Democratic caucus and convention nominee automatically secured the office sought. The voter having given his total commitment to the Democratic party merely ratified the convention choice when he appeared at the polls in the regular election. Parties in one-party states showed some tendency to ignore general considerations for immediate internal party interests. Voters in one-party states with no choice but to ratify became restive. In other words, the direct primary in a one-party state gave the voter an element of choice which he had lacked. Whether the popular pressures for choice might eventually have given all states a generally two-party system if the direct primary had not been invented cannot be asserted with absolute assurance, but the proposition seems reasonable. At least the states which failed to adopt the direct primary have been and are competitive two-party states.

In one-party states primaries are of the utmost significance because most of the candidates who win are assured of election to office. On a state level, winning the Democratic primary in the South almost invariably means winning the final election. Similarly in some Northern and Western states, winning the Republican primary practically assures victory. Below the state level, the primary usually has been even more important. Even in competitive, two-party states, smaller political units of the state frequently have a one-party bias which places the voter's choice in the primary rather than the general election. Probably a majority of legislative seats of the country are primarily contested in the primaries, not at the general election, because these constituencies are either strongly Republican or strongly Democratic. Certainly a majority of county posts are decided, in effect, in the primaries, and in many cities this is also the case.

The direct primary may be defined as an official preliminary election conducted not to elect men to office but to select the few leading candidates who shall have their names printed on the final election ballot. Such a system is "direct" and "primary" because the voters themselves make the nominations without the intermediation of delegates or representatives acting in nominating conventions. The direct primary is, of course, an election and not a meeting, and hence it lacks the possible deliberative element of the caucus or convention.

In a general way, direct primary systems may be classified as follows:

I. Partisan direct primaries
   A. Open
   B. Closed
II. Nonpartisan direct primaries
III. Supplemental use of primaries

Naturally a partisan primary would be followed by a partisan election, a nonpartisan primary by a nonpartisan election. (This would seem "natural" but there are exceptions. Arizona follows a partisan judicial primary nomination with a "nonpartisan" general election of judges.)

A partisan direct primary is a preliminary election in which each party is permitted to have its candidates for office nominated by the voters of the party at a regular official preliminary election, conducted by public authorities just like any other election, and usually at public expense, except in some Southern states. Ordinarily the several party primaries are held on the same day and at the same polling places, although several Southern states permit a party to choose between a direct primary and nomination by convention and hence perhaps only a Democratic primary will be held. With the exception of primaries in the state of Washington, the voter receives a partisan primary ballot with separate columns or separate sheets on which he must indicate his choice of candidate for each office in one party only. The names printed on the ballot represent the individuals who have filed nomination papers with the requisite number of voter signatures as required by law.

Open partisan primaries. An open primary permits a voter to keep his party preference secret and to vote in whatever party primary he believes his vote will do the most good. Three methods have been developed in the quarter of the states that have this system. (1) A voter may be given a series of ballots, one for each party, listing the candidates for nomination by office. The voter then marks the ballot of the party of his choice and deposits it in an appropriate ballot box, depositing the unmarked ballots in another one set aside for this purpose. (2) Another method is to have a single consolidated ballot for all parties with the candidates for nomination of each of them listed in separate columns. The voter chooses which column or party he wishes, but he must not cross over and mark part of the ballot for one party primary and part of it for another. (3) A third method, used only in the state of Washington, is the "wide-open" or blanket primary. Each voter is given a single ballot, but the candidates are grouped by office, not by parties. The candidates seeking nomination for the governorship are all listed together, Republicans as well as Democrats, the party affiliation of each being indicated after his name. The voter simply votes for one of the candidates for each of the offices listed and therefore may vote Republican for governor, Democratic for attorney general, and so forth.

Closed partisan primaries. A closed primary does not permit a voter to keep his party affiliation secret. It is primarily designed to protect a political party against voters who are not sympathetic to it. In an open primary there is nothing to prohibit a Republican from voting in a Democratic primary and vice versa. This practice, called cross-voting, is frequently motivated by a voter's desire to have the party other than that of his first choice choose a nominee more in line with his thinking. On the other hand a political leader might encourage some of his following to vote in another party's primary so that the weakest possible candidate will be nominated, thus making victory in the regular election almost certain for his own group. Whatever the motives for cross-voting, it exists most frequently when there is a sharp contest in one party's primary and virtually no contest whatever in the other's. It also occurs in states and localities where one party is very strong or dominant and the other quite weak. Voters from the weakest party usually cross over, unless there is no contest. A closed primary helps to protect a party against such practices. It is founded on the theory that some important degree of political-party responsibility is desirable; this requires that a party be able to prevent outsiders from determining its nominations and actions.

In law and in theory a closed partisan primary is one that is definitely restricted to members of the party. This result is usually accomplished, as far as it is accomplished, by printing separate primary ballots for each party and by requiring each voter to declare his party affiliation to the election officials to obtain his ballot. In case a voter's declaration of allegiance is challenged, he may in some states be required to swear or affirm that he voted for the candidates of this party at the last election and that he intends to do so at the next. In some places the voter must state his party affiliation at the time of registering; he is then entered as a member of that party, and he cannot claim to vote any primary ballot other than that of his party, although at appropriate times he may change his party registration. Of course, the laws differ greatly from state to state.

In practice, many a so-called "closed" party primary is actually open. A strict law rigidly enforced might succeed in preventing the infiltration of outsiders into the primary of a party, but the cases in which this is fully accomplished are probably rare. In the first place the oath or declaration required in many places relates to matters of which only the voter himself has any knowledge. If X swears that he voted for Republican candidates in the last election, who could possibly prove the contrary? The laws of all the states require secret voting. In the second place, the oath is flexible in some places. The elector must swear that he voted for a majority of the candidates of the party, or that he voted for them "generally." He may have voted against the most important party candidates and still be able to qualify as a partisan without straining his conscience. Then, too, election officials may enforce the law carelessly, and unless the parties are exceedingly well provided with challengers, they will be unable to prevent voters from crossing party lines in this way. For example, in a state where a closed party-primary law exists, many elections officials may never ask the voter at the primary, "What party do you belong to?" but simply "What ballot do you want?" These two questions do not mean the same thing.

Nonpartisan primaries. In keeping with the old American tradition that there is something bad about politics in general and political parties in particular, a movement of large proportions (at least in its effect on local government) developed during the early years of the twentieth century. This is the movement for the nonpartisan primary, *nonpartisan* in that no party designation of candidates is permitted on the primary ballots. Instead, the candidates who file for each office are listed together without indication of party preference. Thus, on a county nonpartisan primary ballot, all candidates for registrar of deeds would be listed together, all candidates for sheriff, all candidates for clerk, and so on. Those two candidates receiving the most votes would win the nomination and their names would appear on the succeeding general election ballot. Both of them might be political independents or might be any conceivable combination of party allegiances. Plurality victories would be entirely possible, especially with many candidates contending for the nominations.

Figure 5. A NONPARTISAN PRIMARY BALLOT

PRIMARY ELECTION BALLOT
CANDIDATES TO BE NOMINATED
WITHOUT PARTY DESIGNATION
Primary Election, Monday, May 14, 1945
CITY OF MINNEAPOLIS
Hennepin County, Minnesota.

CITY CLERK

Put a cross (X) opposite the name of each candidate you wish to vote for in the square indicated by arrow.

For Mayor

Vote for One

- S. C. BOLSTAD
- GIL CARMICHAEL
- T. A. EIDE
- ROLAND L. HILL
- HUBERT H. HUMPHREY, JR.
- JALMER O. JOHNSON
- MARVIN L. KLINE
- LEWIS E. (SCOOP) LOHMANN
- FRANK J. MILLER
- JOHN J. O'BRIEN
- OLAF PEDERSON
- HARRY J. TODD
- EDWARD J. TOOHEY
- OLAV S. WINTHER

For City Treasurer

Vote for One

- AL. HANSEN
- GLADYS E. MILLER
- DEWEY C. YOUNGQUIST
- A. L. FREEBERG

For City Comptroller

Vote for One

- FRANK V. RANDALL
- O. J. TURNER
- RUSSELL S. ACKERMAN

For Member, Board of Estimate and Taxation

Vote for One

- C. F. E. PETERSON
- ARTHUR D. RUSSELL
- STEVEN E. BROOKS

For Park Commissioner

Vote for Four

- CLIFFORD C. PETERSON
- REUBEN H. STORCH
- HAROLD H. TEARSE
- MAUDE D. ARMATAGE
- ANDY CAMPION
- REGINALD FARAGHER
- HOFF HEIBERG
- GEORGE M. JENSEN
- L. W. (LES) JOHNSON
- PAUL C. JOHNSON

For School Director

Vote for Three

- MRS. HAROLD F. WAHLQUIST
- ROY W. WIER
- FELTON COLWELL
- MRS. ALICE GATES FABIANKE
- OLIVER E. JOHNSON
- MRS. GLADYS HOLT PETERSON
- JACOB REMER
- DOUGLAS FORD ROBBINS
- L. F. SCHOBER

For Library Director

Vote for Two

- MRS. B. G. DAHLBERG
- EARL GILBERT
- MILDRED DAUNT HAGLIN
- HOFF HEIBERG
- RUBIN LATZ
- BEN W. PALMER
- NELLIE STONE

For Alderman—First Ward

Vote for One

- STANLEY EDWARD (RED) CIESLA
- LOUIS J. JAROS
- HAROLD J. KAUTH
- PHILIP SABA

The reasoning behind the nonpartisan primary is of the "moral man, immoral society" variety. If only political parties could be eliminated along with their evils or at least have their influence kept to a minimum, local government would probably prosper. Good men would be able to put themselves forth for public office without becoming subservient to political leaders. Furthermore, political parties are inappropriate instruments for local government. They inject partisan and national issues where nonpartisan and local matters should be the determining factors, it is said. We have suggested before that this rationale for nonpartisanship is at least open to question. In predominantly Republican areas and in predominantly Democratic areas, politically sophisticated citizens may refer laughingly to our "nonpartisan Republican candidates" or our "nonpartisan Democratic candidates." Nonpartisanship may cover up more than it reveals and make the possibility of intelligent selection by the voter more difficult.

Supplemental use of primaries.   Direct voting or direct primaries are combined with party convention systems in several states. A number of states use a preprimary convention (see p. 190). New York provides for the popular election of delegates to its state-wide nominating conventions. Maryland and Georgia Democrats use a convention to make final the nominations from their direct primaries (see p. 192). South Dakota and Iowa resolve plurality nomination problems through party conventions when no candidate receives at least 35 percent of the primary vote. Connecticut modified its steady loyalty to the convention-nomination method in 1955 by permitting persons who received at least 20 percent of the convention vote to challenge the convention nominee in a direct primary. Provisions for petition filing and a deposit were made in order to secure a primary election. However, no convention-defeated state-wide candidate has as yet sought a primary in Connecticut.

★ *The direct primary in practice*

The direct primary has been in operation in so many states and localities and under such diverse conditions that the results it has achieved have varied widely. If the end product of the primary system is thought of as the nomination of well-qualified candidates, it has been notably successful in some instances and notably unsuccessful in others. The direct primary is neither under serious assault today nor supported as the great cure-all of political evils. Modifications in practice and occasionally by statute have affected the operation of the direct primary in a number of states. A summary of some of the areas of controversy and debate over the direct primary will help to indicate its strengths and weaknesses.

Figure 6. ONE VIEW OF THE LONG BALLOT
LOOK WHO'S HERE!
THE STOWAWAYS

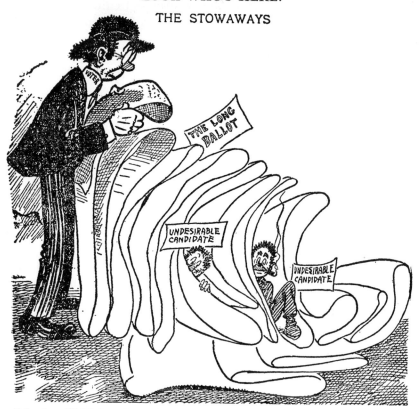

Columbus (Ohio) *State Journal*

1. The long ballot. The direct primary cannot be analyzed as if it existed by itself. Its operation is conditioned by many factors, one of the most important of which is the existence of the long ballot in almost all states and counties and in a number of cities. Recent extreme examples of the long ballot were in Cleveland and in Little Rock. Voters going to the polls in November 1956 were faced with ballots containing 50 positions in Cleveland and 169 positions in Little Rock! [1] It is sometimes difficult to determine to everyone's satisfaction what good or poor choices at an election are, but if good choices presuppose some knowledge about the candidates, long ballots cannot be so productive of them as the short variety (see Fig. 6).

Most local politicians could tell you of names which have had a peculiar fascination for voters when they have inadequate knowledge of the

[1] *National Municipal Review,* April 1957, p. 173.

merits of individual candidates. Wisconsin voters have seemed to like the names Smith, Martin, and Zimmerman for a decade and more. The fact that the original Smith, Martin, or Zimmerman had either died or ceased to be a candidate failed to change voting patterns for minor offices. Voters in other states have clung to other names and voting practices.

A good example of the effect of the long ballot and numerous candidates in the direct primary occurred in Minnesota in 1950. Even though the partisan direct primary is in effect for many state-wide elective offices, the Democratic-Farmer Labor party makes it a practice to endorse a slate of candidates before the primary. The endorsed slate in 1950 was not as strong as it might have been, but each individual endorsed was at least as capable and in most instances much more so than other candidates who filed for the eight state-wide offices. Of the eight endorsed candidates, two, those running for state auditor and secretary of state, were unopposed and hence automatically nominated. A number of candidates filed for the other six nominations. Some of these filings were bona fide—that is, serious— and others were not. Among the latter were at least two groups of people: those who wanted a bit of publicity and those who were entered as opposition candidates to the endorsed slate merely because of their surnames. If any of the latter group were nominated, the Republicans would be assured of victory in November because of the group's obvious lack of qualifications. The Democratic-Farmer Labor endorsed candidate for the nomination for governor was Peterson, and hence a number of other Petersons were convinced by a dissident Democrat to file in the hope of confusing the voters. A very popular Democratic-Farmer Labor Congressman from St. Paul was named McCarthy, the same name as a rather publicized Senator from Wisconsin, and so a Joe McCarthy was entered in one of the state-wide races. The Congressman did not have primary opposition, so this strategy did not directly affect him. A Gallagher was also entered, since this name has had a peculiar fascination for Minnesota voters ever since a Gallagher had sat on the state supreme court as a very respected member. The filings were completed with a sprinkling of Irish and Scandinavian names.

The usual moderate interest was shown by the voters in the primaries in 1950. A number of them stayed at home and confined their activities to the main election. Others went to the polls, but when confronted by a list of thirty or more candidates for six state-wide jobs, plus a complete list of county, judicial, legislative, and Congressional candidates, they found that they did not have adequate information about those for whom they were to vote. The Democratic-Farmer Labor results in the Minnesota primary were as follows: The endorsed candidate for governor was nominated, but not too handily. The endorsed candidate for attorney general was nominated in a very close race, primarily because he was the former party chairman and had conducted an unusually active and vigorous campaign. The party's endorsees for the other four positions were defeated, some of them very severely. The party had put up a well-qualified candidate for membership on a state-wide utility regulating body. He was defeated, and a McCarthy nominated instead. The same fate occurred to the other three indorsees: a Gallagher was nominated as supreme court clerk, a Fitzgerald as treasurer, and a Murphy as lieutenant governor. Of these four successful candidates, only Murphy was known to Democratic-Farmer Labor party leaders, and he was not in agreement with majority sentiment in the party. Fitzgerald turned out to be a rather aged political maverick, and it took two or three days after the primary to find out who McCarthy and Gallagher were—a sacker-handyman at a soy-bean factory and a truck driver. Both were complete unknowns, had no organizational support, had made no speeches, had no cards or literature printed, no campaign workers, and no platform whatsoever, and no obvious qualifications for a regulatory commissioner or clerk to the supreme court. As McCarthy put it after the primary, "I've got a lot of ideas, but this thing [his victory] came up so sudden I don't just know what to say I'm going to do if elected. But I guess I'm as smart as the people that voted for me." [2] As was to be expected in such circumstances, the Republicans swept the state offices in the November election.

2. Party responsibility.   The case just cited is also a good example of how impossible it is to have much party responsibility if the active party members cannot control the nominations. However, the direct primary does not always prevent a party from controlling its own nominations. The results may be determined partly by whether a primary is open or closed and partly by the character of the parties in a state. If a party is organized as vigorously as a few are in the South and in the East, it may be able to control the primary easily. In contrast, a rather loosely organized party, such as the Democratic-Farmer Labor party in Minnesota, will on occasion have great difficulty in nominating its preferred slate, even though no important organized opposition exists within the party.

Primaries may be the scenes of bitter intraparty disputes such as have occurred in a number of states between the old guard of a party and newer and younger elements, usually more liberal. When such contests occur, the direct primary can be an effective mechanism to determine the outcome, but serious difficulties may still arise. The long ballot frequently interferes

[2] Minneapolis *Morning Tribune*, September 15, 1950.

with a clear-cut decision, one faction of the party winning the governorship, for example, and another winning the less important nominations.

As the first state to adopt the direct primary on a state-wide basis, Wisconsin has experimented in practice (with few changes in the governing statutes) with a variety of tools for keeping the primaries open for voter revolt and yet giving the parties a measure of control. Both the Republican and Democratic parties in the state today hold preprimary conventions. Typically the Republican party preprimary convention endorses a slate of candidates for state-wide offices and uses the organization and funds of the party to convince Republican primary voters that these candidates should be nominated.[3] The alert voter has no difficulty knowing in advance which candidates the party prefers. The party's success in the primary with its endorsed slate has varied, but the leaders show no disposition to do away with endorsement. The Democratic party preprimary convention indicates the lines of party programs and usually indicates the relative party strength of particular primary candidates. Some Democrats would like the formal endorsement procedure of the Republicans but have been held back by traditions in the state. The Democratic organization then remains neutral in the primary and supports the primary winners in the general election.[4] Parties in some states, for example, Massachusetts, not only use the Wisconsin Republican-party preprimary-convention endorsement system but have secured authority to show this fact on the primary election ballot.

California (until 1959) and Washington have had special problems in securing party responsibility. From 1913 to 1959 California permitted cross-filing which enabled a candidate to file for the nomination of his own party and also for that of any other party he desired.[5] Whereas the open primary and sometimes even the so-called closed primary invites voters to ignore their dominant party allegiance and to aid in the nominations of the opposing party, the cross-filing system invites a lack of party responsibility from candidates. In California almost all serious candidates for state legisla-

[3] Technically the preprimary conventions of Republicans and Democrats are not statutory party meetings but meetings of associations of Republicans and associations of Democrats. The distinction has importance in control and in avoidance of specific statutory provisions on party organization and finance.

[4] Occasionally Democrats having opposed preprimary party endorsement but disliking the results of the primary election have not given organization and fund support to particular primary winners. Such action constitutes a rather backhanded negative use of the Republican endorsement system.

[5] A number of states do not forbid *cross-filing* in their primaries. New York permits conventions of more than one party to nominate the same individual and the New York Liberal party frequently has endorsed candidates of the Democratic or Republican parties rather than nominate a candidate of its own. California, however, was the outstanding example of general use of cross-filing (or as in New York "cross-endorsement").

ture or state-wide offices cross-filed. Until 1954 when new legislation required the ballots to show the party identification of each candidate, the
cross-filing system seemed exclusively to benefit the incumbent Republicans. With cross-filing the primary ceases to be a contest merely among a
party's own supporters and takes on the aspect of a general election, even
more than Washington's wide-open primary, since at least in Washington
there are two nominees selected for each position in the primary. Party
responsibility is difficult to secure if a candidate is, practically speaking,
elected at the primary before organized party support or opposition can
form. Furthermore, with cross-filing it is always possible for unscrupulous
individuals or groups to enter a number of "dummy" candidates to split the
vote of the opposing party, and thus secure the nominations of all parties
for their favorite candidates.

Party responsibility is least recognized in states and localities that follow the *nonpartisan primary* system. Two states, Nebraska and Minnesota,
nominate and elect their legislators on nonpartisan ballots, and the nonpartisan primary is widespread in school districts, municipalities, and judicial nominations, and somewhat less common for county nominations. The
appropriateness of nonpartisanship is discussed elsewhere (see Ch. 8).
Here it is well to emphasize that parties in some form or other do exist in
all states and most localities, and that they do try to exercise some control
over nominations and elections even in localities having nonpartisan ballots. It has often been argued that partisan primaries make parties more
responsible, but, while partly believable, this has never been proved or
documented adequately. Even with nonpartisan primaries, strongly organized political parties can nominate their preferred candidates, although
weaker parties may have much difficulty. The nonpartisan primary for the
legislature in Minnesota has resulted in poor party responsibility and considerable dissatisfaction.

3. Majority decisions. Direct primaries, whether partisan or nonpartisan,
do not necessarily ensure majority decisions if three or more candidates
contend for a nomination. Except in the state of Washington the marked
ballots in a partisan primary are counted separately for each political
party. In most states a simple plurality of votes is enough for the nomination. Thus Jackson, Johnson, and Thorson might receive 200,000, 110,000,
and 55,000 votes each for governor in the Republican party, and Bulwinkle,
MacWinkle, and Van Winkle 100,000, 75,000, and 53,000 votes each for the
Democratic nomination. Jackson and Bulwinkle would be the nominees
for each party. The results seem reasonable enough in the case of Jackson,
who polled much more than his combined opposition within the Republi-

can party, but Bulwinkle was a plurality, not a majority winner, since his two opponents, MacWinkle and Van Winkle polled between them 128,000 votes. It is possible that the supporters of both these men saw eye to eye on most matters and would have preferred either one of the two to Bulwinkle. One of the difficulties with primaries is plurality nominations if many candidates file. Nevertheless, each party is entitled to one nominee, no matter how many or how few voters cast ballots in its primary. If there are more than two parties, a plurality vote may be sufficient to win in the final election because the several nominees will split the votes.

The most extensively used system in operation today designed to secure majority nominations is the *run-off primary* provided for in eleven Southern states. Since the Democratic nomination is tantamount to election in the South, the problem of plurality nominations may indeed be a serious one. The run-off primary has provided a solution. In case a candidate does not receive a majority of the votes in the Democratic primary, a supplementary primary is held a few weeks later in which those two candidates receiving the highest number of votes in the original contest vie for the nomination.

Majority votes are not the determinants of nomination for the governorships and certain other offices of Maryland and Georgia. These states operate under varying systems that give rural counties more weight per voter than urban counties in determining the outcome of the nomination. This is done in both states by a unit-vote system, in which each county is assigned a number of unit votes and the candidate receiving a majority of the popular votes gets all the unit votes of a county to his credit. Furthermore, rural counties have a greater proportion of the total unit votes than they have of the population or of those who cast ballots. The official nomination of candidates takes place in party conventions following the primaries, and it is in the conventions that the unit vote system pays off. In both Georgia and Maryland, the successful nominee for such an office as governor or U. S. Senator has on occasion received fewer popular votes in his party's primary than his unsuccessful opponent.

4. General evaluation. The direct primary came into existence as a device for reducing the power of the party organization and increasing the direct control of the voters over the nomination of candidates. Desirably or not, it probably achieved this result in most states. Party organizations, however, are tough and increasingly they have adapted to the exigencies of the primary. Their adaptations have received encouragement as more and more leaders in and out of politics have come to believe that strong competing parties, rather than weak parties, may contribute most to democracy.

Whether the direct primary has delayed the rise of competing parties in one-party areas is not established, but it seems plausible. To offset this effect of reduction of party responsibility, it might be argued that (1) the direct primary provided voters with choices which they previously lacked in one-party situations; (2) the threat of the direct primary forced reforms in some state party organizations even where the full use of the primary has never been adopted; and (3) with some modifications, such as use of preprimary conventions, the direct primary may allow voters to enjoy *eating* their cake of an ultimate popular control of nominations and still *having* their cake in providing for significant party responsibility.

Campaigns

Until President Truman's 1948 political upset victory, there were many who looked on campaigning as a ritual with little direct effect on the election results. Neither political analysts nor politicians would be willing to assert specifically what kind of a campaign is most effective or how many votes different types of campaigns will produce. Many citizens are indissolubly attached to one of the parties or to one candidate. No type of campaign would affect their decision. However, it is essential to remember certain points: (1) It is necessary for a campaign to combat the opposition's campaign if the election result is at all in doubt. (2) Campaigning helps to bring out the vote. (3) While campaigning may not change many people's minds, in a close election it may change enough people's thinking or bring out just enough supporters to determine the result. (4) If startling revelations take place during a campaign, a major shift in thinking may take place. Likewise, if during the campaign great differences in the opinions or abilities of the candidates show up, public reaction may be rather extensive. (5) While pressure groups are very important in politics, they seldom can "deliver" the votes of their members as a *bloc*; the members of a certain organization may be influenced by what their leader tells them, but he is definitely limited in his ability to deliver the votes of any substantial number of them. Members of a labor union may vote Democratic to a greater extent than the general population, but in any large union a substantial percentage will vote Republican, and labor-union leaders may have had little to do with the Democratic voting tendency of a union's members anyway. Even if the leaders are responsible, they could not quickly change the vote of their members to the Republican party, as if the members had no ideas of their own.

Much of the literature and political analysis of campaigns have covered Presidential campaigns and have paid less attention to the campaigns of individuals seeking state election.[6] State campaigns involve fewer individuals, less organization, less money; they are frequently affected (but not necessarily won or lost) by the national political situation; and they show up some of the differences in cultural patterns and traditions among the states. California parties and candidates, for example, have used rather flamboyant billboards in some elections, whereas Michigan has prohibited political billboard advertising.

★ *Money*

Even in small states, campaigning is expensive. The amount of money available to a candidate, as well as the effective use of that money, may mean success or failure. A single mailing of literature to half a million voters (and over half the states have more than this number) represents a postage expenditure of $15,000. Newspaper advertising, radio talks, and television appearances vary in cost with communities but universally they are expensive. The candidate's own travel expenses as well as his living expenses during the months when he may have little income from his normal situation (a Rockefeller or Harriman or even a Kohler is saved these worries) mount up. A campaign office in one or more major cities of the state, clerical assistance in the office, numerous telephone calls, probably at least a few part-time campaigners to whom travel expenses if not salaries must be paid—all of these add to the minimal campaign costs of the candidate today.

Where does a candidate get money to cover such costs? Frequently he begins by using his own money and money that personal friends donate. Individuals soliciting in his name will seek to secure additional sums from people or groups likely to be sympathetic to him, to the issues which he supports, and to his party. If he is running with party support, the regular finance organization of the party will assist in securing moneys. A portion of funds raised by Lincoln or Jefferson-Jackson Day dinners (Republican and Democratic annual affairs) may be made available to the candidate. Some money will come from those who hope personally to gain from his success, some will come from committee party members, a little may come from citizens who see the party system as necessary to democracy and who

6 See, for example, V. O. Key, Jr., *Politics, Parties, and Pressure Groups*, 4th ed. (New York: Thomas Y. Crowell, 1958), Ch. 17, "Campaign Techniques." Studies of state campaigns would include: Rhoten A. Smith and Clarence J. Hein, *Republican Primary Fight: A Study in Factionalism* (New York: Henry Holt, 1958) and Joseph P. Lyford, *Candidate* (New York: Henry Holt, 1959). Both are from the Eagleton Foundation series of Case Studies in Practical Politics.

believe small contributions keep the candidate and party from too entangling alliances.

State corrupt-practices laws which attempt to regulate campaign expenses usually limit expenditures in amount, in type of item, and in sources of funds, and require reporting.[7] Limitations on the amount of expenditures have tended to be unrealistic and to invite avoidance. Limitations on sources of funds such as prohibiting contributions from corporations, banks, and in some states from labor unions have been somewhat more enforceable. Reporting requirements, if well established and enforced and if publicized by newspapers in the state, may achieve the most results in advertising the candidate's possible obligations to individuals or groups.

The necessary yet possibly corrupting role of money in campaigns has troubled Americans for 75 years or more. The fears generated by the excessive use of moneys have failed to halt steady increases in the cost of campaigning. Suggestions that candidates' expenses as a part of the costs of democracy be paid for through taxation have floundered for years. States have taken only halting steps in either controlling or assisting campaigns. Oregon mails out to every voter, at state expense, a pamphlet covering certain state issues with a page devoted to each statewide candidate for public office. Wisconsin gives time on its state radio network to every state-wide candidate. Minnesota allows an income tax deduction for modest political contributions. Newspapers sometimes give space for candidate questionnaires which they devise and at times to the candidate questionnaires of such voluntary organizations as the League of Women Voters. In some cities the League occasionally distributes its questionnaires from door to door. A number of voluntary organizations have conducted "get-out-the-vote" campaigns. But a gubernatorial candidate who relied solely on the assistance of government and voluntary organizations to present his case is not likely to occupy the governor's mansion after the election.

★ Organization

To use money effectively, to use volunteer workers, and to make his own efforts most meaningful, a candidate needs an organization. "Lone-wolf" candidates, with a minimum of organization and a maximum of personal effort, only occasionally have succeeded. Incumbent candidates may need less organization (and less money) since they have opportunities for keeping their name in front of the public. The usual new candidate, however, needs an organization to assist him. Again, if he is a party candidate and

[7] See *Book of the States* for a summary table of state restrictions on campaign expenditures (in the 1958-59 edition, on pp. 18 and 19).

the party is reasonably solvent, it will likely provide him with office space in party headquarters in one or more cities of the state. The party will have lists of party supporters who will contribute time or money. The party will have some experienced workers or consultants to advise on the most productive use of radio, television, mailing materials, and special techniques in campaigning. Coordinating the campaigns of several candidates may be mutually advantageous to the candidates and to the party. A candidate of an impoverished, minority party (and minority parties traditionally are impoverished) or without party support is severely handicapped in such simple matters as finding a place to store materials, keeping track of and answering correspondence, and maintaining a list of friends who have offered to give time to the campaign.[8]

Elections

The kind of elections that are held and the way in which elections are administered have a crucial influence on the results. For example, the honesty of election administration, the type of ballots used, and the time of year and frequency of elections may play some role in determining final results. They are far from being the sole determinants of who comes out the victor, but they, along with hundreds of other factors, have some effect.

★ Election timing

It is a matter of some importance whether or not state and local elections are held at the same time as Congressional and Presidential elections. The importance results from two facts: voter turnout is larger for Congressional, Presidential, and gubernatorial elections, and partisan issues important on one level may also affect the results on another. County elections are usually held at the same time that state and national elections occur, and as a result many more people cast their ballots for county positions than would normally be the case. In contrast, most cities usually hold their elections at times when they will not coincide with state and national elections; voter turnout is lower on the average for such cities than for comparable county elections, although voter interest is probably greater in municipal than county affairs.

---

[8] It should be made clear that the amount of money and organization needed varies with states and exceptional cases can be cited. Wisconsin Democrats gained control of state government in 1958 (after 25 years absence) on the proverbial shoestring of money and organization. The governor's campaign manager was a university student. There was money for almost no paid help; organizational confusion seems to have been widespread. But the gubernatorial and U. S. Senatorial candidates personally put in enormous numbers of hours campaigning for several years before they succeeded.

Spring and fall are the most popular times for elections, although there is not a single month in which some election does not occur. State and county elections are commonly in the fall in even-numbered years along with the Congressional and Presidential elections. Primaries may precede the general election by a few weeks or several months. Township, school-district, and municipal elections are frequently held in the spring, although fall dates are common.

The frequency of elections varies all the way from annual elections in the townships and many school districts to the typical every two- or four-year elections that cities, counties, and states usually have. Frequency is important from the standpoint of the voter's burden and also from the standpoint of making government sufficiently responsible at the same time that it is experienced and stable. For the country as a whole there has been a very gradual trend toward elections every four years, but biennial state elections are still common, following the Congressional pattern. While four-year terms for a legislative body may be provided in a state, they may be overlapping terms and so necessitate biennial elections. Elections every four years seem to be about the best compromise between lessening the voter's burden and keeping government responsible and responsive.

★ The administration of elections

The primary purposes of election administration are to secure honest and efficient election processes. Details of this character may at first seem insignificant, but to a candidate or party at election time they may mean victory or defeat.

Putting yourself in the position of a party leader for a moment, what would you want provided in election administration to assure you an honest result? It is obvious from the outset that the persons handling the registration lists and the ballots or voting machines must be either friends or supporters of your campaign or trustworthy nonpartisans. This is the first point of frustration for you, since if you are not in control of the county or city board of elections or governing body or some similar group, you are not likely to have much to say about the appointment of the three or more people who handle election administration in each precinct, since they are usually appointed by such bodies. Although most state laws prescribe that precinct election officials shall be representative of more than one party, appointments are usually based upon patronage considerations. Under such a system it is always possible to find someone who is technically a member of an opposite political party but who agrees, essentially, with the party in control. As a party leader you may find that only your political opponents are represented by election officials. A few states have moved toward selection of precinct election officials by the merit system, but this is still a very limited tendency.

Since you cannot be sure that the election officials will guarantee an honest result for you, you will want some assurance that your representatives can watch all the actions of these persons. In most states there are "watchers." Any political party or candidate may appoint watchers who can be present at the polling place from the time it is open in the morning until the last ballot is counted or the last voting machine checked at night. Of course, securing this number of faithful poll watchers is a very difficult task and in actual fact in many parts of the country where political parties are not extensively organized on precinct levels, very few poll watchers are ever appointed.

Despite the many opportunities for dishonesty in the administration of elections, its quality has improved markedly during the last fifty years. Not dishonest officials but tired, unskilled, careless election officials no doubt account for most errors in ballot counting today. The recording and counting of votes after the polls have closed by workers tired from their earlier efforts and unused to such detail in their normal lives produce a significant number of errors which show up in election recounts. Untrained election officials may unwittingly violate election laws by making prohibited statements such as "Don't forget to vote on the school-bond referendum." More or less unconscious partisan biases tend to show up in the bases on which ballots are disqualified by election officials, in the manner in which voters are informed of the election procedure, and in the actual counting of the votes. Under circumstances which suggest carelessness rather than fraud, ballot boxes sometimes have disappeared by the time the recount is made. Voting machines reduce the chances of counting errors and the normal questions as to the propriety of the ballot cast. A guaranty of accuracy and competency as well as honesty in elections suggests the desirability of checking the minimal qualifications of poll officials and orienting them on their duties.[9]

★ *Polling procedures*

The procedure of casting a ballot—of voting—is a simple one. First, a prospective voter must identify himself, and in areas that require advance registration, this may mean checking the signature of the voter with that of his registration card. Once identified, the voter receives a ballot and pro-

---

[9] A good study of election errors is found in the report by Samuel J. Eldersveld and Albert A. Applegate, *Michigan's Recounts for Governor, 1950 and 1952: A Systematic Analysis of Election Error*, Michigan Governmental Studies No. 30 (Ann Arbor, Mich.: University of Michigan Press, 1954).

ceeds to a booth that is curtained off to provide privacy. There he marks the ballot in secret and folds it appropriately. He leaves the voting booth and deposits the ballot in the box provided for that purpose, or one of the election judges deposits it. When voting machines are used, the voter, after identifying himself, goes to the voting machine, pulls a lever that draws a curtain across the booth, providing privacy, and unlocks the machinery, and proceeds to pull down the appropriate levers of the candidates or party that he favors. When he is through voting, he pulls back the lever that opens the curtain; his vote is automatically recorded at the same time; the levers are raised; and the machine is ready for the next voter.

★ *Types of ballots*

Whether paper ballots or voting machines are used, there is a variety of ballot types. The type of ballot has an important influence on election results: The traditional long ballot sometimes confuses the voter. A straight party ticket is much simpler to use than one which requires that the voter pick and choose among many candidates individually. If only one or two or even three or four offices were to be filled at an election, the type of ballot used would not be very important as long as secrecy was provided.

While there are numerous subvarieties, ballots may be grouped into two types: party-column ballots and office-group ballots. The former is the most common in state elections. The names of the candidates are arranged by the parties that have nominated them, each party's candidates being in a separate column. This type of ballot encourages straight party voting by the very arrangement of the candidates' names. In order to split the ticket, the voter must go from one column to another, a rather inconvenient system. Furthermore, most of the states using this type of ballot provide a circle or lever that may be marked or pulled by which a voter casts a straight party vote (see Fig. 7). The convenience of such an arrangement is tempting to the voter confronted with a long ballot.

Not quite so frequently used as the former in state elections is the office-group ballot. This ballot is adaptable for both partisan and nonpartisan elections. Candidates are grouped according to the office for which they are running, and the voter has no alternative but to mark an **X** or pull a lever next to the candidate of his choice for each office. This ballot arrangement encourages a voter to cross party lines from time to time and vote for a Republican for one office, a Democrat for another, and so on. While candidates in partisan elections have their party affiliations stated after their names, this is much less prominent than the display the parties receive in the party-column ballot. Naturally, in all nonpartisan elections an office-group ballot is used, the only difference being that party identifica-

Figure 7. A PARTY-COLUMN BALLOT, CITY OF LANSING, MICHIGAN, 1958

OFFICES / STRAIGHT PARTY LEVERS	1 Governor	2 Lieutenant Governor	3 Secretary of State	4 Attorney General	5 State Treasurer	6 Auditor General	7 United States Senator	8 Representative in Congress Sixth District	9 State Senator 14th District	10 State Representatives First District (Vote for Two)	11	12 Prosecuting Attorney	13 County Sheriff	14 County Clerk	15 County Treasurer	16 Register of Deeds	17 Drain Comm'er	18 Coroners (Vote for Two)	19	20 Surveyor
Democratic	1 A G. Mennen Williams	2 A John B. Swainson	3 A James M. Hare	4 A Paul L. Adams	5 A Sanford A. Brown	6 A Frank S. Szymanski	7 A Philip A. Hart	8 A Don Hayworth	9 A	10 A Elizabeth L. Belen	11 A Thomas C. Walsh	12 A William G. Jenkins	13 A Thomas C. Wolven	14 A Dona D. Williams	15 A Edward J. Boucher	16 A Mable Culpepper	17 A Howard L. Jones	18 A Joseph R. Gutstein	19 A Arthur W. Jewett	20 A
Republican	1 B Paul D. Bagwell	2 B Donald A. Brown	3 B Raymond A. Plank	4 B Jason L. Honigman	5 B Allan G. Weatherwax	6 B John V. Clements	7 B Charles E. Potter	8 B Charles E. Chamberlain	9 B Paul C. Younger	10 B Willard I. Bowerman, Jr.	11 B Harold W. Hungerford	12 B Jack W. Warren	13 B Willard P. Barnes	14 B C. Ross Hilliard	15 B Laurence D. Parker	16 B Mia Bell Humphrey	17 B Gerald L. Graham	18 B Dorwin E. Hoffmeyer	19 B Jack B. Holmes	20 B William C. Berryman
Socialist Labor	1 C Ralph Muncy	2 C James Horvath	3 C Charles Schwertz	4 C Albert Mills	5 C William Walbridge	6 C Frank Troha	7 C James Sim	8 C	9 C	10 C	11 C									
Socialist Workers	1 D Frank Lovell	2 D Larry Dolinski	3 D Robert Himmel Jr.	4 D Rita Shaw	5 D	6 D	7 D Evelyn Sell	8 D	9 D	10 D	11 D									
Prohibition	1 E Rollin M. Severance	2 E Herbert E. Crouter	3 E Alfred T. Halsted	4 E	5 E Wendell J. Goodwin	6 E William J. Persons	7 E Elmer H. Ormiston	8 E Ernest H. Gorton	9 E Paul H. Kyburz	10 E	11 E									

tion is omitted after the candidate's name. Generally speaking, party leaders prefer the party-column ballot, and independents, reformers, and academics prefer the office-group ballot, for fairly obvious reasons.

★ *Election results*

Election results are officially reported some days or weeks after an election, as soon as an official canvass of voting can be completed. However, newspapers and radio stations usually pool facilities to bring their readers and listeners election results the evening of the election and early the next morning. They send reporters from precinct to precinct, or have friends among poll watchers or election officials who send results to a central location. With voting machines, the problem is less extensive, since an accurate count can be had as soon as the polls are closed by unlocking the voting machines.

Conclusion

Relatively few citizens actively participate in politics other than by voting periodically. And only approximately 60 percent of Americans vote even in Presidential elections—usually the greatest incentive for many voters. Of the voters, considerably fewer than 50 percent believe their actions at the polls can have a significant effect on the direction of governmental policies.

Repeated studies of voters in this country and abroad find that voting is positively correlated with higher incomes and higher education; that businessmen, white-collar employees, government employees, commercial crop farmers, and miners show a higher voting turnout than unskilled workers, servants, and subsistence farmers. Jewish citizens vote more frequently than Protestants, and Protestants more frequently vote than Catholics. Whites show a higher voting turnout than Negroes (even where Negroes are not disfranchised by a variety of means). Men vote more frequently than women; middle-aged people, more often than older people; and older people, more than young people. Old community residents are more likely to vote than newcomers. National or community crises will usually bring out more voters than periods of calm.

The reasons for voting and nonvoting by the above groups are a function of the relation of government activities to each group, the ability of each group to recognize the relation of government action to his welfare, and the absence of conflicting desires or pressures in voting choices. The individual working for government or the individual who receives direct economic assistance will vote more readily than the individual who sees government only as a distant "they" with little impact on his daily sorrows and happiness. When government is a "they" and moreover a "they" about which the individual can do nothing, then the incentive for political activity, even the act of voting, is negligible. The citizen who in business and social life learns to understand the working of government and the opportunities, especially through group action, to influence government is most likely to vote and eventually to pursue other political activity.

Voters from larger cities, larger industrial plants, and areas of high unemployment, or voters from minority ethnic or religious groups or voters in such occupations as mining, commercial farming, shipping, stevedoring, and fishing, are more likely to vote for parties and programs which emphasize greater economic and social equality than are voters from other types of areas, in other occupations, or from majority ethnic or religious groups.

The legal and administrative provisions for carrying out elections determine the limits of the voting population. Sociological factors suggested above help to determine the actual individuals who vote, their concept of the importance of their vote, and their view of issues and parties. Not all of the conclusions as to who votes or the general direction of voting apply without modification in all of the states. For one thing voters have a great tenacity in maintaining older patterns. The changed relation of their interests to the parties and candidates must be especially clear-cut before a shift occurs. The blurred lines of our parties in the several states as well as the low visibility of party activities to many voters may delay a change in voting behavior in some states as compared with other states.

Studies of election behavior give us much more understanding than in the past of why people vote as they do.[10] The best election polls use this increasing knowledge to improve the accuracy of their sampling and forecasting.

REFERENCES

Baker, Gordon E., and Bernard Teitelbaum, "An End to Cross-Filing," 48 *National Civic Review* (formerly *National Municipal Review*) (June 1959), 286-291.
Burdick, Eugene, and Arthur J. Brodbeck, *American Voting Behavior*. Glencoe, Ill.: The Free Press, 1959.
Eulau, Heinz, Samuel J. Eldersveld, and Morris Janowitz, (eds.), *Political Behavior, A Reader in Theory and Research*. Glencoe, Ill.: The Free Press, 1956.

[10] Ch. 30 "The Psychology of Voting: An Analysis of Political Behavior," in Gardner Lindzey, ed., *Handbook of Social Psychology*, Vol. II (Cambridge, Mass.: Addison-Wesley, 1954).

Fenton, John H., and Kenneth N. Vines, "Negro Registration in Louisiana," 51 *American Political Science Review* (September 1957), 704-713.

Harris, Joseph P., *Election Administration in the United States.* Washington, D. C.: The Brookings Institution, 1934.

Hyman, Herbert H., *Political Socialization: A Study in the Psychology of Political Behavior.* Glencoe, Ill.: The Free Press, 1959.

McCormick, Richard P., *The History of Voting in New Jersey; A Study of the Development of Election Machinery, 1664-1911.* New Brunswick, N.J.: Rutgers University Press, 1953.

Ranney, Austin, *The Doctrine of Responsible Party Government, Its Origins and Present State.* Urbana, Ill.: University of Illinois Press, 1954.

Schubert, Glendon A., Jr., *The Michigan State Director of Elections.* Inter-university Case Program. University, Ala.: University of Alabama Press, 1954.

Sekulow, Eugene A., *Monkey Business at the Polls; A Guide to Election Frauds and How to Prevent Some of Them.* Government Research Association Reporter No. 2, 1959.

Simon, Herbert A., "Bandwagon and Underdog Effects and the Possibility of Election Predictions," *Public Opinion Quarterly* (Fall 1954), 245-253.

See also references at end of Chs. 7 and 8.

PART THREE

State Organization

CHAPTER 10

Composition and
Election of State
Legislatures

IN MANY PRIMITIVE SOCIETIES a separate function of legislating as distinct from judging cases and enforcing laws was not known. Indeed, the very idea of changing or abolishing old rules and of making new ones for future application did not clearly exist in such societies, where custom and taboo were the principal regulators of conduct, and where perhaps only the gods were considered to be sources of law. The ruler or the public assembly simply declared the law as it was supposed already to be and applied that law to the case in hand. At some point in their development, communities became more self-conscious, more sophisticated, and, shall we say, more civilized, and the idea of the lawgiver or lawmaker as a wise human being or group of human beings empowered to change old laws and to make new ones for the community came into existence and then proceeded on its own course of development. This course was different in every country, and the developments in the idea stand at different points of advancement in different places.

Before the present states were organized, the English colonies in North America had their colonial legislative assemblies with substantial powers of lawmaking. The first of these appears to have been Virginia, founded in 1607 by the Virginia Company. In 1618 the reforms decreed by the company included the grant of a right to the colonists to hold an annual assembly, consisting of two burgesses elected from each plantation, plus the governor and council. The first assembly, held in 1619, lasted only six days and acted as both a court and a legislative body. In the latter capacity it legislated on idleness, gambling, drunkenness, agriculture, defense, contracts, and other subjects, and also passed the first tax law in North America—a poll tax.[1]

Later other colonies, one by one, received and used the power to hold legislative assemblies, to pass laws on various subjects, and to provide punishments for violations thereof, up to and including the death penalty. These legislatures, the direct forerunners of the state legislatures of today, to some extent set the patterns for later legislative organization and procedure.

Unicameralism and Bicameralism

★ Development of bicameralism

Legislatures may consist of one, two, or more bodies of members, each organized under its own officers and meeting by itself in its own chamber. The Canadian provinces have one-chambered or unicameral legislatures. The strong preference of the American states for two-chambered legislatures antedates the United States Constitution. Most of the colonies that preceded the states had had a sort of two-chambered arrangement. One house consisted of representatives elected by the qualified voters. The other was an appointive body consisting of residents of the colony appointed by the king, one of whose main functions was to advise the royal governor on appointments and executive matters, but which also consulted with him and acted on bills passed by the elected assembly. Thus it had a sort of legislative function. Inasmuch as the framers of the original state constitutions intended to keep the chief executive, called governor or president, under strict control, they must have thought a small second chamber, chosen by the electorate and composed of leading citizens, would perform this function most satisfactorily. There was also the precedent of the two chambers of parliament for legislative purposes. In these two houses were represented different elements in the population—the wealthy, land-owning nobility in the House of Lords, and the more middle-class element of the cities and counties (boroughs and shires) in the elective House of Commons.

The desirability of such a "mixed constitution" was generally conceded by the leaders in the early American states. There would be two sepa-

[1] See *The Oldest Legislative Assembly in America and Its First Statehouse*, revised (pamphlet), National Park Service Interpretive Series, History No. 2, Washington, 1947.

rate considerations of every legislative proposal, check and doublecheck. Nothing would be done that would be harmful to any important class in the state. When the framers of the United States Constitution came forward with a bicameral plan for Congress, one house to represent states equally, the other to represent populations proportionately, the upholders of the bicameral system were re-enforced in their faith. The United States Senate is supposed to represent states, and the House represents people, although in some earlier theories both houses of colonial legislatures presumably represented different classes of people. In New York, for example, voters had to meet a higher property qualification to be permitted to vote for the upper house of the legislature. In Massachusetts those elected to the lower house had to possess a certain amount of property, and those chosen for the upper house had to own three times as much. Thus it was intended, at least in some of the early states, that, while both houses would be conservative, the smaller or upper house would be more conservative or property-minded than the other.[2]

In the United States, of the original thirteen states, eleven entered the union with two-chambered or bicameral legislatures; Georgia and Pennsylvania had one-chambered bodies. Vermont later came in (1791) with a one-house legislature which had been functioning since 1777, but thereafter all new states entered the union with bicameral bodies. Georgia and Pennsylvania soon adopted bicameral systems; Vermont did so in 1836. The conservative pressure in favor of bicameralism and the desire of each state to be like the United States in organization were powerful incentives toward this change. It was not until a century after Vermont abandoned the one-house system that Nebraska broke away from tradition to establish a unicameral system.

Bicameralism has not worked out entirely as expected. The state senates as such do not ordinarily serve as advisers for the governor even when they are small enough to do so, and it depends upon the methods of election and the constituencies represented whether the house or senate is the more conservative body. In many states there is little choice between them in this respect. The same body of voters now elects members of both houses, so that class representation no longer prevails. Careful studies reveal, too, that in age and experience state senators have little advantage over house

[2] On the general question of unicameralism and bicameralism and the role of second chambers, see W. F. Willoughby, *Principles of Legislative Organization and Administration* (Washington, D. C.: Brookings Institution, 1934), pp. 213-238, and *The Government of Modern States*, revised ed. (New York: Appleton-Century-Crofts, 1936), pp. 334-348; James W. Garner, *Political Science and Government* (New York: American Book, 1928), pp. 601-624; John P. Senning, *The One-House Legislature* (New York: McGraw-Hill, 1937); Belle Zeller, ed., *American State Legislatures* (New York: Thomas Y. Crowell, 1954), pp. 47-60.

members, and that the parties are about equally represented in the two houses, except where there is gross overrepresentation of rural districts in one or the other. It is, however, commonly felt by observers that upper-house members usually have greater average ability than do those in the lower house.

★ Present arguments for bicameralism

Since some of the old reasons for two-chambered legislatures are no longer so valid as they once seemed, other considerations now receive more emphasis. It is sometimes argued that the mere fact of having two bodies to consider each bill is a good thing in itself. This is a variation of Washington's little argument concerning the pouring of one's tea from the cup into the saucer before drinking it—"to cool it," he said, but today men say "to improve it." This argument is a relatively old one. The facts show that each house does defeat a number of bills passed in the other and amends a considerable number of others. How much improvement results from these amendments no one can say; it is likely that in many cases the bill is improved and in other cases it is weakened or made worse by compromise provisions and "weasel words."

Another argument, already mentioned, that states need two legislative chambers so that, like Congress, one can represent *areas* and the other represent *people* will be dealt with under the subject of apportionment later in this chapter.

Under the impact of nineteenth-century democratic ideas, property tests for voting and officeholding were generally abandoned by the states. Furthermore, a number of new constitutions made population the sole basis of apportionment in both houses, ignoring areas or units of government. With the same body of voters choosing members of both houses on a mere population basis, the need for two houses began to be seriously questioned.

★ Unicameralism

A sort of nation-wide movement for one-chambered state legislatures had been under way for some time when Nebraska in 1937 put the plan into effect. The Nebraska unicameral legislature has forty-three members elected by single districts for two-year terms on ballots without party labels. The preceding bicameral body had had 133 members. The unicameral body has now held many sessions. Following the first one, its chief sponsor, U. S. Senator George W. Norris, said that it had "demonstrated beyond the possibility of a doubt the great superiority of the one-house legislature," and that its record was "far superior to the record made by any previous legislature in the history of Nebraska." While other comments were not so enthusiastic, they were generally favorable. From the beginning no serious charge of incompetence has been brought against it. In general it has borne out the main arguments for unicameralism: (1) Since the members of both houses in most bicameral state legislatures represent the same people and the same interests, have almost identical qualifications, and have the same duties with minor exceptions, a single body can provide adequate representation of interests and do all that needs to be done; (2) with only one chamber there can be no shifting of responsibility from house to house, and no deadlocks such as now mar many legislative sessions; (3) critical decisions will be made more in the open rather than in conference committees between the two houses where interhouse dispute settlements have sometimes left the two houses little option other than rubber-stamping the result; and (4) the delays and excessive expense of bicameral legislatures will be reduced.

After two and a half decades of experience, Nebraska voters appear satisfied with one house.[3] The National Municipal League sponsors the unicameral system as part of its *Model State Constitution*. Forty-nine states in the union, however, have not jumped on the band wagon. States such as Massachusetts and Wisconsin have had relatively little difficulty in avoiding deadlocks, excessive use of conference committees, and the like with a two-house legislature. Many other states have failed to redistrict or reapportion seats for at least one of the two houses so that the same vested interests which oppose redistricting or reapportionment would necessarily oppose a one-house legislature chosen on a population basis. And the very failure to reapportion contributes to the differences and deadlocks between the two houses. In other words, in many states any consideration of a one-house legislature runs into the same barriers as consideration of population representation in both houses of the legislature.

An advantage of the unicameral legislature that has been little discussed is its unified power and responsibility. The ordinary bicameral legislature has no effective common organization. (One reason Massachusetts

[3] There are many short articles on the Nebraska experience. Among them are: John P. Senning, "Unicameralism Passes Test," 33 *National Municipal Review* (February 1944), 60-65; Lane W. Lancaster, "Nebraska's Experience with a One-House Legislature," 11 *University of Kansas City Law Review* (1942), No. 1, 24-30, and other articles in this issue. Much interesting material and comment will be found in Oklahoma State Legislative Council, Constitutional Study No. 8 (May 1948), entitled *Legislative Organization and Procedure (Part B: Bicameralism and Unicameralism)*, by H. V. Thornton and Betty Quinlan.

and Wisconsin succeed as well as they do is that Massachusetts uses joint committees of its two houses for almost all legislative business, and Wisconsin, for more than a century, has had a joint committee on finance which is the most powerful committee in the legislature.) Each house is a separate entity and can go its own way. This gives the separate houses of the legislative branch some added capacity in ordinary times to delay and obstruct action, and to confuse the public by one house doing this and the other doing that, and it weakens the legislature as a whole when it comes to taking constructive and positive action.

The Size of Legislative Bodies

The efficiency of legislative bodies is dependent in part upon their size. There is a tendency for party discipline to become more necessary as numbers increase. A house of a thousand members in which everyone was a free lance would be chaos, bedlam, but if there were only a dozen members, much freedom of individual speech and action could be tolerated. Any increase in the number of members, intended to increase popular representation in the legislature, defeats its own end when it is carried so far that either business is obstructed or an iron discipline must be introduced to make the body get its work done.

By foreign standards, American state legislatures are relatively small. State senates average about 38 members each, the largest being that of Minnesota with 67 members and the smallest those of Delaware and Nevada with 17 members each. The lower houses in the states average over 119 members each. The New England states with town representation have the largest lower houses: New Hampshire, 400, Connecticut, 280, and Vermont, 246 (a representative in New Hampshire or Vermont represents less than 1500 people). The smallest lower houses are those of Delaware, 35, and Alaska, 40, and Nevada, 47, but Nebraska with 43 members in its unicameral body has actually the smallest state legislature in the country (see Table 5).

There is a great deal of hit-and-miss and what looks like mere historical accident in many of these differences, but once a pattern has been set, even by historical accident, it is very hard to change. One thing appears to be certain: no state other than Nebraska has in recent times reconsidered its legislature's size and structure and then deliberately remodeled it to meet the requirements of a modern state legislature. When other states come to do this the factors they will need to consider are representativeness, attractiveness to men of ability, and effectiveness in legislative work.

Table 5. NUMBER AND TERMS OF STATE LEGISLATORS

State	Senate		House or Assembly		Total number of legislators
	Total	Term	Total	Term	
Alaska	20	4	40	2	60
Alabama	35	4	106	4	141
Arizona	28	2	80	2	108
Arkansas	35	4	100	2	135
California	40	4	80	2	120
Colorado	35	4	65	2	100
Connecticut	36	2	280	2	316
Delaware	17	4	35	2	52
Florida	38	4	95	2	133
Georgia	54	2	205	2	259
Hawaii	25	4	51	2	76
Idaho	44	2	59	2	103
Illinois	58	4	177	2	235
Indiana	50	4	100	2	150
Iowa	50	4	108	2	158
Kansas	40	4	125	2	165
Kentucky	38	4	100	2	138
Louisiana	39	4	101	4	140
Maine	33	2	151	2	184
Maryland	29	4	123	4	152
Massachusetts	40	2	240	2	280
Michigan	34	2	110	2	144
Minnesota	67	4	131	2	198
Mississippi	49	4	140	4	189
Missouri	34	4	157	2	191
Montana	56	4	94	2	150
Nebraska[a]	..	2	Unicameral	..	43
Nevada	17	4	47	2	64
New Hampshire	24	2	400	2	424
New Jersey	21	4	60	2	81
New Mexico	32	4	66	2	98
New York	58	2	150	2	208
North Carolina	50	2	120	2	170
North Dakota	49	4	113	2	162
Ohio	34	4	139	2	173
Oklahoma	44	4	121	2	165
Oregon	30	4	60	2	90
Pennsylvania	50	4	210	2	260
Rhode Island	44	2	100	2	144
South Carolina	46	4	124	2	170
South Dakota	35	2	75	2	110
Tennessee	33	2	99	2	132
Texas	31	4	150	2	181
Utah	25	4	64	2	89
Vermont	30	2	246	2	276
Virginia	40	4	100	2	140
Washington	46	4	99	2	145
West Virginia	32	4	100	2	132
Wisconsin	33	4	100	2	133
Wyoming	27	4	56	2	83
Total	1855		5852		7750

Source: Adapted from *The Book of the States, 1958-59,* p. 35.

[a] Nebraska's one house of 43 is included in totals only.

★ *Importance of size*

The size of a legislative house or body has some importance in several directions. The following propositions about relative size are probably approximately true.

1. Representation of groups.   While perfect representation of all people in the state is impossible, democratic theorists agree that there should be some representation in the legislature for each major interest group and region in the state. What is the minimum needed for this purpose is unknown. Experts in sampling agree that the number in proportion to population can be very small if only a good approximate result is needed. The major groups that constitute a society are not infinite in number. Vocationally they are agriculture, labor, industry, business, the professions, and public servants. The principal religious organizations can usually take care of themselves by electing men of their primary vocational group, and so can the principal regions. Thus a farmer can represent his people as farmers, as residents of a certain area, and as Protestants or Catholics, as the case may be. At any rate, the more than 1,300,000 Nebraskans have not raised any serious objections that the 43 members of their unicameral legislature are not enough to represent their major interests. An even smaller number would probably suffice.

The question whether a legislature adequately and proportionately represents all major interest groups is not, then, primarily one of total numbers of representatives, but of apportionment and methods of election, two questions to be discussed later in this chapter.

2. Experience and ability.   The more the number of members is increased, the more persons of little experience in public affairs and low ability have to be elected to fill all the places. The number of citizens of outstanding ability who are willing to seek legislative office is never too large and is usually too small. Legislative positions lose their attraction for men of ability, also, when the number of such positions is so large that no member counts for very much in the voting. Of course, a few able manipulators of men will turn up in any large organization. In Nebraska the general judgment is that with the reduction in the number of legislators there came a noticeable increase in their average ability. Whether a still greater rise in the level of ability would follow a further reduction is not known. Here a question of political ideals is involved. Should not a legislature be a real cross section of the people, representing all levels of ability as well as all major groups and interests? Some persons seem to hold that only in this way will there be real democracy. The view taken by the writers is that public affairs are so important that every effort should be made to attract the most able leaders into office and to prevent the dilution of the more able with the less able, especially in policy-making positions. If keeping down the number of legislators will help to achieve this result, and if a relatively small number of legislators can represent all major interests and do the necessary work of a legislative body, then the smaller number should be preferred.

3. Responsibility and personal recognition. The larger a legislative body becomes, the more obscure and unimportant is each member, the less personal opportunity for service and recognition he has, and the fewer are the incentives for hard work and responsible public action. It is well known that in the United States House of Representatives many members become discouraged from the start because of a feeling of unimportance and ineffectiveness. The same is unquestionably true in state legislatures of large size. The smaller the number of members, on the other hand, the more each one counts, the more chance he has to be heard and to do something useful and satisfying. Here again it is not possible to set an exact figure as to the best size, but the argument points toward smaller rather than larger legislatures.

4. Size and number of committees. Large legislative bodies in the United States tend to have many and large committees. This is one way to give members something to do. It is now generally recognized that the multiplication of committees went too far in many legislatures. The work was split up too much, and committees even duplicated each other's investigations and activities. Furthermore, the more committees there were, the less publicity each received, so that many things were decided in more or less secret, unpublicized meetings. Attempts to reduce the number of committees without reducing the number of legislative members have been only partly successful. On the other hand, a substantial reduction in the number of members is soon followed by a reduction in the number of committees.

5. Legislative expense. The cost of operating a state legislature is one of the smaller items in any state budget. By reducing its membership, a legislature may be able to save the public a little money, as was done in Nebraska when the one-house legislature was established, but this cannot be made into a principal argument for such reduction. The fact is that when there are fewer members to do the work each must be paid more; more able and responsible men find ways to improve their services but not without spending money. The saving in Nebraska under the unicameral system is hard to calculate exactly, but it probably was about 15 percent of the legislative expense, even more if certain new expenses like those for the Legislative Council be excluded. Just eliminating the second chamber and its expense must explain in large part the saving made in Nebraska.

Legislative Membership Qualifications and Conditions

★ Legal qualifications

Each state by its own constitution establishes the minimum qualifications for membership in its legislature. In many states any citizen or person qualified to vote is eligible for legislative office. Elsewhere there are slightly higher age standards, such as in Alabama, senators, 25 years of age; Hawaii, senators, 30 years of age, representatives, 25; Kentucky, 30 and 24 years, respectively; Tennessee, 30 and 21 years respectively, and so on. Residence within the district is a common requirement. Some state constitutions also provide for special disqualifications.

The low age limits for membership help to open the door for young people to enter the state legislature and after every biennial election one reads of "youngest" representatives and senators in various states, some of whom have just turned twenty-one. The practical effects of these low requirements have been rather slight. It appears that in most legislatures there are very few members in their twenties. The bulk of the membership ranges between 30 and 60 years of age, with an average usually about 50 or above.

The constitutions empower each house to pass on the qualifications and election returns of its own members, and also to expel members by a two-thirds vote. As there is practically no judicial control over this power, legislative houses have in some instances exceeded their apparent powers by excluding or expelling socialists and others whose views the requisite majority has not favored.

★ Terms and tenure

The states have now given up the former one-year terms and a few three-year terms and have agreed upon two- and four-year terms as most suitable to the American political calendar. In thirty-five states the senators are elected for four-year terms, and in the other fifteen, including Nebraska, their terms are two years. In four states having four-year terms for senators, the members of the lower house also have four-year terms, while in the other forty-five states that have a second or lower house the terms are two years. Such trend as there is seems to be in the direction of four-year terms. Two-year terms appear to be too short. The more frequent the need for campaigning for re-election, the more time and money a legislator must spend at it and the more he is distracted from his duties. Besides, a two-year term is too short to give a man enough experience and knowledge of his duties to do much good. As in industry and civil service, a rapid rate of turnover among legislators is not in the public interest.

Since re-election is not forbidden, there are many state legislators, especially in the senates, who have served many successive terms, running to forty years in a few instances. Thus, there is always at least a nucleus or a minority of members who have had long legislative experience. On the other hand there is a considerable and rapid turnover in most of the seats, especially in the lower house. Legislative service interrupts the progress of members in their businesses and professions. For very few does it offer a satisfying career.[4]

As in the Congress, the degree of two-party competition also affects legislative turnover. One-party states or states with a number of one-party legislative districts typically have more legislators with long service records than more competitive two-party states or legislative districts. The long-time legislator offers experience, but in a period of change may be less representative of the voters' current thinking and preferences.[5]

A factor in legislative tenure, and possibly in prestige, is the salary paid legislators. The very large cities in several states pay their city councilmen more than these states pay their legislators.[6] Maryland, in 1958, paid its legislators $3600 for the biennium, whereas Baltimore paid its councilmen $6500 annually or $13,000 for a two-year period. Wisconsin paid its

[4] Zeller, *op. cit.* Chapter 5 discusses legal and other characteristics of legislative membership.

[5] This paragraph is illustrated in the national Congress where Democrats from the one-party South typically control committee chairmanships when the Democrats have a majority in Congress. Republican committee chairmen likewise tend to come from one-party Northern states or Northern Congressional districts and often again to be somewhat out of step with a Republican President or the apparent dominant group in the Republican party which produced the election victory. Analysis of state legislatures would show similar situations but with the probability of shorter tenures due to personal decisions not to continue in the state legislature.

[6] There are frequent comments that the big-city legislative delegations do not measure up to the quality of representatives from other sections of a state. It is difficult to establish objectively the accuracy of such characterization; but assuming at least some degree of truth to it, the explanation may lie in part in the greater salary and local prestige and power in membership in the big-city council as compared to the state legislature. The city council is usually smaller in numbers; in large city affairs, it may be more significant than the state legislature; metropolitan newspapers may give the council more attention; and individual council members may be able to carry on their personal business without excessive absence. These and other assets combined with the sometimes higher pay of city councilmen may attract the individuals who in smaller cities and rural communities would seek legislative seats.

legislators $7200 for the biennium, and Milwaukee paid city councilmen $7500 *annually* in 1958. California legislators received $12,000 for two years, whereas Los Angeles paid its councilmen $12,000 for a single year (though San Francisco paid annual council salaries of $4800).[7] In 1958, only Illinois, Massachusetts, New York, Michigan, New Jersey, Ohio, and California paid their legislators better salaries than Wisconsin's $7200 for a biennium. At the other extreme, North Dakota paid a $5.00 per-diem salary for a maximum of 60 legislative days of a biennial session. Rhode Island paid the same rate but held annual sessions. A Rhode Island legislator could regularly expect about $300 annually, but a North Dakota legislator would receive a maximum salary of $300 only every other year unless the governor called a special session.[8] In addition to their regular remuneration, of course, legislators receive compensation for transportation and more than one half of the states pay additional allowance for expenses during sessions. (Either salary per diems or per-diem expense allowances, or both, may be set with maximums which may limit the length of legislative sessions.)

About half of the state constitutions still establish legislative salaries, at least in part. Whether changes come by constitutional amendment or by statute, legislators frequently feel reluctant to face the public tendency to criticize salary increases. Looking at the pay rates for salaries, travel expenses, and other allowances, one gets the feeling that in total they are too low rather than too high. The dilemma is to avoid attracting candidates interested primarily in the salary without making the salary so low that many desirable candidates find legislative service financially impractical.

★ *Privileges and immunities*

Taking pages from British and colonial experience and later copying the words from the United States Constitution, the framers of the state constitutions have set forth with considerable uniformity the privileges and immunities of state legislators in the performance of their duties. A fairly typical provision is that of Kentucky, as follows:

> SECTION 43. The members of the General Assembly shall, in all cases except treason, felony, breach of surety of the peace, be privileged

---

[7] All three of these states also provided expense allowances for their state legislators, whereas councilmen acting in their home communities would not have such allowances nor would they have the expense of the state legislators. New York City in 1958 paid its councilmen $7000 annually whereas New York State paid legislators $15,000 *biennially*. Boston councilmen received $5000 annually, while Massachusetts paid $10,400 *biennially*. Salaries of councilmen taken from *Municipal Year Book 1958* (Chicago: The International City Managers Association, 1958), table on pp. 70-71.

[8] For further details of salaries and expense allowances of state legislators, see *The Book of the States, 1958-59*, the table, "Salaries and Compensation of Legislators," on pp. 36-37.

from arrest during their attendance on the sessions of their respective houses, and in going to and returning from the same; and for any speech or debate in either house they shall not be questioned in any other place.

This is substantially the same provision as that which protects members of Congress and has in general received the same interpretation. Originally developed in England as a means of protecting members of Parliament from arrest and interference by the king, it has been broadened to protect legislators against private suitors who claim to have been slandered or libeled by words spoken in the legislature. The courts will not entertain such suits, but if a member makes his slanderous or libelous remarks outside legislative halls or committees his legislative privilege will not protect him.

Methods of Electing Legislators

There are a number of ways in which men may be chosen for membership in legislative bodies: by birth to a hereditary right as in the English House of Lords, by right of other office, by appointment, by lot, and by election, to name some of the principal methods. The democratic theory that prevails in the United States requires that legislators who are to make laws to govern the people shall be chosen by the voters in free elections at regular and fairly frequent intervals. It would be interesting to discuss other methods of choosing legislators, but the following pages will deal primarily with the methods actually used for choosing American state legislators. There is a high degree of uniformity in the methods, but still there is enough variety to call for several comments. It perhaps goes without saying that the methods of both election and apportionment have some effect on the result obtained—that is, on the membership of state legislatures. Methods of election will be discussed first, and then the question of apportionment.

In almost all cases American state legislators are elected by the regular list of voters, at two- and four-year intervals, at the general elections in November in the even-numbered years when other state and national officials are being chosen. As a rule, also, these final elections are conducted with ballots that carry party designations, and the elections have been preceded by direct primary nominations also with party designations on the ballots.

★ Size of districts

The legislative districts from which the members are elected and in which they are expected to live frequently coincide with the areas of counties, towns or townships, cities, or similar local-government areas. But many of the more populous counties and cities are divided into two or more districts. The areas of many of the less populous counties and cities are combined with those of surrounding units to make a more adequate district. These districts vary in population from a low average of about 1500 in towns that form districts for lower-house elections in Vermont and New Hampshire up to senate constituencies in New York and California that average about 250,000 in population.

The principle of the "wieldy district" so long espoused by Richard S. Childs of short-ballot and city-manager fame is carried out in most state legislative districts.[9] A *wieldy district* is one that is small enough in area and population so that an independent candidate with a volunteer committee can challenge the regular-party-organization candidate or candidates with good prospects of success. The larger the district the greater the cost of campaigning and the difficulty of meeting the voters face to face. In most state legislative districts, especially for the lower house, an active candidate can actually get around to most of the homes on foot or by using his car. If the argument presented earlier for smaller legislatures gains public acceptance so that smaller legislatures and larger districts result, this face-to-face contact may be partly lost, but with the modern means of publicity (radio, television, movie shorts, phonograph records, newspapers, and other printed matter) plus a sufficient number of public meetings, a candidate could still reach most of the people in the district. Furthermore, the advantages of the wieldy district must be balanced against the disadvantages of oversized legislatures. To divide New York, California, or any other large state into small enough legislative districts to meet the test of wieldiness would produce state legislatures with hundreds of members in each house.

★ Nominations and elections

Candidates for the legislature usually are nominated by partisan primaries and elected by plurality votes. One deviation from standard practice not discussed previously is the election of the lower house in Illinois. With the founding of the Republican party, northern Illinois became rather solidly Republican, while the southern part of the state was as completely Democratic. Thus party lines and regional lines coincided in large part. Northern Illinois sent Republicans and southern Illinois sent Democrats to the legislature. At the same time there were substantial minorities of Demo-

9 R. S. Childs, *Short-ballot Principles* (Boston: Houghton Mifflin, 1911), pp. 51-58.

crats in the northern counties and Republicans in the southern counties who had no direct representation in the legislature. To overcome this difficulty, at least in part, the Illinois Constitution of 1870 provided (Art. IV, secs. 7, 8) for cumulative voting for the lower house. This original plan, slightly modified in 1954 to reduce representation inequities, provides for the establishment of fifty-nine representative districts. Each district elector votes for three representatives by cumulative voting. In effect each voter has three votes for representatives which he may use as he pleases. He may vote all three for one candidate or two for one and one for another, or spread his three votes over three candidates. What seems to happen in practice is that each major party, acting through its local committee in the district, after carefully estimating its relative voting strength in the district, decides to run one, two, or three candidates, depending on how many it feels sure it can elect, and then instructs its voters to act accordingly. Minority parties of small size have very little chance under this system. In most districts one major party elects two and the other elects one representative. This has resulted in both major parties being represented in the lower house in proportion to their total votes in the legislative election, but it has greatly changed the character of the legislative election campaign. Candidates conduct promotional campaigns for themselves rather than hard-fought contests with rival party candidates.

Although they do not use the cumulative voting system, Washington and Maryland, like Illinois, elect all members of the lower house of their legislature from multimember districts. Arizona and Hawaii elect all members of their legislative upper houses from multimember districts. Contrary to a frequent assumption, a majority of states use multimember districts at least in part.[10] Only nine states (California, Delaware, Kansas, Kentucky, Missouri, Nebraska, New York, Rhode Island, and Wisconsin) elect all legislators from single-member districts. A check in 1954 showed 221 senate seats (out of 1841) in sixteen states chosen from multimember districts.[11] In state legislative lower houses, the figures were 2616 (out of 5762) in thirty-six states. In other words 12 percent of state senators and 45 percent of state representatives (or whatever the name used by the state for its lower house) came from multimember districts. The question of multimember vs. single-member districts has significance in state legislative apportionment and in the operation of political parties.

10 For a current and historical analysis of the use of single-member and multimember election districts for state legislators, see Maurice Klain, "A New Look at the Constituencies: The Need for a Recount and a Reappraisal," *American Political Science Review,* Winter 1955.
11 *Ibid.*

Apportionment, Districting, and Gerrymandering

The state constitutions lay down the basic rules by which representatives and senators are distributed to various parts of the state. The state legislatures have power to supplement these rules in various ways, and to see to it that the rules are either enforced or ignored, according to their own thoughts and feelings on the subject. In effect the legislators in a great majority of the states determine the distribution of representation, since the courts will not interfere to command the legislature in this matter. The judges say that the constitutional provisions on this subject are merely directory, telling the legislators what ought to be done, and not mandatory.

Apportionment and districting are two phases of the process of distributing representation. *Apportionment* is the act of assigning to established areas such as counties, townships, towns, and cities, one or more members of the legislature, either arbitrarily and finally, as in the Delaware Constitution (Art. II, sec. 2) or according to some rule. *Districting* is the act of either combining or dividing such existing units in order to form areas to elect one or more members each. An apportionment can be changed by reapportionment—that is, the giving of more or fewer representatives to existing local government areas without changing the boundary lines; but if new districts or areas are formed it is called redistricting. The two processes go together, and the words are in fact used somewhat interchangeably.

★ *Constitutional rules of apportionment*

In the state constitutional rules for apportioning members in state legislatures, two factors are usually given primary consideration: (1) population and (2) certain established areas such as counties and townships.[12] Twelve states mention only population or some close equivalent (male inhabitants over twenty-one, legal voters, population excluding aliens, white population) as the sole consideration in apportionment for both houses.[13] Sixteen others do so for one house, but assure each county or town or some other geographical unit some representation in the other. The remaining states generally provide for county or township representation in both houses. For example, Vermont assures each county of one state senator and each town of one and only one member of the lower house; New York guarantees each county except Hamilton at least one member of the lower house, and forbids any two adjoining counties to have over half the sena-

---

[12] See the table of these provisions in *The Book of the States, 1958-59*, pp. 52-56. Alaska and Hawaii are considered under their new state constitutions.
[13] Included in this twelve is Nebraska with only one house.

tors; Texas forbids any county to have more than one state senator; and Pennsylvania assures every county of one member in the lower house. In several New England states besides Vermont (New Hampshire, Connecticut, and Rhode Island) the representation of towns in the lower house is so arranged that the cities and larger towns are grossly underrepresented as compared with many almost unpopulated rural towns. In the states where each county is entitled to a member in one house or the other, very little allowance is usually made for extra representatives for the larger places, with resultant serious underrepresentation of the populous urban counties.

Where constitutional provisions do not directly create rural overrepresentation and urban underrepresentation, the rural-dominated legislatures frequently achieve it by refusing to enact redistricting (or reapportionment) laws, even when new censuses reveal the continued and increasingly striking violation of the constitutional requirements. Alabama, Connecticut, Delaware, Maryland, New Jersey, South Carolina, Tennessee, and Vermont have not reapportioned or redistricted one or both houses of their legislatures for more than fifty years.[14] Idaho, Iowa, Mississippi, Nevada, and New Hampshire have not done so for more than forty years.[15] (See Table 6 and Fig. 8 for state-by-state detail of legislative representation.) Constitutional amendments to assure population representation face the same legislative bottleneck as reapportionment or redistricting acts. When voters and taxpayers in underrepresented areas appeal to the courts for redress, the latter uniformly have refused to interfere with legislative control.[16] In effect the members who currently occupy seats in the legislature sit as judges in their own case, to hold onto what they have and to prevent larger and more rapidly growing centers of population from being represented according to their populations. The large cities used to be the major victims of urban underrepresentation. With the rapid rise in suburban areas around large cities and a decline in growth if not in absolute numbers of the central cities, it is suburbia which is becoming most underrepre-

[14] Technically, Connecticut, Delaware, Maryland, New Jersey, South Carolina, and Vermont are not specifically required to do so by their constitutions.
[15] Again, Idaho, Nevada, and New Hampshire are not constitutionally bound to do so.
[16] The general judicial response has been that they will not mandamus a coequal branch of the government to act. Recently, a group of Minnesota taxpayers and voters appealed to the federal district court to require state legislative reapportionment on the grounds that their federal right of equal protection under the 14th Amendment was being violated. The court did not throw out the case but said in effect that it felt certain the state legislature would see its duty and act in the 1959 session; but if it did not, the court implied it would hear the case. The 1959 Minnesota legislature did reapportion both houses. Using the 1950 census figures, already substantially out of date, it increased the representation of the Twin City Metropolitan area considerably in both houses, but did not achieve equality for all districts in proportion to population.

Table 6. EXTREMES IN REPRESENTATION

Lower House					Upper House			
Total Membership	Average Pop. per Rep.	Smallest Pop. per Rep.	Largest Pop. per Rep.	State	Total Membership	Average Pop. per Senator	Smallest Pop. per Senator	Largest Pop. per Senator
106	28,884 *a*	8,027	79,846	Alabama	35	87,478 *a*	18,018	558,928
40	2,706	1,187	3,972	Alaska	20	5,412	3,424	26,602
80	9,357	6,402	27,767	Arizona	28	26,735	4,672	165,385
100	19,095	5,978	32,614	Arkansas	35	54,357	43,114	65,562
80	132,327	62,975	200,750	California	40	264,656	14,014	4,151,687
65	20,386	9,362	27,843	Colorado	35	37,860	19,438	56,602
280	7,195	130	88,699	Connecticut	36	55,758	24,309	122,931
35	9,088	1,321	35,762	Delaware	17	18,711	3,496	57,179
95	29,171	2,199	165,028	Florida	38	72,929	10,413	495,084
205	16,803	2,494	157,857	Georgia	54	63,788	16,237	473,572
51	9,800	6,747	12,590	Hawaii *b*	25	19,992	8,797	37,769
59	9,976	918	17,865	Idaho	44	13,379	918	70,649
177	49,221	39,809	68,655	Illinois	58	150,210	17,063	383,803
100	39,342	15,674	68,353	Indiana	50	78,684	39,592	122,717
108	24,269	8,753	113,005	Iowa	50	52,421	21,173	226,010
125	15,242	2,010	74,097	Kansas	40	47,631	20,018	222,290
100	29,448	12,890	50,373	Kentucky	38	77,495	51,992	104,254
101	26,569	6,244	79,118	Louisiana	39	68,808	25,326	158,236
151	6,051	2,372	11,090	Maine	33	27,690	16,053	42,300
123	19,049	6,136	44,894	Maryland	29	80,793	12,272	269,362
240	19,544	2,870	28,675	Mass.	40	117,263	92,216	164,334
110	57,925	32,469	94,994	Michigan	34	187,405	61,008	396,001
131	22,767	7,290	107,246	Minnesota	67	44,513	16,878	153,455
140	16,383	4,966	57,235	Mississippi	49	44,468	17,869	96,910
157	25,189	4,777	48,432	Missouri	34	116,313	87,559	136,687
94	6,287	1,026	10,366	Montana	56	10,554	1,026	55,875
	(Nebraska has only senate)			Nebraska	43	30,826	21,579	40,998
47	3,406	614	6,037	Nevada	17	9,417	614	50,205
399	1,336	16	2,179	N. Hampshire	24	22,218	12,051	34,368
60	80,589	34,423	135,910	New Jersey	21	230,254	34,423	905,949
66	12,385	3,013	16,186	New Mexico	32	21,974	3,013	45,673
150	94,960	14,066	167,226	New York	58	244,887	146,666	344,547
120	33,849	5,048	71,220	N. Carolina	50	81,239	48,375	197,052
113	5,484	3,180	16,609	N. Dakota	49	12,909	5,405	38,766
139	59,303	10,759	98,920	Ohio	33	240,807	163,335	395,551
121	18,457	4,589	46,479	Oklahoma	44	50,758	15,898	251,286
60	26,230	12,740	48,313	Oregon	30	50,711	26,317	67,362
210	49,991	4,944	77,106	Pennsylvania	50	209,960	78,181	442,516
100	7,919	732	14,810	Rhode Island	44	19,315	732	55,060
124	17,073	9,577	23,173	S. Carolina	46	46,022	9,577	168,152
75	8,703	4,046	21,044	S. Dakota	35	19,198	10,450	35,455
99	33,250	3,948	75,134	Tennessee	33	99,748	40,416	208,255
150	51,408	29,192	100,837	Texas	31	248,748	136,756	806,701
64	10,934	364	15,437	Utah	25	27,554	9,642	45,812
246	1,505	49	33,155	Vermont	30	12,592	3,406	17,027
100	33,187	19,218	60,994	Virginia	40	82,967	55,637	135,449
99	24,030	12,994	39,383	Washington	49	48,550	18,935	82,732
100	21,335	5,119	37,540	W. Virginia	32	62,672	30,646	119,814
100	34,346	18,840	51,657	Wisconsin	33	104,078	73,301	128,970
56	5,188	2,481	7,943	Wyoming	27	11,174	2,481	23,831

Source: From *The Christian Science Monitor*, October 2, 1958. Part of a series of articles published October 2, 6, 9, 13, and 16, 1958 on reapportionment and redistricting. Reprinted by permission.

a Figures in second and seventh columns show how many people would be represented by each legislator if states were evenly apportioned on a strict population basis. This theoretical situation bears comparison with the actual present-day figures in the adjoining columns to the right, showing extremes of overrepresentation and underrepresentation. All statistics are based on the 1950 federal census.

b Table has been adjusted to include Hawaii. Calculation of data for the Hawaiian representative districts in Honolulu is approximate as the detail of the published census data does not provide a sufficiently fine breakdown for all city districts. Such data would probably increase the figure for column 4.

sented. In Maryland, for example, Baltimore, Montgomery, and Prince Georges County are becoming more underrepresented than the city of Baltimore.

A few states have achieved a reasonable relationship between population and representation in both houses of the legislature—for example, Massachusetts, Maine, Oregon, Wisconsin, and now Minnesota. In Massachusetts, it takes 48.76 percent of the voters to elect a majority of members of the upper house and 42.15 percent of the voters to elect a majority of members in the lower house. Maine figures are 39.71 percent and 39.12 percent; Oregon, 42.18 percent and 45.42 percent; and Wisconsin, 47.53 percent and 38.87 percent. After gross urban underrepresentation in the Illinois legislature for years (no reapportionment or redistricting from 1901 until 1955), the forces for better population representation succeeded in passing a constitutional amendment which brought the lower house to 46.02 percent but the upper house has 29.42 percent.[17]

★ Lines of cleavage and conflict

The question of fair representation in accordance with population touches many vested interests and can be traced along various lines of cleavage in the body politic. In many states outside the South the cleavage between Republicans and Democrats corresponds roughly with the cleavages between rural and urban, between city laborers and farmers, between property-owning, taxpaying interests and tax-spending, social-service interests on the other. In some states, too, there is a north-south, or upstate-downstate cleavage, as in California, Illinois, and New York. The big-city or metropolitan interest is sometimes opposed also by the smaller cities and towns rather than by strictly rural interests. These various cleavages and conflicts are so interlaced and overlapping that it is difficult to disentangle and appraise them. Each state has its own peculiar situation.

When the question of reapportioning and redistricting to give fairer representation arises, certain other factors enter into the calculation. Many a legislator seems to look upon his existing district as more or less a personal bailiwick, a pocket constituency, and refuses to permit it to be joined with another in which he would have to compete for office with some other member of either the same or a different party. Party leaders themselves are conscious of this situation. They cannot afford to lose able legislators of

---

[17] For the story of the Illinois campaign for reapportionment see John E. Juergensmeyer, *The Campaign for the Illinois Reapportionment Amendment*, (mimeo.) (Urbana: The Institute of Government and Public Affairs, University of Illinois, 1957). The unusually complex story of the 1952 redistricting in Wisconsin is told by William H. Young, "Court Settles Apportionment," *National Municipal Review*, September 1956. See summary in Ch. 1 of this text.

Figure 8. HOW YOUR LEGISLATURE IS ELECTED

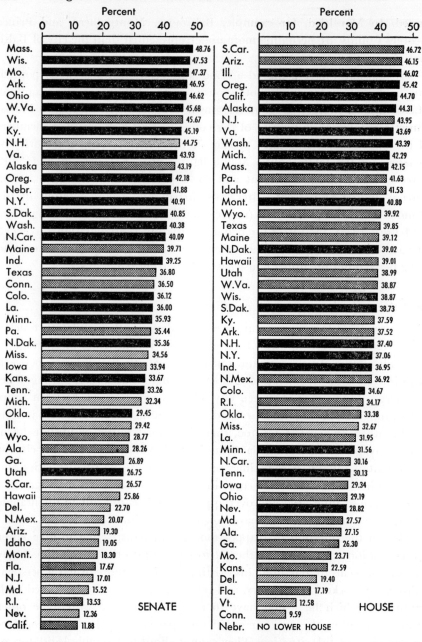

SENATE	Percent		HOUSE	Percent
Mass.	48.76		S.Car.	46.72
Wis.	47.53		Ariz.	46.15
Mo.	47.37		Ill.	46.02
Ark.	46.95		Oreg.	45.42
Ohio	46.62		Calif.	44.70
W.Va.	45.68		Alaska	44.31
Vt.	45.67		N.J.	43.95
Ky.	45.19		Va.	43.69
N.H.	44.75		Wash.	43.39
Va.	43.93		Mich.	42.29
Alaska	43.19		Mass.	42.15
Oreg.	42.18		Pa.	41.63
Nebr.	41.88		Idaho	41.53
N.Y.	40.91		Mont.	40.80
S.Dak.	40.85		Wyo.	39.92
Wash.	40.38		Texas	39.85
N.Car.	40.09		Maine	39.12
Maine	39.71		N.Dak.	39.02
Ind.	39.25		Hawaii	39.01
Texas	36.80		Utah	38.99
Conn.	36.50		W.Va.	38.87
Colo.	36.12		Wis.	38.87
La.	36.00		S.Dak.	38.73
Minn.	35.93		Ky.	37.59
Pa.	35.44		Ark.	37.52
N.Dak.	35.36		N.H.	37.40
Miss.	34.56		N.Y.	37.06
Iowa	33.94		Ind.	36.95
Kans.	33.67		N.Mex.	36.92
Tenn.	33.26		Colo.	34.67
Mich.	32.34		R.I.	34.17
Okla.	29.45		Okla.	33.38
Ill.	29.42		Miss.	32.67
Wyo.	28.77		La.	31.95
Ala.	28.26		Minn.	31.56
Ga.	26.89		N.Car.	30.16
Utah	26.75		Tenn.	30.13
S.Car.	26.57		Iowa	29.34
Hawaii	25.86		Ohio	29.19
Del.	22.70		Nev.	28.82
N.Mex.	20.07		Md.	27.57
Ariz.	19.30		Ala.	27.15
Idaho	19.05		Ga.	26.30
Mont.	18.30		Mo.	23.71
Fla.	17.67		Kans.	22.59
N.J.	17.01		Del.	19.40
Md.	15.52		Fla.	17.19
R.I.	13.53		Vt.	12.58
Nev.	12.36		Conn.	9.59
Calif.	11.88		Nebr.	NO LOWER HOUSE

BASIS OF APPORTIONMENTS

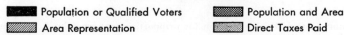

- Population or Qualified Voters
- Area Representation
- Population and Area
- Direct Taxes Paid

NOTE: These charts show the percentage of each state's total population (based on 1950 federal census figures) living in the least populous election districts from which a

their party by pitting two or more of them against each other in any reorganized district. This helps to account for some of the curious boundaries
that result when redistricting takes place—for the boundary lines must be
drawn if possible to keep every representative unopposed in his own district.

Another striking fact is that when redistricting and reapportionment
measures are put to a popular vote, many voters in urban places vote
against increasing and even in favor of decreasing their local representation. The 1952 referendum which redistricted Wisconsin on the basis of
1950 population census received a considerable number of opposition votes
in Milwaukee County! (The redistricting referendum succeeded, however.)
Similar reports come from the Los Angeles area of California and elsewhere; many voters vote against giving themselves more representation.
Some of this voting can no doubt be attributed to ignorance. Some is
strictly a party vote—if your party is likely to lose strength in the legislature, vote against redistricting. Another factor is that conservative people
in large cities are fearful that any additional representation from the cities
will go to labor. Such people appear to believe in a rural preponderance
in the legislature as a check on the radical, antiproperty tendencies that
might come with more urban representation. Indeed much of the argument used in California in 1948 against a proposed amendment to increase
the Los Angeles representation in the state senate made this appeal. Attention was called to organized labor's sponsorship of the proposal and to the
danger that the big-city political "bosses" in four populous counties
would dominate the legislature. The appeal was openly made to keep the
senate under rural control.

★ *Theories against equal representation on a population basis*

Democratic theory is based on the equality of men at least within the same
body politic. Every man, it is said, shall count as one, and no one shall
count as more than one. Many persons do not believe in this proposition,
and there are many departures from it in political practice. Permitting

---

majority of the state senators and state representatives are chosen. Legislatures are arranged in order of representativeness. Note that in all states a majority of the legislators
in both houses come from districts which comprise a minority of the state's population.
Shading indicates on what basis legislative seats are apportioned. (The figure has been
adjusted to include Hawaii. Calculation of data for Hawaiian representative districts in
Honolulu is approximate as the detail of the published census data does not provide a
full breakdown for the city districts. The discrepancies, if any, would not significantly
affect the relations shown.)

Source: *The Christian Science Monitor,* October 2, 1958. Part of a series of articles published on October 2, 6, 9, 13, and 16, 1958, on reapportionment and redistricting. Reprinted by permission.

legislative districts to become so grossly unequal in population that a voter in one district counts for many times more than a voter in another is a striking example.

Even in the early state constitutions there were provisions by which counties and towns as such were to have representation, without regard to population. Recently this has been developed in some states into a "federal-analogy" theory. The counties in the state are likened to states in the Union and are said to be entitled to equal representation as such, despite the fact that counties are legally mere creatures and agents of the state and never had any other status or any part as such in forming the state.

More persuasive to many people is the argument in favor of a "balanced system" of representation. This argument, as used in an election handbill in California in 1948, is that since the three metropolitan counties already had at that time over 59 percent of the state's registered voters,

> . . . these three counties alone now have the voting strength to elect a governor and all other state constitutional officers, both of our two United States Senators, 13 of our 23 Congressmen, 46 of our 80 assemblymen. They likewise have a majority voting control over all referenda of acts of the legislature, as well as laws proposed by the initiative process. Only the state senate retains any real representation for the residents of the other 55 counties. This measure would do away with this check and balance.

This idea of a balance between rural and urban interests is something like the "concurrent-majority" theory of John C. Calhoun that a government should be so organized that each major interest would have a check or veto upon the others. Thus no public action could be taken until all the major interests agreed. The result might be a slowing down of action by government, a check by a large minority upon majority action, but not the complete domination of one over the other. A number of the state constitutions in effect embody this idea of balancing interests, giving *areas* (primarily rural counties or towns) a predominance in one chamber and giving *populations* equality of treatment, with the possibility of urban predominance in the other. The two interests thus balanced against each other can then make trades on the passage of legislation. A number of constitutions, including that of Missouri adopted in 1945, make varying provisions for this balance.

Space limitations preclude a thorough analysis of these new theories of how state legislators should be apportioned, but a few remarks are pertinent. First, the theory of a balance of interests in the legislature is a recent reaction against the democratic constitutional theory of a century ago, which in effect set a straight population basis for representation in both houses (constitutions of Colorado, Illinois, Kansas, Michigan, Minnesota, Nevada, and a number of other states both as early as these and later). Second, while cities were small there was no theory to give them control of one legislative house in order to protect themselves against rural domination. The theory has been developed more or less as a justification for non-reapportionment by the legislature in accordance with constitutional requirements. Third, the theory of balancing interests assumes that the main or only line of cleavage is urban *versus* rural, and that if the people resident in cities were given increased representation in proportion to their population, all the urban legislative delegations would vote as a unit against the rural members of the legislature on major issues. This assumption is not supported by the facts. Fourth, the balance theory cannot justify discrimination against proportionate representation for urban people in states where rural population predominates, and where even with proportionate representation the urban places could not dominate either house.

★ Effects of unfair apportionment

The finding of some fair, satisfactory, and workable scheme for reapportioning legislative seats from time to time is one of the more important issues in state government and politics. For any large number or class of citizens to be treated as less than first-class citizens in the apportionment of representation is recognized by most people as a violation of democratic principles. It creates a sense of injustice and a certain amount of frustration in those so discriminated against. When the constitution calls for reapportionment according to population after each census but no reapportionment is made for decade after decade, while cities grow larger and larger but keep only their old meager representation, it is hard to convince thoughtful urban people that constitutional morality has not reached a low ebb.

The above are essentially moral objections, to be sure, but there is always a close connection between morals and politics. There are also solid economic and political arguments against having legislatures dominated by minorities. (1) Unrepresentative legislatures frequently stand at odds with the governor elected at large. Recent Democratic governors in Michigan and Minnesota have operated under the handicap of Republican and conservative control in one or both houses of their legislatures. However, Republican Governor Theodore McKeldin (1950-1958) in Maryland faced a Democratic-controlled legislature. In all three states, more equitable population representation in the legislatures would probably have given the governors cooperative majorities. A Democratic governor in New York must almost always work with a Republican-controlled state legislature. Stalemate or at least limited action typically results.

(2) At times the rural-urban conflict appears to produce irresponsible government rather than the balance of the Calhoun theory. In some areas of government in which urban interests are concerned and rural interests are not engaged, rural representatives are easily swayed in voting by pressure groups opposed to the particular urban interests. Thus rural legislators may oppose appointment of an effective public-utility commissioner simply to do a favor for a utility lobbyist and because utility regulation generally concerns them very little. Much of the central city-suburban conflict has been exacerbated by the willingness of rural legislators simply to vote against the big cities.

(3) Representing preponderantly the rural areas, a number of legislatures find ways to place a very large part of the tax burden on people in urban places and to channel off the money so raised through grants-in-aid very largely to rural counties and school districts while denying financial relief to urban communities. Shared taxes may be shared more heavily with rural places.

Whether minority control produces a gubernatorial-legislative stalemate, legislative irresponsibility in voting, statutory inequities in apportioning state financial burdens, or all three, the large cities have frequently sought federal action to offset some of their difficulties in the state capitols. Thus some of the most ardent states-rights enthusiasts by their own intransigence have brought on the very federal action they claimed to oppose.[18]

★ What can be done about reapportionment?

Following the 1960 census there will undoubtedly be a new wave of proposals in the states for legislative redistricting or reapportionment in accordance with the state constitutions as well as suggestions for revising the constitutional apportionment provisions. To get the legislatures to live up to their obligations to reapportion under the constitution will certainly require considerable public education and agitation. Candidates for the governorship may be induced to come out for reapportionment, especially in those states where the urban population is a majority, and in some situations a governor might be willing to work actively for the change. In states

[18] This point was emphasized by the Commission on Intergovernmental Relations, *A Report to the President for Transmittal to the Congress* (Washington, D. C.: Government Printing Office, 1955), pp. 40, 41.

that have the "initiative," the voters themselves may organize to put reapportionment before the people for action.

The Model State Constitution and a few states have attempted to remove reapportionment or redistricting from the exclusive control of the legislature. The Missouri constitution of 1945 puts reapportionment for the house under a strict quota rule to be administered by the secretary of state, who merely calculates and announces the results according to the census and the constitutional rules. For the senate a commission of ten chosen by the governor, five from each major political party from panels submitted by the party state central committees, is to make new districts after each census. If the ten commissioners do not produce and announce a result within six months, all senators are to be elected at large—something that no responsible party leader would want ever to happen. In the event the legislature fails to act on reapportionment, Illinois has established a system for both houses rather like the Missouri Senate system and has included election at large as the ultimate sanction. The new Alaskan constitution provides for an advisory board to be appointed by the governor and reporting to him. The governor with the advice of this board reapportions legislative seats after each census (Alaskan Constitution, Art. VI). Any qualified voter is authorized to apply to the courts either to compel the governor to act or to correct any error in redistricting or reapportionment. Hawaii provides for the governor to reapportion the House of Representatives and permits any registered voter in the state to bring suit before the state's supreme court to compel the governor to act or to correct any error in redistricting or reapportionment (Hawaiian Constitution, Art. III, sec. 4).

★ *Redistricting and gerrymandering*

When following or in connection with a reapportionment new legislative districts must be made, other questions affecting the representativeness of the legislature arise. A political party can win a majority in a legislative body without having a majority of the total vote. Thus, if a party averaged 55 percent of the votes in 60 percent of the districts and had no other votes, its total vote would be 33 percent of the total, but it would elect three fifths of the members. This is an unlikely occurrence, to be sure, but something approaching it can occur. In short, the single-member district system does not guarantee majority rule or full minority representation.

Party leaders who control legislative bodies at the time of redistricting have found ways to make use of this principle that a majority of majorities may be a minority. The object of such leaders in redistricting probably will be to assure their party of certain majorities in a majority of the districts, and thus gain or retain fairly permanent control of the legislature. The problem is then one of the most effective use of their scattered popular vote. A study of recent election returns and voter registrations—precinct by precinct, town by town, and county by county—will show where the party voters live in fairly compact masses, and also where the major rival party has its strength. With this knowledge, some tables of figures on votes and registrations, a map, and a little hard work, district lines can be drawn by a party committee that will embrace enough friendly voters to win one district after another by 55, 60, or 65 percent each, while lumping the main areas of opposition strength in a smaller number of other districts which the opposition can carry by large majorities, say 70 or 75 percent.

This is *gerrymandering*, and it has been practiced for a long time in the making of state legislative districts. The old rule for making Congressional districts was that districts should be compact, contiguous, and of substantially equal population, and the same rule has recently been written into the Missouri constitution for the division of counties into state senate districts. In gerrymandering the rule of contiguity, that all parts of a district shall be connected, can hardly be ignored, but the rules of compactness and substantial equality of population may go unheeded. A gerrymandered district may have a very curious shape, indeed, and be far from compact. Also the areas that the opposition party is likely to win can be combined into a few large and populous districts, while the gerrymandering party creates for itself a large number of relatively small districts. By later failure to redistrict following a new census, the inequalities between districts may be permitted to become even greater.

The abuses connected with both apportionment and districting are something of which even the party leaders are not proud. Indeed, they do not like to talk about them. The abuses achieve or help to perpetuate a party's dominance but cannot stand indefinitely against substantial changes in public sentiment.

REFERENCES

Blair, George S., "Cumulative Voting: Patterns of Party Allegiance and Rational Choice in Illinois State Legislative Contests," 52 *American Political Science Review* (March 1958), 123-130.

Council of State Governments, *American Legislatures: Structure and Procedures: Summary and Tabulations of a 1955 Survey.* Chicago: Council of State Governments, 1955.

————, *Book of the States, 1958-59,* pp. 29-71. Also see references at end of Ch. 11.

Johnson, Alvin W., *The Unicameral Legislature.* Minneapolis: The University of Minnesota Press, 1938.

CHAPTER 11

Legislative Organization and Procedure

THE PROCESS by which decisions are reached to establish new public policies in legal form may be called, for short, the legislative process. A new law may simply repeal or modify an old one, or it may deal with a subject not previously covered by an express law, for example, atomic energy, when it was first thought to call for legislation. In either case the decision reached is a new act of lawmaking, a result of the legislative process.

In all countries the legislative process is continuous; it goes on throughout the year. This is especially noticeable in rapidly changing societies, where the output of legislation is sometimes almost frightening to contemplate. In the legislature of the American states the process comes to a peak of feverish activity once a year or once in two years. But the work that is done in state legislative sessions is only a part of the process, and the products thereof are only a part of the total output of new laws.

In democratic nations such as the United States, uncounted numbers of individuals and groups take part in the legislative process. The right to propose improvements in laws and government belongs to everyone. Organized groups of every kind have an interest in the laws that affect them. Labor unions, farmers' organizations, professional societies, bankers, insurance companies, public utilities, horticulturists, cattle raisers, good-roads associations, welfare societies, civil servants, and various units and branches of government—need we name more to indicate the wide range of groups that have legislative programs and actually formulate bills for enactment? By formulating desired policies through conferences and committees, and getting them drafted by lawyers and others into forms acceptable for presentation to lawmaking authorities, all interest groups and public agencies play a part in the legislative process.

In formulating a policy and a bill on any subject, the sponsors have in mind some ideas on who is to enact it and in what form. Some proposals take the form of constitutional amendments. Others go to Congress or to national administrative agencies, or even to the Supreme Court, if they involve the rule-making power of that tribunal for the courts of the United States. In any state men are likely to think first of the state legislature as the most appropriate enacting agency, because of its wide range of lawmaking power, and because they want the law when enacted to apply throughout the state. However, if it is a matter concerning the public health, for example, it may be found that the state board or department of health has ample sublegislative authority to enact what is needed as a rule or regulation and that it is not necessary to approach the state legislature. Other state administrative agencies have similar powers. On the other hand, if it is a matter of more local concern, perhaps the city or village council, the town board or town meeting is the proper agency to put the policy into effect, by ordinance or resolution.

In short, legislation takes place in many places, at various levels of governmental authority, and for many different areas or jurisdictions. It appears in completed written form in written constitutions, statutes, administrative rules and regulations, local ordinances, judicial decisions and court regulations, and no doubt other forms. This chapter will be devoted primarily to that part of the legislative process that comes to fruition or takes place in the fifty state legislatures.

The Changing Role of State Legislatures

The history of state government could well be written around the changing role and activities of the state legislatures. What the legislatures were in the beginning (1776 onward) and what they are now seem poles apart, and many major changes in state government are connected with this great transformation.

Briefly, the original state legislatures were revolutionary conventions that took over the state governments about 1776 after ousting the governors, other colonial officers, and many judges. To assist and advise them on legislation, the original legislatures had little or no organized body of civil servants (bureaucracy) and only a few, not-too-well organized interest or pressure groups. Except for war purposes there was, however, relatively little state government activity. Legislation was largely a matter of deciding a few broad questions of policy, taking over in whole or in part the English common law, and copying out of colonial laws such statutes as seemed most suitable. With the convention or legislature acting nearly alone as a large part of the government, the governors and judges being practically subordinate, a vague theory developed that the legislature was the government, and that it could within its mixed but mostly amateur membership find all the talents and initiative needed to formulate and draft the laws and largely put them into effect. In those days of important beginnings individual legislators and legislative committees no doubt did initiate and draft or copy from other sources much of the important legislation, although experience suggests that they probably were waited upon by numerous individuals and small delegations of citizens who had ideas about legislation.

The situation today is markedly different. Society has become highly organized. Government at all levels is active and is taking on new functions from time to time. Every large interest group and countless small ones have their recognized organizations to speak and act for their interests in the rush for new legislation. The beekeepers and the applegrowers, the automobile builders and the road builders, the professions and the civil servants (again naming but a few out of many) are all prepared with ideas about laws and specific drafts thereof to help the legislators make up their minds. Now, also, there is an organized bureaucracy—national, state, and local—with a wealth of ideas and hosts of competent members who know how present laws are operating and how they might be improved. The governors have risen from their early position of subordination to a role of legislative leadership, which is implemented in large part by the drafts of bills prepared in state and local government agencies and in the offices of large private organizations with whose ideas the governor is sympathetic. To some extent even the agencies of the national government come in with ready-prepared bills for enactment, and so do drafting committees of the Council of State Governments, the National Conference of Commissioners on Uniform State Laws, and other semiofficial agencies.

Thus the initiative in the proposal of bills has passed largely out of the hands of the legislators and into those of the governor, the heads of government agencies, local governments, and the organized private interest groups. Studies made in New York, Ohio, and other places reveal that the great majority of important legislative bills come from the executive agencies of the state government, just as the budget does, and that other sources of bills are local governments, the courts and the bar associations, civil servants, semipublic organizations, and private organizations. Some bills do originate with individual members of the legislature, and a few with committees thereof. In many instances a committee bill is only a rewriting of a bill from another source, or a combination of several such bills into one, while many private members' bills are pressed upon the sponsoring members by insistent citizens.

To a degree, then, the legislature has become a sifting, educating, harmonizing, and retarding agency—not too unlike the British Parliament. From the many hundreds or thousands of bills that are presented to the average legislative session, many are selected for favorable action; others are fused or combined before action is taken; some are delayed from session to session; and others are simply pigeonholed in the hope that they will not appear again at any later session.

Legislative Sessions

If legislatures exist to pass necessary laws and if they require time for careful consideration of measures, why is it that the drafters of state constitutions have exercised so much care to limit the length and frequency of legislative sessions? In the days of the American Revolution democratic theory insisted upon legislative sessions being frequent, not less than one a year and down to quarterly meetings, while time limits on sessions were not considered necessary. Unfortunately the times were hard, and those early legislatures showed radical and irresponsible tendencies in trying to legislate better times. Conservative men, and they were influential, began to think that legislatures were somewhat inconvenient, disturbing to business and society. Among the various restrictions placed upon them were the abolition in many states of annual sessions in favor of biennial sessions, and the placing of time limits on sessions.

★ Annual and biennial sessions

At the present time, sixteen states provide for annual sessions (Alaska, Arizona, California, Colorado, Georgia, Hawaii, Kansas, Louisiana, Maryland, Massachusetts, Michigan, New Jersey, New York, Rhode Island, South Carolina, and West Virginia), but in seven (California, Colorado, Hawaii, Kansas, Louisiana, Maryland, and West Virginia) the sessions in the even-numbered years are supposed to deal primarily with budget, revenue, and tax matters. All other states now provide for biennial sessions, thirty-one of these meeting in the odd years (mostly in January) and in three Southern states in the even years (Kentucky, Mississippi, and Virginia).

★ Time limits on sessions

Thirty-three states limit the length of regular legislative sessions, and twenty-three limit the length of special sessions. The time limits for regular sessions vary from 36 days (biennial, Alabama) to 150 days (biennial, Connecticut and Missouri; time expressed as adjournment by first Wednesday after first Monday in June for Connecticut and May 31 for Missouri). Most of the states with time limits set 60 days—calendar days in some, legislative days in others. The usual limits on special sessions are 20 or 30 days, but the range is from 15 to 60.

All legislatures have a similar experience—a fairly slow start, with committee hearings and conferences taking much time; then the passage of a number of minor and mostly noncontroversial bills; and later a rush of activity. Where legislatures operate under strict time limits, the final rush may be feverish indeed. Legislators so limited may adopt the expedient of stopping or covering the clock so that the last "legislative day" may cover a number of the usual 24-hour variety. The number of bills passed goes up steeply in the last few days, and the governor receives a great pile of passed and enrolled bills.

★ Calling of special sessions

The governor in every state is empowered to call special or "extraordinary" sessions of the legislature, and in seven states (Alaska, Arizona, Georgia, Louisiana, Nebraska, Virginia, and West Virginia), it is his duty to do so if he receives a petition to that effect from a specified extraordinary majority of each house. In addition, Connecticut, Florida, Massachusetts, New Hampshire, and New Mexico authorize their legislatures to call special sessions at such times as they judge necessary.

In practice it is the governors who call special sessions. Under the constitutions of more than half the states, also, the governor may designate the subjects to be dealt with in special sessions, and the legislature is presumably limited to those subjects. Governors often need legislative support and legislators are ingenious in subject classification so that some leeway exists between what the governor would like to limit the session to and what the legislators actually will consider.

★ Split and adjourned sessions

In the effort to overcome some of the time wasting and final rush of time-limited sessions and to achieve other objectives, various states have experimented with split sessions and adjourned sessions. The California split-session arrangement is best known. After spending thirty days in getting organized and receiving the great bulk of the proposed bills, the houses adjourn for thirty days to enable members to study the bills and to consult with their constituents about them. Then they reassemble for another ninety days to complete their work, but no member may introduce more than two bills in this part of the session, and no bill may be introduced without the consent of three fourths of the house concerned. To avoid being blocked by these requirements, members have developed the practice of introducing many bills in the pre-recess session in skeleton form—with a title, enacting clause, and some sections of text, perhaps—the idea being to expand and perfect the measure by later amendments. This partly defeats the purpose of the recess and the bill limitation, because members do not have the full text of bills to study during the recess. The objective of allowing time to consult with constituents has also been achieved only in part. On the other hand the state printer appreciates the thirty-day recess and so does the legislative council's bill-drafting service. Thus there seem to have been some gains from the splitting of the session but not enough to warrant a widespread adoption of the plan. West Virginia has abandoned a similar arrangement, but New Mexico has adopted one.[1]

The usual adjourned session is determined not by constitutional requirement but on the initiative of the legislature. (Legislatures with time limits would not usually find this feasible.) Some legislatures have used the technique of the adjourned session as a means for reviewing all vetoes by the governor. Thus the Republican majority in the Wisconsin legislature did not have full confidence in the Republican governors and, after completing the bulk of their lawmaking about the end of June, adjourned to a fixed day in the fall in seven out of the eight sessions from 1943 to 1957. At that point they took up a few legislative loose ends, perhaps a revenue measure, and reviewed all vetoes of the governor. The new Hawaii constitution provides that the adjourned legislature "may convene at or before noon on the forty-fifth day in special session, without call, for the sole purpose of acting upon any such bill returned by the governor" (Hawaiian Constitution, Art. III, sec. 17).

Legislative Aids

The reasonably conscientious legislator faces tremendous difficulties. Even a legislature which tries to avoid passing detailed laws for the running of

[1] The Wisconsin Legislative Reference Library, *The Split Session in American State Legislatures* (Madison, April 1958). California abandoned its split session in 1959.

state and local government must decide through the budget or otherwise how much the economy and voters of the state can satisfactorily stand in taxes; who ought to pay what taxes; whether it is more important to spend an extra million dollars for highways or for research in mental health; whether local guidance clinics or state institutions with more elaborate facilities will meet mental-health needs more adequately at a particular point in time; which state institutions and services should have priority in appropriations during the next budget period; whether some amount of coercion or strictly educational efforts alone will best meet racial and other biases in employment and generally in public facilities. To make satisfactory decisions, a modern legislator needs to be a generalist, well-versed in many areas. The willingness of the individual legislator to work to inform himself, his basis of value judgments—personal background, party decisions, community interests, his career intentions—and so forth will affect the manner in which he uses the aids available to him. The legislators and the publics of many states believe in education, research, and technical assistance as tools.

★ State legislative reference bureaus

To meet the obvious needs of legislators in his own state, Charles McCarthy, a man with advanced training in economics and government, began in 1901 a legislative information service for the Wisconsin legislature. He was alone; he had a single desk, and a small collection of borrowed books, but he knew how to find the answers to many legislative questions and how to work with legislators. The legislators liked the new service so well that they made provision for it by law, and so was born the first Legislative Reference Bureau in the American states.[2] Soon the movement for such services spread also to other states, until today most state legislatures have made definite provision for legislative reference services.

The function of a legislative reference service is not to tell members what legislation they should enact but to have available for the members concise, pertinent, and reliable information on any given subject. Their libraries contain some books but are mainly composed of special reports, articles, newspaper clippings, pamphlets, and other materials that summarize the desired information. Their staffs usually include competent persons who know how to find the desired information quickly. The work of gathering and compiling information goes on throughout the year, but during the legislative session it increases tremendously. Because most of the questions that come before one legislature also come before others, the Council of State Governments, with headquarters in Chicago, provides for

2 E. E. Witte, "Trail Blazer," 3 State Government, No. 1 (April 1930), 1-2.

the clearance of information among all the state legislative reference services.

★ Legislative councils

The Book of the States lists thirty-seven states as having legislative councils and council-type agencies.[3] (California and New York are among the minority without legislative councils.) Following the lead of Kansas, thirty-six states have generally reduced or eliminated their use of interim legislative committees and in their place have established legislative councils. These consist of leading legislators appointed by the houses themselves to give continuous study to the legislative problems of the state. Appropriations, a research staff, and headquarters are provided and a program of research is carried on. Most of the work of the staff consists in studying and reporting on special problems. In some states, the legislators before adjourning state in formal resolutions many of the problems they expect the council to study. In other states, the council members largely decide the areas of study. Councils may publish research information on the problems studied, may make formal recommendations as a result of their consideration, and/or may draw up bills incorporating their views with the hope of legislative action. If council members enjoy the confidence of their fellow legislators, council-recommended bills receive special consideration for adoption.

★ Budget and audit aid

Legislators often appear most baffled in dealing with executive budgets. Even if the legislature accepts as desirable or necessary the conception that the governor shall draw up the state budget, present it in general terms, and leave only broad decisions of over-all expenditures to the legislature, how does the legislature or its finance committees make any meaningful review? California in 1941 established a joint legislative budget committee and hired a full-time legislative analyst and staff to assist the committee. The analyst sits in on the governor's budget hearings, investigates specific department expenditure requests, and prepares a detailed analysis of the governor's budget for the legislature. Several states have adopted some version of the California system. Whether such an institutional arrangement really gives the legislature more budgetary control or merely divides budgetary control and responsibility between the governor and a hired employee of the legislature needs more study.[4]

3 *The Book of the States, 1958-59,* pp. 70, 71.
4 Wisconsin has a special type of legislative budget assistance in the instance of new bills. Legislators may appraise thoughtfully the governor's budget but then add new programs or tax exemptions without relation to the gross expenditures and revenues of the state.

A number of states have established the position of auditor to review expenditures of state agencies. In theory the auditor presumably is accountable only to the legislature and makes his report for legislative consideration with at least three points in mind. Has the agency properly accounted for all moneys? Did the expenditures, not only in the technical sense but in the policy sense, match the intentions of the legislature? What improvements might be made in the operation of the agencies to secure more effective carrying out of legislative policies? At least twenty of the states have something in the nature of a legislative post-audit agency.

★ Bill-drafting services

Most states have made special provision for legislative drafting services; the other states either designate the attorney general to assist in this matter or make no special provision. The drafting of legislation is, of course, no easy matter. Every bill to be effective must have the correct form, its provisions must conform to the constitution, and its wording must be such that it will accomplish the desired result. Most law schools do not as yet teach the subject of legislative drafting, so that it is not to be assumed that any lawyer will be competent for this purpose. Indeed, bill drafting is becoming more and more a special branch of learning. In those states where a special staff for this purpose has been at work over a period of years, the technical qualities of legislation are being steadily improved.

★ Reviser of statutes

It is desirable not only that every bill be correctly drawn and workable in itself, but also that its relation to the other laws on the same general subject be known. Every new law should be dovetailed with other laws on the subject, by the legislature itself, in a way that cannot be misunderstood. For this purpose a number of states have provided another officer, the reviser of statutes, who is to keep the statutes revised up to date. A permanent system of numbering all sections of the revised statutes is generally adopted, so that any act passed can be fitted properly into the entire code of laws of the state.

Legislative Procedure and Organization

To perform their functions even in a routine way, legislatures need leadership, organization, means by which the majority may act and minorities be

Beginning with experiments in 1953 Wisconsin eventually established the "fiscal note." Every bill must indicate the estimated effect it would have on state revenues and/or expenditures. M. G. Toepel, "Putting a Price Tag on Legislation," *State Government* (May 1958).

heard, and a regularized process for perfecting bills as fully as is easily possible before they become laws. For these and similar purposes there are rules governing procedure and organization.

★ Legislative rules

Sources of rules. State constitutions in all cases contain the fundamental rules that guide the legislature as a whole and its separate houses. There are also a few statutes to be consulted, and the separate rules that each house has power to adopt and alter from time to time. Precedents arising out of the rulings of the presiding officers and the houses are not so thoroughly compiled and indexed as is the case with Congress, but usually the chief clerk or secretary holds over from session to session and keeps records of what has been decided. The one-house legislature of Nebraska has an excellent short manual of procedure, and a number of the bicameral bodies have also prepared good ones. The ordinary "legislative manual" or "bluebook" contains much miscellaneous political information and is devoted only in small part to the rules of the legislature.

The rules deal with several closely interrelated matters: the organization of the legislative chambers and their interrelations; the rights of members; and the procedures to be followed in daily business and in the enactment of bills into laws or resolutions.

Order of business. At the beginning of each day in most legislative bodies, there is a period of an hour, more or less, when routine things are done. The daily "order of business" may be illustrated by the rather detailed one laid down for the Nebraska legislature:

a. Prayer by the chaplain
b. Roll call
c. Call for correction of the journal
d. Petitions and memorials
e. Notice of committee hearings
f. Report of standing committees
g. Report of select committees
h. Resolutions
i. Introduction of bills
j. Bills on first reading by title
k. Bills on second reading by title
l. Bills on third reading

m. Special order of the day (with preference given to the unfinished business of the preceding day)
n. Consideration of bills on select file
o. Consideration of bills on general file
p. Unfinished business, including messages on the president's desk
q. Miscellaneous business[5]

[5] *Nebraska Legislative Manual*, 1937, p. 24, Rule VIII.

In this list from *d* to *m*, as a rule, the speaker or clerk merely gives notice of new petitions, bills, and other matters before the house, and members rise to offer resolutions or to make reports from committees and other announcements. Many questions may also be asked and answered, and comments are made on matters connected with the procedure of the house.

★ *Presiding officers*

Following to some extent the President-Vice President pattern of the United States Constitution, all but eleven of the states provide for lieutenant governors as well as governors. Lieutenant governors succeed to the governorship in case of a vacancy in that office. They are elected by state-wide popular vote, and in all cases but one they preside over the state senate and are addressed as "Mr. President." State senates limit lieutenant governors in their powers to name committees and in their general control over the operation of the senate more than the lower houses do their speakers. The lieutenant governor is not the choice of the senate and may be of a party other than that of the senate majority. In the states where the senate chooses its own president, he represents the dominant party, and his powers are more like those of the speaker of the house.

The office of the speaker of the lower house is much like that of the speaker of the House of Representatives in Congress. The speaker is elected by the members at the beginning of the term or session, usually on a straight party or factional vote, and he represents the majority party or faction in the administration of the office. That is to say, he is not a strictly impartial presiding officer, such as certain other English-speaking countries normally have in their legislatures. His powers usually include that of appointing the house committees, a function in which he definitely represents the majority caucus for all majority-party appointments, but normally accepts without question the minority caucus' list for the minority positions on committees.

In addition to whatever powers they have in appointing committees, the presiding officers of both houses have usually the normal powers attached to the office. These include (1) the right to rule on motions and questions of order and procedure, a function in which they generally follow the precedents as known by the clerk or secretary, and in which they are subject to being overruled by the members; (2) the recognition of members on the floor, which frequently involves a choice among several who are on their feet asking recognition at the same time; and (3) the power to assign bills to committees, a subject on which some legislative bodies have committees and on which the presiding officer can be overruled by the members.

★ Clerks, secretaries, and minor officers

Every legislative chamber has, in addition to its presiding officer, a clerk or secretary who has charge of the records, assistant clerks, and secretaries for various functions such as calling the roll and checking the accuracy of enrolled bills, a sergeant at arms and his assistants, various pages, and other minor officers and employees. These are for the chamber as a whole; in addition there are clerks, stenographers, and other employees for various committees. The total numbers of such personnel are considerable, particularly in the legislatures of the larger and wealthier states, and the common method of selecting them is through a sort of patronage or spoils system controlled by the majority caucus.

Typically legislators have been more willing to provide for merit-system selection of executive and administrative personnel than for their own assistants. Only Wisconsin requires a qualifying examination for appointment. The general absence of any merit-system selection has sometimes resulted in abuses: nepotism (the employment of near-relations), sinecures (the giving of jobs and pay without any duties), and other sloppy, wasteful, if not corrupt, ways of spending public money. The legislators have, of course, been poorly served.

★ Party organization

Mention has already been made of the partisan organization of state legislatures. The members are elected on a partisan basis, with party names on the ballots in all but two states. In Minnesota and Nebraska the ballots carry no party designations, and the election is carried out like a local or judicial nonpartisan election. This does not mean that there is no party organization in the two houses or that the legislature is "nonpolitical." Far from it. In Minnesota the conservative members, mostly Republicans, with a few right-wing Democrats caucus in advance of each session and agree upon a slate of officers. The so-called liberals, mostly members of the Democratic-Farmer Labor party, set up a rival organization. In the most recent sessions, the conservatives have controlled the upper house and the liberals the lower with resulting problems for the Democratic governor.

In all other states the party affiliation of the members is known, and outside the South the division is normally between the Republicans and the Democrats. In 1957, six Southern states had no Republican legislators in either house. Legislatures in the South organize along the lines of factions within the Democratic party, with somewhat different results in each state. The degree of two-party competition in states outside the South differs. To some extent the differences reflect the results of electoral good and bad fortune, but they may represent the consequences of gerrymandering and apportionment of legislative members.

The party organization of a legislative chamber does not ignore but rather controls and works through the formal organization that was outlined above. Party votes, directly or indirectly, determine the presiding officer and the committee chairmen. These individuals normally try to protect the majority's control and to carry out the majority's policy. To keep its control, the majority party in each house holds caucuses from time to time, although the practice is by no means uniform, and operates an organization of its own consisting of a floor leader and various lieutenants called "whips" who keep the party members lined up in support of measures that the caucus has agreed upon. The majority floor leader and various leading committee chairmen and whips in most party-controlled legislatures also dominate the committee on rules, a committee that is empowered to bring in special resolutions from time to time concerning the order of business. Through these and other arrangements and pressures, the majority usually manages to keep control of what the chamber does on at least the bills of great importance to the party.

At times the majority leadership in some legislative chambers becomes highly autocratic even to the point of disregarding the rules and the rights of the minority as well as of individual members. The "short roll-call" method used by the majority in the New York legislatures in counting the votes on bills is a travesty on the rules—the legislature always comes up with the constitutional majority, even though it does not have that many members present.[6]

Of course, the minority party has a floor organization corresponding to that of the majority, ready to catch the majority napping at any time and always busy with obstructionism and criticism.

★ Bill procedure

Since laws are the final product of most legislative activity, bill procedure has relevance. Bills may be introduced by any member or group of members in conformity with the constitution and rules of the house. In some states bills may not be introduced after a certain time in the session. The act of introducing a bill is usually a simple one, such as depositing it in a box or handing it to the clerk. So-called "readings" of the bill often mean merely announcement of title.

Either the presiding officer or a special committee assigns each bill to

[6] Warren Moscow, *Politics in the Empire State* (New York: Alfred A. Knopf, 1948), pp. 175-177.

a committee for consideration. Depending on state custom, the committee may hold a hearing, discuss it, vote on it, and advise the legislative house its recommendation; or the committee or its chairman may decide to set the bill aside and do nothing with it; or the committee or chairman may on his own or after consultation with a few others, but without a public hearing, make a recommendation to the house (or after these steps make no recommendation). In some states an unfavorable committee may bottle up a bill as successfully as Congressional committees do on occasion.

Legislative committees.   To foreign observers, the committee system is one of the most striking features of American legislatures. National, state, and local legislative bodies all employ numerous committees and entrust them with powers almost of life or death over bills. In state legislative practice there are a number of different types of committees, such as:

1. Standing committees of each house separately;
2. Standing joint committees of the two houses (most numerous in Connecticut, Maine, and Massachusetts);
3. Special committees of each house, but in some instances joint committees, for inquiries during the session;
4. Interim committees, either separate or joint, for investigations between sessions.

Outside Maine, Massachusetts, and Connecticut, which use mainly joint committees, the separate standing committees of the lower houses number from eight in South Carolina and fourteen in Maryland and Nebraska up to sixty-five in Arkansas and sixty-three in Missouri. In the upper houses, the numbers vary from seven in New Mexico, eleven in Wisconsin, and fourteen in Maryland up to thirty-nine in Iowa, forty in Florida, and forty-six in Mississippi. Unicameral Nebraska gets along with fourteen standing committees, while Connecticut, Maine, and Massachusetts use very few separate house committees and assign most of the bills to twenty-eight, twenty-four, and thirty-one joint committees, respectively (see Table 7).

The existence of many committees may reflect subdivisions of work by subjects (education, health, finance, roads, and so on), but the establishment of many committees may also reflect the desire of more individual legislators for committee chairmanships. At least there is no necessary parallel between the number and diversity of committees and the number and importance of bills handled by the several state legislatures. Massachusetts with twenty-four joint standing committees and six house and four senate committees had 8324 bills introduced in the two sessions in 1956 and 1957. Mississippi with fifty house, forty-six senate, and five joint standing committees handled 1587 bills in its 1957 biennial session.

Table 7. STANDING COMMITTEES IN THE STATES

Number of States in Each Range

Number of Standing Committees	House 1946	1957	Senate[a] 1946	1957	Joint 1946	1957
10 or under	0	4	0	4 [b]	23	23
11-20	2	16	8	18	0	0
21-30	9	10	15	17	0	2
31-40	15	7	13	8	2	1
41-50	12	7	9	1	1	0
51-60	7	1	2	0	0	0
61-70	2	2	1	0	0	0

Source: Adapted from *The Book of the States, 1958-59.* For a full listing of committees by states, see *The Book of the States.*

a Nebraska is included only under "Senate."
b Includes Maine and Massachusetts which use largely joint committees.

Committee organization, structure, and operation significantly affect the accomplishment of business of the legislature. (1) Who appoints the committees? Are they influenced by individual leaders, the party, or pressure groups? What is the seniority factor? (2) Are there differences in influence among committees? Is there a limited number of reasonably sized committees or a large number of rather large committees? Do all committee members attend most committee sessions? Which committee or committees have most substantial control over measures? In Wisconsin, for example, the most powerful committee is the Joint Committee on Finance, made up of both senate and assembly members and through which all revenue and appropriation measures must pass. (3) Does a multitude of overlapping committees and the rules permit the house or senate officer to assign bills to committees on the basis of their presumed competence or on the basis of their bias for or against the bill in question? (4) Do most or all bills receive a public hearing? Who appears at public hearings? Besides public hearings on what do committee members base their decision? On studies available to them? As a result of interest-group activities? On party decisions? At the governor's request? From influence of administrative department heads? (5) Are most or all bills reported out of committee? How frequently and under what circumstances does one or both houses reverse committee recommendations? Many of these questions require answers to other subquestions, but only through analysis of information for these and other questions can one trace and understand the lawmaking process.

Debate and passage. After a committee reports out a bill, it must be placed on a calendar. When its turn is reached, legislators have the opportunity for general discussion.

Legislatures vote on bills, resolutions, and motions in a variety of ways. These may be listed as follows:

1. Unanimous consent, where no member raises his voice in opposition, and the chairman declares the bill carried.

2. *Viva voce*, where the members call out in unison their Yes or Yea, and their No or Nay votes. There is then no recorded roll call, but the chairman declares the measure carried if he judges that it had a majority.

3. Division and count by tellers. When there is doubt as to the result of a *viva-voce* vote, tellers may be appointed by the chairman to represent each party, and the members for a bill walk past those on one side, and those opposed walk past the tellers on the other. The tellers then report their count to the chair, and the result is announced.

4. Show of hands. Where there is doubt as to result of a *viva-voce* vote, a show of hands is often called for, and the clerk and presiding officer make the count.

5. Roll call, with Yeas and Nays or Ayes and Noes. In this case the roll is called, and every member present is expected to respond and be recorded.

6. Electric voting device, used now in a number of state legislatures, whereby the member has on his desk three electric buttons to press, to indicate approval, disapproval, or present but not voting. An electric scoreboard shows the result in such a way that each member can see if his vote is correctly recorded. A photograph then is taken to make a permanent record of the result. This takes only a very few minutes.

Most state constitutions authorize a defined number of members to require a roll call on any measure. The salutary purpose of this rule is to put members on public record as to their votes. Under a show of hands or a *viva-voce* vote, for example, no record is made of any member's vote. Roll calls take much time, and for this reason the electrical voting device, which gets exactly the same result but far more quickly, may some day be adopted by most legislatures.

When a bill has passed both houses but not in identical form, a conference committee of the two houses usually irons out the differences, and identical bills are then passed in both houses. In any case where both houses have passed the same measure, the two texts are then compared by clerks and an enrolling committee, the original is signed by the presiding officers of both houses, and the "enrolled bill" is sent to the governor for signature.

Executive action on bills. In all states except North Carolina the governor has a veto power, but the terms in which the constitution states this power are not the same in all states. The general veto powers of state governors do not differ materially from the President's. All but nine state governors, however, also have the power to veto items in appropriation bills, while approving the rest of the items. The majorities required for passage over the veto in the states vary considerably. In some cases, a simple majority of all elected members is sufficient. In others it is three fifths of those elected, but in most cases it is two thirds of those present and voting or two thirds of all elected members.

Governors may have significant influence through the veto. If legislators believe the governor may veto a bill if it contains particular provisions, they may try to modify the bill to meet the governor's objections. In several states, in fact, governors sometimes return bills during sessions with suggested amendments and with the implied or express assurance that a bill amended to suit them will receive their approval. Where the legislature hands over a mass of bills to the governor and then adjourns *sine die,* the governor usually can veto bills without stating his reasons and with no chance of being overruled by the legislature. The Illinois legislature has passed only three bills over the governor's veto since 1870. Most vetoes in Illinois come after the legislature has adjourned.[7]

Nonlegislative Work

State legislatures do not have only legislative powers. Indeed, a purely legislative body is hard to find. The following kinds of nonlegislative work are commonly imposed on state legislative bodies: (1) approval of appointments made by the executive, usually by the senate; (2) direct appointments or elections by the legislature of various state officers and boards, such as boards of regents; (3) impeachment and removal of officers, both executive and judicial; (4) investigations of the executive and judicial branches; (5) audits of public funds; and (6) direct legislative administration.

These powers in a general sense follow similar powers of the United States Congress. Traditional practices of each state, together with the particular political situation at a given time, affect the probabilities of

[7] Coleman Ransone, *The Office of Governor in the United States* (University, Ala.: University of Alabama Press, 1956), p. 182. See p. 238 for the use of the adjourned session by the Wisconsin legislature to review the governor's vetoes. See also the unusual provision of the Hawaiian constitution on this subject discussed here on p. 238.

differences and dissension between the legislative body and the executive or among legislators. For example, normally the U. S. Senate almost automatically approves nominations of the President to his Cabinet, but three times (one man twice) in the last four decades the Senate has refused to approve and has spent substantial time in producing its refusal. In the same sense, the Wisconsin State Senate has usually approved the governor's nominations to head state departments; but in 1959, the Senate refused to approve a nominee to the Public Service Commission. Although in both situations the senates were controlled by a party other than that of the chief executive, more than narrow partisan issues were involved in the refusal. It is not possible to generalize on whether nonlegislative functions will take much or little time during a regular session.

Legislative Process

To comprehend the legislative process requires simultaneous attention to a great many different matters. There are legal and objective facts such as what formal officers are provided for by legislative rules, who formally selects the committees, whether there are joint committees or a full set of committees for each house, and so forth. There are the formal institutional arrangements, described in the last chapter, as to one house or two; the number of legislators in each house; the legal qualifications of legislators; and the methods of electing legislators by types of districts. Even in the formal institutional and legal arrangements, the "facts" do not necessarily correspond to the constitutional or statutory provisions. Thus a state whose constitution appears to require reapportionment every ten years may not have had legislative reapportionment or redistricting for fifty years. Even more important, legislators, governors, and others use the formal rules and organization to ratify decisions made elsewhere—by the political party, community leaders, interest groups, and the like.

The intelligent citizen, the successful lobbyist, the government official needs to understand the formal institutions, organization, and rules within which the legislature operates. He must also know who the leaders are, what their background and general preferences are, what influence they have, and who or what can influence them. Final legislative votes which defeat or pass a measure do not come from isolated individuals, prettily following a set legislative ritual after having conscientiously studied and thought about the issues in solitude. Yet the legislative ritual may affect the form, the timing, and even the outcome of the group struggle in any particular case.

★ Case study of a bill [8]

Assemblyman Wilder Crane, Jr., a first term Republican from Chippewa Falls, was invited to speak at the annual ladies' night banquet of the Lions Club in Cornell, a city in his district, early in February 1957. At this meeting, he talked briefly with Mr. Harrison Towle, chairman of the Town of Birch Creek, a rural district near Cornell. Mr. Towle complained that the electors present for the annual town meeting in Birch Creek had voted to reduce his salary after he had served one year of his two-year term. Towle explained that conflicts about road-building policies in the town had resulted in considerable opposition to his administration, and his opponents had come to the annual town meeting in such force as to command a majority which voted to reduce his salary. Towle felt that the state legislature should take action to prevent what he regarded as a great injustice.

Assemblyman Crane raised the question whether the town meeting could legally reduce the salary of an incumbent town officer and suggested that Towle consult an attorney on this issue. Crane came to Cornell again a week later to hold his regular office hours in that city, and Towle reported that his attorney advised that there was nothing in the statutes to prohibit the reduction of town officials' salaries during their term. Towle urged that there should be a statutory prohibition of such action and asked his assemblyman to introduce a bill to accomplish this objective.

Thus, on February 27, Assemblyman Crane introduced Bill 303A, the title of which was "A bill to create 60.60 (4) of the statutes, relating to salary or compensation of town officers." The text of the bill was "No salary or compensation rate shall be reduced during the term of town supervisor, clerk, treasurer, assessor, or constable."

Upon introduction, the bill was read twice by title by the clerk and referred by the speaker to the committee on state affairs. In March a public hearing was held by this committee on a number of minor bills, including Bill 303A. Crane explained the plight of Harrison Towle to the committee and urged a favorable recommendation of the bill. Ben Hanneman, secretary of the Wisconsin Towns Association (and a registered lobbyist), also spoke briefly and informed the committee of the approval of his organization of the bill. Hanneman had previously informed Crane that he had taken notice of the bill when it was introduced and would support it. Nobody spoke against the bill.

Although there was no opposition to the bill, the majority of the committee felt that the problem was not sufficiently important to require legislative action. Thus, after the committee's executive session, Bill 303A was recommended for indefinite postponement on March 26.

The bill was not discussed at the Republican caucus.

[8] This short report and analysis of a bill becoming a law was written by Wilder Crane, Jr., from his personal experience as a member of the Wisconsin State Legislature in 1957. Mr. Crane is now an instructor at Vanderbilt University. He has authorized use of his statement in this text.

When the bill came before the Assembly on March 28, the question before the house was "Shall Bill 303A be indefinitely postponed?" in accordance with the committee recommendation. Crane was the only person to speak on the bill; he urged that the principle of the bill was sound and that it was an important problem for those few people who would be affected. Crane requested a roll call. (Wisconsin rules provide that there shall be a roll call if one sixth of the one hundred members support a roll-call request). At least sixteen members stood to second the request although Crane, as a freshman, had neglected to speak to other members before the session to secure their support.

The roll call resulted in a vote of 46 for indefinite postponement to 48 against indefinite postponement. The question then became "Shall Bill 303A be engrossed and read a third time?" This motion carried on a voice vote with no audible opposition. The Assembly then took up the next bill on the calendar.

One roll call was, therefore, the crucial step in the passage of the bill. An analysis of this roll call reveals no obvious patterns of votes for and against the bill. Thirty-four Republicans voted for the bill and 32 Republicans voted against it, while 14 Democrats voted for the bill and 14 Democrats voted against it. Some who had rural towns in their districts voted for the bill and others against it. Those who represented only cities also split in voting for and against the bill. Those who voted for the bill included every assemblyman in counties contiguous to or near the author's own Chippewa County, every Republican who had been active in suporting the defeated candidate for speaker whom Crane [the author] had supported, the majority of the education committee on which Crane served, those Democrats with whom Crane had voted on the previous roll call that same day, and some others with whom Crane regularly ate lunch. Those who voted against the bill were generally assemblymen with whom Crane was not acquainted.

Having been given preliminary approval, the bill was given routine treatment when it appeared with nine other bills for final Assembly passage on April 4. On that day, Bill 303A was read for the third time by title, given final approval, and messaged to the Senate by unanimous consent.

On April 5, 303A was received by the Senate and referred to its committee on governmental and veterans affairs. Thereafter, Crane became involved with a number of other bills of greater importance, and he forgot Bill 303A. He did not speak to the Senate committee chairman to make certain that the committee would act nor did he speak to any other senators about the bill. Crane was surprised when Ben Hanneman, the lobbyist for the Towns Association, asked him why he had not come to the Senate hearing on the bill. Hanneman explained that he made the sole appearance for the bill at the Senate committee hearing and had later reminded the chairman about the bill to make certain that it was reported out.

The Senate Committee recommended concurrence on May 29. In a few minutes on June 6, with the Republican Senate floor leader making the necessary motions, the bill was given preliminary approval, the rules were suspended, the bill concurred in and ordered immediately messaged back to the Assembly. Bill 303A was one of many bills rushed through without discussion or roll calls at this session of the Senate.

Bill 303A was one of several hundred bills which were sent to the Governor after the Legislature adjourned in June. Although the constitution provides that the Governor has only six days in which to take action on bills once he has received them, it does not specify when they must be sent to him. Thus, the legislative clerks keep the bills and send a few a day to the Governor. Bill 303A was sent to the Governor and approved by him on July 5th. It was published in the *Wisconsin State Journal* in Madison as Chapter 324 of the Session Laws of 1957 on July 12 and became law the next day.

Assemblyman Crane received a letter from Governor Thomson after the bill was published to notify him that his bill had become law. Crane informed Harrison Towle of this fact by letter and received his thanks some weeks later at a meeting at the Chippewa County Court House in Chippewa Falls.

★ *Comment on case study*

"How Bill 303A Became A Law" reflects a number of significant aspects of the legislative process:

1. Many of the bills passed by a legislature are minor and affect very few people.

2. The ideas for most bills emanate from administrative agencies, constituents, and interest groups rather than from the legislators. The contacts between Towle and Crane suggest the immediate, personal relations between state legislators and constituents, especially in small rural districts.

3. The critical roll-call vote reflected personal support for the bill's author rather than divisions by party lines, factional lines, or rural-urban cleavages.

4. This account reflects one role of the lobbyist. The secretary of the Towns Association made certain that the bill was not overlooked in the Senate.

5. In quantitative terms, the story of this bill is probably typical of state legislative bills. Of the major pieces of legislation in any session, the description is not typical.

This bill did not bring into play lobbyists for opposing interest groups, party-leadership support or opposition, or support or opposition from the governor. No general citizen group showed interest. With the exception of the statutory check and the drafting of the bill by the Legislative Reference Library, no particular use was made of library or research facilities.

The case study suggested elements of legislative behavior—friendship, acquaintance, constituent relations, previous voting agreement—in a simple incident where pressure-group and party interest were low. Other studies have tended to show that in American states with a strong two-party system, reasonably reflected in the legislative membership, partisan considerations importantly influence voting on certain issues. Legislative procedure and organization votes regularly call forth party voting loyalty. Particular issues —administrative fiscal programs, economic and social issues—draw partisan voting. Party voting will also occur on matters reflecting on the prestige of the administration. Governors, however, differ in the leadership they exert and in the degree to which they are able to influence the legislators of their own party. Larger, more urban and industrial states especially exhibit party voting patterns.

Lobbyists for major interest groups typically find they must win over only a limited number of legislators—the uncommitted members—on the particular issue. For many legislators, party platform, personal beliefs, and/or constituency characteristics have determined their votes before lobbyists approach them in the legislature. Only when following these guides results in conflict on an issue or provides no answer is the legislator likely to listen to a lobbyist.

The *legislative role* has the highest priority. A newcomer to the legislative body (and this is especially illustrated in the United States Senate) learns a set of relations with his fellow legislators—both in his own party and in the opposition. Violation of these relationships can be more costly than a wrong vote in the eyes of the party, constituency, or pressure group. Fortunately the legislator finds that on most issues he can satisfy his legislative role, his constituency, his party, and the interest groups of concern to him. When these interests conflict, however, the indicated priorities come into play. Additional studies of legislative voting patterns should contribute to measuring the influence of all of these factors more exactly.

REFERENCES

Belknap, George M., "A Method For Analyzing Legislative Behavior," II *Midwest Journal of Political Science* (November 1958), 377-402.

Davey, Harold W., "The Legislative Council Movement in the United States, 1933-1953," 47 *American Political Science Review* (September 1953), 785-797.

Derge, David R., "The Lawyer As Decision-maker In The American State Legislature," 21 *Journal of Politics* (August 1959), 408ff.

Eulau, Heinz, Samuel J. Eldersveld, and Morris Janowitz (eds.), *Political Behavior.* Glencoe, Ill.: The Free Press, 1956, especially pp. 253-264; 308-317; and 317-324.

Gove, Samuel K., and Gilbert Y. Steiner, *The Illinois Legislative Process*. Urbana, Ill.: The University of Illinois, June 1954.

Wahlke, John C., and Heinz Eulau (eds.), *Legislative Behavior*. Glencoe, Ill.: The Free Press, 1959.

Wilbern, York Y., "Pre-Legislative Conferences in Indiana," 32 *State Government* (Winter 1959), 43-46.

C H A P T E R   1 2

The Governor—Office and Powers

FROM GEORGE CLINTON (1777) to Nelson Rockefeller (elected in 1958), forty-nine men have served New York as governor. With only two or three exceptions, every governor of New York in the twentieth century has been a serious contender for the Presidential nomination of his party. Theodore Roosevelt, Charles Evans Hughes, Alfred E. Smith, Franklin D. Roosevelt, and Thomas E. Dewey, were the nominees of their parties on one or more occasions. The two Roosevelts served in the Presidency for a combined total of almost twenty years. Other states have had distinguished (as well as some not so distinguished) governors, but none can compete with New York. In each state, the present significance of the office of governor is made up of many things: the constitutional and statutory powers assigned to the office; the caliber of the men who have served as governor, what they have made of the office, the popular image of the governor, and the political (in the widest meaning) forces currently operating. A historical review of the development of the office, together with some analysis of problems associated with the office today, will give a background for some examination of the role of the individual governor in the individual state.

The Development of the Governorship

★ Colonial governors

The reorganization of the London Company's government of Virginia, which gave rise to the first legislative assembly in the English-speaking colonies in 1619, also brought changes limiting the governor's term to three years and his total tenure to two terms. His formerly broad veto power was reduced at the same time. The Massachusetts Bay Company in 1629 provided for a governor to serve for only one year, gave powers not so much to the governor alone as to the governor and council, and so arranged things that the governor soon became elective by the freemen of the colony, a close approach to modern popular election. He could call special sessions of the legislature (general court), but, unlike present governors, he and his council sat in on, and he presided over, the general court. He voted only in case of a tie and had no veto power. In colonial Rhode Island the governor, his deputy, and the assistants were chosen annually by the freemen assembled in general court. Connecticut had much the same arrangement, including popular election, a one-year term for governor, and a prohibition against any governor serving two successive years. These provisions may help to show that even in early colonial times there was some suspicion of executive powers and of long tenure by governors.[1]

After about 1660, the year of the restoration of monarchy in England, there came many changes in the colonial governments. Attempts were made from England to strengthen the executives, somewhat at the expense of the elected assemblies. The governors in most colonies received the veto power and also had powers to enforce, or to see to the enforcement of, substantially all laws passed by the people or their representatives. Thus executive responsibility was centered mainly in one man. It was some of the governors in this period of 1660-1776 who especially aroused the ire of the assemblymen and their supporters in the colonies by highhanded methods of law enforcement, in which they represented the crown. The revolutionary movement was directed in part against these later developments in the governorship, and the early state constitutions, drafted in 1776, returned to the pre-1660 type of governor's position.

★ Governors under the first state constitutions

The three original charter colonies, Connecticut, Rhode Island, and Massachusetts, at the beginning of the Revolution (1775-1776) either continued

1 On the early colonial period, see especially Percy Lewis Kaye, *The Colonial Executive Prior to the Restoration* (Baltimore: The Johns Hopkins University Press, 1900).

under or revived and used their colonial charters as their constitutions. These provided for short-term, elective governors of very limited powers. In the other colonies the revolutionary conventions (legislatures) drew up the constitutions. Most of them provided for governors (some called them presidents) to be chosen by the legislatures for a term of one year, but South Carolina allowed a two-year term, and Delaware and New York (1777) specified three years. In what was a clear case of reaction against the powerful colonial governors of the decades before the Revolution, the legislatures thus tried to make the governors weak and dependent on the legislature. This was not a separation of powers but the reverse. The governor was given no veto power at all in ten states, and in three only a limited one. His appointing powers were practically nil; the legislature appointed the judges and a number of other officers. An executive or advisory council was placed alongside the governor to check him in all that he could do, and in a few states this council practically was the executive. Thus the office of governor began under the new states at a very low point.

But there were sincere believers in a separation of powers who advocated a strong executive to balance the legislature, and who had influence in the framing of the New York constitution (1777) and the Massachusetts constitution (1780). In the meantime under the stress of war conditions several legislatures admitted their own failures as heads of the executive branch and delegated to the governor various dictatorial emergency powers, an action that brought strong protest from Thomas Jefferson in Virginia. Despite the written constitutions and in the face of theoretical objections, it appears that the state legislatures of necessity entrusted much authority to their governors and chose some of the ablest citizens for the position.[2]

★ Early developments

Under the New York constitution of 1777 the governor was elected by the voters for a three-year term. He was associated with a number of judges in a council of revision with the power to veto legislative acts, subject to being overridden by two thirds of both houses. The appointing power, which was fairly considerable, he shared with a council of appointment, consisting of himself and four state senators elected by the lower house. He was commander in chief of the state militia, had power to call and to prorogue legislative sessions, and to recommend legislative action; he could grant pardons and reprieves, except in the most important cases; and he was authorized to take care that the laws be faithfully executed. In short, under this constitution the governor had a position and powers foreshadowing a

2 Allan Nevins, *The American States during and after the Revolution, 1775-1789* (New York: The Macmillan Co., 1924), pp. 206-207.

little of what we expect today, but he was still too much controlled by councils in his veto and appointing powers.

The Massachusetts constitution of 1780 gave the governor only a one-year term, but he was made elective by the voters and he received a veto power of his own in what came to be standard terms—that is, subject to the repassage of vetoed acts by a two-thirds vote. Part of the appointing power was exercised directly by the legislature; the rest went to the governor, but each appointment was subject to approval by a council composed of the lieutenant governor and nine senators. In other respects the Massachusetts governor had powers similar to those of the governor of New York. Thus the first steps were taken toward a more effective separation of powers and a more adequate set of powers for the chief executive.

The trend thus begun was slow in gaining headway, but the ice of suspicion against executive power was beginning to melt and break up. Several factors helped the movement along. (1) As constitutional conventions like that of Massachusetts succeeded the legislatures as the authors of state constitutions, legislators were no longer able to write in their own desires for dominance over the state government. The conventions provided a somewhat more impartial tribunal for considering the proper balance between the legislative and executive branches. (2) When governors were subjected to popular election, and able, reliable, and popular men were chosen, the suspicions of executive power that had been engendered when the English kings appointed colonial governors were obviously outmoded, although much suspicion still lingered on. (3) The United States Constitution, adopted in 1788, and the calm, firm administration of the executive office by men like Washington and Jefferson soon developed assurances in the minds of men that executive power adequately controlled was not greatly to be feared. Indeed, some of the clauses on the President's powers in the United States Constitution were soon paraphrased and written into state constitutions to describe the powers of the governors.

It would be wrong, however, to think of the trend toward strengthening the governor's position as a rational, nation-wide movement directed toward a fixed and ideal goal. Every decision has been a local one. Time, place, and circumstances have affected each change of a constitution. Countermovements, like that for the direct election of more public officials, have deflected the main trend. It is only when the whole pattern of state constitutional development is considered that a trend toward a general strengthening of the executive can be seen; and no two states have reached exactly the same point in the development. The governor's position and powers differ from state to state, and there are states in which the office is still relatively weak. The ideal espoused by some of a long-term, elected governor with a strong veto power and full authority to appoint, direct, and remove all top state administrative officers is not accepted by everyone and has certainly not been fully attained anywhere.

★ Steps toward a stronger governorship

Some of the main steps taken in the states in the past 150 years affecting the governorship may be summarized as follows:

1. Separation of powers. The theory of the separation of powers has been generally accepted, so that in all states the executive department stands on a constitutionally equal plane with and separate from the legislative and judicial departments. To the extent, then, that the governor is the real head of the executive department, his position benefits from this separation.

2. Direct election. For a long time now the governor has been directly elected by the voters in all states. Thus he gets his moral and political authority from the electorate as a whole. Along with this goes a high degree of independence from legislative interference. Although the legislatures generally have the power to impeach and remove the governor and other state officers, this power is rarely used because it is so hard to make it effective. The popular recall, which exists in a small number of states, is even less effective. For the two or four years for which he has been elected, a governor who does not openly violate laws is secure in his position, and backed up by those who elected him.

3. Party leadership. In the great majority of the states the sharp struggle between two major parties for control over the state government forces the governor into being a leader of his party, so that as party leader he actually receives considerable support from fellow party members in the legislature, in the leading local government offices, and in boards and commissions dominated by the party, even if they are not under his direct control.

This party leadership could not, of course, be provided for in any constitution. It arose with the development of political parties in the nineteenth century and was effective in some instances under some vigorous governors even when the powers of the governor's office were rather limited. Both voters and legislators welcomed leadership in matters of policy and legislation, and it was in this area rather than in administration proper that the governor's leadership was first felt.

The effectiveness of party leadership depends upon a variety of personal and other factors. Sometimes the majority of the legislature is of one party and the governor of another. Not every candidate for the governorship has the necessary qualifications, and in many cases the party bosses choose men who would follow them rather than exert independent leadership. Nevertheless, there have been enough instances of candidates taking over the party leadership on assuming the governorship for it to become the expected thing.

4. Veto power. The power to veto legislation was conferred on the governors by the state constitutions during the nineteenth century in all states except North Carolina. A 1950 computation showed twenty-nine states with "strong" veto provisions, fourteen with "medium," four with "weak," and one without a veto clause. All except nine governors have the *item* or *partial veto* for appropriation measures as well as the general veto.

5. Messages. Along with the veto power has come the more constructive power of the governors to send messages to the legislature at the opening of each session and later from time to time, and thus to focus both legislative and public attention upon the state's needs and the governor's proposals. The governors' messages, even more than the party platforms, become the program of the state.

6. Appointing power. As noted above, the appointing power of the governors in the first state constitutions was distinctly limited, and was hedged in by the requirement of the advice and consent of some executive council for each appointment. One by one the states dropped the requirement that an executive council approve the governor's appointments before they become effective, but the governor often did not gain greatly in control. In the nineteenth century, a rival theory of government was being tried out, of which many traces remain today.

★ Disintegration of executive departments

Early in the nineteenth century the idea spread that voters could and should elect all their more important public officials. It seemed like an affront to the voters, a sign of distrust in democracy, to have the legislature elect or the governor and council appoint certain state-wide officers such as the secretary of state, treasurer, auditor, and even the judges, when they could just as well or better be elected by the voters. It was hard for political leaders, themselves dependent on popular support, to stand against this democratic theory. As a result, the early and middle nineteenth century saw a number of state constitutions adopted in which not only the governor but also a number of other state officers and the judges of the leading state courts were made elective by the voters. Later, by constitutional amendments, other officers, such as the state superintendent of public education and the members of the railroad and public utility commission, were added to the elective list.

Toward the end of the nineteenth century, rapidly expanding governmental functions brought a great increase in the number of state agencies. The legislatures generally followed consistently neither the theory that the governor as the responsible head of the state should have the authority to appoint and remove these new officials, nor the view that they should be elected. Some agencies had single heads and some plural heads (boards and commissions), some officers had long terms and some short terms. The legislature permitted the governor to appoint some of these agency heads. Others were elected. A few were appointed by the legislature itself. Even where the governor could appoint, he had to get senate approval in most instances, and in many cases he could not remove the officials at all, or could remove them only with senate consent.

Qualifications, Terms, and Salaries

Let us now take a closer look at certain conditions affecting the office of governor today.

★ Qualifications

The constitutions set a few minimum qualifications for eligibility to the governorship. The required age is thirty years in thirty-six states, thirty-one in Oklahoma, thirty-five in Hawaii, twenty-five in four states, and unstated in eight others except that to be eligible one must be an elector or twenty-one years of age. Since the requirement of being a voter also implies United States citizenship, the requirement of citizenship probably is an actual requirement in all states, although only thirty-eight state constitutions expressly mention it. A few states require United States citizenship for as long as twenty years (Hawaii, Mississippi, and New Jersey), fifteen years (Georgia), twelve years (Delaware), and ten years (Alabama, Arizona, Florida, Louisiana, Virginia). Nineteen constitutions also require a number of years of residence or citizenship in the state, up to as high as ten years (Louisiana, Maryland, Oklahoma).

★ Terms of office

Although just a few years ago the majority of states still gave their governors only two-year terms, thirty-five states now elect their governors for four years and the number grows with each election.[3] Lengthening the

---
[3] The Book of the States, 1958-59, p. 519.

term of the governor carries two ideas: (1) the desirability of having a chief executive with a program to undertake and carry through and (2) the need of assisting him to do this by making it unnecessary for him to start immediately after inauguration to work for re-election.

Re-eligibility. But the length of term is not more important than the question of re-eligibility. Twenty-three states limit service either by a provision limiting a governor to two terms or prohibiting him from serving two *successive* terms or, as in the case of Alaska, more than *two successive* terms. Although voters make mistakes in selection of governors and a few governors have built strong machines, emphasis today tends to be more on the need for good, experienced governors than on constitutional limits restricting the voter's choice. Three of the most populous states—California, Illinois, and New York—have not limited gubernatorial terms and have managed at least as well as the states which do. New York, in 1960, was enjoying only its sixth individual in the governorship since 1922. Michigan in 1958 elected G. Mennen Williams to his sixth two-year term. Re-eligibility limitations in the South reflect again the one-party situation. Just as Southern Senators and Representatives secure re-election term after term, so might a Southern governor, without the constitutional limitations. Two-party competition places effective limits on terms of governors in most states outside of the South.

Salaries and perquisites. Not only do the states appear to wish to give their governors additional status in recent years through lengthening their term of office, but most states have been raising gubernatorial salaries. (For one thing, of course, the salaries of governors often tend to place ceilings on salaries of other state officials. The continuing need to raise salaries of others has been an important pressure in raising salaries of governors.) New York leads with a salary of $50,000 plus the executive mansion and some expenses. The other extreme are the $10,000 and $12,000 paid by ten states. Whether set by the constitution, as in some states, or by statute, the salaries of the governors lag considerably behind the changes in cost of living, the salaries paid to executives in large corporations, and the earnings of the more successful practitioners of law, medicine, and engineering.

Election and Removal of the Governor

Much of the party system and activity of each state coalesces in the election of the governor. Even the weakest governors have power through the prestige of the office, and a strong governor (personally and in the state's institutional terms) may affect the direction of state policy for years. All groups interested in directing the political power in one or another direction attempt to influence the selection of the governor. Political parties, whether in conventions or through primaries, do not give their nomination for governor lightly. The governor "heads the ticket"; he may determine the party's general fortunes in the election, and, if successful, he may bid for higher national office.

★ Election

There is direct popular partisan election of governors in all fifty states, but there are certain differences. Maryland and Georgia through their "county-unit" system in the nomination of candidates by the Democratic party for state-wide offices have sometimes thwarted the majority in their choice by convention electoral systems which reward the rural areas at the expense of urban representation. Whether a governor can succeed himself and whether he serves a two- or four-year term varies among the states as we have seen.

A major election question for the thirty-five states which elect governors on a four-year basis is that of setting the governor's election in the same year as the Presidential election or in the "off-year." The problem revolves around many party issues: Do "off-year" elections aid in keeping one-party states one-party?[4] Do "off-year" elections undesirably separate state and national issues in times of more and more interweaving of state and national problems? Or do "off-year" elections desirably keep the voter from making his voting decision in national Presidential terms when his state problems are different? Do voters split their tickets between Presidential and gubernatorial parties when this makes good sense in the state situation? Or are "off-year" elections scheduled largely for the benefit of gubernatorial candidates and parties which wish to compete in the Presidential election? Certainly New York and California governors gain some advantage in the fact that they can show off their voting strength in their own states just two years before a Presidential election; can attend the national party convention with the prestige of a state governor; and can return safely to their office of governor if they fail to win nomination or election. The Illinois governor on the other hand is elected governor when the President is elected. His state electoral victory is four years old. If he decides to seek the party's Presidential nomination, he must also decide to give up the state race for the governorship.

4 V. O. Key, Jr., *American State Politics, An Introduction* (New York: Alfred A. Knopf, 1956). Mr. Key generally believes so and analyzes the problem on pp. 42-48.

★ *Vacancies and succession*

Vacancies in the office of governor are defined in various ways in the state constitutions. Many states face the same problems as the national government in determining the disability of the President. Louisiana had a well-publicized experience in 1959 when Governor Earl Long became ill. In the eleven states that have no lieutenant governor, eight arrange for the president pro tempore of the senate to succeed, and four (as in the new Alaskan constitution) give the first succession to the secretary of state. Arrangements are made by statute in a number of states for second, third, and other officers in the line of succession.

★ *Removal of the governors*

The impeachment power in the states follows that in the United States Constitution. The lower house of the legislature brings the charges of impeachment and through a committee acts as prosecutor in the case. The senate, with the president pro tem in the chair, hears the charges and votes for or against conviction on each charge separately. A vote of two thirds is usually required for conviction, and the penalty is removal from office, with certain attendant disqualifications. Few legislatures have impeached governors.

About a quarter of the states permit the voters to remove a governor by recall. Only one governor has been removed by this method (Lynn J. Frazier of North Dakota in 1921), and the voters promptly elevated him to the United States Senate (election of 1922).

The Governor as Leader and Manager

Early suspicions of executive power led to attempts to make the governor a nonentity, a mere agent of the legislatures. Popular election of state officers, emphasized in the Jacksonian era, made the governor only one member of a panel of elected state constitutional executive officers. Situations, individuals, governors, parties, and a variety of groups have gradually pushed the office to the forefront of attention and influence in state government and politics.

The theory of the governor as leader and manager of the state's administrative organization came largely after the Civil War and especially as the number and size of state functions increased. State institutions, departments of health, railroad and utility commissions, bureaus and departments of agriculture, labor, conservation, highways, and others were created one upon another, with cumulative effect. Budgets and payrolls began to get out of hand. Waste and corruption were widely suspected and occasionally found. Separate departments might have overlapping and conflicting statutory responsibilities with no one in authority to take action. Neither legislators nor department boards, commissions, or directors readily acknowledged the need for the governor to lead. Beneficiaries of the various services built up pressure groups around these agencies to protect them against change. To give the governor budgetary, personnel, and policy controls over state government interfered with established methods of conducting affairs and aroused the opposition of legislators, officials, and those who influenced or received services from the agencies.

On the side of making the office of governor the center of control have been: (1) the theory of the separation of powers by which the state executive (modeled after the President) should be responsible for the governing of the state and, therefore, should have control over the administration; (2) the economy and efficiency pressures which saw (and see) state government as a large business with the governor as managing director; (3) the opportunities of the governor with mass communication to personalize government for voters; (4) the opportunities of the governor to be party leader and to influence party groups and the legislature.

In theory state governors today are business managers, party leaders, legislative leaders, law enforcers, and ceremonial representatives of the state. The latter function may seem the least important. It is regularly the most time consuming. Citizens and groups expect the governor to grace many occasions. The governor finds these opportunities to campaign for reelection or gain support for his program. State organization and constitutional and legal practices, time, and the personality and ability of each governor modify and limit the degree to which any governor fills all these roles.

★ *Gubernatorial-legislative relations*

As a single individual, the governor has advantages in relation to the multimember legislature. He may consult with many individuals, but at some point it is he who acts and expresses policies. The strongest legislative leaders usually find the governor stiff competition in the party and before the public. Governors have many roads of access to the legislature itself—formal messages, vetoes, party and personal influence. Governors frequently have sanctions of rewards and penalties. Many legislators do not disdain eventual appointment under the governor, or as in many states, the governor's approval of an individual legislator as his successor.

The governor has the resource of the state's experts to aid in devising his program. His messages may marshal all the available research on a special problem. To supplement the messages, some governors submit through legislative leaders various fully drafted bills—administration bills—for legislative action. A few governors succeed in securing executive review of all departmental bills before they go to the legislature. The total of administration and departmental bills will usually exceed the total of bills received by legislators from any other general source—lobbyists, constituents, or their own. Administration bills do not all get adopted, and especially not without amendment but they have a priority in consideration.

The governor's messages and activities almost always receive newspaper, radio, and television attention. His vetoes can call public attention to discrepancies in legislative action and force legislatures to reconsider earlier decisions. The threat of a veto alone may prevent legislative action. The so-called *partial veto* of some governors (for example, in Wisconsin) has permitted the governor not only to veto specific appropriations but also to modify the purpose for which the appropriation is made.[5]

★ Party leader

We have already indicated that the party does not choose its candidate for governor lightly. The man who secures the confidence of his party sufficiently to get the nomination has qualities which assure him a role in its leadership. If he wins the governorship, he automatically has a post from which he can add to his position of influence and control in the party. The governor who succeeds in his party leadership eases legislative and administrative relations. And the governor who makes a success of legislative and administrative relations adds to his stature in his party.

★ State administrative authority

Appointing power.   State governors seldom enjoy the appointing authority of the President. Apart from the generality of state employees hired under a merit system or a patronage system of sorts, many governors come into office to find (1) major department heads with longer terms than the governor's, (2) a majority of commissioners and board members with longer terms than the governor's, (3) perhaps a few boards or commissions appointed directly by the legislatures, (4) possibly a few departments headed by individuals hired under the merit system and with protected tenure, and (5) at least a few administrators or department heads elected at large.

[5] The Wisconsin Legislative Reference Library, *The Operation of the Executive Veto in Wisconsin, 1937-1955, With Special Reference to the Partial Veto,* Information Bulletin (Madison, January 1957).

The new Alaskan and Hawaiian constitutions (as well as established practice in New York, New Jersey, and Virginia) accept the premise that the governor alone has the executive power of the state and should have the authority to appoint his own department heads and secure the praise or blame for the quality of programs these men carry out. Even in other states, the formal limitations on gubernatorial appointment may be more formidable than the reality. Although the states average to elect five officials besides the governor and lieutenant governor, some of those elected have routine, ministerial functions which affect the reality of the governor's control of program little. Department heads appointed by previous governors or under merit-system rules may be prickly thorns on occasion, but even a thorn bush needs cooperation of soil and weather to live. Departments normally need funds which may be available only through the budget recommended by the governor. Greater centering of appointing authority in the governor would smooth his life at times, but the absence of full appointing authority does not necessarily make the governor powerless in great areas of government.

Removal power. The power of removal of state officers is generally held not to be an incident of the governor's executive or appointing power. If he has a power of removal, it must be stated in the constitution or the statutes. Under some constitutions and statutes, the governor has a wide power of removal extending even to elective officers (other than judicial and legislative) at the state and county level. In some instances, an appointee serves "at the pleasure" of the governor as technically the members of the President's cabinet serve. Such provision gives the governor wide discretion. More normally the constitution or the statutes give the governor the removal power only in case of "incompetency, neglect of duty, or malfeasance in office" or "gross neglect of duty or corrupt conduct." Such provisions make it necessary for the governor ordinarily to file charges against the offending official, to hold a hearing, and to make the removal for one or more of the causes legally recognized. Governors will often suffer undesirable officials to avoid the time and effort (as well as the problematic political impact) involved in hearings. Occasionally constitutional and statutory limitations on removal have reached such inflexibility that a governor and legislature have cooperated to reorganize an administrative agency for the sole purpose of removing an undesirable individual.

Financial powers. Later chapters will take up the detailed fiscal and budgetary powers of the governor. Governors today, in contrast to the nineteenth century, typically present a recommended budget of expenditures and revenues to the legislature. Legislative budget review often results in more sound and fury than in major revision of the governor's financial proposal, and this priority of standing of the governor's budget aids the governor's relations with departments. Again in the execution of the budget, the governor and his fiscal advisers may have a superintending authority.

Centralization of architectural, engineering, and purchasing facilities for all agencies also has often helped a governor to get cooperation for his programs from the departments.

Prestige of the office as power. A New York governor, with his wide appointing, removal, and budgetary authority and his substantial political influence will add the *prestige of the office* to his power and can expect significantly to control the administration and affect the state's program and policy. In states which give the governor few direct controls of administrative agencies (for example, restrict his appointing and removal of personnel, limit his budgetary and fiscal powers, and restrain his possible political influence through giving him only a two-year term or placing limitations on the number of terms he may serve), the governor's greatest asset may be this *prestige of the office.* On a state occasion or where ever the governor appears, he is first. Few state department heads, regardless of the extent of legal control in the governor's hands, wish to appear in opposition to the state's chief executive. After all, the governor is the state-wide elected head of the government. Despite the attitude at times of the administration that "governors come and go, we stay on," agency directors at least in the less controversial areas recognize the headship of the governor. Some individual governors have used this "prestige of office" to gain programs and to build their own position and that of their party.

Law-enforcement powers. Many governors may find the phrase "take care that the laws are faithfully executed" more constitutional rhetoric than the reality of power. Except as he works through the several state agencies, the elected attorney general, the bureau of traffic control, or the state crime bureau (if such exists), the governor takes little part in direct law enforcement. Governors can and, in emergencies, do call out the state militia. The national Constitution (Art. IV, sec. 2, par. 2) gives governors the power to demand the return of criminals who have fled to other states.

In a considerable majority of the states, the governor has the power of pardon, subject to regulation by law. His authority includes usually the powers of outright pardon, reprieve, commutation or reduction of sentence, and parole, and extends to all persons convicted of any crime or misdemeanor under the state laws, but it does not extend to cases of impeachment. Greater knowledge of criminology, psychology, psychiatry, and other fields has led many governors to depend increasingly on the recommendations of specialists in the departments controlling the state's criminal institutions.

The Governor and the Office

While it is helpful for analytical purposes to pick the governorship apart and to examine separately the various pieces and powers, it is also desirable to try to see the office as a whole and the man who occupies it, as a combined entity. Particular powers may be inadequate for this and that purpose, but put together the various powers, the prestige of the governorship, the leadership that is expected from its incumbent, and a shrewd, genial, dynamic man in the office, and the combination becomes an engine of public power that can accomplish great things. Theodore Roosevelt, Charles Evans Hughes, and Al Smith of New York, Woodrow Wilson of New Jersey, Robert M. La Follette of Wisconsin, and many others have shown the potentialities of the office. It is, after all, one of the greatest offices within the gift of the American people, a challenge and an opportunity to men of the highest talents.

REFERENCES

Council of State Governments, *The Governors of the States, 1900-1950*. Chicago: Council of State Governments. Governors' Conference, *Proceedings* (annual). Chicago.

Highsaw, Robert B., "The Southern Governor—Challenge to the Strong Executive Theme?" 19 *Public Administration Review* (Winter 1959), 7-11.

Kammerer, Gladys M., "The Governor as Chief Administrator in Kentucky," 16 *Journal of Politics* (May 1954), 236-256.

Lipson, Leslie, *The American Governor from Figurehead to Leader*. Chicago: University of Chicago Press, 1939.

Ransone, Coleman B., Jr., *The Office of Governor in the United States*. University, Ala.: University of Alabama Press, 1956.

Young, William H., "The Development of the Governorship," 31 *State Government* (Summer 1958), 178-183.

CHAPTER 13

State Courts

IN EVERY STATE there are two systems of courts, those established by the Constitution and the laws of the United States, and those provided for by the constitution and laws of the state. The United States courts are represented in each state primarily by the federal district courts, but the United States Courts of Appeal and Supreme Court also reach into each state to bring up and try cases on appeal.

Each state also has a full system of courts from a state supreme court down perhaps to the justices of the peace. Although citizens often think of county and municipal courts as "local courts," in a constitutional sense all the so-called local courts authorized by state law are state courts. Justices of the peace and municipal judges, for example, perform their functions within prescribed local areas such as counties and cities and are locally elected. In law, however, they are only parts of the state court system, their decisions are subject to review by higher state courts, and they can be reorganized or abolished by state law without any veto by local city or county authorities. It is probably only because they are politically so well entrenched that the local courts in many states have not been more substantially reorganized by state authority.

271

★ Dual system of courts

There are various relationships between the federal courts and the state and local courts, as in the removal of certain cases from state to federal courts, federal-court application of state laws, and state-court cooperation in the enforcement of United States laws.[1] In certain types of cases litigants have a choice between the two sets of courts. This raises the question of jurisdiction.

The term *jurisdiction* as applied to the courts means basically the right to speak the law or to say what the law is. In the theory of the separation of powers, the judicial branch of government, comprising the regular courts, merely ascertains what the existing law is and applies it to specific "cases or controversies" that come before the courts in a prescribed manner, whereas the legislative branch makes new laws, and the executive branch enforces statute laws and judicial decisions. Although this theory breaks down somewhat in practice, it is sufficiently accurate for present purposes as indicating the primary role of the courts. They do handle cases and they do say what the law is when they decide cases.

The jurisdiction of a given court is further defined in two ways. First, there is a territorial limitation to jurisdiction: a state court ordinarily has no jurisdiction outside the state; a county court usually has none outside the county. Secondly, the jurisdiction is defined in terms of the types of cases that may be decided by a court. A probate court, for example, is usually limited by law to deciding cases of wills, estates, guardianships, and closely related matters.

★ State and federal division of jurisdiction

The Constitution and laws of the United States set the outside limits of the jurisdiction of the state courts. Under acts of Congress the federal district courts have exclusive jurisdiction over practically all crimes committed against the United States, and thus the state courts are without authority to try them. On the other hand, cases involving charges of crime against a state are usually tried in the state's own courts, but in some instances (as where an official of the United States is involved) such cases may be removed to a federal court for trial. In civil matters—that is, where no crime or misdemeanor is charged—most cases arising under United States laws are tried in federal courts, but there are many exceptions. Cases under the Federal Employers' Liability Act (injuries to railroad employees), fed-

---

[1] See Mitchell Wendell, *Relations between the Federal and State Courts* (New York: Columbia University Press, 1950); and Forrest Talbott, *Intergovernmental Relations and the Courts* (Minneapolis: University of Minnesota Press, 1950).

eral rent-control and public-housing laws, to give a few examples, are handled in large numbers in state and local courts. This means that the state judges have to be familiar with much United States law in addition to state law.

Where there is "diversity of citizenship"—that is, where persons from two or more states are involved in a suit—and the amount in controversy is more than $10,000, the parties may have the case tried in a federal district court, even though only state law is involved. The act of Congress on this subject is supported by the Constitution and by long usage. It was feared that the state courts would show bias against the rights of persons from other states, and it was felt that only a federal court would provide an impartial trial in such cases. Such a case may start in a state court, but, if it does, the defendant usually can have it removed to a United States district court. On the other hand, if the amount involved is valued at less than $10,000, the case remains in the state courts. Furthermore, when a United States court handles such a "diversity case," it must apply the state law as declared by competent courts of the state concerned, but if the issue is one on which no important state court has made a decision, the federal court must decide it as a matter of state law to the best of its ability. In this way and to this extent the federal district court merely serves as another court of the state in which it sits.[2] Clearly, then, the federal judges have to know the state laws as well as the United States laws, just as the state judges to some extent have to know and apply both bodies of law.

★ Other intercourt relations

Appeals may be made to the United States Supreme Court from the highest state courts in which the decision can be made on all questions involving the interpretation of the United States Constitution, laws, and treaties. In the decision of cases and the development of law, therefore, the United States and state courts are interdependent and complementary—but more or less at arm's length. The United States judges do not really supervise the work of the state judges, nor do the higher state courts supervise the lower courts, in the sense in which there is supervision in the administrative branch of government. Each court works by itself, deciding the cases that come to it, and when a case has been decided a court is usually done with it, except as the parties or attorneys may act to get a retrial or to take an appeal.

In the early years of the United States, it was hard for the state judges to accept the idea of federal judges coming into their territory to decide cases, and their own decisions being appealed on federal questions

[2] Erie Railroad Co. v. Tompkins, 304 U. S. 64 (1938).

to the United States Supreme Court. There was, indeed, a good deal of bitterness in the intercourt relations of those days. If this has not been entirely eliminated, it has at least been reduced. In most states the federal and state courts work side by side in fairly complete harmony. Congress deserves much of the credit for this result; it has been very careful to define the jurisdiction of the United States courts so as not to encroach unduly upon the rights claimed by the states.

The Organization of State and Local Courts

The central hierarchy of courts, from the highest state appellate court down, is set forth for each state in its constitution. The legislature is generally empowered to create other minor or special courts as needed, such as the municipal courts that are set up in urban areas. The general legislative power extends also to the enactment of supplementary general laws on the election and payment of judges, on various court employees and courthouses, on rules of evidence, practice, and procedure, and even to some extent on the jurisdiction of courts within the constitutional limits and on the power of the courts to issue various writs or orders. The statutory and constitutional provisions are amplified and interpreted by many supreme court decisions, and therefore the highest judges are to some extent masters of what the state court system shall be.

The state court systems present many variations in details and in names, but certain features are common to all.[3]

★ A supreme appellate court

In each state there is usually a single highest court of appeals for all kinds of state cases. This is generally called the state *supreme court,* and so here, but in Kentucky, Maryland, and New York it is named the court of appeals, and in Maine and Massachusetts the supreme judicial court, and there are other minor variations in its title. In Texas a separate court of criminal appeals has the final decision in criminal cases, while the supreme court has like authority in civil cases.

The usual supreme court consists of from three to nine justices, five and seven being the most common numbers. Normally it sits at the capitol, but about one sixth of the states provide for it to hold sessions also at a few other leading centers. In over one third of the states, also, the court is organized into divisions that meet separately to hear and decide cases,

[3] The best current source of information on court organization in the states is *The Book of the States.* See, for example, the 1958-59 volume, pp. 95-108.

three justices constituting the usual number for a division. Each supreme court has a chief justice, who is the highest judicial officer of the state. In nine states the chief justice is elected directly to that post; in fourteen the position goes by seniority, usually seniority in service; in another ten states the governor appoints or designates the chief justice; in fourteen states the justices elect him; and the remaining states follow a variety of other practices. The terms of the justices vary generally from six to twelve years, six being the most common, but Vermont sets a two-year term, and several states run above twelve years up to life or "good behavior." The salaries of the justices are relatively high. In most states the justices are elected by the voters, on either a party ballot or on a ballot without party designation, but in Alaska, Hawaii, New Jersey, Delaware, and many of the New England states they are appointed by the governor, and there are other methods of selection in several states.

The jurisdiction of the supreme court is limited almost entirely to deciding cases on appeals from the lower state courts, primarily from the courts of general original jurisdiction, to be discussed below. In some states they also decide questions of law on direct appeal from state regulatory bodies, and they also have a little original jurisdiction here and there in cases of great public importance. In such cases they may have to decide matters of fact as well as law, and without the aid of a jury. Apparently, however, over 99 percent of their work consists in deciding cases on appeals, and in these cases they are concerned mainly with questions of law. The state supreme court is, therefore, the final interpreter in the *legal* sense of the meaning of the state constitution, of the state statutes, of subordinate legislation such as administrative regulations and city ordinances, of the common law, and also of its own previous decisions. As already indicated, even the United States courts are bound by state supreme court decisions when passing on questions of state law. Because of their great importance, state supreme court decisions are printed and published in all states, whereas lower court decisions as a rule are not published. For many of the basic courses in the law schools, the state supreme court decisions supply the most extensive materials.

★ Courts of general original jurisdiction

Below the highest courts of appeal each state has a tier of trial courts of general original jurisdiction in which practically any type of case may be begun and tried. These courts, sometimes called general trial courts, are given different names, such as *district, circuit,* and *superior* courts, but in New York this level of trial courts is called the supreme court. These courts serve districts that may embrace only a single county, and large urban counties will have a number of judges. But generally the districts consist of several counties, so that the judge has to go on circuit from one county courthouse to another, holding "terms" of court a few days here, and a few weeks there, according to a schedule or calendar enacted by the legislature. At each county courthouse where court is held there is, as a rule, a resident clerk. A single judge holds court, but juries are impaneled to pass on the facts in criminal and civil cases, as required by the constitution and laws. In most states the judges of these courts are elected by the voters, but they are appointed in about the same states that appoint supreme court justices. Their terms are most commonly six or four years but vary from two years to life, being only a little shorter on the average than the terms of supreme court justices. In salaries they fall below the supreme court justices but rank high among state officers generally. The judges of these courts and of the state supreme courts are required to be lawyers ("learned in the law"), whereas in many minor courts there is no such general requirement.

Many of these courts take certain small cases on appeal from the justice of the peace and municipal courts, but their main work is the trial in the first instance of the more important civil and criminal causes. The dividing line between their jurisdiction and that of the minor courts varies from state to state, and between rural and urban places within the state. The minor courts (to be discussed below) handle most of the smaller cases, both criminal (misdemeanors) and civil. In the rural districts and villages, for example, the justices of the peace may have jurisdiction to decide misdemeanor cases where the penalty is not over $100 fine or ninety days in the workhouse, and civil cases where the amount in controversy is not over $100 and where the title to real estate is not involved. In many cities, however, the municipal courts handle civil cases involving up to $500, $1000, or even more, depending on the state law. All cases involving more severe penalties or involving larger amounts in controversy, ordinarily will go to the general trial courts here being discussed, except as there may be separate courts for domestic relations and other special fields. Cases involving property rights, business and other contracts, damage suits, divorce, and many other important subjects are decided in these courts in the first instance. Lawyers generally are more interested in these courts and in the state supreme court than in any others, because in and through them they do most of their trial business. The states themselves provide more financial support for these courts of general original jurisdiction than for almost any other class of courts, except the state supreme courts which are supported entirely from the state treasury.

★ Other state courts

Between their supreme courts and their courts of general original jurisdiction, ten of the more populous states have intermediate courts of appeal. These are designed both to relieve the supreme court of a great burden of cases and to save time and expense by having appeals decided closer to the origin of the suit.

Some Southern or Eastern states also have separate "chancery" courts with original jurisdiction in equity cases and certain related matters, leaving the courts of general original jurisidiction in those states to concentrate primarily on criminal cases and on civil common law and statutory actions. The branch of law known as *equity* was developed in England long ago to provide substantial justice in cases where the common-law rules, which had become highly technical, could not afford relief. Certain agreements that fell short of being contracts could be enforced in equity or chancery but not in common-law courts. Furthermore, equity rules provided preventive measures in some instances, the writ of injunction being a well-known equity writ to prevent irreparable damage. One who violates an injunction becomes punishable by the judge for contempt of court. In most states equity and common law have been incorporated into the same general code of laws and entrusted to the same judges, but the states with separate chancery courts still keep to some extent the old separation.

Nearly half the states also have probate or surrogate courts for cases of wills, estates, guardianship, and the administration of estates. These courts are at the county level. In the other states, such cases and administration are handled by courts of general original jurisdiction or by county courts. Whatever court does the work, the administration of wills, estates, and guardianship is different from ordinary trial work. It involves much follow-up to see that guardians and administrators do their work properly and do not enrich themselves at the expense of the wards and the estates entrusted to them.

★ Justices of peace and other minor courts

At the bottom of the judicial hierarchy is a wide array of courts that handle minor cases in small communities, ranging from counties and cities down through villages, towns, and townships to various other sub-divisions of counties called justice precincts, magisterial districts, judicial townships, and so on. Many of these courts have jurisdiction in both civil and criminal cases, where the amount in controversy or penalty is small. The names of these courts vary—justice or justice-of-the-peace courts, municipal courts, small-claims courts, police courts, and so on. Most of these are not "courts of record." This does not mean that they do not keep records, but rather that they are not all separately established by law with the full complement of judicial attributes and powers as a court according to the common law. A justice-of-the-peace court, for example, is practically the same as the justice himself. It exists or not according to local choice, and it does not exist at all if no one is elected to the office—nor is any great harm done to the public by the failure to elect. Municipal courts in many cities, on the other hand, have almost as important a status as the district or circuit courts in the state, and have rather full complements of supporting officials such as a clerk, a reporter, and a bailiff. In the minor courts many cases, such as traffic-ordinance violations and small claims, are settled without the intervention of lawyers, although at any time a party may employ one.

The judge or justice of a minor court is ordinarily chosen by popular election for a relatively short term. Justices of the peace are generally paid by fees, while municipal judges receive salaries for part or full-time service. Justices of the peace are generally not required to be lawyers, nor are judges of municipal courts in some states.

The number of justices of the peace is larger than the number in any other category of judges, but everywhere it falls short of the potential or legally authorized number. In many small communities there is too little judicial business to keep a justice even moderately occupied. On the other hand, municipal courts (of various names) in the larger cities are among the busiest courts in the land. They handle an astounding number of petty cases along with some of considerable importance. Misdemeanors, including infractions of city ordinances and traffic laws, rent and ejectment cases, and numerous small claims bulk large in the statistics of these courts.

★ Multiplicity of courts

Besides these more common types of courts there are many courts of other names and types, such as domestic relations, small claims, and juvenile courts, that occur in some states. The fact seems to be that the states have not only many types of courts for various purposes but also considerable numbers of separate units in their court systems. Wherever this situation prevails there is some difficulty in keeping clear the jurisdictional boundaries and even more in obtaining enough competent judges and court officers to perform the judicial functions satisfactorily. Full statistics on all the fifty state-local court systems are not available, but it seems probable that the average number of courts in each of the states exceeds eight hundred. The largest number would be the widely scattered justice courts, but usually each county and each city of any size have separate courts plus the general trial courts and the supreme court.

In general the development of court systems has been similar to that of state and local administrative systems. Every new judicial need, whether local or state-wide, has usually been met by the creation of a new court with its own limited jurisdiction. The early state constitutions seemed to provide for rather simple judicial systems, but with the passage of time and the creation of new courts the arrangements became more complex and apparently less systematic. Jurisdictional overlappings between courts were not entirely avoidable, and even the lawyers have difficulty threading their ways through the judicial mazes.

Court Procedures

Courts deal primarily with law, and from one viewpoint laws may be classified into *written* and *unwritten*. The written laws—legislation in a broad sense—include written constitutions, statutes, treaties, administrative rules and regulations, and local ordinances and bylaws. These vary in their degree of authority, and the higher generally prevail over the lower levels in cases of conflict, but any one of these classes of written law may be passed upon, interpreted, and applied, in any court from the justice of the peace to the Supreme Court. In addition to these classes of written laws, there is a large body of court-made unwritten law to be found in the decisions of the judges not only in recent time but back through the centuries. It is not at all unusual even today to have the judges refer to some rule made in English or American courts a century or more ago as applicable to a modern case. This body of old rules, including the principles of certain statutes no longer in existence and embracing also what is known as equity, is sometimes called the "common law," although this is a broad and loose use of the term. Many court rules of procedure stem from the common law.

★ *Sources of procedural rules*

The rules of procedure applied in state and local courts are derived principally from four different sources: (1) written constitutions, (2) statutes, (3) judicial decisions, and (4) formal court-made rules.

The United States Constitution makes a general requirement applicable to all courts that they shall conform to "due process of law" (5th and 14th Amendments), but it does not lay down any specific rules for state and local court procedure. The Supreme Court has held, however, that a state court trial does not accord with due process if the procedure used violates "that fundamental fairness essential to the very concept of justice." [4] For example, to deny the accused the right of counsel in criminal cases involving capital punishment, or to permit the use of confessions extracted from the accused by torture, is not due process.[5] In most matters, however, a state may decide its own rules of procedure in both civil and criminal cases.[6]

The state's own written constitution sets forth a number of the basic rules of court procedure, particularly in its bill of rights and judiciary articles. Here such matters as the right of jury trial and the rules against unreasonable searches and seizures, self-incrimination, and double jeopardy are usually stated. State statutes have also from the beginning of American independence regulated state and local court procedures. Both the constitutional provisions and the statutes have in turn been interpreted by the state courts. The common law has been for the courts "the grand reservoir" of procedural rules. State legislation on court procedures has, in general, been interpreted and applied by the courts in the light of the common law that the judges learned in their first study of law and accepted as the basis of their practice as lawyers. Since every court in a sense has made its own interpretations, uniformity of procedure and practice does not exist even in a single state, much less from state to state, where constitutions and statutes also differ.

To provide greater uniformity of procedure within each state and to eliminate various archaic procedures that cause delay and expense have become two objectives of modern judicial reform. But such reforms are not readily forthcoming from state legislatures, where very few members are expert in judicial procedures and where other issues usually dominate thinking and action. It has seemed logical, therefore, to confer the rule-making power on the courts themselves, and particularly on the supreme court or a state judicial council speaking and acting for the whole state. One distinguished jurist argued, indeed, that the rule-making power over judicial procedure belongs inherently to the courts and that the legislature, federal or state, "exceeds its constitutional power when it attempts to impose upon the judiciary any rules for the dispatch of the judiciary's duties; and that therefore all legislatively declared rules for procedure, civil or criminal, in the courts, are void, except such as are expressly stated in the Constitution." [7] This truly astounding doctrine rests upon

---

4 Lisenba v. California, 314 U. S. 219 (1942).
5 Powell v. State of Alabama, 287 U. S. 45 (1932); Brown v. State of Mississippi, 297 U. S. 278 (1936).
6 Palko v. State of Connecticut, 302 U. S. 319 (1937).
7 John H. Wigmore in 20 Journal of the American Judicature Society (1936), 159-160; 24 ibid. (1940), 70-71.

the theory that, under the separation of powers, since the courts may not tell the legislative branch how it shall proceed, the legislature shall not dictate to the courts, and that the judicial power vested in the courts includes the entire power to make rules of procedure. If this contention is sound, then presumably the legislative branch has no power to regulate the procedure of the executive branch either, since it also is one of the three equal branches of the government. Such a doctrine, if put into effect, would not only wipe out hundreds of pages of state and federal legislation regulating judicial procedure but would also inferentially split the state's legislative power among the three branches instead of leaving the legislature as the main source of written law under the constitution. Logic, long usage, and acquiescence by the courts fully support the power of the legislative branch to make rules of judicial procedure.[8] Furthermore, the best argument for letting the state supreme court make the rules of judicial procedure is that the court can do the job better than the legislature, being more expert and more closely in touch with procedural problems, and it is not necessary to assert an inherent power in the courts to make the rules.

Today the states are moving toward the delegation of this power to the state supreme court, although there is much to be said in favor of vesting the power in a state judicial council that represents all important levels in the court system. California entrusts the power to its judicial council. New Jersey, whose 1947 constitutional provision was quoted above, vests it by constitutional provision in the state supreme court, and so do Maryland, Michigan, and Texas—the latter as to civil actions only. Numerous other states now delegate the power to the state supreme court by statute, and this would seem to be the preferable method, since it leaves the legislature as the source of state legislation with a potential revisory power over the rules made by the court.

We now turn from the sources and nature of the rules of judicial procedure to a summary statement of the content of the rules in ordinary practice. The variations from state to state are, as usual, very considerable.

★ Civil procedure

In civil cases, the parties appear as private individuals. The government may be one of the parties, but if so, it presents itself as any individual before the court and expects only a civil judgment or decree if it wins.

The plaintiff is, of course, the party that brings the suit; the defendant, the one that defends. When the plaintiff is the winner, there may

---

[8] Charles H. Beardsley, in 24 *ibid.*, 115-117, also 101-102; Silas A. Harris, "The Rule-making Power," American Bar Association, *Judicial Administration Monographs*, Series A, No. 1.

be a judgment requiring payment of money, but that will depend on the way in which the plaintiff's case was formulated and the remedy available to him. In matters of civil litigation, the true functions of the government (except where it is a party) are simply (1) to provide an impartial and competent tribunal to settle the case, (2) to provide an economical, expeditious, and reliable procedure so that the time and money of the litigants will not be wasted, and (3) to provide means of enforcing the decisions reached.

Beginning of civil cases. Although the law permits individuals to appear for themselves in civil as well as in criminal cases, for important litigation the individual employs an attorney. The latter is considered to be, in a sense, an officer of the court and is obligated to see that the case is properly conducted and that the fullest possible light is thrown on the facts and the law involved to procure a legal and just decision. He has a confidential relation to his client and an obligation to do his best, in good faith, for the client's interests. Following adequate consultation with his client, the attorney for the plaintiff draws up the complaint, bill, or petition to the court and deposits it with the clerk. Notice is thereupon served upon the defendant in the suit, who, if he has not already done so, also employs an attorney to represent him. The latter draws up an answer to the complaint. There may be several exchanges, all in due legal form and through the medium of the clerk of the court and those who serve papers for the court. A difference or "joinder of issues" is presently reached that gives a basis for the suit. If no settlement is reached out of court, the clerk of court lists the case for trial.

There is today a growing emphasis in the courts upon pretrial conferences between the judge and the attorneys for the parties in an endeavor to reach an agreement on all the undisputed facts and even on a settlement without trial, if that proves possible. The courts that have seriously experimented with pretrial conferences have generally reported favorable results with a considerable saving of time and expense for the court and the parties.

Jury trial in state courts. State constitutional provisions also usually guarantee the right of jury trial in civil cases, as that right previously existed or as it existed at common law. By court decisions or by constitutional provision, a waiver of the right is permitted. Many states have also provided for juries of small size (six to eight men) in minor civil cases, and even in some important ones, and some states have provided that if three fourths or five sixths of the jury can agree, they can render a verdict. Most civil cases in both state and federal courts are tried without a jury. The expense of the jury procedure, which falls upon the parties, the loss of time in getting a decision, the difficulty of explaining the facts to the ordinary jury (particularly where rather intricate technical or financial matters are involved) make it undesirable to use a jury. Indeed, jury trial in civil cases is generally on the wane. Certain types of lawyers, with a power to sway juries, still like to use them, however, especially in motor-vehicle accident and other personal-injury cases.

Decision and enforcement. When a jury has rendered its verdict in civil cases, the judge gives the decision of the court. If the jury finds for the defendant, the case is ended, except for possible appeals. If it finds for the plaintiff, a judgment is given in his favor. The *judgment* is a court order that authorizes the sheriff or other officer, after certain formalities, to force the defendant to pay or otherwise satisfy the plaintiff. He may seize and sell the goods of the defendant, if necessary, in order to raise the money needed. Of course, the defendant may have little or nothing, and then the judgment is defeated.

Civil cases in minor courts. Hundreds of thousands of small civil suits are settled every year in the minor courts, such as justice and municipal courts. If treated like more important cases, the expense of handling such a small case as that involving a grocery, fuel, or rent bill, wages, or a similar item would be practically prohibitive. For this reason state laws provide for the larger cities special branches of the municipal court known as "small claims courts." In these, individuals are assisted to make out their own papers; and the judge, sitting frequently in the evening, is able to dispose quickly and inexpensively of a considerable number at one sitting. The fees for such service are kept at the minimum. However, in magistrates' courts and justice-of-the-peace courts in the industrial districts and in the neighborhood of large cities in several states, civil justice is a very different thing. The judges in some of these courts, profiting by the fees from every case brought before them and sometimes in league with the attorneys for the plaintiffs, have been found to render more than 99 percent of the decisions in favor of the plaintiffs—and in such districts, "J. P." has come to mean "judgment for the plaintiff." [9]

Such obvious abuse of power at the expense of the poorer classes is paralleled by the handling of traffic cases and other minor infractions of the law in certain small towns and suburban places where the "joy rider"

[9] W. Brooke Graves, *American State Government,* 4th ed. (Boston: D. C. Heath, 1953), p. 596.

from the city or the tourist from another state is an easy victim. In many states the local treasuries benefit from all fines imposed, while the justices of the peace and the constables who bring in those charged with misdemeanors also get their fees. These occasional scandals in the administration of justice at the bottom of the judicial ladder are exceedingly hard to eliminate. One alternative is, of course, to abolish such courts and to turn all such cases over to a municipal or county court, with a salaried judge and constable, preferably working on a full-time basis.

Equity procedure. The United States Courts, and those states that have adopted codes in which common law and equity are combined, have reduced but not entirely eliminated the distinction between law and equity procedure. In general, equity is available to the litigant only when he can show the court that he has no adequate remedy at law. It can be used to prevent or ward off injuries where the damage would be irreparable. The proceedings are largely if not entirely in writing. There is no jury. The plaintiff through his attorney presents a bill stating his case and the remedy to which he thinks he is entitled. This bill is served on the other party or parties, and the latter makes reply. A definite conflict upon any particular point is not necessary, and the judge is not limited to awarding any specific remedy. Writs of mandamus (compelling action) or injunction (preventing action) are two of the best-known reliefs an equity court can extend a plaintiff.

★ Procedure in criminal cases

The criminal law, in the broad sense, may be thought of as covering both felonies or the more serious criminal offenses, and misdemeanors or the less serious, with an intermediate class of gross misdemeanors in most places. Felonies are usually punishable by a year or more of imprisonment or by a high fine or both. There is no single body of criminal law for the United States as a whole. Congress has defined a series of specific crimes against the United States, such as counterfeiting, robbery of the mails, using the mails to defraud, and taking stolen motor vehicles from one state into another. Each state defines for itself the more common crimes, such as murder, manslaughter, robbery, and arson, and where the state statutes fail to cover a crime adequately, the common-law definitions are used.

Classes of crimes. Since there is no single, unified body of criminal laws, with uniform definitions for the same crime in each state, the Federal Bureau of Investigation in the United States Department of Justice has prepared, with the aid of the International Association of Chiefs of Police, its own classification of certain types of crime in the United States, as follows: "criminal homicide, including (*a*) murder, non-negligent manslaughter, and (*b*) manslaughter by negligence; rape; robbery; aggravated assault; burglary—breaking or entering; larceny—theft; and auto theft." It may be noted that this classification does not include forgery, embezzlement, destruction of public property, election frauds, and various other crimes. In total numbers ordinary larcenies or thefts come first, followed by burglaries, automobile thefts, robberies, and aggravated assaults.

First steps in criminal procedure.   A crime is "known to the police" when it has been reported by a citizen or a police officer and recorded in some police-department complaint book. Arrest of the suspected person may accompany or immediately follow the report, but more commonly a search for the culprit is necessary. The first step in the legal procedure that follows is making out a formal complaint. This can be done by the person who has suffered as a result of the crime, or it can be done by the police officer or the prosecuting attorney or other officer. In earlier times the citizen himself was both complainant and prosecutor, but provision is now made for a public prosecutor in every county or judicial district, and that officer (called county attorney, district attorney, or prosecutor) now bears the brunt of the prosecution.

When the suspect has been arrested, he has a brief hearing before a justice of the peace, municipal judge, or other judicial officer having the powers of a *committing magistrate* to determine whether there is enough evidence to justify holding him for indictment and trial. If there is, bail is usually arranged; but in cases of murder and other *capital cases*, bail may be refused and the suspect jailed. At this stage he is entitled to get in touch with an attorney to defend him, and there may be a habeas corpus proceeding before some higher judge to determine whether he is being legally detained.

The grand jury.   The next stage in the process is the preparation of an information, presentment, or indictment—these being various forms of legal documents in which formal accusation is made that the person named, or Joe Doe, has committed a certain crime at a specified time and place. Indictments and presentments are products of the work of grand juries. The grand jury hears enough of the evidence to convince it that there is a good case against the person accused, and then by a majority vote authorizes the indictment, which is signed as a *true bill* by the foreman of the jury. This formal accusation on the part of the state against the person accused furnishes the basis for the trial. When the jury on its own responsibility presents an accusation against any person, the document is called a *presentment*.

The grand jury originated as a means of getting the opinion of the community as to whether a crime had been committed and if so, by whom. It gave and still gives considerable power to the lay public over the prosecution of criminals. In its original form the grand jury was a fairly large body, and it still consists of from sixteen to twenty-three members in some states, with smaller numbers authorized in others. Its proceedings are secret and necessarily limited to hearing primarily one side of the case. It calls in witnesses, but the accused person and his attorney are not heard.

Procedure by information. Because of the expense, the delay, and the frequent obstruction of justice resulting from the use of the grand jury (obstruction arising, for example, when community opinion is such that no grand jury will indict violators of liquor laws, or persons of great political influence), about a quarter of the states have made the system optional, not compulsory. Where the grand jury is not required, the prosecuting attorney formulates the accusation in criminal cases in a form known as the "information." Some states have gone very far in substituting informations for indictments. The indictment procedure is reserved for very serious cases like murders. It is not unconstitutional for the states to use the information method instead of indictment, but this change of method puts tremendous power into the hands of the prosecuting attorney.

Arraignment and trial. Following the filing of the indictment or information with the clerk of the proper court, on a day set the criminal case comes on for trial. The accused person is then "arraigned" before the court, the indictment is read or summarized by the clerk, and the accused person makes his plea of guilty, not guilty, or one of the less important alternative pleas allowed by the law. The attorney for the defense may promptly "demur" to the indictment, alleging that it is defective or stating that the facts are insufficient to warrant the prosecution, and in some cases the charge will be thrown out by the judge at this point. This is a rare occurrence, but defense attorneys, using every trick of the game, are not deterred by the prospect of being overruled by the judge. Some cases are dismissed at the suggestion of the prosecutor, who finds that his case is not strong enough or that his key witnesses have died or disappeared. Far the most common disposition, however, is through the plea of guilty—over half of all cases in some states. The remaining cases go to trial.

Jury trial in criminal cases. The state constitutions guarantee the right to a jury trial in felony cases, with very few exceptions. As a rule, however, the accused person has a right to waive jury trial. Where the jury is employed in federal criminal cases, it must be a twelve-member jury, and it must reach a unanimous verdict if it is to convict a person. The states also generally follow this old common law rule, except, as already noted, in some states for certain less important cases.

Juries in civil and criminal cases, and grand juries as well, are impaneled or drawn by summons from the proper officer of the court: a clerk of court, jury commissioner, or sheriff, for example. Tax lists and the registers of voters are used, and the names are presumably drawn at random. It is very certain, however, that in some places there are abuses. Persons to whom the daily fee of $2 to $4 means a living often find ways of getting on the panels; in some places it has even been considered proper to use the lists of the unemployed, in order to reduce relief expenditures by giving jury work to the indigent. Such practices are not common, but they serve to lower the level of ability of important bodies that at best do not draw the most outstanding persons in the community. On the other hand, New York has a so-called "blue ribbon" jury law for a more selective drawing of jurors, and it is noticeable that in many communities a more substantial class of citizens is drawn for grand-jury than for petit-jury service.

When a jury case, either criminal or civil, is begun, names are drawn one by one from the panel that has been summoned. There follows a certain amount of questioning to determine the fitness of each potential juror. Sometimes in criminal cases the selection of the jury takes a very long time; each side is allowed a certain number of "peremptory challenges" or refusals to accept jurors without cause given, while the number of "challenges for cause" is practically unlimited.

Procedure in misdemeanor cases. The foregoing discussion of criminal-court procedure relates almost entirely to felony cases. Of course, the great majority of offenses are less serious and are designated as misdemeanors. At the common law, it was not necessary to have a jury for each misdemeanor case, and the same rule prevails generally today. It makes no difference whether the offense is one against state law (such as petty theft) or against some local ordinance (such as disorderly conduct or a traffic violation). Misdemeanors which include many traffic offenses, generally may be tried by "summary process," without indictment by a grand jury, and without trial by a petit jury. The number of such cases is astonishingly large. In most cities these cases are settled with the utmost expedition—and a cash register. In some a check by mail covering the fine is sufficient. Prosecutions are handled by the police alone, or by the city attorney, and the decisions are made by a single judge in each case. The majority of citizens receive their impressions of justice through experiences in such courts.

The Movement for Judicial Reform

In 1906 a young Nebraska lawyer, Roscoe Pound, who later became dean of the Harvard Law School, addressed the American Bar Association on the subject: "Causes of Popular Dissatisfaction with the Administration of Justice." [10] His address, which was a devastating arraignment of archaic court organization and procedures in the American states, appears to have had tremendous influence. Other critics followed in his footsteps, and soon a great movement for judicial reform was begun. Though the results in the following years were rather meager, the movement has grown and spread. From coast to coast leading lawyers, judges, and law teachers have taken up the challenge and are working valiantly and intelligently for the reform of the courts and their procedure. Legislative action looking toward the improvement of judicial procedure and administration is enacted in ever-increasing volume. The American Judicature Society and the American Bar Association, to mention only two, have brought forward numerous proposals to make the courts more efficient, more speedy, and more just.

For at least two decades before his death in 1957, Arthur T. Vanderbilt, for a time chief justice of the New Jersey Supreme Court, wrote, lectured, and worked for reforms in the administration of justice in this country. A recent summary of his essentials of sound administration of justice included: (1) A simple system of courts; (2) competent judges and jurors; (3) effective use of judicial manpower through the administrative head of the courts; (4) simplified procedures to secure decisions on the merits, without delay, technicalities or surprise; and (5) an effective appellate practice.[11] The Model State Constitution and the new constitution of Alaska probably come closest to setting out a judicial structure which meets Justice Vanderbilt's idea for the necessary reforms. Many states, however, have looked at their court organization and operation in late years and have made some adjustments—California, Missouri, New Jersey, and Wisconsin among others.

[10] This address was reprinted in 20 *Journal of the American Judicature Society* (1937), 176-187. See also in the same issue pp. 223-236, an article by William L. Ransom, another former president of the American Bar Association.
[11] *The Book of the States, 1958-59*, p. 95.

★ Meeting the objectives of judicial reform

1. A simple system of courts.   Just as the administrative side of government tended to become very complex and agencies tended to have overlapping responsibilities, so have most judicial systems with the great increase in population and types of cases. The standard original court system of the nineteenth century of local justices of the peace, a county probate court, a general trial court, and a supreme court has been added to. The resulting multiplicity of courts with overlapping jurisdiction has produced confusion for the individual and for his attorney on occasion. Not fewer judges but fewer courts is the need.

2. Competent judges.   The complexity of cases appealed to state and national supreme courts demands long judicial experience and training, and many of our highest court judges well meet these standards. At the lower court levels however (where most citizens have experience with the judicial system), the judges sometimes are inexperienced and fail to provide the standards of justice needed.

Competence in judges presumably includes (*a*) integrity and independence, (*b*) technical ability and learning, and (*c*) social vision and grasp of the problems of justice as distinguished from law. As in many human matters, these are necessarily relative virtues. In approaching a judicial problem, a judge can no more divorce himself from his own background than can a highly conscientious legislator or executive. Within these terms, however, independence from pressure and broad social vision have some objective meaning as do technical ability and learning. A judge must be free to decide cases according to law where the law is clear, and according to law, reason, and justice where the law needs to be supplemented. If he is subject to political pressures because he owes his office to a political boss or ring, if he is controlled by powerful interests in the economic world, whether of capital or labor, or if he is threatened by the executive or legislative branch of the government, he will find it hard to give honest, even-handed justice.

Argument continues whether appointed or elected judges are typically most competent. Actually the term of office ("good behavior," or ten- and twelve-year terms in contrast to two or four) and the traditions of the state or community as to judicial partisanship, re-election of sitting judges, prestige of judicial office, and salary may be of equal importance in procuring competent judges. A major question of each state's system would seem to be, "Do most lawyers of outstanding legal ability with high reputations for personal integrity seek and serve in the state's judicial posts?" If the majority of lawyers highly regarded in the profession do not serve in judicial posts during their lifetimes, judges in the state will not measure up to the standard indicated—whether the selection is by appointment, election, or some combination of the two.

Hawaii constitutionally sets up only a supreme court and circuit courts (giving the legislature authority to establish others) and provides:

> The governor shall nominate and, by and with the advice and consent of the senate, appoint the justices of the supreme court and the judges of the circuit courts. No nomination shall be sent to the senate, and no interim appointment shall be made when the senate is not in session, until after ten days' public notice by the governor. (Hawaii Constitution, Art. V, sec. 3.)

Alaska provides for a supreme court, a superior court, and such other courts as may be established by the legislature (but all the courts constitute a unified judicial system). Appointment by the governor is provided for but under control by the voters as follows:

> The governor shall fill any vacancy in an office of supreme court justice or superior court judge by appointing one of two or more persons nominated by the judicial council.

> Each supreme court justice and superior court judge shall, in the manner provided by law, be subject to approval or rejection on a non-partisan ballot at the first general election held more than three years after his appointment. Thereafter, each supreme court justice shall be subject to approval or rejection in a like manner every tenth year, and each superior court judge, every sixth year. (Alaska Constitution, Art. IV.)

The Hawaiian system of judicial selection approximates the national government's system of appointment by the President with Senatorial confirmation, although the federal judges and those in Massachusetts, Rhode Island, and New Jersey (after a trial period) receive tenure for life or good behavior. California and Missouri provide for appointment to their highest courts by methods not unlike Alaska's.

Nonpartisan judicial selection is a matter of degree. Some states provide for direct partisan election of judges. Some which elect judges on a nonpartisan final ballot authorize or permit a nomination by a partisan primary, or the judicial candidates receive the endorsement of one or the other party. Governors and Presidents in appointing judges do not always overlook the partisan or ideological attachments of candidates. And, of course, a lawyer who never concerned himself with political questions until his appointment to the bench is hardly likely to meet the criterion of "broad social vision."

3. Competent jurors. The United States uses its jury system inherited from England much more extensively today than England. The idea of trial by one's peers and justice tempered with understanding and knowledge of customs and practices is old. Jury service constituted an obligation of the citizen even centuries ago. Present-day society hampers this ideal in operation. First, the normal pay of jurors, the interruption to business and living by serving on a jury, and the unpleasantness of some cases have led many citizens to seek to avoid service. Wisconsin law (and unfortunately such provision is not rare) now provides:

> The following persons shall be exempt from serving as jurors:
> (1) All officers of the United States; elective state officers; members and officers of the legislature during the session thereof; judges and clerks of courts of record; city and county officers; constables; officers and employees of the several state institutions; officers of fire departments and active members of fire companies organized according to law; members of Wisconsin National Guard, and members thereof who are honorably discharged after five years' service, or by reason of injury received in line of duty.
> (2) Attorneys at law; practicing physicians; surgeons; dentists; ministers of the gospel or of any religious society; the president and cashier of any state or national bank.
> (3) The president, professors and instructors of the universities and their assistants; and of the several colleges and incorporated academies; teachers in normal, public or private schools.
> (4) One miller to each gristmill; one head sawyer and engineer in each steam sawmill and shingle mill; one foreman and engineer in each factory and machine shop.
> (5) One dispensing druggist in each prescription drug store; one embalmer holding license issued by the state board of health in each undertaking establishment.
> (6) Telegraph operators, superintendents, conductors, collectors, engineers, firemen, brakemen, and station agents of any railroad or express company, while in actual regular employment as such.
> (7) Any person over 65 upon his request to the court or judge, or upon the judge's own motion. (*Wisconsin Statutes*, 255.02)

Individuals who actively seek jury service either for the money or for the excitement seldom bring to their decisions the experience and judgment needed for justice. Even for the jury of unusual quality, the questions or issues presented may be of too technical a nature.

Legal writers see improvement through (1) clarification and limitation of questions put to the jury while the judge decides the more technical, legal issues after the jury reports its verdict; (2) improved jury selection systems, for example, the Cleveland system of random selection from voting lists followed by a literacy test and brief interview to attempt to establish at least average intelligence and emotional stability; (3) arrangements in time and money for jurors to minimize the hardships of service.

4. Effective use of judicial manpower. At the same time that many judges and many courts are one or more years behind in hearing cases, other judges and other courts may work only a day or two a week. An *integrated court system* (note Alaskan constitutional wording, p. 64) is designed to eliminate overlapping of judicial responsibility and to distribute the judicial load evenly among the judges. This proposal contemplates enabling the individual litigant or his lawyer to go to one central clerk-of-court office in his county, district, or large city, which would inform him about the handling of his case. In each place there would be one court and one panel of judges, not separate county, municipal, probate, and other judges. And these judges, organized under one chief judge, with the assistance of a sort of judicial business manager, would classify the cases and docket them so that each judge on the panel could be assigned to one or another type of work; when he had worked through all the cases of that kind, he could be assigned by the chief judge to assist in some branch of the court that was behind schedule. This single panel of judges would, then, have jurisdiction to hear originally all types of cases arising in the city or county; there would be no confusion as to jurisdiction; and all the judges would be working cooperatively to expedite cases as rapidly as possible.

With an integrated court system, there might or might not be an appellate layer of courts between the court of original jurisdiction and the state supreme court. If there were, it would be organized similarly to the first pattern except that there would be somewhat fewer judges and they would typically serve larger population and geographic areas.

The chief justice, at the top of the entire state court system, would not only preside over the supreme court but would have responsibility for the effective working of the entire system. He would be assisted by a small staff engaged in administering the finances and business operations of the whole court system and by other staffs engaged in studying the dockets, the flow of cases, and further aspects of judicial operations. He would, of course, have authority to assign judges from their normal area of activity to any other area if case loads made this desirable.

A *judicial council*, composed of leading judges, lawyers, and a few laymen would assist the chief justice through constant review of the state's judicial system. Even without an integrated court system, states have established judicial councils. The usual judicial council collects statistics on the number and types of cases handled by the several judges and courts, the backlog of cases of any judge or court, the number and types of appeals, the cost of administering the courts, and similar information. With these data, judicial councils have recommended to the judges, the legislatures, and the public changes in the organization of the courts, changes in procedures, changes in salaries and administrative personnel arrangements, and the like.

5. Simplified procedures.   Courts have historically clung to procedures from tradition as much as from need. In part, frequent changes could work injustices to parties (and might make the lawyer's life difficult). But infrequent changes also affect the cost and reality of justice.

6. Effective appellate practice.   In the development of our court system over the years and in the provisions for review of administrative agency decisions by the courts, there has been a tendency to increase the number of appeals open to the parties in civil cases. This adds greatly to the amount of court work without necessarily increasing justice. Even a somewhat unjust decision may be preferred to uncertainty and delay. Appeals are costly to plaintiff and defendant alike. The cost is represented not only in legal fees and court costs but in the delay in settlement. Sometimes the party with the weak case takes the appeal, perhaps in the hope of discouraging the opponent and forcing him to a smaller settlement for the sake of settlement.

A lower court, of course, may make a mistake. Anglo-Saxon law has assumed this possibility and for centuries provided for redress through the appeal process. Judicial writers urging fewer levels of appeal want to assist justice not by eliminating appeals but by giving the parties one or two appeal opportunities to courts with (a) judges of experience and ability and (b) current calendars so that cases will be disposed of within reasonable time periods.

Conclusion

Federalism in the United States has given us two sets of courts that have some parallel as well as hierarchical jurisdiction. In addition time and changes in our society have added to the complexities of the state court system. Frequently state legislators have met the increased case load of our courts by simply adding a new court here or there without always fitting it carefully into the system. Many states today find their court systems cumbersome because the variety of courts have overlapping and competing jurisdiction; some courts are overloaded and understaffed while other courts do not need to operate on a full-time basis; and the quality of justice is otherwise strained for a variety of reasons. The court reform movement —with bar association, judicial, and citizen backing—attempts to reorganize the court system to improve the quality of justice for all citizens. Court reorganization plans, like administrative reorganization plans, find opposition from individuals and groups (some special groups, some lawyers, some judges, some citizens) satisfied with the present system or skeptical or fearful of the particular proposals. Each state's situation differs somewhat and general "reform" proposals may be inappropriate or at least politically unacceptable in an individual state.

REFERENCES

The Annals of the American Academy of Political and Social Science, No. 285 (May 1953). Issue devoted to "Judicial Administration and the Common Man."

Doyle, Meredith H., "The Administrative Officer of the Courts: His Role in Government," 30 *State Government* (December 1957), pp. 261-263.

Schubert, Glendon A., *Quantitative Analysis of Judicial Behavior.* Glencoe, Ill.: The Free Press, 1959 (a new approach to judicial research).

Talbott, Forrest, *Intergovernmental Relations and the Courts.* Minneapolis: University of Minnesota Press, 1950.

Vanderbilt, Arthur T., *Judges and Jurors: Their Functions, Qualifications, and Selection.* Boston: Boston University Press, 1956.

———, *Men and Measures in the Law.* New York: Alfred A. Knopf, 1949.

Several states have examined their court systems recently and issued reports. For example, *1956 Report of the Temporary Commission on the Courts to the Governor and the Legislature of the State of New York.* Albany: Williams Press (February 15, 1956); and Assembly of the State of California, *Report of the Assembly Interim Committee on Judiciary,* Vol. 20, No. 20, Assembly Interim Committee Reports, 1953-55 (March 1955).

Organization, Personnel, and Finance

PART FOUR

Organization, Personnel,
and Finance

CHAPTER 14

State Administrative Organization

LEGISLATIVE BODIES pass laws, but the existence of legislation on the statute books does not automatically bring acceptance and obedience. Many laws, moreover, tend to state general policies but require specific application and interpretation for specific cases. The laws may be enforced and administered by the governor and department heads responsible to him, by individuals, boards, or commissions reporting to the legislature directly, by the courts, by local officials, or by elected state department heads. Some law is enforced through all these methods and much law will involve the governor, state agencies, the courts, and finally the legislature.

Chapter 12 reviewed the changing theory of the role of the governor in the states. Much of the interpretation of the governor's role revolves around his relation to administration. From an early trend to limit the governor either through placing authority in the legislature or dividing the governor's authority with a number of elected officials, analyses of expanding government operations in the twentieth century have tended to emphasize the need for a hierarchy of responsibility which gives the governor alone more and more direct supervision and control of administration of state laws. The voters and the legislators are expected to review the results and call the governor to account. To give the governor practical control and responsibility for carrying out the state programs, recommendations frequently include: (1) reduction in the number of state departments; (2) organization of departments around broad functional purposes, such as education, social welfare, and public works; (3) development of a clearly defined hierarchy of authority from the governor down through the department heads, bureau heads, division heads, and so forth, to the bottom levels of the administration; and (4) staff organizations such as budget, personnel, purchasing to assist the governor in control of the administrative management and policies of the departments.

This chapter broadly describes the usual administrative arrangements in the states. Succeeding chapters describe in more detail major staff and program agencies of the state governments.

Present State Administrative Organization

To draw a complete picture of American state administration today is not easy, and for several reasons. There are fifty states, and each has its own combination of administrative agencies, although there are some features that are found in all or nearly all. Many older features are found mixed up with newer ones—that is, the states are administratively now as always in a period of transition.[1] The reader should also keep in mind that similarly designated agencies and organization structures may show quite different results among the states. Administration depends on people, traditions, political practices, and voter and legislative response to its activities.

Assignment of Administration

★ *The governor as chief administrator*

In the administration of state affairs in New Jersey, New York, and Virginia the governor has powers as head of a relatively integrated state administrative system. New York generally led the way, especially in the 1920s, in placing the governor at the head of its state administration. Virginia followed. The 1947 constitution of New Jersey and the new Alaska and Hawaii constitutions put the governor in a strong position to control the administration. The Alaska constitution reads:

> Sec. 22. All executive and administrative offices, departments, and agencies of the state government and their respective functions, powers, and

[1] Many of the states have made one or more studies of their administrative organization during the 1950s. Bibliographies of such studies may be consulted. See also the regular articles on state administrative organization in *The Book of the States*, of which the latest now available is in the 1958-59 volume, pp. 111-114.

duties shall be allocated by law among and within not more than twenty principal departments, so as to group them as far as practicable according to major purposes . . .

Sec. 23. The governor may make changes in the organization of the executive branch or in the assignment of functions among its units which he considers necessary for efficient administration. Where these changes require the force of law, they shall be set forth in executive orders. The legislature shall have sixty days of a regular session, or a full session if of shorter duration, to disapprove these executive orders . . .

Sec. 24. Each principal department shall be under the supervision of the governor.

Sec. 25. The head of each principal department shall be a single executive unless otherwise provided by law. He shall be appointed by the governor, subject to confirmation by a majority of the members of the legislature in joint session, and shall serve at the pleasure of the governor . . .[2]

In the other states there are frequently numerous departments with varying degrees of independence from the governor. Seldom has he any authority to rearrange responsibilities of these departments, and reorganization proposals to the legislature stir up many antagonisms. The governor's appointing powers over administrative department heads created by statute sometimes are extensive but his removal power is in most cases limited to removals "for cause." "Cause" usually means *legal* cause only and not because of differences over policies or lack of cooperation. In forty-two states, the governor prepares and presents to the legislature the regular state budget, annually or biennially, and even in the other eight states he has a budget role. In most of the states he has some powers to enforce the budget. He serves ex officio on various state boards and commissions.

In several states, the governor has the assistance of a department of administration. In Minnesota this agency has existed since 1939 when a general state reorganization was made; it is headed by a Commissioner of Administration appointed by and fully responsible to the governor. In this department are divisions of the budget, administrative management, purchasing, public properties, and architectural engineering. The department has the power to prepare the biennial budget, maintain a quarterly allotment system for expenditures by the various agencies, keep expenditures from exceeding revenues, control purchasing for the state, control the letting of contracts for buildings, highways, and other improvements, supervise the construction of buildings for the state, inspect and keep an inventory of state properties, establish regulations for travel at state ex-

2 Constitution of Alaska, Art. III.

pense, and transfer employees from agency to agency to meet seasonal demands—all subject to the governor's approval. In short, this department is
the governor's principal agent for the control of state business and finances,
and it is generally recognized as a success.

★ The constitutional elective officers

Reaching back into the past, most state constitutions continue to provide
for the election of four or five officials in addition to the governor. Apart
from the lieutenant governor with his traditional role of presiding over
the upper house of the state legislature and succeeding to the position of
governor in the case of disability, death, or absence, state constitutions frequently provided for electing a secretary of state, a state auditor, a state
treasurer, and an attorney general.

1. A secretary of state.   The secretary of state, usually created by the state
constitution and elected by the voters, was responsible for attesting, preserving, and publishing the state laws; for preparing the state election ballot
and publishing the notices of state elections (mostly through official newspapers) and helping to canvass state election returns; for receiving and
filing notices of incorporation of both private and municipal corporations;
for issuing certificates of election, certified copies of public laws, and other
similar public documents; and for performing various other similar duties,
including the preservation of a great many public documents.

  With such an officer at hand, legislatures were inclined in later years to
give him additional minor functions from time to time in order to avoid
the necessity of creating additional clerical officers and not to increase the
power of the governor. The registration of motor vehicles and the issuance
of motor vehicle licenses, for example, were later devolved upon the secretary of state in many states.

2. A state auditor.   A state auditor or officer of similar title was set up by
the constitutions of most states to keep the principal or controlling accounts
of the state's finances, to audit the accounts of all officers who either received or spent state money, and to countersign all vouchers for the expenditure of state funds. In some states he also was given supervision of
state lands and other property. In the earliest years he was usually elected
by the legislature, but later he became elective by the voters in most states.

3. A state treasurer.   Established by the constitution, and made elective first
by the legislature and later more commonly by the voters, a state treasurer
was made responsible for receiving all taxes and other moneys due to the

state, for keeping them safe, and for paying them out on proper vouchers signed by the auditor. He and the auditor participated also in the issuance and redemption of state bonds when the state borrowed money. In the early years when the property tax was the main source of state tax revenue, the state treasurer had no important tax-collecting functions. Property taxes were collected locally by county, town, and municipal officials, and the state's share was turned over by the local collectors to the state treasurer. Later, when the states took to levying taxes on corporations, on inheritances, and on other subjects beyond the reach of local collectors, many states conferred some tax-collecting functions on their treasurers.

4. An attorney general. An attorney general became a constitutional officer in every state and subject to popular election in most. His duties were to advise the legislature and the state officers about their powers and duties, to help draft bills and prepare contracts, bond forms, and other legal documents for the state, to represent the state in suits brought by it against others and (more rarely) in suits against the state, and to perform a variety of other legal services for the state.

These four constitutional state officers, though described here in the past tense, are still the most common constitutional officers of the states and are almost everywhere subject to popular election. Their central functions, as summarized above, are essentially of a housekeeping or overhead nature for the state. They do not reach out and render services that redound directly to the benefit of people throughout the state's area in the same sense that a highway department or a public-health department does. They illustrate what state administration was in the days of minimum government.

Overhead and Housekeeping Agencies

In the state capitols and state office buildings will be found a number of agencies, bureaus, and offices that are engaged primarily in looking after the *means* with which state administrations work. These agencies have arisen as the volume of different types of work increased and as the standards of service rose, so that specialists were called for. Among these agencies the following may be mentioned:

Personnel:
> Civil service commission or director of personnel
> Retirement and pension boards

Finance:

    Treasury, fund management

    Auditor, comptroller, accounting

    Revenues, tax collections

    Budgeting, expenditure controls

    Purchasing, central purchasing office, stores management

    Property management and accounting

    Debt management, sinking funds

    Investment of endowment and trust funds

Public Buildings:

    Capitol, office building, institutional structures

    Supervising architect or engineer, repairs, maintenance

Public Relations:

    Informational services, public printing, government reports.

Each state has somewhat different arrangements for handling these functions. In an administration that is integrated under the governor, as we have seen above, the financial management functions may be grouped in a department of administration. On the other hand, most states keep the administration of the civil service and personnel laws under a separate commission. Both finance and personnel administration are discussed later.

Major Service Departments

Whether set up under single heads or under boards, a number of principal state departments appear in some form, separately or in combination with others, in every state administration. Since we examine the conditions that affect the major services in later chapters, we will only outline here the major functional fields, indicating the usual names and types of the administrative agencies that handle them.

SOCIAL AGENCIES:

Education, primary and secondary:

    Under State Department of Education, and a State Superintendent of Public Instruction elective by voters in thirty states

Education, higher:

    State University—Board of Regents

    Teachers colleges and other state colleges—often under separate boards

    Technical institutions—agriculture, forestry, mining, technology—often under separate boards

Social welfare:

    Relief, old-age assistance, aid to dependent children, aid to the blind, etc.—State Department of Welfare

Hospitals and institutions:
　For dependent and defective classes—Department of Institutions
Correctional institutions:
　Separate boards, or combined with other institutions under one
　　board
Veterans' affairs:
　Soldiers' homes, hospitals, veterans' organizations—Veterans Ad-
　　visory Board
Public health:
　Communicable diseases, health education, etc., environmental sani-
　　tation—Department of Health, under a board in most states

REGULATORY OR PROMOTIONAL AGENCIES:
Labor:
　Employment security, employment offices, workmen's compensation,
　　wages and hours, child labor, industrial safety, industrial disputes
　　—State Department of Labor, Industrial Commission, State Con-
　　ciliator, and other agencies
General law enforcement:
　Highway patrol, state police, fire marshal—various state bureaus
Liquor control:
　Liquor Control Commission
Defense:
　National Guard, training, armories—Adjutant General under gov-
　　ernor
Business regulation and promotion:
　Railroad and public utility regulation, rates, service, etc.—Public
　　Utilities Commission, Railroad Commission

　Corporations, chartering, licensing, taxing—some states have Corpo-
　　ration Commission or Commissioner, and some of these cover
　　railroad and utility regulation

　Banking—State Banking Department or Commission

　Insurance—State Insurance Commissioner

　Securities—issue and sale of, State Securities Commission or Com-
　　missioner ("Blue Sky" Commission)

　Savings and loan associations—state commission

　State business development, attracting new business to state—State
　　Department of Business Development

Professions and vocations:
　Licensing and regulation of—separate board for each specialty,
　　such as architects, barbers, beauticians or cosmetologists, chiro-
　　practors, dentists, doctors, embalmers, engineers, nurses, optome-
　　trists, osteopaths, pharmacists, podiatrists, public accountants,
　　real estate agents, veterinaries

Agriculture:

Promotion, regulation, research—State Department of Agriculture, also boards or bureaus for separate products (livestock sanitation, poultry, horticulture, bee culture, etc.); aid to agricultural organizations, like State Agricultural Society, and societies for special crops

PHYSICAL AND NATURAL RESOURCE AGENCIES:

Natural resources:

Conservation and development—one Department of Conservation, or a number of separate ones (some under boards), such as Forestry, Game and Fish, Mines and Minerals, Oil and Gas, Water resources

State parks and monuments:

Separate department in some states

Drainage, irrigation, flood control:

Separate departments in some states

Highways:

Construction and maintenance—State Department of Highways, some under boards

Miscellaneous Agencies

Historical and local interest account for the existence of special agencies in some states. Many of these spend only a little money and perform only small services. Thus Texas had in 1945 a Board of Mansion Supervisors, a Cigarette Tax Stamp Board, a Board of Managers of State Iron Industries. a Texas Naval Board, and a Pink Bollworm Commission. In a 1946 list, Kansas had a Port of Entry Board and a Murals Commission (for murals in the statehouse rotunda) and had just recently transferred the work of a State Brand Board to the Kansas Livestock Commission. These are not presented as oddities but as examples of unusual agencies to be found in every state, as each tries to respond to its state and local needs.

★ *Semipublic agencies and societies*

Also frequently included in the long lists of state administrative agencies or agencies that receive state funds, are a number of semipublic agencies like state historical societies, art societies, scientific bodies, state promotional groups, and welfare organizations working among veterans, the blind, and other special groups. The importance of these varies considerably, but none of them ranks with such great departments as highways, education, and social welfare. These agencies on the borderlands of government, half in and half out, nevertheless constitute an interesting study by themselves.

Reorganization Surveys and Legislation

How far can the existing state administrative organization be reorganized along modern lines? The work of President Taft's Commission on Economy and Efficiency in the national government (1911) set a number of states to surveying their administrative organizations with a view to reform, and recently the Hoover Commission study of the national government (1947-1948) apparently helped to start another wave, for nearly *half the states* initiated surveys of their own in 1947-1949.[3] In the intervening decades there were many other surveys and reports. Most of the reports moved in the direction of more modern state administrative organization, but some were only halfhearted and piecemeal in their proposals.

Naturally the governors have been most active in proposing reorganizations, but legislators, other officials, and leading laymen have also taken part. The surveys that precede specific reorganization proposals have been handled by legislative committees, mixed commissions of legislators and appointed members, and lay commissions, as provided by law or a governor's act of appointment, and the actual studies have been conducted under such committees and commissions in a variety of ways—by professional survey organizations, local talent, and the staffs of legislative research councils. Special libraries now contain a wealth of materials on state administration arising out of these surveys.

The recommendations of these surveys in some instances call for changes in the state constitution, such as the transfer of the constitutional officers from an elective to an appointive basis. Most of the changes require changes in the statutes, and some can be carried out by administrative action. In any case, a sweeping reorganization such as has been carried out in a few states will call for many changes in the laws and, usually, the enactment of a new administrative code.

Even before the proposals appear in final form the lines of battle begin to form. The governor, some leading legislators, students of public administration, taxpayers' associations and governmental research bureaus, some commercial organizations, leagues of voters, some newspapers, and

[3] See Hubert R. Gallagher, "State Reorganization Surveys," IX *Public Administration Review* (Autumn 1949), pp. 252-256. The second Hoover Commission, reporting in 1954, and the pressures for expanded state functions and higher state taxes brought a second flurry of state reorganization surveys.

various leading citizens are likely to favor the proposals in general, and occasionally even a political party will do so. The opposition also lines up rather quickly and is likely to include many small groups and individuals who oppose specific changes with especial vehemence. The beneficiaries of various services and their pressure groups are likely to be strongly opposed to changes in their favored agencies, and behind the scenes, if not openly, leading public officials and their staffs of employees may work hard against changes that endanger their independence. As a result of opposition, parts of the program may not be enacted at all, while other features have to be modified before passage. In other words, what is enacted is seldom the whole program of reorganization but rather a reduced and somewhat watered-down version.

Following enactment of any part of the program comes the effort of putting it into effect. At this stage the support of a vigorous, able, and popular governor with a fairly long term of office ahead of him is almost indispensable to success. Governors elected after the reforms have been initiated are not likely to be such ardent supporters of them.

Despite the many obstacles to change, considerable progress has been made in some states. New York, Virginia, and now New Jersey are generally recognized as having gone far toward reorganization, while other states follow, one or more steps behind. Alaska and Hawaii begin with constitutions incorporating most of the administrative reform ideas.

REFERENCES

Bell, James R., "A Coordinator for State Agencies," 18 *Public Administration Review* (Spring 1958), 98-101.

Daland, Robert T., and Raymond Wickham, "States Seek Efficiency," 47 *National Municipal Review* (April 1958), 166-170.

Eley, Lynn W., "Executive Reorganization in Michigan," 32 *State Government* (Winter 1959), 33-37.

Landers, Frank M., and Howard D. Hamilton, "State Administrative Reorganization in Michigan: The Legislative Approach," XIV *Public Administration Review* (Spring 1954), 99-111.

Schuck, Victoria, "Massachusetts Audit of State Needs: A New Kind of Planning Agency," 32 *State Government* (Winter 1959), 38-42.

See also individual state reports of reorganization commissions.

CHAPTER 15

State Government Personnel

AT THE BEGINNING of 1958 all governments in the United States employed 8,300,000 people in civilian capacities. Somewhat over 2,000,000 were employed by the national government, and over 6,000,000 by state and local governments.

Extent of State and Local Employment

State and local governments alone now employ more people than the total population of the United States—men, women, and children of all races —at the first census of 1790. Separately organized school districts lead all classes of governmental units in total employees (see Table 8), and this total of 1,750,000 does not include the 225,000 school employees in places where the city government controls the school system. City governments of the United States come next in total employment, with state governments a close third. This makes three levels of governmental units with more than one million employees each. Counties, although to some extent they serve nearly the entire United States population, run a poor fourth, while all other units (towns, townships, incorporated places with a population under 2500 and hence classified as nonurban, and all special districts other than school districts) bring up the rear with about 9 percent of the total state and local employees.

Table 8. NUMBER OF STATE AND LOCAL EMPLOYEES, OCTOBER 1958

Unit of Government	School[a]	Nonschool	Total
State	467,000	1,002,000	1,469,000
City	225,000	1,369,000	1,594,000
County	147,000	532,000	679,000
School district	1,750,000	....	1,750,000
All other	....	549,000	549,000
Total	2,589,000	3,452,000	6,041,000

Source: U.S. Bureau of the Census, *Public Employment* series. Adjustments have been made in totals to make columns add which result in 149,000 more nonschool and total than census reports. Alaska and Hawaii were not states in 1958 and were not included in census figures.

a School employees include not only teachers and supervisors but also clerks, janitors, and other employees.

Considering only the civilian employments in government as shown in Figure 9, we note that over 12 percent of the persons gainfully employed in 1958 were in government employment, 8 million out of 65 million. The National government accounted for over 3 percent, state and local (including school) for 9 percent. These total figures show from a numerical and economic viewpoint the relative importance in the national economy of public employment, but they cannot possibly reveal the dependence of the public on the maintenance of high public personnel standards.

Neither do the total national figures throw much light on the problem of personnel administration. The total figures are mere sums of the employment figures in thousands of employing units. Great states like New York, Illinois, California, and Pennsylvania, and the correspondingly great cities of New York, Chicago, Los Angeles, and Philadelphia, each employ many thousands of personnel. Their problems of personnel management are large and complicated. On the other hand some smaller states and localities employ more persons per 10,000 inhabitants (see Fig. 10). Then there are thousands of small local employing units with only one or a few employees each. Although the same merit principles probably should apply in all public employment, the methods used to get and retain meritorious employees vary with the size and circumstances of different places and so do the levels of ability that can be procured. Large and wealthy units of government can and do attract into their service some of the most able people in the land.

While this chapter does not pretend to discuss the many details of state and local government personnel, it does examine the development of personnel policies and the spread of the merit system, civil-service laws and agencies, and some of the special problems that have arisen.

Figure 9. PUBLIC EMPLOYMENT AND PAYROLLS, 1948 TO 1958

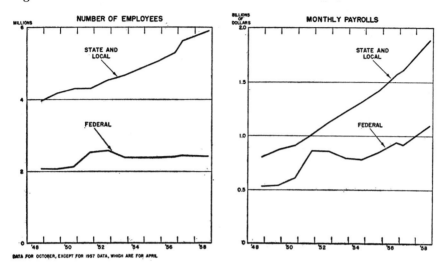

Source: U. S. Bureau of the Census, *State Distribution of Public Employment in 1958* (1959), p. 2.

Development of Personnel Policies

In the early days of the United States, when the services of state and local governments were very few and limited and not so highly specialized as to call for specially trained persons, many local public functions were performed by citizens without pay under the compulsion of state laws and local ordinances. In the New England towns and in many cities and boroughs elsewhere there were specific offices, such as weighers, measurers, fence inspectors, pound masters, "hogreeves," and so on, to which men could be elected by their fellow townsmen and in which they would have to serve a term without pay or be fined. Local citizens in rotation performed the night watch; every householder helped to fight fires by keeping a rope and bucket handy and responding to the call of the bell. Roads and streets were built, maintained, and cleaned under various systems by householders and farmers who spent several days a year, or certain hours each week, joining their neighbors in the work, or were fined or taxed for nonperformance. "Working out the road tax" was a common experience. (Some of the more prosperous citizens paid the tax and thus avoided work.) Naturally the services for a whole county or state could not be performed

Figure 10. NUMBER OF FULL-TIME EQUIVALENT EMPLOYEES OF STATE AND LOCAL GOVERNMENT PER 10,000 POPULATION, OCTOBER 1958

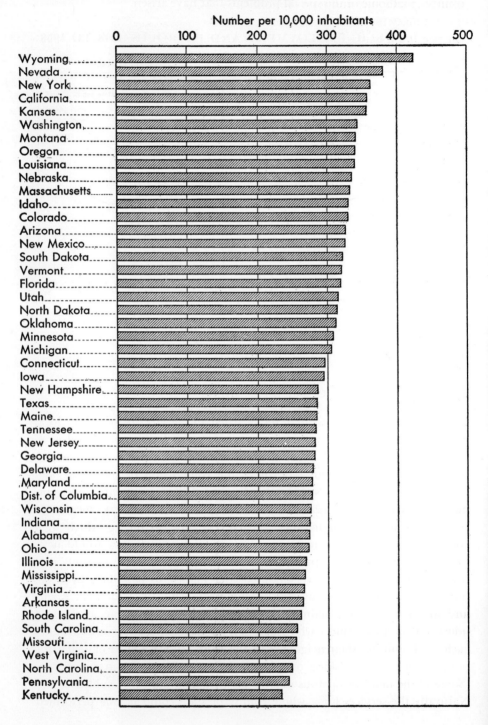

in this way, so that a few officers paid by fees or salary would be found in county courthouses and state capitols.

Changes in public personnel policies often paralleled changes in theory of administrative organization and for many of the same reasons. Early governmental personnel were either elected by the voters or selected by officials on the basis of their personal knowledge of the applicant's qualifications. As government grew larger, officials needed to rely on the judgment of others for selection. "Others"—including political bosses, legislators, governors—might emphasize friendship, party service, competence, or other characteristics in making their recommendations. The rather strong sense of service of many of our earliest government employees gave way to theories of democracy which argued not only that every citizen was capable of working for government but ought to be given a job for at least a year or two if he wanted it. The extremes of patronage and spoils systems, together with expansion of government service, brought demands for reform. "Throw the rascals out" was an accepted slogan.

Reform in its earliest stages emphasized selection solely on the basis of tests of competence. Its supporters frowned upon any party-membership, religious-affiliation, or other tests that was unrelated to loyalty to the government or ability to perform the duties of office or employment. They opposed any intrusion of partisanship in the public service and stood for a public service that was politically neutral. Only governments with merit systems deserved praise. Somewhat later, from about 1910 or so, the national government and several states led or were pushed by citizen groups to add ideas of scientific management (then being introduced into industry by Frederick Taylor and others) to the negative goal of "keeping out the rascals." States interested in improved personnel management established central personnel departments to assist in selecting more competent employees and to aid departments in making the best use of those hired.

More recently research and writing in the personnel field suggest that the "efficiency" and "merit-system" concepts may be too mechanical. Government employees are human beings who perform well or poorly not only as indicated by tests of ability and training but in terms of a variety of incentives in the organization and personal relations of the department in which they work. The religious ethic "to do unto others as you would have them do unto you" has application in the working world of government or private industry. An experiment at the Hawthorne Plant of the Western Electric Company in the late 1920s showed that employees in routine work produced more on the job when they were conscious of supervisory interest

Source: U. S. Bureau of the Census, *State Distribution of Public Employment in 1958* (1959), G.GE58, No. 1, Fig. 2, p. 4.

in their welfare as individuals and were given a sense of status on the job.[1]

Recent personnel writers have also called attention to the fact that as government expands its functions, policy decisions are made at fairly low levels of the hierarchy. If we really want an active government with program and policy adjustments in line with the voters' broad selections at the polls, it may be necessary to permit political considerations to have a somewhat greater force than was advocated by many of the civil-service reformers. If as voters we choose to change from a "conservative" Republican governor to a "liberal" Democratic governor (or vice versa or any variation), ought this not to mean that state agencies should modify their programs to match the new governor's policies? Can we expect personnel at the top of the agency easily to adapt to the new regime? If we cannot, how can we secure expertness and policy orientation with little guarantee of tenure? These questions and the problems raised occur in much of the recent personnel literature.[2]

The Merit System in the States

The year 1883, when Congress passed the Pendleton Act for the reform of the national civil service, is usually accepted as marking the beginning of effective merit systems in the United States. The state of New York adopted a similar law in 1883, and Massachusetts followed suit in 1884. Then there was a long wait until the days of the Progressive movement, when Wisconsin and Illinois (1905), Colorado (1907), New Jersey (1908), and California and Ohio (1913) adopted state civil-service laws. Thus, before World War I leading states from coast to coast had merit-system legislation. Then the movement lagged for a time, with a few state adoptions here and there, until the late 1930s and 1940s when a considerable forward movement took place. This movement was related to a nation-wide "united-front" drive for the merit system in which a national Commission of Inquiry on Public Service Personnel played a leading part.[3]

[1] F. J. Roethlisberger and William J. Dickson, *Management and the Worker* (Cambridge, Mass.: Harvard University Press, 1939).
[2] In addition to the regular section on personnel in *The Book of the States,* the following references may be particularly helpful: Felix A. Nigro, *Public Personnel Administration* (New York: Henry Holt, 1959), especially Ch. 1; and Paul P. Van Riper, *History of the United States Civil Service* (Evanston, Ill.: Row, Peterson, 1958). Both of these books have extensive bibliographies. A reference valuable especially for its comments on the need for recognition of politics in bureaucracy is Paul T. David and Ross Pollock, *Executives for Government* (Washington, D. C.: Brookings Institution, 1957).
[3] See the several volumes of studies and hearings published by the commission (New York: McGraw-Hill, 1935), and especially its summary of findings and programs for change in *Better Government Personnel,* Vol. I in the series.

By the end of the 1950s twenty-nine states had legislation in effect for general programs of personnel recruitment and administration under a merit system administered by a state personnel agency.[4] These states were well distributed among the various regions of the country, but they were most commonly in the more populous, urban states. Some of these states have old, well-established, and well-run merit systems. In other states of this group, the legislature has written general merit-system legislation and established a state personnel agency but either the legislature or the governors or both have failed to provide adequate funds or other support to give the state full merit-system selection. On occasion states have withheld merit-system application from one or more major programs (for example, highways in Illinois). Such limitations on merit-system use may also affect the quality of the general personnel program in the state.

There is some merit-system selection in the twenty-one states not included above. Since 1939, for example, the national Social Security Act has required that any state receiving grants—and they all do—must administer its part of the social-security program (old-age assistance, aid to dependent children, and so on) through personnel employed under a merit system. As a result all states lacking general merit-system laws have "merit-system councils" or similar agencies in the social-security field. Experience with the merit system in the social-security program seems to have been an important factor in the adoption of general merit systems in some states. In several states which did not choose to give up patronage-selection practices, standardized leave, classification, and compensation statutes followed from their experience with the social-security merit system.

In summary, a third or more of the states still attempt to conduct much of the state's business with nineteenth-century spoils and patronage systems. Even states which technically select personnel through a merit system differ greatly in the number of employees covered and the general quality of their merit system. In other words, a number of states are not troubled by the problems to which current personnel writers have referred since they still do not use a merit system for selection. The personnel problems of these states frequently are of the older type—selection on the basis of party affiliation with little regard to competence; general inefficiency within state service; low prestige for state employment which limits the number and quality of individuals willing to consider state service; greater tendencies toward a variety of types of corruption; and the like.

[4] *The Book of the States, 1958-59,* pp. 140-143. These twenty-nine states were Alaska, Alabama, California, Colorado, Connecticut, Florida, Georgia, Hawaii, Illinois, Kansas, Louisiana, Maine, Maryland, Massachusetts, Michigan, Minnesota, Nevada, New Hampshire, New Jersey, New York, North Carolina, Ohio, Oregon, Rhode Island, Tennessee, Vermont, Virginia, Wisconsin and Wyoming.

314 - ORGANIZATION, PERSONNEL, AND FINANCE

Civil-service Laws and Agencies

General merit-system laws for states have substantially the same content. A number of states (Alaska, California, Hawaii, Michigan, and New York, among others) provide for state merit systems in their constitutions. On the other hand the majority of states, including Massachusetts and Wisconsin which have two of the oldest merit systems, have statutory authorization only. It is sometimes thought that constitutional provision gives greater assurance of integrity. Yet constitutional provisions, for example, in Georgia and Louisiana, have sometimes remained unimplemented and ineffective, whereas Wisconsin's more-than-fifty-year-old statute receives all the veneration of constitutional law. The state's traditions, political experience, public opinion, and administrative experience with the merit system influence the depth of support. A merit system adopted when one party is in power receives its test only after the other party has gained control and accepted general merit selection.

The New York provision, which has been widely studied and to some extent copied into other state constitutions and laws, has benefited from two-party and public support. Its basic provision reads that:

> Appointments and promotions in the civil service of the state and all of the civil divisions thereof, including cities and villages, shall be made according to merit and fitness to be ascertained, as far as practicable, by examination, which, as far as practicable, shall be competitive . . . (Art. V, sec. 6, New York Constitution)

A subsequent amendment to this clause now provides for preference to disabled veterans.

The California constitution carries a rather detailed summary of the civil-service law. The Colorado and Michigan provisions are somewhat shorter than that of California but longer than those of New York and Ohio. In Michigan the constitution itself defines the civil service, establishes the civil-service commission, wipes out all previous personnel agencies, authorizes the commission to make and enforce the rules of civil service, guarantees the commission an adequate beginning budget (not less than $\frac{1}{2}$ of 1 percent of the last preceding aggregate annual payroll of the state), and makes unlawful any payment of wages or salaries by the state until the constitutional provision has been complied with in all respects (Art. VI, sec. 22). While the governor might presumably fail to appoint civil-service commissioners, and the legislature fail to appropriate sufficient funds, the Michigan provision can be circumvented only if the courts fail to do their duty, because any citizen of the state may get from the court an injunction or a writ of mandamus to prevent such evasion.

★ *Agency heads*

Most of the state civil-service laws provide for a department to be headed by an appointed commission of three members, although some commissions number from two to five. The governors normally make the appointments, subject to senate or council approval as in the case of other appointments. The commissioners' terms of office are fairly long, four and six years being rather common, and they are usually staggered for the purpose of maintaining some continuity of membership. In Maryland there is a single commissioner of state employment under the governor; in Connecticut, a director of personnel and an advisory committee; and in Virginia, a division of personnel under a director appointed by the governor. The Michigan constitutional amendment vests the administration of the commission's powers in a state personnel director who is to be chosen by it through a competitive examination. Wisconsin, Minnesota, and several other states with recent or revised laws make substantially the same arrangement, so that the commission members, who are unsalaried, exercise only general policy-making and control powers. The older idea of a salaried commission whose members gave part or full time to the work and tried to administer the department as well as to decide policies, make rules, and decide cases is now definitely on the wane in the states. The inefficiency of administration by a board of untrained citizens and the division of responsibility that results from board administration have led everywhere to an increasing demand for one-man responsibility in personnel administration.

The Model State Civil Service Law, prepared by the National Civil Service League includes a commission whose members are appointed by the governor with the responsibility of advising the personnel director and the governor, making necessary investigations, and making regular reports of personnel progress. The Model Law provides for a director of personnel to head the personnel department.

> Upon recommendation of the Civil Service Commission, the Governor shall appoint a Director of Personnel, who shall be experienced in the field of personnel administration, and who is in known sympathy with the application of merit principles in public employment.

The argument is made that a competitive examination is more likely to select a technician than the man of the experience, imagination, and policy orientation needed to head the state's personnel agency. And the same argument also reasons that the governor with his general responsibility for the executive branch of government should have the authority to appoint the director of the state's personnel department. The authors of the Model Law recognize that state practices may limit the desirability of their proposal.

> There are those who advocate that personnel administration should be taken out of the control of the political chief executive and placed in the hands of a separate body; and that the Civil Service Commission should appoint the Director after competitive examination. This has sometimes been found desirable in jurisdictions with a strong political patronage tradition.[5]

★ *Internal organization*

State departments of personnel usually have divisions or units which follow closely the functional division of the agency's work, such as classification, examination, recruiting, training, and personnel relations. In the smaller agencies a single personnel officer will handle all phases of the work, with the aid of a secretary and perhaps an examiner or two. Outside specialists must be used even by large agencies in examining for the more professional and specialized positions.

★ *Coverage of civil-service laws*

Every civil-service law exempts almost completely from its provisions certain public positions, including always those of elective officers and the appointive members of boards and commissions, and usually a number of department headships, positions of confidential secretaries, teachers, and librarians—the latter groups because they are covered by professional certification schemes. These are the *exempt positions.*

Under the law in the fullest sense are positions in the *classified service.* In fully developed systems this is by far the largest group of positions.

Under the law to some extent but not for all purposes of examination, recruitment, and tenure, for example, are the positions in the *unclassified service.* Some positions are in this category only temporarily, until a classification is made. Others, such as those of unskilled laborers, may be in the unclassified service permanently. Field services may remain unclassified for a considerable period. Temporary and seasonal jobs may also be

---

[5] Part of "comment" within sec. 4 of A Model State Civil Service Law prepared by National Civil Service League and National Municipal League. This Model Law with its internal comments quoted in full in Appendix A in Nigro, *op. cit.*

essentially unclassified. To some extent the designation means only "miscellaneous."

Major Personnel Functions

No attempt will be made here to present more than a condensed conspectus of the work of public personnel agencies.

★ Classification

The only proper basis for examinations, promotions, and pay plans is a thorough description and classification of all positions coming under the civil-service law. Classifications are based upon the nature of the duties and the degree of responsibility that attaches to each post. Specialists in classification usually survey all positions with the assistance and advice of the incumbents (who fill out questionnaires about their work and duties), their immediate supervisors, and department heads. When the paper work has been done and the hearings have been held on different positions, a classification scheme is worked out, and then usually more hearings are held. Naturally almost every employee wants his position given as high a rating as possible. The classification scheme finally adopted by the commission or department may have to be approved by higher authorities in the government concerned, by the governor or city council, for example. It is then embodied in the civil-service rules. All new positions are supposed to find a place in the classification, and reclassifications are made of particular positions when the duties have sufficiently changed. Classification is, therefore, a continuing function. General revisions of classifications also have to be made from time to time.

The main classes are based upon services, vocations, and professions —clerical, fiscal, administrative, medical, engineering, law enforcement, for example. Within each service there are various levels or classes of positions —junior clerk-stenographer, clerk-stenographer, senior clerk-stenographer, secretary, to take a rather familiar illustration. These steps provide a sort of ladder for promotions and a basis for examinations and pay scales.

★ Examinations, eligible lists, and recruiting

When the duties of the various positions are known, the personnel agency is in position to undertake its central function, that of devising and administering practical tests of fitness for all applicants in the different categories. All the examinations tend to be practical, but they take many forms—competitive written examinations, actual performance tests, oral examinations, noncompetitive tests for certain high professional and technical posts, only medical and physical examinations for unskilled laborers, and so on. There have been extensive developments in testing methods, and the tests are selected and grouped for the different types of positions as determined by experience.

In addition to the information about each applicant that is derived from his or her performance in the examinations, the personnel agency records information about each applicant such as his age, sex, citizenship, education, work experience, military service, and other factors that are pertinent to his or her right and ability to serve the public in the work applied for. Questions about political affiliations, religion, color, and race are generally forbidden by law.

A candidate's performance on the different tests, his experience, and other factors are given appropriate weights, and his total score is then computed and recorded. This much having been done, a register is prepared of all eligibles (those who have an agreed passing score) for the specific position or type of position, the eligibles with the highest scores being listed first. This is the "eligible list" or eligible register for that type of work from which appointing officers are required to make appointments in accordance with the law.

An alert personnel agency that has sufficient funds and staff endeavors to anticipate demands for employees by holding examinations and preparing eligible lists well in advance of need. This necessitates keeping in close touch with all employing agencies in the governmental unit that it serves.

★ Making and enforcing regulations

Every civil-service law contains provisions for the improvement of the public service and for the protection of civil servants. These provisions have to be supplemented by rules and regulations adopted by the personnel agency itself. The laws and rules cover the political activity of civil servants; partisan interference with them and assessments upon them; veterans' preference in appointments, promotions, and layoffs; vacations, sick leaves, promotions, demotions, and dismissals; and various other conditions of work and tenure.

These rules the personnel agency must try to enforce, at least in the first instance. This in turn necessitates hearings and decisions upon a considerable variety of complaints, from those of persons who have been refused the right to take an examination to those of employees threatened with dismissal. In this work the personnel agency, or more commonly the commission itself or special trial panels, exercise judicial and law-enforcing functions.

★ *Pay scales*

In recent public personnel laws, personnel agencies have been saddled with the responsibility of preparing or helping to prepare suitable rates of pay for the different classes and grades of employees. The resultant "pay plans," which must stay within the appropriations, usually set minimum and maximum pay rates for each defined type of position, with possible increases at the end of each year or similar period for employees within a grade, up to the maximum. Recently some of these pay plans have provided also for "cost-of-living" increases and decreases which are tied to various cost of living indexes, such as that of the United States Bureau of Labor Statistics. Once a pay plan has been approved, the personnel agency may also have some responsibility for its observance, although the main burden of this is likely to fall on fiscal agencies.

★ *Training, recruiting, and morale*

Public personnel agencies, especially in the more populous states and cities, are more and more becoming responsible for in-service training programs and for the general promotion of training for the public service. This ties in with another development, that of actively endeavoring to interest people of training and ability to apply for public positions. The old idea of merely sitting back and giving examinations to those who happen to apply has been giving way to a more active and constructive type of recruiting policy designed to tap other and higher levels of ability.

Another factor in improving the public service is raising and maintaining the morale of the employees. About this the early civil-service commissions seem to have done little or nothing. Careful studies have indicated that in the minds of many citizens, service with state and local governments is a rather low and "political" form of employment. No doubt this widespread feeling has been associated with the patronage and spoils systems in appointment, the undistinguished character of many persons who were recruited under those systems, and the frequent exposures of state and municipal inefficiency and corruption from the days of the Tweed Ring in New York after the Civil War down through the muckraking of the early part of the twentieth century. At the same time the public attitude probably reflected a lack of pride and a somewhat low state of morale within the service. To overcome these attitudes, to make state and local public service more attractive to outsiders and more satisfying and desirable to those within, have become important objectives of modern public personnel agencies. Improvements in efficiency, in working conditions, and in *esprit de corps*, fair and adequate reporting of service achievements to the public, and special awards for outstanding service are among the means being employed.

Thus the general purposes of public personnel work are changing from the older negative ones of keeping out incompetents and spoilsmen to positive ones of recruiting the best available, encouraging adequate education and training, and in general raising the entire tone and outlook of the civil service.

Employee Unions and Political Activity

During the last thirty years there has been a considerable increase in the number of public-employee unions and of their members. Some of these unions are affiliated with the American Federation of Labor-Congress of Industrial Organizations, and some are independent. A number of the unions, such as those for painters or plumbers, are not composed solely or even primarily of public employees, although they do have some public-employee membership. The growth of unions in the state and local public services has been a part of the nation-wide movement toward unionization, the objectives of which are to protect employees against arbitrary action, to lobby for their special interests, and to promote their vocations and professions.

★ Unionism

Two special problems have arisen with the growth of unionism in the public services: the right to strike and the right to bargain collectively. There have never been very many public-employee strikes due in large part to a strong no-strike policy on the part of public-employee unions. However, state legislatures increasingly have been banning strikes by state or local employees as being against public policy. State or local government, it is contended, cannot tolerate a challenge to its authority that a strike might entail. Furthermore, certain services of government are essential to the health, welfare, and safety of the citizens, and these services should not be interrupted.

Although nationally the Tennessee Valley Authority has engaged successfully in collective bargaining over hours, wages, and working conditions, state agencies have used the technique little even where state law does not prohibit collective bargaining. All the arguments for employee rights and the general right of employees to organize run up against the right and duty of the state legislature, representing all citizens, to make decisions on conditions of employment and on budget and salary matters.

The state legislature has a claim to sovereignty which is quite different from the status of the ordinary private company with which a union may bargain. Both legislators and government employees normally try not to reach the impasse of each pressing its rights to the utmost. Employee-union representatives lobby before the state legislature, and the legislators attempt to appraise their claims reasonably.

★ Ban of certain political activity

Because the spoils system involves coercing public employees to engage in political activity for the candidates or party responsible for their hiring, such coercion is banned by national, state, and local laws in many instances. Frequently these laws are not enforced strictly, but where they are enforced they limit the political activity of state and local employees rather severely.

The so-called Hatch Acts, passed by Congress in 1939-1940, affect all state and local employees whose employment is in connection with any activity financed in whole or in part by loans or grants made by the United States. This would include most state employees in such departments as highways, health, welfare, and agriculture and many local government employees. Elective officers, certain department heads, and employees of state or local educational institutions are exempt from the law. The acts provide that no employee shall

> (1) use his official authority or influence for the purpose of interfering with an election or a nomination for office, or affecting the result thereof, or (2) directly or indirectly coerce, attempt to coerce, command, or advise any other such officer or employee to pay, lend, or contribute any part of his salary or compensation or anything else of value to any party, committee, organization, agency, or person for political purposes.

This part of the law seems totally unobjectionable and has helped to curb gross abuses.

However, the law also provides that "no such officer or employee shall take any active part in political management or in political campaigns." This impinges rather severely on the political activity of an employee during his leisure hours and is opposed by many people, including a number of public-employee unions. Their opposition has been accentuated by the passage of some state laws, board of regents' resolutions, and city-charter provisions paralleling the Hatch Acts.

Public employees must not be allowed to engage in partisan political activity during their working hours nor should they campaign as representatives of the agencies for which they work. Yet in those areas in which the merit system is rather firmly established, two things should be possible:

(1) to ensure an employee a leave of absence without prejudice if he wants to engage in political action that would encroach upon normal working hours; (2) to permit an employee to engage freely in any partisan action outside the normal working hours, provided he does not do so as a public employee or use his employment for partisan advantage.

The Future of the Merit System ·

Since states have accepted the idea of merit-system selection in varying degrees, discussion of the future of the merit system necessarily generalizes inexactly for some states. States which still select employees as a reward for routine party work or on the basis of personal friendship with little regard to competence have many steps to take before they can be included in much of this summary of the future. On the other hand, the national requirement of merit selection in the social-security program, the increased number of functions and specializations in state programs, general full employment in the economy, and other factors have forced all states to give more attention to means of positive recruitment and retention of employees. Every state has raised its salary scales, most have developed retirement systems and placed their employees under national old-age and survivors' insurance, several have partially removed residence requirements, most have extended the number of days of available sick and vacation leave, and in other ways generally have attempted to attract and to retain capable employees for careers in state service.

Probably the majority of states continue to find the national government and private industry tough competitors. Highway departments seeking engineers, tax departments looking for auditors, and health departments recruiting doctors and psychiatrists often find all their efforts futile in the face of relatively low state salaries, uncertain conditions of employment, and the lesser status of state employees. Perhaps states succeed best where they establish good working conditions in all aspects and then emphasize to potential employees the opportunities for service in working for the state. Many individuals are willing to make reasonable economic sacrifices if they can definitely give service. The general quality of state employees in New York, California, Oregon, Wisconsin, and some other states shows that it is possible to give stature to state employment.

States with entrenched merit systems would do well not only to continue research and activity in all the established lines but increasingly to recognize the function of personnel agencies and the personnel process as service to the operating agencies of the state. Many governors and administrative agency heads want competent employees and recognize that narrow party loyalty and activity is an insufficient test. These governors and administrators share the general goals of the merit system agency. But the governors and administrators also want employees who sympathize with their general policy goals. If the personnel agency clings too stubbornly to technical provisions of the civil-service laws and regulations and fails to provide the quality of employees needed, the public may lose respect for the principles of the merit system.

REFERENCES

Appleby, Paul H., *Morality and Administration in Democratic Government*. Baton Rouge, La.: Louisiana State University Press, 1952.

"A Code of Public Ethics for Arlington County, Virginia," XIII *Public Administration Review* (Spring 1953), 120-122. A number of communities have adopted such codes. The New York City Code was approved by the Mayor and the City Council in 1959.

Commission on Organization of the Executive Branch of the Government, *Task Force Report on Personnel and Civil Service*. Washington, D. C.: Government Printing Office, 1955. The report for the Second Hoover Commission which discusses personnel questions from the national-government point of view.

Fabricant, Solomon, *The Trend of Government Activity in the United States Since 1900*. New York: Bureau of Economic Research, 1952.

Holloway, W. V., *Personnel Administration in the States*. Oklahoma City: Oklahoma Legislative Council, 1948.

Janowitz, Morris, and Deil Wright, "The Prestige of Public Employment: 1929 and 1954," XVI *Public Administration Review* (Winter 1956), 15-21.

National Civil Service League and National Municipal League, *Model State Civil Service Law*, New York: National Municipal League, 1946.

New York State Civil Service Commission, *Civil Service Administration in the Empire State*, Albany, 1949.

Personnel Review (quarterly).

Sorauf, Frank J., "Patronage and Party," III *Midwest Journal of Political Science* (May 1959), 115-126.

Wilbern, York, "Professionalization in the Public Service: Too Little or Too Much?", XIV *Public Administration Review* (Winter 1954).

CHAPTER 16

State Revenues

BEFORE ANY LEVEL of government can perform the services demanded of it today, that government must raise the moneys it spends. Plato and Aristotle apparently began the Western tradition of writing books on politics and government without considering how governments are financed. Many books in political theory, constitutional law, and governmental organization are still written that way, but when government is dealt with realistically as a practical operating thing, public finance becomes one of its more important aspects.

Alexander Hamilton gave a vigorous and incisive analysis of money as the "vital principle" of the body politic in *The Federalist*.[1] To call revenue, as some do, either the life blood or the food supply of the state is figurative rather than scientific, but certain it is that much of the state's organization is built around and modified by the functions of drawing in revenue and sending it out again as expenditure. Moreover, there are few issues of politics that arise more frequently and persistently than questions of taxes and public expenditures.

As the revenue needs of government have increased with the expansion of governmental services, the three levels of government have become more and more competitive in their struggle for revenue sources. Out of

[1] No. 30.

this competition, in turn, has come increasing interdependence. Situated in the middle, between the other two levels, the states have become involved in their financing with both the national government and the local governments, while in practice a few connecting lines run directly from the national to the local treasuries. The fiscal interconnections take many different forms: taxation of the same persons and things by national, state, and local governments; grants-in-aid and loans from higher to lower levels; gifts; sharing of costs of joint services; and so on. But when we say "interconnections" and "interdependence," we in effect say "changes in the form of organization and in the functioning of governments." National, state, and local governments are, as it were, consolidating or growing together into a more integrated form, largely because of financial and functional connections and joint activities.

In addition to taxation, governments have various sources of revenue: income from investments and rents of property, fees and charges for a variety of services (such as educational tuition fees and charges for street and highway services), sales of products from prison industries and farms, and various others. These can be increased to some extent but usually not enough to meet increasing public needs. In 1958, for example, all government revenues amounted to $130 billion, of which taxes produced $98 billion and all other revenue sources only $32 billion, or about 25 percent of the total. It is only by taxing that governments can obtain the large sums they need each year to cover their expenditures. Furthermore, there is little or no conflict among governments over miscellaneous revenues, while the struggle over tax resources is keen and unabating. For these reasons, among the sources of revenue, it is taxation that will receive the most attention.

The Taxing Power of the States

★ Constitutional limits on state taxing powers

In Chapter 3 we gave passing notice to the constitutional limitations on the taxing powers of the states. We now analyze these a little more fully so as to show the legal boundaries and extent of state tax resources. The local governments are, of course, under the same United States constitutional tax limitations plus a number of additional ones, so that this discussion applies as much to local as to state governments.

Express limitations. The states, as noted in Chapter 3, are forbidden to levy import, export, and tonnage taxes. For practical purposes these prohibitions are more important as trade regulations than as sources of revenue, and therefore we need not discuss them at length here.

Implied prohibition against taxing national government. In general the states may not tax the property, functions, activities, or instrumentalities of the national government without the consent of Congress. That consent has been given rather sparingly. National banks, though privately owned, are instrumentalities of the nation, and Congress could exempt them from state taxation more than it has. In practice it permits the states to tax their real estate like any other privately owned property, and also their capital, provided the tax rates imposed are not higher on national banks than on other private capital used for lending purposes. In general Congress does not permit the states to tax national public lands and buildings, or national postal or other facilities and services.

It is impossible to calculate how much revenue the states might get if they could impose such taxes, but several points are fairly clear. (1) If Congress permitted such taxation of the national government's property and services, it would also have to increase its own tax revenues by an amount equal to the state taxes thereon, so that on a nation-wide basis there would be no saving to the taxpayers. (2) Unless Congress regulated uniformly the rates of state taxes on its property and services, there would be great inequalities in such taxes from state to state, so that some states would be taking an unfair advantage of others through taxes on the national government. (3) An unlimited power in the states to tax the national government, if it had been used without restraint, might have destroyed the national government in its infancy. From that viewpoint Chief Justice Marshall's "The power to tax involves the power to destroy" was undoubtedly right.[2]

Instead of permitting state taxation of national public lands, buildings, and services, Congress has provided for certain limited payments to state and local authorities in lieu of such taxes, and has also provided greater grants-in-aid (under the federal aid for highways laws, for example) for states in which there are unusually large amounts of United States public lands. To give but one example of a sort of in-lieu payment, a part of the revenue from the United States forests is paid to the governments of the states and local units in which the revenue arises; such payments are generally thought of as being in lieu of state and local taxes on the forests and to help support local public services. Because the present in-lieu payment arrangements are scattered throughout the laws and do not conform to any clear general principles, representative officials of the state and national government have been studying the whole problem for some time

[2] McCulloch *vs.* Maryland, 4 Wheat. 316 (1819).

with a view to proposing general legislation. In the meantime such in-lieu payments from the United States to the state and local governments, while important in some regions, are a very small factor (less than 1 percent) in the revenues of state and local governments. Grants-in-aid present a separate subject matter to be considered later.

Taxes that burden interstate commerce. If each state could tax freely and in its own way the interstate commerce that flows into, out of, and across it, states would develop great inequalities in taxing the same business (a railroad operating in many states, for example) and the same type of business. Agricultural, industrial, and mining states would follow different policies, according to their separate judgments as to their own interests. In addition, the total tax burden on interstate commerce might in some states and on some types of commerce be more than the commerce could bear.

In the absence of specific action by Congress, the Supreme Court has developed the doctrines (1) that it is the intent of the commerce clause of the Constitution that interstate commerce shall be free from burdensome state and local taxes and restrictions, and (2) that "the silence of Congress" on the subject indicates that Congress also expects such commerce to be unburdened, and does not by its silence grant the state or local authorities a right to burden commerce with taxes. It happens, however, that a great deal of all commerce is now interstate, and that farmers, miners, manufacturers, publishers, and others produce largely for interstate commerce. Does it follow that state and local governments may not tax anything or any person that is engaged in or that contributes to interstate commerce? Their taxing powers would indeed be seriously restricted if this were the situation, but fortunately for them it is not so.

With respect to taxes on or affecting interstate commerce the Supreme Court follows several major principles. One is that state and local taxes must not discriminate against interstate commerce in favor of local commerce or business. Taxes upon nonresident merchants, peddlers, or salesmen that are not matched by corresponding taxes on local or resident competitors are examples of legislative acts that will be held unconstitutional because they are discriminatory. The methods of taxing need not be exactly the same but there must be substantial equivalence of burden on out-of-state and in-state dealers and businesses if ths laws are to be sustained. A second principle is that the state or local tax on or affecting commerce should not be directly or unduly burdensome. The movement of persons, goods, or communications into or through a state may not be directly taxed, but when goods have come to rest within a state they may be taxed the same as other comparable goods. Since Congress is empowered to regulate interstate commerce, its legislation concerning the taxation of commerce by the states will be respected by the courts. If Congress wants to let down the bars that ordinarily restrict the states, it may do so.

Within these limitations the states may tax corporations and other persons engaged in commerce within the state (1) upon their real estate (railroad rights-of-way) within the state; (2) upon the proportion of their movable property (railroad cars) used within the state; (3) upon their gross or net income earned within the state; (4) upon their sales within the state (under a general sales tax); and so on. The courts will pass upon the reasonableness of such state taxes in proper cases but will not rewrite the laws that the legislatures enact. Furthermore, a state may tax (5) the entire business and income of a manufacturing or mining company located wholly within the state, even though most or all of the product is shipped out; and a state may tax (6) corporations that it has chartered upon their net worth as represented by stock values, again provided that it does not directly discriminate against interstate commerce as such but taxes alike all the corporations it has chartered.

There are two fields of great importance in a revenue sense in which the state taxing powers are especially broad. (7) Since the 21st Amendment repealed the 18th or Prohibition Amendment, the power of the states to tax, regulate, or even to prohibit the liquor business is almost unlimited. A state may, for example, place heavier taxes on liquor produced outside and brought into the state than it imposes on liquor produced in the state. (8) Because the highways are acquired, constructed, and maintained largely at the expense of the states, the power of the states to tax motor vehicles, including trucks and buses, using the state highways and to tax motor fuel is subject to very few constitutional restrictions. The states practice reciprocity to a considerable extent, as shown by their not charging license fees on out-of-state cars that are in the state for only short periods, but the power to charge such fees still exists though unused. Trucks and buses that operate regularly in several states must obtain licenses and pay their taxes in all the states concerned.

Due process in taxation. Under what is known as "substantive due process," the courts have laid down several restrictions on state taxing powers. One is the rule that a state may not tax what is not within its jurisdiction— that is, not within its reach constitutionally. The clearest illustration is that a state may not tax real estate in another state. On the other hand, movable things (items of personal property) are supposed to follow the person and to be taxable against him where he resides, no matter where they are. But of course a state may also tax the movable things themselves (stocks, bonds, and so forth) that are found within its limits. Thus it happens that several states may tax the same parts of an inheritance—the state where the stocks and bonds are being held and the state where the deceased owner lived may both tax these movables.

Another substantive restriction is that taxes may be levied only for public purposes. For the legislature to levy a tax on one man in order to give the money raised to another would not be for a public purpose. In this connection poor relief is considered a public purpose, and therefore to tax those who have money or other wealth in order to provide relief for those in want is to tax for a public purpose. The same is true of public education, public housing, and a whole range of other services. Indeed, many functions are now conceded to be for a public purpose that only a few decades ago were not so considered.

Importance of Constitutional restrictions. The Constitutional restrictions on their taxing powers are far from being fatal to the state and local governments. Indeed, the rules are more like a common-sense code that merely keeps the states from encroaching on each other and on the national government. They do not prevent the states from levying any important type of tax whatever. Property taxes, income taxes, inheritance taxes, sales taxes, occupation taxes, and other types of levies are all within the powers of the states, and legally, at least, without any limits as to rates or amounts. Practically all forms and types of business and production are subject to state taxation. In recent years the United States Supreme Court has been usually solicitous of the states' taxing interests. If the states have any grievances on the score of taxation, therefore, they must be found not in the Constitutional law of taxation but in other directions.

★ Practical limits on state taxing powers

Priority of United States tax claims. In law and in fact the taxes levied by the national government enjoy a priority over state and local taxes. This confronts the states with their first substantial difficulty. They are members of a union, not wholly independent states. In that union the national government is responsible for national defense against foreign aggressors and is primarily responsible also for waging war against disasters and depressions at home. Because national defense is the first responsibility of governments, and by far the most urgent and expensive one, the member states in a federal system simply have to concede the priority of national needs over state and local. The framers of the Constitution took care of this to some extent by making the United States Constitution and laws the "supreme

law of the land," and Congress has added laws that definitely give national taxes priority in collection over state and local. World-wide conditions in recent decades, with two world wars, a great depression, the continuance of the cold war, and a change in government-spending policy
have made the fiscal needs of the national government overwhelmingly
greater than those of state and local governments combined. On the other
hand, state and local governments have been increasing their expenditures
faster than has the national government for its expenditures apart from
national defense. In 1958, the national government was taking over $68
billion in taxes, the states had come up to $15 billion, and local govern-
ments, $15 billion. State and local taxes combined thus amounted to about
31 percent of all taxes collected, national taxes about 69 percent.

Limitations of economics and politics. The economic and political limitations of taxation have been debated for centuries. It is reasonably clear
that no formula exists which establishes that if you raise taxes to such and
such a limit that either the economy will collapse or that the party in
power will be turned out of office. In periods of crisis, such as war, citizens
are willing to be taxed heavily to protect their country and the objectives
for which it stands. Government expenditures can contribute to a satisfactory economy for all citizens just as does private industry. It all depends
on what government uses the tax money for and how badly citizens want
the services that the government is providing with the taxes.

In state terms, each individual state's leaders tend to worry about their
tax system in relation to the tax systems of their neighbors. Despite the lack
of full evidence, many state leaders believe that a tax system with a "heavy"
impact on business may drive industry into states with a more favorable
tax climate. Much pointing of fingers goes on in Wisconsin, for example,
to argue that the greater industrial prosperity of Illinois is related to absence of an income tax in Illinois. (Wisconsin relies heavily on income
taxes and does not use the general sales tax of Illinois.) The opposing argument runs that the income tax is a more equitable tax (based on ability to
pay) than the sales tax; and anyway, not taxes but quality of government
services, transportation, labor, and raw materials determine industry location.

To take 100 percent of the people's income and leave them nothing to
live on is the outside limit that no government even closely approaches.
On the other hand specific taxes, as on liquor for example, may be so high
that there is a great deal of tax evasion. People will also reduce their consumption of liquor, and the net revenue becomes less at the higher rates.
These are economic limitations, but usually before they are reached the

political considerations begin to operate. Legislators and councilmen refuse to risk the great unpopularity they would probably suffer if they were to vote ever higher taxes. But again, the politically acceptable height of taxes is closely related to the intensity of popular demand for government services.

Territorial and administrative limits.   Because each state is limited to taxing only within its own area, although most business is done on an interstate or nation-wide basis, states cannot reach considerable taxable wealth and income. Theoretically they should be able to do so, especially if they cooperated fully with each other. In practice, fifty state governments operating under territorial limitations and conforming to different tax theories and laws, simply cannot do to the large taxable aggregations of wealth what one national Internal Revenue Service with nation-wide power can do.

Mutual forbearance and recognition of needs.   In his discussion of the concurrent taxing powers of the national and state governments, Alexander Hamilton argued that when one level of government imposed a certain tax, the other would probably forbear to use the same tax, out of consideration for the needs of the other.[3] The national government has not shown this predicted forbearance toward the states—perhaps it has not been able to do so. Similarly many states have invaded the tax fields already occupied by the national government. The states generally took up the taxation of tobacco after the national government, and the latter began to tax gasoline after most of the states. Other examples could be given. In 1958, 93 percent of combined national and state tax revenues came from tax categories used by both levels of government.

The state governments have been in the more difficult position because they must look after not only their own needs but also those of their local units. Many states have given up the ordinary property tax entirely to their local units, and having done so, they are simply compelled to find more revenue from other tax sources, some of which, like personal and corporate income taxes, are already being used by the national government.

Congress has power to regulate its tax relations with the states and has done so to some extent, notably in the case of inheritance taxes. In this field the problem was to stabilize national revenues and to protect the majority of the states against a few states that advertised themselves as havens for the wealthy, without inheritance taxes. To these ends, Congress enacted a tax law with certain rates and exemptions under which any taxpayer who

[3] *The Federalist*, Nos. 33, 34, 36. "Reciprocal forbearance" is the phrase used in No. 36.

could show that he was paying a state inheritance tax could deduct the amount thereof up to 80 percent of his United States inheritance tax, when paying the latter. This act showed considerable Congressional forbearance toward the states. Residents of states without inheritance-tax laws paid 100 percent of all their inheritance taxes due into the United States treasury. States without inheritance taxes lost revenue and their taxpayers gained no advantage by the absence of such a tax; as a result most states adopted the tax. Later, however, Congress imposed additional taxes on inheritances over the original rates, and these added sums all go into the United States treasury. Congressional forbearance toward state taxes in this instance is, therefore, somewhat limited, but the experience shows what may some day be done with other taxes—possibly with income taxes—although the states would have to be in extremely dire need before Congress would take so drastic a step.

Clearly, then, the state and local governments are in an inferior fiscal situation as compared with the national government. Only world-wide peace and security and a substantial reduction of military expenditures can do much to begin to correct the balance. For example, the many proposals that have been made for Congress to repeal its taxes on gasoline and admissions to places of amusement, in order to relinquish these tax sources to the states, will probably have to wait until more peaceful times.[4]

Taxing Powers of Local Governments

Local units of government do not have any inherent taxing powers of their own. They are creatures and agents of the state and have only such powers as the states confer upon them. Some state constitutions contain charter provisions or tax-limitation clauses that appear to give local units some taxing power, but in most states the local units have only such taxing powers as the legislatures delegate to them. The latter arrangement is probably the most logical, since it enables the legislature to adjust the entire tax system of the state to the needs of both the state and local governments.

In practice the states confer upon local governments the right to tax property, but this right is hedged about with many restrictions that determine the basis of property valuation, the rates of tax that may be levied, and the methods of collection and enforcement. The local authorities can do very little except to influence slightly the increase or decrease of valua-

[4] A good discussion of national-state tax relations is found in U. S. Congress, House of Representatives, Committee on Ways and Means, *Coordination of Federal, State, and Local Taxes* (Washington, D. C.: Government Printing Office, 1953), House Report 2519.

tions and to set tax rates for local purposes up to but not beyond what the law allows. A number of states have left the property tax entirely to local governments, and in all states this tax provides the great bulk of local tax revenue.

Many states have also conferred upon cities and other local units the power to levy taxes upon one or more of the following: local businesses and occupations, admissions to places of amusement, utility bills, retail sales, liquor and liquor establishments, cigarettes and other tobacco products, motor vehicles and motor fuel, parimutuel betting, and incomes.

The New York and Pennsylvania laws of 1947 gave their local governments unusual taxing powers. When the property tax failed to yield enough revenue (a common experience of local units) New York, in the depression of the 1930s, authorized New York City to levy various new taxes, such as a 2-percent retail sales tax, a general business gross-receipts tax, and a public utility gross-receipts tax. In 1947 the state extended authority to counties and cities over 25,000 to levy a variety of nonproperty taxes. New York local governments have used only the following: (a) 1 to 3 percent on retail sales and use; (b) 5 percent on restaurant meals, if the charge is $1 or more; (c) 3 percent on utility bills; (d) 15 to 30 percent on admission to harness races and flat races; (e) 5 percent on admissions; (f) ¼ of 1 percent on gross receipts from businesses or professions (⅖ of 1 percent on the gross income of financial businesses), and (g) 5 percent on occupancy of hotel rooms if the rent is $2 or more per day.[5] New York City used a few additional taxes including a 1¢ per-pack tax on cigarettes.

Pennsylvania more than ten years ago went even further in some respects, although it had previously been reluctant to grant "home-rule" tax powers to localities. By its famous Act 481 of 1947, it authorized all cities except Philadelphia, all school districts except those of Philadelphia and Pittsburgh, and all boroughs and first-class townships to tax anything not taxed by the state, with a few exceptions stated in the law, and subject to the proviso that the total taken by any community from the new taxes should not exceed what could be raised by a real estate tax at the maximum allowable local tax rate.[6] Although the state courts have not ruled in detail on the matter, it is believed that home rule for Wisconsin cities extends to giving them all taxing powers not prohibited to them by state statutes or the constitution.

The legislation in most other states has been more piecemeal and limited, but in all states there is a trend toward granting more taxing pow-

5 The New York State and Local Tax System 1958, Department of Taxation and Finance, Albany, 1958, pp. 26, 27.
6 See David H. Kurtzman, "Pennsylvania's Home Rule Tax Law," I GRA Reporter, No. 2 (March-April 1949), 1, 7-8.

ers to local governments. The revenue from the new sources does not any-where near equal that from the property tax, but time may bring a fuller utilization of the new powers. Experience has already revealed, however, that many taxes are not highly suitable for local administration. The ex-pense of administering them in small units is disproportionately high. Then, too, the rate of evasion may be rather considerable, especially in the case of local sales taxes. People tend to buy their cigarettes and other commodities where there is no tax, and to enforce a "use tax" on goods bought elsewhere is not easy. The "home-rule" idea in local taxation leads to differences in the taxes employed from place to place, with attendant confusion. More experience with such home-rule laws may lead to more general adoption of a few standard taxes and, possibly, to some state as-sistance in their administration.

In general, however, the local governments are in the poorest position of all with respect to freedom to work out their tax difficulties and increase their revenues. They are forced to go to their state legislatures, session after session, to get increased taxing powers, and the legislatures, with the competing claims of state departments and institutions to consider, are generally more tightfisted than the local authorities like. County, township, and school-district taxing powers are restricted almost everywhere to the levying of property taxes, but counties and school districts receive con-siderable state aid. States differ greatly in their degree of generosity with grants-in-aids and shared taxes to urban places (villages and cities). Chap-ter 6 indicated that state-local fiscal arrangements is often the critical problem in metropolitan areas.

Principal Tax Sources

Every state and locality has its own financial peculiarities, for each has developed its own fiscal policy and system of taxation according to local conditions, taxable resources, and the ideas of those who successively domi-nated state politics.[7] The question of tax policy is always a major issue in every government, because there is a direct relationship between what is taken in taxes and what is left over of personal and corporate incomes for private expenditure. Taxpayers' associations struggle against tax increases generally but usually are especially concerned about property-tax rates. Manufacturing and mining interests, agricultural and labor interests fight the tax changes that they think will adversely affect them. The line is

[7] *The Book of the States* and annual reports of the Bureau of the Census show types of taxes employed by the states. Some changes take place almost every legislative session.

now drawn in most states between those who favor a sales tax and oppose progressive income taxes, and those who want progressive income taxes to bring in the bulk of state revenue and oppose all general sales taxes as being especially burdensome on people of small incomes. Subsidiary conflicts exist over whether the gasoline tax should all go into highway work, how the local governments shall share in gasoline and income taxes, what the liquor and tobacco taxes shall be and how shared, and so on. In the struggles over tax policy the states have developed a considerable number of different taxes, but as these appear in divergent forms and combinations in different states, no two states are strictly comparable.

★ *Shift from the state property tax*

One rather general tendency in all states has been the attempt to limit the tax burden on property and to shift the property tax more and more to the local units. Some states have abandoned it as a source of state revenue and reserved it under limitations for the local governments. To fill the gap in their revenues, the states have developed and more or less reserved for themselves a variety of other taxes.

Table 9. STATE TAX REVENUES IN MILLIONS OF DOLLARS, 1959

Sales, use, and gross receipts		9,289
General sales, use, and gross receipts	3,694	
Motor vehicle fuels	3,048	
Alcoholic beverages	599	
Tobacco products	680	
Other	1,269	
License and privilege		2,310
Motor vehicles and operators	1,381	
Other	929	
Individual income		1,778
Corporation income		979
Property		565
Death and gift		349
Other		562
Grand total		15,831

Source: U. S. Bureau of the Census, *State Tax Collections in 1959*, G-SF59-No. 3, August 23, 1959.

NOTE: Because of rounding, the items do not always add up to the totals. Hawaii tax revenues not included.

It will be noted in Table 9 that the property tax which had once been the principal source of state revenue was in 1959 producing only 3.6 percent of the total revenue of the states, although it was still an important producer in a small number of states. For *general* state purposes, the general

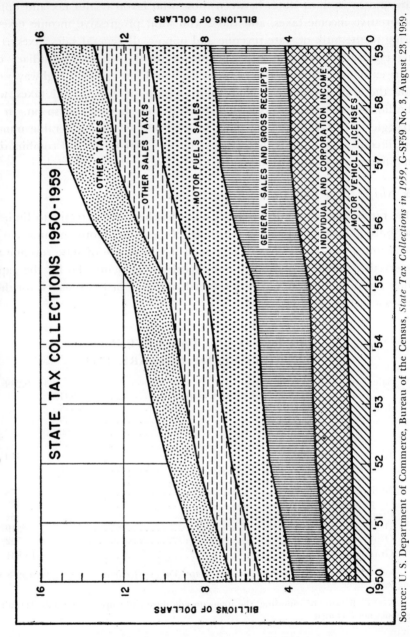

Figure 11. STATE TAX COLLECTIONS, 1950-1959

Source: U. S. Department of Commerce, Bureau of the Census, *State Tax Collections in 1959*, G-SF59 No. 3, August 23, 1959.

sales, use, gross-receipts, and income taxes were far out in the lead, and even liquor and tobacco taxes separately exceeded the property tax as producers of state revenue. Leading "income tax states" included New York, California, Wisconsin, Massachusetts, Minnesota, North Carolina, Oregon, and Pennsylvania (corporate income tax only), but California, North Carolina, and Pennsylvania also had general sales taxes or the equivalent. Outstanding general sales-tax states were California, Florida, Georgia, Illinois, Indiana, Michigan, Missouri, Ohio, Pennsylvania and Washington.

The taxes that are devoted primarily to highway purposes, namely, the gasoline, motor-vehicle, and motor-vehicle-operator taxes, together produced about $4.2 billion or almost one fourth of all revenues.

Although the property tax has shrunk *proportionately* as a producer of state revenue, it is providing more dollars to the state treasuries than in many earlier years. In 1890 it yielded the states only $69 million, but this was over 90 percent of all state taxes then. As the property-tax revenue increased in absolute amounts, it fell behind in its percentage of the total. What has happened, in short, is a tremendous increase in the scale of state revenues and expenditures, an increase so great that the property tax alone was insufficient to carry the load.

★ Local tax sources

If we go back again to 1890 we find that local taxes then exceeded state taxes by more than 4 to 1, or $405 million against $96 million. Since then and down through 1957 local taxes had increased 43 times, while state taxes had jumped all of 145 times.[8] By 1942 the tax revenues of the forty-eight states, which had been lagging so far behind local taxes, had passed all the tax revenues of the over 155,000 local units of government (see Table 10). During the subsequent years the tax revenues of the states and local governments have remained roughly equal, with the states collecting slightly more tax revenues in total.

As the result of state restrictions and administrative difficulties local governments have not been able to enter freely into the rich fields of income, sales, payroll, and other forms of taxation. They were left with just one basic tax, the property tax. In 1890 it was yielding them $374 million or 92 percent of all their tax revenue. In 1946 it produced thirteen times as much for the local governments, or $4904 million, and this was still a little over 92 percent of all local tax revenue. Since 1946 a number of new local taxes have been introduced here and there, as mentioned above, but

8 Bureau of the Census, *Historical Review of State and Local Government Finances,* June 1948, p. 13; *Governmental Finances in the United States 1902 to 1957,* March 1959; and *Compendium of State Government Finances in 1958* (Washington, D. C.: Government Printing Office 1959).

even in 1958 property taxes accounted for 80 percent of all local tax revenue ($14,273 million out of $17,865 million).

Table 10. COMPARISON OF STATE AND LOCAL TAX REVENUES, SELECTED YEARS, 1902-1957

Govern-ments	1957	1956	1955	1954	1953	1952	1942	1932	1922	1913	1902
State	14,531	13,375	11,597	11,089	10,552	9,857	3,903	1,890	947	301	156
Local	14,511	12,992	11,886	10,978	10,356	9,466	4,625	4,274	3,069	1,308	704
Total	29,042	26,367	23,483	22,067	20,908	19,323	8,528	6,164	4,016	1,609	860

Source: U. S. Department of Commerce, Bureau of the Census, *Governmental Finances in the United States, 1902-1957* (Washington: Government Printing Office, March 1959). Hawaii and Alaska were not states in 1957 and their revenues are not included.

The fact is, of course, that both state and local governments in recent decades have come to rely more and more on revenues other than their own taxes, and largely on revenues that they do not themselves raise.

Nontax Revenues

★ *Grants-in-aid and shared taxes*

One of the most obvious changes in state and local finance in recent decades is the rapid increase of grants-in-aid—from the national government primarily to the states but also to local units, and from the states to their local governments. Most grants-in-aid are regular, recurrent payments that are tied to expenditure on specific services, like highways, relief, and education. The receiving government is usually required to match the grants dollar for dollar or in some other ratio, and then to spend both the grant and its own matching contribution on the service concerned. Grants-in-aid have been introduced by higher level governments, national and state, in recognition of their own responsibilities and superior financial resources, as a means of establishing new public services, raising the standards of services especially in the poorer areas, providing for more uniformity of services over large areas, helping to equalize the tax burden among governmental units of very unequal financial capacity, and for other purposes.

In 1958 the states received grants-in-aid from the national government in the amount of $4461 million, which was over 17 percent of all state revenues.[9] In 1902 there was only $7 million of such aid reported, and this was less than 1 percent of all state revenue.

[9] Bureau of the Census, *Compendium, op. cit.*, p. 6.

But in 1958 the states aided local governments in the amount of $7943 million, or almost twice as much as the states received from the national government (grants-in-aid and shared taxes). A part of this money came from the national government and was handed on down to the local units, as for old-age assistance. The total of state aid to local governments has increased rapidly in recent years, and now averages nearly 30 percent of all local revenues. This average contribution is very unevenly distributed, however. Some states give very little aid to their local units, others a great deal. Among units of government, school districts and counties receive the bulk of state aid, because they are primarily responsible for the most-aided functions—public education, public assistance (primarily old-age assistance), and highways. The general functions of cities, villages, and towns are definitely the "stepchildren" when it comes to grants-in-aid from the states.

Governments have almost complete control over revenues that they raise for themselves within their own territory and from their own people. This is not true of grants-in-aid, since the acceptance of grants always implies the acceptance of conditions. An outside will, that of another government, has something to say about how the money shall be spent. There must be negotiation, agreement, supervision, and auditing if the granting authorities and the receiving authorities are both to be satisfied. Several of the states (but not the national government) make some of their assistance available in the form of shared taxes. States share a specified portion of a state-wide income and sales or other taxes with local governments. The local government recipient may use the shared tax money for any expenditure purpose. *No* supervision and audit follows by the state. The receiving government is, however, not guaranteed a particular amount (as is usual with grants-in-aid) and must depend on the amount the tax happens to yield each year.

★ *State borrowing and debt*

If a state government wishes to spend in excess of tax and other revenues, the constitution usually gives some power to borrow. The exact policies permitted by the constitution and pursued by states in borrowing and long term debt differ greatly. In some instances low current per-capita taxes are bought at the price of high per capita long term debt. In other states almost no borrowing has been undertaken and even long-use capital items have been paid for currently. Constitutional debt limits may be high or low and even where the limit is very low in terms of modern expenditure levels many states have found it possible to avoid the constitutional specifications through the establishment of separate "authorities" or "corporations" which borrow and spend for the state without technically using the state's credit. Wisconsin, for example, has established building corporations which borrow to build structures needed by the state; charge the state rent for the use of the completed buildings; use the rent to pay off the bonds issued; and eventually turn the debt-free building over to the state. This and other measures of avoiding constitutional debt limits in Wisconsin and other states have received the blessing of state supreme courts.

Students of public finance formerly worried a great deal about the borrowing and debts of state and local governments. City debts in particular were a cause of concern. In 1890 state and local gross debt exceeded that of the national government—$1137 million as against $1122 million.[10] This excess continued to increase until in 1913 state and local gross debt was over three times that of the national government—$3822 million as against $1193 million. In World War I the trend was sharply reversed, and in 1919 the national debt jumped ahead—to over $25,000 million. But by 1932 state and local debt had almost overtaken the national debt—$17,577 million (a great state and local increase) as against $19,487 million (a substantial decrease from the wartime peak). Thereafter the national debt pulled ahead steadily, especially during World War II. In 1949 the national debt of $252 billion was twelve times the state and local debt of nearly $21 billion, or over 92 percent of the total public debt. Today the difference is so great, and men think in such utterly different terms about debt, that state and local indebtedness no longer causes as much concern. Furthermore, besides being widely distributed, state and local bonds now issue at such low rates of interest that the tax burden to support the debt is proportionately smaller.

State Tax Administration

There was a time when the states did very little directly in the administration of taxes. Relying as they did almost entirely on the property tax, they simply determined once every year or two, through legislative action, how much property-tax revenue was to be collected for state purposes by or in each town, city, and county. They then waited for the local tax officials to levy and collect the tax and to turn over to the state treasury (which had a first claim on collections) the amount to which the state was entitled. Lawsuits were employed when necessary to make the local officials do their

[10] Bureau of the Census, *Historical Statistics of the United States, 1789-1945* (Washington, D. C.: Government Printing Office, 1949), pp. 306, 314.

duty, to collect the money from them, or to punish them for "nonfeasance" or "misfeasance." The local property-tax officials—assessors, tax collectors, treasurers, and auditors—were elected or appointed in each town or city, or in the larger units, the counties. The assessor listed the values of the various properties subject to taxation; the tax collector collected the amounts calculated to be due from the taxpayers to the state, the county, and the other local units; the treasurer received and accounted for the money; and the auditor audited the books and official performances of all concerned. Thus local officials administered the state's principal tax. Early legislatures made various attempts to equalize the valuations of property in all towns or counties, so that taxpayers in one place would not have to pay state taxes out of proportion to those elsewhere. They entrusted some authority in this matter to the state auditors and treasurers, but they were slow to set up separate state administrative officers for the purpose of equalizing taxes. Later they created state boards of equalization and state tax commissions for this purpose.

Still later, when the legislatures began to add new taxes, they assigned the work of administering them to various officials, such as the treasurer, secretary of state, attorney general, board of equalization, or state tax commission—each one on the basis of some special decision (this official was unpopular or of the wrong party; that one was not efficient, or he knew too little about tax law, and so forth). Whatever the reasons, the work of state tax administration was scattered around the state capitol in different offices, a little here and a little there. Much of this condition still prevails in some states, but nowadays the trend is toward setting up one state department of taxation to administer most or all the state taxes. The ideal of some students and administrators is to have one all-inclusive finance department, which will collect all taxes.

The creation of various central state-tax-collection departments has resulted in a considerable increase in efficiency in tax administration. It is generally agreed that several states do excellent work in administering their income, sales, gross earnings, and other state-wide taxes. There are always some difficulties such as the import of gasoline and various consumers goods from other states without payment of the state taxes, but the Supreme Court has upheld the requirement that shippers in interstate commerce (mail-order houses, for example) must cooperate with the tax authorities in collecting sales taxes for the states into which they send taxable goods, and direct cooperation between tax officials in the various states also helps to plug some of the leaks.

A typical system of state tax administration would today be hard to find.[11] In each state there is usually one state agency for taxation or revenue purposes that is called the department of taxation, department of revenue, department of finance, tax commission, or something like that, which exercises a rather broad authority in the administration of state revenue laws. This agency may be headed by a commission, usually of three salaried members who actually engage in its administration, or by a single person called commissioner or director. These officers are generally appointed by the governor with senate or council approval. In addition to this general revenue agency, one or more other offices usually collect a special tax, such as that on motor-vehicle licenses. Under the recent New Jersey constitution, provision has been made by the legislature for a department of the treasury, headed by an appointed state treasurer, which is responsible for all the state's fiscal affairs, including the collection of all revenues. This appears to be a more complete integration of fiscal functions than any other state has yet achieved. If such a department had responsibility for all the revenue functions of an average or large state, as in the case of the United States Treasury Department for the national government, it would have a great deal to do. The average state today collects over $450 million annually from a great variety of taxes and nontax sources, borrows and repays borrowings in considerable amounts, supervises local tax assessment and administration, and performs a number of other revenue functions. In administering several of its taxes it may seek and receive assistance from the Internal Revenue Service.

State Expenditures

As we turn away from revenue and income to the expenditure side of state and local finance, let us try to grasp once more the significance of what we are dealing with. Everyone knows that in dollar amounts the figures are tremendously greater than they used to be, and in general continue to increase (see Table 11). In 1890 state and local governments combined spent less than $9 per capita for all purposes except debt retirement. The amount increased slowly but steadily for the next three decades. Then in the depression decade of the 1930s, when relief and public works spending took so much money, it rose in 1932 to over $67 per capita and kept going up. Today the amount spent annually, including what comes through federal aid, is about $240 per capita. In 1957, state and local governments in five states spent less than $160 per capita and from that minimum the

11 *The Book of the States 1958-59*, pp. 126-127 lists the state "revenue" and "taxation" departments.

range of expenditures extended upward to four states which spent in excess of $300 per capita.

★ Increases in expenditures

When compared with the increases in national government expenditures, state and local increases do not loom so large. The same is true when the amounts are compared on a per-capita basis with the estimated incomes of the people. In fact, it is debatable whether recent years have shown much increase in the percentage of the national income taken for all state and local public purposes. In 1932, when incomes were almost at their lowest for many years and relief and public works were being provided on a large scale, state and local revenues took nearly 18 percent of the total income. By 1942 this figure was down to 8.3 percent, and by 1946 down to 7.5 percent.[12] In 1957, state and local revenues represented almost 10 percent of the total national income.

A comparison of gross national product with state and local expenditures is also striking. "Gross national product" is an inclusive concept of all production (which we will not try to explain here) which is widely used for statistical purposes. In 1932 all state and local government expenditures amounted to 12.7 percent of the gross national product; from that year they declined, until in 1944, about the middle of World War II, they accounted for only 3.6 percent of the gross national product. From that point they increased slightly in the postwar years to take 5.4 percent in 1947.[13] These figures do not include federal grants-in-aid which would raise the percentages about one tenth, but the percentages are still low in view of the fact that they cover all state and local services, rural and urban, including education, highways, social-welfare work, public health, law enforcement, and general government. With an estimate of $442.5 billion gross national product in 1957, all state and local general expenditures in that year, including grants-in-aid from the national government, were about 8.6 percent of the total.[14]

The absolute increase in expenditures from about $1 billion in 1902 or $7.8 billion in 1932 to $40.4 billion in 1957 reflects many things: the increased population; the decreased purchasing power of the dollar; the increased cost of living and the change in salary levels; the shift from a rural

12 Bureau of the Census, *Historical Review, op. cit.*, June 1948, p. 14; and *State and Local Government Finances in 1957* (Washington, D. C.: Government Printing Office, February 1957).

13 Tax Foundation, *Facts and Figures on Government Finance, 1948-49*, p. 17. Data from U. S. Department of Commerce. U. S. Department of Commerce, *Survey of Current Business*, July 1959, p. 9.

14 Bureau of the Census, *Historical Statistics, op. cit.*, p. 67.

Table 11. GENERAL EXPENDITURES OF STATE AND LOCAL GOVERNMENT BY FUNCTION FOR SELECTED YEARS, 1902-1957

General Expenditures (in millions of dollars)

	1957	1956	1955	1954	1953	1952	1942	1932	1922	1913	1902
Education	14,501	13,220	11,907	10,557	9,390	8,318	2,586	2,311	1,705	577	255
Highways	7,762	6,953	6,452	5,527	4,987	4,650	1,490	1,741	1,294	419	175
Public welfare	3,411	3,139	3,168	3,060	2,914	2,788	1,225	444	119	52	37
Health and hospitals	3,137	2,772	2,524	2,409	2,290	2,185	591	456	258	108	60
Police and fire	2,271	2,067	1,923	1,783	1,636	1,525	630	528	348	165	90
General control	1,712	1,560	1,452	1,375	1,263	1,193	578	470	313	211	141
Sanitation	1,405	1,326	1,142	1,058	908	992	229	223	189	97	51
Interest on debt	1,094	986	838	718	614	552	565	741	382	147	68
Natural resources	1,002	906	793	762	705	776	214	165	61	14	9
All other	4,143	3,782	3,525	3,452	3,203	3,117	1,082	686	549	274	127
Total	40,438	36,711	33,724	30,701	27,910	26,098	9,190	7,765	5,218	2,064	1,013

Source: U. S. Department of Commerce, Bureau of the Census, *Governmental Finances in the United States, 1902-1957* (Washington, D. C.: U. S. Government Printing Office, March 1959). Because of rounding, details may not add to the totals. Neither Alaska nor Hawaii was a state in 1957 and their expenditures are not included.

to an urban society with its greater governmental demands; the great increase in use of the automobile; and the like. The increase also reflects that we are a wealthier nation today with higher personal standards of living that demand higher standards in governmental services. We can afford to send more children to state colleges and universities. We buy more automobiles to use up the highways. We insist on higher minimum standards of health and welfare for all. We want parks and public recreational opportunities. We live longer and we want the higher living standard from birth to death.

★ *Areas of expenditure increase*

More meaningful in many ways than gross expenditure increases is an analysis of expenditure trends by major functions (Table 11). The three most costly functions of state and local government—education, highways, and public welfare—have been the most costly functions and in the same rank order since the enlarged public welfare programs in the 1930s. Health and hospitals have tended to come fourth and police and fire protection fifth. General government, or general control, is about sixth today, substantially lower than the leaders.

Taxes and Expenditures as Politics and Policy

Governors and legislators frequently look at taxes and tax administration with considerable interest. What income levels in the population or what economic sectors pay what proportions of state taxes are matters of high policy and politics. The decision to date of New York State to utilize the income tax heavily in state revenues and not to use a general state sales tax and the rather opposite decision of Illinois to rely on a general state sales tax but not to use either an individual or corporate income tax are a measure of many aspects of the politics and economies of the two states. Perhaps no decision in a state legislature lines up more active interest groups or party loyalties and more opposition than taxes—whether they shall be raised or what taxes shall be emphasized. Both the governor and the legislature also interest themselves in taxes from the point of view of appraising the possible level of expenditure programs. Governmental functions cost money. Many states can not borrow for general expenditures. The estimate of tax revenues for the coming fiscal year or biennium then sets a ceiling for state expenditures unless the governor and legislature agree to add new taxes or higher tax rates. Budgets, discussed in the next chapter, provide plans of state expenditures and revenues as a basis for appraising the desire for expenditures as against the opposition to taxes.

REFERENCES

Anderson, William, *Intergovernmental Fiscal Relations*. Minneapolis: University of Minnesota Press, 1956.

Council of State Governments, *Public Authorities in the States: A Report to the Governors' Conference*. Chicago: Council of State Governments, 1953.

Frank, Henry J., "Measuring State Tax Burdens," 12 *National Tax Journal* (June 1959), 179-185.

Lawrence, Leonard A., "State and Local Governmental Revenue Structures—A National and Regional Analysis," XI *National Tax Journal* (March 1958), 67-77.

Morrow, Glenn D., "State Constitutional Limitations on the Taxing Authority of the State," IX *National Tax Journal* (June 1956), 126-133.

Myers, Eugene A., "Revenue Estimation and State Fiscal Management," 11 *National Tax Journal* (December 1958), 347-353.

Penniman, Clara, and Walter W. Heller, *State Income Tax Administration*. Chicago: Public Administration Service, 1959.

CHAPTER 17

Budgets and State Controls

TAXES AND EXPENDITURES are the two sides of the state's financial plan. For state governments taxes are normally determined exclusively in terms of expenditures. Fifty years ago when states largely used the property tax and seldom had advance spending plans, it was common practice for the state legislature to pass a long series of appropriations. At the end of the session the many appropriation bills would be totaled, and a state property tax set to cover this total. Today most governors have at least some responsibility for presenting a budget to the legislators which shows a plan of recommended expenditures and a plan of recommended revenues which will meet these expenditures.

Changing Concepts of Budgets

As in many other areas of our discussion, the states have not changed their practices uniformly. In the following consideration of developing budget practices, we are really reviewing the changing literature and ideas in the field of budgeting. A few states still operate in the prebudget or nonbudget stage. Others are in more advanced stages, or in a combination of stages,

347

and a few have taken leadership in devising new ways to make the budget serve more and more purposes.

★ Financial procedures in the nonbudget era

Before integrated budgets became the rule, and even now to some extent in some places, different state agencies and pressure groups brought in proposals for expenditures to their respective committees in the legislature, and these, with committee revision and approval, came before the legislature separately. Later on, all appropriations bills also went to the committee on appropriations in each house, and still later in the nineteenth century in some states an officer like the state auditor or comptroller was expected to collect all agency requests in advance of the session and print them in one document for the legislators. This service, performed rather perfunctorily, provided useful information, but it was not planning nor was it budget-making. There was no serious advance study of the requests by a responsible executive officer, no attempt to bring income and outgo into balance, no planning of the whole state's finances and work program for the year. The legislature enacted separate appropriation bills, and only in the closing days of the session could the finance committee or ways and means committee figure out even approximately how much money would have to be raised by taxing and borrowing. Since that was the era of state dependence on the property tax, one of the last-minute acts of the legislature before adjournment was to fix the state property tax for the next year or biennium at such a rate as would presumably bring in the needed revenue to cover the appropriations.

Even today, with more adequate advance budget planning, some state legislatures follow much the same course in handling money bills, but in most states from the beginning of the session the legislature has a much clearer conception of the state's financial needs and resources, and it has a planned financial program that has been submitted by a responsible executive.

★ Efficiency and reform movement

With the turn of the century the growing demand for public services and the insistence of taxpayer groups upon economy in government led to careful study of the budget problems of state and local governments (beginning especially at the Bureau of Municipal Research in New York City about 1906) and the formulation of the idea of financial planning and budgeting for all units of American government. This phase of the general planning movement began to produce results before World War I, just when the city-planning movement was well started. Several states had adopted budget laws and imposed budget requirements on some of their local governments before the United States Budget and Accounting Act was passed in 1921. These early budget laws—and there were a number of them before the great depression—were naturally incomplete and rather experimental, but they laid the groundwork for testing out the budget idea. Today every state makes provision for an annual or biennial budget, and in addition most large cities, many counties, and considerable numbers of other governmental units also operate under budget laws.

The earliest arguments for budget practices emphasized efficiency and control. Although these words appear in contemporary budget literature, the meaning has grown. Often the earlier view of efficiency seemed to assert that by knowing and showing totals of moneys spent by each department for the detail of personnel, supplies, equipment and other items of expenditures, it would be possible for the governor and the legislature to recognize waste. Recognition of waste would bring efficiency. Inadequate attention was given to the fact that efficiency has meaning only in terms of specific objectives and that many might disagree as to these objectives.

★ Executive budget

Earlier chapters stressed the increasing functions in government and the accompanying demands for more centralization and control in the governor's hands. The idea that the budget should be an instrument of policy and control for the governor was a part of the efficiency and reform movements. If the governor was to be responsible for the general running of the government and all its programs, then he needed to plan and control the budget for the state. It was also assumed that the governor's budget would be an inclusive plan of *all* expenditures and revenues (*no* segregated or dedicated funds). A well-planned and presented budget gives the governor, the legislature, and the public a comprehensive view of state operations. It is possible for a budget to present an excellent picture of (1) the general financial health of the state government; (2) the types of programs carried on by the state; (3) the future needs of these programs, documented as to population or other trends which would affect the functions involved; (4) the relative costs of all programs; and (5) the governor's view of programs to be emphasized through expenditures and revenues to be raised to meet these expenditures.

The executive budget theory (especially in the first decades of this century) often attempted to argue for the governor a role similar to that of the prime minister in the British Parliamentary system where the budget of the Government in power is reviewed and debated by the Parliament but never changed. American legislators have not chosen to abdicate their reviewing power to that extreme.[1]

★ Program and performance budgeting

Although not unknown before, the first Hoover Commission Report (1949) popularized the use of program and performance budgets. Program and performance budgets simply represent techniques of presenting the budget to permit more analysis of expenditure goals and the methods of reaching these goals than the standard budget presentation which identified the things bought—personal services, typewriters, cement, and so on. When we carefully set out our broad objectives in a program budget, indicate the steps toward these objectives and cost of performing the necessary parts to accomplish these steps and then the whole goal, we are in a better position to judge the efficiency of the use of public moneys.

As an example of program and performance budget, we might think of a highway-department budget. Under the older budget system, the governor and the legislature would receive a statement of the number of persons required; the amount of supplies of paper, pencils, gravel, and cement needed; the estimated expenditure for telephone calls; and the estimates for all the other type of expenditures which would be made. Under a program budget, there would be a few lines stating the number of miles of particular types of highways which are to be built and the over-all cost of these highways. The more detailed performance budget would show that for a mile of Class A highway, on the average, it takes $X of planning and research personnel time and related costs; $Y of cement at $a per ton; $Z for purchase of the right of way and land for the highway; $C for grading and preparing the roadbed; $D for laying the cement. Other costs might also be shown. The total cost of building a mile of Class A highway would then be calculated and that figure mutliplied by the total number of miles to be built. The governor and legislature have the specific decision to make of whether they want to spend such and such an amount to secure fifty miles of Class A highways or whether they wish to reduce the highway expenditure and consequently the number of miles of highways built. Are highways being built efficiently in the state? Usually comparisons need to be made as to whether the costs of highway construction in one state compare favorably with the costs of similar highway construction in other states. Is the state paying the usual amount for cement, for preparing the

[1] One legislative response to placing budget authority in the governor has been the establishment of a legislative analyst and staff to assist the finance committees of the legislature (see p. 240).

roadbed, for research, and so forth? No absolute answer of efficiency can be established but an approximation is possible.[2]

State Budgeting Today

An examination of what some of the states do in an effort to develop a plan of expenditures and matching revenue should assist in a further understanding of budgeting.

★ *Legal provisions*

Early state constitutions made no provisions for regular financial planning or budgeting. A typical state constitution today (which was written fifty years or more ago) does not mention the word budget and the typical constitutional provisions in the general finance and expenditure area (listed below) give little guidance for budget planning.

> Revenue measures shall originate in the lower house.
> Appropriations shall be made only by bills that are to be passed through the usual stages like other laws.
> The governor shall have a veto, which covers financial measures as well as others. (In many states he has, in addition, an item veto on appropriations.)
> Various taxes and other revenues shall be segregated for specified uses (gasoline and motor-vehicle taxes for highways, school trust funds for public education, certain percentages of other funds for education, and so on).
> The state shall not "loan its credit" to others, and as a rule, shall be severely restricted in the amounts it may borrow (except for stated and favored functions, such as highways).

The new Alaska constitution illustrates the trend in contemporary thinking on state financial management. Having elsewhere provided for appropriations and a line-item veto for the governor, the constitution devotes Article IX to finance and taxation. Here the legislature is given some leeway in borrowing; the establishment of segregated funds is limited; and both executive budgeting and legislative post-audit are provided. The budget section reads:

[2] The student seriously interested in program and performance budgeting should seek more extensive statements than are possible here. The references are numerous but one of the best is Jesse Burkhead, *Government Budgeting* (New York: John Wiley, 1956), esp. Chs. 5, 6, 7.

It is also, of course, recognized by all writers in the field that performance budgeting can be a greater cost than it is worth in some areas. Exhaustive cost accounting as a basis for performance budgeting may not pay for itself. Some functions, moreover, do not readily permit the use of performance budget. This is especially true where the end product is one of service rather than a product such as miles of highway.

The governor shall submit to the legislature, at a time fixed by law, a budget for the next fiscal year setting forth all proposed expenditures and anticipated income of all departments, offices, and agencies of the State. The governor, at the same time, shall submit a general appropriation bill to authorize the proposed expenditures, and a bill or bills covering recommendations in the budget for new or additional revenues. (Art. IX, sec. 12)

The slightly older Missouri constitution has a somewhat similar budget statement:

The governor shall, within thirty days after it convenes in each regular session, submit to the general assembly a budget for the ensuing appropriation period, containing the estimated available revenues of the state and a complete and itemized plan of proposed expenditures of the state and all its agencies, together with his recommendations of any laws necessary to provide revenues sufficient to meet the expenditures. (Art. IV, sec. 24)

These provisions cover only the minimum essentials of a public budget: one budget for an entire governmental unit for a whole fiscal period, submitted by a responsible chief executive to the legislature, covering both proposed expenditures and revenues, and including his recommendations for bringing them into balance. What they do not state fills numerous books and articles on the subject of budgeting: the organization and staffing of the budget agency, the large amount of research, inquiry, and planning that must go into budget planning, the steps in the procedure by which the budget becomes law and is converted into practice, and the various ways in which responsible officials try to make the budget binding and effective throughout the fiscal period. Some of these added details are supplied by statutes on the subject. Even the states with constitutional provisions for budgeting have additional laws on the subject, while the great majority of the states rely entirely on statutes and custom.[3]

★ Administrative organization

The governor.   Only one state seems to exclude the governor entirely from the budget-making process—Arkansas assigns the budget-making authority to its Legislative Council. Five states have administrative budget boards, with the governor as chairman and other officers such as auditor and treasurer as members of the board. North Dakota has a budget board with

[3] Alaska, California, Hawaii, Maryland, Massachusetts, Missouri, New York, Texas, and West Virginia constitutions include sections dealing with state budgets. Other states have provided for their budgets through statutes.

the governor as chairman and with both legislators and administrative officers in the membership, while in South Carolina the governor presides over a budget board consisting of himself and the chairmen of the senate finance committee and the house ways and means committee.[4]

The other forty-two states make the governor responsible in one way or another for preparing and presenting the budget. These states have what is called the "executive budget system." This puts the planning of the budget in the hands of the man who is primarily responsible for the state's administration, and who is in the best position to get first-hand and reliable information about it. Then, too, the system results in proposals from the chief executive, whom the voters expect to assume leadership in policy matters, while leaving the legislature free to pursue its useful role of critic of the administration.

State budget bureaus. As the governor more and more becomes the administrative head and business manager in the states, the tendency is to equip his office with various staff agencies to assist him. These deal with budgeting, revenue, accounting and control of expenditures, management of state-owned buildings and motor vehicles, purchasing, planning, personnel, reporting, printing, and information, among others. More and more states beginning with Minnesota and Michigan have combined substantially all the agencies dealing with financial and business operations and, in one or two cases, have even included the state personnel function in this single staff agency to the governor.[5]

To perform their work most effectively, budget bureaus need a number of trained, experienced persons who are thoroughly familiar with certain branches of the state or local service and know something not only about public finance but also about administrative organization, procedures, and relative costs and efficiencies. Although its approach is from the financial side, a budget-bureau staff comes to know more than any other agency of government about administrative management practices. A few bureaus have separate units for studies in that direction.

[4] See table of state budgetary practices in *The Book of the States, 1958-59*, pp. 122-123.
[5] It might be assumed that if the budget bureau (or management agency) is to assist the governor directly, at least the head of the bureau or agency would be the governor's man —appointed by the governor and removable by him. This is true in New York and several states. On the other hand, the Michigan Department of Administration is headed by an ex-officio board, the members of which may or may not be sympathetic to the governor. Some other states give the agency head a term longer than the governor's or in other ways make the degree of the governor's control uncertain. For a discussion of the Michigan Department of Administration see: Ferrel Heady and Robert H. Pealy, "The Michigan Department of Administration: A Case Study in the Politics of Administration," *Public Administration Review*, spring 1956, pp. 82-89.

★ Budget agency procedure

In all governments—national, state, and local—budget-making and budget enforcement are woven into the annual cycle and the recurrent minor cycles of financial procedure. The annual cycle of events is based upon the official fiscal year, which may be the calendar year (January 1 to December 31) or any other twelve-month period, quite commonly July 1 of one year to June 30 of the next. In the latter case "fiscal 1960," for example, was the fiscal year that ended in June 1960.

Preparations for the next annual or biennial budget are more or less continuous in the budget bureau and in other agencies of government. The formal process begins some months before the completed budget document is to go before the legislative branch for approval, and legislative action in turn must be geared to the tax and expenditure calendars.

By a certain date the various agencies of government receive from the budget office the forms for estimating their financial needs and their expected revenue for the next fiscal year. These are accompanied by suggestions from the chief executive or budget officer as to the general policy to be followed respecting proposed increases, decreases, and new projects. Returned to the budget office by a certain date, the agencies' estimates and requests are scrutinized by the budget agency for conformity to (1) the general budget policy, (2) previous suggestions to an agency as to its expenditures, business methods, and other matters, and (3) any studies the budget bureau has made of the agency's work during the year. The purpose is not simply to find ways in which agency requests can be reduced, but rather to see that each agency has presented a defensible work program for the ensuing year and that its financial proposals make sense in terms of what it hopes to achieve.

Following its preliminary inspection of budget requests, the bureau holds hearings for one agency after another, trying to elicit further information and to get the agency heads to modify their requests to conform more nearly to the chief executive's stated budget policies. As the hearings proceed, the budget agency also goes ahead, in consultation with the chief executive, with formulating the complete budget proposal. This may depart in many particulars from the various original requests and is usually considerably lower than the total of the requests.

The essential idea of budget-making is to bring into rational relationship the total need for expenditure on one side and the responsibility for raising the necessary money on the other. Current revenues do not always have to equal exactly the appropriations made. During World War II many states budgeted to accumulate surpluses for use in the postwar period, while both state and local governments contrived to pay off larger amounts than usual of their indebtedness. Normally, current revenues do little more than meet operating expenses, leaving permanent improvements and acquisitions and large nonrecurrent expenditures (such as soldiers' bonuses) to be financed from borrowing; in times of emergency, some money may even be borrowed for current expenses. Whatever the circumstances, well-advised budget procedures bring all the facts together, so that those who make the policy know precisely what they must do to finance the appropriations that they make. In many instances it is necessary to recommend not only adjustment of tax rates or even the adoption of new taxes but the borrowing of certain amounts during the year or biennium.

When all is finished, with the chief executive's approval, the budget is printed or otherwise duplicated as a proposal for legislative action. It is usually accompanied by the chief executive's budget message, as in the case of the United States budget.

One of the strongest arguments for annual legislative sessions and four-year terms for governors comes out of the budget-making procedure. New governors often find that they are faced with budget hearings almost the day after they know they are elected. For the new governor with only a two-year term and a biennial budget to prepare immediately, such timing gives him little opportunity to do the extensive planning which budgeting presumes. In large part he must rely on the budget technicians and others who have reviewed the agency requests. Only in the case of a few special programs on which he may have made campaign promises or in the matter of tax policy is such a new governor likely to feel he can make the kind of impact on the budget he would like to make. If the governor has a four-year term and the state is on an annual budget basis, the governor may find it possible to submit a "hold-the-line budget" the first year as he is learning and then in subsequent budgets attempt to direct program expenditures and tax revenues the way he wishes.

Not only does the *new* governor have a special problem, but the *biennial* budget creates difficulties for all governors, administrators, and legislators. Biennial estimates of departmental needs frequently are made three years in advance of the end of the biennium for which the budget applies. Thus in the summer of 1958, Minnesota and Wisconsin agencies prepared estimates of expenditures for the biennium ending June 30, 1961. In the fall of 1958 and the early winter of 1959, the governors of these states reviewed the expenditure estimates and made recommendations to the legislators who, in turn, approved expenditure maximums by the late spring of 1959.

Sometimes accurate estimating of tax revenues exceeds in difficulty the estimating of state expenditures. The general health of the national economy as well as the health of particular sectors of the economy will significantly affect revenues. A national steel strike will idle the iron mines in Minnesota which produce an important amount of that state's taxes. The 1958 recession reduced the public demand for cars in the United States and significantly affected the income of Michigan workers. Reduced incomes meant reduced purchasing power and less sales-tax revenue to the state. Michigan, with its annual budget, has more opportunity for accurate estimating of revenues than does Minnesota with its biennial budget; but it did not escape difficulties. Accuracy in estimating is always a matter of degree, but long-range estimating generally is more complex than short-range estimating.

★ The budget document

For those who know how to read them, the printed (proposed) budgets of American units of government are mines of codified information about what government is and does. Many state and local budgets are very large documents, and all contain tables on revenues, appropriations, expenditures, and debts for recent years and proposed appropriations and estimated revenues for the year ahead. The document enables legislators and other citizens to see trends and to compare one agency with another. Recently budgets have begun to show by actual operating units (named institutions, schools, plants, offices, and so forth) how much goes into each and what service each is performing. Graphs, curves, bar diagrams, and even photographs are introduced to make the information easier to visualize. Consequently, a well-prepared budget can be a report of achievements as well as a list of proposed expenditures and revenues.

★ Special budgeting problems

Budgeting procedure is constantly altered by the presence of special problems.

1. Deficiencies and surpluses. Despite the most careful estimates, revenues sometimes are less than appropriations, whereas in other cases, by design or otherwise, surpluses are created. The revenues from sales, income, inheritance, and even property taxes can never be accurately gauged a year or two in advance. On the other hand, even under careful controls, expenditures will sometimes exceed appropriations, especially in times of emergency or of rapidly rising prices. Hospitals and institutions, for example, cannot be closed just because their appropriation has run out. State and local legislative bodies are therefore called upon frequently to make "deficiency appropriations," to cover expenditures already made for which there were not adequate appropriations. Short-term borrowing may be necessary if revenues fall off. Surpluses in revenue, much less common, create a different kind of problem, because then the legislators are importuned by various pressure groups to spend the surplus for their pet projects. Careful budgeting and expenditure controls help to make deficiency appropriations unnecessary and to provide sound plans for the use of surpluses.

2. Grants-in-aid. A government that makes grants-in-aid can budget for them just as it does for other expenditures, but the many governments that receive grants-in-aid have difficulty in calculating revenues from this source and hence are at a loss as how to budget them. Federal grants to the states are based upon different legal provisions, are paid at different times and in various ways, and depend upon a variety of distribution formulas and matching provisions. If Congress were to guarantee every state in advance certain definite sums, it would lose most of the advantages of the grants-in-aid system. The same is true of the states in making grants to local governments. For completeness of information, every state and local legislative body needs to know at least approximately how much will be received from grants-in-aid, and some budgets now include such estimates, together with data on past receipts from this source. At best, however, there will always be an element of uncertainty about such revenues.

3. Earmarked or dedicated revenues. Practically all money received by the national government is subject to Congressional appropriation, although obviously postal revenues and taxes paid into trust funds, like those for old-age and survivors' insurance and railroad-retirement benefits, are in effect committed to these particular uses. State and local governments generally are in a different situation. Certain taxes such as those on gasoline and motor vehicles may be pledged by the state constitutions for use only upon the highways, while others are earmarked for schools. By statutes, also, hunting- and fishing-license revenues may be pledged entirely for game and fish conservation. In such cases separate "funds" are set up in the books into which all such earmarked funds are put. Behind these earmarked funds stand strong pressure groups to make life unpleasant and uncertain for executives and legislators who would like to see more freedom for the legislatures to raise money where they can and to spend where needed. Especially in times of emergency, tying up money in funds for purposes of no immediate need does not seem to be sound financing. As matters now stand, state legislative bodies have substantial budgetary control over only a part of the annual revenue of the governmental unit—a part that may be as small as 20 or 25 percent of the total. State legislatures are legally empowered to modify or repeal all earmarking that is set up in the statutes. Of course, earmarking is not fatal to the budget-making process, but it is a handicap. It stems from a time of limited government functions and a great distrust of legislative bodies and is encouraged by many special interests. With the growth of more responsible government there seems to be less need than before for the numerous dedications of revenue that still exist.

When it comes to eliminating segregated funds, a doctrinaire approach is pointless. The value judgment which emphasizes the oneness of the budget in planning by the executive and in reviewing by the legislature is clear. The groups, however, which push for segregation of funds will push for the particular expenditures in which they are interested if no segregated fund exists. It is at least not certain that less money would be spent on highways and more on education if the highway segregated funds (so common among the states) were eliminated.

4. Capital budgeting. Budget writers normally examine the desirability of setting up a separate budget for major capital expenditures. Neither the United States national government nor the states generally have established separate capital budgets but have included expenditures for buildings, purchases of land, building of highways, and the like on a more or less current basis. A few cities have established separate capital budgets. Since capital items are expected to last for many years, there is a rational argument that this particular year's taxpayers should not bear the burden for the full cost. Others will enjoy the highways, the school buildings, or whatever over the years and these subsequent taxpayers should share in the cost. The inclusion of capital items in the ordinary budget, moreover, exaggerates the expenditures in the particular year and the governor and legislature may find this such a political burden that they will postpone capital expenditures that are currently needed. If capital expenditures can be maintained at a rather steady growth rate, then the taxpayers of any year are not unfairly burdened and the political disability drops.

A few states have established building-reserve funds into which particular moneys are placed. Many states used some of their World War II surpluses in this manner. Others, following business practices, have continued to put aside a set percentage, such as 1 or 2 percent, of the total value of their buildings, as a depreciation reserve. A separate appropriation appears in the regular budget for this depreciation reserve.

The Legislature and the Budget

Legislators generally recognize their action on the state budget as one of their supreme political jobs. Citizens, singly and in groups, press them to provide money for this or that program. Some of these same citizens, quite inconsistently, will also press them to lower taxes or at least not to raise them.[6] We all want the states to spend for the things in which we are interested, and we all want to pay less taxes if possible. Typically the legislature listens to the governor's budget message and receives his recommended budget rather early in the session. From then on almost to the close of the session, one or more committees are reviewing aspects of the expenditures and revenues proposed.

Although both houses of the state legislature have appropriations committees (Massachusetts and Wisconsin use a joint committee of their two houses) to pass upon all requests for funds, the usual practice has been to let other legislative committees also consider the budget requests pertinent to their fields, so that they might give their views to the appropriations committees.[7] Furthermore, the practice in making appropriations has been to enact several measures, such as one for education, one for state institutions, and so on. The committees hold public hearings, cross-examine administrators, and in the states with a strong executive budget listen to a defense of the governor's budget from the budget officer or a member of his or the governor's staff. Interested individuals may also appear. A considerable amount of checking of administrative agencies and their actions occurs at such time.

The progress of the proposed budget in committees and the degree of adjustment is related to the state's politics and practices. In a state with a competitive two-party system where the governor and a majority of each house belong to the same party, the governor's budget normally is passed with few changes. If party control is divided, a budget stalemate (either

6 One of the authors of this text once listened to an irate citizen before a legislative committee complaining about the height of the state's taxes and the audacity of the legislature even to consider raising them. When he had completed his statement, the legislative committee chairman mildly inquired: "Weren't you down here last week asking us to appropriate funds for an airport in your community?" There was some confusion and a mumbled, "yes."

7 This is an instance where state practices differ considerably. In Wisconsin the governor's proposed budget goes to the Joint Committee on Finance. It is in this committee only that the budget programs are reviewed through hearings and any studies the committee wishes to make. The Joint Committee on Finance then makes its recommendations on the total budget to the lower house of the legislature which acts on the bill and sends it on to the Senate. Only in the cases of appropriations outside the executive budget—new programs, for example—do the bills go to the interested committees for hearing and then to the Joint Committee on Finance.

on expenditures or revenues or both) may develop as occurred in Michigan and Minnesota in 1959. In states with weak party organization and control, the legislature is more likely to feel free to adjust the governor's budget. Assuming that committee majorities reflect legislative party majorities, the entire legislative body is likely to accept the budget recommendations of its committees with little debate.

Appropriation acts are authorizations to the agencies to spend the amounts appropriated to them—frequently with legislative restrictions on the spending. Not until all appropriations have been passed is the total amount of authorized expenditure known exactly. Legislative bodies sometimes reduce the amount allowed below what the executive's budget proposes, but frequently legislatures increase the amounts (or at least add new items which make the total larger). Increases above executive requests (but not new items separate from the budget) are forbidden by the constitution in Maryland (Art. II, sec. 52), except that executive requests for the legislative and judicial branches may be increased, and the governor may modify his own requests before passage of the budget to meet legislative demands. Some persons believe that the Maryland plan of prohibiting legislative increases in appropriations makes for sounder public finance and greater executive care and responsibility in proposing expenditures. Maryland also provides for a single, comprehensive appropriation bill to be prepared and submitted by the governor.

The budget bills of New York and Wisconsin governors are supposed to receive legislative consideration ahead of all other appropriation measures. In this fashion, a legislature does not pass a miscellany of appropriation bills in which individual legislators are interested and then find these have adversely affected the state's revenues for covering the executive budget proposals.

Expenditure Controls and Accounting

The printed budget document is a mere proposal, full of details, but not binding as such on any agency of government. It is the appropriation acts subsequently passed, the legislative authorizations to the spending agencies to spend the amounts appropriated, that are legally binding. At the same time, if tacit or express agreements have been made during the budget hearings that expenditures will follow this course and not that, ways of holding the agencies to their agreements will usually be found. Agencies that fail to keep such agreements may have their appropriations requests for the next year scrutinized with double care; they may even be subjected to new restrictive legislation.

★ Expenditure controls

State and local governments have various officers, usually called auditors and controllers, whose function it is to keep the money-spending agencies within the bounds of law and appropriations. Spending follows appropriations, of course, and is the actual laying out of the money appropriated to pay for personal services, materials, supplies, utilities, land, buildings, rents, and other necessities of government. Normally the money is in the treasury (though largely deposited in banks) and is subject to checking out by the treasurer, with the approval of an officer such as the controller or auditor.

Requisitions and other business forms are supplied to the spending agencies, and the latter must fill out and sign the proper forms in order to have their payrolls, purchases, and other expenditures approved. The appropriate officer, usually the auditor or controller, sets up accounts for each agency based on and itemized in accordance with the appropriations made to it, so that when requisitions are approved, entries can be made on the books showing that such and such parts of the appropriation are encumbered to pay the sums called for in those requisitions. Thus an agency will presumably be prevented from spending more for office help, labor, supplies, and so on, than its appropriation.

How complete the appropriation itemization shall be is a matter of debate. There is some advantage in allowing each agency some freedom in expenditure (for example, more for personal services, less for supplies) when the exigencies require a change from the original estimates. Nevertheless, the appropriations allowed an agency should be the outside limit of its expenditure, unless arrangement has been made for emergency additions from some general fund controlled by some higher authority.

★ Pre-audit and post-audit

The modern conception is that pre-auditing, or the controlling and checking of expenditures before they are made, belongs in the executive branch under a controller within the finance department. Since the governor is fully responsible for his administration to the voters or the legislative body or both, he needs someone of competence in the finance department to improve the accounting system and to prevent illegal and improper expenditures, without being obstructed by an outside officer. On the other hand, the legislative body needs to have full authority, through an auditor appointed by it, to post-audit all accounts, to report to it on all expenditures after they have been made, and if necessary to bring actions at law to recover money illegally or improperly spent. This seems to be the practice in various foreign governments, but its progress in this country is rather slow. In some states auditors are elected. In others, the governor appoints the auditor (with senate approval). Only in about a fourth of the states is the post-audit conducted by an official appointed by the legislature, by one house of it, or by a legislative committee. Some of the state auditors have both pre-audit and post-audit authority.[8]

★ Allotment systems

The practical development of state and local budgeting has led to a number of changes at various stages in the procedure. One is the institution of allotment controls over expenditures. A principal reason for the frequent departmental deficits that had to be made up by deficiency appropriations was the habit of spending the entire departmental appropriation before the end of the fiscal year (sometimes just before the election). Such bad management has been checked in many places by the establishment of monthly or, more commonly, quarterly allotment systems. The budget bureau itself sometimes administers these allotments. In effect, these plans divide up annual appropriations into quarters or other fractions, and only that fraction is released for expenditure in the given period. Even to get these allotments, the agencies must submit periodic verified requests and justifications.

These systems are interesting because they introduce additional checks upon expenditure and entrust the enforcement of them to an agency *under the chief executive*. At times when economy has been especially urgent, such allotment systems have been accompanied by the requirement that the budget bureau withhold 5 or 10 percent of each allotment, leaving the agencies to find ways of economizing to that extent. In this way surpluses might be built up, or deficits avoided if revenues fell off. The next step may be to authorize and require the executive to make economies in total expenditure, below the amounts appropriated.

★ Purchasing and contract-letting

Other means of keeping expenditures down and of increasing the economies of operation have been the provisions for central purchasing and central control of the letting of contracts. Money that has been appropriated is to be spent only in accordance with principles of good management. If every agency of a government buys its own supplies, printing, and other items,

---

[8] *The Book of the States 1958-59*, p. 131, identifies the officials in the states responsible for pre-audit and post-audit.

there will be no common standards of quality and the prices paid will vary considerably and will mostly be too high, because purchases are made in small quantities by various inexpert part-time purchasing agents. Centralizing the major staple purchases in one purchasing department for each state (sometimes with separate divisions for very large departments) has been found to produce economies.

A number of states have now also centralized the letting of contracts for highway and building construction in order to enforce the laws on bids for contracts and to obtain lower prices and better work.

Fiscal Interdependence

At the beginning of these two chapters on state and local finance we called attention to the fiscal interdependence of all units of government in the United States. They draw their revenues in general from the same stream of popular income; they borrow in the same markets; and they compete with each other for revenues and also aid each other in many different ways. This interdependence is clearly not that of equals. The national government dominates almost completely the financial lives of state and local governments, while the states in turn authorize, regulate, and supervise local fiscal operations in a conscious effort to protect their own financial resources and credit. If time permitted us to do so, we might trace out in detail the numerous financial connections between the state and local units. The interdependence of the state and national finances, and the subordination of the states, have caused concern in Congress, in the national executive branch, and in other places as well as in the states themselves. Numerous studies have been made, some of which are listed in the readings for this and the foregoing chapter. Most recently the Joint Federal-State Action Committee (members appointed by the President and the chairman of the Governors' Conference) has studied and made recommendations on federal-state financial relations.

In all such efforts to understand and to remedy the situation, the plight of the local governments needs most careful attention. They are at the bottom of the pyramid and least able to help themselves.

REFERENCES

Bell, George A., *State Budget Administration in Maryland.* College Park, Md.: Bureau of Government Research, University of Maryland, 1957.

Burkhead, Jesse M., *Government Budgeting*. New York: John Wiley and Sons, 1956.

Harton, William R., and others, "Performance Budget in Public Health Management," 43 *American Journal of Public Health* (March 1953), 259-264.

Report of the Legislative Analyst, Budget for 1959-60. Sacramento, State of California, 1959.

Schubert, Glendon A., Jr., and Donald F. McIntyre, "Preparing the Michigan State Budget," XIII *Public Administration Review* (Autumn 1953), 237-246.

See also current state budgets (a few states also have "budgets in brief") and governors' budget messages. The budget message of Governor Orville Freeman to the Minnesota Legislature in 1959, for example, provided an unusual amount of detail for an understanding both of the state's expenditure and revenue programs.

PART FIVE

Public Services and the
Democratic Process

CHAPTER 18

Law Enforcement

CHAPTER 13 discussed issues of justice in terms of court organization. Justice is many-faceted. Highly respected judges often depend on legislative action and law enforcement for the quality of justice they can provide. Law-enforcing officers of government are primarily in the executive branch of government but have many contacts with the courts and legislative members in their work. They cooperate with the courts as a rule, and the courts cooperate normally with them. At times, however, the courts serve as a check upon law-enforcing officials, and at other times they spur them on to greater activity. It is one of the basic understandings of all governments in the United States that the executive branch of government and all its appropriate officials will carry out the orders of the courts, but sometimes they neglect to do so. On the other hand, the judges sometimes fail to support the law-enforcement officers.

The relations of law-enforcing officers to legislative bodies exist largely because the legislatures pass upon basic law enforcement policies from time to time and also control appropriations. On occasion, these relations can be nefarious. A legislator may ask the state police "to take it easy" on a friend of his who is violating the law; a city alderman may be involved in vice and gambling in his ward and may see to it that the police do not interfere. More commonly legislators indicate their attitude on law enforcement by such means as approving or failing to approve funds for additional law-enforcement personnel.

In our thinking we usually limit law enforcement to the criminal branch of law—the most serious offenses that carry the death penalty or life imprisonment down to petty traffic offenses where the penalty is a fine of a dollar or two. Actually there is a large area of law enforcement in connection with civil matters. One thinks at once of the collection of delinquent taxes, the ejection of undesirable tenants from rented property, and the collection of civil judgments rendered by the courts. These and others fall mainly in the field of protection of property rights and the enforcement of public duties.

Another important area is that of personal rights, divided into civil liberties and civil rights. *Civil liberties* include personal rights such as freedom of speech, press, religion, and assembly, which are protected by constitutional bills of rights against invasion by governments and public officials. The rights of equal participation in elections and in public education by all qualified citizens are primarily civil liberties that are guaranteed by the equal-protection and due-process clauses of the Constitution. *Civil rights*, on the other hand, include rights of equal access to hotels, theaters, restaurants, and similar public places by all citizens, without regard to race, color, or religion. Fair-employment-practices laws in some states have added certain rights to equal treatment in employment to the list.

Police departments and law enforcement officials seldom develop positive programs to protect and strengthen the major freedoms. They have, in fact, accepted local pressures and prevented or broken up meetings of unpopular groups in violation of constitutional guarantees of freedom of speech and freedom of assembly. Liberal, labor, and socialist groups especially have been the victims of such actions as well as certain religious sects. The police have prevented the distribution of religious or political literature, again directly against constitutional provisions. Perhaps more frequent are the illegal actions of police departments in arresting people without just cause, treating prisoners cruelly in order to force confessions, and denying prisoners access to attorneys or outside help.

Any government needs order to exist. Democratic government needs order, but if it buys order at the expense of basic liberties, it loses its democratic character.

Intergovernmental Relations

Our federal system in law enforcement both aids and retards democratic law enforcement. The division of labor among national, state, and local authorities prevents an all-encompassing police net acting on the command of a few individuals and without consideration of local differences and desires. The federal system can also provide avoidance opportunities for the guilty or permit local communities to violate national standards of personal rights and liberties. The development of national and international crime syndicates and the general ease of crossing state lines to avoid prosecution have helped to bring about interstate and national-state joint efforts. As in many other areas of government, intergovernmental cooperation has encouraged professionalization and reduced (although by no means eliminated) differences in standards of law enforcement.

★ The laws to be enforced

The division of powers and functions between the national and state governments, and the exercise of law-making powers at both levels, result in producing two primary bodies of law to be enforced in each state—United States laws and state laws. Local governments that are possessed of ordinance-making powers produce additional laws, applicable in the local units concerned and necessarily subordinate to both state and national laws. Of course, all laws in the United States must conform to the federal Constitution.

These various bodies of law are interdependent, and it sometimes happens that a person arrested can be charged under several different laws and jurisdictions for essentially the same act. In the days of national prohibition and the Volstead Act, a single act of selling liquor would, in most states and many cities, be an offense against national, state, and local laws at the same time.

To assist the states in enforcing their laws or to deter people from breaking them, Congress has passed a number of acts under its commerce and postal powers that, in effect, provide additional penalties and federal punishment for what are primarily offenses against the state. Thus there is federal legislation against the interstate transportation of stolen automobiles: when an offender is caught, he is liable to the state penalty for stealing the car in the state where he stole it and the federal penalty for transporting it across state lines. This type of situation necessarily brings national and state police officers into frequent contact and has resulted in the establishment of regular methods of cooperation.

★ National-state relations

In almost everything that state and local governments do, the federal system must receive some consideration. In criminal matters the national government normally enforces its own laws through its own courts and executive agencies. The latter include the United States district attorneys and United States marshals resident in each state and a number of law-enforcement units that are centered in Washington, D. C., and have agents located in cities here and there throughout the nation. Of these units the Federal Bureau of Investigation (FBI) is the largest and has the most inclusive array of law-enforcement duties, covering bank robberies, motor-vehicle thefts and transportation, white-slave traffic, and many other offenses. Also important are the Immigration and Naturalization Service which has extensive control over aliens, the Alcohol Tax Unit which helps to enforce the nation's taxes and regulations on liquor, the Bureau of Narcotics which has similar duties in its field, the United States Secret Service which helps to enforce the counterfeiting laws, and the Postal Inspector services which help to enforce the laws concerning the use of the mails.

Thus, in every state and in most cities there are United States officers who make investigations and arrests right alongside the state and local police. As previously stated, many criminal acts are violations at one and the same time of national, state, and even local laws (as in cases of stealing and transporting automobiles and in violations of the narcotics and liquor laws), so that the same offenders may be wanted by the officers of all three levels of government. There is, consequently, some unavoidable overlapping of jurisdiction and the need for a great deal of understanding and cooperation among the various law-enforcing agencies. The degree to which such cooperation exists and the forms that it takes vary from place to place and from time to time. At all times, however, the FBI cooperates with state and local police through its nation-wide fingerprinting service and its training schools, which regularly admit selected state and local police officers.

The special United States Senate subcommittee on investigation of interstate crime (1950-1951), headed by Senator Estes Kefauver of Tennessee, is a good example of Congressional-state relations in the law-enforcement field. The committee toured the country, held hearings, and conducted investigations. As a result of its efforts, many friendly relations between state and local law-enforcement officials and those controlling gambling, rackets, and vice were revealed; the outcome of some state and local elections was probably altered, particularly in Cook County (Chicago), Illinois; and a few personnel changes took place in police departments. In part as a response to committee disclosures, Congress passed a law prohibiting slot machines from being shipped in interstate commerce, despite the objection of a Senator from Nevada that such action was a violation of "states rights"! This law was designed to help those state and local governments that wanted to abolish slot machines.

★ State-local relations

In a constitutional sense the fifty states have the primary responsibility for ordinary law enforcement, outside of offenses against the national government. Thus, murder, manslaughter, robbery, burglary, and the rest of the common-law offenses and many statutory offenses are offenses against the state and punishable by it. Historically, and to a large extent in practice even today, the states have left law enforcement very largely to local officers, elected in or appointed by the counties, cities, villages, and towns. While the governor is required "to see to it" that law is enforced, city police departments are under the control of the mayor, or manager and council; county sheriffs and the constables in the towns and townships are locally elected.

Though locally elected, constables and sheriffs are held to be officers of the state. The Alabama constitution declares that the sheriff of each county is a part of the executive department of the state (Art. V, sec. 112). In Arkansas the sheriff along with other county officers is commissioned by the governor (Art. VII, sec. 48), and in Mississippi the sheriff and the rest of the elective county officers are provided for in the executive article of the state constitution (Art. V, sec. 138). Governors are quite commonly given the power of removing sheriffs. Such provisions only recognize more or less explicitly what the courts have often said: that sheriffs and other county officers, along with police officers generally, are state officers in the legal sense. They enforce state laws primarily, and they are subject to regulation by state law.

However, their local political ties and responsibilities have prevented the states from assuming much active control over them. If a governor tries to remove a sheriff it may cost the governor thousands of votes in the county concerned because of the sheriff's local popularity. In the course of normal law enforcement, the sheriff or local police officials need never take very seriously any suggestion from the state. Legally they may be state officials, but in the eyes of the local populace, and in their own estimation, they are local officials, responsible to local pressures and desires.

In spite of the feeling of local pride and independence, local law-enforcement officials cooperate extensively with their state counterparts. For example, state police agencies help train new sheriffs or other local police personnel. There may be joint investigation of certain crimes, joint raids, or a scheme for a division of labor worked out for some phases of their work. Frequently the state has skilled and specialized personnel and facilities that it makes available to all local law-enforcement officials. A spirit of cooperation usually prevails, and through the International Association of Chiefs of Police and other organizations, state and local police work is becoming more and more professionalized.

State Organization for Law Enforcement

The states began to assume a large degree of direct responsibility for law enforcement at the time that the automobile and the modern highway greatly increased the mobility of criminals, enabling them to live in one place and to engage in crime in other places, whether urban or rural and whether in the same or some other state. Rapid urbanization and the increasing density of the population in most states tended to wipe out the differences between the urban places and those that were previously rural, so that the latter also needed more effective and more pervasive police protection.

★ Rise of state police

It is generally believed that the semimilitary Texas Rangers, established in 1835 before Texas was admitted to the Union for the purpose of patrolling the Mexican border, were the first state police. In 1865 Massachusetts provided for a few "state constables" for the suppression of vice throughout the state, and in 1879 these became a sort of state detective force called the "district police." Connecticut soon followed Massachusetts' lead, while Arizona and New Mexico followed that of Texas. In 1905 Pennsylvania established the first modern system of state police in the United States. The purpose of this new force was to patrol the rural areas, a thing no state had done systematically before; to maintain order and enforce law during strikes and other industrial disturbances; and to be an arm of the state governor for general law-enforcement purposes. During World War I and just after it, other states such as New York, Michigan, and Colorado also established state police forces.

During this period organized labor developed strong opposition to state police forces on the ground that they might be used against labor during strikes, and many states were deterred from creating full-fledged state police forces all at once. However, the then-rapidly expanding state highway systems seemed to call for centralized traffic-law enforcement. Consequently state highway patrols with primarily traffic-control functions were established in a number of states. These did not meet the needs for general law enforcement, however; and since the law-enforcing responsibilities of the governor and the attorney general were increasing, various states that were not prepared to create complete state police systems established small investigating or detective bureaus under various titles. These were designed to assist the governor and attorney general in ordinary law enforcement, to conduct investigations for the local police especially in rural areas, to establish fingerprint and other systems of records of criminals, and to facilitate local police work generally through radio broadcasting and other means, but not to make arrests by themselves.

★ State fire marshals

Fire marshals are to be found in over three fourths of the states. Their function is to investigate all cases of suspected arson throughout the state and to bring about the arrest and prosecution of those accused. In addition they to some extent inspect important buildings for fire safety and issue both general regulations and specific orders on this subject. Their staffs are rather small, and they confine their work largely to places that do not have adequate local fire protection and fire-marshal service, including rural areas, but they are free also to investigate fires in cities that have their own fire marshals. It is not surprising that the organizations of fire insurance companies and such affiliates of theirs as the National Fire Protection Association are especially interested in the work of these state agencies. Almost half the states with state fire marshals place them in the state insurance department. The other states make a variety of different arrangements.[1]

★ State militia or national guard

As previously noted, the organized portion of the state militia (now called the national guard) is available for state law-enforcement duties in emergencies. At times when the national guard is engaged in regular military duties under the President, the states provide in various ways for "home guards" to take its place. The governor, as commander in chief of the national guard in his state, appoints an adjutant general to exercise active control over it and other top guard officers on the recommendation of the adjutant general.

As a state law-enforcement agency, the national guard is usable primarily in emergencies such as insurrections and extensive disorder during strikes and lockouts, when the ordinary local police are unable to control the situation. It is customary for the governor to wait for a request from the local sheriff or chief of police before calling out the guard, but this is not necessary. The most appropriate use of the guard even in emergencies is to lend support to the regular courts, the sheriff, and the police. In some

[1] *The Book of the States 1958-59*, pp. 380-381.

instances the mere show of force is enough to re-establish order. In a number of instances, however, governors have declared martial law in such emergencies. In effect this meant that they set aside the ordinary courts and law-enforcing agencies, made arrests through the militia itself, and tried those arrested in military courts or even locked them up for days and weeks without trial. This amounts to a suspension of the writ of *habeas corpus*— that is, suspension of a man's right when arrested to be heard promptly in an ordinary court—and is generally considered to be unconstitutional. Circumstances alter cases, however, and situations in which the regular courts simply cannot function call for drastic measures like martial law.

The states that have large forces of state police can handle most local disturbances without resort to the national guard, but there are disadvantages attendant upon such action. To use the state police extensively in strikes, for example, is not only to call them away from their ordinary patrol duties but also to antagonize large sections of the population. In most states the need for the national guard as a "stand-by" law-enforcement agency is likely to continue.

Police Organization Locally

Law enforcement in the United States, as remarked earlier in this chapter, has been widely diffused among local officers under local political control, and it still is so to a preponderant extent. County sheriffs and prosecutors, local constables and marshals, and urban police account for the largest numbers of law-enforcing officials in the nation. With local courts to try most offenders and local juries to express local opinions on convictions and punishment, American communities have so far kept law enforcement very largely in their own hands. It is to be noted, however, that some urban police systems, like those of Boston, Baltimore, St. Louis, and Kansas City, are under state control, and that the rise of state police systems has proportionately reduced the importance of local rural police like sheriffs and constables.

★ County sheriffs

Practically all counties, as the major territorial divisions of the states, have sheriffs, and through them each state can reach into all parts of the state's area for law-enforcement purposes. They have in general the old common-law duty and power to keep the peace and maintain law and order within the county, to make arrests, and to execute and enforce the orders of the courts and of other lawful authorities in the county. In addition to these central law-enforcing powers, they have a variety of other duties imposed upon them by statutes in different states, such as: to serve as jailer for the county; to produce accused persons in court for trial and to transport those convicted to prison; to summon citizens for jury duty and to watch over the judge and the jurors of the major trial court while they perform their duties; to execute death sentences; to serve various summonses and other legal papers issued by the court, in civil as well as criminal cases; to collect delinquent taxes, and to sell property that is tax delinquent; to conduct elections and to perform a variety of other functions, varying from state to state. These miscellaneous duties occupy much of the time of any sheriff's office, and where they bring in fees they are likely to receive a good deal of attention. In urban centers the work of law enforcement in the ordinary sense may fall almost entirely on the city police, while the sheriff's office devotes itself to the other duties; but some sheriff's offices do provide limited patrol service on the county highways and in the rural fringes of the urbanized counties.

In rural counties, on the other hand, the force of deputies is usually so small in proportion to the area and population of the county that there can be no thought of regular patrol service by the sheriff's staff. An elective officer with no special training for law enforcement, the sheriff is not as a rule an ideal police officer, nor can his deputies generally claim much more special skill. By experience they do acquire special competence in particular functions like delinquent-tax collection. The modern developments in law-enforcement methods have largely passed by the sheriff's office, to become centered in the headquarters of the state police and of the larger city police departments. While the sheriff is there at the county seat, equipped with an automobile and other facilities, on call when a crime is reported, more and more he needs the help of other agencies for his work. It is not likely, either, that any large number of trained police officers will seek election as sheriffs in the majority of the rural counties. The pay is small, the hours may be long and are always uncertain, and the chance of being elected and re-elected is never better than 50 percent at best.

★ Coroner

If the office of sheriff is, in a sense, on the wane, it is not, like the ancient office of coroner, actually being eliminated in a number of places. Originally established in England as an officer both to aid and serve as a check upon the sheriff, and at various times endowed with a variety of powers, the county coroner has been limited in the United States to essentially one regular function: to conduct inquests into the causes of deaths that occur by violence or under suspicious circumstances. The coroner orders the inquest and presides over it. The county prosecutor presents the evidence, and a jury (usually of six men) may be impaneled to hear the evidence and reach a verdict. If the verdict is death by a criminal act, the coroner must order the arrest of the person or persons suspected. Aside from this regular duty, the coroner in various states acts in place of the sheriff when the latter is unable to perform his duties by reason of absence or disability.

Elected by the voters of the county for a term of two, three, or four years as a rule, and paid but a small salary in most counties, the coroner is usually a physician, although this is not everywhere required by law. Whether physician, undertaker, barber, or something else by profession or vocation, the elected coroner is not usually the expert in legal medicine, autopsies, or criminal investigation, cross examination, and judicial proceedings that the office seems to require. In many counties the coroners are distinctly unlearned men who, far from being helpful in getting at the truth about a death, bungle the facts, compel the prosecutor to divulge his case against suspected persons, and otherwise make more difficult the later prosecution of the accused. Some states have abolished the office and substituted appointed medical examiners at reasonably good salaries and for long terms. The county attorney then assumes the more legal and judicial parts of the coroner's work.

★ *Prosecuting attorney*

The county attorney, county prosecutor, or district attorney (the titles vary) is in most states elected by the voters for a two- or four-year term, and is expected to be a lawyer. In the large urban counties his office carries a fairly high salary, as county salaries go, and he usually has a comfortably large staff of assistants. In the smaller and more rural counties, on the other hand, his official salary is on a part-time basis and not high, and he may not have a single assistant except a secretary. Often county attorneys serve several successive terms, but rarely does one make a career of being county attorney. Many young lawyers use the office as a political stepping stone.

The fact that the office is a sort of political stepping stone means that at any given time numerous relatively inexperienced county attorneys are likely to be holding office, and that the office is used to some extent by the incumbent for self-advertising purposes. The dramatic cases, those in which the public has taken a great interest, are seized upon for prosecution, while the more humdrum cases may be neglected. What is more, among all cases, those that are most likely to result in easy convictions are put first, because a record of a high percentage of convictions obtained by a county attorney is known to be a strong argument not only for his re-election but also for advancement to higher political office.

The county attorney, especially in large urban centers, wields great power. It is he who must present evidence to grand juries to bring about indictments for crime or formulate and present information to the court as the basis for criminal trials. And it is he also who must later prosecute the offenders before the court. Whether he prosecutes or not is largely for him to decide, since there is no higher official who has direct supervision over him. He is in his county the prosecutor for the state in all serious cases and practically the only one. The power of the state attorney general directly to undertake prosecutions is rather limited. Sometimes his office is called in by a county attorney to give help, but his staff is rather small, as a rule, and generally busy with giving legal advice to state and local officers. Thus the states are dependent for most prosecutions for crime upon locally elected county attorneys who naturally conform to local sentiment in much that they do, and are in a better position than most officials to use their offices for personal political advantage. Since the elective county sheriff is also in somewhat the same position, and also has to conform to local sentiment and yield to local pressure, it can be understood why state law enforcement is so uneven over the state. The state police themselves must work with the county attorneys in the counties where they make arrests in order to obtain convictions.

The idea of a state department of justice under a long-term attorney general, with authority to supervise local sheriffs and prosecutors and to tone up the entire system of law enforcement, has not made notable progress.

★ Public defender

Under American standards of justice, an accused individual is entitled to counsel if he wishes. The defendant with funds normally secures an attorney to represent him. Many defendants have inadequate funds and no acquaintance with attorneys. To meet this situation, courts have assigned counsel or in a few jurisdictions the legal aid society has taken criminal cases. Assigned counsel, lawyers appointed by court (usually without pay) to represent the defendant, have differed greatly in ability and in willingness to devote their efforts to the defendant's interests. Criticism of the quality of assigned counsel in particular cases and the further criticism that the system frequently gives the defendant no legal advice until he has come into court have resulted in the adoption of the public defender system in some jurisdictions.[2] Where the public defender is used his services may be limited to felonies or special situations in criminal cases. Where the pub-

[2] California, Connecticut, Indiana, Minnesota, Nebraska, Oklahoma, Rhode Island, and Virginia have authorized use of the public defender system in the state. Individual counties or communities in a few other states also use it. Institute of Judicial Administration, *Public Defenders* (mimeographed), May 18, 1956.

lic defender is given general responsibility for defense of indigents charged with criminal offenses, he has a counterpart position to that of the presecuting attorney.[3]

★ Constable and marshal

In the states that have town or township organization, each organized town or township usually elects one or two constables, while the organized villages choose marshals to patrol their streets at night and perhaps to control traffic by day. These scattered, unsupervised, and mostly untrained and poorly equipped officers of the law, paid only by fees in most cases (although marshals usually get small salaries), simply cannot function effectively as officers of general law enforcement. They serve the justice courts by serving legal papers; in the vicinity of large cities they arrest numerous offenders of traffic laws. Otherwise the constables are mostly on call and not always easy to find, because necessarily they have other employment. Every small community needs one or more local residents who are empowered to make arrests in local emergencies and to serve the local courts as process servers. At the same time the law-enforcement functions of small communities are likely to contract slowly, as the state police systems improve.

★ Urban police

Primarily urban places of over 2500 inhabitants have regular organized police patrols, and generally the larger cities have made the greatest progress in local police administration. The system of full-time uniformed urban police began to replace the older citizen night-watch system over a century ago, when the spoils system had come to prevail in the larger cities. Thus the uniformed police systems became from the first the spoils and the tools of the victorious urban political parties. Policemen were hired and fired for personal and partisan reasons, and they hardly expected to stay in office when a new party came into power, especially in the large cities. Despite these and other serious handicaps, the idea of a regular, full-time police force grew from city to city. For urban communities under modern industrial conditions there is no logical substitute.

The urban police have, of course, the powers of arrest entrusted to constables and sheriffs by the common law; and though they are employed and paid by municipalities, they are legally officers of the state. Thus we can say that all the police of counties, cities, and other local units are parts of the same police system, although it is not a thoroughly integrated one.

[3] David Mars, "The Public Defender System in Connecticut," *State Government*, February 1954.

Since all major crimes and many minor ones are crimes against the state, the local and state police functions are combined in these local police forces, who enforce local ordinances along with state laws.

Taken all together, the urban police forces outnumber by a wide margin the combined strength of the sheriffs and their deputies and all the state police forces. New York City alone has had about 25,000 men on its force in recent years. In general the city police forces in cities of 500,000 and over have averaged recently well over two policemen for every 1000 inhabitants. From this high point the average drops to about 1.88 in cities of 250,000 to 500,000, and goes down to 1.58 for cities of 10,000 to 25,000. Thus an average city of 10,000 would have a force of about 16, one of 50,-000 a force of 86, and one of 300,000 a force of 564. In most of the larger cities police officers are selected on a merit basis, given at least some police training, and paid reasonably good salaries for a median work week of forty-eight hours.

Direct responsibility for the police is vested in the mayor in most mayor-council plans of city government. In council-manager plans of organization the manager usually controls the police, whereas in commission-governed cities either the mayor or a commissioner of public safety generally does so. There are many exceptions, however.[4] In some cities a locally constituted board appoints the chief (Los Angeles, San Francisco, Milwaukee); in others a board appointed by the state governor chooses the chief (St. Louis, Kansas City); and in two major cities (Boston, Baltimore) the governor appoints the chief directly. To a large extent control over the police goes with the power of appointing the chief.

It goes without saying that the police departments of cities and villages provide a large portion of the law enforcement for the entire nation. Although the sheriff's jurisdiction usually extends over the entire county, he frequently leaves to the local police all law enforcement within the cities of his county. Indeed, the state police and even the federal law-enforcing agencies usually respect city police jurisdiction to the extent of getting the city police to help them in making local arrests. The Uniform Crime Reports put out by the FBI are based almost entirely on the "offenses known to the police" that are recorded by city police forces—arrests made by urban police for serious crimes run to hundreds of thousands per year.

Fairly steady improvement in law enforcement and the policing of cities has been made for the past half century, if not longer. Many difficul-

---

[4] See the *Municipal Year Book 1959*, Table XVIII, pp. 414-434, for police-department data on cities of over 10,000 population. Each annual issue of this yearbook includes an excellent section on urban police administration, with bibliography.

ties remain. Among these are the relatively short tenure and the initial in-
experience of police chiefs and commissioners; the difficulties of recruiting
enough really able young men for the force (considering education and
brains as well as brawn) in the light of the pay scales available and certain
public attitudes of cynicism toward police work; the tendency in some cities
for law enforcement to be a constant issue in party politics; the constant
temptations from illicit gambling, liquor, and vice interests, which in many
places are allied with the party machines; and the complications inherent
in law enforcement in cities with their populations compounded of several
races and many national and religious groups, their areas of slum conditions, and their groups of vagrants and criminals moving in and out.

Policing and law enforcement have improved more or less in step with
the rise of what is called with some accuracy "police science." The public
press tells daily about some of the methods, inventions, and "gadgets" that
this science has developed—fingerprinting, the lie detector, tests for drunkenness, and so on. Another branch of this science deals with police administrative organization and procedures—selection of personnel, types of
central and precinct organization, training in police methods, police records,
and presentation of evidence in court, one-man versus two-man cars for
patrol duty, and many other points. It is now possible for a city of 50,000 or
over, with a force of, say, 100 men and a police budget of $500,000 to $600,-
000, to have most of the advantages in organization, equipment, specialized
personnel, and scientific methods that even the largest cities can afford.

Attention has been turning also to preventive police work in cities and
to preparation for emergency needs including civil defense. Work with boys'
groups, work with educational and recreational agencies to prevent juvenile
delinquency, attempts to improve understanding between racial and other
groups, school traffic police, junior police—these suggest some of the new
activities of the more advanced police departments.

Conclusion

The nature of law enforcement varies with different societies and cultures.
Technological changes in the United States have changed law enforcement
from almost totally a local matter in the eighteenth and much of the nineteenth centuries to a matter of substantial state and national concern. The
state nature of local law-enforcement officers shows up more today as state
police forces, state crime laboratories, state traffic patrols take over formerly local duties or assist local officials. Even the national government

through the FBI and other agencies significantly aids in "local" law enforcement.

Law-enforcement needs have greatly changed. Before 1900, there was hardly any need for traffic regulation in the United States whereas today probably no police activity takes as much time. Juvenile delinquency, narcotics control, and gambling regulation all require new approaches and new techniques for old problems.

One of the unsettled questions of understanding law enforcement is why some states and communities have a tradition of order, respect personal rights, and avoid police corruption whereas other states or communities appear to invite disorder, police corruption and violation of personal rights. Population density and tradition are factors, but some rural communities have enforced law at the expense of personal rights or have allowed extensive illegal activity to develop.

To answer "tradition" merely pushes the question back. How does tradition start? How can a new tradition be inaugurated? For decades Milwaukee has rated high among large cities in the quality of its general city government and law enforcement. Despite numerous reform attempts, neighboring Chicago has not established a similar reputation for law enforcement or general integrity of government. Size alone does not explain the difference. Most characteristics usually mentioned account only in a surface sense for the present problems without explaining why such developed originally or why it is so difficult to change the direction. Anthropologists, sociologists, psychologists, political scientists, and other specialists need to work together to assist in answering this question.

REFERENCES

Camp, Irving, *Our State Police*. New York: Dodd, Mead, 1955.
Council of State Governments, *The Handbook in Interstate Crime Control*, rev. ed. Chicago: Council of State Governments, 1955.
U. S. Federal Bureau of Investigation, *Uniform Crime Reports* (semiannual). Washington, D. C.: Government Printing Office.
Votaw, Roy C., "Programs for Delinquency Prevention," **XXXI** *State Government* (June 1958), 110-113.
See also references at end of Ch. 23.

Highway and Air-Transportation Policies

THE RELATIONSHIP OF GOVERNMENT to technology has received much public discussion as a result of the development of atomic energy, but actually the relationship is an old one. State and local governments have performed services for many decades, even centuries, that require technological competence. Highways and streets, public utilities, conservation, airports, housing, public planning, and university teaching and research are a few of them. While social and economic policies inevitably are conditioned by technology, there are important differences in the policy-making and administering processes between the services we are about to examine and those that directly deal with individuals (discussed in Chapter 23) or those that are motivated primarily by economic considerations (discussed in Chapter 22).

Technology is a conditioning factor in policy formation that is often not directly present in social and economic decisions. It is a matter of technical competence, specialization, and exactness, and a general administrator or legislator is not likely to feel qualified to make judgments on technological details. The building of a bridge, the construction of a hydroelectric plant, or the layout of an airport are all subject to engineering principles, and if the principles are not followed, disaster or the waste of public funds is likely to be the net result. Therefore, policy decisions in the public-works and conservation fields must take principles of engineering, physics, and chemistry into account. In contrast economic- and social-policy decisions seem conditioned by factors not so precise. The breakdown of an economic theory is not as demonstrable as the cracking of a highway or the failure of a municipal water-supply system. Precision can be obtained to a greater degree in the physical and natural sciences than in the social or economic sciences, and this fact is recognized by legislators, administrators, and the general public. Therefore, the role of the expert is much greater in the public services depending heavily upon technology.

The differences between public works and conservation policies and other areas of public policy are not based solely upon the scientific exactness of some of the conditioning factors. There is a great difference in the kind of matter with which an administrator or legislator must deal. In the one case he is dealing with a service that directly affects individuals, whereas in another he is dealing with something that rather indirectly affects them. The former is a highly controversial field, the latter much less so. An administrator need be much less careful with mortar and brick than with human beings, and while there will be human beings using the physical structure after it is erected, the fact remains there is a nonanimate intermediary between the administrators and consumers of technological services of government.

Of course there are many nonscientific factors that condition policy decisions on public works and conservation. Cries of socialism are often heard in the fields of public planning, housing, and utilities, and basic economic interests might be affected by almost any physical service of state and local governments. Highway policy affects the competition of trucks and buses with the railroads, and airlines and railroads disagree on airport policy. Conservation policy involves many economic interests. No area of government policy is completely removed from human beings or value judgments, certainly not the fields of public works and conservation. Engineers can report what will be the approximate cost of a power dam and what will be the results of erecting it in terms of amount of power produced, effect on fishing in the river, floods, and many other details. They cannot remove interstate jealousies, private power interests, or difficulties of raising the necessary money.

Of increasing importance is the question of the relation of a scientist to government. A scientist frequently feels a special obligation to mankind in general in addition to the obligation to the unit of government he serves. When the two obligations are in harmony, no special problem arises, but many times they conflict. A county governing-body member wants a black-topped road running past his house, even though traffic surveys show that this is not a pressing need. What should the engineer do, fabricate his records or findings, offer no opinion whatsoever, or oppose the favorite project of a powerful governing-body member? It is easy enough to favor the latter as a theoretical proposition, but in actual practice an engineer may not feel free to oppose a project that will injure his rapport with the governing body and may cost him a raise in salary or even his job at some future date. Furthermore, technology has not arrived at the point where there are no disagreements, and there may be some engineers who would favor such a project, others who would oppose it.

It would seem highly important to permit engineers and other scientists who are employed by governmental units great leeway in making their recommendations so that a report will contain basic truths rather than primarily political views. The recommendations made in a report do not always have to be accepted. At the same time it may be necessary to try to broaden the training of engineers to include an understanding of the human relations in government. They also need to recognize the boundary between technology, economics, and politics. In the area of physical services of government a knowledge of technology, economics, and human relations is needed by administrators, and legislators need to have a grasp of the proper role of a scientist.

★ Highways

At first glance there seems to be nothing controversial about highways or streets; no important policy questions seem to be involved. What can be controversial about pouring concrete, smoothing gravel, or plowing snow? The answer is: Almost everything! Once the surface of highway policy is scratched, many controversies appear. The following pages will indicate some of these.

Furthermore, highway policy has very often been a part of spoils politics. Even today this is true of some state highway agencies, and a number of counties operate their highway departments much as they did thirty years ago, except that they now have engineers who conform to whatever standards were previously in effect. With the exception of police administration, no field of government has had a greater tendency to corruption than highway administration. Large contracts must be let; expensive equipment purchased; land for rights-of-way condemned; and many seasonal unskilled employees obtained. There is opportunity to play spoils politics in each of these steps. Yet despite the possibilities of abuse of the taxpayers' money, many state and local highway departments today perform their services efficiently and with little or no evidence of corruption or spoils politics.

★ *Influences and pressures*

A new highway engineer soon becomes acquainted with the many political considerations that enter into highway policy. An early aspect of state highway policy illustrates the point well. When state trunk highways were established in the early 1920s with the aid of grants from the national government, a serious problem arose as to what highway mileage should be included in the state system. Each locality brought pressure to bear upon its state legislators to get extensive road mileages within its area designated as trunk highways. Local antagonisms were aroused, and any compromise that was reached at the beginning of state highways was soon forgotten; the localities continued to ask legislatures at virtually every session to extend the trunk highway system. The reasons why political pressures have been so great on the state trunk highway system are that, first of all, a locality may hope to prosper economically if an important highway is routed through it, and, secondly, the transfer of the maintenance and construction of a highway from a township or county to a state relieves the local taxpayers of a financial burden. To accomplish their objectives, local groups work primarily through their state legislative delegations, although they also try to obtain support for their ideas from the state highway agency. Similar relationships are present in states that have both counties and townships as highway units, the townships petitioning the counties to take over additional mileage.

An urban-rural split on some aspects of highway policy has occurred. Rural-dominated state legislatures have had more sympathy for trunk highways and farm-to-market roads than they have for highways and expressways in metropolitan areas. Even state highway agencies have been traditionally rural-oriented because the tasks assigned to them in the past have largely involved highways in rural areas. Much of the controversy has concerned the relative amount of use urban and rural populations received from particular types of highway mileage. Many of these arguments turn largely upon point of view. For example, it is frequently said that farm-to-market roads benefit the urbanites, since farm products are necessary for the city's survival. But it can also be said that such roads are necessary for the economic well-being of the farmer. Urban expressways obviously help the urban driver, but farmers also need ready access to the centers of large cities.

Highway finance is the center of attention of many highway pressure groups.[1] State administrators and legislators also play a crucial role in this aspect of highway policy. As a whole, all those who are interested in high-

[1] For statistics on state highway expenditures see Figure 12 in Chapter 16.

ways tend to be for the widespread practice of state-dedicated revenue. All highway-user fees and taxes, such as those from car licenses, drivers' licenses, and motor-fuel taxation, go into a special fund that can be used only for highway purposes. Administrators generally like this system because it assures them of certain revenues, no matter what action the legislature takes, and gives them a measure of independence from both governor and legislature. Highway-user pressure groups favor this system, because all the money they contribute through the dedicated taxes goes for the upkeep and extension of the highways they use. The alignment of both commercial and private users together with administrators has been too much for the legislature to withstand.

Users do not always agree among themselves as to policy. Commercial and private highway users have frequent conflicts among themselves and with administrators. Commercial truckers demand full use of the highways, while private groups sometimes try to limit their use. The many restrictions states have on the types of trucks that may travel over their highways are examples. Traffic composed of unusually heavy trucks tends to break up pavements as well as to slow up traffic. Railroad interests also lobby against the bus and truck interests' demands for unlimited use of the highways. The former feel that the states are subsidizing these competitors of the railroads by providing them with a highway system for which everyone helps to pay.

One special problem state and county highway officials have in states in the snow belt is the control of highway use during the annual spring thaw and breakup. Along certain stretches of highway, it is necessary to limit the weight of vehicles that may pass over the road. Truckers and bus companies object to any limitation of their rights of free passage, but the major pressures come from school districts and farmers. School buses and milk and oil trucks are heavy vehicles, but many a county engineer has discovered that the combined influence of school and farm groups has been too great to resist, even if roads are damaged by inadvisable use in the spring. Here is a case of conflicting values; damaged roads versus curtailed schooling and economic hardship or inconvenience.

Highways illustrate the effect that technological progress can have on a function of government. The necessity for any large-scale highway system at all stems primarily from the modern automobile, bus, and truck, and as the character of these vehicles has changed, highway policy has had to be responsive. Highways require great attention in the spreading metropolitan areas as well as the frequently overcrowded downtown centers. The failure to anticipate the increasing volume and speed of traffic led to street plans in the 1920s and 1930s which are totally unsuited to the present. Great additional expense occurs in buying land in dense use for homes and business in order to add to the width or length of streets or to change the design. (The question of the future of the helicopter for commuter traffic may be overlooked too much in present planning.) Wider highways, four and six lanes, and straightening of curves in rural areas to permit higher speeds and more traffic have also been necessary. Engineering progress has made possible the building of better highways and bridges that can withstand greater use. However, scientific progress has had some rather indirect effects on highway problems. For example, the perfection of engines that get more miles to the gallon has meant that highway revenue from gasoline taxes has decreased in relation to the use made of the highways. Again, the perfection of more and more complicated and refined motor vehicles has resulted in a product that runs best on well-maintained modern highways. While the total cost of highway maintenance and construction is great, the total social cost would be still greater if only poor highways were available. It is estimated that it costs about one cent a mile more to drive a car on poor roads than on good roads. These are costs not to the person as a taxpayer but to him as a driver. The demand for good highways is therefore in part a demand to transfer personal cost to government; there it is paid by taxpayers, generally, in return for which more convenient services are made available.

★ Legislative-executive relations and highway policy

Many of the pressures and influences in the field of highways come to bear on the legislature. Highway policy, in fact, has always remained quite closely controlled by legislative bodies. Whether the state legislature is examined or the county governing bodies, town boards, or city councils, the conclusion is always the same: highways are woven into legislative activity. The desire to control the routing and surfacing of highways and streets is one thing that motivates members of legislative bodies to pay close attention to highway policies, although spoils politics may also be a factor. If an alderman can obtain the paving of a street in his district at general city expense, he can expect more support at the next election. If a legislator secures a rerouting of a state highway so that it serves the convenience of a group of his constituents more effectively, he also may expect extra votes at the polls. Sometimes local groups do not want improvements to come near their property, in which case councilmen may work for an expressway to go through another part of town, or a state legislator may push legislation for a bypass around a city.

Control over the highway committees of state legislatures and local governing bodies may be the determining factor in influencing highway policy. Control is vested in the political party in power, and as much as possible each member of that party in the legislative body is considered a special spokesman for highway policy affecting his district. His advice is almost always taken, if it does not conflict with that of his fellow partisans. On a county level similar conditions exist if the governing body is very large, but in those units with governing agencies of three or five members, committees may be dispensed with or the entire governing body may be ex officio a highway committee. The county commissioner or supervisor may be in effect a road commissioner for his district, taking an active part in administration of roads as well as in road policy decisions. He may hire all help and supervise the building and maintenance of roads in his district. Road administration is most primitive in some Midwestern townships, where one of the members of the town board may house a piece of road equipment in his barn or yard and have a hired hand grade the roads each summer and plow the snow in the winter.

What about the governor? The usual segregation of highway revenues, the intense local concern for many aspects of highway policies, the importance of federal aids and standards, and the technical professionalism of the highway-department personnel appear generally to have limited the influence of governors. In most states, the governor has less control over the highway budget than over general state revenues and expenditures. Frequently his appointing powers are restricted in regard to the top officials of the highway department. His signature on highway contracts may often be perfunctory. The highway department or the department and the highway committees of the legislature generally determine highway location. The National Bureau of Public Roads largely determines the minimum standards for federally-aided highways. Exceptions to this evaluation of the governor's influence appear either (1) under circumstances of possible major changes in highway policies or (2) where patronage in highway personnel or in contract awards contributes to the governor's party or personal position.

★ Administration of highway programs

The pattern of responsibility for highways is fairly uniform throughout the country, with states administering primarily the main trunk highways (about 500,000 miles), counties the bulk of rural roads (about 1,700,000 miles), and municipalities urban streets (about 300,000 miles). There are a few variations from this pattern, such as in New England (where towns or the states generally have principal responsibility for rural roads) and in North Carolina, Virginia, West Virginia, and Delaware (where state agencies have control of all rural highways and roads). In a few Eastern and Midwestern states, townships have a role to play in maintaining many miles of minor rural roads. All town and township road mileage (including New England) totals about 700,000 miles. While the general outlines of program responsibility in the highway field are fairly clear, there are many overlappings and many relationships among units of government that pose problems of policy and administration.

Administrative agencies in the highway field vary not only in formal organization, but very importantly in the degree of professionalization of their staff members. Formally, highway organization on a state level takes two principal forms, a highway commission or a single-headed state highway department. State highway departments center their programs on the trunk highways, although they deal with many other aspects of highway policy. Usually they have divisions of road maintenance and road construction. Both divisions must have regional or district offices at convenient locations in order to perform their tasks adequately and promptly. In addition to divisions of maintenance and construction, a department is likely to have divisions of administration (with perhaps public information, organization and management, office-services, and personnel units); planning and reasearch (with economic studies, programming, and mapping units); and finance (with accounting and auditing, budgetary control, and payroll units).

Traditionally construction is handled by contract with private companies, while maintenance is by state-employed highway crews. The kinds of pressure exerted upon these divisions is reflected by their functions. Private contractors become eager to have "influence" with those in charge of supervising construction as well as those who draw up construction contracts. The latter function is usually handled by the department's legal staff. Opportunities for spoils and patronage jobs occur largely in maintenance operations.[2]

Almost 18 percent of all state employees in October 1958 were employed by state highway agencies (and this figure does not include employees of private firms with state highway contracts). Only state hospitals and state institutions of higher learning had larger numbers of personnel on their payrolls. Highway departments hire skilled and unskilled labor, clerical personnel, accountants, highly trained engineers, economists, statisticians, and administrators. Often the more professionally trained the personnel in the state highway department, the closer the relations that exist with the United States Bureau of Public Roads and its technically trained staff.

Highway administration frequently tests or shows up the general characteristics of the state's government. Are merit tests applied in hiring the

2 Frank J. Sorauf, "State Patronage in a Rural County," L *American Political Science Review*, December 1956, pp. 1046-1056.

great bulk of employees in highways or is it whom you know that counts? Does the highway department make every reasonable attempt to secure contracts most advantageous to the state for the building of the roads? What is the timing of contracts? How are specifications for the contracts handled? Is the bidding open and competitive? Are research efforts used in determining road materials? Does the highway budget show up clearly costs of highways for types of highways and under varying conditions? How is road location determined? What is the procedure for valuing land and paying owners for land needed for highways? These questions should assist in suggesting some of the characteristics of highway administration which affect the standards of the state's government.[3]

★ Intergovernmental relations

National leadership. Beginning with the Federal Aid Road Act in 1916, the national government has been active in trying to shape state and local road policy through a system of grants-in-aid. In this it has been notably successful, although interstate cooperation has also produced results. For example, uniform numbering of the so-called "U. S." highways was a project of interstate cooperation, and highways so numbered are not necessarily federal-aid roads. Similarly, interstate agreement as to the routing of highways has prevented a highway ending abruptly at a state border or a paved highway turning into a narrow dirt road where an artificial legal boundary is reached. But, while interstate cooperation has made important contributions, the national government has taken the leadership in most aspects of highway planning and standards.

Highways are one of the two most expensive services of state and local governments, and national grants for this purpose have provided the states with substantial revenue. The grants have recently been for four purposes—trunk highways, farm-to-market or secondary highways, urban extensions of federal-aid highways and the interstate highway system. The national government thus has four areas of highway policy in which it has tried to determine state and local policies by insisting on minimum standards if grants-in-aid are to be distributed. The minimum standards are actually enforced, and funds have been withheld at least temporarily from recalcitrant states. National grants are for construction, and a state must maintain its nationally aided highways in good condition or else forfeit future grants. Most states would maintain their highways fairly reasonably whether any national aid were involved or not, but occasionally an economy

[3] Illinois, for example, does not include highway personnel under its general civil-service merit-system laws.

wave or a special revenue problem will cause a legislature or governor to slight this aspect of government. National requirements therefore limit the discretion of state authorities. Outside of highway maintenance, national requirements concern the location of highways, their engineering details, and supervision over their construction. One objective of national aid is to create an extensive system of interregional highways, a system that is free from toll roads and bridges.

As a whole, national-state relations in the highway field have been very smooth and friendly. The main controversy, and even this is a rather minor one, has been between the national government and the governors or legislatures because national regulations tend to limit their policy powers over highways. Maintenance requirements are one example. Another is the stipulation that to be eligible for aid the states must continue to apply as great an amount of the state's highway-user taxes for highway purposes as was applied on June 18, 1934. This, the so-called diversion clause, was passed in the depression era to prevent states from allocating highway-user taxes for welfare or other pressing needs. User pressure groups were largely instrumental in getting this clause inserted into the law and have vigorously defended it. Regardless of its merits, it effectively curtails the over-all financial control that the legislature or governor can exercise over the highway department, and some of the governors and their budget directors particularly have objected to it as unnecessary and as an invasion of states' rights.

National system of interstate and defense highways. In 1956 Congress added a fourth federal-aid highway program when it designated approximately 41,000 miles of proposed highway routes in the United States as a network of interstate roads linking all state capitals and all major population centers as well as providing links for the projected inter-American route from Alaska to the tip of South America. For the purpose of putting these 41,000 miles of highway in top condition and insuring generally at least four lanes, a construction able to withstand the heaviest trucks operating, and an engineering design aimed to improve safety, Congress appropriated money beginning in 1956 for grants to the states for a speeded-up thirteen-year program of construction on the interstate system. The national government expects to provide 90 percent of the cost of the roads and the states the other 10 percent and thereafter the maintenance of roads within their boundaries. (Most other highway grant-in-aid programs have been on a fifty-fifty matching basis.)

State-local programs. Most state highway departments are both supervising and operating agencies. For the most part they supervise county road administration, although they have some relationships with municipalities. The states have developed a fairly extensive pattern of grants-in-aid for rural roads, and in order to qualify for this aid counties must meet a number of minimum conditions. These standards pertain to such matters as road materials, width and grades, and general minimums of maintenance. The state-local relationship is not just one of direction and inspection on the part of the state agency. It is also one of advice and mutual help. County engineers do not have large staffs of experts to conduct research or keep up on the many new developments in highway engineering. They therefore look to the state for much technical advice. To facilitate state-local relations, some highway departments have established spearate bureaus or divisions that handle all contacts with counties.

Grant-in-aid formulas. The formulas for apportioning highway grants-in-aid among the states by the national government or among local government units by the states represent another area of important political decision-making in the field of highways. Most apportionment formulas take some account of the number of motor vehicles registered in the area, the number of miles of highways, the population of the area, and possibly other factors such as total land area. If the formula emphasizes number of miles, rural areas generally gain in aid. If the formula emphasizes population and number of vehicles, urban areas are likely to gain. Such results are especially likely where, as is common, the cities, villages, and towns accept most responsibility for construction and maintenance of purely local road systems. To the extent to which population is emphasized in national apportionment formulas, the Eastern states tend to gain at the expense of the mountain and Western states. If mileage outweighs population, the mountain and less populated states gain in the apportionment of moneys. (*Note.* Most of this discussion is in relative and not absolute terms or in terms of amount of grant moneys apportioned per mile of roads in a given area or state. How much more per mile should the state or national government pay in grants to communities with heavily traveled roads—identified by population density and motor-vehicle registration—over communities with less traveled roads? [4])

---

[4] Apart from the interstate and defense highway grants, Congress has provided for the distribution of highway grants to the states on the following general statutory formulas: Appropriations to be used on the *primary system of highways* is distributed as follows: one third, land area; one third, total population; and one third, mileage of rural delivery and star routes. No state is to get less than ½ of 1 percent of the available funds in this category. Appropriations to be used for a *secondary system* are to be distributed on same basis as for the primary system. Appropriations to be used for *urban extensions* are to be distributed on the basis of population in cities and other urban places of 5000 or more.

★ *Fiscal aspects of highways*

Governments have usually found highways costly. With more and more cars and trucks being driven faster and faster and carrying heavier and heavier loads, highway costs have jumped. In 1920 there were nine million motor vehicles registered in the United States. Now there are about seven times as many. The 1965 estimate is at least eight times the 1920 figure. Americans have multiplied their use of the highways more spectacularly than the increase in car numbers. A 1965 estimate of 800 billion vehicle miles is roughly sixteen times the number of miles driven in 1920.

The states reported total state and local highway expenditures (including federal grants) of $3 billion in 1948, whereas the 1957 figure was $7.8 billion. Each subsequent year has seen a significant increase. As a percent of total state and local expenditures, only education exceeds highways. Since highways represent roughly one fifth of all state and local expenditures, highway financing necessarily looms large in every state budget. Questions involve such issues as who should be taxed for highways and in what relation, whether highway-user taxes should be segregated, whether toll roads are desirable and can be financially solvent, and how to apportion moneys among areas and types of roads of the state. These questions involve issues which have been generally discussed elsewhere. The first point especially raises the issue of the distribution of highway costs among the trucker, the passenger-car operator, and the general taxpaying public. In all states, at least residual costs of highway and motor-vehicle operation (the cost of courts used for accident suits, enforcement of traffic laws in the courts, often some city street costs, and so on) rest on the general taxpayer. Toll roads involve all of these issues: What should be the amount of the tolls and to whom should they be charged? Are the toll rates low enough to attract travelers and high enough to cover the costs of construction and maintenance? Finally, how much are citizens willing to spend for highways in total and in relation to expenditures for other functions of government. Significant improvements in optimum use of moneys for highways could assist state budgets.[5] Many suggestions for making state governments more

[5] Savings may come from such items as prices paid for rights of way, methods of advertising bids to achieve the lowest possible contract prices, the development of engineering methods which reduce the cost of construction, and the related development of road materials which will hold up under heavier traffic use. States which carelessly or intentionally permit highway contracts and maintenance work to be available for spoils naturally pay a heavy penalty in increased tax costs. The great differences among the states in the cost per mile of highway building reflect differences in topography (e.g., mountains or swamps increase road costs), use of highway programs for spoils, and efficiency of state highway departments. Indiana and Illinois, among other states, have had publicized scandals involving excessive payments to owners of land acquired for highway purposes, excessive contract payments, and embezzlement of tolls.

Figure 12. A FAMILIAR SCENE: ROAD BUILDING

Source: Maryland State Roads Commission.

efficient concern matters which by themselves appear to be insignificant. (Probably no taxpayer, for example, would notice in his tax bill either an increase or decrease in the salaries paid to the governor or state legislators.) But when it is recognized that one mile of a four-lane highway may cost $1 million or more, management or technical improvements to reduce this amount by 1 percent or more mean real taxpayer savings.

★ The future of highways

The foregoing summary of governmental fiscal aspects of highways suggests the present impact of highways on state budgets and should also suggest that there is little likelihood of substantially reducing this impact. Highways have significance for the economy in general not only in terms of their use and their impact on governmental budgets but also in terms of the industries which provide materials for their construction and maintenance. *U. S. News and World Report* (June 29, 1956) reported an estimate of the American Road Builders' Association which listed the probable consumption of the following materials in highways built in 1961: 113,100,000 barrels of cement; 662,911,000 tons of stone, gravel, and sand; 9,236,000 tons of asphalt and tar; 680,800,000 board feet of lumber; 22,173,200 linear feet of timber piling; 3,672,000 tons of steel; 4,380,800 tons of concrete pipe; 15,032,600 linear feet of clay pipe and tile; 1,069,339,600 gallons of oil products; 152,563,000 pounds of explosives; and 662,200 signs!

The problem of highways for urban areas has received greater emphasis in recent national grant programs and from legislators in states with large urban centers. Without necessarily neglecting rural highways, this recognition has funneled an increasing proportion of funds to city "beltlines," expressways, and bypasses. So far the city highway problem seems to grow faster than the willingness of state and national governments to provide assistance. Can the central-city business section flourish if all passenger traffic except by public transportation (buses, monorails, and so forth) is barred? One or two cities are experimenting with this procedure. Will helicopter use develop to permit significant numbers of commuters to avoid clogging streets with private cars? Or is the only solution either great superhighways into the city (which frequently blight surrounding areas) or planned dispersion of joint living and working areas? The more adequately we investigate these possibilities and forecast the future, the more effectively we can plan the highway systems we build now.

Motor-vehicle Regulation

Intimately related to highways is the whole subject of motor-vehicle regulation. Most highway departments directly or in concert with a state motor-vehicle department have discretion in establishing regulations for speed limits on certain stretches of road and in prohibiting or limiting the use of roads by certain types of vehicles at particular times or on certain highways. Regulation is intended to protect the state's investment in highways, to protect drivers from accidents, and to protect car owners against theft. Individual car owners sometimes desire all of these protections for themselves but resent enforcement when it is used to protect others from them.

Highway accidents between 1900 and 1955 killed more Americans (1,149,414) than our eight wars between 1775 and 1955 (1,130,393).[6] Speed which is excessive for the driving conditions continues to cause a large proportion of the accidents. A disproportionate number of accidents involve youths under 25. A study in Pennsylvania reported that some accident-prone youthful drivers looked upon driving as an activity to relieve their mental tension.[7] Improved highway engineering and automobile design can

6 *U. S. News and World Report*, February 3, 1956.
7 The study by Robert C. S. Rommel of Pennsylvania State University was reported in the *Wisconsin Traffic Safety Reporter*, September 1958. Rommel also found that accident-

Figure 13. HIGHWAY DEATHS: MORE LIVES WERE LOST

Reprinted from *U. S. News & World Report* (Feb. 3, 1956), an independent weekly news magazine published at Washington. Copyright 1956 United States News Publishing Corporation.

and have improved safety. On the other hand, the development of bigger and more powerful automobiles together with straighter and smoother roads have often worked in the opposite direction.

State legislators and governors have expressed great concern for the "slaughter" on the highways.[8] Money has been spent for driver-training courses in schools, larger state traffic patrols, and accident research. State laws have placed higher and higher (sometimes unenforceably high) penalties on drunken drivers and repeated highway violators. Connecticut,

prone youths frequently experienced one or more of the following: a desire to leave home; an urge to do something shocking; association with friends to whom parents objected; a desire to frighten others for the fun of it; suspicion of overfriendly people; a tendency to be easily influenced by others; difficulty with the police.

[8] The Governors' Conference in 1956 appointed a Committee on Highway Safety. The recommendations of this Committee are summarized in *The Book of the States, 1958-59*, pp. 297ff.

IN AUTOMOBILE ACCIDENTS THAN IN ALL U. S. WARS

1900 - 1955

1,149,414
AMERICANS DIED
IN
U. S. HIGHWAY
ACCIDENTS

with one of the best safety records in the country, has enforced strict traffic laws and gives safe drivers recognition by issuing personalized license plates. State speed limits vary from 40 miles an hour to "reasonable and prudent," which puts the burden of proof for excessive speed on the state and has often been found to mean no speed limit. No state as yet has required cars to have speed governors which mechanically prevent the driver from going above a specified maximum.

Aviation

Although state governments regulate railroads they have not built either their roadbeds or terminals.[9] The trucking and bus industries and individual car owners have received through tax moneys thousands of miles of highways. Aviation has had free skyways but national subsidies such as mail

[9] It is recognized, of course, that nineteenth-century America at the state- and national-government levels provided substantial subsidies in land and money to the railroads.

contracts have helped to develop the industry and national, state, and local money has helped to build airport facilities and terminals. In part because of the military implications, the national government has taken the lead in regulating and assisting aviation. The states have held back in both regulation and assistance. In the ten post-World War II years of 1947 to 1957, federal funds to state and local agencies totaled $314 million and matching state and local public funds slightly exceeded this amount.

As aircraft have become more versatile, productive, and dependable, they have shown growth records similar to the automobile. In 1936, there were five million take-offs and landings at the nation's airports. Twenty years later, there were 65 million with 115 million forecast for 1975.[10] The future use of commercial passenger planes, freight planes, private planes, helicopters and vertical take-off-and-landing aircraft will have an effect both on state airport and highway needs. An expansion of air travel will bring more government activity at all levels into the regulation of airlines and the development of airports. The airlanes, once considered more or less unlimited, are becoming crowded. Part of the overcrowding stems from the diversity of planes—small and large, relatively slow and fast, commercial, private, and military.

Legislators, governors, and administrators will have to deal with many of the same pressures in airline regulation and assistance as they have in the highway field. Even more than in the case of highways, rural-oriented legislators in the past have tended to ignore urban needs for airports.[11] National grants have in part been made directly to cities for airports and more or less bypassed state governments. Governors and legislators have complained of this development in the distribution of federal aid. As more states assume supervisory functions over aviation, the administration of federal grants may assume the more usual pattern of national-state-local relations. With jet flights across the country from Washington to San Francisco in approximately five hours, however, much regulation will necessarily remain with the national government.

Conclusions

Government becomes larger and more expensive in the field of transportation as the number of automobiles and airplanes increases. Much of the

10 See "Aviation among the States," *The Book of the States, 1958-59*, pp. 304ff.
11 Rural constituents have frequently not assisted urban areas in their desire for large airport-terminal facilities to be financed in part from state funds. On the other hand the use of aircraft by farmers and ranchers has increased and at least small rural landing fields have been needed. "Approximately one in every seven cultivated acres in the United States, along with millions of acres of forest land, were seeded or treated in 1956 by some form of aerial chemical application." *Ibid.*, p. 306.

regulation and highway or airport building depends on technical knowledge. Yet with the new technical knowledge remain many of the old political and administrative questions. Spoils politics may increase the tax cost of transportation, decisions on location of highways and airports may affect the industrial health of a community or the desirability of particular areas (the choice between the noise of jet planes landing or huge trucks shifting gears is no choice for the individual wishing quiet around his home). The political process of determining who gets what, how and when affects these and other decisions in regard to the regulation of and assistance to transportation.

REFERENCES

Chapman, A. L., "An Epidemiological Approach to Traffic Safety," *Public Health Reports.* Washington, D. C.: Government Printing Office, August 1954, pp. 773-775.

Due, John F., "The Rise and Decline of the Toll Principle in Highway Finance—1940-1957," X *National Tax Journal* (June 1957), 97-113.

Gomez, R. A., *Intergovernmental Relations in Highways.* Minneapolis: University of Minnesota Press, 1950.

House of Representatives, Committee on Interstate and Foreign Commerce, *State Taxation of Interstate Trucking and the Reciprocity Problem.* House Document No. 449, 84th Cong., 2d Sess., 1956.

Martin, James W., "Administrative Dangers in the Enlarged Highway Program," XIX *Public Administration Review* (Summer 1959), 164-172.

Moses, Robert, "The New Super-Highways: Blessing or Blight?" *Harper's Magazine* (December 1956), 27-31.

National Highway Users Conference, various publications.

Netzer, Dick, "Financial Policy for Highways: Impact of the 1956 Federal Legislation," X *National Tax Journal* (June 1957), 114-125.

Scheffer, Walter F., "Reciprocity in the Taxation of Interstate Trucks," IX *National Tax Journal* (March 1956), 75-83.

State Government, various articles. For example, W. L. Haas, "How Wisconsin Trains Highway Engineers and Aides," 28 *State Government* (July 1955), 159ff.; and Carl E. Fritts, "Solving the Engineering Problems in State Highway Construction," 30 *State Government* (December 1957), 258-261.

State Highway Department reports.

Study Committee on Federal Aid to Highways, Commission on Intergovernmental Relations, *A Study Committee Report on Federal Aid to Highways.* Washington, D. C.: Government Printing Office, June 1955.

The Research and Policy Committee of the Committee for Economic Development, *Modernizing The Nation's Highways.* New York: Committee for Economic Development, January 1956.

U. S. Department of Commerce, Bureau of Public Roads, *Annual Report.* Washington, D. C.: Government Printing Office.

CHAPTER 20

Agriculture and Natural Resources

THE AMERICAN CONTINENT in the seventeenth and eighteenth centuries offered the great attraction of virgin soil and increased food production to Europe which was using overworked lands to feed a growing population. Even as late as the early nineteenth century, Malthus believed that starvation for many, as the result of insufficient food supplies, was a normal state of affairs. Although periodically such is the case (and in Asia it is prevalent), the enormous advances in agriculture have reduced the specter of starvation in most Western countries. Whereas the economy required almost 80 percent of the population to be farmers in 1790 to feed the 20 percent who lived in urban areas, the figures have more than reversed. In 1950, only 16 percent of the population of the United States lived on farms. This 16 percent fed the nation in a superior fashion, exported agricultural products, and sought government assistance to curb production, dispose of surpluses, and keep up prices.

Technological improvements have given the farmer a variety of machinery to reduce the harshness of his life in earlier centuries and to permit him to plant and harvest beyond the ability of the farm family and its hired help of the past. Commercial fertilizers, improved land practices, improved seed, the development of hybrids have contributed to a productivity per acre unimagined even in 1900. A 1954 report on Midwestern agriculture stated:

> Possibly no measure of increased efficiency is so spectacular as that which shows the rise in output per man-hour. *Since 1940*, for example, the total production of corn and other feed grains has increased about one-fifth, the man-hours used to produce them have been reduced by more than one-half, and the output of feed grains per man-hour has increased nearly threefold.[1] [Italics added.]

And research, development, farming practices add annually to the productivity not only of corn and feed grains but of almost every agricultural item. Beef cattle produce more pounds of good beef. Milk cows produce more milk. And so on.

Agricultural policy is shaped by all levels of government.[2] Reflecting this, the farmers (or at least some of them) are organized on a county, state, and national basis, and they may well claim the largest and most effective pressure groups. Agricultural policy is influenced not so much by farmers in general as by organized farmers, and especially by organized farmers' paid lobbyists. This is the nongovernmental side of agricultural policy. On the other side are county governing-body members, state legislators, governors, and agricultural administrators and experts who are variously influenced by, deal with, and are a part of the farm pressure groups.[3] At some point in between are the political parties.

Governmental Agricultural Programs[4]

Nations typically have recognized large economic groups in their programs and policies. With more than 50 percent of the American people living on farms until the last quarter of the nineteenth century, farmers and their problems received attention to some degree from the beginning. Government land prices and homestead grants took account of farmers' demands. Water transportation, roads, and railroads developed in part to meet the

---

[1] Federal Reserve Bank of Chicago, *Annual Report 1954*, p. 6.

[2] On this point, and on agricultural policy in general, see Charles M. Hardin's excellent article, "Reflections on Agricultural Policy Formation in the United States," *American Political Science Review*, October 1948, pp. 881-905; and by the same author, the book, *The Politics of Agriculture* (Glencoe, Ill.: Free Press, 1952).

[3] *Agricultural policy* in which farmers and farm groups have interested themselves extends beyond policies that directly affect agricultural production. Farmers have used their influence and their organizations to work for farm-to-market roads, to adjust school-district consolidation to their desires, and to oppose redistricting and reapportionment that might limit their influence in state legislatures and in Congress. Our discussion in this chapter is limited to the development and administration of farm programs in the narrower sense.

[4] There is no intent here to list and identify all agricultural programs of American government today. The discussion should be only suggestive.

needs of agricultural interests. The United States Department of Agriculture was established as early as 1862. Lands were given the states for agricultural colleges, and in 1887 national grants for agricultural experiment stations became available. The Department of Agriculture began its own experimental work in the nineteenth century in an effort to improve the quality of seed, discover the best planting conditions, and in all ways assist in the greater productivity of American farms. The department also began rather early to gather some statistics on agricultural production and by the twentieth century to provide weather and marketing information.

The increase in agricultural programs in the 1930s as part of the New Deal's effort to assist the farmer in the depression expanded some programs long in operation and put into existence others long discussed. Research to improve production was continued along with programs to take land out of production and to raise the depressed farm prices which resulted from overproduction. Dust storms and other evidence of land damage brought soil conservation programs—assistance and direction in contour plowing, strip planting, repair and preventive work for gullying and erosion. Some farmers received assistance in leaving submarginal lands and getting a fresh start on lands more suitable for farming. Crop and farm mortgage loans assumed large proportions during the 1930s. Crop mortgage loans have continued in importance and are sometimes tied to price-guaranty programs.

Overlapping the federal Department of Agriculture in origin and sometimes in content, state departments of agriculture conduct some research, collect agricultural data, publish marketing information, assist in the eradication of plant and animal diseases, and carry out inspection activities in such fields as weed control, milk and food sanitation, and plant and animal diseases. State colleges of agriculture together with their experiment stations and extension-work divisions engage in agricultural research (scientific, economic, and social research), put out agricultural publications, and do other educational work. Through county agricultural agents, agricultural colleges have spread their findings in research to the individual farmer.

The scope of a state's agricultural program necessarily differs with the type of agriculture found in the state. Ranchers in Colorado will seek to have their department and college of agriculture emphasize problems of irrigation, dry farming, possibly wheat or fruit farming, sheep, and cattle. New York and Wisconsin farmers have sought primary emphasis on dairy farming. Soil conservation may receive greater attention in the hills of North Carolina than in the flat Illinois prairies.

The reduction in the farming population and the consequent lesser need for some of the past activities of the agricultural extension services have turned the attention of agricultural colleges and county agents to urban or at least suburban interests. The county agricultural agent in Milwaukee County (Wisconsin), for example, spends significant amounts of his time on the horticultural problems of suburban homeowners. In 1957, the U. S. Department of Agriculture reported that only 62 percent of the members of the Four-H clubs served by the county agents of the nation actually lived on farms.

★ *Administrative organization*

The national government centralizes most agricultural programs within the United States Department of Agriculture. The states have frequently had much more complex arrangements. With only a few exceptions, every state has a department of agriculture and a state agricultural college.[5] No exact demarcation line divides the responsibilities undertaken by each, and there is much competition in programs and appropriations, as well as cooperation. The state college of agriculture with its protective board of regents, substantial grants from the U. S. Department of Agriculture, and "field men" (the county agricultural agents) is less subject to control and supervision by the governor and legislature than is the state department of agriculture. In some states, the agricultural department achieves a measure of isolation from legislative and executive control either through an elective head for the department or a board appointed by the governor whose members serve long overlapping terms.

In every state, the U. S. Department of Agriculture has established many state and county committees of farmers and farm experts. Most of them have no formal relationship to state or county agricultural agencies, but frequently some of the employees of these agencies, such as the county agent or the head of the state extension service, serve on them in an ex-officio capacity. At any one time the agricultural agencies working in a state present a confusing array of national, state, and local authorities plus a number of special farmer groups and organizations. The possibilities of competition among the several agencies do not necessarily give the legislature and the governor a particularly free hand in their direction. Agricultural employees frequently have been trained in the state college of agriculture and share a common background and experience. Some are members of one or more of the principal farmers' pressure groups. All deal with pressure-group representatives. The legislature and governor may find

[5] In Arkansas and New Mexico the state agricultural colleges have been assigned functions more usually allotted elsewhere to separate state departments of agriculture. A few other states combine agriculture with another function, such as the Kentucky Department of Agriculture, Labor, and Statistics or the Mississippi Department of Agriculture and Commerce.

themselves consulted only when a particularly heated controversy develops in which the agencies and the farm interest groups have already chosen sides.

★ Agricultural finance

The U. S. Department of Agriculture carries on many farm programs directly. Cooperative assignment of personnel and exchange of information continue in others. The largest agricultural grants occur in the traditional programs—agricultural experiment stations and cooperative agricultural extension work.[6] National grants in agricultural work vary from something like 10 percent to 50 percent of the cost of running agricultural experiment stations and extension work. Federal grant money also supports the crop-marketing, and weather-reporting programs and some livestock and plant disease-control activities. Apart from the expenditures for soil and water conservation, states spent $388 million or only 1.6 percent of their total general expenditures in 1958 for agricultural activities. The national government provided $78 million or 20 percent of the cost of the programs.

★ Interest groups in agriculture

Americans have generally taken a protective interest and concern in farmers and farming even when many individual Americans have not the slightest interest in being farmers. Thomas Jefferson wrote distrustfully of city mobs and placed his faith in democracy with the sturdy yeoman of the farms. All of the folklore of the nineteenth century admired the virtues of the farmer and condemned the city and its inhabitants, stereotyping the laborer as poor and undeserving and the successful man of business or finance as crafty. Sin, shrewdness, and poverty were associated with the city; virtue, bravery, and self-reliance, with the farm. The fact that the farmer in the nineteenth century and today normally operates as a businessman—sometimes speculating in land, borrowing to expand his operations, hiring labor at the lowest wage rates, and generally entering into and dependent upon the market— has not affected the traditional picture. A nostalgia for the past and the folklore that identifies agriculture with democracy have given farmers a distinct political advantage.

Numerous and diverse farm pressure groups operate on the national, state, and local levels. Some pretend to be general farm organizations, while others are frankly devoted to the interests of the milk producers, the wool growers, or some other limited category of farmers. Farm cooperatives also are highly organized on local, state, and national levels. Many farmers be-

[6] See Chapter 21 for a discussion of national grants for agricultural and home economics training in high schools and for underwriting the school lunch program.

long to two or more of these associations. Their objectives sometimes clash as the leadership of the several associations may have different goals. Farm groups help form farm opinion as well as government opinion on agricultural policy. Public officials normally deal with these groups, especially their leaders and representatives.

By far the most powerful farm pressure group is the American Farm Bureau Federation. Organized only in 1919, it was born of mixed parentage, including semiofficial sponsorship by certain states and the national government together with some previously existing farm groups. Much of its power has stemmed from its ability to become the official or at least the semiofficial representative of the farmers for agricultural extension work at the county level. Its importance has been highlighted by the fact that it has inevitably been concerned with agricultural policy and has taken definite stands with which some farmers disagree. In general the Farm Bureau has been characterized by a rather conservative farm and social policy, some antagonism to labor groups, and an affinity for the more prosperous and large-scale farmer.[7] There are notable exceptions to this statement, the Ohio Farm Bureau perhaps being the most outstanding.

The major opposition to the Farm Bureau and several of its important policies has come from the Farmers Union and the farmer-consumer cooperative movement. These are characterized by a more liberal social philosophy; frequently they cooperate with labor unions, and they attempt to represent the smaller and poorer farmers. They are far less effective and have fewer members than the Farm Bureau in most states, but in some states and a number of counties, particularly those that are poor and have traditions stemming back to radical agrarian movements, the Farmers Union-cooperative movement alliance predominates.

Farm Bureau and TVA. The position of the Farm Bureau and other groups relative to the agricultural extension system has imporatnt implications for such appealing phrases as the "grass-roots" approach. In a study of the Tennessee Valley Authority's grass-roots approach in the field of agriculture, it was found that many national policy objectives were abandoned

---

[7] Some years ago, the head of the American Farm Bureau Federation specifically disclaimed interest in the nonmarket farmer: "Many actual farmers are included (in Census definition) who produce little more than enough to feed themselves and their families.

". . . their problem is not primarily a farm problem, and the answers are not to be found in farm costs or farm prices. . . .

"The farmers about whom this article is written are the approximately two million who sold farm commodities worth $2,500 or more in 1949, producing over 80 per cent of all farm commodities sold." Allan B. Kline, "What the Farmers Want," *The Annals of the American Academy of Political and Social Science*, September 1948. Quoted by Henry A. Turner in *Politics in the United States, Readings in Political Parties and Pressure Groups* (New York: McGraw-Hill, 1955), pp. 111-112.

or altered because of the nature of existing agricultural leadership on a state and county level.[8] TVA's primary policy was a grass-roots approach— that is, working with and through existing state and local agencies whenever possible. In the field of agriculture this meant that TVA would work through the state extension services and county agents. Since the Farm Bureau was very influential in extension work, and since, in general, state and local agricultural personnel were rather conservatively oriented in such matters as soil conservation and the position of tenant farmers, the result was that a New Deal agency, the TVA, thwarted some of the more liberal objectives of other New Deal agencies as well as its own. Therefore it was decided to establish a grass-roots pattern of national-government contacts with the farmers in the Tennessee Valley area. Whether decisions are actually decentralized in such a grass-roots approach is open to doubt, since the farmers at the county level frequently take their cues in farm policy from the *national* farm group to which they belong. The Farm Security Administration and the Soil Conservation Service were two New Deal organizations which came in conflict with TVA over the matter. In the 1940s the Farm Bureau openly opposed the Agricultural Adjustment Administration and demanded that its educational activities be funneled through the extension system.[9]

Oleomargarine. The dairying interests have long carried on a fight against margarine, colored or uncolored. For years the dairy pressure groups relied upon both the national and state governments in their attempt to have margarine sales either prohibited or taxed to death. In 1950, when all discriminatory taxes of the national government against margarine were lifted, twenty Northern and Western states still had laws that continued such discrimination within their borders.

The oleomargarine fight brings many interests into play. Dairy farmers are not the largest segment of agriculture. Growers of soybeans and cottonseed are farmers too. The split of agricultural interests appeared repeatedly when the oleomargarine issue came up in Congress. With the decrease in the number of dairy farmers, improvements in production of margarine and the increased public knowledge of margarine, groups interested in soybeans and cottonseed overcame the dairy farmer in Congress and then in most of the states. Only Minnesota and Wisconsin still prohibit the sale of colored margarine within their borders. As Wisconsin attempts to expand its milk market into the South, it finds barriers in these states that are

---

[8] Philip Selznick, *TVA and the Grass Roots* (Berkeley, Calif.: University of California Press, 1949).
[9] *Ibid.*, pp. 157-164.

defended in part on the grounds of Wisconsin's discrimination against the sale of margarine.

Conservation

European immigrants to the United States in the eighteenth and nineteenth centuries found a land of plenty—inexhaustible supplies of rich farm lands, timber, mineral deposits, pure water, game, fish, and birds. Everyone might take and use the resources at his own discretion; there was always more. Only toward the close of the nineteenth century did individuals and groups begin to sense the limits. From the days of Theodore Roosevelt conservation became a fighting cause. Much of the vigor of the conservation movement has stemmed from a love of nature and its beauties, and as a result its participants have had a fervor and a determination not unlike certain religious cults. To some, the destruction of trees and game by a forest fire or the elimination of the productiveness of land by a flood or soil erosion seems equivalent to violating quasi-religious commandments. Each generation has received a heritage in the form of natural resources that it has a solemn obligation not to waste but to pass on to the next generation.

The original conservation movement was in part an attack on rich timber barons and mine owners. Men felt that a few enriched themselves at the expense of the many. The cry against the exploiters and for conservation was taken up by the liberal movements early in the century and has been a part of the liberal tradition ever since. Population growth and industrial expansion have made exploitation profitable at the same time that the consciousness of limitations has grown. "Bottomless" iron mines no longer produce high-grade iron. State and national parks, once considered too large, often seem crowded to the thousands of motorists camping there with their families. Water polluted from industrial and human wastes of cities reduces fishing and recreational opportunities as well as the beauty of surrounding areas.

Conservation Programs

Natural resources and their relation to our economy and peoples are so all inclusive that it is difficult to identify all governmental conservation activities. The more usual lists, however, include soil conservation (sometimes identified with agriculture); forests; parks; fish and game regulation; water; regulation of extractive industries such as coal, iron, copper, and oil.

Both the national and state governments and some local governments have acquired lands for forests as a long-term crop; cutting of mature trees goes on while new trees are planted. Very little virgin timber still remains. Research is undertaken to identify growth of different species of trees under different conditions; to identify tree pests and diseases and means of controlling them; to find substitutes for wood or to find uses for wood products formerly discarded.

All modern methods of communication and fire equipment are used to protect forests from fire. A recent report showed the states owned 10,000 radios, 3000 transportation trucks, 1600 tanker trucks, 1500 plows, 1900 power pumps, 1200 tractors, 350 jeeps with plows or tanks, 40 airplanes, 3300 lookout towers for forest-fire detection, and 24,000 miles of telephone lines for communication. Experimental activities in cloud seeding, lightning dispersal, Detecto-Vision using television for detecting fires, measuring weather, and rating fire behavior have aided.[10]

The automobile has greatly increased the demands on parks. Millions of Americans wish to spend their two or three weeks of vacation away from the city, close to nature with plenty of green grass, trees, clear water, perhaps some fish and game, and not too many other people. State and national park facilities were not built for the present number of visitors, and annual increases in facilities and acreage are sought.[11]

The first conservation efforts of most of the states involved fish and game regulation. Fish and game programs today usually go far beyond the old negative programs of limiting the season and catch; they include research into diseases of fish and game and desirable natural-habitat conditions and the raising of fish and game under controlled conditions—sometimes for eventual supplementation of fish and game in the natural areas. At times, in the case of commercial fisheries or of game in particular resort areas, substantial economic interests as well as the interests of the sportsman come into play.

Water conservation activities embrace many things: antipollution, irrigation, dams and power development, transportation, flood prevention, and others. Again the national, state, and local governments have all acted at one time or another in this area. Each individual government has sometimes found coordination of water policies difficult, and coordination and cooperation among states and among local governments as well as between the national and state governments finds many barriers. Upstream pollution from industries, cities, or resorts or commercial use of ports may seriously

10 *The Book of the States, 1958-59*, p. 409.
11 In 1956, 12.6 million Americans used *state* parks overnight and over 200 million spent some time in state parks.

reduce or destroy a thriving oyster business in the bay. Water-power needs may reduce the natural beauty of an area and affect fish and wildlife deleteriously for the nature lover and sportsman. Too generous use of water in areas of plenty may bring drought and disaster to farmers elsewhere. Population growth and the great increases in water use in modern living have forced supposedly water-rich areas to examine their water policies.

★ *State organization of natural-resource conservation*

Diversity of interests in conservation as well as the inevitable overlapping of programs makes a neat assignment of the conservation function to a single department impossible. Even states with supposedly general conservation departments in fact assign related functions to other departments. Where should state control of water be placed? In the health department for pollution control to assure safe and sanitary water for drinking purposes? In the public service commission or utility regulatory commission for the control of power development and hence the control of utility rates? In the department of agriculture in the interest of farm irrigation? Few states have given total control of water policy to a single department; generally they have assigned areas of water policy at different times to agencies with responsibilities related to the most pressing water-policy problems. In recent years several states have then attempted to coordinate a general water policy or at least to eliminate the more obvious inconsistencies of state water policies through an interdepartmental committee. Other areas of conservation show up similar difficulties. A general department of conservation is likely to include: forests, parks, fish and wildlife, and possibly separate divisions on water (pollution control or whatever segment has been assigned) and mines and minerals. A majority of states do not have so comprehensive a department. Some will have separate departments of forestry, fish and wildlife, mines and minerals, and so forth.

Where conservation departments are headed by boards or commissions, the elected governor has all the usual difficulties of effective direction. All states have some segregated funds at least for fish and wildlife programs. In accord with the provisions of the federal Pittman-Robertson and Dingell-Johnson acts, all fish-and-game-license moneys must be earmarked for the exclusive use of fish and wildlife resources. Neither the governor nor the legislature can appropriate such moneys otherwise without the state's forfeiture of national grants-in-aid. In states where such license revenues are extensive, the state agency tends to assert a greater freedom from legislative and executive control.[12]

[12] The Conservation Commission in Wisconsin in the summer of 1959 asserted its right to ignore an executive decision for the department to change quarters on the ground

Governors may also find that the conservation controls they have take more time and make more enemies than issues of much greater worth. It is, for example, impossible to establish a deer season satisfactory to all. The hunter usually wants a fairly long one. The summer resort owner wants plenty of deer left to attract customers next year. The farmer wants a small deer herd to avoid crop depredation, but then he may find hunters do even more damage. Those interested in forests often want the deer herd cut down to avoid extensive young-tree damage (especially if it proves to be a hard winter). On the other hand, hunters may start forest fires. And then there are the pro-deer citizens who wish no deer to be shot. If the governor listens to any number of the representatives of these interests and tries to establish the public good, he will have consumed hours of time he had planned for other parts of the state's business.

Few state programs have developed so many interstate agreements. Northeastern, Southeastern, South Central, and Middle Atlantic forest-fire compacts have been signed by the area states. *The Book of the States* lists twenty-five interstate water compacts dealing with apportionment of water, pollution control, flood control, and multipurposes.[13] Other water compacts are under consideration. There is a Mississippi Valley Flyways Council working on problems of migratory birds. Several states have interstate park agreements. Thirty-one states have signed the interstate oil compact. Natural resource planning and control has national meaning.

★ *Financing conservation*

Currently about 2 percent of state expenditures are for conservation activities apart from agriculture. We have already noted that an important source of state conservation funds are revenues from fish and game licenses. Special forestry taxes exist in some states, and recently several states including Minnesota, Nebraska, and Illinois have established small fees for state-park use. These revenue assignments together with national government grants (national grants average about 7 percent of state conservation expenditures—$36.6 million of $510 million) give conservation departments relative fiscal independence for a number of their programs. States receive national grants for fish and wildlife preservation and research, for water-pollution control, for forest-fire control, insect and disease control, reforestation, and some forest research. In addition, many of the national gov-

---

that previous rentals paid from license revenues gave it a claim to remain in the state office building. Governor Nelson publicly denied the Commission's authority in the matter. Whatever the outcome, the incident illustrates the difficulties of executive control over state programs with agencies headed by commissions and with fiscal independence through segregated funds.

13 *The Book of the States, 1958-59*, p. 393.

ernment programs in forestry, soil conservation, and parks supplement state programs.

★ *Interest groups in conservation*

The conservation movement is represented today by a large number of groups. In total they are extremely powerful, although their power ranges from near dictation of conservation policies in some states to almost no influence in others. Sportsmen's clubs are perhaps the most extensively organized conservation associations, and their power is usually commensurate with their numbers. One of the peculiar advantages that sportsmen's clubs have in making their voice heard in public policy is that generally they are allied with the sports writers of the major newspapers. Whenever the conservation department or the legislature takes or even contemplates taking some action that the club members think undesirable, a flood of articles and editorials appear on the sports pages, almost always favoring the sportsmen's point of view. If the head of the fish and game division is not in accord with these groups, the result is a series of bitter disputes that sap the energy and popularity of the division and the governor. Sometimes commercial fishermen will oppose the recommendations of sportsmen's groups, and if fishing is an important industry in the state, a continual tug-of-war may be carried on between the pressure groups, with the conservation department as the prize.

The regulation of *extractive industries* such as coal, iron, copper, and oil is a phase of conservation that is intertwined with economic policy. If there is large-scale state or local ownership of land that has valuable mineral or other subsurface properties, public agencies may receive large amounts of revenue in the form of royalties. Some Southwestern universities have prospered from the oil land they own. As a whole, the states have not been very effective regulators of extractive industries. Rather, they have tended to represent the interests of their own extractive industries before Congress and the national administrative agencies. Both state agencies and the extractive industries have argued for "states' rights" in such matters as tidelands oil. From the standpoint of the industries affected, state regulation has generally meant friendlier and more favorable regulation.

Conclusion

The regulation, control, and development of natural resources have grown in dimensions as governmental functions from a time when there was apparently no limit to the lands available for agriculture and other natural resources to today when the possibilities of exhausting particular resources are widely recognized. The public's emotional responses to farmers, farming, and nature's gifts do not necessarily provide practical, consistent policies for government to follow. Groups interested in the exploitation of particular resources or conservationists who see only special aspects of the whole problem are well organized to push their policies. Governors and legislators at their best find it difficult to pursue the public interest. Interstate relations, interdepartmental cooperation requirements, national grants, and segregated funds help to restrict the governor and legislature in the pursuit of any given policy.

REFERENCES

Benedict, Murray R., *Can We Solve the Farm Problem?* New York: Twentieth Century Fund, 1955.

Council of State Governments, *State Administration of Water Resources.* Chicago: Council of State Governments, 1957.

Dewhurst, J. Frederic, and associates, *America's Needs and Resources; A New Survey.* New York: Twentieth Century Fund, 1955.

McConnell, Grant, *The Decline of Agrarian Democracy.* Berkeley: University of California Press, 1953.

"Migratory Farm Labor, The Problem and Proposals for Improvement," 31 *State Government* (May 1958), 94-99.

Ostrom, Vincent, "State Administration of Natural Resources in the West," 47 *American Political Science Review* (June 1953), 478-493.

Study of State Recreation in Connection with Federal Reservoirs. Chicago: Council of State Governments, 1951.

"Water Supply and Use in the States," 30 *State Government* (September 1957), 204-206.

CHAPTER 21

Education

EVERYONE IS AGAINST SIN; everyone is for education. Democracy requires some level of education for its existence. An industrial society would collapse without general education. Modern military science requires a minimum education for the common soldier as well as the most advanced education and training for men working on space, missile, and atomic problems. Acceptance of the desirability of education does not define and identify the content of education, the responsibility of the schools for children and young adults, or the direction, support, and control of the schools.

The conventional, ostrich theory (held by many educators and some other groups in our society) maintains that education is a nonpartisan activity because every "good" person is for it, and education must be kept from the ravages of politics. To underwrite this theory, the state department of education should not be directly responsible to the governor but separately elected or insulated by a board of education whose members have long overlapping terms. Preferably some revenue sources are dedicated to education, so the legislature need not be regularly consulted. Locally, schools must be administered by independent school boards— boards that have policy and financial control of education. Traditional theories of public administration do not apply to education.

States and local governments generally have accepted this approach

413

but they still find that separatism does not solve all problems. Somehow politics is still injected into the problems of education. Even where everybody is for education, differences exist as to its content. Taxpayers at some point look at their *total* tax bill. Governors and legislators are pressed to put additional moneys at the disposal of the schools. The school problem exacerbates the metropolitan problem. Conservatives in the South may prefer private schools and providing an inferior education for some children in order to avoid racial integration. Conservatives in another community may prefer fewer "frills" for education in order to avoid higher property taxes. Whether party labels are used or not, there are differences in attitudes concerning the content and conduct of education. Industrialists may want to emphasize vocational training; farmers, agricultural and home economics training. Recent demands for mathematics and scientific training do not fully recognize language and social-science needs. Individual pressure groups press for their particular interests. To a degree attitudes toward education correspond to general political philosophies toward government and its several functions. Political parties and concepts of legislative and executive control are not irrelevant. But few would wish to place school teachers on party patronage lists any more than they would highway engineers, welfare case workers, or doctors at state institutions. Democratic control may well require party politics for deciding major policy issues in education, and permit the professional education administrator and teacher to carry out the programs.

Interest Groups in Education

★ *Educator groups and the desire for independence*

Part of the fear of American educators for injecting politics into education no doubt traces back to the influence of nineteenth-century spoils politics on personnel and management. (Yet in the awarding of school-building contracts, the purchase of school books and equipment and the hiring of local teachers, the independent school board has sometimes had its own spoils system.) Part of the desire for separatism rests on the assumption that a group can get more money and has more control when it is apart from the whole. Nearly every group of specialists, be they in the field of education or in such fields as public health, welfare, or conservation, desires to have the same degree of independence from the governor, the legislature, and local governmental units that education now has. The only difference is that education has been far more successful in achieving the goal. All these functional specialists feel that their programs are somewhat unique, are highly important, and should be left to those having a special interest and skill in the matter, rather than at the mercy of general political control. Professionalization of personnel in the public service has brought many advantages, but it has also resulted in a feeling of separateness, a feeling that the function and not the unit of government is the important thing. Therefore, two educational administartors operating on two different levels of government are likely to have more in common than one of them has with the governor and the other has with the county governing body. The training of the two administrators is probably similar and their objectives are quite alike—an excellent public education system. They feel little loyalty to county or state governments as a whole; they have much more loyalty to the function that they are administering. Education is not the sole example of a separatist philosophy in state and local government, but it is a very good one.

Those functions that have the strongest clientele groups supporting them are usually found to be the most independent. Education ranks high on this score. Parent-Teacher Associations are effective means of bringing teacher and parents together for the benefit of the children's education. They are also powerful pressure groups in support of public education. Almost always they support dedicated revenue for schools on a state level and in most areas they vigorously defend the independence of local school districts. PTAs are stanchly pro-education, and they work toward the end that the entire community will also view education favorably. Backing up the PTAs are the National Education Association and the various state education associations, members of which are largely teachers and educators. School-board members have their National School Boards Association. These education associations carry on important activities designed to influence public and legislative opinion; as a whole they have played a powerful role in shaping public-education policy.

★ Other organized groups in the education field

Apart from organized educators in the public schools, church groups, taxpayers groups, racial groups, certain patriotic groups, and other interest groups attempt to influence education. To the extent that schools are separated from the general political organization, the group conflict occurs within PTAs, school boards, or school administrations. Opposition to school bond issues may come not only from economy-minded taxpayers but from churches with parochial schools where the parishioner may not send his child to the church school if his public school taxes are high. Federal and state school-aid proposals that do not include private schools may be opposed. The issue of released time for religious instruction arises in many states and communities. The separation of church and state is provided for in the state and federal constitutions, but legal prescriptions do not always end social controversies. Some states permit school districts to support bus services for parochial as well as public school children. Louisiana purchases school books for children in parochial and public grade schools.

Legal prescriptions also have not easily settled the issue of segregation in the public-school system. Whereas *local* control of education in a democracy is sometimes emphasized as a supreme value (opponents to federal aid use this issue on occasion), governors and legislators do not always trust local control. Several Southern states have acted to prevent local communities from making their own decisions on local integration.[1] Other states have sometimes found local control of education at times has worked at odds with opinion generally in the state. States have used grant-in-aid formulas and other means to dissolve small school districts, to set minimum standards of education, and otherwise to force some norms.

Organization of Elementary and Secondary Education

★ State level

Only four states (New Jersey, Pennsylvania, Tennessee, and Virginia) accept the thesis that the governor should have the power to appoint the superintendent of public instruction. Thirty states permit the governor to appoint members of a school board (usually the members have terms which overlap and exceed the governor's in length) that in nineteen states names the chief school officer.[2] The state departments of public education have differing degrees of control over local schools and educational policies. They may certify the eligibility of teachers, distribute funds under state formulas to school districts, approve school-building plans, and periodically check whether all schools of the state meet some minimal requirements. State education departments may also gather statistics, make reports, and undertake some research as to the educational policies and needs of the state. Only in the way of finance or occasional major changes in educational

[1] State legislation in Arkansas, Georgia, and Virginia, among others, might be cited. The argument, of course, could be made that the state is merely assisting the local governments to fight the United States Supreme Court, but the actions of local school boards and some of the division in legislative votes and the attitudes of governors suggest that there is a fear of local community acceptance of integration. The limitations on population representation in state legislatures, such as Georgia, affect the outcome.
[2] *The Book of the States, 1958-59*, p. 272.

policies do either the governor or the legislators typically participate in the general control and supervision of schools.[3]

★ *Local government*

Day-to-day control of education remains in most states with locally elected school boards for each school district. In 1957, the Census reported 50,446 school districts and 2467 municipal school systems. One sixth of the school districts did not actually operate schools but arranged to send children in the area to other schools where they paid nonresident tuition.[4] The school district may or may not coincide with any municipality (town, village, or city); and even when it does, the municipality may have neither the fiscal or general control over the decisions of the school board that it might have in the case of the health or welfare function.[5] The school board and school administration usually determine the curriculum, hire and fire the teachers, determine the need for new buildings. In the usual pattern of the larger school systems at least, professional educators through the superintendent of schools bring policy matters before the board of education. The board more or less automatically approves the recommendations if it has confidence in the superintendent and enough money to afford the programs suggested.

School curriculums may represent major policy decisions. Is vocational education stressed at the expense of general education? How do languages and social sciences fare in comparison with mathematics and the natural sciences? Are extracurricular activities emphasized more than studies? What is provided to meet the needs of the bright child and the intellectually limited child? What is the political (partisan or nonpartisan) interest of the community, state, and nation in the making of these decisions? Again professional educators, through the superintendent of schools and the school board, have commonly made the decisions. Often, too, the PTA has represented at most a sounding board for educators and frequently an easy source for support for any desired change. The general political interests of the community, state, or nation enter only occasionally.[6]

[3] The minimum age at which a child may leave school is usually stated in a general state law. A few states require the teaching of one or more particular subjects. Policy standards such as the diversity of curriculum, number of children per teacher, and the professional training of teachers may be included as basic requirements for receipt of state aid.

[4] A considerable campaign of the last decade and more has emphasized the desirability of eliminating small school districts in order to achieve schools of an economical size to operate and with reasonable breadth to the curriculum. School districts have dropped in number from 108,579 in 1942 to 50,446 in 1957.

[5] County school districts are uncommon, although some states have county superintendents of schools to supervise noncity school districts.

[6] It has already been indicated that school policies normally are kept apart from the general political bodies of the country—city councils, state legislatures, and Congress as well

★ *Intergovernmental relations and education*[7]

The national government, through the U. S. Office of Education in the Department of Health, Education, and Welfare, has assisted the schools in the collection of statistics, in some research and experimental programs, as a point of clearance and, sometimes, in giving broad guidance. The U. S. Department of Agriculture has administered the school lunch program, originally designed to use agricultural surpluses for lunches for children unable to pay for them.

The absence of national grants for education, substantial differences in wealth among the states, and differences in educational preferences have produced significant differences in educational standards. States do not agree, for example, on (1) qualifications required of teachers, (2) the number of years (or even the number of days in each year) that a child should attend school, (3) the enforcement of school attendance laws, or (4) the variety of offerings in a minimum curriculum. Lack of uniformity is not necessarily unfortunate, but wide differences in *minimum* standards may be. The educational standards of some states may cause citizens to fail to meet voting literacy requirements of the same states. The military services have rejected more men from some states than others as the result of inadequate minimum education. Population mobility brings adults into states with far higher educational standards than those of their state of origin.

School Finance

Education uses more state and local tax revenues than any other function and accounts for a large part of the present pressures on tax revenues. Whereas state and local education expenditures were $5.4 billion in 1948, they totaled $14.5 billion in 1957. State and local governments employed the equivalent of 2,270,000 full-time persons in all phases of education in October 1958. In addition to the decision of how much money should be put into education, other questions arise: (1) How much money should be raised locally for schools? (Most local school revenues come from the prop-

---

as the elected executive at each governing level. When some major event raises a question about the education system, however, the general political bodies or more of an active public may bring pressure on school authorities. The Russian launching of Sputnik in advance of our own space satellite activated individuals and groups not normally in the education field.

[7] See Chapter 5 for a survey of interstate compacts in higher education. At least one interstate compact (Illinois and Wisconsin) has been signed to permit a common school district for two border communities.

erty tax.) (2) How much money should the state raise? (3) What should be the basis of distribution of moneys for education from the state? (4) Should a minimum local tax effort be required? (5) Should a minimum standard or education be required? (6) How much of the state funds should be used in flat grants on a per pupil (or some other basis) to all school districts? (7) How much of the state funds should be used to equalize school costs among districts? (8) How much of the state funds should be used to encourage educational standards above the minimum? (9) Should there be general federal grants for public education? These are not questions that can be answered in a paragraph or a few pages. Many informed citizens and professional educators would disagree on the detail of any set of answers. The questions should help to identify the issues that many legislators and governors are studying, answering in part in each session of the legislature, and making speeches about in each campaign.

Major questions of policy have arisen over proposals for general national grants-in-aid to education such as exist in health, welfare, and highways. Historically, the national government beginning with the Ordinance of 1787 made land grants available to the states for local schools. Not only lands but funds were given to the states for university agricultural and engineering programs in the nineteenth-century. In the twentieth, education aids to higher education have been extended in a number of directions. For grade and high school students, however, little federal money has been available except for vocational schools, the teaching of agriculture and home economics in the high schools, school lunches, some schools built in the 1930s, and for areas of large increased school populations as the result of a federal military base or special project.

If educational groups could agree on the desirability of federal grants-in-aid for elementary and high schools, it seems clear Congress would be at least as willing to assist in this field as it has been in the case of higher education or health or welfare. At least three issues have divided citizens on every national grant-in-aid bill—fear of centralized control and the questions of aid to private schools (usually parochial schools) and to racially segregated schools. If the Southern states achieve an adjustment of their school systems satisfactory to the Supreme Court, they would also overcome a major obstacle to federal school aid. Currently the Congress will not pass federal school-aid bills that insist on integration or permit segregation. An unwillingness exists to use federal funds on either side of the controversy. The question of assistance to nonpublic schools raises the nineteenth-century argument of sectarian education. The sides drawn up on this issue probably would not involve the degree of bitterness of the segregation-integration dispute.

Figure 14. JUST ONE SCHOOL PROBLEM

"Let's Come To Order, Class. The Next Shift Is Waiting"

By permission of Herblock and *The Washington Post*

Most difficult of appraisal is the issue of national control of education. Some people who oppose federal aid because of their views on religious or racial issues cite the bad aspects of federal control in their argument. Some taxpayer groups, fearing the possibility of larger tax bills, also use the control issue. Other individuals and groups, however, genuinely fear the possibility of federal control. Dictatorships and totalitarian governments have used school systems for their own purposes. In a democracy as large as the United States a centralized educational system would seem to be highly undesirable if not outright dangerous. Mistakes in local control of education have none of the potential for disaster of mistakes in Washington. The only answer is one of history and faith. Neither in state nor in federal grant-in-aid programs in other functions has control been taken over completely by the grantor. Federal grants to institutions of higher learning have not resulted in dictation. State grants to local school districts have not eliminated local freedom in the determination of the content of most courses and curriculums, or the many "extras" in modern education. All the equalizing functions of federal grants in other fields would seem to carry special weight in the field of education.

Organization of Higher Education

College enrollments have shown a long-run upward trend that has resulted in greatly expanded teaching facilities. The general increase in standards of living, the greater demands of business and society for college-trained individuals, the G.I. Bill of Rights, and the increasing birth rate of the last two decades are placing demands for higher education beyond the bounds of present campuses.

In 1950, some 2,175,000 students were enrolled in colleges or professional schools—1,275,000 in public institutions. The figure for college students for 1955 (despite the low birth rates of the 1930s) was 1,533,000 and the 1965 estimate is 3,011,000. Except for the original states of New England and the Middle Atlantic area with their early tradition of private colleges, most of the states early established state universities and normal schools with the blessing of federal land grants. Especially in the Middle and Far West the state universities assumed the intellectual leadership role of the Harvards, Yales, and Columbias in the East. Most of the older normal schools are now state colleges.

Some states support two major universities run by separate boards of regents, teachers colleges run by a third board, and a number of junior colleges that are attached to the larger city school systems. The regular state departments of education have little or no supervision over any of these, except possibly in the case of the junior colleges. Typically the governor and legislature have control over higher education only through appointment and approval of appointments of members to long-term boards of regents and through budget review and appropriations. Even budget review may be restricted by the constitution.

The movement for consolidation and elimination of small, local school districts has been paralleled in time by a movement for single state boards of regents for institutions of higher learning or at least for a coordinating arrangement of some type. States with separate boards of regents for one or more universities and for their college systems and with little direct control by the legislature or executive found little planned, over-all educational policy for the state. The several state educational institutions competed through their boards of regents for operating appropriations, buildings, and research moneys. Such pressure on tax revenues as well as the absence of an over-all state higher educational plan have led a number of states to accept the theory of a single board of regents of higher education or at least a reduction in the number of boards controlling higher education. Most states have achieved some more planning and coordination of post high-school education in the 1950s. Governors and legislators have had a somewhat larger voice in the state's general policies of higher education in this period of organization change and appropriation increases.

The line between academic freedom and democratic control is fine indeed. Universities exist for basic research and the advancement of knowledge as well as for teaching purposes. The very idea of progress in a democracy is predicated on freedom to find the truth, wherever truth may lead. Restrictions on research or teaching can make a university an instrument of propaganda. Restrictions can arise from university administrations, boards of regents, governors, state legislators, and pressure groups. Most higher educational policy is decided by boards of regents and university presidents with some faculty consultation and controlled somewhat by state legislative and executive approval of funds. Academic freedom is not violated where the governor and the legislature exercise their general responsibilities to determine the broad type of educational program to be carried out or the general size of the program. Usually state universities and colleges can satisfactorily follow state procedure in the hiring of administrative, clerical, and maintenance personnel; in the purchase of equipment and materials; in the letting of contracts for building; and in many of the other management tasks common to other departments of the state. Only in the hiring and firing of faculty members and in the determination of course and research content do academic freedom problems normally arise.

Financing of Higher Education

Most state universities have a variety of sources of income—student fees, grants for general or specific purposes from private or governmental sources, business income (e.g., dormitory rents), contracts for research from private business or governmental agencies, federal grants, income from university investments (the original source of investments may have been private or governmental), and state taxes. The state taxes may be dedi cated tax revenues or general tax revenues. The university competes not only for a share of the tax revenues for operating expenses but in the present period of growth presses hard for large sums for building programs.

Apart from the original land grants, the national government has aided state higher education through moneys for agricultural college programs and experiment stations, large grants for contract research, tuition funds for World War II veterans, and special defense grants for the expansion of particular programs.

Federal moneys available to universities (public and private) today are large, but there are no *general* federal grants-in-aid for higher education.

The problems of financing higher education raise many questions. What type of higher education program can the state afford? Should the university, like most other state departments, come to the legislature for funds or should tax revenues be segregated for its use? Should the national government make larger, more general grants to the states for higher education? Should state students pay a larger portion of the cost of their education or should higher education be available to all as is elementary and secondary for little or no charge?

Future

The questions of control and funds clearly will continue to be of significance in the educational field at every level. How much separation of educational policy from general governmental policy decisions is desirable? In the problem of funds, the level of appropriations and the possibility of federal grants take precedence.

In higher education, at least, coordination of state policies may precede coordination with private institutions but the separatism of the two programs can not justify their ignoring one another's existence. Some private institutions have had a distinguished tradition and by their presence have helped in the building of standards of state universities. Possibly the most difficult question for higher education is who should go to college. Should state higher education facilities be expanded to accept *all* high school graduates or should there be more strict entrance requirements? Should a junior college, two-year terminal program be made a substitute for college for the intellectually less prepared?

REFERENCES

Brown, Robert H., "A New Study of the Composition of School Boards," *American School Board Journal* (August 1954), 23, 24.

Burke, Arvid G., *Financing Public Schools in the United States*. New York: Harper and Brothers, 1957.

Committee on Education beyond the High School, *A Report to the President*. Washington, D. C.: Government Printing Office, 1957.

Committee on Government and Higher Education, *The Efficiency of Freedom*. Baltimore: The Johns Hopkins Press, 1959.

Committee for White House Conference on Education, *A Report to the President*. Washington, D. C.: Government Printing Office, 1956.

Council of State Governments, *Higher Education in the 48 States: A Report to the Governors' Conference*. Chicago: Council of State Governments, 1952.

———, *The Forty-eight State School Systems*. Chicago: Council of State Governments, 1949.

Moos, Malcolm, and Francis E. Rourke, *The Campus and the State*. Baltimore: The Johns Hopkins Press, 1959.

Morlan, Robert L., *Intergovernmental Relations in Education*. Minneapolis: University of Minnesota Press, 1950.

State Higher Education Study Commissions, *A Summary of Their Organization, Staff Activities, and Financing*, RM325. Chicago: Council of State Governments, June 1959.

Thurston, Lee M., and William H. Roe, *State School Administration*. New York: Harper and Brothers, 1957.

U. S. Department of Health, Education and Welfare, *Biennial Survey of Education in the United States*. Washington, D. C.: Government Printing Office.

CHAPTER 22

Government and the Economy

No ECONOMIC laissez-faire theory ever has been extended to the point that business and industry have refused to ask favors of government. In the nineteenth century, many business leaders proclaimed the desirability of freedom from government interference while at the same time seeking protective tariffs, government assistance to railroads, a national bank or friendly legislation for banks generally. As long as American business was relatively small and the opportunities for the employee to become the owner were plentiful, government was looked to for general favors but not for regulation. Post-Civil War America soon had a different look. Large industries, some bordering on monopolies, developed in most fields. The "poor boy who became rich" story seemed more and more a myth. Workers saw employers continuing to gain, while they had difficulty meeting modest family budgets. Injuries, layoffs, or illnesses created major crises in many families. Farmers often bought supplies from monopolistic concerns; and then after producing in uncontrolled conditions found their railroad rates and market prices fixed to their disadvantage by the large business concerns. At the same time in the last seventy-five years that business and industry have continued to seek and to receive favors from government, other groups in the economy have sought and achieved some regulation of industry.

The relations of government, at all levels, to business are many and

425

complex. The trilogy of agriculture, business, and labor neither includes all of America's citizens nor suggests adequately the enormous differences that occur within each class. An oilman and a railroad executive may each be a businessman, but the governmental action for which each will press is likely to be quite different, if not contradictory. Importers and exporters are likely to press for opposite tariff policies. A state chamber of commerce, dominated by industry, may seek a state sales tax. Retail store owners, with the problem of collecting and handling the sales tax, may prefer income taxes. Labor, too, is far from a cohesive unit. There are differences between unionized and nonunionized labor, between the American Federation of Labor-Congress of Industrial Organizations and the Railroad Brotherhoods, and between strong national unions and small company unions. Some large national unions and some large industries will find points of greater agreement than those perhaps between large and small industry or large and small unions.

Self-employed persons, teachers, the professional groups generally, and servants—among others—do not fit neatly into any of the three categories above and, of course, do not make another class. A member of the American Medical Association may hold opinions quite contrary to those of a social science professor. Similarly a governmental employee may differ in his outlook from an employee of a private concern, a coal miner from a painter, and so on indefinitely. There is no certainty that two auto workers or two businessmen or two lawyers will agree on matters of government economic policy. There is every chance that they will disagree in one or more important respects.

Each group within the community—retail merchants, automobile manufacturers, steel industrialists, laborers within large unions, utilities, organized consumers, and professional people—has sought assistance for itself or regulation of others from that level of government most sympathetic to its problem. State regulation of business in the last century and in the beginning of this often exceeded that of the national government. Farmers and laborers found state governments listening to them and giving them either direct assistance or regulation of an adversary. With the 1930s and to an extent ever since, the roles have seemed to be reversed. Farmers and labor unions often have found the national Congress, the President, and the national administrative agencies more sympathetic. Business has become "states rights" and pushed its case before state legislatures and governors. Cities, perhaps, have been most conscious of consumer interests over the years with their municipally owned utilities, inspectional services of many kinds, and official pressure on state governments for a variety of programs of interest to consumers.

The States and Business and Industry

To discuss in a few pages state government policies as they affect the many different kinds of business and industry may give the erroneous impression that policies are everywhere similar. Quite the contrary is true. Some state administrations have had a business orientation for many decades, just as others have looked upon agriculture or labor for their principal support and direction.

★ *Business interest groups*

In contrast to labor pressure groups, both business and farm organizations have been notably successful in identifying themselves with the local community. Local chambers of commerce are so identified with city governments at times that high school seniors have listed the chamber of commerce as a regular city department. In medium-size and small cities the chambers of commerce may be the single most important pressure group influencing administrative and legislative action.

In addition to the chambers of commerce and the state and national associations of manufacturers, business groups are organized into an amazing array of temporary and permanent organizations to promote and oppose certain governmental policies. The National Tax Equality Association is essentially a group organized to oppose cooperatives, for example, while other associations generally seek to promote their own business interests. Name a line of business and there will almost surely be an association of those engaged in it—existing in part to influence public policy. Most of the associations of businessmen have rather specific objectives, and the largest of them are rather powerful in attaining them. The oilmen of Texas, Oklahoma, or California, for example, greatly influence state and local economic policies on oil. Similarly there are states that favor silver (Nevada) or copper (Montana) or some other localized business or industry in their legislation and administration. The influence of a particular industry on a city or county is likely to be more pronounced than on a state level, since there are "one-industry" localities but no "one-industry" states. One cannot understand a coal-mining town or an oil city (Long Beach, Calif.) or an automobile manufacturing community (Detroit or Flint) without tracing the preponderant influence the major industry has on all types of public issues and on all candidates for elective office. The future of such communities is intimately tied to the future of the specific industry, and unusual public policies and political alignments result.

Businessmen, like members of other economic groups, are for fewer governmental regulations that affect them adversely and for more that affect the other person. Chain stores bitterly fought the attempts of independent grocers to obtain state approval of anti-chain-store laws; cut-rate druggists have long fought the attempts of manufacturers to have states pass and enforce so-called fair-trade laws, prohibiting retailers from selling certain products at less than prescribed prices. Generally speaking, businessmen are for bigger and better cities and states, hoping to increase the volume of their business thereby. This emphasis upon public relations and a general expansionist attitude leads businessmen to support widespread advertising of a state's or locality's advantages by governmental agencies. Businessmen generally also desire an ample, cheap, and cooperative source of labor. They may threaten to move from a locality if labor conditions are not improved, and they usually will try to be influential in shaping public policies that affect the nature of their labor supply.

Businessmen and business groups have close relations with legislative and administrative agencies. Presidents or other representatives of important corporations have a prestige that is a great asset in dealing with governmental agencies. Governors frequently choose top state administrators from business in part because of their qualifications, in part because of past political support. While two or more businessmen do not always instinctively agree, there is a community of feeling among many of them, and this helps to determine the course of public policy from time to time. Business lobbies in state legislatures have been traditionally well financed, whether representing truckers and other utilities concerned with the scope of the state's regulation of their business or manufacturing industries seeking stricter regulation of labor or seeking airports well situated to their needs.

★ State administrative organization and business

On a state level several key departments usually carry on programs that closely concern business. Most businesses are incorporated by one state or another, and generally the secretary of state handles incorporation. The privilege of incorporation is one of the most valuable that states confer, and they may make their conditions for incorporation one means of regulating business. Delaware is famous for its easy incorporation laws, but it does not stand alone.

In the several states, departments of banking and of insurance are common; occasionally they are combined. The national government has so far left insurance regulation to the states, and although it regulates national banks and inspects and audits state banks and savings and loan associations under the Federal Deposit Insurance program, the states have not turned over all bank-audit responsibilities to the national government. State banking departments normally check state banks for the safety of deposits and their conformity to general banking regulations and enforce the state's interest regulations against banks, other loan organizations, and individuals. State insurance departments regulate insurance companies as to their rates, policies, and financial solvency. The absence of national regulation of insurance companies places a special burden on the states. Reciprocal and retaliatory legislation have been common. Many of the states provide tougher regulation for out-of-state insurance companies unless the home state of the company gives out-of-state insurance companies relief from stringent regulation.

A public utilities commission is a third common business regulatory agency among the states. States differ greatly in the degree of regulation of service and rates they have established for intrastate transportation companies (bus, trucks, railroads, possibly planes) and telephone, light, gas, and water utilities. Where the utilities commission has extensive control and regulatory authority, it will employ numbers of trained accountants, engineers, lawyers, and other specialists to carry out its functions. Regulated utilities seek authority to build dams, to expand or contract operations, to change the quality of service upwards or downwards, and to hold or adjust rates. Commission employees examine the facilities and records of the companies, listen to the testimony of consumers and company officials, and attempt to determine the public interest within the statutory standards.

In a sense the existence of government makes business possible, and all agencies of government aid business. The very quality of government has its own impact on business. Such broad definitions of business aid are seldom used, but it has something of the same meaningfulness as the slogan of the National Association of Manufacturers that "What is good for business is good for you." Specifically, on the business-service side, states provide a hiring market through their employment services; provide substantial information on the general conditions of the labor market and its future prospects; advertise at least some aspects of the state through slogans on motor-vehicle license plates, displays or advertisements on something approaching a nation-wide basis; and provide a variety of research services through special state departments or through a bureau of business research in the state university.

Few national grants-in-aid and almost no segregated funds, but not necessarily fewer boards and commissions, give the legislature and the governor more immediate control of agencies regulating or servicing industry than is usual in highways or conservation or education. Businesses regulated or serviced by state departments may have great influence in the legislature, the governor's office, and the administrative agency; but they do not usually have the protection of national grants that lay down conditions or segregated funds that remove areas of programs from normal review by the legislature and governor. A governor and legislature determined on stricter regulation of the state's utilities, for example, may proceed without the barriers to change that are common in the conservation or highway field.

★ Intergovernmental relations

Most regulation of business and much of the direct assistance to business have proceeded apart in the national, state, and local governments without the coordination and cooperation involved in grants-in-aid programs. In some areas—for example, banking, securities regulation, and antimonopoly legislation—several of the states initiated programs; then the national government entered the field; and the state programs generally lost significance although they may supplement the national regulation at times. State utility regulation applies only to intrastate operations, whereas the work of the Federal Power Commission and Interstate Commerce Commission reaches interstate business that the states cannot control. In a few states, part of the utility regulation is still at the local level. Minnesota communities still establish rates to be charged for electricity through contracts with the utilities. In some situations, the Minnesota Railroad and Warehouse Commission may determine the type of service.[1] Insurance regulation has been a state function exclusively. Licensing and inspection may be federal, state, or local. In the interests of public health, meat in interstate commerce is inspected by the national government. States or local governments may provide for inspection of meat sold within the state. The employment services are the unusual example of a state business activity with national grants. Public employment offices to assist labor and business were initiated in some of the states but became a necessary part of the operation of the unemployment insurance program and hence expanded and received national grants from the 1930s on.

The States and Labor

Distinguishing between government and business and government and labor necessarily involves some artificiality. In the first place, many programs benefiting labor mean government regulation of business. Secondly, some

[1] One economist has asserted that such decentralization of rate making has worked satisfactorily primarily because of the strict state regulation and rate making in neighboring Wisconsin. The pressure of reasonable rates next door makes possible reasonable rates in Minnesota. See *The Book of the States, 1958-59*, p. 457, for the scope of regulatory power of the state utility commissions.

programs initiated to benefit labor have worked so satisfactorily that the aid to labor *and* business became mutual. Workmen's compensation, for example, came into being in the face of business and industry opposition. The evident benefits have brought industrial acceptance and almost elimi nated any desire for repeal.

The states have always given some attention to labor and its problems. The policies that have emanated from the several states have varied greatly depending upon control of the legislatures and the governorships. In the early decades of this century a few states, notably Wisconsin under the influence of the La Follette Progressive movement, experimented with policies that would be more favorable to labor. Wisconsin was one of several states that passed a workman's compensation act in 1911. It led the states in establishing an unemployment compensation program (1932). With other states, including Massachusetts, New York, and Oregon, it established maximum working hours for women, minimum pay scales, and limitations on child labor. During the 1920s the national government took a few steps in these directions, and the states served as testing grounds for economic policies. After 1933 the political situation changed, and the national government evidenced an increasing concern for labor and its problems. Since the end of the 1930s, some states have experimented with labor laws ("right-to-work" laws, for example) more restrictive in nature than those of the national government. In other words, the states have been used by the party out of power nationally as suitable units to enact their party's labor policies. Other states, especially when the dominant party is the same as in Washington, have shown tendencies to copy the policy laid down by the national government. Several states in the wake of the 1957 and 1958 McClellan Committee reports on labor racketeering and corruption have provided for state regulation of employee welfare funds.

★ *Labor departments*

Most states today have departments or commissions of labor or of labor and industry, although their duties do not always include all the labor activities of the respective states. The idea of a single labor department appeals to those interested in reducing the number of agencies reporting to the governor. Organized labor generally has supported a single agency at both the state and national government levels. A separate labor department presumably gives recognition and status to labor and promotes the appointment of a "labor" director or "labor" commission members, just as departments of agriculture and commerce gives status and normally receive directors from agriculture and business.

Whether organized in a single department or separately, state labor programs normally include workman's compensation, safety and sanitation, employment service, unemployment compensation, collection of labor statistics, probably regulation of hours and wages in work, mediation and arbitration of industrial disputes, and possibly fair-employment-practice laws and laws restricting unions.

All states have workman's compensation laws. These laws provide compensation to workmen who are injured or who contract an occupational disease while employed. Generally an employer must insure with a private concern or with the states or have a satisfactory self-insurance scheme. Closely related to workman's compensation are many of the safety and sanitation laws. Employers, in effect, are required to provide a safe and sanitary place of employment. When accidents occur or employees develop occupational diseases, the employer is presumed to be at fault and collection can be made from the insurance.[2] In most states if the employee has failed to use safety devices provided in accord with law, his insurance payments will be reduced.

Although Wisconsin had adopted unemployment legislation before the national act of 1935 and some other states were interested in doing so, the national government virtually assured nation-wide adoption through the tax-offset device.[3] All states then provided for some measure of insurance payments to employees involuntarily laid off from their job who are unable immediately to find comparable employment either on their own or through the efforts of the state employment service where they have registered. In the 1950s four states—California, New Jersey, New York, and Rhode Island—added temporary disability insurance to their unemployment insurance programs. California provides a maximum weekly benefit amount of $50 and hospital payments of $12 a day for twenty days.

The pressures of ideologically opposite groups have led a number of states to adopt either restrictive legislation controlling unions or fair-employment-practice laws or both. At least eighteen states have adopted right-to-work laws that bar union membership as a condition of hiring or holding

2 The philosophy of workman's compensation is almost the exact opposite to that existing under the common law. Before workman's compensation laws, an injured employee could sue for damages; but the employer was free to claim (1) that the accident occurred because of the fault of a fellow employee; (2) that the employee in accepting employment had assumed the risks of the job; or (3) that the employee had been at least a little negligent.
3 Under the national government's taxing powers, buisness and industry in all states were to be taxed at 3 percent of their payrolls. If the state passed an appropriate unemployment insurance act, 90 percent of the tax collected would be made available for the payment of unemployment compensation in the state. The other 10 percent of the tax was to be used to cover the cost of administration of the program—both the claims taking and determination and the employment service for the registration and placement of the unemployed. The government won the constitutional test of its taxing powers and the tax-offset device. Steward Machine Company v. Davis, 301 U. S. 548 (1937).

employment.[4] At least fourteen states prohibit discrimination in employment on account of race, creed, color, national origin, or ancestry. Both types of legislation represent policies for which no national legislation is presently attainable.

★ Pressure groups and labor legislation

Whether a state has restrictive union legislation or a fair-employment act and whether benefits under workman's compensation and unemployment compensation programs reasonably reflect current wage levels or medical costs, the content of numerous administrative regulations and the effectiveness of enforcement are the stuff of politics in labor. Two opposing groups of organizations—business and labor—point up the conflicts more strongly than is true in many fields of government where a clientele group supports a particular program and the opposition, if any, seems dispersed and disorganized.[5]

Two main national union groups, with their state affiliates, normally present labor's case in the states. The American Federation of Labor-Congress of Industrial Organizations and the Railroad Brotherhoods seek benefits from government for organized labor and, incidentally, for unorganized labor too. In some states the United Mine Workers or one or another unaffiliated union group may have an influence. Labor groups more often (or at least more often, more openly) than many other interest groups work to affect the political process in the grass-roots political education of their own members and in publicizing support of individual political candidates. Most large locals, together with city and state labor councils, have political committees that endorse candidates for office, list candidates to be defeated, suggest specific platforms or policies for adoption by the union as a whole, and in general give political campaign leadership to the group. Within individual union groups, there is probably less toleration of political views contrary to the majority than in comparable farm and business organizations. For example, members of a city-wide union political committee—probably

---

[4] *The Book of the States, 1958-59,* pp. 418-449, summarizes labor legislation in the states during 1956-1957. Labor legislation for 1958-1959 will be similarly summarized in *The Book of the States, 1960-61.*

[5] Hunters and fishermen, for example, may have to settle some intergroup differences; but when they appear as an organized group to secure advantageous policies, the opposition (which might, in fact, represent the "public interest") seldom is in agreement or has significant backing. Similarly, the "public interest" in agriculture or even a real opposition to the policies of organized agriculture achieves little hearing. Union labor policies on the other hand normally find ready-made opponents in business. Some opposition in legislative and administrative halls, however, is merely shadow boxing with agreements actually reached in official or unofficial ways elsewhere. The Railroad Brotherhoods and the state railroad associations, for example, may publicly appear on the same side of issues or one or the other withhold public opposition.

numbering several hundred and including all the important labor leaders in the area—are usually forced to support the union-endorsed slate 100 percent or lose their membership on the committee.[6] Those who disagree with the slate must bow to the majority and simply wait their time to secure converts for a more acceptable slate on the next occasion.

Labor unions do not confine their attention to political campaigns and elections in their attempt to influence public policy. Most large union groups have paid legislative lobbyists who try to determine the course of labor legislation in the labor committees of each house and before the two houses and with the governor. Labor appointments to the state's labor agency will be sought, and the labor agency importuned from time to time to see labor's side of each issue. Labor's success as a lobbyist in administration does not equal that of farm or business groups. Agricultural extension and business bureaus in state universities have only recently seen some parallel developments in labor bureaus or "schools for workers." Few city or state government officials accept labor union leaders as advisors in the same matter of fact manner as chamber of commerce representatives. The relative youthfulness of organized labor and the general absence of labor organization background and experience among city and state officials probably account for much of the distance between labor and government.

★ Intergovernmental relations

Labor necessarily finds much of concern at every level of government. Do the local, state, and national governments and their agencies permit labor to organize government employees? Is each level sympathetic to a role for organized labor? Is much of the apparent sympathy of the national and/or state governments dissolved in the face of local opposition so that the city police take a narrow view of labor's rights in a strike? Does labor find discrimination in other services of government that a businessman would not face?

Although there are few grants-in-aid in the labor field, federal-state relations are important. Experience at either level frequently has influenced policies at the other. Many of the published statistical reports of the U. S. Department of Labor are secured in part through the cooperation of all of the state labor agencies. Costs of state employment services and unemployment insurance agencies are met through budgets approved by the Department of Labor from funds set apart and appropriated by Congress for this purpose. In the labor relations field, confusion as to state and national roles has sometimes occurred. For much of the last decade, the Supreme

---

[6] This statement says nothing about the acceptance of the union-endorsed slate by rank-and-file union members. Control here is by no means so complete.

Court has frequently held that the Congress has acted in areas of labor disputes to the exclusion of the states. At the same time, the National Labor Relations Board has had calendars too full to hear cases that the state boards formerly considered.

Without the pressure of national grants-in-aid and with a wide difference in traditions and industrial development among the states, labor legislation—both regulatory and assistance—has grown at an uneven pace among the states. The states, however, copy from the national government and from each other. Interstate competition has an impact for uniformity on labor policy as on tax policy of the states. If business is subjected to more regulation in the interests of labor in State X than in State Y or if State Y writes tougher and more restrictive labor regulation laws than State X, the latter state may fear the loss of new industrial development. This fear, however well or ill founded in the particular instance, may restrict the influence of labor groups in legislation and administration.

Professions

★ Licensing

The practice of requiring licenses in order to engage in certain kinds of business is well developed and extends far beyond the limits of what is normally included in the professions. Cities, counties, and New England towns all license taxicabs, beer and liquor stores, and similar businesses for purposes of regulation and revenue. When a license is required for doing business, its granting or withholding may become a highly contested process, particularly if there is some limitation on the number of licenses that will be issued. This explains why the licensing of liquor stores and taxicabs has so frequently become a factor in local corruption. Any government-created monopoly or restriction on competition is highly prized, since it may enrich a few at the expense of the many if it is not properly regulated.

More frequently licensing comes under a plan whereby any person who possesses minimum qualifications may engage in certain trades or professions. Barbers, commercial fishermen, beauty operators, morticians, and weighmasters are examples in nonprofessional occupations, while architects, public accountants, civil engineers, dentists, physicians, and lawyers are commonly licensed in the professional sphere. As the country becomes more and more educated and professionalized, the list of fields in which licenses are required will grow steadily. Most of the licensing of trades and professions is done on a state level by boards appointed specially for this purpose, one for each field.

Professional licensing has several purposes. The most frequent argument is that it is needed to protect the public. Laymen are not presumed to be able to distinguish between qualified and unqualified doctors, lawyers, and other professional people, and licensing guarantees minimum training, ability, and standards. In critical areas licensing undoubtedly is necessary to protect the public from quacks and incompetents. But professional licensing may also give status, restrict entry into the field, and permit higher charges for services. House painters, watchmakers, and many others have sought and sometimes secured professional licensing for their own private interests as much as for the protection of the public.[7]

★ *Administration of licensing*

Not only do many professions seek state licensing in their own or the public's interest but having secured it, they successfully insist on making the licensing board or commission an adjunct of their professional society. Normally the state medical society, the state bar association, or the state dental society officials recommend members for appointment to the licensing boards to the governor. The licensing boards need not regularly go to the governor and the legislature for appropriations, as typically the original statutes gave them the state license fees for administrative expenses. The ability to secure appointments by the professional society's official hierarchy, the independence from the legislature for administrative costs, and technical specialization have given the state's name and official status to licensing boards more or less privately controlled. This hybrid state-private system tends to work satisfactorily ordinarily but in a crisis may show a strong bias for the elite group of the profession. Higher and higher entrance requirements may serve the income interests of those in the profession more than the public. Revolutionary new practices (lauded in the future) may be accepted only after great delay.

★ *The doctor in politics: An example*

A number of studies have shown something of the significant influence the American Medical Association and its various state and county affiliates have had on public health legislation and professional regulation. In one such study some years ago, two economists analyzed AMA policy-making in restrictions for entrance into the profession.[8] In 1904 the AMA created a permanent Council on Medical Education. Since that time, this council has been remarkably successful in convincing state legislatures, state boards

[7] Ruth B. Doyle, "The Fence-Me-In Laws," *Harper's Magazine*, August 1952, pp. 89-91.
[8] The following discussion is taken primarily from M. Friedman and S. Kuznets, *Income From Independent Professional Practice* (New York: National Bureau of Economic Research, 1945), pp. 8-20, 118-136. All statistics and conclusions apply only to 1945.

of medical examiners, medical schools, and hospitals to adopt certain restrictive regulations concerning entry into the medical profession. Medical
licensing was in operation in all the states in 1904, but almost anyone could
take the examination. Little or no prior education was required. Similarly,
the standards of medical schools were very low. The Council therefore
adopted a policy of approval of medical schools, and succeeded in having
the legislature or board of medical examiners in forty-five states require
that all applicants for the licensing examinations be graduates of approved
medical schools. Thus a private group, the Council on Medical Education
of the AMA, has life or death control over medical schools in at least
forty-five states by approving or not approving them, and this control is
made effective by state requirements.

The basic pattern thus established, the Council proceeded to place progressive restrictions upon the medical schools of the country. Most of these
restrictions have been in the form of "suggestions," but with the control the
Council has, its suggestions have more the force of regulations. Medical
school personnel probably agree with the Council most of the time anyway.
The results of the Council's progressive insistence upon higher and higher
educational standards in medical schools from 1904 on were to reduce
greatly the number of physicians in proportion to population and to raise
their quality.

All this has been possible because of the official recognition given the
Council on Medical Education by the several states. The most questionable
use of the control of entry into the medical profession by the AMA came
during the 1930s in its attempt to prevent students denied access to American medical schools from getting foreign degrees and then returning to
practice in the United States. Also some foreign medical men were immi-
grating to this country because of persecution abroad. To meet these threats
to its monopoly on entry into the medical profession, the AMA again
turned to the states and the medical schools. It was successful in getting
sixteen states to refuse to recognize foreign medical degrees altogether. Of
the remaining thirty-two, twenty require full citizenship (the acquisition of
which takes at least five years) plus a foreign degree, and twenty-one require
additional work in this country before permission to take the state licensing
examination is granted—usually a year's internship or the senior year of
medical school or both. These restrictions did not satisfy the AMA, and
in 1936 its House of Delegates urged the states that still recognized foreign
degrees to do so only if the recipient of the degree had secured a license in
the country in which it was granted, a procedure that would have required
an American studying abroad to renounce his American citizenship, become
a citizen of the country in which he received his medical degree, return to

the United States and go through the process of becoming a citizen again, plus taking additional training in American medical schools and an internship. Two years later the Council suggested to the hospitals training interns (it "approves" hospitals for this purpose) that they should take foreigners as interns only if Americans did not fill their quota and only then if they had passed certain parts of the state medical exam, this no matter how well trained they were.

The results of restricting entry in this fashion have been fortunate for the medical profession, no matter what its motives. The income of physicians, it has been found, is over 32 percent larger than that of dentists, and 15 of the 32 percent is probably due to the restrictions on entry that the AMA has sponsored but which the dental association has not.[9] The remainder of the difference is probably due to the longer and more expensive training physicians must have. A second result was some embarrassment on the part of all concerned after World War II when certain displaced persons were brought to this country to practice medicine in communities lacking physicians, only to find that they could not be licensed until they became citizens and had taken additional training in American medical schools. Under great public pressure in some states, the legislatures or boards of examiners relaxed the requirements for admittance to the licensing examination, at least temporarily.

This example of the American Medical Association merely illustrates some of the many techniques that pressure groups use to influence public policy.

Conclusion

When examining the expenditures of state and local governments or the number of their employees, the field of economic policies does not loom large, with the exception of unemployment compensation. Administered with relatively few employees and without large outlays of tax funds, the economic policies of state and local governments nevertheless may be very expensive in terms of social cost and highly important in terms of personal income. The cost to the consumer of a government-protected monopoly, for example, can be very great indeed. The incomes of those who control it are likely to be much enhanced. The reverse may occasionally happen, also, with a utility being so restricted in the rates it can charge that it loses money while the consumers gain at least temporarily. In the field of labor legislation, well-organized groups of business and labor may contest strongly

9 *Ibid.*

for the adoption and practice of their views. In many other areas, the immediately interested groups may face little organized opposition.

REFERENCES

Becker, Joseph M., S. J., *Shared Government in Employment Security, A Study of Advisory Councils.* New York: Columbia University Press, 1959.

Bernstein, Marver H., *Regulating Business by Independent Commission.* Princeton: Princeton University Press, 1955.

Commission on Intergovernmental Relations, *Unemployment Compensation and Employment Service.* Washington, D. C.: Government Printing Office, 1955.

Council of State Governments, *Occupational Licensing in the States.* Chicago: Council of State Governments, 1952.

Dahl, Robert A., and Charles E. Lindblom, *Politics, Economics and Welfare.* New York: Harper and Brothers, 1953.

Diamond, Norene M., *A Guide to State Mediation Laws and Agencies,* U. S. Bureau of Labor Standards, Bulletin 176, Washington, D. C.: Government Printing Office, December 1958.

Millis, Harry A., and Royal E. Montgomery, *Organized Labor.* New York: McGraw-Hill, 1945.

Redford, Emmette S., *Administration of National Economic Control.* New York: The Macmillan Company, 1952.

——— (ed.), *Public Administration and Policy Formation: Studies in Oil, Gas, Banking, River Development, and Corporation Investigation.* Austin, Tex.: University of Texas Press, 1956.

Rourke, Francis E., *Intergovernmental Relations in Employment Security.* Minneapolis: University of Minnesota Press, 1952.

Van de Water, John R., and Harold C. Petrovitz, "Federal-State Jurisdiction and the Constitutional Framework in Industrial Relations," *Southern California Law Review* (February 1958), 111-149.

CHAPTER 23

Health and Welfare

THE NATIONAL CONSTITUTION and the several state constitutions written before the last decade or so failed either to mention health and welfare or simply declared "to promote the general welfare" to be one of the justifications of government. The constitution of Hawaii contrasts sharply:

> SEC. 1. The State shall provide for the protection and promotion of the public health.

> SEC. 2. The State shall have power to provide for treatment and rehabilitation, as well as domiciliary care, of mentally or physically handicapped persons.

> SEC. 3. The State shall have power to provide assistance for persons unable to maintain a standard of living compatible with decency and health.

> SEC. 4. The State shall have power to provide for or assist in slum clearance and the development or rehabilitation of substandard areas, including housing for persons of low income.[1]

The national government and the other forty-nine states, of course, have given attention to the health and welfare needs of their citizens; but the Hawaii statement in contrast to earlier omissions indicates the change in

[1] Constitution of Hawaii, Article VIII.

440

public philosophy toward government and the health and welfare function in its direct charge of responsibility to the state government.[2]

Welfare

The term "welfare" has always had a broad meaning (for example, the national Constitution lists "to promote the general welfare" as a reason for the Constitution and includes "to provide for the general welfare" as an expenditure purpose for which taxes might be levied), and has included within its scope both physical and spiritual or mental conditions of living. Welfare within this context may be provided by government simply because a democratic government exists and gives individuals opportunities for freedom. Or welfare may demand that government provide a direct service. In current terms of action, we usually think of a variety of social services as welfare functions—assistance to the physically or mentally handicapped; assistance to children and aged who are limited in the ways that they can help themselves; assistance to those who need help to adjust to society; assistance to individuals and families without adequate income for subsistence.

For approximately a century and a half from 1776 to the 1930s, our state and national governments assumed little responsibility for the social welfare needs of citizens. State and local budget items, often labeled "charities and corrections," covered costs of prisons and related institutions, insane asylums (a very literal designation), poor houses or poor farms, and occasionally in the twentieth century mother's pensions, pensions for the blind, and even more rarely old-age pensions. Local governments provided a measure of relief to individuals or families in economic distress. Until 1911 or later, no workmen's compensation plan carried families when the wage earner had been injured in an industrial accident; until the 1930s, no unemployment insurance carried families over periods of temporary unemployment and no national social security system provided insurance benefits for the aged or for dependents. Personal hospital and health insurance was almost unknown. Private retirement plans were few. Relatives, neighbors, friends, and organized private charity attempted to meet some of the most pressing needs. The lack of classification of causes of relief (to a degree, our modern system of programs separates those who are in difficulty without personal responsibility—unemployment, injury, age, blindness, and

---

2 Every state under its present constitution has been able to provide areas of health and welfare services for its citizens, but some states have found their constitutions more inflexible in the matter of housing.

so forth—from those on general relief who may have a more direct responsibility in their situation) added to the distress of those who needed assistance.

The readiness with which government in the nineteenth century and early twentieth century left most of the social welfare work to private individuals or groups reflected (1) philosophical assumptions of individual and family responsibility, (2) assumptions of a largely rural or small-business economy where neighbors, employers, and community groups tended to be personally acquainted with individual and family problems and assumed a responsibility, and (3) an absence of recognition of the diverse causes of social welfare needs and some of the modern understanding of assistance apart from or in addition to the mere provision of physical necessities. The Great Depression of the 1930s brought a revolution in government, particularly state and national government, assumption of responsibility. The older assumptions changed or were modified as citizens and governmental leaders recognized the development of an increasingly industrialized and urbanized society in which seemingly impersonal forces created unemployment and took almost every resource for self-maintenance from millions of citizens. Impersonality characterized relations in large cities, and problems were beyond individual assistance. Studies in sociology, psychology, and mental and physical health provided further foundation for the acceptance of a growing role for government in the social welfare of its citizens.[3]

The growth of government in the welfare field has not eliminated private welfare agencies. United Givers Funds in almost every city collect millions of dollars each year for a variety of agencies designed to prevent juvenile delinquency; to give assistance to young people and adults in trouble where guidance or other temporary aid may help; to provide mental health clinics, maternal and child clinics, summer camps for children. Private agencies frequently meet specific needs that governmental agencies are not equipped or not authorized to meet; sometimes private agencies provide services over and above what government can do or sometimes they work in fields not yet fully accepted as proper social welfare work by government agencies. Christmas baskets and Christmas gifts for children illustrate an-

[3] John Maynard Keynes, English economist, also had an important effect on attitudes toward government public works and welfare for the unemployed in his emphasis on the consumer as the key to prosperity. In his view not saving and investment so much but high levels of consumption gave full employment and hence prosperity to an industrial society. When the economy falters, government, using its borrowing powers, should step in with large public works and immediate assistance so that citizens will continue and increase their consumption habits. As they buy manufacturing will necessarily expand again to meet the demand. Keynes published his major study in 1936 and the leaders of the industrial nations have accepted and practiced many of his conclusions.

other type of service from private rather than public agencies. Extensive medical care sometimes can be more readily covered by private rather than public resources.

★ Welfare programs

What are the welfare functions of government? Clearly the exact scope of welfare functions changes with time and the fullness of programs varies among the states. Today we would begin by including the so-called categorical aid programs: old-age assistance, aid to the blind, aid to dependent children, and aid to the permanently and totally disabled. The national government has established old-age and survivors' insurance (commonly called social security) covering more than 90 percent of the labor force. General assistance or "general relief" is available when the foregoing programs either do not apply or are inadequate. The modern "poor farm" is normally a home or a hospital that would be unrecognizable in nineteenth-century terms.[4]

Whereas, the social security program is financed through employer-employee payroll taxes, the other programs above are covered by tax revenues by the national, state, and often local governments. The categorical aid programs provide in effect that individuals with needs beyond their own resources who are dependent children, old, blind, or disabled may seek on that basis monthly assistance. The social worker in the welfare department will appraise the resources and needs of the individual or family in terms of community standards and within the general provisions of the state law. On occasion, an aged individual or couple may receive a social security check, an old-age assistance check, and a general relief check. The social security check, based on earnings in the past, may be inadequate to cover regular expenses of food, shelter, and clothing. The addition of the state's maximum allotment under old-age assistance may be inadequate to meet the difference plus medical and other needs so that further financial aid is given through general relief. The adequacy of the social security check is likely to depend on the level of past earnings of the recipient and the related level of his own savings. Inflation and major medical expenses may make a social security check insufficient even when reinforced with personal savings. In 1958, 2,452,465 individuals received old-age assistance and 2,850,440 children and their guardians, 109,831 blind individuals, and 327,763 permanently and totally disabled individuals received aid.

Our present use of the term "welfare" often includes both the "chari-

---

[4] See Will Carleton's poem, *Over the Hill to the Poor House*, and the short story, "The Town Poor" from the collection *The Country of the Pointed Firs* and *Other Stories* by Sarah Orne Jewett (New York: Doubleday, 1955).

ties" and the "corrections" of the older classification. Thus an integrated state welfare department will likely have among its functions the operation of state prisons, state prison farms, correctional institutions for youths and substantial probation and parole programs to assist in the rehabilitation of individuals who have failed to adjust to society's standards. A division of children and youth will attempt to meet the problems of children whose parents have died, have deserted them, or are unfit to guide them and the problems of delinquents in or out of institutions. Governmental (and private) welfare services usually include a further broad responsibility that may be variously discharged in practice:

> Provision to all of the opportunity to receive through professional services, the corrective, protective, and preventive advice and assistance which will minimize social maladjustment and increase individual and family well-being. The advice and assistance of trained personnel are essential to the welfare of both children and adults.[5]

★ Organization of welfare functions

National. The establishment in 1949 of a cabinet Department of Health, Education, and Welfare recognized the role the national government began assuming in welfare after 1932. The old-age and survivors' insurance program is a wholly national responsibility that underpins many aspects of welfare programs throughout the United States. Beginning as a part of the same Congressional act, the national government also accepted a responsibility for providing funds through grants-in-aid for the categorical aids and in effect nationalizing the adoption of these programs and setting minimum standards for their operation. One unusual provision in the grant-in-aid area is that states receiving welfare grants may employ only individuals hired under a merit system for their grant-in-aid programs.[6] The U. S. Department of Health, Education, and Welfare provides a further important service function to the states in its collection of welfare statistics and in its studies of nation-wide welfare problems.

State. Each state government typically has a single department of welfare that may or may not include responsibilities for the correctional institutions. An occasional state includes all of the functions described above and adds others such as mental health or at least the state's mental hospitals and

5 Study Committee on Federal Aid to Welfare, *A Study Committee Report on Federal Aid to Welfare*, submitted to the Commission on Intergovernmental Relations (Washington, D. C.: U. S. Government Printing Office, June 1955).
6 See Chapter 15.

institutions for both the mentally deficient and mentally ill children and adults.[7] On the theory of separating welfare and institutions from politics, a number of states have continued to use a board or commission to head their welfare departments. A full-time director may manage the welfare department with or without an overhead or advising board.

With the possible exception of a few of the World War II years, governors and legislators have seldom found it possible in the last thirty years to ignore the state's welfare programs. Since the crisis of the 1930s, public interest and sympathy have brought demands for increasing the number and quality of welfare services. Inflation has continued to make each earlier maximum assistance payment out of date and inadequate. Population growth, not only because of an increasing birth rate but also because of longer life expectancy, has added to the number of aged persons and children needing special services. Juvenile delinquency and crime rate increases have raised the demands on the correctional institutions and probation, parole, and other special services. Any state that failed to meet some of these problems on its own initiative found the national government nudging it forward through grant-in-aid program changes. Few states have segregated funds for welfare, and governors and legislators have opportunities for directing state welfare policies *where the state has undertaken responsibilities above the minimum standards* of federal grant-in-aid arrangements.

Local. The shift of welfare responsibilities from private to public agencies and from local to state and national levels has not eliminated either local governments or private agencies from welfare roles. Private social work continues to be an important supplement to public agencies: disaster relief, family case work, adoptions and foster-home care, psychiatric case work, services for unwed mothers, and a wide variety of group work in settlement houses and elsewhere. The type and amount of private social work depends in part on the adequacy of public welfare work in terms of the standards of the community.

In a minority of states, including Wisconsin, county welfare departments actually carry on the personal work with welfare clients under the categorical aid programs. Most states leave general relief responsibilities either with the county or with smaller local units. Larger cities often supplement state welfare programs in some of the same ways as private groups. Cities usually look after welfare needs of their newest citizens whether or not they meet specific residency standards of the state for assistance. Large cities frequently have public clinics for family case-work and mental and physical health needs.

[7] Mental health programs will be discussed in the later health section of this chapter.

★ Welfare finance

Federal grants to the states for welfare exceeded all other such grants in 1958 and were 40 percent of the total ($1.8 billion out of a total of $4.5 billion). Welfare has ranked third in cost among state and local functions for a quarter of a century. Since the 1930s the largest federal grants have been in welfare, and welfare programs have been the third costliest to state and local governments. (Highways have been the only competitor with federal welfare grants in size. It is possible that with the large federal grants for the interstate highway system with a 90-10 matching requirement highway grants will overtake federal welfare grants. In 1958 the national government provided $1.5 billion in grants for highways and $1.8 billion for welfare.)

The purposes of federal grants in general and in welfare in particular have been debated many times. Is the basic purpose to stimulate state action? Is it to aid the state that does not have the resources to undertake the program otherwise? Is it to equalize governmental burdens among the states? Is it to provide a minimal standard of services for all Americans regardless of the state in which they live? Is it some combination of all of these or something else in addition? Answers to these questions have significance in most programs but particularly in the field of welfare.[8] If the purpose of federal grants-in-aid is merely to aid states that have insufficient resources, then presumably Mississippi would receive grants and New York would not. The same answer might be true if the purpose were to stimulate state action. In fact, our federal system seems to preclude such specific answers. New York Congressmen and Senators are willing to assist Mississippi by voting grants-in-aid for programs that New York taxpayers will pay for to a higher degree than Mississippi taxpayers in federal taxes, but they are not willing to provide programs of grants-in-aid for Mississippi and none for New York. Or at least so it seems.

Welfare grants in practice have been made on rather elaborate formula bases that perhaps assist the poorer states at the most needed points but also assist the more well-to-do states. The formula for public assistance grants illustrates the point.

The national grant formula is intended to (1) assure $30.00 per month

---

[8] The United States government has not employed bloc grants as has the British and some others. Under a bloc-grant system, funds are made available (usually on some tax-burden-equalizing basis) without designation as to use. The receiving government uses the grants as it finds best. It would be possible to have bloc grants for welfare without designating the program or bloc grants to the states without designating highways, welfare, education, or whatever, as at present. Despite discussion of bloc grants in this country, the Congressional leaders and Presidents have shown little desire to change from our practice of specific purpose grants.

as the minimum assistance payment; (2) encourage states to make at least $65.00 per month as the assistance payment; and (3) permit states that can afford to do so to increase their maximum payments over this figure. Application of the formula does not necessarily result in equalizing burdens among the states. The comparatively wealthy state of California, for example, received national grants to cover 72.3 percent of its old-age assistance program in 1956, whereas the much less wealthy state of North Carolina received national grants to cover only 40.1 percent of its program. In part the formula used may be faulty and in part no clear determination has been made either as to the desirability of equalizing burdens or as to defining in practice what is meant by equalizing burdens.[9]

The increasing numbers of older citizens in the population together with greatly rising medical costs have added a special burden that government frequently has had to assume. Recipients of social security may find their monthly checks, even when supplemented by their own savings or by old-age assistance, inadequate in periods of prolonged illness. Rising medical costs may also make inadequate the usual aid to the blind, dependent children, or the totally and permanently disabled. National, state, and local governments have recently made special provisions for attempting to meet such medical costs.

States, such as Wisconsin, that continue to leave the immediate administration of welfare programs to the counties usually use formulas somewhat similar to those of the national government in transferring national and state assistance. The counties then finally determine the amount of assistance over and above the national and state minimums that they will pay to their citizens requiring assistance. Many states leave payment of general relief for individuals not qualifying under any of these programs (or requiring assistance in an amount above that available in the programs) to their counties or municipal governments.

State governments alone bear most costs of correctional administration whether institutional or related. States also assume most other costs of their general welfare programs, although urban communities may supplement with further programs to meet the special needs of their citizens.

★ *Special interest groups*

One basic issue in welfare policy is: To what extent shall public funds be used to furnish security for the individuals in society? Different answers have been returned to this question in different states. Social philosophy, inter-

[9] See the discussion on federal aid formulas for public assistance: *A Study Committee Report on Federal Aid to Welfare, op. cit.*, pp. 16-35; also see tables on aid payments, *The Book of the States, 1958-59*, pp. 338-344.

governmental relations, and special interest groups are all bound up in this controversy. Essentially, those groups with rather conservative and individualistic philosophies have made much of states' rights in welfare. They have argued that excessive security leads to lack of progress, since incentive is lost. Seeing that the national government has not accepted this view they have also resorted to the states'-rights argument that welfare policy-making should be a state, not a national, responsibility—or at least more than it is now. Their defense of state prerogatives is probably motivated primarily by two considerations. First, it is becoming increasingly obvious that the states are not able to handle the welfare problem alone. The causes of insecurity are mainly national, and nation-wide policies are needed to minimize their effects. Therefore, no national action may be equivalent to no effective action whatsoever, which is what some of the conservative groups desire. Secondly, those defending an extreme states'-rights position in welfare feel that at least some state legislatures, governors, and administrators (especially the first two) are more conservatively minded than their national counterparts, and hence state policy decisions, if made independent of the national government, would be more in line with a conservative philosophy. Liberal groups generally take an opposite viewpoint, namely that the national government is the only level that can take adequate steps in the welfare field, and therefore a large measure of centralization is called for.

Welfare policy therefore raises this further question: Has the defense of states' rights and local self-government, long-cherished liberal principles, become almost exclusively the concern of the conservatives? Except for relatively few people, an affirmative answer must be returned. In the struggle over welfare policies, national, state, and local governments are merely means to ends. If the ends a group desires to achieve cannot be accomplished through one level of government, another is employed. The level of government that is able best to accomplish the ends sought is defended in both practical and philosophical terms. The relation of local self-government and states' rights to democracy seems of less importance today, because government is first of all expected to be able to meet the problems that confront society and these problems are increasingly national. If government can meet social needs successfully, many contend, it will at the same time be doing the most that can possibly be done to preserve democracy. Substance, not form, has become primary in national-state-local relations.

Administrators of welfare agencies find themselves surrounded by special-interest groups that try to influence welfare policies in every way possible. Among the most powerful of these have been old-age-pension groups. Their power stems from their large numbers and the permanence of their individual security problems. Other categories of welfare clients, such as those on general relief, are composed of individuals who hope some day to find security through adequate employment. Permanent organizations of people on relief are therefore difficult to form, although in periods of deep economic depression relief recipients may assume political importance. The numbers of the blind are small, and they are interested in only a small part of welfare policy, yet their power relative to that part is even greater than the power exercised over old-age-security policies by old-age groups. Children have the weakest position among the categories of welfare clientele. Unable to make their voices heard at the polls directly, they must rely upon adults to take whatever action is needed.

Pressure-group tactics are clearly reflected in welfare policies. Part of the reason for the *categorical-aid* program and not a *general* welfare grant policy is that old-age and blind groups are strong enough politically to force special recognition of their welfare needs. They do not want to have to depend upon the separate and unguided actions of all the states, and the passage of the Social Security Act assured at least a nation-state program. Many groups interested in welfare services might prefer a straight national program, eliminating the states, particularly if through their influence on Congress and administrative agencies they could help write such a program. There were doubts based on Constitutional grounds that this would be possible in 1935, and so a grants-in-aid program was established instead. Without discarding their desire for a uniform nation-wide program, old-age and blind pressure groups have concentrated their efforts on the states in an attempt to secure state and not state-local administration of the categorical-aid program. Aid to dependent children is also a categorical aid, and one reason for including it in the Social Security Act was to make sure that the states, under pressure from other welfare pressure groups, would not neglect the needs of dependent children.

In contrast, some states have taken leadership in new youth programs. Certain humanitarian groups or public officials have tried to dramatize the waste of human resources that occurs when juvenile delinquency is allowed to run rampant. The traditional method of dealing with juvenile delinquents has been to have the police or prosecuting officials bring the offenders to juvenile court (in rural areas commonly the probate court) and the judge to punish the offenders as he sees fit, putting them on probation or committing them to state reformatories. In the last few years leading states have set up special administrative agencies to handle juvenile delinquents, to which judges must refer cases if the youths are found guilty. Employing trained psychiatrists, social workers, and counselors, these agencies have tried to get at the cause of each individual's delinquency and, by helping to remove it, aid the youth to become a useful member of society. Investigations by these agencies have frequently found home and family conditions that have caused maladjustment, and an attempt is made to alleviate them. At the same time, conditions in reformatories as well as prisons have greatly improved, mere punishment being more and more replaced or supplemented by special treatment for each individual prisoner in order that his future adjustment to the outside world may be satisfactory. Prison alumni seldom can lobby to influence increased appropriations.

Health

National public health services had their origin in a Marine Hospital Service founded in 1798 for the care of ill sailors. From this beginning the United States Public Health Service assisted the armed forces, the states, and the nation in controlling epidemics, aiding in the development and enforcement of quarantine regulations at ports of entry, and investigating the causes, methods of transmission, and cures of communicable diseases. It was the United States Public Health Service that won an enviable place in its investigation and control of malaria and yellow fever when the United States built the Panama Canal at the beginning of this century. In more recent years, the United States Public Health Service has had added to its work by acts of Congress the task of assisting the states in improving their public health services through exchanges of information and several grant-in-aid programs.

State public health departments often began as statistics-gathering agencies. Until the advent of modern medicine after Pasteur's work of the 1870s, community and state public health work generally consisted of rudimentary sanitation and sewage arrangements in cities, occasionally isolation of the sick, and some gathering of vital statistics of births and deaths. In handling mentally ill patients, governments undertook custody only. And custody might mean poorer physical surroundings than the worst prisons of the period.

From their beginnings when they merely collected statistics of births, deaths, and disease, state health departments today will handle a wide range of services from research into special health problems, investigations of outbreaks of illness, operation of state hospitals for the mentally and physically ill, and the administration of grant-in-aid programs for the building of community hospitals to maintenance of traveling buses to provide free chest x-rays. Public clinics may be operated for babies and small children or for adults without adequate financial resources. Special campaigns have been undertaken against tuberculosis, venereal disease, poliomyelitis, and others. State health laboratories maintain checks on water supplies and food. Training is given to professional health workers, health information is made available to the public, and new methods and techniques for control of disease and promotion of health are demonstrated to local health officers, nurses, and doctors.

★ Organization

Health programs are not necessarily located in a single agency in the state. At least some food inspection (for example meat and dairy products) may be in the hands of the agricultural agency. Water-pollution control may be in conservation. State hospitals may be in a separate agency, in the welfare department, or attached to the state university. But whatever the distribution of health functions, there is also a department of health in the state with a director and quite possibly a board setting general policy.

Health shares with education and welfare some of the public attitudes of being "above politics." Boards of health are rather common both in local and state governments. A majority of board members frequently come from the medical profession, and the development of public health services has probably been both helped and hindered by this close association. On the negative side, private doctors on the board have tended to reflect attitudes of the American Medical Association and to oppose expansion of public health services that other segments of the population might desire. Devoted doctor members of boards have, of course, assisted in carrying major health campaigns to the public and in securing greater funds for the total health program.

State health departments have had difficult staffing problems for at least a decade. The continuous growth in incomes for doctors and psychiatrists in private practice has widened the economic gap between private and public practice. Salaries of around $20,000 for the state's chief health officer (paid by a few states only) are well below the successful income level in private practice, and most health officers, other doctors, and psychiatrists on the staff receive considerably less than a $20,000 annual salary. Medical schools, special public health programs, and universities are graduating fewer professional and technical personnel than the growth in population and increased standards of medical service require. Salary differentials lessen the competitive attractiveness of the public health service for this inadequate supply of graduates.

Although a board may separate the governor from immediate direction of the state health department and the professionalism of doctors on the board in the department may keep any layman at arm's length in health matters, the agency must normally come to the governor for budgets and otherwise report to the governor and legislature. Critical health needs have brought the active support of many governors. It was a Conference of State Governors, for example, that helped to dramatize the plight of the mentally ill in this nation. And a study sponsored by the governors aided in providing the factual information for securing action in a number of states.

★ *Special health programs*

Emphases in health programs necessarily change over time and even among states. At the beginning of most state health departments tuberculosis was the leading cause of death in the nation. The work of health departments in public information on the disease, in early identification, and in the development of treatment has contributed importantly to eliminating tuberculosis as one of the first ten causes of death. Heart disease and cancer now lead as causes of death in the nation, and state health departments have turned their attention here to diagnostic, research, and public information efforts. Air-pollution control, chronic-disease programs, and dental, radiological, and mental health programs have been added or given increased emphasis recently. Air pollution and radiology are health hazards that require state, national, and international action. About a quarter of the states have written legislation in the air-pollution field. New Jersey and New York have agreed on a joint study of smoke and air pollution in the New York City metropolitan area. The National Committee for Radiation Protection has recommended comprehensive radiation regulations that some states have adopted. An Advisory Committee of State Officials, appointed by the United States Atomic Energy Commission, is considering federal-state radiation protection programs.

★ *Mental illness*

Although scientists have not solved all physical health problems, they seem closer to solutions or at least understanding in the physical-health sphere than in the mental-health field. The very idea of who are the mentally ill has not been answered identically in all societies. More primitive societies sometimes have seen the gods embodied in the mentally ill, others have seen mental illness as incorporating the devil. In the former situation, the individual might become the priest or priestess of the group. In the latter, he might be tortured or burned at the stake. After the witchburning episodes of the seventeenth century, Americans seemed to accept mental illness as an unfortunate fact about which little could be done. Under the best of circumstances, the community or state incarcerated the individual in prison or prisonlike institutions. The seriously mentally ill did not grow well under either treatment.

"A person can be mentally healthy in the deepest sense of the term only if he realizes his own values and establishes the kind of relationships to people, to his culture, to nature, and to the spiritual universe which are truly his own." [10] Not many of us achieve this state of health, although our deviations may not require treatment.

On any given day, more hospital beds in the nation are likely to be occupied by the mentally ill than by the physically ill. Many more such individuals are receiving treatment outside hospitals. One estimate places the total number of Americans suffering from mental illness at any one time as 1 in 10.[11] Common mental illnesses include neuroses, psychoses (includes schizophrenia), senility, and a variety of physiological brain disorders. The first two classes are usually designated as functional disorders; senility is a result of aging and is characterized largely by loss of memory that may be so extensive as to require hospitalization and custody; physiological brain disorders may arise from injuries to the brain, infection, and metabolic disturbances. As a generalization, neuroses and physiological brain disorders respond best to treatment.

State governments have led in the last two decades in undertaking a wide variety of medical research in mental health problems as well as vastly improving facilities for treatment. The development of tranquilizers and stimulant drugs has made it possible to control behavior and treat formerly "hopeless" cases. Public discussion and understanding of mental illness together with greatly improved facilities for treatment have brought individuals to seek help at earlier stages of their illness. Community clinics have been established to give assistance while the patient pursues many of his usual activities. Greater attention has been given to assisting patients who have been hospitalized to adjust to the community when they have recovered. The shift from custody to treatment and the hope of continuing advances in understanding of the nature of mental illness have opened a widely different perspective not only for the patient and his family but for the responsibility of government.

[10] Fred H. Blum, "Mental Health and Ethics," *Society's Stake in Mental Health* (Minneapolis: Social Science Research Center of the Graduate School, University of Minnesota, 1957), p. 9.
[11] Those who are mentally ill are to be distinguished from the mentally retarded or the mentally defective. A child born without an arm can receive help to adjust to the difficulty but can never engage in sports or activities requiring full use of both hands. Our present understanding suggests that the mentally retarded child can be helped in some instances to live satisfactorily in the society even though he can never enjoy the intellectual pursuits of citizens of normal intelligence.

★ Health and finance

As in every other area of government expenditure, the legislature, governor, and public must decide how much they can afford to spend for health (perhaps how much they can*not* afford *not* to spend) in relation to tax revenues and in relation to other demands on government. The state and local governments supply the larger part of their own direct health-program costs. National-government grants on the average cover approximately 20 percent of total expenditures. National grants are available for programs in the fields of maternal and child health, venereal disease, poliomyelitis, public health training, and others. The Federal Hospital Survey and Construction Act has aided greatly in stimulating the expansion of hospital facilities in many communities. Federal funds have represented slightly less than one half of the almost $2 billion expenditure in about ten years.

Local governments carry on local health programs with some direction and guidance but not too much money from the states. County nurse programs usually receive some state aid; recent programs for establishing community health centers have included state aid to the locality. Many of the state's health services are carried out in the field by state agency personnel.

★ Health and interest groups

American medical societies, much more than their British counterparts, have feared "socialized medicine" and have actively opposed expansion of public health services that would compete with the private doctor's practice. Research and services such as tuberculosis sanitoria or mental hospitals have not normally come under the ban. Apart from this general opposition that frequently extends to members of boards of health, health advisory committees, and some of the professional staff members of the health agency, health departments may face specific opposition from individual members or groups of the medical profession on particular issues. The issue of fluoridation of the water supplies brought almost hysterical opposition from various other groups in some communities.

One of the most difficult interest-group situations that governments face is that of the competition of local chapters of the cancer society, the polio society, the heart society, and others. A tendency has existed to single out one disease as *the* enemy and insist on pouring most of our private contributions and public health tax revenues into it to the great neglect of other areas of health. Polio, for example, was a disease easy to dramatize; and the question at least arose whether too much money was not poured in at times for efficient use. Both mental and physical health have many interrelations. Research into particular diseases is necessary. But we also need funds and services to provide general health for all citizens.

Conclusion

The changing characteristics of our society have brought changes in the role of government in welfare and health. Change seems evident for the future. The preferred term for individuals over 65 is now "senior citizens," not aged. The acceptance of this term into our vocabularies (along with the disappearance not only of "aged" but of "poor farms" and similar designations) ratifies a significant change in attitudes. As senior citizens they have an implied claim on government not only for assistance in maintaining an income level and physical and mental health but for programs of education, recreation, and housing. Several universities in the nation, including Illinois and Michigan, are attempting to carry out research into the needs of the aging and to train personnel for work in the field. Child welfare services are another area of change and development. Family patterns have changed not only to make family care of aged relatives less practical today, but working mothers may leave children inadequately supervised and make them candidates for delinquency. The resulting social problems again are bringing in government.

The rush to construct new, enlarged, and better buildings for mental hospitals, general hospitals, and other institutions has slowed somewhat. Buildings were and are needed. Greater success in treatment of many patients has reduced hospital days for each patient and hence reduced some of the pressure for rooms. Even in the field of corrections, greater use of probation and parole and new ideas in correctional administration has reduced the earlier estimates for maximum security institutions.

REFERENCES

Bennett, James V., "Probation and Parole among the States," 30 *State Government*, June 1957, 130-133.
Bloch, Herbert A. and Frank T. Flynn, *Delinquency: The Juvenile Offender in America Today*. New York: Random House, 1956.
Commission on Intergovernmental Relations, *Federal Aid to Public Health: A Study Committee Report*. Washington, D. C.: Government Printing Office, 1955.
————, *Federal Aid to Welfare: A Study Committee Report*. Washington, D.C.: Government Printing Office, 1955.
Corson, John J., and John W. McConnell, *Economic Needs of Older People*. New York: The Twentieth Century Fund, 1956.

Council of State Governments, *The States and Their Older Citizens*. Chicago: Council of State Governments, 1955.

——, *Training and Research in State Mental Health Programs, A Report to the Governors' Conference*. Chicago: Council of State Governments, 1953.

——, *The Mental Health Programs of the Forty-eight States; A Report to the Governors' Conference*. Chicago: Council of State Governments, 1950.

Daland, Robert T., *Government and Health: The Alabama Experience*. University, Ala.: Bureau of Public Administration, University of Alabama, 1955.

Juvenile Delinquency. A report by the Subcommittee on Juvenile Delinquency of the U. S. Senate Committee on the Judiciary. Washington, D. C.: Government Printing Office, 1957.

Keith-Lucas, Alan, "The Political Theory Implicit in Social Casework Theory," 47 *American Political Science Review*, December 1953, 1076-1091.

Kieve, Rudolph, "The Chemical Revolution in Psychiatry: Its Effects on Care of the Mentally Ill," 32 *State Government*, Spring 1959, 104-108.

Powers, Sanger B., "Elements for Advance in Our Correctional Programs," 32 *State Government*, Summer 1959, 174-178.

Raup, Ruth, *Intergovernmental Relations in Social Welfare*. Minneapolis: University of Minnesota Press, 1952.

Robinson, Jerome, "The Maryland Approach to Defective Delinquent Criminals," 32 *State Government*, Summer 1959, 179-187.

Wyatt, Laurence, *Intergovernmental Relations in Public Health*. Minneapolis: University of Minnesota Press, 1951.

Ylvisaker, Paul N., *Intergovernmental Relations at the Grass Roots: A Study of Blue Earth County Minnesota to 1946*. Minneapolis: University of Minnesota Press, 1956.

CHAPTER 24

Problems of Change in State Government

WE LIVE in a dynamic society. Change is ever present. People themselves change—their age, their numbers, their religious affiliations and racial compositions. The values and objectives that human beings hold are seldom constant. Bringing about the many changes in values and in the people themselves are a host of dynamic factors—technological and social progress, environmental change, such as the weather, accretion or depletion of natural resources, wars, and depressions—the list is without end.

Democratic theory normally has held the ability to change without revolution to be one of the great achievements of democracies. Democratic governments are supposed to have a resiliency and responsiveness to the needs and aspirations of people that achieve continuing adjustment without the violent bursting of old bonds as has been true under monarchies and dictatorships or as predicted by Marxist theory. American state and local governments, as well as the national government, have a never-ending challenge to meet.

Areas of Change

★ Intergovernmental relations

Our experiment in federalism may succeed or fail as much by intelligent transfers of responsibility to the national government in some fields and a sharing with the national government of responsibility in other fields as by insistence on measuring whether the states have relatively a greater or lesser role now than in the past. Our continually growing interdependence in economic, social, and military ways can not but affect governmental institutions and ways. And the question keeps recurring year after year, how can federalism operate meaningfully today? The difficulty is that the answer changes. The division of labor does not remain the same. Participation shifts.

The states, moreover, do not work with the national government on equal terms. Not only does the national government have a superior position from the Constitution but the states vary among themselves in their ability to contest differences with the national government. Wealthy and moderately wealthy states may accept national grants-in-aid without any sense of pressure. Such states either are already carrying on the programs or are ready to do so on a scale frequently higher than the national minimums. Few national standards for grant-in-aid programs match those present in California, New York, and a number of other states. Differences in detail between these states and the national grant-in-aid agency are negotiable on rather even terms. At the other end, however, are the Mississippis. Here the states may accept the federal grants-in-aid as a defensive measure to assure receipt of federal moneys but without enthusiasm for the program. Both the much lower wealth and differences in political attitudes may make the state also accept of necessity the minimum standards of the national government without attempting state individualization of the program. Each change in program standard is then accepted under much the same forced circumstances. The fiscal pressures to meet minimum federal standards in particular programs may delay or prevent use of tax moneys in programs that the state might develop otherwise on its own. Is there any way to give a policy-contributing role to the states of lesser resources and differing philosophies without sacrificing minimum program standards desired for the nation as a whole?

The evidence is not complete as to the lot of the Mississippis, indicated above in the grant-in-aid program area, and it is even less certain in other types of negotiations with the national government and its agencies. In the cases of transfers of Indian reservations to the states, of the in-lieu tax payments where the national government has taken over substantial areas for defense facilities or for TVAs, of mutual agreements on tax information exchange, how important are the caliber of professional negotiations in the state agencies concerned? How important is the strategic importance of the state's Congressional representation? Again there would seem to be differences among the states. The more the national government and the states work together in numerous ways, the more important for federalism that the states come to the negotiations with some measure of equality. The national interest may be involved not only in the equity of the outcome for the nation but also in the method by which it is arrived at. Can the states meet this challenge? Is there a feasible contribution by the national government?

Are improvements in interstate relations another part of the answer to successful federalism? The increased use of interstate compacts in substantive programs suggests that some regional problems and some needs for uniform legislation can be met through united action of some or all of the states. But only foolhardiness would lead anyone to crusade for interstate compacts and other forms of interstate cooperation as *the* answer. Some interstate compacts tangle with questions of the desirability of functional versus area government. The deficiencies or differences in states that make national grants-in-aid a barrier to state individuality create problems in interstate cooperation. In the field of tax administration, greater cooperation exists in practice between the national and state governments than among the states. Certainly more cooperation exists between the national and state governments in income tax administration and the exchange of audit information. Among other reasons, states with effective income tax auditing have not wished to carry the burden of cooperation with states with decidedly inferior administrations.

★ *Metropolitan problems*

Intergovernmental relations do not run merely between the states and the national government or among the states. Many similar problems, in fact, are present in the different setting of the states and their local governments. State grants-in-aid with their concomitant standards reduce some opportunities for local decisions and this may especially be true in less wealthy communities. The interests of the state necessarily override in some instances. Both grants-in-aid and shared taxes pose questions of the degree of responsibility of the state for equalizing tax burdens among its citizens.

One of the most pressing problems for state governments lies in the developing metropolises. State after state finds one or a dozen or more population concentrations within its borders where the people within each of these centers share common economic and social community ties but are separated by governmental divisions. Large city governments have normally experienced problems of greater complexity than small cities. With the present tendency for clusters of cities and villages to develop with only artificial map lines separating them, many of the older difficulties assume new and worsened shapes.

The state has several opportunities to aid or hinder in metropolitan problems. Is the state legislature sufficiently representative of population to give the peoples of the metropolises a reasonable hearing and voice? Does state legislation encourage separatism or unification of the governmental divisions that separate otherwise common economic and social communities? Where should the state step in to limit home rule and local self-determination on behalf of the general interests of the state? Can governments along functional lines serve citizens and respond to the whole body of citizens as well as governments by area? How do our findings here affect our approach to federalism at the state and national level?

★ *Functions*

A prediction of great certainty asserts that governments in general will undertake more functions and will continue most of their present functions in greater depth as the years go on. Increasing populations require more of everything now being done. With changing (and so far increasing) standards of personal living, demands on government programs have grown. Whether future transportation is by automobile or by air, governments will provide a large part of the facilities. Each generation of Americans has attempted to enlarge the educational opportunities of their children. Our scientific age has added further pressures for education, and the number of children has increased. With the greater awareness and recognition of mental illness has come also the increasing knowledge of how to treat it. The number of community and state mental health clinics, hospitals, and professional personnel grow each year. Neither the Southern states nor the Northern states have solved problems of race relations and the sometime separate, sometimes related problems of law enforcement. We have much to learn and to do to understand about juvenile and adult delinquents and criminals. Mental illness, community attitudes, living conditions, opportunities, and individual development all play a part. Some things we understand but then fail to act on our knowledge. Other things in the field of criminology we do not understand, and if we act, we act blindly.

Predictions as to probable areas of government activity could be discussed in page after page. What state governments do depends on the findings in the physical and social sciences, on the citizen's attitude toward government acting, and on the citizen's willingness to pay for government services.

★ *Administration and organization*

The citizen's attitude toward government acting may depend on how well government meets its present jobs and each additional job. We noted earlier that the states that undertake the fewest programs tend to be the states with the least well-organized governments. There seems a reasonable presumption that citizens do not add further programs to governments when these governments fail to handle well those they now have. If the need for the program is intense, then the states or local governments have at times been bypassed to secure action at the next level.

Reformers have lost some of their earlier faith that a change in organization structure to meet a model will bring *good* government. Increasingly people have recognized that efficiency and economy are not goals standing alone but must be defined only in terms of other objectives sought. Nevertheless government organization may aid or impede. Efficiency and economy, redefined, have meaning. Improved budget and personnel administration have brought understanding, greater productivity, and a renewed sense of service. Coordination of state programs normally increases as the lines to the governor's office become disentangled.

Constitutional provisions, like organization, may impede good government but a model constitution does not provide a guarantee of good government. A flexible constitution following most of our model-constitution thinking gives the legislative majority an opportunity to meet problems with greater ease. A detailed and badly outdated constitution hampers the most active and intelligent citizen majority by giving a minority opportunities for obstruction. Needed constitutional amendments, new apportionments or redistricting for legislative or congressional purposes, tax legislation, and program legislation may stumble on electoral minority tactics. The state of Washington has witnessed repeated successes of minority interest groups operating through the courts and through a nonrepresentative legislature to prevent the apparent desire of the majority of voters to redistrict the state for population representation in the legislature, for the use of a state income tax, and for other matters. Yet the constitutional difficulties of the state have not produced on balance either poor government in an administrative sense or a government generally failing to meet the program needs of the citizens. If these dire results had come about, constitutional change might be easier!

★ Politics

Active state participation in federalism no doubt requires organizational, administrative, and constitutional reforms in the states. But it requires more than these. And it is this "more" that seems most difficult to identify. The goal of reasonable prosperity with a reasonable distribution of the prosperity among the state's citizens has been discussed earlier. Too great differences in wealth among the states may mitigate against a meaningful federalism for the lower quarter of states just as a minimal economic base appears necessary for democracy in nations.

A political leadership with a sense of responsibility and with dreams for the future can give state government quality and a glow that encourages citizen participation. States such as California, New York, Oregon, Washington, and Wisconsin that were touched in varying ways by the Progressive-Populist-reform movements during the early decades of this century, have never lost a sense of leadership, a sense of a job to be done, and a tradition in the carrying on of state services.

Two-party competition, or even continuing, competing factions within one party, to secure the interest and support of voters for major programs and policies widely discussed and debated characterizes the leading states. As in the national government, significant programs passed by one party and accepted by the voters as desirable soon receive the acclaim of the opposition who wish merely to administer them better. When parties or factions debate endlessly over small issues and, instead of providing the voters with forward-looking leadership, show a willingness to pay off in patronage and corruption, voter interest is low. Then state-elected and -appointed positions are low in prestige, service opportunities, or professional career development. The failure of a state's leadership to develop a reasonably distinguished state government affects the state's federal relationship with the national government and the ability of its local governments to perform their roles.

How does the state establish a tradition for good government? What has been the combination of forces that has given some states a forward-looking political leadership and other states a normally petty, self-seeking leadership? As political scientists and as citizens, we need to search for answers to these crucial questions.

Groups and Change

Since changes often produce other changes, have events in our several states assumed a predetermined course that has not been shaped or molded or willed by organizations of human beings? In part, yes, but it also seems evident that many groups and individuals have altered many aspects of state and local government materially. Reform succeeds here and fails there as a result of the differences in activities of groups supporting and opposing it. And these groups have been of all varieties, organized on a national, state-wide, or local basis.

★ National organizations

Although there are many nationally organized pressure groups and several national political parties, the organization that has led the field in state and local government reorganization has been the National Municipal League. Never having had a large budget nor many thousands of members, the League has nevertheless achieved widespread recognition for the reforms it suggests and promotes. Its name is deceiving, it being neither a league of civic groups nor interested solely in municipal government. It is largely an organization of forward-looking citizens who wish to promote better state and local government within the framework of democratic ideals. The League's program has been broad, but perhaps it is best known for its Model City Charter and Model State Constitution, and its monthly periodical, the *National Civic Review* (formerly the *National Municipal Review*). Together the model charter and constitution spell out what the League thinks are desirable basic laws for city and state, including basic organization, powers, and procedures. The council-manager plan for cities and more responsible state government under a strong governor and a unicameral legislature have been some of the notable features of these documents.

The model law program of the League, a program of drawing up what League members consider "model" laws, has gone much beyond the model charter and constitution, however. Election laws, civil service laws, budget acts—these and many more are numbered among the League publications of model laws. In addition, the League sponsors annual national conferences on government; it acts in an advisory capacity to countless civic groups throughout the country who have been engaged in campaigning for government improvements; and in general it is in the forefront of state and local reform, acting in the role of a guide and stimulator.

Many a political party has sponsored changes in state and local government, but seldom have they originated the movements for change. The very nature of state and local parties in the United States assures to other groups or individuals the task of suggesting initially the desirable change. After a sufficiently large movement has developed in support of a proposal, some political party, frequently both major parties, will adopt it in their platforms. At other times when party support for a suggested change is not forthcoming, interested pressure groups work directly on the legislators, the voters, or other appropriate groups or persons to accomplish their aim.

There are dozens of important national organizations of state or local officials that play a major part in adapting state and local government to new conditions. The Council of State Governments, an organization of the several state governments, has come forth with many excellent suggestions for the reorganization of state and local government and the improvement of state-local relations. It leans toward a states'-rights viewpoint, and as a result it occasionally comes in conflict with the national government's policies and also with organizations of local government officials. Capably led, and relatively well financed, it is by far the most powerful of the many national organizations of state officials.

Whereas the Council of State Governments purports to speak for the several state governments as a whole, numerous associations of functional officials try to promote the interests of their particular activity as they see them. Virtually every public function is represented by at least one association—welfare, health, education, highways, agriculture. The goals of such groups are quite limited. Most of them attempt to improve the professional standards in their fields by raising the educational requirements for employment or by extending university education and courses in their fields. Frequently they are solicitous to prevent encroachments by others on their own field, and occasionally they work at cross-purposes to the Council of State Governments or to each other. Most typically they desire their function of government to be better financed, better administered, and better appreciated, and they seek maximum freedom from over-all control by legislature or governor to this end.

On a local level, likewise, there are national organizations of officials. The American Municipal Association, which is the national federation of leagues of municipalities, labors continually for increased powers for city governments, including enlarged sources of revenue. The International City Managers Association is more interested in the broader problems of administrative management on a city level, and especially in assuring that city managers everywhere will be men of high professional standards and ability. Similar in interest to the American Municipal Association is the United States Conference of Mayors, while an organization of city councilmen was created in 1950. The law officers, finance officers, public relations officers, and other municipal officials also have their associations.

County officers have been somewhat slower to organize, and the relatively young National Association of County Officials has not yet reached the strength in membership, leadership, publication, or research that has characterized the municipal league movement for many years. Some county department heads belong to specialized associations, however. Some of these on a national level combine in their membership national, state, and county officials. An example would be the American Public Welfare Association, to which county welfare executives commonly belong side by side with city, state, and national welfare workers. Many county health officers belong to the American Public Health Association, together with health officials of other levels and private individuals interested in public health activities. Superintendents of schools, county agriculture agents, engineers, and sheriffs all have associations. Policy questions concerning the particular function of interest to these groups are debated, resolved upon, and translated into action if at all possible.

In the field of private organizations, there are numerous national associations that lobby for, or in some way promote, change. The Governmental Research Association stimulates research, particularly on subjects concerning state and local finance. Since research may bring forth action in legislative halls and administrative offices, the influence of such a group can be considerable. Not concentrating its activities on research is the national League of Women Voters. It does carry on some background research but is mainly interested in a broad educational program on public policies. Most of its publications are devoted to this end. Through its many tireless workers in local and state chapters, the League has been involved in nearly every major campaign for better state and city government and in many a county fight as well.

Some organizations have more specialized purposes, such as the National Civil Service League, interested in improving and extending the use of the merit system. The Proportional Representation League has carried on a program of education and promotion of action for the adoption of the Hare system of voting. There truly seems to be an organization for every purpose, as the long list of associations contained in the standard directory will testify.[1]

★ State and local organizations

Many national associations have chapters or counterparts that carry on more or less complementary activities at state and local levels. In several functional fields, associations of state and local officials in individual states parallel the national spiderweb of organizations. Education is a field that almost always has one or more such groups (e.g., state education associations), and they are to be found in welfare, health, law enforcement, and other areas of governmental activity. There are, of course, many local officer groups organized on a state level, including county government asso-

[1] For a list of organizations and a brief statement of their activities and publications, see Public Administration Clearing House, *Public Administration Organizations, A Directory, 1954* (Chicago). A directory of research organizations is published by the Governmental Research Association, *GRA Directory*, issued biennially (New York).

ciations, leagues of municipalities, and county, municipal, and school-district groups, more specialized than the former two. The end in view of most of these organizations is to promote legislation of interest to them before the state legislature, to represent their members before state administrative agencies on occasion, and further to interchange technical information and the administrative experiences of the various units of local government. Sometimes state agencies are instrumental in organizing state-wide associations of local officials as a means of promoting state-local contacts.

Taxpayer groups, chambers of commerce, labor unions, and farm associations all have special organizations on all levels of government—national, state, and local. None of these organizations as such has distinctive programs for general state or local reform, although they join in campaigns for better government from time to time as the exigencies of the situation seem to warrant. Perhaps because of their older status as associations, their more secure positions and their greater concern over tax burdens, taxpayer groups and chambers of commerce have shown more interest in general reorganization questions than have labor and farm groups. Most of the energies of all these associations are consumed in advancing political and legislative action of special concern to them, action that has a special functional slant such as labor regulation, farm supports, and business legislation.

Political parties are generally present in greater or lesser strength on state and local levels, but few party organizations have taken up the banner of reorganization, unless it be an "out" party that wants to embarrass the "ins" in order to obtain political preferment. The most active leaders of general reform on a state-wide or local basis have been nonparty groups such as the League of Women Voters, local civic and good-government organizations, and occasionally professors of political science and public administration. The latter have given mostly of their technical knowledge, the former two groups, of their organizing drive and enthusiasm.

No list of active associations supporting or opposing changes in state and local government could be complete except for a limited area and a short period of time. New ones constantly arise, and old ones drop out or change their programs. A different set of organizations supports each proposal for change. It is not unusual for one group to oppose one reform measure and vigorously favor another. In a country crisscrossed with thousands of special pressure groups, it is only natural that few general-interest organizations should exist and that they should attract relatively few members. The practice of such general-interest groups is to amalgamate with special pressure groups from time to time to effect change in directions they desire.

★ Resistance to change

Neither the forces of continuing technological and environmental changes nor the forces of groups organized to bring about change readily bring change nor melt all the forces of resistance to change.

★ Need for variation

We pride ourselves on the values of state and local government to a democratic society. One of these values inheres in the fact that groups that are minorities in the large national scene may become majorities in smaller units of state and local government. A minority may wish to effectuate or resist certain changes, and if the decisions thereon are left to state and local units some will decide one way and some another. In a sense the state and local governments constitute a vast governmental laboratory. While all the experiments and variations may not be worth copying, lack of uniformity is an unavoidable result. Consequently, we can point to some very efficient and progressive states and localities, especially certain cities and a few states, and we also may point to some very inefficient and unprogressive units, especially certain counties. Then again a unit that is modern and progressive in one or a few respects, may be the opposite in others.

The very variety of people and conditions would lead one to conclude that a uniform solution for all state and local governments is not acceptable. Federalism in fact was adopted to permit differences. One can only label as "unfortunate" the tendency among reformers and among firms of consultants who advise our civic and official groups, to recommend a uniform pattern of organization and procedure for every agency they visit or investigate. Just as in baseball each individual adapts his own stance in the batter's box, deviating a little this way or that from what are considered to be the best basic principles, so in government we must recognize that each state and locality has peculiar circumstances and must choose or invent its own solutions to many of its governmental problems. Adoption of rigid patterns may increase the resistance to change.

★ Dynamic forces

Resistance to change in cities and counties is heightened by the fact that, taken separately, each of these units of local government is affected by fewer dynamic forces in our society than is the nation. The states are in an intermediate position in this regard. As a whole, the nation is becoming more integrated. Social and economic changes are taking place on a nation-wide or at least on a region-wide scale. As a result, the adaptations of government to meet economic and social changes must be made primarily on a national and only secondarily on a state or local level. It is possible that certain states or localities may be quite isolated from rather general nation-wide phenomena. For example, while the population of the nation as a whole may grow tremendously, the population of several states and many localities could decrease. The services demanded by the citizens of their government may not be altered in the slightest by depression or inflation in certain areas, while on a national scale the services demanded enlarge very greatly. More and more the role of the national government has been to cushion the shock of social and economic changes on state and local govern-ments, and the states, in turn, must labor to assist all of their local govern-mental units.

To the extent that this has been successfully accomplished, this prac-tice has unwittingly perhaps but nevertheless actually discouraged changes in state and local governments. One of the most important contributors to change in states, cities, and counties—indeed in any social institution—is the pressure of numerous social and economic changes of all varieties. Change does not take place in a vacuum. It is part of a chain reaction. To the extent that the national government and state governments are creat-ing a semivacuum of constancy for state or local governments, they dis-courage the forces making for reform in these units.

★ Role of the expert

Resistance to change has also been increased by a lack of appreciation in some state and local governments of the role of the expert. Professionaliza-tion of personnel has been a driving force for change on the national level, but the lack of professionalization in many local governments and some states, whether through ignorance or lack of need, is striking. To put the matter another way, the idea that a man can be jack of all trades including that of public administration implies a type of governmental organization unlike that implied in a theory that values the role of the expert in execut-ing policies democratically arrived at. In many localities small government, indeed petty government, still exists. There are no experts, there are no professionally competent individuals employed, and as a result problems of professionalization or of bigness have not forced a change, since the theories of Jacksonian democracy first were popular. When technical advice is essential, most localities depend on the states. In cases where the states fail to render such help, or where local needs are so insistent that experts must be employed, problems of governmental reorganization have arisen al-most immediately. It is not surprising that state and local government re-form has proceeded at a rapid pace in those states where changes in popula-tion and environmental factors are great and hence the need for experts and professionalism important. California is an excellent example; so are many of the cities in Texas.

★ Tradition and vested interests

Tradition does not always produce vitality in government and a professionalism that examines new ideas and anticipates changes. Tradition can mean an apathetic acceptance of the way things always have been done, a feeling of "live and let live," a fear of change and possible displacement of long-held privileges.

Vested interests are innumerable. The position of employees under the existing governmental arrangements, the prerogatives of political parties or political groups in connection with spoils and election systems, the stake of certain people in maintaining the current plan of rural-urban relations or of property tax assessment—all these situations and many more contribute to a feeling on the part of certain individuals that they have a personal stake in maintaining the present local system, whatever that may be. At any rate, whenever a change is proposed in a state or local government a number of persons benefiting from the present system resist the proposal.

The desire to resist is reinforced if the proposal is made by someone from outside the present system. It may seem as if external forces are trying to obtain a change for their own interests as against those who have some position in the present system. Furthermore, many changes are likely to ignore or to go contrary to some of the established patterns in the unit of government. Consequently, those who have power under the present system may feel that a proposal for change made by any group other than their own is a personal attack on them and hence to be opposed. It may be that they lack adequate information or they may simply have unwarranted fears, but nonetheless their beliefs are very real.

These factors explain why many public employees frequently resist change in the government they serve. They are asked to give up certainty for at least some uncertainty. Similarly, the factors enumerated explain much of the resistance of certain labor unions and other organized groups to changes in governmental procedure and organization; any group that is in power in a particular unit is likely to feel that any change may result in its being ousted. There are instances where chambers of commerce have opposed modifications in city government that are generally conceded to be desirable simply because the proposals emanated from labor and the businessmen were afraid that the net result of the change might be a labor victory at the polls.

Such fears are not ill founded. On a local government level changes in organization and procedure are frequently followed by a shift in actual political control. As a matter of fact, one of the best ways to get a change in the personnel of public officialdom in a city is to have an all-out charter campaign. The civic interest stirred up by a charter campaign frequently results in new people running for office, and hence further change is promoted. This factor is especially true of local government reorganization as compared with state and national, since most city and some county reform must be effected by means of local referendums. Unlike most reform on the higher levels of government, local government reform is therefore a matter for the average man on the street to be concerned about.

Conclusion

Work and research are needed to answer the questions of what changes are needed and how to bring about these changes in state and local government with the general goals of making our democracy and our federal system operate effectively in a changing world. To quote the *Report* of The Commission on Intergovernmental Relations:

> The strengthening of State and local governments is essentially a task for the States themselves. Thomas Jefferson observed that the only way in which the States can erect a barrier against the extension of National power into areas within their proper sphere is "to strengthen the State governments, and as this cannot be done by any change in the Federal Constitution . . . it must be done by the States themselves. . . ." He explained: "The only barrier in their power is a wise government. A weak one will lose ground in every contest." [2]

2 The Commission on Intergovernmental Relations, *A Report to the President for Transmittal to the Congress* (Washington, D. C.: Government Printing Office, June 1955), p. 37. The quotation from Jefferson is cited as: Letter to Archibald Stuart, Dec. 23, 1791, from Paul L. Ford (ed.), *The Writings of Thomas Jefferson*, Vol. V (New York, 1892), pp. 409-410.

Appendix

THE CONSTITUTION OF THE
STATE OF ALASKA

Agreed upon by the
DELEGATES OF THE PEOPLE OF ALASKA
University of Alaska
February 5, 1956

PREAMBLE

We the people of Alaska, grateful to God and to those who founded our nation and pioneered this great land, in order to secure and transmit to succeeding generations our heritage of political, civil, and religious liberty within the Union of States, do ordain and establish this constitution for the State of Alaska.

ARTICLE I
DECLARATION OF RIGHTS

SECTION 1. **Inherent Rights.** This constitution is dedicated to the principles that all persons have a natural right to life, liberty, the pursuit of happiness, and the enjoyment of the rewards of their own industry; that all persons are equal and entitled to equal rights, opportunities, and protection under the law; and that all persons have corresponding obligations to the people and to the State.

SECTION 2. **Source of Government.** All political power is inherent in the people. All government originates with the people, is founded upon their will only, and is instituted solely for the good of the people as a whole.

SECTION 3. **Civil Rights.** No person is to be denied the enjoyment of any civil or political right because of race, color, creed, or national origin. The legislature shall implement this section.

SECTION 4. **Freedom of Religion.** No law shall be made respecting an establishment of religion, or prohibiting the free exercise thereof.

SECTION 5. **Freedom of Speech.** Every person may freely speak, write, and publish on all subjects, being responsible for the abuse of that right.

SECTION 6. **Assembly; Petition.** The right of the people peaceably to assemble, and to petition the government shall never be abridged.

SECTION 7. **Due Process.** No person shall be deprived of life, liberty, or property, without due process of law. The right of all persons to fair and just treatment in the course of legislative and executive investigations shall not be infringed.

SECTION 8. **Grand Jury.** No person shall be held to answer for a capital, or otherwise infamous crime, unless on a presentment or indictment of a grand jury, except in cases arising in the armed forces in time of war or public danger. Indictment may be waived by the accused. In that case the prosecution shall be by information. The grand jury shall consist of at least twelve citizens, a majority of whom concurring may return an indictment. The power of grand juries to investigate and make recommendations concerning the public welfare or safety shall never be suspended.

SECTION 9. **Jeopardy and Self-Incrimination.** No person shall be put in jeopardy twice for the same offense. No person shall be compelled in any criminal proceeding to be a witness against himself.

SECTION 10. **Treason.** Treason against the State consists only in levying war against it, or in adhering to its enemies, giving them aid and comfort. No person shall be convicted of treason, unless on the testimony of two witnesses to the same overt act, or on confession in open court.

SECTION 11. **Rights of Accused.** In all criminal prosecutions, the accused shall have the right to a speedy and public trial, by an impartial jury of twelve, except that the legislature may provide for a jury of not more than twelve nor less than six in courts not of record. The accused is entitled to be informed of the nature and cause of the accusation; to be released on bail, except for capital offenses when the proof is evident or the presumption great; to be confronted with the witnesses against him; to have compulsory process for obtaining witnesses in his favor, and to have the assistance of counsel for his defense.

SECTION 12. **Excessive Punishment.** Excessive bail shall not be required, nor excessive fines imposed, nor cruel and unusual punishments inflicted. Penal administration shall be based on the principle of reformation and upon the need for protecting the public.

SECTION 13. **Habeas Corpus.** The privilege of the writ of habeas corpus shall not be suspended, unless when in cases of rebellion or actual or imminent invasion, the public safety requires it.

SECTION 14. **Searches and Seizures.** The right of the people to be secure in their persons, houses and other property, papers, and effects, against unreasonable searches and seizures, shall not be violated. No warrants shall issue, but upon probable cause, supported by oath or affirmation, and particularly describing the place to be searched, and the persons or things to be seized.

SECTION 15. **Prohibited State Action.** No bill of attainder or ex post facto law shall be passed. No law impairing the obligation of contracts, and no law making any irrevocable grant of special privileges or immunities shall be passed. No conviction shall work corruption of blood or forfeiture of estate.

SECTION 16. **Civil Suits; Trial by Jury.** In civil cases where the amount in controversy exceeds two hundred fifty dollars, the right of trial by a jury of twelve is preserved to the same extent as it existed at common law. The legislature may make provision for a verdict by not less than three-fourths of the jury and, in courts not of record, may provide for a jury of not less than six or more than twelve.

SECTION 17. **Imprisonment for Debt.** There shall be no imprisonment for debt. This section does not prohibit civil arrest of absconding debtors.

SECTION 18. **Eminent Domain.** Private property shall not be taken or damaged for public use without just compensation.

SECTION 19. **Right to Bear Arms.** A well-regulated militia being necessary to the security of a free state, the right of the people to keep and bear arms shall not be infringed.

SECTION 20. **Quartering Soldiers.** No member of the armed forces shall in time of peace be quartered in any house without the consent of the owner or occupant, or in time of war except as prescribed by law. The military shall be in strict subordination to the civil power.

SECTION 21. **Construction.** The enumeration of rights in this constitution shall not impair or deny others retained by the people.

ARTICLE II
THE LEGISLATURE

SECTION 1. **Legislative Power; Membership.** The legislative power of the State is vested in a legislature consisting of a senate with a membership of twenty and a house of representatives with a membership of forty.

SECTION 2. **Members: Qualifications.** A member of the legislature shall be a qualified voter who has been a resident of Alaska for at least three years and of the district from which elected for at least one year, immediately preceding his filing for office. A senator shall be at least twenty-five years of age and a representative at least twenty-one years of age.

SECTION 3. **Election and Terms.** Legislators shall be elected at general elections. Their terms begin on the fourth Monday of the January following election unless otherwise provided by law. The term of representatives shall be two years, and the term of senators, four years. One-half of the senators shall be elected every two years.

SECTION 4. **Vacancies.** A vacancy in the legislature shall be filled for the unexpired term as provided by law. If no provision is made, the governor shall fill the vacancy by appointment.

SECTION 5. **Disqualifications.** No legislator may hold any other office or position of profit under the United States or the State. During the term for which elected and for one year thereafter, no legislator may be nominated, elected, or appointed to any other office or position of profit which has been created, or the salary or emoluments of which have been increased, while he was a member. This section shall not prevent any person from seeking or holding the office of governor, secretary of state, or member of Congress. This section shall not apply to employment by or election to a constitutional convention.

SECTION 6. **Immunities.** Legislators may not be held to answer before any other tribunal for any statement made in the exercise of their legislative duties while the legislature is in session. Members attending, going to, or returning from legislative sessions are not subject to civil process and are privileged from arrest except for felony or breach of the peace.

SECTION 7. **Salary and Expenses.** Legislators shall receive annual salaries. They may receive a per diem allowance for expenses while in session and are entitled to travel expenses going to and from sessions. Presiding officers may receive additional compensation.

SECTION 8. **Regular Sessions.** The legislature shall convene each year on the fourth Monday in January, but the month and day may be changed by law.

SECTION 9. **Special Sessions.** Special sessions may be called by the governor or by vote of two-thirds of the legislators. The vote may be conducted by the legislative council or as prescribed by law. At special sessions called by the governor, legislation shall be limited to subjects designated in his proclamation calling the session or to subjects presented by him. Special sessions are limited to thirty days.

SECTION 10. **Adjournment.** Neither house may adjourn or recess for longer than three days unless the other concurs. If the two houses cannot agree on the time of adjournment and either house certifies the disagreement to the governor, he may adjourn the legislature.

SECTION 11. **Interim Committees.** There shall be a legislative council, and the legislature may establish other interim committees. The council and other interim committees may meet between legislative sessions. They may perform duties and employ personnel as provided by the legislature. Their members may receive an allowance for expenses while performing their duties.

SECTION 12. **Rules.** The houses of each legislature shall adopt uniform rules of procedure. Each house may choose its officers and employees. Each is the judge of the election and qualifications of its members and may expel a member with the concurrence of two-thirds of its members. Each shall keep a journal of its proceedings. A majority of the membership of each house constitutes a quorum to do business, but a smaller number may adjourn from day to day and may compel attendance of absent members. The legislature shall regulate lobbying.

SECTION 13. **Form of Bills.** Every bill shall be confined to one subject unless it is an appropriation bill or one codifying, revising, or rearranging existing laws. Bills for appropriations shall be confined to appropriations. The subject of each bill shall be expressed in the title. The enacting clause shall be: "Be it enacted by the Legislature of the State of Alaska."

SECTION 14. **Passage of Bills.** The legislature shall establish the procedure for enactment of bills into law. No bill may become law unless it has passed three readings in each house on three separate days, except that any bill may be advanced from second to third reading on the same day by concurrence of three-fourths of the house considering it. No bill may become law without an affirmative vote of a majority of the membership of each house. The yeas and nays on final passage shall be entered in the journal.

SECTION 15. **Veto.** The governor may veto bills passed by the legislature. He may, by veto, strike or reduce items in appropriation bills. He shall return any vetoed bill, with a statement of his objections, to the house of origin.

SECTION 16. **Action upon Veto.** Upon receipt of a veto message, the legislature shall meet immediately in joint session and reconsider passage of the vetoed bill or item. Bills to raise revenue and appropriation bills or items, although vetoed, become law by affirmative vote of three-fourths of the membership of the legislature. Other vetoed bills become law by affirmative vote of two-thirds of the membership of the legislature. The vote on reconsideration of a vetoed bill shall be entered on the journals of both houses.

SECTION 17. **Bills Not Signed.** A bill becomes law if, while the legislature is in session, the governor neither signs nor vetoes it within fifteen days, Sundays excepted, after its delivery to him. If the legislature is not in session and the governor neither signs nor vetoes a bill within twenty days, Sundays excepted, after its delivery to him, the bill becomes law.

SECTION 18. **Effective Date.** Laws passed by the legislature become effective ninety days after enactment. The legislature may, by concurrence of two-thirds of the membership of each house, provide for another effective date.

SECTION 19. **Local or Special Acts.** The legislature shall pass no local or special act if a general act can be made applicable. Whether a general act can be made applicable shall be subject to judicial determination. Local acts necessitating appropriations by a political subdivision may not become effective unless approved by a majority of the qualified voters voting thereon in the subdivision affected.

SECTION 20. **Impeachment.** All civil officers of the State are subject to impeachment by the legislature. Impeach-ment shall originate in the senate and must be approved by a two-thirds vote of its members. The motion for impeachment shall list fully the basis for the proceeding. Trial on impeachment shall be conducted by the house of representatives. A supreme court justice designated by the court shall preside at the trial. Concurrence of two-thirds of the members of the house is required for a judgment of impeachment. The judgment may not extend beyond removal from office, but shall not prevent proceedings in the courts on the same or related charges.

SECTION 21. **Suits against the State.** The legislature shall establish procedures for suits against the State.

ARTICLE III
THE EXECUTIVE

SECTION 1. **Executive Power.** The executive power of the State is vested in the governor.

SECTION 2. **Governor: Qualifications.** The governor shall be at least thirty years of age and a qualified voter of the State. He shall have been a resident of Alaska at least seven years immediately preceding his filing for office, and he shall have been a citizen of the United States for at least seven years.

SECTION 3. **Election.** The governor shall be chosen by the qualified voters of the State at a general election. The candidate receiving the greatest number of votes shall be governor.

SECTION 4. **Term of Office.** The term of office of the governor is four years, beginning at noon on the first Monday in December following his election and ending at noon on the first Monday in December four years later.

SECTION 5. **Limit on Tenure.** No person who has been elected governor for two full successive terms shall be again eligible to hold that office until one full term has intervened.

SECTION 6. **Dual Office Holding.** The governor shall not hold any other office or position of profit under the United States, the State, or its political subdivisions.

SECTION 7. **Secretary of State:**

Duties. There shall be a secretary of state. He shall have the same qualifications as the governor and serve for the same term. He shall perform such duties as may be prescribed by law and as may be delegated to him by the governor.

SECTION 8. **Election.** The secretary of state shall be nominated in the manner provided by law for nominating candidates for other elective offices. In the general election the votes cast for a candidate for governor shall be considered as cast also for the candidate for secretary of state running jointly with him. The candidate whose name appears on the ballot jointly with that of the successful candidate for governor shall be elected secretary of state.

SECTION 9. **Acting Governor.** In case of the temporary absence of the governor from office, the secretary of state shall serve as acting governor.

SECTION 10. **Succession: Failure to Qualify.** If the governor-elect dies, resigns, or is disqualified, the secretary of state elected with him shall succeed to the office of governor for the full term. If the governor-elect fails to assume office for any other reason, the secretary of state elected with him shall serve as acting governor, and shall succeed to the office if the governor-elect does not assume his office within six months of the beginning of the term.

SECTION 11. **Vacancy.** In case of a vacancy in the office of governor for any reason, the secretary of state shall succeed to the office for the remainder of the term.

SECTION 12. **Absence.** Whenever for a period of six months, a governor has been continuously absent from office or has been unable to discharge the duties of his office by reason of mental or physical disability, the office shall be deemed vacant. The procedure for determining absence and disability shall be prescribed by law.

SECTION 13. **Further Succession.** Provision shall be made by law for succession to the office of governor and for an acting governor in the event that the secretary of state is unable to succeed to the office or act as governor. No election of a secretary of state shall be held except at the time of electing a governor.

SECTION 14. **Title and Authority.** When the secretary of state succeeds to the office of governor, he shall have the title, powers, duties, and emoluments of that office.

SECTION 15. **Compensation.** The compensation of the governor and the secretary of state shall be prescribed by law and shall not be diminished during their term of office, unless by general law applying to all salaried officers of the State.

SECTION 16. **Governor: Authority.** The governor shall be responsible for the faithful execution of the laws. He may, by appropriate court action or proceeding brought in the name of the State, enforce compliance with any constitutional or legislative mandate, or restrain violation of any constitutional or legislative power, duty, or right by any officer, department, or agency of the State or any of its political subdivisions. This authority shall not be construed to authorize any action or proceeding against the legislature.

SECTION 17. **Convening Legislature.** Whenever the governor considers it in the public interest, he may convene the legislature, either house, or the two houses in joint session.

SECTION 18. **Messages to Legislature.** The governor shall, at the beginning of each session, and may at other times, give the legislature information concerning the affairs of the State and recommend the measures he considers necessary.

SECTION 19. **Military Authority.** The governor is commander-in-chief of the armed forces of the State. He may call out these forces to execute the laws, suppress or prevent insurrection or lawless violence, or repel invasion. The governor, as provided by law, shall appoint all general and flag officers of the armed forces of the State, subject to confirmation by a majority of the members of the legislature in joint session. He shall appoint and commission all other officers.

SECTION 20. **Martial Law.** The governor may proclaim martial law when the public safety requires it in case of rebellion or actual or imminent invasion. Martial law shall not continue for longer than twenty days without the approval of a majority of the members of the legislature in joint session.

SECTION 21. **Executive Clemency.** Subject to procedure prescribed by law, the governor may grant pardons, commutations, and reprieves, and may suspend and remit fines and forfeitures. This power shall not extend to impeachment. A parole system shall be provided by law.

SECTION 22. **Executive Branch.** All executive and administrative offices, departments, and agencies of the state government and their respective functions, powers, and duties shall be allocated by law among and within not more than twenty principal departments, so as to group them as far as practicable according to major purposes. Regulatory, quasi-judicial, and temporary agencies may be established by law and need not be allocated within a principal department.

SECTION 23. **Reorganization.** The governor may make changes in the organization of the executive branch or in the assignment of functions among its units which he considers necessary for efficient administration. Where these changes require the force of law, they shall be set forth in executive orders. The legislature shall have sixty days of a regular session, or a full session if of shorter duration, to disapprove these executive orders. Unless disapproved by resolution concurred in by a majority of the members in joint session, these orders become effective at a date thereafter to be designated by the governor.

SECTION 24. **Supervision.** Each principal department shall be under the supervision of the governor.

SECTION 25. **Department Heads.** The head of each principal department shall be a single executive unless otherwise provided by law. He shall be appointed by the governor, subject to confirmation by a majority of the members of the legislature in joint session, and shall serve at the pleasure of the governor, except as otherwise provided in this article with respect to the secretary of state. The heads of all principal departments shall be citizens of the United States.

SECTION 26. **Boards and Commissions.** When a board or commission is at the head of a principal department or a regulatory or quasi-judicial agency, its members shall be appointed by the governor, subject to confirmation by a majority of the members of the legislature in joint session, and may be removed as provided by law. They shall be citizens of the United States. The board or commission may appoint a principal executive officer when authorized by law, but the appointment shall be subject to the approval of the governor.

SECTION 27. **Recess Appointments.** The governor may make appointments to fill vacancies occurring during a recess of the legislature, in offices requiring confirmation by the legislature. The duration of such appointments shall be prescribed by law.

ARTICLE IV
THE JUDICIARY

SECTION 1. **Judicial Power and Jurisdiction.** The judicial power of the State is vested in a supreme court, a superior court, and the courts established by the legislature. The jurisdiction of courts shall be prescribed by law. The courts shall constitute a unified judicial system for operation and administration. Judicial districts shall be established by law.

SECTION 2. **Supreme Court.** The supreme court shall be the highest court of the State, with final appellate jurisdiction. It shall consist of three justices, one of whom is chief justice. The number of justices may be increased by law upon the request of the supreme court.

SECTION 3. **Superior Court.** The superior court shall be the trial court of general jurisdiction and shall consist of five judges. The number of judges may be changed by law.

SECTION 4. **Qualifications of Jus-**

tices and **Judges.** Supreme court justices and superior court judges shall be citizens of the United States and of the State, licensed to practice law in the State, and possessing any additional qualifications prescribed by law. Judges of other courts shall be selected in a manner, for terms, and with qualifications prescribed by law.

SECTION 5. **Nomination and Appointment.** The governor shall fill any vacancy in an office of supreme court justice or superior court judge by appointing one of two or more persons nominated by the judicial council.

SECTION 6. **Approval or Rejection.** Each supreme court justice and superior court judge shall, in the manner provided by law, be subject to approval or rejection on a nonpartisan ballot at the first general election held more than three years after his appointment. Thereafter, each supreme court justice shall be subject to approval or rejection in a like manner every tenth year, and each superior court judge, every sixth year.

SECTION 7. **Vacancy.** The office of any supreme court justice or superior court judge becomes vacant ninety days after the election at which he is rejected by a majority of those voting on the question, or for which he fails to file his declaration of candidacy to succeed himself.

SECTION 8. **Judicial Council.** The judicial council shall consist of seven members. Three attorney members shall be appointed for six-year terms by the governing body of the organized state bar. Three non-attorney members shall be appointed for six-year terms by the governor subject to confirmation by a majority of the members of the legislature in joint session. Vacancies shall be filled for the unexpired term in like manner. Appointments shall be made with due consideration to area representation and without regard to political affiliation. The chief justice of the supreme court shall be ex officio the seventh member and chairman of the judicial council. No member of the judicial council, except the chief justice, may hold any other office or position of profit

under the United States or the State. The judicial council shall act by concurrence of four or more members and according to rules which it adopts.

SECTION 9. **Additional Duties.** The judicial council shall conduct studies for improvement of the administration of justice, and make reports and recommendations to the supreme court and to the legislature at intervals of not more than two years. The judicial council shall perform other duties assigned by law.

SECTION 10. **Incapacity of Judges.** Whenever the judicial council certifies to the governor that a supreme court justice appears to be so incapacitated as substantially to prevent him from performing his judicial duties, the governor shall appoint a board of three persons to inquire into the circumstances, and may on the board's recommendation retire the justice. Whenever a judge of another court appears to be so incapacitated as substantially to prevent him from performing his judicial duties, the judicial council shall recommend to the supreme court that the judge be placed under early retirement. After notice and hearing, the supreme court by majority vote of its members may retire the judge.

SECTION 11. **Retirement.** Justices and judges shall be retired at the age of seventy except as provided in this article. The basis and amount of retirement pay shall be prescribed by law. Retired judges shall render no further service on the bench except for special assignments as provided by court rule.

SECTION 12. **Impeachment.** Impeachment of any justice or judge for malfeasance or misfeasance in the performance of his official duties shall be according to procedure prescribed for civil officers.

SECTION 13. **Compensation.** Justices, judges, and members of the judicial council shall receive compensation as prescribed by law. Compensation of justices and judges shall not be diminished during their terms of office, unless by general law applying to all salaried officers of the State.

SECTION 14. **Restrictions.** Supreme

court justices and superior court judges while holding office may not practice law, hold office in a political party, or hold any other office or position of profit under the United States, the State, or its political subdivisions. Any supreme court justice or superior court judge filing for another elective public office forfeits his judicial position.

SECTION 15. **Rule-making Power.** The supreme court shall make and promulgate rules governing the administration of all courts. It shall make and promulgate rules governing practice and procedure in civil and criminal cases in all courts. These rules may be changed by the legislature by two-thirds vote of the members elected to each house.

SECTION 16. **Court Administration.** The chief justice of the supreme court shall be the administrative head of all courts. He may assign judges from one court or division thereof to another for temporary service. The chief justice shall, with the approval of the supreme court, appoint an administrative director to serve at his pleasure and to supervise the administrative operations of the judicial system.

ARTICLE V
SUFFRAGE AND ELECTIONS

SECTION 1. **Qualified Voters.** Every citizen of the United States who is at least nineteen years of age, who meets registration requirements which may be prescribed by law, and who is qualified to vote under this article, may vote in any state or local election. He shall have been, immediately preceding the election, for one year a resident of Alaska and for thirty days a resident of the election district in which he seeks to vote. He shall be able to read or speak the English language as prescribed by law, unless prevented by physical disability. Additional voting qualifications may be prescribed by law for bond issue elections of political subdivisions.

SECTION 2. **Disqualifications.** No person may vote who has been convicted of a felony involving moral turpitude unless his civil rights have been restored. No person may vote who has been ju-dicially determined to be of unsound mind unless the disability has been removed.

SECTION 3. **Methods of Voting; Election Contests.** Methods of voting, including absentee voting, shall be prescribed by law. Secrecy of voting shall be preserved. The procedure for determining election contests, with right of appeal to the courts, shall be prescribed by law.

SECTION 4. **Voting Precincts; Registration.** The legislature may provide a system of permanent registration of voters, and may establish voting precincts within election districts.

SECTION 5. **General Elections.** General elections shall be held on the second Tuesday in October of every even-numbered year, but the month and day may be changed by law.

ARTICLE VI
LEGISLATIVE APPORTIONMENT

SECTION 1. **Election Districts.** Members of the house of representatives shall be elected by the qualified voters of the respective election districts. Until reapportionment, election districts and the number of representatives to be elected from each district shall be as set forth in Section 1 of Article XIV.

SECTION 2. **Senate Districts.** Members of the senate shall be elected by the qualified voters of the respective senate districts. Senate districts shall be as set forth in Section 2 of Article XIV, subject to changes authorized in this article.

SECTION 3. **Reapportionment of House.** The governor shall reapportion the house of representatives immediately following the official reporting of each decennial census of the United States. Reapportionment shall be based upon civilian population within each election district as reported by the census.

SECTION 4. **Method.** Reapportionment shall be by the method of equal proportions, except that each election district having the major fraction of the quotient obtained by dividing total civilian population by forty shall have one representative.

SECTION 5. **Combining Districts.**

APPENDIX - 481

Should the total civilian population within any election district fall below one-half of the quotient, the district shall be attached to an election district within its senate district, and the reapportionment for the new district shall be determined as provided in Section 4 of this article.

SECTION 6. **Redistricting.** The governor may further redistrict by changing the size and area of election districts, subject to the limitations of this article. Each new district so created shall be formed of contiguous and compact territory containing as nearly as practicable a relatively integrated socio-economic area. Each shall contain a population at least equal to the quotient obtained by dividing the total civilian population by forty. Consideration may be given to local government boundaries. Drainage and other geographic features shall be used in describing boundaries wherever possible.

SECTION 7. **Modification of Senate Districts.** The senate districts, described in Section 2 of Article XIV, may be modified to reflect changes in election districts. A district, although modified, shall retain its total number of senators and its approximate perimeter.

SECTION 8. **Reapportionment Board.** The governor shall appoint a reapportionment board to act in an advisory capacity to him. It shall consist of five members, none of whom may be public employees or officials. At least one member each shall be appointed from the Southeastern, Southcentral, Central, and Northwestern Senate Districts. Appointments shall be made without regard to political affiliation. Board members shall be compensated.

SECTION 9. **Organization.** The board shall elect one of its members chairman and may employ temporary assistants. Concurrence of three members is required for a ruling or determination, but a lesser number may conduct hearings or otherwise act for the board.

SECTION 10. **Reapportionment Plan and Proclamation.** Within ninety days following the official reporting of each decennial census, the board shall submit to the governor a plan for reapportionment and redistricting as provided in this article. Within ninety days after receipt of the plan, the governor shall issue a proclamation of reapportionment and redistricting. An accompanying statement shall explain any change from the plan of the board. The reapportionment and redistricting shall be effective for the election of members of the legislature until after the official reporting of the next decennial census.

SECTION 11. **Enforcement.** Any qualified voter may apply to the superior court to compel the governor, by mandamus or otherwise, to perform his reapportionment duties or to correct any error in redistricting or reapportionment. Application to compel the governor to perform his reapportionment duties must be filed within thirty days of the expiration of either of the two ninety-day periods specified in this article. Application to compel correction of any error in redistricting or reapportionment must be filed within thirty days following the proclamation. Original jurisdiction in these matters is hereby vested in the superior court. On appeal, the cause shall be reviewed by the supreme court upon the law and the facts.

ARTICLE VII
HEALTH, EDUCATION, AND WELFARE

SECTION 1. **Public Education.** The legislature shall by general law establish and maintain a system of public schools open to all children of the State, and may provide for other public educational institutions. Schools and institutions so established shall be free from sectarian control. No money shall be paid from public funds for the direct benefit of any religious or other private educational institution.

SECTION 2. **State University.** The University of Alaska is hereby established as the state university and constituted a body corporate. It shall have title to all real and personal property now or hereafter set aside for or conveyed to it. Its property shall be administered and disposed of according to law.

SECTION 3. **Board of Regents.** The University of Alaska shall be governed by a board of regents. The regents shall be appointed by the governor, subject to confirmation by a majority of the members of the legislature in joint session. The board shall, in accordance with law, formulate policy and appoint the president of the university. He shall be the executive officer of the board.

SECTION 4. **Public Health.** The legislature shall provide for the promotion and protection of public health.

SECTION 5. **Public Welfare.** The legislature shall provide for public welfare.

ARTICLE VIII
NATURAL RESOURCES

SECTION 1. **Statement of Policy.** It is the policy of the State to encourage the settlement of its land and the development of its resources by making them available for maximum use consistent with the public interest.

SECTION 2. **General Authority.** The legislature shall provide for the utilization, development, and conservation of all natural resources belonging to the State, including land and waters, for the maximum benefit of its people.

SECTION 3. **Common Use.** Wherever occurring in their natural state, fish, wildlife, and waters are reserved to the people for common use.

SECTION 4. **Sustained Yield.** Fish, forests, wildlife, grasslands, and all other replenishable resources belonging to the State shall be utilized, developed, and maintained on the sustained yield principle, subject to preferences among beneficial uses.

SECTION 5. **Facilities and Improvements.** The legislature may provide for facilities, improvements, and services to assure greater utilization, development, reclamation, and settlement of lands, and to assure fuller utilization and development of the fisheries, wildlife, and waters.

SECTION 6. **State Public Domain.** Lands and interests therein, including submerged and tidal lands, possessed or acquired by the State, and not used or intended exclusively for governmental purposes, constitute the state public domain. The legislature shall provide for the selection of lands granted to the State by the United States, and for the administration of the state public domain.

SECTION 7. **Special Purpose Sites.** The legislature may provide for the acquisition of sites, objects, and areas of natural beauty or of historic, cultural, recreational, or scientific value. It may reserve them from the public domain and provide for their administration and preservation for the use, enjoyment, and welfare of the people.

SECTION 8. **Leases.** The legislature may provide for the leasing of, and the issuance of permits for exploration of, any part of the public domain or interest therein, subject to reasonable concurrent uses. Leases and permits shall provide, among other conditions, for payment by the party at fault for damage or injury arising from noncompliance with terms governing concurrent use, and for forfeiture in the event of breach of conditions.

SECTION 9. **Sales and Grants.** Subject to the provisions of this section, the legislature may provide for the sale or grant of state lands, or interests therein, and establish sales procedures. All sales or grants shall contain such reservations to the State of all resources as may be required by Congress or the State and shall provide for access to these resources. Reservation of access shall not unnecessarily impair the owners' use, prevent the control of trespass, or preclude compensation for damage.

SECTION 10. **Public Notice.** No disposals or leases of state lands, or interests therein, shall be made without prior public notice and other safeguards of the public interest as may be prescribed by law.

SECTION 11. **Mineral Rights.** Discovery and appropriation shall be the basis for establishing a right in those minerals reserved to the State which, upon the date of ratification of this constitution by the people of Alaska. were subject to location under the federal mining laws. Prior discovery, location, and filing, as prescribed by law, shall establish a prior right to these minerals and also a prior right to permits, leases, and transferable licenses for their extraction. Continuation of these rights shall depend upon the performance of annual labor, or the payment of fees, rents, or royalties, or upon other requirements as may be prescribed by law. Surface uses of land by a mineral claimant shall be limited to those necessary for the extraction or basic processing of the mineral deposits, or for both. Discovery and appropriation shall initiate a right, subject to further requirements of law, to patent of mineral lands if authorized by the State and not prohibited by Congress. The provisions of this section shall apply to all other minerals reserved to the State which by law are declared subject to appropriation.

SECTION 12. **Mineral Leases and Permits.** The legislature shall provide for the issuance, types and terms of leases for coal, oil, gas, oil shale, sodium, phosphate, potash, sulfur, pumice, and other minerals as may be prescribed by law. Leases and permits giving the exclusive right of exploration for these minerals for specific periods and areas, subject to reasonable concurrent exploration as to different classes of minerals, may be authorized by law. Like leases and permits giving the exclusive right of prospecting by geophysical, geochemical, and similar methods for all minerals may also be authorized by law.

SECTION 13. **Water Rights.** All surface and subsurface waters reserved to the people for common use, except mineral and medicinal waters, are subject to appropriation. Priority of appropriation shall give prior right. Except for public water supply, an appropriation of water shall be limited to stated purposes and subject to preferences among beneficial uses, concurrent or otherwise, as prescribed by law, and to the general reservation of fish and wildlife.

SECTION 14. **Access to Navigable Waters.** Free access to the navigable or public waters of the State, as defined by the legislature, shall not be denied any citizen of the United States or resident of the State, except that the legislature may by general law regulate and limit such access for other beneficial uses or public purposes.

SECTION 15. **No Exclusive Right of Fishery.** No exclusive right or special privilege of fishery shall be created or authorized in the natural waters of the State.

SECTION 16. **Protection of Rights.** No person shall be involuntarily divested of his right to the use of waters, his interests in lands, or improvements affecting either, except for a superior beneficial use or public purpose and then only with just compensation and by operation of law.

SECTION 17. **Uniform Application.** Laws and regulations governing the use or disposal of natural resources shall apply equally to all persons similarly situated with reference to the subject matter and purpose to be served by the law or regulation.

SECTION 18. **Private Ways of Necessity.** Proceedings in eminent domain may be undertaken for private ways of necessity to permit essential access for extraction or utilization of resources. Just compensation shall be made for property taken or for resultant damages to other property rights.

ARTICLE IX
FINANCE AND TAXATION

SECTION 1. **Taxing Power.** The power of taxation shall never be surrendered. This power shall not be suspended or contracted away, except as provided in this article.

SECTION 2. **Nondiscrimination.** The lands and other property belonging to citizens of the United States residing without the State shall never be taxed at a higher rate than the lands and other property belonging to the residents of the State.

SECTION 3. **Assessment Standards.** Standards for appraisal of all property assessed by the State or its political subdivisions shall be prescribed by law.

SECTION 4. **Exemptions.** The real

and personal property of the State or its political subdivisions shall be exempt from taxation under conditions and exceptions which may be provided by law. All, or any portion of, property used exclusively for non-profit religious, charitable, cemetery, or educational purposes, as defined by law, shall be exempt from taxation. Other exemptions of like or different kind may be granted by general law. All valid existing exemptions shall be retained until otherwise provided by law.

SECTION 5. **Interests in Government Property.** Private leaseholds, contracts, or interests in land or property owned or held by the United States, the State, or its political subdivisions, shall be taxable to the extent of the interests.

SECTION 6. **Public Purpose.** No tax shall be levied, or appropriation of public money made, or public property transferred, nor shall the public credit be used, except for a public purpose.

SECTION 7. **Dedicated Funds.** The proceeds of any state tax or license shall not be dedicated to any special purpose, except when required by the federal government for state participation in federal programs. This provision shall not prohibit the continuance of any dedication for special purposes existing upon the date of ratification of this constitution by the people of Alaska.

SECTION 8. **State Debt.** No state debt shall be contracted unless authorized by law for capital improvements and ratified by a majority of the qualified voters of the State who vote on the question. The State may, as provided by law and without ratification, contract debt for the purpose of repelling invasion, suppressing insurrection, defending the State in war, meeting natural disasters, or redeeming indebtedness outstanding at the time this constitution becomes effective.

SECTION 9. **Local Debts.** No debt shall be contracted by any political subdivision of the State, unless authorized for capital improvements by its governing body and ratified by a majority vote of those qualified to vote and voting on the question.

SECTION 10. **Interim Borrowing.** The State and its political subdivisions may borrow money to meet appropriations for any fiscal year in anticipation of the collection of the revenues for that year, but all debt so contracted shall be paid before the end of the next fiscal year.

SECTION 11. **Exceptions.** The restrictions on contracting debt do not apply to debt incurred through the issuance of revenue bonds by a public enterprise or public corporation of the State or a political subdivision, when the only security is the revenues of the enterprise or corporation. The restrictions do not apply to indebtedness to be paid from special assessments on the benefited property, nor do they apply to refunding indebtedness of the State or its political subdivisions.

SECTION 12. **Budget.** The governor shall submit to the legislature, at a time fixed by law, a budget for the next fiscal year setting forth all proposed expenditures and anticipated income of all departments, offices, and agencies of the State. The governor, at the same time, shall submit a general appropriation bill to authorize the proposed expenditures, and a bill or bills covering recommendations in the budget for new or additional revenues.

SECTION 13. **Expenditures.** No money shall be withdrawn from the treasury except in accordance with appropriations made by law. No obligation for the payment of money shall be incurred except as authorized by law. Unobligated appropriations outstanding at the end of the period of time specified by law shall be void.

SECTION 14. **Legislative Post-audit.** The legislature shall appoint an auditor to serve at its pleasure. He shall be a certified public accountant. The auditor shall conduct post-audits as prescribed by law and shall report to the legislature and to the governor.

ARTICLE X
LOCAL GOVERNMENT

SECTION 1. **Purpose and Construction.** The purpose of this article is to provide for maximum local self-government with a minimum of local government units, and to prevent duplication of tax-levying jurisdictions. A liberal construction shall be given to the powers of local government units.

SECTION 2. **Local Government Powers.** All local government powers shall be vested in boroughs and cities. The State may delegate taxing powers to organized boroughs and cities only.

SECTION 3. **Boroughs.** The entire State shall be divided into boroughs, organized or unorganized. They shall be established in a manner and according to standards provided by law. The standards shall include population, geography, economy, transportation, and other factors. Each borough shall embrace an area and population with common interests to the maximum degree possible. The legislature shall classify boroughs and prescribe their powers and functions. Methods by which boroughs may be organized, incorporated, merged, consolidated, reclassified, or dissolved shall be prescribed by law.

SECTION 4. **Assembly.** The governing body of the organized borough shall be the assembly, and its composition shall be established by law or charter. Each city of the first class, and each city of any other class designated by law, shall be represented on the assembly by one or more members of its council. The other members of the assembly shall be elected from and by the qualified voters resident outside such cities.

SECTION 5. **Service Areas.** Service areas to provide special services within an organized borough may be established, altered, or abolished by the assembly, subject to the provisions of law or charter. A new service area shall not be established if, consistent with the purposes of this article, the new service can be provided by an existing service area, by incorporation as a city, or by annexation to a city. The assembly may authorize the levying of taxes, charges, or assessments within a service area to finance the special services.

SECTION 6. **Unorganized Boroughs.** The legislature shall provide for the performance of services it deems necessary or advisable in unorganized boroughs, allowing for maximum local participation and responsibility. It may exercise any power or function in an unorganized borough which the assembly may exercise in an organized borough.

SECTION 7. **Cities.** Cities shall be incorporated in a manner prescribed by law, and shall be a part of the borough in which they are located. Cities shall have the powers and functions conferred by law or charter. They may be merged, consolidated, classified, reclassified, or dissolved in the manner provided by law.

SECTION 8. **Council.** The governing body of a city shall be the council.

SECTION 9. **Charters.** The qualified voters of any borough of the first class or city of the first class may adopt, amend, or repeal a home rule charter in a manner provided by law. In the absence of such legislation, the governing body of a borough or city of the first class shall provide the procedure for the preparation and adoption or rejection of the charter. All charters, or parts or amendments of charters, shall be submitted to the qualified voters of the borough or city, and shall become effective if approved by a majority of those who vote on the specific question.

SECTION 10. **Extended Home Rule.** The legislature may extend home rule to other boroughs and cities.

SECTION 11. **Home Rule Powers.** A home rule borough or city may exercise all legislative powers not prohibited by law or by charter.

SECTION 12. **Boundaries.** A local boundary commission or board shall be established by law in the executive branch of the state government. The commission or board may consider any proposed local government boundary change. It may present proposed changes to the legislature during the first ten days of any regular session. The change shall become effective forty-five days after presentation or at the end of the session, whichever is earlier, unless disapproved by a resolution concurred in by a majority of the members of each house. The commission or board, subject to law, may establish procedures whereby boundaries may be adjusted by local action.

SECTION 13. **Agreements; Transfer of Powers.** Agreements, including those for co-operative or joint administration of any functions or powers, may be made by any local government with any other local government, with the State, or with the United States, unless otherwise provided by law or charter. A city may transfer to the borough in which it is located any of its powers or functions unless prohibited by law or charter, and may in like manner revoke the transfer.

SECTION 14. **Local Government Agency.** An agency shall be established by law in the executive branch of the state government to advise and assist local governments. It shall review their activities, collect and publish local government information, and perform other duties prescribed by law.

SECTION 15. **Special Service Districts.** Special service districts existing at the time a borough is organized shall be integrated with the government of the borough as provided by law.

ARTICLE XI
INITIATIVE, REFERENDUM, AND RECALL

SECTION 1. **Initiative and Referendum.** The people may propose and enact laws by the initiative, and approve or reject acts of the legislature by the referendum.

SECTION 2. **Application.** An initiative or referendum is proposed by an application containing the bill to be initiated or the act to be referred. The application shall be signed by not less than one hundred qualified voters as sponsors, and shall be filed with the secretary of state. If he finds it in proper form he shall so certify. Denial of certification shall be subject to judicial review.

SECTION 3. **Petition.** After certification of the application, a petition containing a summary of the subject matter shall be prepared by the secretary of state for circulation by the sponsors. If

signed by qualified voters, equal in number to ten per cent of those who voted in the preceding general election and resident in at least two-thirds of the election districts of the State, it may be filed with the secretary of state.

SECTION 4. **Initiative Election.** An initiative petition may be filed at any time. The secretary of state shall prepare a ballot title and proposition summarizing the proposed law, and shall place them on the ballot for the first statewide election held more than one hundred twenty days after adjournment of the legislative session following the filing. If, before the election, substantially the same measure has been enacted, the petition is void.

SECTION 5. **Referendum Election.** A referendum petition may be filed only within ninety days after adjournment of the legislative session at which the act was passed. The secretary of state shall prepare a ballot title and proposition summarizing the act and shall place them on the ballot for the first statewide election held more than one hundred eighty days after adjournment of that session.

SECTION 6. **Enactment.** If a majority of the votes cast on the proposition favor its adoption, the initiated measure is enacted. If a majority of the votes cast on the proposition favor the rejection of an act referred, it is rejected. The secretary of state shall certify the election returns. An initiated law becomes effective ninety days after certification, is not subject to veto, and may not be repealed by the legislature within two years of its effective date. It may be amended at any time. An act rejected by referendum is void thirty days after certification. Additional procedures for the initiative and referendum may be prescribed by law.

SECTION 7. **Restrictions.** The initiative shall not be used to dedicate revenues, make or repeal appropriations, create courts, define the jurisdiction of courts or prescribe their rules, or enact local or special legislation. The referendum shall not be applied to dedications of revenue, to appropriations, to local or special legislation, or to laws necessary for the immediate preservation of the public peace, health, or safety.

SECTION 8. **Recall.** All elected public officials in the State, except judicial officers, are subject to recall by the voters of the State or political subdivision from which elected. Procedures and grounds for recall shall be prescribed by the legislature.

ARTICLE XII
GENERAL PROVISIONS

SECTION 1. **State Boundaries.** The State of Alaska shall consist of all the territory, together with the territorial waters appurtenant thereto, included in the Territory of Alaska upon the date of ratification of this constitution by the people of Alaska.

SECTION 2. **Intergovernmental Relations.** The State and its political subdivisions may cooperate with the United States and its territories, and with other states and their political subdivisions on matters of common interest. The respective legislative bodies may make appropriations for this purpose.

SECTION 3. **Office of Profit.** Service in the armed forces of the United States or of the State is not an office or position of profit as the term is used in this constitution.

SECTION 4. **Disqualification for Disloyalty.** No person who advocates, or who aids or belongs to any party or organization or association which advocates, the overthrow by force or violence of the government of the United States or of the State shall be qualified to hold any public office of trust or profit under this constitution.

SECTION 5. **Oath of Office.** All public officers, before entering upon the duties of their offices, shall take and subscribe to the following oath or affirmation: "I do soldemnly swear (or affirm) that I will support and defend the Constitution of the United States and the Constitution of the State of Alaska, and that I will faithfully discharge my duties as .... to the best of my ability." The legislature may prescribe further oaths or affirmations.

SECTION 6. **Merit System.** The legislature shall establish a system under which the merit principle will govern the employment of persons by the State.

SECTION 7. **Retirement Systems.** Membership in employee retirement systems of the State or its political subdivisions shall constitute a contractual relationship. Accrued benefits of these systems shall not be diminished or impaired.

SECTION 8. **Residual Power.** The enumeration of specified powers in this constitution shall not be construed as limiting the powers of the State.

SECTION 9. **Provisions Self-executing.** The provisions of this constitution shall be construed to be self-executing whenever possible.

SECTION 10. **Interpretation.** Titles and subtitles shall not be used in construing this constitution. Personal pronouns used in this constitution shall be construed as including either sex.

SECTION 11. **Law-making Power.** As used in this constitution, the terms "by law" and "by the legislature," or variations of these terms, are used interchangeably when related to law-making powers. Unless clearly inapplicable, the law-making powers assigned to the legislature may be exercised by the people through the initiative, subject to the limitations of Article XI.

SECTION 12. **Disclaimer and Agreement.** The State of Alaska and its people forever disclaim all right and title in or to any property belonging to the United States, or subject to its disposition, and not granted or confirmed to the State or its political subdivisions, by or under the act admitting Alaska to the Union. The State and its people further disclaim all right or title in or to any property, including fishing rights, the right or title to which may be held by or for any Indian, Eskimo, or Aleut, or community thereof, as that right or title is defined in the act of admission. The State and its people agree that, unless otherwise provided by Congress, the property, as described in this section, shall remain subject to the absolute disposition of the United States. They further agree that no taxes will be imposed upon any such property, until otherwise provided by the Congress. This tax exemption shall not apply to property held by individuals in fee without restrictions on alienation.

SECTION 13. **Consent to Act of Admission.** All provisions of the act admitting Alaska to the Union which reserve rights or powers to the United States, as well as those prescribing the terms or conditions of the grants of lands or other property, are consented to fully by the State and its people.

ARTICLE XIII
AMENDMENT AND REVISION

SECTION 1. **Amendments.** Amendments to this constitution may be proposed by a two-thirds vote of each house of the legislature. The secretary of state shall prepare a ballot title and proposition summarizing each proposed amendment, and shall place them on the ballot for the next statewide election. If a majority of the votes cast on the proposition favor the amendment, it shall be adopted. Unless otherwise provided in the amendment, it becomes effective thirty days after the certification of the election returns by the secretary of state.

SECTION 2. **Convention.** The legislature may call constitutional conventions at any time.

SECTION 3. **Call by Referendum.** If during any ten-year period a constitutional convention has not been held, the secretary of state shall place on the ballot for the next general election the question: "Shall there be a Constitutional Convention?" If a majority of the votes cast on the question are in the negative, the question need not be placed on the ballot until the end of the next ten-year period. If a majority of the votes cast on the question are in the affirmative, delegates to the convention shall be chosen at the next regular statewide election, unless the legislature provides for the election of the delegates at a special election. The secretary of state shall issue the call for the convention. Unless other provisions have been made by law, the call shall conform as nearly as possible to the act calling the Alaska Constitutional Convention of 1955, including, but not limited to, number of members, districts, election and certification of delegates, and submission and ratification of revisions and ordinances. The appropriation provisions of the call shall by self-executing and shall constitute a first claim on the state treasury.

SECTION 4. **Powers.** Constitutional conventions shall have plenary power to amend or revise the constitution, subject only to ratification by the people. No call for a constitutional convention shall limit these powers of the convention.

ARTICLE XIV
APPORTIONMENT SCHEDULE

SECTION 1. **Election Districts.** Members of the house of representatives shall, until reapportionment, be elected from the election districts and in the numbers shown below:

Number of District	Name of District	Number of Representatives
1	Prince of Wales	1
2	Ketchikan	2
3	Wrangell-Petersburg	1
4	Sitka	2
5	Juneau	2
6	Lynn Canal-Icy Straits	1
7	Cordova-McCarthy	1
8	Valdez-Chitina-Whittier	1
9	Palmer-Wasilla-Talkeetna	1
10	Anchorage	8
11	Seward	1
12	Kenai-Cook Inlet	1
13	Kodiak	2
14	Aleutian Islands	1
15	Bristol Bay	1
16	Bethel	1
17	Kuskokwim	1
18	Yukon-Koyukuk	1
19	Fairbanks	5
20	Upper Yukon	1
21	Barrow	1
22	Kobuk	1
23	Nome	2
24	Wade Hampton	1

SECTION 2. **Senate Districts.** Members of the senate shall be elected from

the senate districts and in the number shown below:

Name of District	Composed of Election Districts	Number of Senators
A. Southeastern	1, 2, 3, 4, 5, and 6	2
B. Ketchikan-Prince of Wales	1 and 2	1
C. Wrangell-Petersburg-Sitka	3 and 4	1
D. Juneau-Yakutat	5 and 6	1
E. Southcentral	7, 8, 9, 10, 11, 12, 13, and 14	2
F. Cordova-Valdez	7 and 8	1
G. Anchorage-Palmer	9 and 10	1
H. Seward-Kenai	11 and 12	1
I. Kodiak-Aleutians	13 and 14	1
J. Central	15, 16, 17, 18, 19, and 20	2
K. Bristol Bay-Bethel	15 and 16	1
L. Yukon-Kuskokwim	17 and 18	1
M. Fairbanks-Fort Yukon	19 and 20	1
N. Northwestern	21, 22, 23, and 24	2
O. Barrow-Kobuk	21 and 22	1
P. Nome-Wade Hampton	23 and 24	1

SECTION 3. **Description of Election Districts.** [*The detailed description of election districts set forth in this section has been omitted.*]

ARTICLE XV
SCHEDULE OF TRANSITIONAL MEASURES

To provide an orderly transition from a territorial to a state form of government, it is declared and ordained:

SECTION 1. **Continuance of Laws.** All laws in force in the Territory of Alaska on the effective date of this constitution and consistent therewith shall continue in force until they expire by their own limitation, are amended, or repealed.

SECTION 2. **Saving of Existing Rights and Liabilities.** Except as otherwise provided in this constitution, all rights, titles, actions, suits, contracts, and liabilities and all civil, criminal, or administrative proceedings shall continue unaffected by the change from territorial to state government, and the State shall be the legal successor to the Territory in these matters.

SECTION 3. **Local Government.** Cities, school districts, health districts, public utility districts, and other local subdivisions of government existing on the effective date of this constitution shall continue to exercise their powers and functions under existing law, pending enactment of legislation to carry out the provisions of this constitution. New local subdivisions of government shall be created only in accordance with this constitution.

SECTION 4. **Continuance of Office.** All officers of the Territory, or under its laws, on the effective date of this constitution shall continue to perform the duties of their offices in a manner consistent with this constitution until they are superseded by officers of the State.

SECTION 5. **Corresponding Qualifications.** Residence, citizenship, or other qualifications under the Territory may be used toward the fulfillment of corresponding qualifications required by this constitution.

SECTION 6. **Governor to Proclaim Election.** When the people of the Territory ratify this constitution and it is approved by the duly constituted authority of the United States, the governor of the Territory shall, within thirty days after receipt of the official notification of such approval, issue a proclamation and take necessary measures to hold primary and general elections for all state elective offices provided for by this constitution.

SECTION 7. **First State Elections.** The primary election shall take place not less than forty nor more than ninety days after the proclamation by the governor of the Territory. The general election shall take place not less than ninety days after the primary election. The elections shall be governed by this constitution and by applicable territorial laws.

SECTION 8. **United States Senators and Representative.** The officers to be elected at the first general election shall include two senators and one representative to serve in the Congress of the United States, unless senators and a representative have been previously elected and seated. One senator shall be elected for the long term and one senator for the short term, each term to expire on the third day of January in an odd-numbered year to be determined by authority of the United States. The term of the representative shall expire on the third day of January in the odd-numbered year immediately following his assuming office. If the first representative is elected in an even-numbered year to take office in that year, a representative shall be elected at the same time to fill the full term commencing on the third day of January of the following year, and the same person may be elected for both terms.

SECTION 9. **First Governor and Secretary of State: Terms.** The first governor and secretary of state shall hold office for a term beginning with the day on which they assume office and ending at noon on the first Monday in December of the even-numbered year following the next presidential election. This term shall count as a full term for purposes of determining eligibility for re-election only if it is four years or more in duration.

SECTION 10. **Election of First Senators.** At the first state general election, one senator shall be chosen for a two-year term from each of the following senate districts, described in Section 2 of Article XIV: A, B, D, E, G, I, J, L, N, and O. At the same election, one senator shall be chosen for a four-year term from each of the following senate districts, described in Section 2 of Article XIV: A, C, E, F, H, J, K, M, N, and P.

SECTION 11. **Terms of First State Legislators.** The first state legislators shall hold office for a term beginning with the day on which they assume office and ending at noon on the fourth Mon-

day in January after the next general election, except that senators elected for four-year terms shall serve an additional two years thereafter. If the first general election is held in an even-numbered year, it shall be deemed to be the general election for that year.

SECTION 12. **Election Returns.** The returns of the first general election shall be made, canvassed, and certified in the manner prescribed by law. The governor of the Territory shall certify the results to the President of the United States.

SECTION 13. **Assumption of Office.** When the President of the United States issues a proclamation announcing the results of the election, and the State has been admitted into the Union, the officers elected and qualified shall assume office.

SECTION 14. **First Session of Legislature.** The governor shall call a special session of the first state legislature within thirty days after the presidential proclamation unless a regular session of the legislature falls within that period. The special session shall not be limited as to duration.

SECTION 15. **First Legislators: Office Holding.** The provisions of Section 5 of Article II shall not prohibit any member of the first state legislature from holding any office or position created during his first term.

SECTION 16. **First Judicial Council.** The first members of the judicial council shall, notwithstanding Section 8 of Article IV, be appointed for terms as follows: three attorney members for one, three, and five years respectively, and three non-attorney members for two, four, and six years respectively. The six members so appointed shall, in accordance with Section 5 of Article IV, submit to the governor nominations to fill the initial vacancies on the superior court and the supreme court, including the office of chief justice. After the initial vacancies on the superior and supreme courts are filled, the chief justice shall assume his seat on the judicial council.

SECTION 17. **Transfer of Court Jurisdiction.** Until the courts provided for in Article IV are organized, the courts, their jurisdiction, and the judicial system shall remain as constituted on the date of admission unless otherwise provided by law. When the state courts are organized, new actions shall be commenced and filed therein, and all causes, other than those under the jurisdiction of the United States, pending in the courts existing on the date of admission, shall be transferred to the proper state court as though commenced, filed, or lodged in those courts in the first instance, except as otherwise provided by law.

SECTION 18. **Territorial Assets and Liabilities.** The debts and liabilities of the Territory of Alaska shall be assumed and paid by the State, and debts owed to the Territory shall be collected by the State. Assets and records of the Territory shall become the property of the State.

SECTION 19. **First Reapportionment.** The first reapportionment of the house of representatives shall be made immediately following the official reporting of the 1960 decennial census, or after the first regular legislative session if the session occurs thereafter, notwithstanding the provision as to time contained in Section 3 of Article VI. All other provisions of Article VI shall apply in the first reapportionment.

SECTION 20. **State Capital.** The capital of the State of Alaska shall be at Juneau.

SECTION 21. **Seal.** The seal of the Territory, substituting the word "State" for "Territory," shall be the seal of the State.

SECTION 22. **Flag.** The flag of the Territory shall be the flag of the State.

SECTION 23. **Special Voting Provision.** Citizens who legally voted in the general election of November 4, 1924, and who meet the residence requirements for voting, shall be entitled to vote notwithstanding the provisions of Section 1 of Article V.

SECTION 24. **Ordinances.** Ordinance No. 1 on ratification of the constitution, Ordinance No. 2 on the Alaska-Tennessee Plan, and Ordinance No. 3 on the abolition of fish traps, adopted by the Alaska Constitutional Convention and appended to this constitution, shall be submitted to the voters and if ratified shall become effective as provided in each ordinance.

SECTION 25. **Effective Date.** This constitution shall take effect immediately upon the admission of Alaska into the Union as a state.

Agreed upon by the delegates in Constitutional Convention assembled at the University of Alaska, this fifth day of February, in the year of our Lord one thousand nine hundred and fifty-six, and of the Independence of the United States the one hundred and eightieth.

WM. A. EGAN
President of the Convention
R. ROLLAND ARMSTRONG
DOROTHY J. AWES
FRANK BARR
JOHN C. BOSWELL
SEABORN J. BUCKALEW, JR.
JOHN B. COGHILL
E. B. COLLINS
GEORGE D. COOPER
JOHN M. CROSS
EDWARD V. DAVIS
JAMES P. DOOGAN
TRUMAN C. EMBERG
HELEN FISCHER
VICTOR FISCHER
DOUGLAS GRAY
THOMAS C. HARRIS
JOHN S. HELLENTHAL
MILDRED R. HERMANN
HERB HILSCHER
JACK HINCKEL
JAMES HURLEY
MAURICE T. JOHNSON
YULE F. KILCHER
LEONARD H. KING
WILLIAM W. KNIGHT
W. W. LAWS
ELDOR R. LEE
MAYNARD D. LONDBORG
STEVE McCUTCHEON
GEORGE M. McLAUGHLIN
ROBERT J. McNEALY
JOHN A. McNEES
M. R. MARSTON
IRWIN L. METCALF

LESLIE NERLAND
JAMES NOLAN
KATHERINE D. NORDALE
FRANK PERATROVICH
CHRIS POULSEN
PETER L. READER
BURKE RILEY
RALPH J. RIVERS
VICTOR C. RIVERS
JOHN H. ROSSWOG
B. D. STEWART
W. O. SMITH
GEORGE SUNDBORG
DORA M. SWEENEY
WARREN A. TAYLOR
H. R. VANDERLEEST
M. J. WALSH
BARRIE M. WHITE
ADA B. WIEN

ATTEST:
THOMAS B. STEWART
Secretary of the Convention

ORDINANCE NO. 1
RATIFICATION OF
CONSTITUTION

SECTION 1. **Election.** The Constitution for the State of Alaska agreed upon by the delegates to the Alaska Constitutional Convention on February 5, 1956, shall be submitted to the voters of Alaska for ratification or rejection at the territorial primary election to be held on April 24, 1956. The election shall be conducted according to existing laws regulating primary elections so far as applicable.

SECTION 2. **Ballot.** Each elector who offers to vote upon this constitution shall be given a ballot by the election judges which will be separate from the ballot on which candidates in the primary election are listed. Each of the propositions offered by the Alaska Constitutional Convention shall be set forth separately, but on the same ballot form. The first proposition shall be as follows:

"Shall the Constitution for the State of Alaska prepared Yes ☐ and agreed upon by the Alaska Constitutional Convention be No ☐ adopted?"

SECTION 3. **Canvass.** The returns of this election shall be made to the governor of the Territory of Alaska, and shall be canvassed in substantially the manner provided by law for territorial elections.

SECTION 4. **Acceptance and Approval.** If a majority of the votes cast on the proposition favor the constitution, then the constitution shall be deemed to be ratified by the people of Alaska to become effective as provided in the constitution.

SECTION 5. **Submission of Constitution.** Upon ratification of the constitution, the governor of the Territory shall forthwith transmit a certified copy of the constitution to the President of the United States for submission to the Congress, together with a statement of the votes cast for and against ratification.

ORDINANCE NO. 2
ALASKA-TENNESSEE PLAN

SECTION 1. **Statement of Purpose.** The election of senators and a representative to serve in the Congress of the United States being necessary and proper to prepare for the admission of Alaska as a state of the Union, the following sections are hereby ordained, pursuant to Chapter 46, SLA 1955:

SECTION 2. **Ballot.** Each elector who offers to vote upon the ratification of the constitution may, upon the same ballot, vote on a second proposition, which shall be as follows:

"Shall Ordinance Number Two (Alaska-Tennessee Plan) of the Alaska Constitutional Yes ☐ Convention, calling for the immediate election of two United States Senators and No ☐ one United States Representative, be adopted?"

SECTION 3. **Approval.** Upon ratification of the constitution by the people of Alaska and separate approval of this ordinance by a majority of all votes cast for and against it, the remainder of this ordinance shall become effective.

SECTION 4. **Election of Senators and Representative.** Two United States senators and one United States representative shall be chosen at the 1956 general election.

SECTION 5. **Terms.** One senator shall be chosen for the regular term expiring on January 3, 1963, and the other for an initial short term expiring on January 3, 1961, unless when they are seated the Senate prescribes other expiration dates. The representative shall be chosen for the regular term of two years expiring January 3, 1959.

SECTION 6. **Qualifications.** Candidates for senators and representative shall have the qualifications prescribed in the Constitution of the United States and shall be qualified voters of Alaska.

SECTION 7. **Other Office Holding.** Until the admission of Alaska as a state, the senators and representative may also hold or be nominated and elected to other offices of the United States or of the Territory of Alaska, provided that no person may receive compensation for more than one office.

SECTION 8. **Election Procedure.** Except as provided herein, the laws of the Territory governing elections to the office of Delegate to Congress shall, to the extent applicable, govern the election of the senators and representative. Territorial and other officials shall perform their duties with reference to this election accordingly.

SECTION 9. **Independent Candidates.** Persons not representing any political party may become independent candidates for the offices of senator or representative by filing applications in the manner provided in Section 38-5-10, ACLA 1949, insofar as applicable. Applications must be filed in the office of the director of finance of the Territory on or before June 30, 1956.

SECTION 10. **Party Nominations.** Party nominations for senators and representative shall, for this election only, be made by party conventions in the manner prescribed in Section 38-4-11, ACLA 1949, for filling a vacancy in a party nomination occurring after a primary election. The names of the candidates nominated shall be certified by the chairman and secretary of the central committee of each political party to the director of finance of the Territory on or before June 30, 1956.

SECTION 11. **Certification.** The director of finance shall certify the names of all candidates for senators and representative to the clerks of court by July 15, 1956. The clerks of court shall cause the names to be printed on the official ballot for the general election. Independent candidates shall be identified as provided in Section 38-5-10, ACLA 1949. Candidates nominated at party conventions shall be identified with appropriate party designations as is provided by law for nominations at primary elections.

SECTION 12. **Ballot Form; Who Elected.** The ballot form shall group separately the candidates seeking the regular senate term, those seeking the short senate term, and candidates for representative. The candidate for each office receiving the largest number of votes cast for that office shall be elected.

SECTION 13. **Duties and Emoluments.** The duties and emoluments of the offices of senator and representative shall be as prescribed by law.

SECTION 14. **Convention Assistance.** The president of the Alaska Constitutional Convention, or a person designated by him, may assist in carrying out the purposes of this ordinance. The unexpended and unobligated funds appropriated to the Alaska Constitutional Convention by Chapter 46, SLA 1955, may be used to defray expenses attributable to the referendum and the election required by this ordinance.

SECTION 15. **Alternate Effective Dates.** If the Congress of the United States seats the senators and representative elected pursuant to this ordinance and approves the constitution before the first election of state officers, then Section 25 of Article XV shall be void and shall be replaced by the following:

"The provisions of the constitution applicable to the first election of state officers shall take effect immediately upon the admission of Alaska into the Union as a state. The remainder of the constitution shall take effect when the elected governor takes office."

ORDINANCE NO. 3
ABOLITION OF FISH TRAPS

SECTION 1. **Ballot.** Each elector who offers to vote upon the ratification of the constitution may, upon the same ballot, vote on a third proposition, which shall be as follows:

"Shall Ordinance Number Three of the Alaska Constitutional Convention, prohibiting the use of fish traps for the taking of salmon for commercial purposes in the coastal waters of the State, be adopted?"

    Yes ☐

    No ☐

SECTION 2. **Effect of Referendum.** If the constitution shall be adopted by the electors and if a majority of all the votes cast for and against this ordinance favor its adoption, then the following shall become operative upon the effective date of the constitution:

"As a matter of immediate public necessity, to relieve economic distress among individual fishermen and those dependent upon them for a livelihood, to conserve the rapidly dwindling supply of salmon in Alaska, to insure fair competition among those engaged in commercial fishing, and to make manifest the will of the people of Alaska, the use of fish traps for the taking of salmon for commercial purposes is hereby prohibited in all the coastal waters of the State."

Index

Index